Child Development

EDITOR IN CHIEF
Neil J. Salkind
University of Kansas

ASSOCIATE EDITOR
Lewis Margolis
University of North Carolina, Chapel Hill

RESEARCH ASSISTANT
Mandy D. Goodnight
University of Kansas

EDITORIAL AND PRODUCTION STAFF

Shawn Beall
Project Editor

Nancy Dziedzic
Dave Salamie
Copy Editors

William Drennan
Rebecca N. Ferguson
Proofreaders

Datapage Technologies International
Compositor

MACMILLAN REFERENCE USA
Elly Dickason, *Publisher*
Jill Lectka, *Associate Publisher*

Child
Development

Edited by Neil J. Salkind

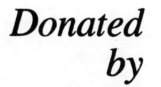
MACMILLAN REFERENCE USA

GALE GROUP
™
THOMSON LEARNING

New York • Detroit • San Diego • San Francisco
Boston • New Haven, Conn. • Waterville, Maine
London • Munich

Macmillan Library Reference USA   Macmillan Library Reference USA
300 Park Avenue South   *27500 Drake Road*
New York, NY 10010   Farmington Hills, MI 48331–3535

Library of Congress Cataloging-in-Publication Data

Child development/ edited by Neil J. Salkind.
     p. cm.—(Macmillan psychology reference series)
  Includes bibliographical references and index.
  ISBN 0-02-865618-0 (hc.)
     1. Child development. I. Salkind, Neil J. II. Series.
HQ772.C436 2002
305.231—dc21   2001037062

Printed in the United States of America

10 9 8 7 6 5 4 3 2 1

DEDICATION

This book is dedicated to the memory of John C. Wright, whose life tragically ended in the summer of 2001. John was a leading researcher and teacher in the field of child development, and an outspoken and passionate advocate for children and other groups who did not have a voice of their own. His legacy is in the hundreds of students he taught and in the colleagues he influenced to be better, more involved, and more concerned people.

The good things in life last for limited days,

but a good name endures forever.

BEN SIRA
from *The Wisdom of Ben Sira*

CONTENTS

PREFACE

Child Development, the first volume in the Macmillan Psychology Reference Series, is an extensive collection of articles about every facet of child development, ranging from adoption and day care to welfare programs and video games. It focuses on topics that are important for the educated parent, pediatrician, teacher, high school and college student, or anyone else interested in better understanding the how's and why's of a child's development.

The 289 articles are organized in a way that will make the Encyclopedia easily understood and accessible. To do this, we organized the collection by creating four separate types of entries:

- Overviews are articles consisting of 3,000 words that provide an in-depth look at a particular topic in child development such as parenting, social development, or child abuse. These articles introduce the reader to all of the important ideas and concepts within the topic and provide an introduction to some of the issues and controversies important to child development specialists.

- The second type of article is about 1,500 words long and serves as an introduction to important topics in child development. These are a bit less ambitious than the overviews, including brief discussions about day care, home schooling, and friendship.

- Definitions are the third article type. These are 150-word definitions of important terms that should be familiar to anyone interested in child development. Altruism, conservation, and bilingual education are examples of such articles. We created definitions of these terms rather than writing 1,500- or 3,000-word articles because we did not feel it necessary to elaborate on these topics to the same extent.

- Biographies are comprised of 400 words and focus on leading characters in the history of child development. These are the men and women who are best known for the lasting and influential effects of their research and writing.

Finally, the appendix is replete with visually interesting and easily understood tables and charts that include topics such as children in various living arrangements, child poverty, and youth participating in volunteer activities.

Each entry is followed by a bibliography.

Who Will Use This Encyclopedia?

This Encyclopedia is for anyone who wants to know more about the field of child development. This includes parents, teachers, professionals in the health fields, such as doctors and nurses, social workers, lawyers, people involved in creating policies that affect children and families, school board members, and high school and college students who are interested in learning more about children or are writing a term paper on an aspect of child development.

The editors emphasized the importance of writing for an educated audience that might not yet be familiar with many of the terms and ideas relevant to understanding a child's development. We tried to make this material informative and approachable, but not overly technical. We hope that we have achieved our goal.

How to Use This Encyclopedia

The topics are organized alphabetically from A to Z. In addition, there are several other ways to locate information.

First, there is an extensive subject index covering every topic mentioned in the Encyclopedia along with corresponding page numbers for that topic. This index is located in the back of the Encyclopedia.

There are also cross-reference terms at the end of the entries. These terms refer to other articles that contain information about the topic. For example, at the end of "Attachment" there is a cross-reference to Parent-Child Relationships.

Who Wrote This Encyclopedia?

The topics in this encyclopedia were selected and organized by Neil J. Salkind and Lewis Margolis (editor and associate editor, respectively), with the help of Mandy Goodnight. Neil J. Salkind is a professor of Psychology and Research in Education at the University of Kansas, while Lewis Margolis is a professor of Public Health at the University of North Carolina in Chapel Hill. Mandy Goodnight is a practicing school psychologist in western Kansas.

All of the entries were written by leading experts in their field or those who were under their supervision. Each author was asked to make a specific contribution. The diversity and excellence of the contributors adds an unmistakable flavor of comprehensiveness and authority to the entries. Speaking for all of the editors, it was a pleasure and an honor to have such a distinguished group of scholars contribute to the volume.

Acknowledgments

No book is ever the product of just editors and contributors. *Child Development* is the result of the hard work put forth by several people. First, we would like to thank Elly Dickason, Publisher, and Jill Lectka, Associate Publisher, at Macmillan for the opportunity to undertake this project. Jill was especially helpful in organizing the team that produced this volume. Second, Shawn Beall was the project manager, and it was because of her flawless organization skills, good nature, and record keeping that we managed to track 289 different articles by almost as many authors. On a daily basis, Shawn was there to answer questions, remind authors of article due dates, and respond to queries about format. We would also like to thank imaging coordinator Dean Dauphinais, permissions associate Julie Juengling, and senior art directors Tracey Rowens and Cindy Baldwin for the page and cover design. Additional thanks goes to managing editor Betz Des Chenes for the time and effort she contributed to writing captions and "putting out fires."

And finally, to our contributors we want to express our heartfelt thanks. The quality and tone of the writing is excellent, especially given the audience to which this volume is addressed. With authors such as these writing about, caring about, and working with children and their families, there is hope for the future and the role that children will play in building a better world.

Neil J. Salkind
Lewis Margolis
August, 2001

LIST OF ARTICLES

LIST OF CONTRIBUTORS

Leonard Abbeduto
University of Wisconsin, Madison
Preschool

Jane L. Abraham
Virginia Tech
Puberty
Sex Education

Maria Adiyanti
Gadjah Mada University
Aggression

Andréa Aguiar
University of Waterloo
Object Permanence

Benjamin Aguilar
Insitute of Child Development, University of Minnesota
Delinquency

Daisuke Akiba
Center for the Study of Human Development, Brown University
Heredity versus Environment

Greg R. Alexander
Department of Maternal and Child Health, University of Alabama, Birmingham School of Public Health
Birthweight
Infant Mortality
Premature Infants

Elizabeth C. Allen
Wake Forest University School of Medicine
Children with Special Health Care Needs

Gary L. Allen
University of South Carolina, Columbia
Three Mountain Task

Virginia D. Allhusen
University of California, Irvine
Stages of Development

Jeannette M. Alvarez
Department of Psychology, New York University
Acting Out
Self-Concept

Lynley H. Anderman
University of Kentucky
Self-Fulfilling Prophecy

Linda J. Anooshian
Boise State University
Poverty

Glen P. Aylward
Southern Illinois University School of Medicine
Learning Disabilities

Don Bailey
Frank Porter Graham Child Development Center, University of North Carolina, Chapel Hill
Fragile X Syndrome

Tracey R. Bainter
University of Kansas
Domestic Violence

Amy J. L. Baker
The Children's Village
Working in Adolescence

Lynne E. Baker-Ward
North Carolina State University
Memory

Dare A. Baldwin
University of Oregon
Motherese

Janet W. Bates
University of Kansas
Play

Daniel J. Bauer
Odum Institute for Research in Social Science, University of North Carolina, Chapel Hill
Day Care

Lisa Baumwell
New York University
Firstborn Children

Sherry L. Beaumont
University of Northern British Columbia
Gesell, Arnold

Debora Bell-Dolan
University of Missouri
Ethical Guidelines for Research

Trude Bennett
University of North Carolina, Chapel Hill
Abortion
Maternal Health

Janette B. Benson
Department of Psychology, University of Denver
Activity Level

Victor W. Bergenn
Council on Education Psychology
McGraw, Myrtle Byram

Jesse M. Bering
Florida Atlantic University
Milestones of Development

Michael D. Berzonsky
*State University of New York,
Cortland*
Social Cognition

Patti Beth
*University of Wisconsin,
Madison*
Preschool

E G Bishop
Naturalistic Observation

Joanne Bitetti
*Teachers College, Columbia
University*
Empathy

David F. Bjorklund
Florida Atlantic University
Milestones of Development

Michael Blank
*Department of Psychiatry,
University of Pennsylvania*
Rural Children

Elaine A. Blechman
University of Colorado, Boulder
Altruism

John D. Bonvillian
*University of Virginia,
Charlottesville*
Sign Language

Anne I. H. Borge
*Institute of Psychology,
University of Oslo*
Antisocial Behavior

Watson A. Bowes Jr.
*School of Medicine, University of
North Carolina, Chapel Hill*
Cesarean Delivery

Rhonda Cherie Boyd
*Society for Research in Child
Development*
Conformity
Defense Mechanism

Robert E. Boykin
*University of North Carolina,
Chapel Hill*
Genetic Counseling
Genotype
Human Genome Project
Mitosis
Phenotype

Rebecca J. Brand
University of Oregon
Motherese

Joanne Bregman
*Department of Pediatrics,
Evanston Northwestern
Healthcare*
Apgar Scoring System

Cornelia Brentano
Tufts University, Medford
Child Custody and Support

Inge Bretherton
*Department of Human
Development and Family
Studies, University of
Wisconsin, Madison*
Ainsworth, Mary Dinsmore
Salter

Pia Rebello Britto
*Center for Children and Families,
Teachers Collge, Columbia
University*
Children's Rights

Gene H. Brody
University of Georgia
Siblings and Sibling
Relationships

David M. Brodzinsky
Rutgers University
Adoption

Jane Brown-O'Gorman
Empathy

Liesette Brunson
University of Illinois, Urbana
Development

Amy Buchanan
Arizona State University
Emotional Development

Richard M. Buck
Creighton University
Locke, John

Martha J. Buell
*Department of Individual and
Family Studies, University of
Delaware*
Montessori Method

Raymond Buriel
Pomona College
Dialectical Perspectives

Don Bushell Jr.
University of Kansas
Behavior Analysis

Kay Bussey
*Department of Psychology,
Macquarie University*
Observational Learning

Natasha J. Cabrera
*National Institute of Child
Health and Human
Development*
Fathers

Emily D. Cahan
Wheelock College
Kessen, William

Yvonne M. Caldera
Texas Tech University
Amniocentesis

Noel A. Card
St. John's University
Social Development

Erin Nash Casler
University of Kansas
Sensory Development

Richard J. Castillo
*Department of Psychology,
University of Hawaii, West
O'ahu*
Egocentrism

Stephen J. Ceci
*Human Development, Cornell
University*
Learning

Elyse Chadwick
*Division of Epidemiology,
University of Minnesota*
Sexual Activity

Xin Chen
*Department of Psychology,
University of Connecticut*
Handedness

Eva G. Clarke
Old Dominion University
Identity Development

Roberta R. Collard
*Professor Emeritus, School of
Education, University of
Massachusetts, Amherst*
Parallel Play

Michael Lamport Commons
Harvard Medical School
Natural Childbirth

Andrew Coulson
Macinac Center for Public Policy
School Vouchers

Martha J. Cox
*University of North Carolina,
Chapel Hill*
Parent-Child Relationships

Donna J. Crowley
Florida State University
American Sign Language

Mary Elizabeth Curtner-Smith
*Department of Human
Development and Family
Studies, University of Alabama*
Anger

Janet Abboud Dal Santo
*UNC Injury Prevention Research
Center, Department of Health
Behavior and Health
Education, University of North
Carolina, Chapel Hill*
Injuries

Thomas C. Dalton
Cal Poly State University
McGraw, Myrtle Byram

Victoria L. Davids
*Basehor Elementary School,
Basehor, KS*
Reading

Donna M. Davis
*University of Missouri, Kansas
City*
Dewey, John

Terri De Ment
Claremont Graduate University
Dialectical Perspectives

Eric Dearing
Harvard University
Attachment

Joan Ziegler Delahunt
*University of Kansas Medical
Center*
Brazelton Neonatal
Assessment Scale
Maturation
Motor Development

Susan Dickstein
Bradley Hospital and *Brown
University*
Postpartum Depression

Janice Dodds
*School of Public Health,
University of North Carolina,
Chapel Hill*
Malnutrition
Nutrition
Women, Infants, and
Children

Esther Dromi
Tel-Aviv University
Babbling and Early Words

Stacy L. Dubit
*School of Public Health,
University of North Carolina,
Chapel Hill*
Nutrition

Jennifer R. Dyer
*University of Michigan, Ann
Arbor*
Cognitive Development

Jacquelynne S. Eccles
*University of Michigan, Ann
Arbor*
Adolescence

Lisa M. Edwards
University of Kansas
Hispanic Children

Meica M. Efird
*Department of Pediatrics,
University of North Carolina,
Chapel Hill*
Fetal Alcohol Syndrome
Phenylketonuria

Byron Egeland
*Insitute of Child Development,
University of Minnesota*
Delinquency

Nancy Eisenberg
Arizona State University
Friendship

Patricia Crane Ellerson
*University of California, Santa
Barbara*
Placenta

Claire Etaugh
*Department of Psychology,
Bradley University*
Androgyny

David W. Evans
*Department of Psychology,
Bucknell University*
Down Syndrome

Richard A. Fabes
Arizona State University
Emotional Development

Anita Farel
*Department of Maternal and
Child Health, University of
North Carolina, Chapel Hill*
Birth Defects
Chronic Illness

Jennifer E. N. Fedie
Growth Rate

Jennifer S. Feenstra
University of New Hampshire
Maslow, Abraham

Xin Feng
University of Connecticut
Swaddling of Infants

Barbara H. Fiese
Syracuse University
Generation Gap

Frank D. Fincham
*University at Buffalo, State
University of New York*
Divorce

Anne C. Fletcher
*University of North Carolina,
Greensboro*
Single-Parent Families

Edward J. Forbes III
*Lock Haven University of
Pennsylvania*
Prosocial Behavior

Martin E. Ford
George Mason University
Selfishness

Laura E. Frame
*Department of Maternal and
Child Health, School of Public
Health, University of North
Carolina, Chapel Hill*
Substance Abuse

Rebecca L. Fraser
Cornell University
Learning

Tierra M. Freeman
University of Kentucky
Self-Fulfilling Prophecy

Marc Fritz
*Department of Obstetrics and
Gynecology, University of North
Carolina, Chapel Hill*
Artificial Insemination

Cynthia A. Frosch
Arizona State University
Emotional Development

Vanessa C. Gallo
Gymboree Play Programs, Inc.
Gifted Children

Gillian S. Garfinkle
*Department of Psychology, New
York University*
Acting Out

Aimee Gelnaw
Family Pride Coalition
Gay- and Lesbian-Headed
Families

Alice Ginott
Ginott, Haim

Laraine Masters Glidden
St. Mary's College of Maryland
Vygotsky, Lev

Rebecca J. Glover
University of North Texas
Dating

H. Wallace Goddard
*University of Arkansas
Cooperative Extension Service*
Ginott, Haim
Inductive Reasoning

LaVell Gold
*Gold Training Group,
Minneapolis, MN*
Physical Growth

Dale E. Goldhaber
*Early Child and Human
Development Program,
University of Vermont*
Theories of Development

Roberta Michnick Golinkoff
*Educational Studies at the
University of Delaware*
Language Development

Roberta Louis Goodman
*Cleveland College of Jewish
Studies*
Religion

Sherryl Hope Goodman
Emory University
Mental Disorders

Mandy D. Goodnight
University of Kansas
Parental Leave

Nathan W. Gottfried
Louisiana State University
Attention Span

Laurie Ann Greco
West Virginia University
Reinforcement

Gwen E. Gustafson
*Department of Psychology,
University of Connecticut*
Handedness

M. Gutierrez
University of Missouri
Imaginary Playmates

Sarit Guttmann-Steinmetz
*State University of New York,
Stony Brook*
Head Start

Michelle de Haan
*Developmental Cognitive
Neuroscience Unit, Institute of
Child Health, The Wolfson
Centre*
Brain Development

Patricia A. Haensly
*Department of Psychology,
Western Washington University*
Bell Curve

Denise Hallfors
*School of Public Health,
Department of Maternal and
Child Health, University of
North Carolina, Chapel Hill*
Substance Abuse

Lawrence D. Hammer
*Lucile Packard Children's
Hospital, Stanford University
School of Medicine*
Obesity

Philip Hannaford
*Department of General Practice
and Primary Care, University
of Aberdeen*
Contraception

Robert C. Hardy
*Institute for Child Study,
University of Maryland*
Bandura, Albert

Kim Harrison
*Special Education Policy and
Leadership, University of
Kansas*
Welfare Programs

Algea O. Harrison-Hale
*Department of Psychology,
Oakland University*
African-American Children

Robin L. Harwood
University of Connecticut
Swaddling of Infants

Theresa Lawton Hawley
The Ounce of Prevention Fund
Homeless Children

Ericka V. Hayes
*University of California, San
Francisco*
Asthma

Nancy Hazen
University of Texas, Austin
Bowlby, John

Matthew J. Hertenstein
*Department of Psychology,
University of California,
Berkeley*
Erikson, Erik
Infancy

Maggie Hicken
*Department of Maternal and
Child Health, University of
North Carolina, Chapel Hill*
Birth Defects

Marianne M. Hillemeier
*University of Michigan, Ann
Arbor*
Teenage Pregnancy

Jim Hillesheim
University of Kansas
Rousseau, Jean-Jacque

John H. Himes
*Division of Epidemiology,
University of Minnesota*
Physical Growth

Kathy Hirsh-Pasek
*Department of Psychology,
Temple University*
Language Development

Ernest V. E. Hodges
St. John's University
Social Development

Lois Wladis Hoffman
*University of Michigan, Ann
Arbor*
Working Families

G. Holliday
University of Missouri
Imaginary Playmates

Alice Sterling Honig
Syracuse University
Harlow, Harry
Hearing Loss and Deafness

Pamela P. Hufnagel
Penn State, Dubois
Retention

Jeffrey W. Hull
*Children's Hospital of Alabama,
Birmingham*
Failure to Thrive

Aquiles Iglesias
Temple University
Black English

Molly Carter Imhoff
North Carolina State University
Memory

Glendessa Insabella
*Department of Psychology, Yale
University*
Blended Families

Jenny Isaacs
St. John's University
Social Development

Mark H. Johnson
*Center for Brain and Cognitive
Development, Birkbeck College*
Brain Development

Howard W. Jones Jr.
Eastern Virginia Medical School
In Vitro Fertilization

Elaine M. Justice
Old Dominion University
Identity Development

Beth A. Kapes
*Medical Writer and Editor,
Cleveland, OH*
Health Insurance
Menstrual Cycle

Dennis H. Karpowitz
*Department of Psychology,
University of Kansas*
Latchkey Children

Heather Kelly
Bethany College
Video Games

Leah M. Kelly
*Department of Psychology,
University of Denver*
Activity Level

Nicole B. Knee
*School of Public Health,
University of North Carolina,
Chapel Hill*
Malnutrition
Nutrition
Women, Infants, and
Children

Michele Knox
Medical College of Ohio
Bullying

Becky Kochenderfer-Ladd
Arizona State University
Separation Anxiety

Dolph Kohnstamm
*Professor Emeritus, Leiden
University, Netherlands*
Shyness

Hideo Kojima
Kyoto Gakuen University
Hall, Granville Stanley

Jonathan Kotch
*Department of Maternal and
Child Health, University of
North Carolina, Chapel Hill*
Title V (Maternal and Child
Health Services Block
Grant)

Milton Kotelchuck
*School of Public Health, Boston
University*
Healthy Start
Prenatal Care

Kristen L. Kucera
*Department of Epidemiology,
University of North Carolina,
Chapel Hill*
Injuries

Evelyn K. Kumoji
*Population and Family Health
Sciences, Johns Hopkins
University*
Street Children

Chris Lalonde
University of Victoria
Piaget, Jean

Garrett Lam
*Department of Obstetrics and
Gynecology, University of North
Carolina, Chapel Hill*
Pregnancy
Ultrasound
Umbilical Cord

Frank J. Landy
SHL: Litigation Support
Cattell, James

Carrie Lazarus
St. Mary's College of Maryland
Vygotsky, Lev

Diane B. Leach
George Washington University
Spock, Benjamin

Anthony Lee
*Tavistock Clinic and University
College*
Hypothesis

Clarese Lemberger
University of Kentucky
Television

Kathryn S. Lemery
Arizona State University
Sickle Cell Anemia
Twin Studies

Laura E. Levine
*Central Connecticut State
University*
Kohlberg, Lawrence

Wing Ling Li
City University of Hong Kong
Employment in Adolescence

Timothy K. Loper
University of Kansas
Crying

Elizabeth Lorch
University of Kentucky
Television

Raymond P. Lorion
University of Pennsylvania
Rural Children

Debbie Madden-Derdich
*Department of Family and
Human Development, Arizona
State University*
Family Size

Jeanna L. Magyar-Moe
University of Kansas
Suicide

Janeen C. Manuel
*Wake Forest University School of
Medicine*
Children with Special Health
Care Needs

Diane D. Marshall
*University of North Carolina,
Chapel Hill*
Respiratory Distress
Syndrome

L. R. S. Martens
University of Kansas
Cognitive Style

Staci Martin
*HIV and AIDS Malignancy
Branch, National Cancer
Institute*
Acquired Immune Deficiency
Syndrome

Jeffrey V. May
*Women's Research Institute,
University of Kansas School of
Medicine, Wichita*
Reproductive Technologies

Linda K. McCampbell
University of Kansas
Social Class

Kathleen McCartney
Harvard University
Attachment

Michael E. McCarty
Texas Tech University
Spatial Abilities

Rebecca B. McCathren
University of Missouri
Imaginary Playmates

Linda J. McGarvey-Levin
Standardized Testing

Shirley McGuire
University of San Francisco
Temperament

Doris McIlwain
*Department of Psychology,
Macquarie University*
Freud, Sigmund

Anne McIntyre
*University of Tennessee,
Knoxville*
Stranger Anxiety

Vonnie C. McLoyd
*Department of Psychology, Center
for Human Growth and
Development, University of
Michigan, Ann Arbor*
African-American Children

Kenneth F. McPherson
Chronological Age

Debra Mekos
*Department of Population and
Family Health Sciences, Johns
Hopkins School of Hygiene and
Public Health*
Street Children

Jean Mercer
Richard Stockton College
Surrogate Motherhood

Laurie L. Meschke
*Division of Epidemiology,
University of Minnesota*
Sexual Activity

Robert Meyer
*Department of Maternal and
Child Health, University of
North Carolina, Chapel Hill*
Birth Defects

Bryan D. Midgley
McPherson College
Skinner, B. F.

Sharon Seidman Milburn
*California State University,
Fullerton*
Internet

Carol A. Miller
*University of California, San
Francisco*
Circumcision
Neonate
Sudden Infant Death
Syndrome

Patrice Marie Miller
*Department of Psychology,
University of Florida*
Natural Childbirth

Kristi L. Milowic
*Clinical Center for Development
and Learning, University of
North Carolina, Chapel Hill*
High Risk Infants

Majka Woods Mitchell
*Department of Educational
Psychology, Baylor University*
Methods of Studying
Children

Kenneth J. Moise Jr.
*University of North Carolina
School of Medicine*
Maternal Age
Rh Disease

Dennis L. Molfese
University of Louisville
Symbolic Thought

Victoria J. Molfese
University of Louisville
Symbolic Thought

Amanda Sheffield Morris
Arizona State University
Friendship

Edward K. Morris
University of Kansas
Classical Conditioning
Skinner, B. F.

David Moshman
University of Nebraska
Tabula Rasa

Ann D. Murray
Kansas State University
Laissez-Faire Parents

Dennie Nadeau
*University of North Carolina,
Chapel Hill*
Abortion

Laura L. Namy
Emory University
Language Acquisition Device

David Nelson
*New Opportunities Education
Project*
Bilingual Education

Eileen Neubaum-Carlan
University of Georgia
Siblings and Sibling
Relationships

Brian Newberry
University of Kansas
Computers
Corporal Punishment

Illene C. Noppe
*University of Wisconsin, Green
Bay*
Death
Gender-Role Development

Donna M. Noyes-Grosser
*New York State Department of
Health, Early Intervention
Program*
Mainstreaming

Larry P. Nucci
University of Illinois, Chicago
Marasmus

Susan L. O'Donnell
*Institute of Child Development,
University of Minnesota*
Class Size

Abigail Tuttle O'Keeffe
*Elementary and Early Childhood
Education, The College of New
Jersey*
Parenting

Patricia Ohlenroth
Sound Content Editorial Services
Homework
Pets

David R. Olson
*Ontario Institute for Studies in
Education, University of
Toronto*
Bruner, Jerome

Deena R. Palenchar
University of Pittsburgh
Teratogens

Mary Ann Pass
*Department of Maternal and
Child Health, University of
Alabama, Birmingham School
of Public Health*
Infant Mortality
Premature Infants

Jennifer Teramoto Pedrotti
University of Kansas
Asian-American Children

David Peres
University of Kansas
After-School Programs

Maria Gabriela Periera
Cornell University
Learning

Vicki Diane Peyton
University of Kansas
Brazelton, T. Berry

Julie Poehlman
University of Wisconsin
Generation Gap

LeShawndra N. Price
*Center for Developmental Science,
University of North Carolina,
Chapel Hill*
Racial Differences

Mitchell J. Prinstein
Yale University
Cliques

Elizabeth P. Pungello
*Frank Porter Graham Child
Development Center, University
of North Carolina, Chapel Hill*
Day Care

Jason D. Rehfeldt
University of Kansas
Home Schooling

Deana Reimer
*New Opportunities Education
Project*
Bilingual Education

Richard Rende
*Department of Psychiatry and
Human Behavior, Brown
Medical School*
and
*Centers for Behavioral and
Preventive Medicine at The
Miriam Hospital*
Conduct Disorder

Gary Resnick
Westat
Mediation

Brady Reynolds
West Virginia University
Personality Development

Danae E. Roberts
University of Kansas
Moral Development

Joanne E. Roberts
*Frank Porter Graham Child
Development Center, University
of North Carolina, Chapel Hill*
Ear Infections/Otitis Media

Julia Robinson
University of Louisville
Symbolic Thought

Katherine M. Robinson
*Campion College at University of
Regina*
Cohort

Ann L. Robson
University of Western Ontario
Critical/Sensitive Periods

Faye B. Steuer
College of Charleston
Midwives

Tanya F. Stockhammer
*New York State Psychiatric
Institute*
Violence

Michael Storr
Queens University
Miscarriage

Ronald P. Strauss
*Department of Dental Ecology,
University of North Carolina
School of Dentistry, Chapel
Hill*
Cleft Lip/Cleft Palate

Anne Dopkins Stright
Indiana University
Stepfamilies

Amy R. Susman-Stillman
*Institute of Child Development,
University of Minnesota*
Co-Parenting

Shawn R. A. Svoboda-Barber
Exercise

John I. Takayama
*Department of Pediatrics,
University of California, San
Francisco*
Lead Poisoning

Marjorie Taylor
University of Oregon
Imaginary Audience

Adrea D. Theodore
*Department of Pediatrics,
University of North Carolina
School of Medicine, Chapel
Hill*
Child Abuse

Evelyn B. Thoman
*Department of Family and Child
Nursing University of
Washington*
Apnea

David W. Threadgill
*University of North Carolina,
Chapel Hill*
Genetic Counseling
Genotype
Human Genome Project
Mitosis
Phenotype

James A. Troha
Baker University
Birth Order and Spacing

Pascal Louis Trohanis
*Frank Porter Graham Child
Development Center, University
of North Carolina, Chapel Hill*
Individuals with Disabilities
Education Act

Alan Uba
*Division of General Pediatrics,
University of California, San
Francisco*
Immunization
Rubella

Derrald W. Vaughn
Bethany College
Video Games

Jo Ellen Vespo
*Department of Psychology, Utica
College of Syracuse University*
Wechsler Intelligence Scale
for Children

Marjorie Erickson Warfield
*University of Massachusetts
Medical School*
Developmental Disabilities

Laura A. Webber
University of Kansas
Intelligence

Scott Weckerly
University of Delaware
Scholastic Aptitude Test

Lisa A. Wertenberger
University of Kansas
Mental Retardation

Sandra J. White
University of Kansas
Attention Deficit
Hyperactivity Disorder

Rosemary C. White-Traut
*College of Nursing, University of
Illinois, Chicago*
Apgar, Virginia

Lori Wiener
*HIV and AIDS Malignancy
Branch, National Cancer
Institute*
Acquired Immune Deficiency
Syndrome

Diane E. Wille
Indiana University, Southeast
Milestones of Development:
Overview

Jennifer D. Wishner
Claremont Graduate University
Binet, Alfred

David C. Witherington
*Department of Psychology,
University of Virginia*
Infancy

Beth K. Yudkowsky
American Academy of Pediatrics
State Children's Health
Insurance Program

Philip Sanford Zeskind
*Neurodevelopmental Research,
Department of Pediatrics,
Carolinas Medical Center*
Touch

A

ABORTION

The technical definition of induced abortion is the removal of products of conception from the uterus of a pregnant woman. Throughout recorded history there is evidence that women have found the means to limit and space their childbearing through the use of induced abortion. Women of all identities and living in a wide variety of conditions all over the world continue to choose termination as one response to unintended pregnancies. In 1997, approximately 20 out of every 1,000 women in the United States aged fifteen to forty-four had induced abortions; this rate has remained stable since 1995. Another way to express the frequency of abortion is the number of induced abortions compared with the number of live births; in 1997 this ratio was 306 abortions per 1,000 live births. These statistics do not include abortions that happen spontaneously, usually called miscarriages.

Who Has Abortions?

Nearly half (49%) of all pregnancies that occur in the United States are not intended, and about half of unintended pregnancies are resolved by abortions. Most (58%) of the women who have abortions had been using some form of birth control but became pregnant because of the failure or misuse of the birth control product/method. By the age of forty-five, about 43 percent of women in the United States have experienced at least one abortion. Among the women choosing to have abortions at a given time, nearly half (43%) have had at least one previous abortion.

There is not one particular type of woman who is likely to have an abortion. More than half (55%) of the women having abortions have had at least one child already. About two-thirds of the women having abortions have never been married. The majority (52%) are younger than age twenty-five, but only 20 percent are teenagers.

Women of all racial and religious groups obtain abortions. The largest number (60%) of abortions are performed on white women, but black women are three times as likely and Hispanic women twice as likely as white women to have an abortion in a given year. Catholic women are equally likely to have abortions as all women nationwide, but the rate of induced abortion for Catholic women is actually 29 percent higher than the rate for Protestant women.

Abortions occur for many reasons, and women tend to have multiple explanations for their abortion decisions. The most common reason, given by three-quarters of women having abortions, is that having a baby at that time in their lives would conflict with major responsibilities such as work or school. Two-thirds of women having abortions give economic reasons for delaying or foregoing parenthood. Half of the women choosing abortion do not have the supportive relationship that they would like for becoming a parent—either they do not want to start out as a single mother or they are having problems in their relationship with a husband or partner. Approximately 14,000 women a year choose abortions to terminate pregnancies resulting from rape or incest.

When Abortion Was Illegal

Major complications from induced abortion are very rare in the United States, occurring in fewer than 1 percent of abortions. The risk of death from childbirth, an uncommon event in industrialized countries, is ten times greater than the mortality risk of abortion. The safety of legal abortion is in stark contrast to the danger women faced before abortion was decriminalized in the United States in 1973. In the 1950s, for example, there were about 1 million illegal abortions every year, with at least 1,000 deaths per year resulting.

Before legalization some courageous and qualified providers took considerable personal risks to offer safe procedures to women in need. Women with adequate financial and social resources were sometimes able to seek safe abortions in legal settings outside the United States. Desperation often drove other women to unskilled abortionists working in unsanitary conditions. Women who survived so-called back-alley abortions of this sort or attempts to self-abort sometimes suffered painful chronic illnesses, lost the ability to have children, or experienced trauma that affected their psychological health and well-being.

Judicial and Legislative Rulings

On January 22, 1973, the U.S. Supreme Court handed down the *Roe v. Wade* decision, which created a legal, though limited, right to abortion. *Roe v. Wade* concluded that the "right of privacy . . . founded in the Fourteenth Amendment's concept of personal liberty . . . is broad enough to encompass a woman's decision whether or not to terminate her pregnancy." Based on their individual right to privacy, women in consultation with their doctors were given the legal right to choose abortion in the first three months (or first trimester) of pregnancy. State laws were permitted to limit second-trimester abortions "only in the interest of the woman's safety." In the final three months (third trimester) of pregnancy, *Roe v. Wade* allowed states to protect the fetus by restricting abortion unless there is potential danger to the life or health of the pregnant woman.

Roe v. Wade granted women the right to early abortion with a physician's consent, but it did not guarantee financial or medical access to abortion. In 1976 the U.S. Congress passed the Hyde amendment to a federal appropriations bill, eliminating federal reimbursement for induced abortions from Medicaid public insurance coverage for low-income women. Through 2001, Congress had annually reinstated this ban on federal funding of abortion, with narrow exceptions for rape, incest, and threats to the life of the woman if she continues the pregnancy. As of 1997 the cost of an abortion in a clinic or doctor's office ranged from $100 to $1,535, averaging between $316 and $401.

Funding issues have been only one arena of debate in the controversy over women's right to abortion. Religious and personal beliefs lead some people to reject abortion as an individual option for themselves. Among those with personal objections to abortion, some advocate for the right of other people to make their own decisions. Others attempt to use the judicial and legislative systems to return to the situation that existed before legalization. Attitudes toward sexuality and women's autonomy, as well as fundamental beliefs about social control over individual decision making, motivate activists on different sides of the abortion issue.

The U.S. Supreme Court heard another major abortion case in July 1992. In *Planned Parenthood v. Casey*, the court reviewed a Pennsylvania statute that required women seeking abortions to receive counseling from physicians in favor of continuing their pregnancies, and then to wait at least twenty-four hours before obtaining an abortion procedure. Notification of spouses and parents about requests for abortions was also required. Only the provision for spousal notification was considered to impose an undue burden on women by the Supreme Court, and this provision was thus judged unconstitutional. The Court acknowledged the situation of women in abusive relationships, with the potential for violence perceived as part of the burden for women wishing to act independently of their partners. Other provisions of the statute were left intact, although most were seen by the Court as medically unnecessary and burdensome to a lesser extent.

Although *Roe v. Wade* was not overturned by the Supreme Court in the *Planned Parenthood v. Casey* decision, the Court's strict interpretation of undue burden set a precedent for states to impose numerous restrictions on women exercising their right to abortion. As of January 2001, the majority (31) of states had parental notification or consent laws in effect for adolescents seeking abortions. The participation of at least one parent is expected in these states. In most states it is possible for a teen to receive a "judicial bypass" of parental involvement, but only if the teen has the information and resources to bring a persuasive request to a court.

Access to Abortion

Restrictions on abortion and lack of broad access to abortion services are unique for a legal medical procedure. The controversy over abortion and associated violence and harassment of patients and providers have resulted in a limited number of active abortion providers, especially in rural areas of the United States. In 1996 out of all U.S. counties only 14 percent had practicing providers, and the number appeared to be declining. Nearly one-third (32%) of women aged fifteen to forty-four were living in counties without local abortion services.

The majority of medical residents specializing in obstetrics and gynecology are not required to perform first-trimester induced abortions as part of their training. In 1995 only 12 percent of obstetrics and gynecology residency programs routinely offered abortion training, though nearly half (46%) reported provision of routine training in 1998 subsequent to new guidelines from the Accreditation Council for Graduate Medical Education. Family practice residents have limited experience with either contraception or abortion. The approval in 2000 by the Food and Drug Administration of pharmaceutical agents to induce abortion medically rather than surgically could increase the number of providers. At the time of approval, however, both women and doctors indicated the importance of maintaining a range of abortion choices, since preferences are influenced by many practical, physiological, and psychological factors.

See also: BIRTH; REPRODUCTIVE TECHNOLOGIES

Bibliography

The Alan Guttmacher Institute. "Facts in Brief." In the Alan Guttmacher Institute [web site]. New York, 2000. Available from http://www.agi-usa.org/pubs/fb_induced_abortion.html; INTERNET.

Almeling, Rene, Laureen Tews, and Susan Dudley. "Abortion Training in U.S. Obstetrics and Gynecology Residency Programs, 1998." *Family Planning Perspectives* 32 (2000):268–320.

American Civil Liberties Union Freedom Network. "Reproductive Rights: Public Funding for Abortion." In the American Civil Liberties Union [web site]. New York, 2000. Available from http://www.aclu.org/library/funding.html; INTERNET.

The Boston Women's Health Book Collective. *The New Our Bodies, Ourselves.* New York: Simon and Schuster, 1992.

Henshaw, Stanley K. "Abortion Incidence and Services in the United States, 1995–1996." *Family Planning Perspectives* 30 (1998):263–270, 287.

Koonin, Lisa K., Lilo T. Strauss, Camaryn E. Chrisman, and Wilda Y. Parker. "Abortion Surveillance—United States, 1997." *Morbidity and Mortality Weekly Report* 49 (SS11) (2000):1–44.

MacKay, H. Trent, and Andrea P. MacKay. "Abortion Training in Obstetrics and Gynecology Residency Programs in the United States, 1991–1992." *Family Planning Perspectives* 27 (1995):112–115.

Steinauer, Jody E., Teresa DePineres, Anne M. Robert, John Westfall, and Philip Darney. "Training Family Practice Residents in Abortion and Other Reproductive Health Care: A Nationwide Survey." *Family Planning Perspectives* 29 (1997):222–227.

Trude Bennett
Dennie Nadeau

Planned Parenthood, headquartered in Boston, Massachusetts, provides abortion counseling at satellite offices across the country. (AP/Wide World Photos)

ABSTRACT REASONING

A child who has developed good abstract reasoning skills easily uses symbols instead of concrete objects when learning new information. The beginning learner usually needs concrete aids. To represent the number "five," for example, the teacher or child might put out five blocks. A child who has made the shift to abstract reasoning, however, understands the concept of "quantity" without relying on objects. So in mathematics, abstract reasoning enables the child to understand that the abstract character "5" might stand for five of any specific object—or just the numerical idea of five.

In reading, abstract characters (letters) are grouped in specific patterns to represent the concrete world. Abstract reasoning allows the child to use phonics to sound out words (e.g., "rock"); form a mental image of a rock; and use that information to understand what is being read. While children can always be taught concretely, the leap to abstract reasoning results in more rapid, efficient learning.

See also: THEORY OF MIND

Bibliography

Cegelka, Patricia Thomas, and William H. Berdine. *Effective Instruction for Students with Learning Disabilities.* Boston: Allyn and Bacon, 1995.

Susan Setley

ACQUIRED IMMUNE DEFICIENCY SYNDROME

The human immunodeficiency virus (HIV) was first discovered in the early 1980s and has now been established as the cause of acquired immune deficiency syndrome (AIDS). HIV works by attacking the immune system, the human body's defense system that fights off foreign invaders, such as germs and bacteria. The immune systems of people with HIV are ultimately weakened to the point that illnesses such as pneumonia and other infections can take over, eventually leading to death.

Epidemiology and Transmission

Since the early 1980s, HIV infection has emerged as a major health problem for children in the United States and many other parts of the world. The Centers for Disease Control and Prevention (CDC) estimated that in 2000 more than 431,000 people in the United States were living with HIV, and that approximately 5,575 of these individuals were children under the age of thirteen. The World Health Organization estimated in 2000 that about 1,600 children around the world were becoming newly infected each day.

HIV lives in body fluids, such as blood and semen, and transmission occurs primarily through unprotected sex (both heterosexual and homosexual) and the injection of illicit drugs. The virus can also be transmitted from mother to child during pregnancy or at the time of delivery, but medical advances have led to a significant reduction in these cases because pregnant women are now encouraged to undergo voluntary HIV testing. If a woman is found to carry the virus, doctors can begin administering medication to her right away and to her infant after birth. The rate of transmission through contaminated blood or blood products (i.e., via transfusions) was high until 1985 when measures were put into place to ensure the safety of the blood supply in North America, Europe, and some other parts of the world. Transmission still occurs from an unsafe blood supply in some underdeveloped countries.

Originally, AIDS was viewed as a death sentence, with only 5 percent to 10 percent of people living for three years after diagnosis. Now, new medications have led to a dramatic decline in AIDS-related deaths. HIV is therefore seen as more of a chronic disease, similar to diabetes or cystic fibrosis. As a result, psychologists are focusing more on psychosocial issues in children who were infected early in life and are now living into adolescence and young adulthood.

Developmental and Social Impact on the Child

How a child copes with his HIV infection depends on his age and developmental stage, cognitive abilities, and general psychological makeup. One must also assess the child's stage of illness and the way in which the parents cope with the illness. Together, these factors determine the meaning the illness carries for the child, and the mental resources they possess to help them deal with each new challenge during the process of learning about their illness.

Infancy through Preschool

Children younger than two years of age are unable to grasp the concept of being diagnosed with a life-threatening disease. As a result, the psychological impact of the diagnosis falls mainly on the child's caregiver(s). Parents may feel horrified at the idea of losing their child to a disease that they essentially "gave" to their children. They may benefit from psychological services that offer support and guidance for coping with these feelings of fear and guilt. Infants and toddlers, on the other hand, are most concerned with immediate events, such as painful procedures and separation from their parents. Psychologists can help parents prepare their child for medical procedures through role-playing, medical play, and coloring books that illustrate the procedure.

Another concern for small children with HIV is that the virus can invade the brain and central nervous system, creating problems with language, motor skills, and general cognitive abilities. For this reason, regular developmental and neuropsychological testing is recommended in order to identify deficits and to assist in obtaining special educational services as needed. These assessments should begin during the first year of life and should continue throughout childhood and early adolescence.

School-Age Years

Diagnosis disclosure and medical adherence are two important issues that arise during an HIV-positive child's school-age years. Nearly all parents struggle with the idea of diagnosis disclosure, the process of telling children that they are living with a life-threatening illness. Research with other diseases has clearly documented the risks of keeping the diagnosis a secret and the benefits of open communication about illness in the family. Because of the stigma attached to this disease, however, disclosure poses unique difficulties in families affected by HIV/AIDS. Parents' concerns include the fear that knowledge of the diagnosis will traumatize the child and the possibility that their child will tell others about their illness, thereby putting themselves at risk for being teased and ridiculed by peers. Thus, the diagnosis frequently becomes a guarded secret that is considered shameful, embarrassing, and potentially explosive if revealed. Maintaining this secret places tremendous stress on all members of the family—especially the infected child. It is primarily for this reason that parents put off sharing information about the virus with their children. But children who are not told about their illness sometimes become increasingly resentful of having to take numerous pills, many of which are large and difficult to swallow. Liquid medications are no better, often tasting extremely unpleasant. This can lead to daily power struggles between the parent and child when the time for medication arrives.

Disclosure best takes place in a supportive atmosphere of cooperation between mental health professionals (e.g., psychologists, social workers) and parents. It should be thought of as a process rather than a single episode. Emotional reactions following disclosure vary but tend to be consistent with the way the child has responded to earlier crises. If disclosure is conducted in a supportive manner, almost all children demonstrate considerable pride with mastery of information about the illness and an improved ability to tolerate procedures such as blood draws and pill swallowing. Many parents report that their child's medication adherence improves following disclosure. Also, participation in support groups, art therapy, and family therapy can help the children to continue processing the information that they have been given.

Preadolescence and Adolescence
Among adolescents infected with HIV, the primary difficulties involve the virus's impact on their social life, medication adherence, and grief over past losses and their own uncertain future. The most damaging result of HIV in a teenager's life is often its effect on relationships outside the family. These adolescents live in fear of others finding out about their diagnosis. In fact, they may fear rejection more than they fear dying from the disease. It may be difficult to form friendships, since they may always feel the shadow of secrecy coming between them and their peers. Dating creates even more anxiety, since they may not know how to handle issues of sexual intimacy, honesty, and trust.

Adherence to treatment remains a problem during adolescence—most of the drug regimens are exceptionally complicated and difficult to follow. The large number of pills, the need for timing meals with medications, and the very specific storage instructions make keeping up with the schedule quite challenging. When considering AIDS-related stigma and adolescents' desire for peer approval, as well as the side effects frequently associated with these drugs (e.g., stomach bloating and diarrhea), one can see how "skipping a few pills" could easily occur. If a patient

does not take his or her medicines consistently, then there will not be enough medicine in the blood to stop the virus from growing. When this happens, the virus becomes stronger, and the medicine loses its ability to fight the virus. In other words, the virus becomes resistant to the medicine. Many anti-HIV medicines are so similar that once HIV becomes resistant to one particular drug, it may be resistant to other drugs that it has not been exposed to yet.

Many of these youngsters have experienced multiple losses in their early years, and they find themselves grieving for their parents, siblings, and/or close friends who did not live long enough to benefit from the drugs currently available. Others have been shuffled between households, schools, and neighborhoods. Depression and anxiety about these multiple losses, their uncertain future, and guilt surrounding survival can lead to disabling mental health problems.

Most HIV-infected teens either have limited access to, or will not participate in, mental health services. If these issues are not appropriately addressed, however, AIDS can affect virtually every aspect of an adolescent's life. Physical symptoms (e.g., fatigue, aches, pains) and psychological symptoms (e.g., depression, anxiety, substance abuse, sexual acting out) may become significant problems. If a strong relationship can be formed with a therapist, issues related to sexuality, disclosure, family conflicts, and future planning can be openly discussed.

Because many teens are reluctant to attend individual therapy, alternatives such as support groups and camping programs have been developed. Support groups offer these teens a sense of belonging and a place where they can undo the shame and stigmatization that has isolated them from their peers. It is also a place where their pain can be validated, their trauma understood, and a deep connection with others made. Camping programs can also be helpful by offering therapeutic activities such as artwork, challenge courses, campfire chats, and rap sessions. Through these activities, connections with repressed emotions and with other people in similar situations can lead to enormous healing and growth.

Prevention

As mentioned previously, medical advances have led to a decrease in the number of infants born with HIV. Despite this encouraging trend, the CDC estimated that more than 5,500 children under age thirteen were living with HIV or AIDS in the United States in 2000. Among adolescents thirteen to nineteen years of age, the number of AIDS cases reported each year has increased from 1 case in 1981 to 310 (3,865 cumulative) in 2000. Of even more concern is

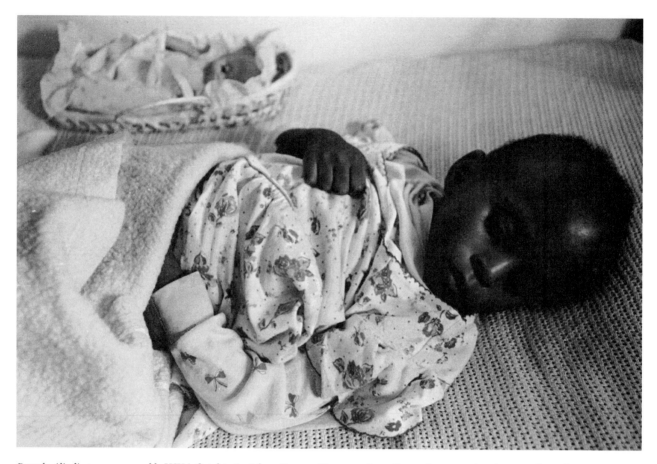

Beverly Alindi, a seven year old, HIV-infected patient from Kenya, appears much smaller and younger than her actual age due to complications from the virus. (AP Wide World Photos)

that many young adults with AIDS almost certainly acquired their infection as teenagers. Throughout adolescence, teenagers often feel a sense of invulnerability and may therefore engage in risky behaviors such as drug use and unsafe sex. Alarmingly, it has been estimated that more than 80 percent of teenagers infected with HIV use condoms inconsistently, and many of these adolescents probably do not tell their partners about their diagnosis. Furthermore, sharing a single contaminated needle can infect many users and, hence, their sexual partners.

Mental health professionals can play an important role in the prevention of HIV by providing information about safer sex, drug use, and other means of transmission. School programs focused on self-esteem building and assertiveness training have been shown to help teenagers navigate the complex interpersonal situations that can place them at risk for acquiring HIV. Mental health professionals can also work with parents, encouraging them to foster an environment of open communication in the home.

The Future Outlook

At the beginning of the 1990s, there was a bleak outlook for those living with HIV. By the start of the twenty-first century, children born with this virus were graduating high school, attending trade schools or colleges, and holding down jobs.

Along with proper medical care, attitude appears to be essential. Those who keep themselves mentally active, have a sense of purpose in their lives, and maintain a sense of humor appear able to successfully adapt to the continued uncertainties inherent in this disease. Despite the many stresses they must face, young adults with HIV need to be given the opportunity to develop and pursue their goals. In an article that appeared in the book *Pediatric AIDS*, Lori Wiener, Anita Septimus, and Christine Grady emphasized that if recognized and nurtured, young people with HIV have the potential to significantly contribute to society. The psychologist working with children and adolescents with HIV can play an essential role in helping these individuals overcome obstacles and achieve their goals. Thus, for patients with HIV and for the mental health professionals involved in their care, the future is looking brighter every day.

See also: BIRTH DEFECTS; PREGNANCY

Bibliography

HIV/AIDS Surveillance Report. 12(1):20. Atlanta. Centers for Disease Control and Prevention, 2000; Washington, DC: U.S. Government Printing Office, 2000.

Kaplan, Edward. "Evaluating Needle-Exchange Programs via Syringe Tracking and Testing (STT)." *AIDS and Public Policy Journal* 6, no. 3 (1991):109–115.

Lemp, George F., Susan F. Payne, Dennese Neal, Tes Temelso, and George W. Rutherford. "Survival Trends for Patients with AIDS." *Journal of the American Medical Association* 263 (1990):402–406.

Lipson, Michael. "What Do You Say to a Child with AIDS?" *Hastings Center Report* 23 (1993):6–12.

Remafedi, Gary. "The University of Minnesota Youth and AIDS Projects' Adolescent Early Intervention Program: A Model to Link HIV-Seropositive Youth with Care." *Journal of Adolescent Health* 23S (1998):115–121.

Stephens Richard C., Thomas E. Feucht, and Shadi W. Roman. "Effects of an Intervention Program on AIDS-related Drug and Needle Behavior among Intravenous Drug Users." *American Journal of Public Health* 81 (1991):568–571.

Wiener, Lori S., Anita Septimus, and Christine Grady. "Psychological Support and Ethical Issues for the Child and Family." In Philip A. Pizzo and Catherine M. Wilfert eds., *Pediatric AIDS: The Challenge of HIV Infection in Infants, Children, and Adolescents*, 3rd edition. Baltimore: Williams and Wilkins, 1998.

World Health Organization. "Global AIDS Surveillance—Part I." *Weekly Epidemiological Report* 72 (1997):357–360.

Lori Wiener
Staci Martin

ACTING OUT

Acting out originally referred to the psychodynamic concept of expressing repressed impulses, but now it more generally refers to maladaptive behavior exhibited by children and adolescents. Rather than coping with the resurfacing of negative emotions (i.e., anxiety, fear) associated with past traumatic experiences or a dysfunctional family environment, the child or adolescent acts out these emotions by engaging in externalizing behaviors. These behaviors range from the less serious (i.e., disobedience, moodiness) to the more severe (i.e., suicidal tendencies, violence). Acting out is often associated with the development of psychopathology, such as antisocial or borderline personality disorder, or is viewed as evidence of a mood disorder; it can also refer to rebellious behavior exhibited by children and, especially, adolescents attempting to assert independence. The interaction of several factors, including ineffective parenting, temperament, and peer rejection can reinforce or exacerbate acting out behavior, leading to delinquency or psychopathology in adolescence or childhood.

See also: ANGER; MENTAL DISORDERS

Bibliography

Forehand, Rex, and Nicholas Long. "Outpatient Treatment of the Acting Out Child: Procedures, Long-Term Follow-Up Data, and Clinical Problems." *Advances in Behavior Research and Therapy* 10 (1988):129–177.

Nielsen, G. *Borderline and Acting-Out Adolescents: A Developmental Approach.* New York: Human Sciences Press, 1983.

Patterson, Gerald, Barbara DeBaryshe, and Elizabeth Ramsey. "A Developmental Perspective on Antisocial Behavior." *American Psychologist* 44 (1989):329–335.

Jeannette M. Alvarez
Gillian S. Garfinkle

ACTIVITY LEVEL

Activity level refers to the relative amounts of motor behavior produced by children and includes everything from a toddler's first steps to a middle-school child's skillful soccer playing. Activity level is measured in a number of ways, ranging from parental observations to computer analysis. Regardless of how it is measured, activity level is usually related to other factors, such as gender, age, and individual differences. Boys are usually more active than girls, and rates of movement are generally the highest between the ages of seven and nine. A child's relative periods of activity and inactivity have been viewed as a stable feature of temperament, suggesting that active infants may become active children, and active children may become extroverted adults. If very high levels of activity accompany poor concentration, disorganization, an inability to "sit still," high levels of distractability, impulsiveness, and little sustained attention, then a diagnosis of hyperactivity with Attention Deficit Hyperactivity Disorder (ADHD) may be indicated.

See also: ATTENTION DEFICIT HYPERACTIVITY DISORDER

Bibliography

Buss, Arnold H., and Robert B. Plomin. *Temperament: Early Developing Personality Traits.* Hillsdale, NJ: Lawrence Erlbaum, 1984.

Janette B. Benson
Leah M. Kelly

ADHD

See: ATTENTION DEFICIT HYPERACTIVITY DISORDER

ADOLESCENCE

Many people imagine an adolescent as being a gangly, awkward, and troublesome individual. Researchers shared this view until quite recently. This period of life (generally considered to run from age ten to age twenty-five) was seen as a time of "storm and stress." But what is adolescent development really like? Clearly it is a time of great change on many levels. Probably most dramatic are the biological changes associated with puberty. These changes include dramatic shifts in the shape of the body, increases in hormones, and changes in brain architecture. These biological shifts are directly linked to changes in sexual interest, cognitive capacities, and physical capacities. There are also major social changes associated with the school-linked transitions and with changes in the roles adolescents are expected to play by all those around them. Finally, there are major psychological changes linked to increasing social and cognitive maturity. In fact, very few developmental periods are characterized by so many changes at so many different levels. With rapid change comes a heightened potential for both positive and negative outcomes. And, although most individuals pass through this developmental period without excessively high levels of "storm and stress," a substantial number of individuals do experience some difficulties.

Adolescence is also a time when individuals make many choices and engage in a wide range of behaviors likely to influence the rest of their lives. For example, adolescents pick which high school courses to take, which after-school activities to participate in, and which peer groups to join. They begin to make future educational and occupational plans and to implement these plans through secondary school course work and out-of-school vocational and volunteer activity choices. Finally, some experiment with quite problematic behaviors such as drug and alcohol consumption and unprotected sexual intercourse. Most of these youth do not suffer long-term consequences for this experimentation, although a few do. Understanding what distinguishes between these two groups is one of the key research issues related to development during adolescence.

Grand Theories of Adolescent Development

Erik Erikson, a German-born American psychoanalyst, proposed the most comprehensive theoretical analysis of development during adolescence as part of his more general theoretical analysis of human development across the life span. He hypothesized that developing a sense of mastery, a sense of identity, and a sense of intimacy were the key challenges for this period of life. He also stressed that these challenges are played out in an increasingly complex set of social contexts and in both cultural and historical

settings. Optimal resolution of these challenges depends on the psychosocial, physical, and cognitive assets of the individual and the developmental appropriateness of the social contexts encountered by the individual across all of the years of adolescence.

Others have expanded these challenges to include autonomy, sexuality, intimacy, achievement, and identity. In many cultural groups, these challenges translate into more specific tasks, including (1) changing the nature of the relationship between youth and their parents so that the youth can take on a more "mature" role in the social fabric of their community (in white American culture this change often takes the form of greater independence from parents and greater decision-making power over one's own current and future behaviors; in other cultures this change can take the form of greater responsibility for family support and increased participation in community decision making); (2) exploring changing social-sexual roles and identities; (3) transforming peer relationships into deeper friendships and intimate partnerships; (4) exploring personal and social identities; (5) focusing some of this identity work on making future life plans; and (6) participating in a series of experiences and choices that facilitate future economic independence or interdependence.

Biological Changes Associated with Puberty

As a result of the activation of the hormones controlling pubertal development, early adolescents undergo a growth spurt, develop primary and secondary sex characteristics, become fertile, and experience increased sexual drive. There is also some evidence that the hormonal changes are linked to behaviors such as aggression, sexuality, and mood swings. These relations are quite weak, however, and are often overridden by social experiences.

In general, pubertal changes begin twelve to eighteen months earlier for girls than for boys. As a result, anyone working with youth in grade six will immediately notice a major difference in the physical maturity between girls and boys. Many girls at this age look and act like fully mature young women, while most of the males still look and act like boys. The impact of these differences on the development of young men and women will vary by cultural group depending on cultural beliefs and norms, such as appropriate roles for physically mature individuals, appropriate heterosexual activities, and ideals related to female and male beauty.

There are also major individual differences in pubertal development within each sex. Some children begin their pubertal changes earlier than others. The impact of these differences depends on the cultural beliefs and norms that relate to the meaning of early maturation for both girls and boys. For example, among white populations, early maturation tends to be advantageous for boys, particularly with respect to their participation in sports activities and their social standing in school. By contrast, early maturation can be problematic for white girls, because the kinds of physical changes girls experience with puberty (such as weight gain) are not highly valued among many white American groups who value the slim, androgynous female body characteristic of white fashion models. In a 1987 study, Roberta Simmons and Dale Blyth found that early maturing white females had lower self-esteem and more difficulty adjusting to school transitions, particularly the transition from elementary to junior high school, than later maturing white females, white males, and both early and later maturing African-American females. Similarly, in a 1990 study in Sweden, Håkan Stattin and David Magnusson found that early maturing girls obtained less education and married earlier than their later maturing peers, because they were more likely to join older peer groups and date older males. In turn, these girls were more likely to drop out of school and get married, perhaps because school achievement was not valued by their peer social network while early entry into the job market and early marriage was. Early maturation does not have these kinds of effects in all cultural groups. For example, African-American females in the United States do not evidence these patterns.

Directly linked to the biological changes associated with puberty are the changes in both body architecture and emotions related to sexuality. Puberty is all about the emergence of sexuality. The physical changes of puberty both increase the individual's own interest in sex and turn the individual into a sexual object in other people's eyes. Both of these changes can have a profound impact on development. Sexual behavior increases dramatically during early to middle adolescence. With these increases go increases in pregnancy and sexually transmitted diseases. Both the frequency of these behaviors and the long-term consequences of these behaviors differ across cultural groups.

Changes in Cognition

Adolescence is accompanied by an increasing ability to think abstractly, consider the hypothetical as well as the real, engage in more sophisticated and elaborate information processing strategies, consider multiple dimensions of a problem at once, and reflect on one's self and on complicated problems. There is also a steady increase in learning strategies, in knowledge of a variety of different topics and subject areas, in the ability to apply knowledge to new learning situations, and in the awareness of one's strengths and weaknesses as a learner. With practice these new cognitive skills can help adolescents become more efficient, sophisticated learners, ready to cope with relatively advanced topics in many different subject areas.

These kinds of cognitive changes also affect individuals' self-concepts, thoughts about their future, and understanding of others. Many theorists have suggested that the adolescent years are a time of change in children's self-concepts, as they consider what possibilities are available to them and try to come to a deeper understanding of themselves in the social and cultural contexts in which they live. In a culture that stresses personal choice in life planning, these concerns and interests also set the stage for personal and social identity formation focused on life planning issues such as those linked to educational, occupational, recreational, and marital choices. Finally, as adolescents become more interested in understanding the psychological characteristics of others, friendships become based more on perceived similarities in these characteristics.

Social Changes Associated with Adolescence in Western Industrialized Countries

There are also major social changes associated with adolescence. Since these vary more across cultures than the biological and cognitive changes just discussed, the following social changes are common in Western industrialized countries.

Friendships and Peer Groups

Probably the most controversial changes during adolescence are those linked to peer relationships. One major change in this arena is the general increase in peer focus and involvement in peer-related social sports, and other extracurricular activities. Many adolescents attach great importance to the activities they do with their peers—substantially more importance than they attach to academic activities and to activities with family members. Further, early adolescents' confidence in their physical appearance and social acceptance is a more important predictor of self-esteem than confidence in their cognitive/academic competence.

In part because of the importance of social acceptance during adolescence, friendship networks during this period often are organized into relatively rigid cliques that differ in social status within school and community settings. The existence of these cliques reflects adolescents' need to establish a sense

During adolescence, many young people attach greater importance to the activities and opinions of their peers than those of family members. (Robert J. Huffman/Field Mark Publications)

of identity; belonging to a group is one way to solve the problem of "who I am." Also, in part because of the importance of social acceptance, children's conformity to their peers peaks during early adolescence. Much has been written about how this peer conformity creates problems for adolescents, and about how "good" children are often corrupted by the negative influences of peers, particularly by adolescent gangs. More often than not, however, adolescents agree more with their parents' views on "major" issues such as morality, politics, religion, and the importance of education. Peers have more influence on such things as dress and clothing styles, music, and activity choice. In addition, adolescents tend to socialize with peers who hold similar views as their parents on the major issues listed above.

Changes in Family Relations

Although the extent of actual disruption in parent-adolescent relations is not as great as one might expect given stereotypes about this period of life. There is little question that parent-child relations do change during adolescence. As adolescents become physically mature they often seek more independence and autonomy and may begin to question family rules and roles, leading to conflicts particularly around such issues as dress and appearance, chores, and dating. Despite these conflicts over day-to-day issues, parents and adolescents agree more than they disagree regarding core values linked to education, politics, and spirituality. Nonetheless, parents and adolescents do interact with each other less frequently than they did in middle childhood. Some researchers have argued that this distancing in parent-adolescent relations has great functional value for adolescents, in that it fosters their individuation from their parents, allows them to try more things on their own, and develops their own competencies and confidence in their abilities. But it is important to bear in mind that, in most families, this distancing takes place in the context of continuing close emotional relationships. And in many cultural groups, adolescents play an increasingly central role in family life and family maintenance.

School Transitions

In most Western countries, adolescents experience at least one major school transition (e.g., the transition into high school) and often two major school transitions (e.g., an additional transition into either middle or junior high school). Several scholars and policymakers have argued that these school transitions are linked to negative changes in the functioning of many adolescents, particularly in the realm of academic achievement. For example, a number of researchers have concluded that the junior high school transition contributes to declines in interest in school, intrinsic motivation, self-concepts/self-perceptions, and confidence in one's intellectual abilities. Drawing upon person-environment fit theory, Jacquelynne Eccles and her colleagues proposed that the negative motivational and behavioral changes associated with these school transitions stem from many junior and senior high schools not providing appropriate educational environments for youth in early and middle adolescence. According to person-environment theory, individuals' behavior, motivation, and mental health are influenced by the fit between the characteristics individuals bring to their social environments and the characteristics of these social environments. Individuals are not likely to do very well, or be very motivated, if they are in social environments that do not fit their psychological needs. If the social environments in the typical junior and senior high schools do not fit very well with the psychological needs of adolescents, then person-environment fit theory predicts a decline in the motivation, interest, performance, and behavior of adolescents as they move into this environment.

Evidence from a variety of sources supports this hypothesis. Both of these school transitions usually involve the following types of contextual changes: (1) a shift from a smaller school to a larger school; (2) a shift to a more bureaucratic social system; (3) a shift to a more controlling social system; (4) a shift to a more heterogeneous social system; (5) a shift to a social context with less personal contact with adults and less opportunity to be engaged in school activities and responsible school roles; (6) a shift to a more rigid, socially comparative grading system; and (7) a shift to a more lock-step curriculum tracking system. Along with these changes, evidence from more micro-classroom-based studies suggests that the teachers in junior and senior high school feel less able to teach all of their students the more challenging academic material and are more likely to use exclusionary and harsh discipline strategies that can effectively drive low achieving and problematic students away from school. Work in a variety of areas has documented the impact on motivation of such changes in classroom and school environments.

See also: DEVELOPMENTAL NORMS; MILESTONES OF DEVELOPMENT

Bibliography

Brooks-Gunn, Jeanne, and Edward Reiter. "The Role of Pubertal Processes." In Shirley Feldman and Glen Elliott eds., *At the Threshold: The Developing Adolescent*. Cambridge, MA: Harvard University Press, 1990.

Brown, Brad. "Peer Groups and Peer Cultures." In Shirley Feldman and Glen Elliott eds., *At the Threshold: The Developing Adolescent*. Cambridge, MA: Harvard University Press, 1990.

Buchanan, Christy, Jacquelynne Eccles, and Jill Becker. "Are Adolescents the Victims of Raging Hormones? Evidence for Activational Effects of Hormones on Moods and Behaviors at Adolescence." *Psychological Bulletin* 111 (1992):62–107.

Carnegie Council on Adolescent Development. *Turning Points: Preparing American Youth for the Twenty-First Century*. New York: Carnegie Corporation, 1989.

Collins, W. Andrew. "Parent-Child Relationships in the Transition to Adolescence: Continuity and Change in Interaction, Affect, and Cognition." In Raymond Montemayor, Gerald Adams, and Thomas Gullotta eds., *From Childhood to Adolescence: A Transitional Period?* Beverly Hills, CA: Sage, 1990.

Eccles, Jacquelynne, Carol Midgley, Christy Buchanan, Allen Wigfield, David Reuman, and Douglas Mac Iver. "Developmental during Adolescence: The Impact of Stage/Environment Fit." *American Psychologist* 48 (1993):90–101.

Eccles, Jacquelynne, Sarah Lord, Robert Roeser, Bonnie Barber, and Deborah Jozefowicz. "The Association of School Transitions in Early Adolescence with Developmental Trajectories through High School." In John Schulenberg, Jennifer Maggs, and Klaus Hurrelmann eds., *Health Risks and Developmental Transitions during Adolescence*. New York: Cambridge University Press, 1996.

Erikson, Erik. *Childhood and Society*. New York: Norton, 1963.

Harter, Susan. "Causes, Correlates, and the Functional Role of Self-Worth: A Life-Span Perspective." In Robert Sternberg and John Kolligian eds., *Competence Considered*. New Haven, CT: Yale University Press, 1990.

Keating, Daniel. "Adolescent Thinking." In Shirley Feldman and Glen Elliott eds., *At the Threshold: The Developing Adolescent*. Cambridge, MA: Harvard University Press, 1990.

Olweus, Daniel, A. Mattssoon, Daisy Schalling, and Hans Loew. "Circulating Testosterone Levels and Aggression in Adolescent Males: A Causal Analysis." *Psychosomatic Medicine* 50 (1988):261–272.

Piaget, Jean, and Bärbel Inhelder. *Memory and Intelligence*. London: Routledge and Kegan Paul, 1973.

Selman, Robert. *The Growth of Interpersonal Understanding*. New York: Academic Press, 1980.

Siegler, Robert. *Children's Thinking*. Englewood Cliffs, NJ: Prentice Hall, 1986.

Simmons, Roberta, and Dale Blyth. *Moving into Adolescence: The Impact of Pubertal Change and School Context*. Hawthorn, NY: Aldine de Gruyler, 1987.

Stattin, Håkan, and David Magnusson. *Pubertal Maturation in Female Development*. Hillsdale, NJ: Erlbaum, 1990.

Steinberg, Lawrence. "Autonomy, Conflict, and Harmony in the Family Relationship." In Shirley Feldman and Glen Elliott eds., *At the Threshold: The Developing Adolescent*. Cambridge, MA: Harvard University Press, 1990.

Sullivan, Harry. *The Interpersonal Theory of Psychiatry*. New York: Norton, 1953.

Susman, Elizabeth, Gale Inoff-Germain, Edith Nottelmann, D. Lynn Loriaux, C. B. Cutler, and George Chrousos. "Hormones, Emotional Dispositions, and Aggressive Attributes in Young Adolescents." *Child Development* 58 (1987):1114–1134.

U.S. Department of Education, Office of Educational Research and Improvement. *Youth Indicators, 1988*. Washington, DC: U.S. Government Printing Office, 1988.

Wigfield, Allan, Jacquelynne Eccles, and Paul Pintrich. "Development between the Ages of Eleven and Twenty-Five." In David Berliner and Robert Calfee eds., *The Handbook of Educational Psychology*. New York: Macmillan, 1996.

Jacquelynne S. Eccles

ADOPTION

Each year, tens of thousands of children are adopted in the United States. The majority of them are placed in their families through licensed adoption agencies. The remaining children are adopted privately, usually with the assistance of attorneys who serve as intermediaries between birth parents and adoptive parents.

The Changing Nature of Adoption

Although historically adoption typically involved the placement of a healthy, newborn, white infant with a middle class to upper middle class, infertile, white couple, the nature of adoption has changed dramatically. Beginning in the 1950s, the number of healthy, white infants available for adoption began to decline in a striking manner. Whereas approximately 20 percent of infants born to unmarried, white women were relinquished for adoption from the mid-1950s to the early 1970s, by 1995 the corresponding rate was less than 2 percent. In contrast, rates of adoption placement during this same period among African-American and Hispanic women were quite low, ranging from 1.5 percent prior to the 1970s to less than 1 percent in the mid-1990s. The overall decline in the number of infants available for adoption has been linked to several factors, including the legalization of abortion, greater availability of contraception, greater societal acceptance of single parenthood, and increased availability of family support programs.

One significant outcome of the reduced availability of adoptable infants was that many individuals began to consider adoption through private placements, which frequently offered greater hope for finding a baby, rather than through licensed agencies. Today, healthier newborn infants are placed for adoption through independent means than through the adoption agency system. In other cases, prospective adoptive parents began looking beyond the borders of the United States in their effort to adopt children. Beginning after World War II and escalating after the Korean and Vietnam wars, international adoption has become a major source of children for individuals wishing to become adoptive parents. In 2000, for example, U.S. citizens adopted more than 16,000 children from other countries, with the greatest numbers coming from Russia, China, South Korea, eastern Europe, and Central and South America. In many cases, these adoptions involved placements across racial lines. Still other prospective adoptive parents began considering adopting foster children whose history and personal characteristics (e.g., older age at placement, minority racial status, exposure to neglect and/or abuse, chronic medical problems, mental and/or psychological problems) were thought, in the past, to be barriers to adoption. Interest in adopting these so-called special needs children grew with the passage of the Adoption Assistance and Child Welfare Act in 1980 and has continued with the passage of the Adoption and Safe Families Act during the Clinton administration.

There also has been considerable change in the types of individuals who are seeking to become adoptive parents. In the past, most adoptive parents were white, middle class to upper middle class, married, infertile couples, usually in their thirties or forties, and free of any form of disability. Agencies routinely screened out older individuals, unmarried adults, fertile couples, individuals with financial problems, homosexuals, and disabled persons as prospective adoptive parents. Even foster parents were seldom approved for adoption of the children in their care. Since the 1970s, however, adoption agency policy and practice has moved in the direction of screening in many different types of adoption applicants as opposed to screening them out. As a result, many of the restrictive criteria for adoptive parenthood have been eliminated, opening up the possibility of adoption to a much larger segment of the population. Adoption has become a remarkably complex social service practice and a highly diverse form of family life.

Psychological and Social Service Issues in Adoption

A number of psychological and social service issues in adoption have arisen since the 1970s. Some of the more important issues include: (1) the psychological risk associated with adoption, (2) special needs adoption, (3) transracial adoption, and (4) openness in adoption.

Historically, adoption has been viewed as a highly successful societal practice for children whose biological parents could not or would not care for them. Evidence of the benefits of adoption is obvious when comparing the more favorable medical, psychological, social, and educational outcomes for adopted children with the increased problems manifested by those children who grow up in institutional environments, foster care, or neglectful and/or abusive homes. Furthermore, adopted children, on average, also have been shown to fare significantly better than those who come from socioeconomic backgrounds similar to the ones of the adopted children's biological families. Yet despite these benefits, many mental health professionals have expressed concern about possible psychological risk associated with adoption. Although research has documented that the vast majority of adopted children are well within the normal range of psychological and academic adjustment, the data also show that adopted children are more likely than their nonadopted age-mates to be referred for mental health services and to display a variety of diagnosable psychiatric conditions. In most cases, these conditions are associated with one or more of the following problems: inattention, impulsivity, defiance, aggressiveness, attachment difficulties, depression, learning disabilities, and substance abuse. Although numerous theories have been offered to explain the adjustment difficulties of adopted children, a common theme that runs through most of them is the psychological impact of adoption-related loss.

Today, a growing number of children are entering adoptive homes after experiencing life within the foster care system. Typically, they are older at the time of adoption placement and have histories of neglect and/or abuse. Some have significant medical problems. Others manifest serious psychological and learning difficulties. Prior to the early 1980s, these special-needs children were considered unadoptable. As a result, agencies did little to find permanent homes for them. Starting in the early 1980s, however, adoption agencies, guided and supported by federal legislation and financial incentives, became much more successful in placing these children with adoptive families. Although research has shown that special-needs adoptions are associated with less placement stability and greater adjustment problems among family members than are infant adoptions, the more remarkable and encouraging finding is that the vast majority of these placements remain intact and family members report a reasonably high degree of satisfaction with the adoption outcome.

Another area that has received considerable attention in the adoption field is the placement of children across racial lines. Critics of transracial adoption have argued that this practice not only undermines children's self-esteem, racial identity, and emotional stability, but also promotes racial and cultural genocide. In contrast, individuals who support transracial adoption emphasize that children's interests are best served by placing them in a nurturing and stable family as quickly as possible, even if the children are of a different race than the parents, rather than waiting until an in-racial adoptive placement can be achieved. Although research has shown that most children who are placed across racial lines show similar patterns of psychological adjustment as those individuals who are adopted in-racially, questions still remain regarding the long-term impact of transracial adoption, especially in relation to the development of a secure racial identity.

Perhaps the greatest controversy in the adoption field since the 1970s has been the emergence of openness in adoption, including the movement toward unsealing adoption records. With the creation of the adoption agency system in the early part of the twentieth century, emphasis was placed on maintaining confidentiality in the adoption process. Adoption records were sealed by law, and birth parents and adoptive parents were prevented from sharing identifying information with one another. As a result, adopted individuals grew up knowing little about their background, having little or no contact with birth family members, and being prevented from having access to their original birth certificate. In the last three decades of the twentieth century, however, there was a

Since the 1970s, many of the restrictive criteria for adoptive parenthood have been eliminated. As a result, adoption has become a remarkably complex social service practice and a highly diverse form of family life. (AP/Wide World Photos)

substantial shift toward greater openness in adoption. It has since become quite common for birth parents and adoptive parents to create an adoption plan in which the two families share information on an ongoing basis and even have periodic contact with one another. A number of states (e.g., Tennessee, Oregon, Alaska, Kansas) have also passed laws allowing adult adoptees access to their original birth certificate. In addition, a growing number of adult adoptees and birth parents are seeking to make contact with one another. Although critics of openness in adoption have expressed concerns that these types of changes in adoption policy, practice, and law will have dire consequences for birth parents and adoptive parents, as well as for adoptees, research has thus far failed to support these concerns. Still, most social service and mental health professionals do not view either open adoption or the unsealing of adoption records as a panacea for the problems experienced by birth parents, adoptive parents, and adoptees. Rather, the movement toward openness is seen as a way of removing the veil of secrecy that has been associated with adoption for some time, thereby offering all parties a greater sense of personal control over their own lives. It is still too soon to know how these changes will influence the lives of individuals who are touched by adoption.

There is no question that adoption, as a social service practice, has become exceedingly complex. In turn, this complexity has given rise to many controversies among social service and mental health professionals, and has fostered a greater degree of challenge for adoptive family members. Yet for all the changes that emerged in this field in the twentieth century, it is important not to lose sight of one important point: Adoption was created, in part, to provide family permanency for children and to foster their physical, psychological, educational, and spiritual well-being. Although certainly not a perfect system, adoption has been quite successful in achieving these goals.

See also: PARENT-CHILD RELATIONSHIPS; PARENTING

Bibliography

Brodzinsky, David M., Daniel W. Smith, and Anne B. Brodzinsky. *Children's Adjustment to Adoption: Developmental and Clinical Issues.* Thousand Oaks, CA: Sage, 1998.

Brodzinsky, David M., Marshall D. Schechter, and Robin M. Henig. *Being Adopted: The Lifelong Search for Self.* New York: Doubleday, 1992.

Grotevant, Harold D., and Ruth G. McRoy. *Openness in Adoption: Exploring Family Connections.* Thousand Oaks, CA: Sage, 1998.

Melina, Lois R. *Raising the Adopted Child.* New York: HarperCollins, 1998.

Register, Cheri. *Are Those Your Kids? American Families with Children Adopted from Other Countries.* New York: Free Press, 1991.

Reitz, Miriam, and Kenneth W. Watson. *Adoption and the Family System.* New York: Guilford Press, 1992.

Sachdev, Paul. *Unlocking the Adoption Files.* Lexington, MA: Lexington Books, 1989.

Schulman, Irving, guest ed. "Adoption" (special issue). *Future of Children* 3, no. 1 (1993).

David M. Brodzinsky

AFRICAN-AMERICAN CHILDREN

African-American children are individuals under the age of eighteen who include among their ancestors individuals who were forcibly brought from African countries to the Americas as slaves beginning in the early 1600s. In 1998, of the 69.9 million children in the United States, 15 percent were African American. Although the majority of poor children in the United States are of European ancestry, annual rates of poverty among African-American children typically are two to three times that of non-Latino European-American children. In 1997, for example, 37 percent of African-American children lived in families with incomes below the official poverty threshold, compared to 15 percent of European-American children. African-American children also are far more likely than non-Hispanic European-American children to experience long-term poverty. Poverty among non-Hispanic European-American children is primarily a transitory phenomenon. An analysis that focused on children who were between birth and five years of age in 1982 tracked these children over a ten-year period (1982–1991). Although 41 percent of the African-American children never experienced poverty during this period, 43 percent were poor for at least three of the ten years, 28 percent were poor for six or more years, and 17 percent were poor for at least nine years. The comparable figures for non-African-American children were 79 percent, 9 percent, 3 percent, and 1 percent, respectively (U.S. Department of Health and Human Services 1999). These racial disparities are alarming because it is well established that experiencing poverty year after year has more detrimental effects on cognitive development, school achievement, and socioemotional functioning than experiencing poverty occasionally (Duncan and Brooks-Gunn 1997).

Equally as striking are racial differences in net financial assets (readily liquid sources of wealth that can be used for a family's immediate needs and desires such as savings accounts, stocks, and bonds) within households at similar income levels. In the late 1980s, African Americans in high-income households (over $50,000) possessed only 23 cents of median net financial assets for every dollar of assets held by European Americans. African-American children are further disadvantaged because they are more likely to live in poor, isolated urban ghettos than European Americans of similar economic status. On average, these communities have fewer social, educational, and occupational resources that enhance children's development (e.g., high quality child care), and in many cases are plagued by high rates of crime and violence related to gang- and drug-related activities. Even when African Americans escape poverty at the family level, they have a 50 percent chance of encountering it in their neighborhoods. The social, educational, and economic resources of neighborhoods can influence children in a multitude of developmental areas. For example, children who grow up in affluent neighborhoods or neighborhoods with a higher percentage of affluent families have higher cognitive functioning, complete more years of school, and have lower school dropout rates than children from economically similar families who grow up in poor neighborhoods or neighborhoods with proportionately fewer affluent families.

Family Structure

In 1998, 51 percent of African-American children lived in mother-only families, compared to 18 percent of European-American children. Two primary events result in female-headed households, namely, births to unmarried women and marital dissolution, and both are more common among African Americans than European Americans. This is partly a consequence of the unfavorable economic status of African-American men relative to European-American men, which reduces their eligibility as desirable mates. African-American men who are stably employed have higher marriage rates and lower rates of divorce and separation than those who are unemployed or have only minimal or unstable attachment to the labor force. Employment factors, however, represent only one set of factors that influence rates of marriage, divorce, and separation among African Americans. Following divorce and separation, African-American children are more likely to fall into poverty than are European-American children because they were less well-off to begin with. In addition, African-American children spend more time than European-American children in a mother-headed family before making the transition to a two-parent family and are far more likely than European-American children to remain in a mother-headed family for the duration of childhood. All of these factors contribute to race differences in long-term childhood poverty.

Nevertheless, the difference in family structure is not the sole factor responsible for the increased prevalence of poverty among African-American children. The expected prevalence of poverty among African-American children living in two-parent families throughout childhood is roughly the same as the expected prevalence among European-American children who spend their entire childhood living in single-parent families. These race differences are fundamentally rooted in structural forces—traceable to longstanding racial discrimination in employment, education, mortgage lending, and housing—that have produced layers of accumulated disadvantages. Racial discrimination is not only individual-level behavior based on negative racial prejudice. It is also a "system of advantage based on race" sustained by institutional practices and policies. It also encompasses behavior intended to maintain racial advantage even though actors may not overtly embrace prejudicial thinking (Tatum 1997).

Academic, Cognitive, and Physical Well-Being

At all levels of family income, African-American children receive lower scores on subtests of IQ tests and on reading and writing achievement tests than European-American children. Several factors contribute to these differences, including cultural bias in IQ tests and differences in school quality, teacher expectancy, the home learning environment, and economic resources not reflected in current income. Racial disparity in children's early physical health status also may be a factor. African-American children, compared to European-American children, have higher rates of iron deficiency anemia, elevated blood lead, and low birthweight (less than or equal to 2,500 grams (5 pounds, 8 ounces) at birth). Racial disparities in anemia and elevated blood lead exist at all income levels but are especially significant among children who are poor.

The adverse effects of these physical health conditions on children's development are well documented. Iron-deficiency anemia in infancy adversely affects brain development partly by affecting the neurotransmitter function and myelin formation; it is consistently associated with poorer scores on cognitive and motor functioning. Children with elevated blood lead levels, compared to those with lower lead burdens, have slightly decreased scores on measures of intelligence, poorer school performance and achievement test scores, shorter attention spans, and increased impulsiveness. Although the vast majority of low birthweight children have normal outcomes, as a group they have more problems in cognition, attention, and neuromotor functioning during middle childhood and adolescence.

Elevated levels of lead in the blood is more prevalent among African-American children because poverty and housing discrimination have relegated African-American families in disproportionate numbers to poor, older, urban neighborhoods. Housing units in these neighborhoods often contain deteriorating lead-based paint and lead-contaminated dust. In addition, these neighborhoods tend to be near industrial areas, which increases exposure to lead gasoline. It remains a puzzle why low birthweight births are more common among African Americans than among any other ethnic group, regardless of the mother's educational level (an indicator of socioeconomic status). Higher teen pregnancy rates among African Americans do not explain this race differential and genetic hypotheses have been discounted (McLoyd and Lozoff 2001).

Socioemotional Well-Being

The self-esteem of African-American children and adolescents is reported to be equal to and oftentimes higher than that of European-American children and adolescents. During the grade school years,

African-American children, compared to European-American children, report more positive attitudes about school and homework, perceive themselves to be more competent in reading and mathematics, hold higher expectations about their future performance in reading and mathematics courses, and are more optimistic that they will attend college. These differential expectations are at odds with racial differences in children's actual performance on school achievement tests and national statistics on rates of high school completion and college attendance, suggesting perhaps that some African-American children do not receive or have not incorporated feedback about their performance in school. These findings also raise questions about why young African-American children's greater fondness for school and higher educational expectations do not translate into higher levels of academic performance and educational attainment. Notwithstanding comparatively high educational expectations, as early as second grade, African-American boys residing in inner city neighborhoods have lower occupational aspirations and expectations than middle class European-American boys, with the gap between aspirations and expectations being larger for the inner-city boys than the other boys. Both groups of boys become more realistic about occupational aspirations and expectations the older they are. For example, the percentage who aspire and expect to be professional athletes decreases with age.

Evidence concerning race differences in rates of depression is mixed, with some studies reporting higher rates among African Americans, others reporting higher rates among European Americans, and still others reporting no racial differences. African-American adolescents, however, have long had substantially lower suicide rates than European-American adolescents. It is thought that suicidal behavior is inhibited among African Americans by extended social support networks that serve as buffers against stressors and by cultural values that proscribe suicide. The racial gap in the adolescent suicide rate has narrowed in recent years, especially among males. Scholars have speculated that the increases in suicide among African-American adolescents are due to African Americans' rise to middle class status and its attendant splintering of community and family support networks, weakening of bonds to religion, and psychological distress resulting from efforts to compete in historically European-American-dominated social circles. Others have suggested that with greater assimilation and contact with European Americans, African-American adolescents increasingly adopt or model European-American adolescents' strategies for coping with depression and other forms of psychological distress. None of these hypotheses has been adequately tested.

African-American male adolescents are more likely than their European-American counterparts to be labeled conduct disordered or antisocial; to be disciplined, suspended, or expelled from junior high and high school; and to be arrested and incarcerated. Some of these differences appear to reflect racial bias resulting in more harsh treatment of African-American adolescents for comparable offenses. Generally, studies of self-reported delinquency find no race differences. For several decades, however, the rate of death from homicide has been higher for African-American male adolescents than European-American adolescents. In annual national surveys conducted since the early 1980s, African-American adolescents, compared to European-American and Hispanic adolescents, consistently reported the lowest level of marijuana use, the lowest prevalence of alcohol use and binge drinking, and the lowest level of cigarette smoking. School-based surveys probably underestimate drug use by African-American and Hispanic youth because of higher dropout rates among these two groups, compared to European-American youth. Nevertheless, this does not fully account for the racial and ethnic disparities. There is some support for the claim that African-American adolescents are less likely to use drugs because they have less exposure to peer and adult drug users and are more religious.

Sources of Strength and Buffers of Race-Related Stressors

Religion and Church Membership

Religion has been theorized to be an adaptive coping mechanism that has enabled African Americans to transcend the limitations and harshness of their social realities and to give meaning and direction to their individual and collective existence. During the 1980s, nearly 70 percent of African Americans reported themselves to be members of a church. Churches provide informal support (e.g., friendship, companionship, advice and comfort, help during illness, financial assistance), formal services (e.g., meals on wheels, transportation, group outings and vacations, ministerial counseling), and moral guidance. Religiosity and church membership enhance self-esteem partly as a consequence of the perception that one is held in high regard by other believers and by an omnipotent divine other who makes his/her presence felt in one's life. Religiosity also buffers the negative psychological effects of stress. Having a mother who seeks spiritual support is one of several factors that distinguishes African-American children who are stress resilient from those who are stress impaired.

Extended Family Relations and Social Support Networks

African Americans are more likely to reside in extended family households than are European Americans. Extended families are close kin relations within and across generations whose members are intensely involved in the reciprocal exchange of goods, services, and ongoing emotional support. As such, they are problem-solving and stress-coping systems. Typically, involvement with extended family is beneficial to young children and adolescents, partly because of increased support, monitoring, and supervision. African-American adolescents whose single parent is involved in extended family activities report fewer problem behaviors.

African-American and Latino adolescent mothers who report higher levels of grandmother support have fewer psychological problems, more positive interactions with their babies, and higher levels of educational attainment. Nevertheless, the impact of grandmother involvement, especially when mother and grandmother are co-residing and/or co-parenting, is not uniformly positive. Researchers do not yet have a good understanding of what circumstances render different types of support from grandmothers helpful versus detrimental or inert. In general, though, parents' support networks reduce emotional strain; lessen the tendency toward punitive, coercive, and inconsistent parenting; and in turn, foster socioemotional development in children.

Racial Socialization

Given the especially virulent and egregious discrimination that African Americans have historically faced and continue to experience, it is not surprising that African-American parents generally provide more extensive racial and ethnic socialization than other parents of color who have been studied. For example, African-American parents are more likely to report talking with their adolescent children about racial and ethnic prejudice as a problem and how to handle it than are Mexican-American parents, who, in turn, are more likely to talk about these issues than are Japanese-American parents.

African-American parents convey messages about children's cultural heritage and the importance of racial pride more frequently than messages about racial discrimination and how to cope with it. Messages intended to promote racial mistrust are a comparatively minor, if not rare, element of racial socialization among African-American parents. It is not yet clear whether racial socialization consistently influences African-American children's racial identity, school achievement, or ability to deal with racial stereotyping and discrimination. There is evidence from studies of African-American adults, however, that both racial socialization and group identity (i.e., feelings of closeness in ideas and affect to one's self-identified racial group; race-linked self-image) protect physical/mental health in the face of perceived racial discrimination and unfair treatment.

Responsive Discipline

Urban African-American and European-American parents modify their strategies for managing their children's lives and behavior in accordance with the risks and opportunities afforded by neighborhood conditions (e.g., resources, level of crime). This responsiveness has positive effects on children's development. For example, parenting characterized by a combination of restrictiveness, extensive rule setting, and warmth appears to be especially beneficial to the cognitive and socioemotional functioning of African-American children living in high-risk, crime-laden neighborhoods. This parenting style shields children from noxious elements and bestows them with a positive self-concept that helps deflect negative influences in their extrafamilial environment.

African Americans are more likely to view physical discipline short of abuse as an appropriate display of positive parenting than are European Americans. African-American mothers consistently report higher frequencies of spanking than European-American mothers, even when socioeconomic status is taken into account (McLoyd, Cauce, Takeuchi, and Wilson 2000). Cultural variation in the acceptability, meaning, and parental attributes associated with spanking also may be the reason that parents' use of physical discipline predicts higher levels of behavior problems among European-American children, but does not among African-American children. That is, because of its commonplaceness in African-American culture, spanking may coexist with high levels of warmth to a greater extent in African-American households than in European-American households. African-American parents also may be less likely to administer spanking in an impulsive or excessively harsh, punitive manner. There is some preliminary support for these claims, but more rigorous evaluation of them is needed. In any case, existing research underscores how critically important it is that parental strictness not be equated with punitiveness and a cold emotional style. The latter qualities are risk factors for behavioral problems in children as indicated by evidence that mothers of stress-resilient African-American children (those exposed to high stress burdens, but who show no clinically significant behavior problems) are less rejecting and aggressive than mothers of stress-impaired African-American children (those exposed to high stress burdens who show clinically significant behavior problems).

See also: RACIAL DIFFERENCES

Bibliography

Duncan, Greg J., and Jeanne Brooks-Gunn, eds. *Consequences of Growing Up Poor.* New York: Russell Sage Foundation. 1997.

McLoyd, Vonnie C., A. M. Cauce, D. Takeuchi, and L. Wilson, "Marital Processes and Parental Socialization in Families of Color: A Decade Review of Research." *Journal of Marriage and the Family* 62 (2000): 1070-1093.

McLoyd, Vonnie C., and Bo Lozoff. "Racial and Ethnic Trends in Children's Behavior and Development." In Neil J. Smelser, William Julius Wilson, and Faith Mitchell eds., *America Becoming: Racial Trends and Their Consequences.* Washington, DC: National Academy Press, 2001.

Tatum, Beverly Daniel. *Why Are All the Black Kids Sitting Together in the Cafeteria? And Other Conversations About Race.* New York: Basic Books, 1997.

U.S. Department of Health and Human Services. *Trends in the Well-Being of America's Children and Youth.* Washington, DC: Child Trends, 1999.

Vonnie C. McLoyd
Algea O. Harrison-Hale

AFTER-SCHOOL PROGRAMS

For a variety of social and economic reasons, after-school programs are greatly needed for school-age children. Approximately 28 million children have parents who work outside the home, and most children return to an empty home after school. Studies indicate that parents find the need for these programs outweighs the current supply. Furthermore, parents support after-school programs in order to provide fun and enriching learning opportunities and activities that are typically viewed as more valuable than watching television or playing computer games.

After-school programs help children in several ways. First, they can keep children safe and out of trouble in a structured environment. Second, they can improve academic performance. Third, after-school programs can raise children's social skills and self-confidence. The goals of most after-school programs generally include: reducing the numbers of latchkey children, providing homework and school support, providing cultural enrichment, providing physical recreation, teaching self-care skills, and broadening community support and ties to the schools.

See also: HOME SCHOOLING; LATCHKEY CHILDREN; WORKING FAMILIES

Bibliography

Chung, A. *After-School Programs: Keeping Children Safe and Smart.* Partnership for Family Involvement in Education, 2000.

Popwell, E. P. *The After-School Program for School-Age Children. A Descriptive Report,* vol. 13, no. 25, 1991.

David Peres

AGGRESSION

Aggression in humans remains a substantial social problem. A number of theories have been constructed to explain aggression, and much research has focused on factors that affect aggressive behavior.

In the ethological approach, aggression is viewed as an instinctual system built into the organism independently of external stimuli. This aggression must be released through an appropriate releasing stimulus. The most influential instinctual theory is the concept of thanatos proposed by Austrian neurologist Sigmund Freud (1856–1939). He theorized that two instinctual drives, eros (love instinct) and thanatos (death instinct), motivate human behavior. Thanatos manifests itself as aggressive behavior in daily living.

The other main theory comes from social learning and focuses on environmental influences. Albert Bandura focused on modeling processes that shape aggressive behavior and direct feedback in the form of reward and punishment. From social cognitive theorists comes the assumption that the social interpretation about which interpersonal behaviors constitute aggressive provocational retaliation is crucial for determining whether children will behave aggressively or not.

Definition

Aggression is defined as behavior aimed at causing harm or pain, psychological harm, or personal injury or physical distraction. An important aspect of aggressive behavior is the intention underlying the actor's behavior. Not all behaviors resulting in harm are considered aggression. For example, a doctor who makes an injection that harms people, but who did so with the intent of preventing the further spread of illness, is not considered to have committed an aggressive act.

Aggression can be direct or indirect, active or passive, and physical or verbal. Using these categories, human aggression can be grouped into eight classes of behavior:

- Punching the victim (direct, active, physical)
- Insulting the victim (direct, active, verbal)
- Performing a practical joke, setting a booby trap (direct, passive, physical)
- Spreading malicious gossip (direct, passive, verbal)
- Obstructing passage, participating in a sit-in (indirect, active, physical)
- Refusing to speak (indirect, active, verbal)
- Refusing to perform a necessary task (indirect, passive, physical)

Direct aggression, especially physically active aggression, is more common among animals. Actors who express indirect aggression usually feel less satisfaction, but they are also less concerned about retaliation. Passive and indirect aggression is the least noxious form. Subordinates rebelling against authority figures often use it. In the family relation it is often used by children against their parents.

The Role of Biological Factors

Some theorists argue that the foundations of aggression are biological. Biological factors that influence aggressive behavior include hormones, physiological illness, and temperament.

Hormones play some indirect role in human aggression. Interaction with external stimuli may affect the threshold of aggressive behavior. Some researchers have concluded that high testosterone levels could be a result of aggressive behavior. In women, premenstrual tension syndrome is associated with a number of aggressive behaviors, such as violent crime.

People with a serious physiological illness, such as cancer, may be affected by negative mood states. These mood states may indirectly affect the aggressive behavior of individuals.

Temperament may be indirectly related to aggressive behavior. People who are impulsive are more likely to be aggressive than people who have a deliberate temperament.

Relationship to Rearing Practices

Although human aggression may have an instinctual component, aggression is modifiable by environmental factors, such as child-rearing practices and parental characteristics.

Aggressive children often develop in families with a low degree of positive interactions and a high degree of punitive reciprocity. Children in such families learn to control other family members through aggression. This model of control behavior in the home is then generalized to peers. This process thus creates aggressive children.

Research focused on parental characteristics found that mothers of nonaggressive girls tended to use the strategy of discussion to solve social problems more often than mothers of aggressive girls. Fathers of nonaggressive girls had more alternative strategies for solving social problems than fathers of aggressive girls.

Influence of Television and Other Media

Of the several different forms of media, television is one of the most influential in terms of child development. The effects of seeing violence on television has been debated among the scientists interested in child development. The main reason why watching violence on television causes violence in real world is the pervasiveness of violent programs.

There are several ways of explaining how the viewing of violence on television affects aggression in young people, including the direct effect, desensitization, and the so-called mean world syndrome. Aggression and favorable attitudes toward the use of aggression will develop if people watch a lot of violence on television. This direct effect has been a focus of research. Ross Parke and his colleagues, working in a natural setting, found that boys who viewed aggressive movies displayed an increased amount of physical and verbal aggression against other children.

According to desensitization theory, people who watch a lot of violence on television may become less sensitive to the various kinds of aggression and violence in the real world.

A third explanation for the link between television and aggression holds that some people suffer from the mean world syndrome, in which they believe that the world is as dangerous as it appears on television.

The effect of television violence on children has been debated. It is important to note that psychologists and psychiatrists involved in media studies do not suggest that violent media are the only causes of violence in society.

The Effectiveness of Intervention to Reduce Aggression

A variety of ways of handling aggression have been suggested over the years. One aspect of social learning that tends to inhibit aggression is the tendency of most people to take responsibility for their own actions. But if this sense of responsibility is weakened, the tendency to act more aggressively will increase. (In one experiment, a researcher demonstrated that persons who are anonymous and unidentifiable tend to act more aggressively than persons who are not anonymous.)

There are a number of ways that an individual can reduce aggression. As long as there is a hope that is unsatisfied, there will be frustration that can result in aggression. Aggression can be reduced by satisfying that hope.

Doing something physically exerting or watching someone else engage in aggression directly or indirectly tends to relieve built-up aggressive energies and hence reduce the likelihood of further of aggressive behavior. This is called catharsis. The catharsis

Aggressive play, like wrestling, can lead to aggressive behavior as children get older. (Nick Kelsh/Corbis)

hypothesis also holds that watching an aggressive behavior on television serves a valuable function in draining off aggressive energy.

It has been argued that it might be possible to reduce aggression by presenting the child with the sight of aggressive models who come to bad ends. The implicit theory is that individuals who are exposed to this sight will in effect be vicariously punished for their own aggression and accordingly will become less aggressive.

Other methods of reducing aggression that have been proposed include defusing anger through apology and providing training in communication and problem-solving skills.

Using punishment to reduce aggressive behavior is tricky. It can be effective if it is not too severe and if it follows closely on the heels of the aggressive act.

Anger Management Programs

In 1997 Albert Ellis and Raymond Chip Tafrate presented an approach to the problem of dealing with anger called rational emotive behavior therapy (REBT). This approach was designed to help people deal effectively with emotional problems and to systematically understand the roots and nature of anger. REBT deals with the problem of anger realistically. The core of REBT is unconditional acceptance of self and then continually maintaining this feeling of self-acceptance.

The Role That Peers Play

Children generally establish strong, stable, mutual affiliations with peers similar to themselves in aggression, but aggressive children have more difficulty establishing such affiliations. The interaction of peer pairs containing at least one aggressive child was characterized by more frequent, lengthy, and intense conflict regardless of the affiliate relationship characterizing the pair. Researchers found that the amount of time children spent interacting with aggressive peers predicted changes in observed and teacher-rated aggression three months later.

Peer estimation of aggression was found to be internally more consistent than self-estimation. This was true of both sexes for both the aggressive and victim version of the test. Participants seem to be more reliable when they estimate the degree to which they are the victims of others' aggression than when they estimate the degree to which they themselves are aggressive. This is particularly true for girls.

Influences of Socialization

Although growing up in a violent community is associated with aggressive behavior, the degree to which this can be considered seriously pathological has been called into question by the results of some research.

See also: ANGER; VIOLENCE

Bibliography

Aronson, E., T. D. Wilson, and R. M. Akert. *Social Psychology.* New York: Longman, 1997.

Baron R. A., and D. Byrne. *Social Psychology: Understanding Human Interaction,* 5th edition. Newton, MA: Allyn and Bacon, 1987.

Betsch, T., and D. Dickenberger. "Why Do Aggressive Movies Make People Aggressive? An Attempt to Explain Short-Term Effects of the Depiction of Violence on the Observer." *Aggressive Behavior* 19 (1993):137–149.

Buss, A. *Psychology: Man in Perspective.* New York: Wiley, 1973.

Dollard, John, L. W. Doof, N. E. Miller, O. H. Mowrer, and R. R. Sears. *Frustration and Aggression.* Westport, CT: Greenwood Press, 1980.

Ellis, Albert, and Raymond Chip Tafrate. *How to Control Your Anger Before It Controls You.* Toronto: Carol Publishing, 1997.

Groves, P. M., and G. V. Rebeck. *Introduction to Biological Psychology,* 4th edition. Dubuque, IA: William C. Brown, 1992.

Österman, K., K. Björkqvist, K. M. J. Lagerspetz, A. Kaukianen, L. R. Huesmann, and A. Fraczek. "Peer and Self-Estimated Aggression and Victimization in Eight-Year-Old Children from Five Ethnic Groups." *Aggressive Behavior* 20 (1994):411–428.

Pakaslahti, L., I. Spoof, R. L. Asplund-Peltola, and L. Keltikangas-Jaarvinen. "Parent's Social Problem Solving Strategies in Families with Aggressive and Non-Aggressive Girls." *Aggressive Behavior* 34 (1998):37–51.

Snyder, J., E. Horsh, and J. Childs. "Peer Relationships of Young Children: Affiliative Choices and the Shaping of Aggressive Behavior." *Journal of Clinical Psychology* 26, no. 2 (1997):145–155.

Maria Adiyanti

AINSWORTH, MARY DINSMORE SALTER (1913–1999)

Mary Dinsmore Salter was born on December 1, 1913, in Glendale, Ohio, the oldest daughter of Charles and Mary Salter. Charles, a successful businessman, moved his family to Toronto at the end of World War I. Their daughter Mary was a gifted child who learned to read at the age of three, and was very attached to her father. During her undergraduate years at the University of Toronto, William Blatz, who had developed "security theory," sparked Salter's interest in psychology. According to this theory, the family is the secure base from which a developing individual can move out to develop new skills and interests. Salter's dissertation, entitled "An Evaluation of Adjustment Based on the Concept of Security," was completed in 1939.

After teaching briefly at the University of Toronto, Salter felt an increasing obligation to contribute to the war effort. She entered the Canadian Women's Army Corps in 1942, attaining the rank of major. In this position, she gained considerable clinical and diagnostic skills. After returning to the University of Toronto as assistant professor in 1946, she co-authored a widely used clinical book, *Developments in the Rorschach Technique,* with Bruno Klopfer.

In 1950 Salter married Leonard Ainsworth, a World War II veteran and graduate student in psychology at Toronto. Both went to London, where Leonard completed his doctoral studies and Mary applied for a research position on John Bowlby's team at the Tavistock Institute for Human Relations. She was offered the position, and her collaboration with Bowlby changed the direction of her career.

Bowlby, together with his collaborator James Robertson, had begun to conduct observational studies of the devastating effects of prolonged separation from the mother on young children who were hospitalized or living in residential nurseries. Robertson's observational methods, acquired while working at Anna Freud's wartime residential nursery, impressed Ainsworth particularly and inspired her later naturalistic studies. At the same time, she was exposed to Bowlby's emerging ideas about the evolutionary foundation of infant-mother attachment, but despite her love for ethology, she did not initially find Bowlby's new propositions particularly convincing. Like most others at the time, she believed that babies came to love their mothers because mothers satisfy babies' needs.

In 1953 Ainsworth's husband accepted a postdoctoral position at the East African Institute for Social Research in Kampala, Uganda. Mary accompanied him and was able to garner funds for a short-term longitudinal study of twenty-six Ganda village families with young infants. It was during her observations of these families that Bowlby's ethological notions began to make sense to her. Thus, the first attachment study was undertaken before Bowlby formally presented attachment theory in 1958. The book, *Infancy in Uganda,* which contains detailed case studies of every

Mary Dinsmore Salter Ainsworth's conceptual contributions and empirical findings revolutionized how psychologists think about infant-caregiver attachment. (R. S. Marvin)

infant-mother pair, was published many years later, in 1967.

In 1954 the Ainsworths moved to Baltimore, Maryland. For a few years, Mary lectured part-time and worked at a psychiatric hospital. It was only in 1958 that Johns Hopkins University offered her a professorship in developmental psychology. During this period, she and Leonard divorced.

The position at Johns Hopkins enabled her to launch a groundbreaking sequel to the Ganda Study. The Baltimore Project was based on monthly home observations of twenty-six families. Home visits began shortly after an infant's birth and were recorded as detailed narratives. The last observation, at twelve months, consisted of a laboratory procedure of mother-infant separations and reunions, devised with Barbara Wittig, and now known as the Strange Situation. The Strange Situation revealed important individual differences in patterns of attachment that were correlated with home observation findings. For this reason, it became tremendously important as a shortcut method of assessing the quality of infant-parent attachment. However, Ainsworth occasionally expressed regret that the Strange Situation stole the limelight from her highly original analyses of feeding, close bodily contact, face-to-face play, and crying observed in the home. These documented that maternal sensitivity to infant signals in the early months leads to a more harmonious mother-infant relationship at the end of the first year. Several influential journal articles and a book, *Patterns of Attachment*, were published over the next decade or so.

From the mid-1960s onwards, Ainsworth attracted many graduate students who made further contributions to attachment theory and research (e.g., Silvia Bell, Mary Blehar, Inge Bretherton, Alicia Lieberman, Mary Main, Sally Wall). Her stimulating lectures influenced undergraduates such as Mark Cummings, Mark Greenberg, Robert Marvin, and Everett Waters, who, as graduate students, took attachment theory to other universities.

When Ainsworth accepted a position at the University of Virginia in 1974, her work was becoming increasingly influential, stimulating longitudinal studies of attachment in the United States and other countries that are still ongoing. In the late 1970s she was elected president of the Society for Research in Child Development. At the same time, many graduate students interested in attachment continued to flock to her (among them Jude Cassidy, Deborah Cohn, Virginia Colin, Patricia Crittenden, Carolyn Eichberg, Rogers Kobak, and Ulrike Wartner). After reluctantly retiring as Professor Emerita in 1984 at the required age of seventy, Ainsworth remained professionally active until 1992. In her later years, until her health began to fail, she retained a deep interest in the work of her former students who had begun to study attachment beyond infancy. A year before her death, she received one of the highest honors psychology can bestow, the Gold Medal Award for Life Achievement in the Science of Psychology from the American Psychological Association. She died of a massive stroke on March 21, 1999, in Charlottesville, Virginia. Her conceptual contributions and empirical findings have revolutionized how psychologists think about infant-caregiver attachment and close human relationships at all ages.

See also: ATTACHMENT; PARENT-CHILD RELATIONSHIPS

Bibliography

Bretherton, Inge. "The Origins of Attachment Theory: John Bowlby and Mary Ainsworth." *Developmental Psychology* 28 (1992):759–775.

Karen, Robert. *Becoming Attached: First Relationships and How They Shape Our Capacity to Love.* New York: Oxford University Press, 1998.

Publications by Ainsworth

Infancy in Uganda: Infant Care and the Growth of Love. Baltimore, MD: Johns Hopkins University Press, 1967.

Ainsworth, Mary D. S., Mary C. Blehar, Everett Waters, and Sally Wall. *Patterns of Attachment: A Psychological Study of the Strange Situation.* Hillsdale, NJ: Lawrence Erlbaum, 1978.

Ainsworth, Mary D. S., Silvia Bell, and D. Stayton. "Intant-Mother Attachment and Social Development." In M. P. Richards ed., *The Introduction of the Child into a Social World.* London: Cambridge University Press, 1974.

"Attachments Beyond Infancy." *American Psychologist* 44 (1989):709–716.

Bell, Silvia M., and Mary D. S. Ainsworth. "Infant Crying and Maternal Responsiveness." *Child Development* 43 (1972):1171–1190.

Inge Bretherton

ALTRUISM

Altruism is unselfish behavior designed to promote others' welfare regardless of harm to self. For example, non-Jewish rescuers of Jews during the Holocaust of World War II behaved altruistically. While prosocial behavior balances own and others' needs, and martyrdom risks death in support of a cause, altruism serves others without expectation of recognition. Altruism requires awareness of one's own needs, empathetic understanding of others' emotions, and action consistent with personal moral standards. At best, children discern their emotions by age three, empathize with others' feelings by age six, understand social interactions simultaneously from their own and others' perspectives by age ten, and base their moral standards on principles they have evaluated rather than on authority by late adolescence. Experiences with parents, siblings, peers, and authority figures who demonstrate, discuss, and reward self-awareness, empathy, and moral reasoning are essential for the development of a sense of altruism. Parents, in particular, stimulate the growth of altruistic behavior by considering their children's needs before their own.

See also: PERSONALITY DEVELOPMENT

Bibliography

Blechman, Elaine A., Jean E. Dumas, and Ronald J. Prinz. "Prosocial Coping by Youth Exposed to Violence." *Journal of Child and Adolescent Group Therapy* 4 (1994):205–227.

Blechman, Elaine A., Ronald J. Prinz, and Jean E. Dumas. "Coping, Competence, and Aggression Prevention. Part 1: Developmental Model." *Applied and Preventive Psychology* 4 (1995):211–232.

Prinz, Ronald J., Elaine A. Blechman, and Jean E. Dumas. "An Evaluation of Peer Coping Skills Training for Childhood Aggression." *Journal of Clinical Child Psychology* 23 (1994):193–203.

Elaine A. Blechman

AMERICAN SIGN LANGUAGE

American Sign Language (ASL) is a manual language that involves the use of hand configurations, facial gestures, body posture, range, direction, and movement in space to exchange meaning between people. This language is primarily used by persons who are deaf and do not use speech to communicate. Once thought of as only "pictures in the air," ASL is recognized as a true language with elaborate linguistic rules.

ASL is used with young children who are deaf as a means of facilitating the natural acquisition of language. When born into families that use sign language to communicate, deaf babies are know to "babble" with their hands in a similar manner as hearing children babble with early sounds. In the presence of fluent users of ASL, deaf children acquire sign as quickly and easily as hearing children acquire speech. English is typically taught as a second language to promote literacy.

Bibliography

Hall, Barbara J., Herbert J. Oyer, and William H. Haas. *Speech, Language and Hearing Disorders: A Guide for the Teacher.* Boston: Allyn and Bacon, 2001.

Padden, Carol, and Tom Humphries. *Deaf in America: Voices from a Culture.* Cambridge, MA: Harvard University Press, 1988.

Paul, Peter V. *Literacy and Deafness: The Development of Reading, Writing, and Literate Thought.* Boston: Allyn and Bacon, 1998.

Paul, Peter V., and Stephen P. Quigley. *Language and Deafness,* 2nd edition. San Diego, CA: Singular Publishing Group, 1994.

Sacks, Oliver. *Seeing Voices.* Berkeley: University of California Press, 1988.

Schirmer, Barbara R. *Language and Literacy Development in Children Who Are Deaf.* Boston: Allyn and Bacon, 2000.

Donna J. Crowley

AMNIOCENTESIS

Amniocentesis is a prenatal diagnostic test in which amniotic fluid is extracted via a long thin needle inserted through the maternal abdomen into the uterus and the amniotic sac. The procedure is usually performed between the fifteenth and eighteenth week of gestation and results can be obtained nine to fourteen days later. Some major medical centers now use a procedure called Fluorescence In Situ Hybridization (FISH) to obtain results within twenty-four hours. It is recommended for women over age thirty-five and those having risk factors for genetic abnormalities. Amniocentesis is a reliable (95% accuracy rate) indicator of chromosomal abnormalities such as Down syndrome, or genetic disorders such as Tay Sachs disease, Hunter's syndrome, or neural tube abnormalities such as spina bifida and others. While usually safe, amniocentesis can trigger cramping, leakage of amniotic fluid, vaginal bleeding, and it may increase the risk of miscarriage by about .5 to 1 percent.

See also: BIRTH; PRENATAL DEVELOPMENT; ULTRASOUND

Bibliography

"Amniocentesis: Indications for Amniocentesis." Available from http://www.stanford.edu/üholbrook/Amniocentesis.html; IN-TERNET.

Epstein, R. H. "Great News about Prenatal Testing." *Parents* 73, no. 6 (2000).

Heller, L. "Genetic Testing." *Parents* 70 (1995):96.

Williams, R. D. "Testing for Birth Defects." *FDA Consumer* 33, no. 2 (2000):22.

Yvonne M. Caldera

ANDROGYNY

Historically, psychologists have viewed femininity and masculinity as opposite poles of a continuum. The more feminine a person was, the less masculine that person could be. In the late 1990s, psychologists, including Sandra Bem, have asserted that femininity and masculinity are independent personality dimensions. Individuals, female or male, who exhibit high levels of both feminine and masculine personality traits are said to demonstrate androgyny. People who have many masculine but few feminine traits are termed masculine; those with many feminine but few masculine characteristics are feminine. People who show few masculine and feminine traits are designated as undifferentiated. Numerous studies indicate that androgynous persons are better adjusted psychologically, more popular, and have higher self-esteem than are masculine, feminine, or undifferentiated persons. In other research, individuals high in masculinity appear as well off as androgynous persons. These results suggest that it is the masculine component of androgyny (e.g., independence, confidence, self-reliance) that is most strongly associated with psychological well-being.

See also: GENDER-ROLE DEVELOPMENT

Bibliography

Bem, Sandra. "The Measurement of Psychological Androgyny." *Journal of Consulting and Clinical Psychology* 42 (1974):155–162.

Claire Etaugh

ANGER

Anger is the experience of extreme displeasure. It is a basic emotion that first appears when infants are three to four months old. Anger among infants is characterized by a facial expression involving eyebrows that are lowered and drawn together, eyes that are narrowed, and a mouth that is opened and angular. Angry infants also engage in an angry cry in which excess air is forced through the vocal cords. Anger during early infancy occurs when parents fail to meet infants' needs. Parents who are inconsistent in responding to infants foster feelings of infant anger. Developmentalists tend to agree that parents should quickly and consistently respond to infant cries, and that an infant cannot be spoiled during the first year of life. In fact, quick, consistent response to infant distress (regardless of whether the distress is due to a physiological status or being unable to exert control over an object or event) facilitates a secure parent-infant attachment. Securely attached infants are more likely to develop skillful emotional self-regulatory behavior because they have been taught that their negative emotions will be soothed (Cassidy and Berlin, 1994).

During the toddler period, anger arises from frustration over children's unsuccessful attempts to control objects or events. Emotional regulation first begins in toddlerhood and involves the suppression or appropriate expression of anger. There are three ways that parents can influence children's development of emotional anger regulation. First, parents cause frustration by barring children's control over objects or events, which leads to children's feelings and expression of anger. Second, parents model expressions of anger and its management. Third, parents directly instruct children in how to recognize when and why they feel angry and offer ways to cope with anger. Effective regulation of anger, or anger management, is related to children's positive relationships with peers throughout childhood and adolescence. Ineffective regulation of anger may result in poor peer relationships, behavior problems, bullying, and deviancy throughout childhood and adolescence. Children who are ineffective at regulating anger may benefit from training in anger management.

See also: ACTING OUT; EMOTIONAL DEVELOPMENT

Bibliography

Cassidy, Jude, and Lisa Berline. "The Insecure/Ambivalent Pattern of Attachment: Theory and Research." *Child Development* 65, no. 4 (1994):971–991.

DeBaryshe, Barbara, and Dale Fryxell. "A Developmental Perspective on Anger: Family and Peer Contexts." *Psychology in the Schools* 35, no. 3 (1998):205–216.

Izzard, Carroll, Christina Fantauzzo, Janine Castle, et al. "The Ontogeny and Significance of Infants' Facial Expressions in the First Nine Months of Life." *Developmental Psychology* 31, no. 6 (1995):997–1013.

Zeman, Janice, and Kimberly Shipman. "Social-Contextual Influences on Expectancies for Managing Anger and Sadness: The

Transition from Middle Childhood to Adolescence." *Developmental Psychology* 33, no. 6 (1997):917–924.

Mary Elizabeth Curtner-Smith

ANTISOCIAL BEHAVIOR

Antisocial behavior in children is associated with social impairment and psychological dysfunction, such as oppositional/defiant disorders, conduct disorders, and antisocial personality disorders. These disorders often involve engaging in delinquent behavior, but they are far from synonymous with criminal activity. In preschoolers, antisocial behavior can include temper tantrums, quarreling with peers, and physical aggression (i.e., hitting, kicking, biting). Parents often report difficulties in handling and controlling the child. Comorbidity (visible problems that may not be the child's only problem) is often found because antisocial behavior is associated with hyperactivity, depression, and reading difficulties. Follow-up studies indicate that antisocial behavior in toddlers often decreases with age, as children learn to control their behavior or benefit from the intervention of professionals in the field. Individual differences dictate the tendency of children to engage in antisocial behavior, and this tendency may change over time according to the overall level of antisocial behavior, situational variations, and the persistence or nonpersistence of antisocial behavior as individuals grow older.

See also: ACTING OUT

Bibliography

McCord, Joan, and Richard Tremblay, eds. *Preventing Antisocial Behavior: Interventions from Birth through Adolescence.* New York: Guilford Press, 1992.

Moffitt, T. E. "Adolescence-Limited and Life-Course-Persistent Antisocial Behaviour: A Developmental Taxonomy." *Psychological Review* 100, no. 4 (1993):674–701.

Rutter, Michael, Henri Giller, and Ann Hagell. *Antisocial Behaviour by Young People.* Cambridge, Eng.: Cambridge University Press, 1998.

Tremblay, Richard. "The Development of Aggressive Behaviour during Childhood: What Have We Learned in the Past Century?" *International Journal of Behavioral Development* 24 (2000):129–141.

Anne I. H. Borge

APGAR, VIRGINIA (1909–1974)

Virginia Apgar, inventor of the APGAR Score for newborn infants, was born in Westfield, New Jersey, on June 7, 1909. Having witnessed her brothers' chronic and deadly childhood illnesses, Apgar chose a career in medicine, like her father before her. She graduated from Mount Holyoke College in 1929 after

Virginia Apgar invented the APGAR Score, a method for assessing newborn infant stability based on five key observation points: Appearance, Pulse, Grimace, Activity, and Respiration. (Bettmann/Corbis)

studying zoology, chemistry, and physiology. She then entered the College of Physicians and Surgeons at Columbia University, earning her medical degree in 1933. After graduation, Apgar accepted a prized surgical internship at Columbia University, during which she studied under Alan Whipple, the chairman of surgery. Whipple encouraged Apgar to study anesthesiology instead of surgery. In 1937 Apgar became the first female board-certified anesthesiologist in the United States, and in 1949 she was the first woman appointed as full professor of anesthesiology at Columbia University.

Later in 1949, Apgar's professional focus shifted to the field of obstetrical anesthesia. During this time, Apgar overheard her colleagues discussing their concerns regarding the difficulty of assessing whether a newborn baby was stable after delivery, and she immediately wrote down the five points now known as the APGAR Score. The APGAR Score consists of five observation points that are evaluated by healthcare personnel at one, five, and ten minutes following birth: Activity, Pulse, Grimace (reflex response), Appearance (muscle tone and movement), and Respiration. The APGAR Score was published in 1953 and is the standard of practice all over the world, as well as an early marker for later developmental outcomes.

In 1959 Apgar left Columbia University to attend John Hopkins University in pursuit of her master's degree in public health; she also studied statistics to improve her research skills. In April of 1959 Apgar was appointed by the director of the National Foundation-March of Dimes (now the Dimes Birth Defects Foundation) to assist in its effort to promote public awareness of birth defects. From 1967 to 1972 Apgar served as Director of Basic Research of the National Foundation. She later co-authored the book *Is My Baby All Right?* (1972), which dealt with birth defects, with Joan Beck. Apgar died August 7, 1974.

See also: APGAR SCORING SYSTEM; INFANCY

Bibliography

"Apgar, Virginia." In the Discovery Channel School [web site]. Available from http://school.discovery.com/homeworkhelp/worldbook/atozscience/a/726460.html; INTERNET.

"Apgar, Virginia." In the Encyclopædia Britannica [web site]. 1999. Available from http://women.eb.com/women/articles/Apgar_Virginia.html; INTERNET.

Calmes, Selma Harrison. "Virginia Apgar: A Woman Physician's Career in a Developing Specialty." *Journal of the American Medical Women's Association* 39, no. 6 (1984):184–188. Available from http://www.apgarfamily.com/Selma1.html; INTERNET.

Publications by Apgar

"A Proposal for a New Method of Evaluation of the Newborn Infant." Available from http://www.apgarfamily.com/drvirginial1.htm; INTERNET.

Rosemary C. White-Traut

APGAR SCORING SYSTEM

The APGAR scoring system is used universally in the delivery room to assess the overall health and integrity of the newborn immediately after birth. A score of zero to two is assigned in each of the five areas at one and five minutes after birth. If prolonged resuscitation is needed, scoring continues at five minute intervals until the infant is stabilized. The five areas are: Activity—from no movement (0) to tone, movement, and flexion (2); Pulse—from absent (0) to more than one hundred beats per minute (2); Grimace—from no reflex irritability (0) to cough or pulling away (2); Appearance—from blue-gray color (0) to normal (2); and Respiration—from absent (0) to regular with crying (2). A score of seven to ten is normal. A score of four to seven signals a need for resuscitation. And a score of three or below signals the need for intense, and sometimes prolonged, resuscitation. A low score (less than three) of long duration (greater than ten minutes) may correlate with future neurological dysfunction.

See also: APGAR, VIRGINIA; BIRTH; INFANCY

Bibliography

Committee on Fetus and Newborn, American Academy of Pediatrics, and Committee on Obstetric Practice, American College of Obstetricians and Gynecologists. Policy Statement. "Use and Abuse of the APGAR Score." *Pediatrics* 98, no. 1 (1996):141–142.

Freeman, John, and Karin Nelson. "Intrapartum Asphyxia and Cerebral Palsy." *Pediatrics* 82, no. 2 (1988):240–249.

Goodwin, T. Murphy. "Role of the APGAR Score in Assessing Perinatal Asphyxia." *Contemporary OB/GYN* (June 1997):80–92.

Nelson, Karin, and Jonas Ellenberg. "Obstetric Complications as Risk Factors for Cerebral or Seizure Disorders." *Journal of the American Medical Association* (1984):251, 1843–1848.

Socol, Michael, Patricia Garcia, and Susan Riter. "Depressed APGAR Scores, Acid-Base Status, and Neurologic Outcome." *American Journal of Obstetrics and Gynecology* 170, no. 4 (1994):991–999.

Joanne Bregman

APNEA

Apnea is a condition when breathing stops during sleep. Since common brain processes regulate both sleep and breath, respiration is controlled differently when we are awake and asleep. Breathing may stop because the brain fails to tell the muscles in the lungs to contract or expand (central apnea) or because of physical obstruction of the upper airway, with breathing muscles in the diaphragm and chest continuing to function (obstructive apnea), or both combined (mixed apnea). Apneic pauses as brief as two to six seconds normally occur in infants and children. If they last longer (say, fifteen to twenty seconds), occur frequently, and are accompanied by lowered blood oxygen levels (hypoxemia), the developing brain is deprived of needed oxygen. If untreated, this Obstructive Sleep Apnea Syndrome (OSAS) places a child at risk for mental deficits, heart and respiratory abnormalities, and even death. This respiratory dysfunction has been associated with snoring, as well as upper respiratory infection, Down syndrome, Prader-Willi syndrome, Attention Deficit Hyperactivity Disorder (ADHD), epilepsy, and sudden infant death syndrome (SIDS). Protection against its effects can be provided by treatment with continuous positive airway pressure (CPAP) during sleeping as well as a number of drugs.

See also: SLEEPING

Bibliography

Carroll, John, and Gerald Loughlin. "Obstructive Sleep Apnea Syndrome in Infants and Children: Diagnosis and Management." In Richard Ferber and Meier Kryger eds., *Principles and Practice of Sleep Medicine in the Child*. Philadelphia: W. B. Saunders, 1995.

Evelyn B. Thoman

APGAR SCORING SYSTEM			
Factor	0 points	1 point	2 points
Heart rate	No heartbeat	Under 100 beats per minute	Over 100 beats per minute
Respiration	Not breathing	Irregular, with weak cry	Regular with strong cry
Muscle tone	Limp, no movement	Limited movement of the limbs	Active movement of the limbs
Color	Completely blue, pale	Pink body with blue hands and feet	All pink
Reflexes	No response to being poked in the nose	Grimace when poked	Cry, cough, or sneeze when poked

A sample of the APGAR scoring system devised by Virginia Apgar (1909–1974). (Standley Publication)

ARTIFICIAL INSEMINATION

Artificial insemination is a procedure in which sperm obtained by masturbation or other methods of mechanical stimulation are deposited in the vagina, cervix, or uterus of the female by means other than natural intercourse, with the specific intent to achieve pregnancy. Artificial insemination is a brief office procedure that may be performed using the fresh sperm of the male partner or the frozen/thawed sperm of an anonymous sperm donor, and involves injection of the sperm into the female through a thin tube. Intrauterine insemination requires preliminary processing of the semen sample to isolate the sperm for insemination since seminal plasma cannot be directly injected into the uterus. To be effective, insemination must be performed in close proximity to the time of ovulation (release of an egg) in the female as both sperm and eggs have a relatively short lifespan. Situations in which artificial insemination may be a recommended procedure include: (1) anatomical problems that prevent effective natural intercourse or interfere with normal sperm movement through the female reproductive tract; (2) poor semen quality with an abnormally low sperm count and/or poor sperm motility (ability to move); and (3) "unexplained infertility" in which the purpose is to increase the probability of pregnancy by introducing more than the usual numbers of sperm, typically in a cycle involving stimulation of the female with fertility drugs in efforts to cause release of more than a single mature egg.

See also: BIRTH

Bibliography

Friedman, Andrew J., Mary Juneau-Norcross, Beverly Sedensky, Nina Andrews, Jayne Dorfman, and Daniel W. Cramer. "Life Table Analysis of Intrauterine Insemination Pregnancy Rates for Couples with Cervical Factor, Male Factor, and Idiopathic Infertility." *Fertility and Sterility* 55 (1991):1005–1007.

Shenfield F., P. Doyle, A. Valentine, S. J. Steele, S. L. Tan. "Effects of Age, Gravidity and Male Infertility Status on Cumulative Conception Rates Following Artificial Insemination with Cryopreserved Donor Semen: Analysis of 2,998 Cycles of Treatment in One Centre Over Ten Years. *Human Reproduction* 8 (1993):60–64.

Wilcox Allen J., Clarice R. Weinberg, Donna D. Baird. "Timing of Sexual Intercourse in Relation to Ovulation—Effects on the Probability of Conception, Survival of the Pregnancy, and Sex of the Baby." *New England Journal of Medicine* 333 (1995):1517–1521.

Marc Fritz

ASIAN-AMERICAN CHILDREN

Asian Americans are a diverse group of individuals made up of several "micro" cultures under the umbrella of a larger shared "macro" heritage. It is important to note this inner diversity—Americans of Chinese, Japanese, Korean, Vietnamese, and other Asian heritages—as the various groups are at times as different as they are similar. Nonetheless, there are some common features that may help in better understanding Asian-American children.

The Shared Asian-American Heritage

Before considering some of the shared values and practices of Asian-American groups, it is necessary to reiterate that these groups are exteremly diverse and that individual differences must be kept in mind as these broad generalizations are discussed. There are, however, some similar threads found in various Asian culutres, including the tendency to be more collectivistic (as opposed to the more individualistic Western orientation), as well as the tendency to view the role of the family as central to existence. In addition, the value given toward preserving honor and harmony may be common across Asian-American individuals. These commonalities will be discussed before attention is turned to some of the differences present between the various Asian-American groups.

Collectivism

Valerie Pang and Li-Rong Cheng have called collectivism "one of the most powerful values" found in Asian-American communities (Pang and Cheng 1998, p. 6). Collectivism is characterized by a value system such that the group has more value than the individuals of which it is made. In this orientation, individuals sacrifice their own goals for the greater good of the community, and norms and traditions are emphasized. Virtually every Asian culture is collectivist in nature, in contrast to the more individualistically oriented American framework. This has special implications for Asian-American children, as they may incorporate both Asian and American value systems into their own beliefs. This can be difficult for them as they straddle both cultures. An example is the extreme focus on independence as a positive quality in Western value systems such as that in the United States. An Asian-American child might allow his family more of a role in decisions regarding career or marriage and may thus be viewed in a negative light because of "dependence" on his family. It is important to understand that collectivist societies such as those in Asian cultures may have different values and priorities than those adhered to by Western societies.

Deep Familial Ties

The role of family as central is another common tenet in most Asian cultures, and this familial devotion is often seen in Asian-American children as well. Brian Leung discusses these deep familial ties, noting that Asian-American parents are often seen as sacrificing their own needs for the needs of their children, and in turn adult children are often expected to care for their elderly parents. Also, respect for elder family members is more common in Asian-American cultures than in Western societies.

It is also important to note that not all Asian-American families are at the same stage in their own process of acculturation to the United States. Leung divides these families into three potential groups: recently arrived immigrant families, immigrant-American families, and immigrant-descendant families. Recently arrived immigrant families may struggle with involvement in educational practices in America because of differences in beliefs about the educational system, language barriers, and employment demands. Immigrant-American families are those that consist of parents born overseas and chil-

dren born in America, as well as entire families born overseas that have lived in the United States for a substantial amount of time (twenty years or more). These parents will most likely have more involvement in their children's education, as they are more accustomed to the culture of America. Differences may exist in opinions and values between parents and children as their levels of acculturation may be at different stages, and this can at times cause conflict in an Asian-American family. Finally, American-born families are those in which all members of the family are American-born. These families may subscribe to many Asian values but may practice them to a lesser extent.

Preserving Honor and Harmony

A third major tenet shared by many Asian and Asian-American cultures is the presence of behaviors designed to "save face" or preserve honor and harmony. Saving face is important not only for oneself but also for others with whom one might be interacting, including groups outside of the ingroup. Disagreements are usually avoided and maintaining a polite and conscientious appearance is more important than winning an argument. This approach must be understood as appropriate in Asian-American children, though it differs from Western viewpoints about asserting oneself. Even children from American-born Asian-American families may retain these types of behavior patterns, as they are central to the Asian value system.

Differences among Asian-American Cultures

There are, of course, many differences between the various Asian-American cultures as well. On one level, traditions and customs, language, and dress differ from group to group, while on another level, differences exist in the immigration practices and regulations of the different groups, as well as in historical experiences. These differences may cause Asian Americans to develop culturally in different ways.

The Effect of Immigration Practices on Asian-American Children

Chinese Americans are the Asian-American group that has been in America the longest. Many Chinese individuals immigrated to the United States to find jobs and fortune in the early 1800s and were welcomed at first because of the cheap labor they provided. Soon sentiments turned negative, however, leading to the Chinese Exclusion Act of 1882. This act prevented immigration from China and lead to discriminatory practices in the United States, including lack of access to certain legal rights and segregation.

In addition, the prevention of immigration created a Chinese-American population comprised mostly of men, leading to lower numbers in subsequent generations. This act was not repealed until 1943 and had extreme influences on both the physical and psychological well being of Chinese Americans. Such practices had an effect on the children of these Chinese immigrants as well, as feelings of shame and the results of discrimination and poverty were passed on from previous generations. Good education is often a main focus for these families and is a key reason for their immigration to the United States. Thus, educational achievement remains an immensely important goal for Chinese-American children.

Korean individuals arrived in America about a century later than the Chinese and also served as laborers. Again, attainment of better education was a major goal of these first Korean immigrants. The anti-Asian sentiments that continued to effect all Asian-American populations at this time in the United States caused many Korean and Korean-American families to settle close to one another, forming tightly knit communities. It is important for those working with Korean-American children to respect these communities and to try to work within them, making attempts to involve parents as much as possible. Though most Korean-American parents are highly respectful of teachers and educational administrators, they may not see it as their place to enter into the educational forum, deferring instead to teachers. Using material in the language of the parent is one way of ensuring more involvement.

Japanese individuals first immigrated to the United States in the late 1800s and early 1900s, with a desire for better education and financial opportunities as the primary force behind their immigration. While welcomed at first, anti-Asian sentiments resulted in the halting of immigration practices from 1931 to 1940. Whereas immigration was prevented quickly for the Chinese, this process took longer with the Japanese, allowing time for both males and females to immigrate to America. Thus, the Japanese-American population was not affected by the same setbacks suffered by the Chinese-American population. As a result, the Japanese-American population continued to thrive with two-thirds of the Japanese population being American-born by the 1940s. The discriminations directed against the Japanese-American population during World War II affected the acculturation of these citizens drastically, however, leading to less identification with America in some and highly overt identification, to the destruction of some of their own customs and practices, on the parts of others. World War II's relative recentness means that many Japanese-American children might come from families directly affected by its events.

The central roles of family and culture are common tenets in most Asian populations. A young girl wearing traditional Southeast Asian clothing holds an American flag for Independence Day festivities in Sheboygan, Wisconsin. (Kevin Fleming/Corbis)

The Effect of Historical Experiences on Asian-American Children

Historical experiences also differ for the various groups of Asian Americans. As mentioned before, during World War II, more than 100,000 Japanese Americans were interned in concentration camps in the United States, an event that continues to affect many Japanese-American families. Though two-thirds of these individuals were Nisei, or second-generation individuals who had been born in America, the U.S. government viewed them as a danger to their country following the Japanese attack on Pearl Harbor. This indignation resulted in most Japanese-American families losing all that they owned, leading to a step backward in their solidification as productive landowners and business owners. Because of the emphasis placed on the tenet of honor in Japanese societies, many of these families did not speak of the internment for many years afterwards, and Japanese-American children might be just beginning to understand the effects of this imprisonment on their own families.

The end of the Vietnam War in 1975 and the immigration that followed provides another example of a historical influence on a different group of Asian Americans. This group of Southeast Asian immigrants came from three different countries: Vietnam, Laos, and Cambodia. Although the first immigrants who came to the United States around 1975 were generally wealthy and quickly established themselves in their new country, immigrants that followed came from more desperate circumstances, escaping refugee camps and war-ravaged conditions in their homelands. Following these immigrants came the people released from reeducation camps and many biracial Asian children whose American fathers were in the service during the Vietnam War. Understanding which group the families of Southeast-Asian-American children are associated with can provide those working with them in schools and elsewhere with crucial information about their backgrounds, value systems, and behaviors. In the Southeast-Asian-American community, there is a high level of respect for education and those who provide it, and thus good grades and hard work are emphasized by these families.

Having more knowledge about the value systems, practices, and histories of Asian-American children can aid all those who work with them in better understanding their differences from and their similarities to non-Asian-American individuals.

See also: RACIAL DIFFERENCES

Bibliography

California State Department of Education. *A Handbook for Teaching Korean-Speaking Students.* Sacramento: California State Department of Education, Office of Bilingual Bicultural Education, 1983.

Leung, Brian. "Who Are Chinese-American, Japanese-American, and Korean-American Children? Cultural Profiles." In Valerie Pang and Li-Rong Cheng eds., *Struggling to Be Heard: The Unmet Needs of Asian Pacific American Children.* Albany: State University of New York Press, 1998.

Pang, Valerie, and Li-Rong Cheng, eds. "The Quest for Concepts, Competence, and Connections: The Education of Asian Pacific American Children." *Struggling to Be Heard: The Unmet Needs of Asian Pacific American Children.* Albany: State University of New York Press, 1998.

Tran, My Luong. "Behind the Smiles: The True Heart of Southeast-Asian-American Children." In Valerie Pang and Li-Rong Cheng eds., *Struggling to Be Heard: The Unmet Needs of Asian Pacific American Children.* Albany: State University of New York Press, 1998.

Jennifer Teramoto Pedrotti

ASTHMA

Asthma is the most common chronic illness seen in childhood, affecting 5 to 15 percent of children in the United States, approximately 3 million children younger than eighteen years of age. One-third of these children have severe asthma. Over the last twenty-five years, there has been an increase in the prevalence of asthma. Although part of this may be attributed to physicians diagnosing asthma earlier in children, there still seems to be a real rise in the number of children worldwide with asthma. In the United States, African-American children are more likely to have asthma and more severe instances of the disease compared to Caucasian children. African-American children under four years of age are hospitalized four times as often for their asthma. Crowded inner city living also has been shown to increase a child's likelihood of having asthma, regardless of race. The inner city environment has particles or allergens such as air pollutants that sensitize these children to develop asthma. Urban settings provide increased allergic exposures and increased viral infections early in life (possibly secondary to earlier daycare placement), and crowding. Furthermore, asthma tends to be more severe among children, resulting in higher death rates for children with asthma. Other associated factors include prematurity, low birthweight, poor nutrition, lack of breastfeeding, and low family income. Genetics also plays a role in developing asthma. If one parent is affected with asthma, the child is three times as likely to develop asthma compared to a child with non-asthmatic parents; if both parents have asthma, the risk increases sixfold.

Asthma is an illness that affects the lungs, specifically the airways. Air enters the body through the nose or mouth. It then enters the trachea, also known as the windpipe. This is the large main airway of the lungs. The trachea then divides into two smaller pipes called bronchi that bring air to both the right and left lungs. These airways then divide into many smaller airways called bronchioles. These small airways eventually bring air (and oxygen) to the smallest sub-unit of the lung called the alveolus. The alveolus is where oxygen enters the blood and where carbon dioxide is released. There are hundreds of thousands of alveoli in each lung.

The airways are made up of three parts. First there are the smooth muscle cells that surround the airway. These cells allow the airway to get bigger or smaller by relaxing or contracting. These muscles are involuntary, meaning that they cannot be consciously moved. They respond to local chemicals and nerves to relax and contract. The second part is the lining of the tube, which is made of normally thin cells called epithelial cells. These cells help to protect the body

Children who suffer from asthma use inhalers, or bronchodilators, which allow them to breathe easier.
(B. S. I. P./Custom Medical Stock Photo)

from particles (such as viruses or bacteria) that may be breathed in but that should not be absorbed into the lungs or the body. The cells do this by trapping particles in mucus and moving them out by a brush border, which acts as a moving carpet by beating and bringing the particle laden mucus back out of the lungs. When the particles get closer to the throat, a person can feel them and is then stimulated to cough to get them out of the lungs. The third part is the lumen, or airway opening through which the air passes on its way to the alveolus to bring oxygen to the lungs (that will then be used by the body). The size of this lumen is affected by the smooth muscle, the lining cells, and by any debris (mucus and particles).

When someone has an acute asthma attack, their airways narrow because of smooth muscles, swelling or edema of the airway lining cells, and production of excessive mucus by these cells, making it more difficult to move air in and out of the lungs. When this happens, the patient will often cough, breathe more quickly than normal, and feel short of breath. People with asthma may also have noisy breathing, or wheezing. Wheezing occurs because the patient must still move the same amount of air through a narrower airway in the same amount of time. This means the air has to move faster to move past these narrow areas. This is heard as wheezing. The process is similar to water flowing through a narrowed pipe or tube; for

example, through a nozzle. Water flow becomes noisy and audible, where it is normally quiet. Wheezing, however, may also occur in patients who do not have asthma but may have airway narrowing for other reasons such as a foreign body in the airway. Very young children may wheeze in response to a cold but may not have asthma when they get older. Patients having an asthma attack also can appear to be breathing hard, using extra muscles like their abdomen, shoulders and rib muscles to breathe. If allowed to continue without treatment, a patient will continue to work harder and harder until the muscles of breathing are exhausted, thus leading to death. Patients with asthma may be mildly to severely ill with an asthma attack, and symptoms can progress very quickly if not treated.

Many things can cause asthma attacks. For some people key triggers can be identified. Triggers are environmental, infectious, or social causes that set off a person's asthma. Common triggers include pollens, cigarette smoking, secondhand smoke exposure, dust mites, molds, pet dander, colds, cold air, exercise, stress, and changes in weather. These triggers are sensed by the lungs and the body over-responds, causing an asthma attack. Some patients have asthma where no clear trigger can be identified. Individuals with many allergies are at higher risk for getting asthma. People with eczema (an itchy dry skin condition often associated with allergies) also are more likely to have asthma.

Treatment of asthma requires a whole life approach. Prevention of attacks is extremely important, especially in children with moderate to severe asthma. This requires a multifactorial approach involving attention to and potential changes in all spheres of a child's life, including home and school. Environmental modification includes elimination of triggers such as cigarette smoke, pet dander, dust, molds, pollens, and insects (especially cockroaches). Special care to avoid colds is also important. Furthermore, some children require preventive or prophylactic medicine daily to decrease the number of attacks. These include anti-inflammatory medications in more severe cases of asthma, to help decrease inflammation and swelling of airway lining cells. Once an acute asthma attack has started, treatment consists of albuterol, which immediately relaxes the smooth muscle to help open the airway. Steroids can also increase airway size by decreasing acute inflammation. Oxygen may also be needed. Education of patient, family, and other caregivers in the early recognition of symptoms is key to successful treatment of an asthmatic attack, and improving baseline lung functioning.

Asthma, like any chronic illness, can have a significant impact on a child's psychosocial functioning and development. Children with asthma exhibit a threefold increase in school absences (on average) when compared to children without asthma. A study by Fowler from 1992 also suggests a potential link between asthma and learning disabilities in children with poor to fair health because of severe asthma with poorer school performance. Children with asthma who come from lower income families (household income less than $20,000 per year) were twice as likely to fail a grade than healthy children from low income homes in this study.

Children with asthma also exhibit increased emotional vulnerability. They may demonstrate anxiety regarding their asthma, and feel physically vulnerable as well, sometimes out of proportion to the severity of their asthma. Anxiety with hyperventilation can be a trigger for stress-induced asthma attacks. Young children with moderate to severe asthma may have great fears and anxieties regarding their health and fear of death at a very young age. In addition to the child, parents also develop fear and anxiety in relation to their child with chronic illness, which also may be out of proportion to the severity of the child's asthma. This can lead to increased parental sheltering and overprotectiveness, giving rise to the vulnerable child syndrome and feeding the child's anxiety.

Asthma can also be an isolating illness for school-age children. Increased school absences take them away from their friends and peers. Having to leave the classroom to receive medicines or treatments also may give the child a sense of being set apart from peers and therefore different. Furthermore, classmates may perceive the child as being "sick" and may treat him differently as a result, further impairing bonding with peers.

In conclusion, asthma is a common illness among children. It affects their physical, psychosocial, and emotional lives. Effective management involves the child, family, pediatrician, school personnel, and when needed, allergy specialists to minimize symptoms and allow children with asthma to thrive.

See also: CHRONIC ILLNESS

Bibliography

Bloomberg, G. R. "Crisis in Asthma Care." *Pediatric Clinics of North America* 39 (1992):1225–1241.

Brugman, S. M. "Asthma in Infants and Small Children." *Clinics in Chest Medicine* 16 (1995):637–656.

Fowler, M. G. "School Functioning of U.S. Children with Asthma." *Pediatrics* 90 (1992):939–944.

Gern, J. E. "Childhood Asthma: Older Children and Adolescents." *Clinics in Chest Medicine* 16 (1995):657–670.

Hoekelman, Robert, Stanford B. Friedman, and Modena E. H. Wilson, eds. *Primary Pediatric Care,* 3rd edition. St. Louis: Mosby, 1997.

Morgan, W. J. "Risk Factors for Developing Wheezing and Asthma in Childhood." *Pediatric Clinics of North America* 39 (1992):1185–1203.

Warner, J. O. "Third International Pediatric Consensus Statement on the Management of Childhood Asthma." *Pediatric Pulmonology* 25 (1998):1–17.

Ericka V. Hayes

ATTACHMENT

Attachment is a strong emotional tie that children develop with the special people in their lives, particularly parents. Attachment figures provide comfort to children in times of stress; in so doing, they serve as a secure base from which children explore the world. Further, attachment figures serve as a source of pleasure and joy for children. Note, however, that parents also play other important roles in their children's lives, including playmate, teacher, and disciplinarian.

The development of attachment follows four phases in infancy. For the first two to three months, young infants do not discriminate among the people who care for them. From three to seven months infants begin to show their preferences for familiar caregivers, such as their parents, by reaching for them, smiling at them, and responding to soothing efforts by them. By nine months, infants show evidence of their attachment relationships. They make attempts to maintain close proximity to their caregivers, and they are distressed by separations from them. Over time, partnerships emerge between children and their caregivers, such that children develop an appreciation of caregivers as separate persons with their own goals, needs, and desires. Attachment relationships with parents and other important caregivers continue throughout the lifespan. Moreover, beginning in adolescence, other attachment relationships develop, including those with romantic partners and close friends.

History of Attachment Theory

The earliest roots of attachment theory can be found in Sigmund Freud's psychoanalytic theory of development, written at the turn of the twentieth century. Freud was the first theorist to propose a stage theory of development. His first stage, the oral stage, presupposed that infants develop relationships with their mothers, because mothers satisfy their hunger. Animal studies, however, provided persuasive evidence that feeding was not a sufficient explanation for attachment. In a series of famous experiments, Harry Harlow and his colleagues demonstrated that infant rhesus monkeys, raised in isolation, preferred the comfort of a cloth-covered surrogate mother to that of a wire-mesh surrogate with an attached feeding bottle. Clearly, the basis for attachment relationships does not reside in feeding alone. Erik Erikson, a student of Freud's, foreshadowed attachment theory by emphasizing the importance of children's ability to trust parents to meet their needs as the basis for later social and emotional development.

World Wars I and II alerted mental health professionals and the general public alike to the importance of close interpersonal relationships in development. Particularly in Europe, where casualty rates were highest, psychological trauma due to the loss of loved ones was common. Therapists, in fact, reported that death of family members was a frequent reason for individuals to seek therapy during the postwar years. In this context, British psychiatrist John Bowlby, while working with children and adolescents in London orphanages, discovered that the most disturbed children were those who had experienced separations from their caregivers, particularly their mothers. Consider, for example, his account of a seven-year-old girl:

> At twelve months she fell ill with bronchitis and was in the hospital for nine months . . . During this time she never saw her parents, who were only permitted to visit her when she was asleep . . . When examined at the Clinic [at seven years of age] she was found . . . to

be a withdrawn, detached, and unemotional child (Bowlby 1940, pp. 159–160).

Bowlby also noted that children who developed behavioral and emotional problems often experienced parenting that was characterized by displays of ambivalence or outright rejection. Based on these observations, he hypothesized that a caregiver's emotional attitude toward a child had direct implications for that child's later mental health. In other words, he believed that mental health is dependent upon a child feeling wanted and loved.

Three Main Propositions of Attachment Theory

Bowlby's seminal three-volume series on attachment and loss and subsequent work by his student, Mary Dinsmore Salter Ainsworth, form the core of attachment theory. There are three main propositions. The first is that infants' emotional ties to their caregivers can be viewed from an evolutionary perspective. Consider, for example, that closeness with adults can be viewed as an adaptive strategy for children because it leads to protection from environmental hazards, such as predators. Throughout the long evolution of human history, children who did not develop close relationships with their parents were less likely to survive and therefore less likely to reproduce. It is difficult to prove this thesis because there is no fossil record for social behavior. Still, it seems likely that attachment behaviors provided an evolutionary advantage.

Second, attachment is grounded in what is called a motivational control system, which organizes children's behavior. Just as physiological control systems are believed to regulate processes such as body temperature, a behavioral control system balances a child's desires to explore the environment and to seek proximity with caregivers, especially in the presence of danger. In this system, the child's primary goal is to feel safe and secure. Feelings of security, however, are dependent on caregivers' responses. When caregivers are sensitive and responsive, children are confidant that their needs will be met and that they may rely on their caregivers in times of stress. In contrast, when caregivers are insensitive and unresponsive, children become distrustful of their caregivers and are unable to rely on them. In the face of insensitive caregiving, infants develop strategies that are adaptive in context, for example avoiding or clinging to caregivers.

Third, early experience guides later behaviors and feelings via internal working models of attachment—"internal" because they reside in the mind, "working" because they guide perceptions and behaviors, and "models" because they are cognitive representations of relationship experiences. In other words, children store knowledge about relationships, especially knowledge about safety and danger, in models that guide their future interactions. Each new interpersonal interaction is processed and interpreted according to children's representations.

These models are assumed to operate, for the most part, outside of conscious experience. Knowledge gained from interactions with primary caregivers, typically parents, is of greatest importance; for example, children with loving parents develop positive models of relationships based on trust. Simultaneously, children develop parallel models of themselves; for example, children with loving parents view themselves as worthy of care. These models are assumed to generalize from parents to other people in children's lives, including friends and teachers. So, a child will assume that a friend or teacher is trustworthy if the child's primary caregiver is trustworthy.

Mary Dinsmore Salter Ainsworth and the Strange Situation

Ainsworth conducted the first observational studies of mothers and children that were rooted in attachment theory, first in Uganda and later in Baltimore, Maryland. Through her careful field notes, she noticed important individual differences among infants. Most appeared soothed by their mothers, while others were not, and still others displayed little emotion to their mothers' presence or absence. Ainsworth moved her work to the laboratory in order to assess the effect of maternal absence on infant exploratory behaviors. Her paradigm, called the Strange Situation, is a thirty-minute procedure that consists of a series of separations and reunions among a caregiver, a child, and a stranger.

Ainsworth and her students identified three patterns of attachment that were particularly evident from children's behavior in the reunion episodes with mothers. Most children displayed a pattern of attachment that Ainsworth and colleagues labeled "secure." When their mothers were present, these children displayed a balance between exploring the laboratory playroom and seeking proximity with their mothers. During separations, secure children displayed some distress as indicated, for example, by crying. When reunited, these children greeted their mothers warmly, often with hugs, and were easily soothed by them. Children classified as "insecure-ambivalent" displayed few exploratory behaviors when their mothers were present, often clinging to them. These children were usually very upset during separations. When reunited, they displayed angry and resistant or ambivalent behaviors toward their mothers. For example, they would cry and raise their arms to be picked up and then push their mothers away while continuing to cry. Children classified as "insecure-avoidant" explored the playroom when their mothers were present. Unlike other children, however, these children paid little attention to their mothers. In addition, these children were usually not upset during separations and snubbed or avoided their mothers during reunions. Mary Main and Judith Solomon identified a fourth pattern of attachment, "insecure-disorganized," characterized by extreme distress over separations and disorganized, disoriented, and confused behaviors during reunions. Specifically, these children displayed frozen postures, repetitive movements, and dazed facial expressions when reunited with their mothers.

Overwhelmingly, the Strange Situation has become the preferred method of assessing attachment in infancy. There is, in fact, considerable evidence that security status in the Strange Situation is related to parenting behaviors, especially maternal sensitivity, which can be defined as the mother's ability to perceive an infant's signals accurately and to respond promptly and appropriately. Children whose mothers are sensitive to their needs are likely to be classified as secure. Children with avoidant patterns tend to have mothers who are either rejecting or intrusive and overstimulating. Children with ambivalent patterns tend to have mothers who are inconsistent in their parenting behaviors; for example, they may be sensitive and responsive some of the time but not always, which makes it difficult for children to predict their behavior. Children with disorganized patterns tend to have mothers who have experienced loss, trauma, or mental illnesses.

Although most of the research that has been conducted on patterns of attachment concerns infants' relationships with their mothers, there is some work that has examined infants' relationships with their fathers. There is no debate that children develop full-fledged attachment relationships with their fathers. In other words, it is clear that children can and do develop multiple attachment relationships. Little is known, however, about how children integrate the knowledge gained from multiple attachment models, especially when the models are different. Yet, there is some evidence for concordance across attachment figures—children who are securely attached to their mothers are also likely to be securely attached to their fathers. Concordance is best explained by shared parenting values, although infant temperament has also been suggested as an explanation.

Child Care

By the twenty-first century, most infants in the United States experienced some form of child care in their first year of life. This represented an enormous shift in how children in the United States were raised, a shift that led to concerns about whether infant child care disrupts mother-child attachment. Some have argued that infants experience daily separations as maternal rejection, which should lead to avoidance, while others have suggested that separations prevent mothers from having sufficient opportunities to develop sensitive caregiving styles. The results of the National Institute of Child Health and Human Development Study of Early Child Care, a study of more than 1,000 infants and their mothers, clearly demonstrated that neither security nor avoidance in the Strange Situation was associated with type of care, amount of care, or quality of care. Instead, security was associated with characteristics of mothering, such as sensitivity. Infants who experienced dual risks, for example poor quality child care and insensitive mothering, were at increased risk for developing insecure attachments. Thus, the effects of child care on attachment depend primarily on the nature of ongoing interactions between mothers and children.

Other Measures of Attachment

The Strange Situation continues to be the benchmark method for assessing attachment security in infancy. Alternatives, however, have been developed. The Attachment Q-sort, developed by Everett Waters, is a method designed to assess attachment security naturalistically in the home environment. Observers sort a set of ninety cards with behavioral descriptions—for example, "Actively solicits comforting from adult when distressed"—from most characteristic to least characteristic of the child. The child's profile is compared to that of a prototypical securely attached child, based on attachment researchers' hypothetical sorts or rankings of the cards.

Methods have also been developed for assessing attachment security in adolescence and adulthood. Preeminent among these is the Adult Attachment Interview (developed by Carol George, Nancy Kaplan, and Mary Main), a semistructured interview in which adults are asked to reflect and report on their early experiences with attachment figures, typically their mothers and fathers. The coding system focuses on the consistency and coherency of responses. Adults are classified as "secure/autonomous" if they express value for their early attachment relationships and are able to report on these experiences in a clear and organized fashion. Adults are classified as "dismissing" if they devalue the importance of early attachment relationships by expressing disregard for negative experiences, by having few memories of childhood, or by having idealized memories of their childhoods. Adults are classified as "preoccupied" if they display confusion or anger regarding early attachment relationships and talk excessively about their early experiences concerning them. Finally, adults are classified as "unresolved/disorganized" if they demonstrate lapses in reasoning during discussions of loss or abuse.

Stability of Attachment and Later Relationship Functioning

There is some evidence that attachment status is a stable phenomenon, as evidenced by concordance between security in the Strange Situation during infancy and in the Adult Attachment Interview during adolescence or early adulthood. Specifically, secure infants become autonomous adults, while avoidant infants become dismissing and ambivalent infants become preoccupied. Instability in attachment classifications over time seems to be linked to salient life events. Events that may redirect secure infants toward patterns of insecurity in adolescence and adulthood include maltreatment, the loss of a parent, parental divorce, or a serious illness for the parent or child.

Strange Situation classifications in infancy are also predictive of later relationship functioning. Infants classified as secure show more positive emotions toward their parents at two years of age and have better communication with their parents during middle childhood than infants classified as insecure. Patterns of attachment in infancy are also predictive of the quality of relationships with people other than parents. For example, children who are securely attached to their caregivers have better relationships with teachers, peers, and close friends.

Clinical Implications

The field of attachment began with Bowlby's clinical work with disordered patients. Since then, researchers have remained interested in links between early attachment history and the development of psychopathology. Work with institutionalized children demonstrates that the failure to form attachment relationships can lead to serious mental health problems. Most research, however, concerns associations between the quality of care children receive from attachment figures and later behavior. For example, infants with ambivalent attachment relationships are more likely to develop later anxiety disorders, while those with disorganized attachment relationships are more likely to develop later dissociative disorders, where individuals lose touch with reality. There is lit-

Attachment figures—such as this teacher—provide comfort to children in times of stress by offering a safe haven from situations that may appear dangerous or unsettling. (Stephanie Maze/Corbis)

tle evidence for specific links between types of insecurity and types of disorders. Instead, insecurity seems to operate as a risk factor that is neither a necessary nor a sufficient cause for disorders. Not surprisingly, there is evidence that a secure attachment relationship functions as a protective factor for children; in other words, security may protect children from the effects of other risk factors associated with psychopathology, such as their own difficult temperaments.

The processes through which early attachment relationships lead to later disorders are not well understood. Most theorists, however, believe that internal working models must moderate any link between the two. Models characterized by anger, mistrust, anxiety, and fear may lead children not only to behave aggressively but also to interpret the behaviors of others, even kind behaviors, negatively. In fact, the early memories of people with personality disorders are characterized by marked distortions and inconsistencies that reflect their negative attributions of themselves and others. More research on internal working models, especially with respect to their resistance to change, could help direct future therapeutic efforts with both children and adults.

Cross-Cultural Research

Because attachment theory is grounded in evolutionary biology, one of its core assumptions is that infant-caregiver attachment is a universal phenomenon. This assumption is controversial. At the very least, however, research from around the world supports the claim that all infants develop attachment relationships, secure or insecure, with their primary caregivers. Beyond this, there is considerable evidence that the number of children who develop a secure pattern of attachment is proportionately similar across cultures. In African, Chinese, Israeli, Japanese, Western European, and American cultures alike, most children, about two-thirds, are securely attached to their caregivers.

The proportion of children who are insecure-avoidant or insecure-ambivalent, however, varies across cultures. Consider that in Japan a higher proportion of children are classified as ambivalent and a lower proportion of children are classified as avoidant than in Western European and American cultures. Japanese infants, in fact, are more likely to be very upset during separations from their caregivers and less likely to explore the environment than American infants. Based on these data and using the Japanese culture as an example, Fred Rothbaum and his colleagues offered a critique of the universality of attachment that focused on cultural variations in caregiver sensitivity and child competence.

Rothbaum and his colleagues argued that caregiver sensitivity in Japan is a function of parents' efforts to maintain high levels of emotional closeness with their children, but that in the United States it is a function of parents' efforts to balance emotional closeness with children's assumed need to become self-sufficient. In fact, Japanese parents spend more time in close contact with their infants than parents in the United States. Regardless, most attachment researchers now agree that caregiver sensitivity is only one important contributor to attachment security. In all cultures, other factors such as how much stimulation parents provide their children, as well as child characteristics such as temperament, are likely to influence the development of attachment.

The link between attachment security and child competence has also received scrutiny from a cross-cultural perspective. Child characteristics that are associated with security in Western cultures, such as independence, emotional openness, and sociability, are less valued in other cultures. Attachment security may lead to social behaviors that vary across cultures but are nonetheless adaptive in context. For example, Japanese secure children may be more likely than Western secure children to depend on others to meet personal needs, because interpersonal dependency is valued in the Japanese culture. In other words, the characteristics of child competence may differ across cultures as a result of culture-specific pressures.

See also: AINSWORTH, MARY DINSMORE SALTER; BOWLBY, JOHN; PARENT-CHILD RELATIONSHIPS

Bibliography

Ainsworth, Mary D. S., Mary C. Blehar, Everett Waters, and Sally Wall. *Patterns of Attachment: A Psychological Study of the Strange Situation.* Hillsdale, NJ: Erlbaum, 1978.

Bowlby, John. "The Influence of Early Environment in the Development of Neurosis and Neurotic Character." *International Journal of Psychoanalysis* 21 (1940):154–178.

Bowlby, John. *Attachment and Loss,* Vol. 1: *Attachment.* New York: Basic, 1969.

Bowlby, John. *Attachment and Loss,* Vol. 2: *Separation.* New York: Basic, 1973.

Bowlby, John. *Attachment and Loss,* Vol. 3: *Loss.* New York: Basic, 1980.

Bretherton, Inge. "Attachment Theory: Retrospect and Prospect." In Inge Bretherton and Everett Waters eds., *Growing Points of Attachment Theory and Research.* Chicago: University of Chicago Press, 1985.

Crick, Nicki R., and Kenneth A. Dodge. "A Review and Reformulation of Social Informational-Processing Mechanism in Children's Social Adjustment." *Psychological Bulletin* 115 (1994):74–101.

DeWolff, Marianne S., and Marinus H. van IJzendoorn. "Sensitivity and Attachment: A Meta-analysis on Parental Antecedents of Infant Attachment." *Child Development* 68 (1997):571–591.

Erikson, Erik. *Childhood and Society.* New York: Norton, 1950.

Fox, Nathan A., Nancy L. Kimmerly, and William D. Schafer. "Attachment to Mother/Attachment to Father: A Meta-analysis." *Child Development* 62 (1991):210–225.

Freud, Sigmund. *An Outline of Psychoanalysis.* New York: Norton, 1949.

George, Carol, Nancy Kaplan, and Mary Main. "The Adult Attachment Interview." Manuscript, University of California, Berkeley, 1996.

Greenberg, Mark T. "Attachment and Psychopathology in Childhood." In Jude Cassidy and Phillip Shaver eds., *Handbook of Attachment: Theory, Research, and Clinical Applications.* New York: Guilford Press, 1999.

Harlow, Harry F. "The Nature of Love." *American Psychologist* 13 (1958):573–685.

Main, Mary, and Judith Solomon. "Procedures of Identifying Infants as Disorganized/Disoriented during the Ainsworth Strange Situation." In Mark Greenberg, Dante Cicchetti, and E. Mark Cummings eds., *Attachment in the Preschool Years: Theory, Research, and Intervention.* Chicago: University of Chicago Press, 1990.

National Institute of Child Health and Human Development. Early Child Care Research Network. "The Effects of Infant Child Care on Infant-Mother Attachment Security: Results of the NICHD Study of Early Child Care." *Child Development* 68 (1997):860–879.

Rothbaum, Fred, John Weisz, Martha Pott, Kazuo Miyake, and Gilda Morelli. "Attachment and Culture: Security in the United States and Japan." *American Psychologist* 55 (2000):1093–1104.

Thompson, Ross A. "Early Attachment and Later Development." In Jude Cassidy and Phillip R. Shaver eds., *Handbook of Attachment: Theory, Research, and Clinical Applications.* New York: Guilford Press, 1999.

van Ijzendoorn, Marinus H., and Abraham Sagi. "Cross-Cultural Patterns of Attachment: Universal and Contextual Dimensions." In Jude Cassidy and Phillip R. Shaver eds., *Handbook of Attachment: Theory, Research, and Clinical Applications.* New York: Guilford Press, 1999.

Waters, Everett. "The Attachment Q-Set." In Everett Waters, Brian E. Vaughn, German Posada, and Kiyomi Kondo-Ikemura eds., *Caregiving, Cultural, and Cognitive Perspectives on Secure-Base Behavior and Working Models.* Chicago: University of Chicago Press, 1995.

Waters, Everett, Nancy S. Weinfield, and Claire E. Hamilton. "The Stability of Attachment Security from Infancy to Adolescence and Early Adulthood: General Discussion." *Child Development* 71 (2000):703–706.

Kathleen McCartney
Eric Dearing

ATTENTION DEFICIT HYPERACTIVITY DISORDER

Attention Deficit Hyperactivity Disorder (ADHD) begins in early childhood and has a significant impact on how children develop and how families function. This disorder affects how information in the brain is processed and is currently diagnosed in 3 to 5 percent of school-aged children. Children with ADHD are easily distracted, impulsive, have difficulty focusing and sustaining attention, and can be easily overstimulated. In addition to these characteristics, some children with ADHD are also hyperactive. While all children can be highly active or lack the ability to stay focused at times, children with ADHD exhibit these behaviors in combination with one another more frequently and with greater severity than other children of the same age.

Identifying ADHD

The primary tool for identifying the symptoms of ADHD is the *Diagnostic and Statistical Manual of Mental Disorders,* published by the American Psychiatric Association. This diagnostic manual specifies three groups of behaviors that are characteristic of ADHD. Children need only demonstrate behaviors in any one group to be diagnosed with ADHD. Children in the first group show signs of being consistently inattentive. Children in the second group will show hyperactive and impulsive behaviors. The third group of children exhibit a combination of behaviors from both groups (inattention, hyperactivity, and impulsiveness).

According to the diagnostic manual, an inattentive type of ADHD child is identified when six or more of the following symptoms have persisted for at least six months to a degree that significant impairments in a child's daily activities are noted. These symptoms must be seen in two or more environments, such as at home, at school, or in social settings. Symptoms include:

- failure to pay close attention to details or make careless mistakes in schoolwork;
- difficulty sustaining attention to tasks or play activities;
- failure to listen when spoken to directly;
- failure to follow through on instructions or complete schoolwork, chores, or duties;
- difficulty organizing tasks and activities;
- avoidance, dislike, or reluctance to engage in tasks that require sustained mental effort;
- frequent loss of things necessary for tasks or activities;
- easy distraction by outside stimuli; and
- forgetfulness in daily activities.

The diagnostic manual identifies the hyperactive/impulsive ADHD child when six or more of the following symptoms have persisted for at least six months to a degree that significant impairment in a child's daily activities are noted. These symptoms must also be seen in two or more environments, such as at home, at school, or in social settings. Symptoms include:

- fidgeting with hands or feet or squirming in seat;
- leaving seat in classroom or in other situations where remaining in seat is expected;
- running about or climbing excessively;
- having difficulty playing or engaging in leisure activities quietly;
- often "on the go" or acting as if "driven by a motor";
- talking excessively;
- blurting out answers;
- having difficulty waiting turn; and
- interrupting or intruding on others.

Possible Causes of ADHD

ADHD has been extensively researched, but its exact cause is unknown. According to the organization Children and Adults with Attention Deficit Hyperactivity Disorder (CHADD), current research suggests a neurobiological basis for this disorder. This means that there may be an imbalance of neurotransmitters or a lack of the chemical dopamine, which is used by the brain to control behavior. When individuals concentrate, the brain releases neurotransmitters that enable them to focus on one thing and block out others. People with ADHD seem to have decreased amounts of these neurotransmitters. Some research suggests that abnormal glucose metabolism in the central nervous system may be a possible cause. Research indicates that the areas of the brain that control attention use less glucose, suggesting that these areas are less active for those with ADHD. Other studies suggest that prenatal drug and alcohol exposure may have an effect. Some doctors believe that environmental toxins and chemical additives in food may be the cause. There is no definite agreement on the neurobiological cause of ADHD. There is, however, widespread agreement among researchers that ADHD tends to run in families.

How Is ADHD Diagnosed?

There is currently no single test that can be given to diagnose ADHD. Since some biological and psychological disorders can appear similar to ADHD, these should be considered and ruled out before a diagnosis of ADHD is made. Conditions such as stress-related anxiety, depression, oppositional defiant disorder, the effects of child abuse or neglect, or obsessive compulsive disorder may look like ADHD but require different treatments.

A comprehensive evaluation is necessary to determine a diagnosis of ADHD. This includes information and observations from parents, teachers, school psychologists, and pediatricians. Parents see their children at home and in small social groups. Classroom teachers can be of assistance since they see how well children perform school work and how children interact with their peers. School psychologists can make behavioral observations in multiple settings and interview the child. Pediatricians provide needed medical information.

Completion of behavioral checklists are part of a comprehensive evaluation. The checklists rate the severity of ADHD symptoms and are completed by primary caregivers such as parents or guardians and classroom teachers. Items on the checklist include behaviors such as having no sense of fair play, temper outbursts, unpredictable behavior, and excessive demands for attention. In addition to this information, a thorough evaluation is needed of the child's current level of academic, social, and emotional functioning. This assessment is used to determine significant impairment in social relationships and academic performance. Careful consideration and review of all the information gathered is needed before the evaluation is complete.

Recommended Treatment for ADHD

Although there is no cure for ADHD, there is a recommended treatment plan that requires parents, educators, and members of the medical profession to work cooperatively. This plan includes parent training in managing behavior, counseling, educational supports, and medication when needed.

The parent training component recognizes how important it is for parents to provide clear expectations for behavior, establish consistent rules, provide positive reinforcement when rules are followed, and provide immediate consequences when rules are broken.

The counseling portion of the treatment plan may include both individual and family counseling. Family counseling may be useful in planning and evaluating workable strategies, such as conflict resolution, and providing needed emotional support. Individual counseling for the ADHD child can provide training in social skills, anger control, and relaxation techniques.

A supportive educational program with regular home-school communication is also needed. An

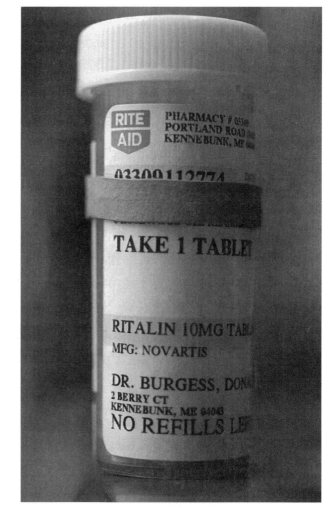

Drugs such as Ritalin are sometimes administered to children diagnosed with ADHD in an effort to provide a decrease in impulsiveness, aggressiveness, hyperactivity, and inappropriate social interaction. (A/P Wide World Photos)

ADHD child benefits when teachers provide structure by clearly communicating expectations, rules, and consequences. The educational program may also include modifications and accommodations such as shortening assignments, allowing more time for work completion or tests, and limiting homework.

The most controversial part of the treatment plan is the decision regarding medication of children with ADHD. When medication is prescribed, it is intended to improve the symptoms of ADHD. The benefits of medication can include a decrease in impulsiveness, aggressiveness, hyperactivity, and inappropriate social interaction. There can also be an increase in the child's ability to concentrate, shut out distractions, and complete schoolwork and jobs at home. The use of medication is controversial, though. Many people believe that schools advocate the use of medication as a way to control unruly behavior in children who do not necessarily have ADHD. The primary reason, however, that parents oppose the use of medication is because of possible side effects. Some children experience weight loss, lose their appetite, or have difficulty falling asleep. Together, parents and doctors should consider the benefits and concerns when making a decision about medication.

The Impact of ADHD on Families

Children with ADHD may have significant impairments that can have a profound impact on their families. Children often forget what they have been told or defiantly oppose what is requested of them. They tend to be demanding, unpredictable, restless, quick tempered, forgetful, inconsistent in their school work, and socially immature. These experiences lead to increased levels of parental frustration. Many parents struggle with deciding on the best methods for disciplining their child. They may question if they are being too strict or too permissive. Parents may feel guilty and at fault for their child's problems. Fair and consistent disciplinary practices can help change behavior in a positive way. When the condition is identified early and adequate treatment plans are implemented, children with ADHD can have successful school experiences and can develop positive relationships with peers and adults.

See also: ACTIVITY LEVEL; MENTAL DISORDERS

Bibliography

Barkley, Russell. *Attention Deficit Hyperactivity Disorder: A Handbook for Diagnosis and Treatment*, 2nd edition. New York: Guilford Press, 1998.

Children and Adults with Attention Deficit Hyperactivity Disorder (CHADD). Available from http://www.chadd.org; INTERNET

Rief, Sandra. *How to Reach and Teach ADD/ADHD Children*. West Nyack, NY: Center for Applied Research in Education, 1993.

Sandra J. White

ATTENTION SPAN

Attention span is the degree to which a child demonstrates sustained focus on designated tasks and activities, especially in school. During the preschool and early elementary school ages, attention span varies with age, gender, and type of activity. A longer attention span is generally found in older children than in younger children, and in girls more often than in boys. Children are usually able to maintain a longer attention span when performing tasks that match their abilities and interests.

An adequate attention span is an important part of learning in a classroom setting, enabling children to organize and consolidate important features of the subjects being studied. Most children develop the expected level of concentration in the course of ordinary school experience. But for those with short attention spans, learning problems sometimes develop, including over-attention to irrelevant details of tasks and general restlessness and overactive movements that distract them from their focus. Attention span problems are frequently reported in children with learning disabilities, such as those diagnosed with Attention Deficit Disorder (ADD) and Attention Deficit Hyperactivity Disorder (ADHD).

See also: ATTENTION DEFICIT HYPERACTIVITY DISORDER

Bibliography

Guevremont, David, and Russell Barkley. "Attention Deficit Hyperactivity Disorder in Children." In Stephen Hooper, George Hynd, and Robert Mattison eds., *Child Psychopathology: Diagnostic Criteria and Clinical Assessment*. Hillsdale, NJ: Erlbaum, 1992.

Hunt, Earl. "Verbal Ability." In Robert Sternberg ed., *Human Abilities*. New York: Freeman, 1985.

Thompson, Ross. "The Individual Child: Temperament, Emotion, Self, and Personality." In Marc Bornstein and Michael Lamb eds., *Developmental Psychology: An Advanced Textbook*, Mahwah, NJ: Erlbaum, 1999.

Nathan W. Gottfried

AUTISM

Autism, a condition more precisely referred to as autistic disorder, is a lifelong developmental disability affecting social and communicative functioning. In the American Psychiatric Association's *Diagnostic and Statistical Manual of Mental Disorders: DSM-IV*, autistic disorder is the main pervasive developmental disorder (PDD), with other disorders in the PDD classification including pervasive developmental disorder, not otherwise specified (PDD-NOS), and Asperger's disorder.

Diagnosis

DSM-IV describes autistic disorder as consisting of twelve possible symptom areas in three areas of development. These include social—marked impairment in nonverbal behaviors, failure at peer relations, impaired sharing of pleasure and lack of socioemotional reciprocity; communication—delay in communication without gesture compensation, impairment in conversational ability, stereotyped and repetitive language, and lack of imaginative play; atypical activities and interests—restricted interests, nonfunctional routines and rituals, and preoccupation with parts of objects. To be diagnosed with autistic disorder, an individual must exhibit at least six out of the twelve symptoms, with at least two being in the social domain, along with one each in the communicative domain and the domain of atypical activities and interests. Individuals with at least one symptom each in the social and communicative domains, but fewer than six symptoms overall, are classified as PDD-NOS as are individuals without symptoms in the domain of atypical activities and interests. The criteria for Asperger's disorder uses the same social criteria as autistic disorder, but requires at least one symptom in the area of atypical activities and interests, as well as normal age of onset for language.

Prevalence of Autism

There is much controversy concerning the prevalence of autism. *DSM-IV* notes a prevalence rate of 4 to 5 cases per 10,000 in the United States, though these data are based on diagnostic criteria from the third edition of the *DSM*, criteria that have been shown to be diagnostically more restrictive. Many investigators have suggested a prevalence rate for PDD of around 1 in 800 cases in the United States, but no definitive prevalence data exist for *DSM-IV* criteria. It is clear, however, that more cases are being diagnosed. Several possible influences include earlier detection, diagnosis of more mildly affected individuals, the use of autism rather than mental retardation as the primary diagnosis in cases of more severe mental retardation, and the preference for this diagnosis in geographic regions where it is associated with higher intensity delivery of services. According to *DSM-IV*, approximately 70 percent of individuals diagnosed with autism have also been diagnosed with mild to severe mental retardation.

Causes of the Disorder

The causes of autism remain incompletely understood, although 40 percent to 60 percent of cases are believed to have a genetic component traced to multiple genes predisposing development of different aspects of autism. Concordance in monozygotic (identical) twins is around 95 percent; in dizygotic (fraternal) twins, around 9 percent; and in siblings, 3 percent. About 15 percent to 25 percent of siblings of individuals with autism have mild to severe language difficulties.

Autism's Clinical Course

Autism is usually detected in the third or fourth year of life. Early hallmarks include a failure to begin pointing, an apparent lack of interest in peers, a disinterest in playing with toys (or a disinterest in playing with them the same way that others of the same age do), and a delay in the development of speech for communicative purposes. Children with autism have a difficult time coordinating verbal and nonverbal forms of communication and therefore often do not mark acknowledgement of being spoken to with a gaze, do not mark their own communicative speech with eye contact directed at the listener, and do not coordinate body gesture with gaze and vocalization in such communicative efforts. Some children with autism develop single words slowly, but then lose these words, seldom use them, or seemingly plateau in language development. Others develop language for the first time around the third or fourth year of life or after initiation of speech therapy. Early language for a child with autism is marked by an instrumental quality with utterances mainly focused on getting needs and wants addressed. There is typically little conversational use of language.

Autism has sometimes been characterized as a primary disorder of failing to develop a theory of mind. Autistic children, especially in the early years, show a fairly universal disability at assuming the perspective of others, engaging in planned deception, or showing empathy or sympathy. The range of emotional recognition and expression is more limited than normal and social-emotional responses are usually severely lacking. When language does develop, it may be characterized by use of immediate or delayed echolalia in the form of repeating what has just been heard (in the case of the former) or repeating something from past experience in its entirety (in the case of the latter). Echolalia often, though not always, serves some abbreviated communicative function resulting in a characteristically stilted manner of discourse.

In addition to social and language deficits, autism is often marked by odd ways of relating to the environment, which may include adherence to unreasonable routines, ritualized ways of carrying out everyday activities, and a general resistance to change. Autistic children may exhibit overly repetitive tendencies in speech and play, and for many, novelty is generally eschewed and exploratory activity is greatly reduced compared to peers. There may be fixations or avoidance of specific sensory stimuli, such as covering the ears to certain kinds of sounds, visually fixating on objects with a strong vertical or horizontal axis, peripheral gazing at objects, sniffing objects not usually smelled, and physical hypersensitivities—a strong aversion to solid foods or certain types of food, or the avoidance of certain types of clothing.

Treatment for Autism

Treatment for autism is mostly based on methods of changing maladaptive behavior and developing

Treatment for autism is primarily based on methods of changing maladaptive behavior and developing learning and communication skills. This line drawing was created by an autistic child, who has identified both himself ("Mike") and his brother ("Kevin") as passengers in the same car. (Gladys Agell and Vermont College of Norwich University)

learning skills. Behavior modification approaches, educationally based approaches, speech therapy, parent skill training, and adaptive skill training are generally part of an individualized multimodal treatment plan. The prescribing of drugs is used as an adjunct to treat specific symptoms, but there is no medication that treats autism as a whole. In the latter part of the 1990s, comparative reviews of model programs have shown that multiple methods are effective and that there is no one behavioral approach that is of singular value. Intensity of treatment, age of initiation of treatment, parent training, high teacher to student ratios, and use of structured intervention procedures all contribute to positive outcomes. Proven treatments include the use of behavior analysis procedures using discrete trial training methods tailored for areas of common autistic cognitive and motivational deficit, and the Treatment and Education for Autistic and Communication Handicapped Children (TEACCH) curriculum for structure with its emphasis on visually based guidance. Other treatment approaches target specific symptom areas such as the Picture Exchange Communication System (PECS), which targets communication. Most treatment programs are eclectic and integrate features of a number of approaches.

The field of autism treatment, both behavioral and medical, has been subject to many treatment fads, all claiming high levels of success that are either invalidated or simply not supported by subsequent controlled studies. On the behavioral side, such putative cures include facilitated communication, holding therapy, auditory integration therapy, and sensory-integration therapy. Putative cures on the medical side include treatment with megavitamins, B vitamins, dimethylglycine, secretin, and elimination diets for gluten and casein. Most families, at least initially, undertake multiple treatments including trials of some unproven treatments, which over time, tend to be tailored by perceived or measurable positive responses.

See also: FACILITATED COMMUNICATION; SOCIAL DEVELOPMENT

Bibliography

American Psychiatric Association. *The Diagnostic and Statistical Manual of Mental Disorders: DSM-IV.* Washington, DC: American Psychiatric Association, 1994.

Bryson, S. E. "Epidemiology of Autism: Overview and Issues Understanding." In Donald J. Cohen and Fred R. Volkmar eds., *Handbook of Autism and Pervasive Developmental Disorders,* 2nd edition. New York: Wiley, 1997.

Green, Gina. "Evaluating Claims about Treatment for Autism." In Catherine Maurice, Gina Green, and Stephen Luce eds., *Behavioral Intervention for Young Children with Autism: A Manual for Parents and Professionals.* Austin, TX: Pro Ed, 1996.

Harris, Sandra, and Jan Handleman, eds. *Preschool Education Programs for Children with Autism.* Austin, TX: Pro Ed, 1994.

Bryna Siegel

B

BABBLING AND EARLY WORDS

A child's entrance into human society begins with the onset of language development. Parents often acknowledge this accomplishment upon hearing their infant's first words. Research on early language has convinced scientists that the emergence of first words is inseparable from important developmental milestones that occur prior to the recording of these words. Pre-speech vocalizations can be examined narrowly within the verbal domain only, or can be explored in a wider scope as related to cognitive and communicative developments that are established during the first year of life. The study of pre-speech vocalizations flourished during the last quarter of the twentieth century. During the late 1970s and early 1980s, most efforts concentrated on describing the sounds infants produce. In the 1990s, study of pre-speech development expanded in several important directions.

The Form of Infants' Pre-Speech Vocalizations

Pre-speech vocalizations are divided into reflexive vocalizations (e.g., cries, coughs, hiccups), which are related to the baby's physical state, and nonreflexive vocalizations (e.g., cooing, playful productions, yelling), which contain phonetic and syllabic features of speech. Both vowels and consonants appear in nonreflexive vocalizations, and the most prevalent syllable structure is a consonant followed by a vowel (CV; e.g., \ba\, \du\, \ke\). The overall composition of

pre-speech vocalizations changes dramatically during the first year of life. In the first six months, babies all over the world sound alike. During this period, vowels predominate and are supported by prolonged back consonants (e.g., \k\, \g\). During the next six months, the sound repertoire significantly expands, with a marked shift toward more frontal consonants. John Locke reported in 1993 that, by their first birthday, American English-speaking infants produce stops (\p\, \b\, \t\, \d\, \k\, \g\), nasals (\m\, \n\), and glides (\w\, \j\).

Stages in the Development of Pre-Speech Vocalizations

Developmental stages of pre-speech vocalizations (e.g., as described by Carol Stoel-Gammon in 1998) are not discrete, and vocalizations from previous stages continue to be uttered subsequently. Novel emergent behaviors define the beginning of a new stage. Ages are assigned to each stage as estimates only, because children differ greatly regarding the timing for recording milestones of early language development.

The first stage (from zero to two months), phonation, is characterized mainly by fussing, crying, sneezing, and burping, which bear little resemblance to adult speech. The second stage (at two to three months), cooing, begins when back vowels and nasals appear together with velar consonants (e.g., \gu\, \ku\). Cooing differs in its acoustic characteristics from adult vocalizations and is recorded mainly during interactions with caregivers. In the third stage (at four to six months), vocal play or expansion, syllable-like productions with long vowels appear. Squeals, growls, yells, bilabial or labiodental trills, and friction noises demonstrate infants' playful exploration of their vocal tract capabilities during this stage.

In the extremely important canonical babbling stage (at seven to ten months), two types of productions emerge: reduplicated babbling—identical, repetitive sequences of CV syllables (e.g., \ma\ma\, \da\da\); and variegated babbling—sequences of different consonants and vowels (e.g., CV, V, VC, VCV = \ga\e\im\ada\). Such productions are not true words, as they lack meaning. Canonical babbling is syllabic, containing mainly frontal stops, nasals, and glides coupled with lax vowels (e.g., \a\, \e\, \o\). The emergence of canonical babbling is highly important, holding predictive value for future linguistic developments. Oller and her colleagues in 1999 argued that babies who do not produce canonical babbling on time are at high risk for future speech and language pathology, and should be carefully evaluated by a language clinician.

In the fifth stage (at twelve to thirteen months), jargon or intonated babble, infants produce long strings of syllables having varied stress and intonation patterns. Jargon sounds like whole sentences conveying the contents of statements or questions, and often co-occurs with real words. Yet, it lacks linguistic content or grammatical structure.

Pre-Speech Vocalizations in Different Target Languages

The early interpretation of similarities in the phonetic structure of babbling among infants who acquire different languages (e.g., Japanese, Hebrew) was that pre-speech vocalizations are universal. This observation was explained by the strong constraints of the mouth's anatomical characteristics and by physiological mechanisms controlling movements of the tongue and palate. Cross-linguistic research in the 1990s revealed, however, that clear influences of segmental and suprasegmental patterns (i.e., intonation and stress) of the input are recognizable in pre-speech vocalizations. This is particularly true during the second half of the first year of life. In a longitudinal comparative study by Bénédicte de Boysson-Baradis (1999) of ten-month-old Spanish, English, Japanese, and Swedish infants, the relative distribution of consonants in their canonical babbling resembled the distribution of these segments in their language. As babies grow, the segmental similarity between their babbling and early words increases. Sever-

al studies by Peter Jusezyk and colleagues on speech perception indicate that infants' sensitivity to the acoustics and phonetics of languages increases with age, influencing their ability to discriminate the sequences of sounds and syllable structures typical to their own language. Indirect evidence for the role of audition in the development of pre-speech vocalizations derives from studies on deaf children, who show significant delays in the emergence of canonical babbling and also a decreased variety of consonants uttered from age eight months onward.

Mutual Imitation within Mother-Child Interaction

In 1989 Metchthild and Hanus Papoušek were among the first researchers to point out that more than 50 percent of two- to five-month-olds' noncrying vocalizations are either infant imitations of mothers' previous vocalizations or mothers' imitations of infants' previous vocalizations. They suggested that this mutual vocal matching mechanism relates to the emotional regulation of communication in the beginning of life. Joanna Blake and Bénédicte de Boysson-Bardies found in 1992 that infants tend to vocalize more while manipulating small objects and especially when adults are present. Edy Veneziano in 1988 analyzed vocal turn taking in pairs of nine- to seventeen-month-old babies and their mothers. She reported that, as children advance toward conventional language, mothers' imitations of what babies say becomes selective. Mothers imitate only those infant vocalizations resembling conventional words, thus signaling to the child what constitutes a linguistic symbol with meaning.

Pre-Symbolic Productions in Hearing and in Deaf Infants

Cumulative research on pre-speech vocalizations clearly indicates that babbling is in fact structurally and functionally related to early speech. Locke argued in 1996 that when variegated babbling emerges, a consistent relation is identified between vocalizations and specific communicative functions (i.e., protest, question, and statement). At around age eighteen months, the child's phonological system is clearly shaped by the target language's phonetic characteristics, and at that time conventional words emerge.

Indirect evidence for the developmental significance of babbling was published in a revolutionary 1991 paper by Laura Petitto and Paula Marentette on hand babbling in two deaf infants of signing mothers. The argument was that these two infants (who were recorded at ages ten, twelve, and fourteen months) produced far more manual babbling than three matched hearing infants at similar ages. The deaf infants' hand babbling also revealed phonetic features of American Sign Language, suggesting that babbling reflects infants' innate ability to analyze phonetic and syllabic components of linguistic input.

Pre-Speech Productions and First Words or Signs

Early words are produced by the child in expected contexts, and hence are recognized by familiar listeners as linguistic units conveying meanings. In 1999 Esther Dromi distinguished between comprehensible and meaningful words. Comprehensible words are phonetically consistent forms resembling adult words that caregivers understand, but that do not yet convey referential meanings. Meaningful words are symbolic, arbitrary, and agreed-upon terms of reference. Considerable variation exists in both the age of speech onset and the rate of early lexical development. Large-scale questionnaire data reported in 1994 by Fenson and his colleagues for English-speaking typically developing children, cited the range of vocabulary size for twelve- to thirteen-month-olds at 0 to 67 different words, and for eighteen- to nineteen-month-olds at 13 to 471 different words. In 2000 Maital and her colleagues reported very similar figures for Hebrew.

Early words are constructed from a limited set of consonants, mainly stops, nasals, and glides. Syllable structures in these words are usually CV, CVC, or CVCV. Several researchers found that during the first few months of lexical learning, many new words are composed from segments that the child is already using in babbling. A number of researchers have proposed that patterns of lexical selection and avoidance reflect the child's production capabilities. When productive vocabularies contain more than a hundred different words, the influences of phonology on the lexicon decline. Nevertheless, children who have relatively larger lexicons of single words also show larger inventories of sounds and syllable structures than children with smaller productive lexicons. Precocious word learners have much larger phonetic inventories than typically developing children at age eighteen months. The major semantic achievement in the first few months of vocabulary learning is the ability to use words referentially. Martyn Barrett and Esther Dromi, who independently carried out detailed longitudinal analyses of repeated uses of the same words over time, have argued that some early words show referential use from their outset, while other words are initially produced only in very specific contexts. Throughout the one-word stage, the phonology of words improves, and meanings become symbolic and

arbitrary. A word initially produced in just one situation is now uttered in a much wider range of contexts, until it becomes completely context free and referential. As words become conventional tools for expressing meanings, the amount of pre-speech vocalizations declines and gradually disappears.

See also: INFANCY; LANGUAGE DEVELOPMENT

Bibliography

Barrett, Martyn. "Early Semantic Representations and Early Word Usage." In Stan Kuczay and Martyn Barrett eds., *The Development of Word Meaning.* New York: Springer, 1986.

Blake, Joanna, and Bénédicte de Boysson-Bardies. "Patterns in Babbling: A Cross-Linguistic Study." *Journal of Child Language* 19 (1992):51–74.

de Boysson-Bardies, Bénédicte. *How Language Comes to Children: From Birth to Two Years.* Cambridge, MA: MIT Press, 1999.

Dromi, Esther. *Early Lexical Development.* Cambridge, Eng.: Cambridge University Press, 1987.

Dromi, Esther. "Early Lexical Development." In Martyn Barrett ed., *The Development of Language.* London: UCL Press, 1999.

Fenson, Larry, Philip S. Dale, Steven J. Reznick, Elizabeth Bates, Donna Thal, and S. J. Pethick. *Variability in Early Communication Development.* Malden, MA: Blackwell, 1994.

Jusczyk, Peter W. *The Discovery of Spoken Language.* Cambridge, MA: MIT Press, 1997.

Locke, John L. *The Child's Path to Spoken Language.* Cambridge, MA: Harvard University Press, 1993.

Locke, John L. "Why Do Infants Begin to Talk? Language as an Unintended Consequence." *Journal of Child Language* 23 (1996):251–268.

Maital, Sharone L., Esther Dromi, Avi Sagi, and Marc H. Borenstein. "The Hebrew Communicative Development Inventory: Language Specific Properties and Cross-Linguistic Generalizations." *Journal of Child Language* 27 (2000):43–67.

Oller, Kimberly D., and Rebecca E. Eilers. "The Role of Audition in Infant Babbling." *Journal of Child Language* 59 (1988):441–449.

Papoušek, Metchthild, and Hanus Papoušek. "Form and Function of Vocal Matching in Interactions between Mothers and Their Precanonical Infants." *First Language* 9 (1989):137–158.

Petitto, Laura A., and Paula F. Marentette. "Babbling in the Manual Mode: Evidence for the Ontogeny of Language." *Science* 251 (1991):1493–1496.

Stoel-Gammon, Carol. "Role of Babbling and Phonology in Early Linguistic Development." In Amy M. Wetherby, Steven F. Warren, and J. Reichle eds., *Transitions in Prelinguistic Communication.* Baltimore: Paul Brookes, 1997.

Veneziano, Edy. "Vocal-Verbal Interaction and the Construction of Early Lexical Knowledge." In M. D. Smith and John L. Locke eds., *The Emergent Lexicon: The Child's Development of a Linguistic Vocabulary.* New York: Academic Press, 1988.

Vihman, Marilyn M. *Phonological Development: The Origins of Language in the Child.* Cambridge, MA: Blackwell, 1996.

Esther Dromi

BANDURA, ALBERT (1925–)

Albert Bandura, who proposed the most comprehensive and widely held theory of modeling, was born in

Albert Bandura proposed the most comprehensive and accepted modeling theory. (Archives of the History of American Psychology)

Mundane, Alberta, Canada, in 1925. He initially termed this social learning theory, but it is now identified as social cognitive theory. Bandura's early school years were spent in a small, understaffed school in which students had to take a great amount of responsibility for their own learning. This style of learning helped to foster his desire for inquiry, which he has maintained throughout his career.

Bandura attended the University of British Columbia, graduating in 1949 with the Bolocan Award in Psychology. He received his master's degree in 1951 and his Ph.D. in 1952 from the University of Iowa, where he was strongly influenced by the work of Neal Miller (1909–), an early proponent of social learning as a way to explain human behavior. Shortly after graduating, Bandura joined the faculty at Stanford University, where he was promoted to full professor in 1964 and awarded the David Starr Jordan Endowed Chair in psychology in 1974.

In collaboration with his first doctoral student Richard Walters, Bandura conducted research into the role of modeling and observational learning in child behavior. In 1963 they published *Social Learning and Personality Development,* in which they stated that an individual could model behavior by just observing the behavior of another. Bandura later developed a comprehensive social cognitive theory of human functioning. In this theory, self-regulatory and self-reflective processes enable the individual to adapt to various situations. This interest in self-efficacy is a central aspect to his theoretical position. This work led to his publication of *Social Foundations of Thought and Action: A Social Cognitive Theory* in 1986 and *Self-Efficacy: The Exercise of Control* in 1997.

Bandura served as president of the American Psychological Association in 1974, and he has earned many awards, including the Distinguished Scientific Contributions Award and the Thorndike Award for Distinguished Contributions of Psychology to Education by the American Psychological Association; the William James Award of the American Psychological Society; the James McKeen Cattell Award; and the Distinguished Scientist Award of the Society of Behavioral Medicine.

Bandura's seminal research on the modeling behavior of children, self-efficacy, and social cognitive theory made him a renowned researcher. His own arduous work adds credence to his theoretical position that belief in oneself can lead to success in life.

See also: PERSONALITY DEVELOPMENT

Bibliography

Publications by Bandura

Bandura, Albert, and Richard H. Walters. *Adolescent Aggression: A Study of the Influence of Child-Training Practices.* New York: Ronald Press, 1959.

Principles of Behavior Modification. New York: Holt, Rinehart and Winston, 1969.

Psychological Modeling: Conflicting Theories. Chicago: Aldine-Atherton, 1971.

Aggression: A Social Learning Analysis. Englewood Cliffs, NJ: Prentice-Hall, 1973.

Social Foundations of Thought and Action: A Social Cognitive Theory. Englewood Cliffs, NJ: Prentice-Hall, 1986.

Self-Efficacy: The Exercise of Control. New York: W. H. Freeman, 1997.

Robert C. Hardy

BAYLEY, NANCY (1899–1994)

Nancy Bayley, an eminent developmental psychologist, made significant contributions to the measurement of infant intelligence and human development. Born in Dalles, Oregon, on September 28, 1899, she is best known for her work leading to the publication of the Bayley Scales of Infant Development in 1968 and the revised edition in 1993. Her career, spanning six decades, may have been influenced by her work on the world-renowned Berkeley Growth Study, a longitudinal study she initiated in 1928 that followed subjects from infancy through adulthood. Her productive career produced more than 200 publications about child development and she received many awards. Bayley was the first woman to receive the Distinguished Scientific Contribution Award of the American Psychological Association in 1966. Other awards included the Gold Medal Award of the American Psychological Association in 1982 and the G. Stanley Hall Award for distinguished contributions to developmental psychology in 1971.

Prior to taking an introductory psychology course with Edwin R. Guthrie, Bayley planned to teach English. With her interest in psychology sparked, Bayley earned her master's degree from the University of Washington just two years after earning her bachelor's degree at the same institution. She earned her Ph.D. at the University of Iowa in 1926.

Bayley was descended from pioneering ancestors including paternal grandparents who sailed around Cape Horn to Victoria, British Columbia, and maternal grandparents who traveled west by covered wagon. Like her ancestors, Bayley has been described as a pioneer who extended the study of human development to a lifespan perspective and meticulously studied a wide range of interests. She demonstrated her adventuresome spirit when she carried out a series of studies measuring fear reactions on a galvanometer. According to a 1930 news account, she shot off a .38 revolver in class to elicit and measure fear response. Most of her studies were concerned with detailed exploration of physical and mental growth and intelligence predictability. She explored relationships among measured characteristics and carefully considered environmental and other influences on her subjects. Bayley's interests included the study of physical maturation, body build, androgyny, and sex differences. By 1962, through her studies of skeletal maturation, she developed a means of predicting adult height within one inch. The tables she developed are still used by endocrinologists.

Bayley's career focused on developing tests for infants and young children that correlate with other measures and/or predict later intelligence. While looking for data trends and groupings, she highlighted individual differences in human development. She did not believe intelligence was fixed and studied the cause of variability in scores across the lifespan. She was ahead of her time when she examined changes in intelligence in adulthood in the 1950s. She was one of the first to consider the impact of child-rearing attitudes and behaviors on child development, and recognized that there are so many factors influencing development that it would be difficult to isolate any

Developmental psychologist Nancy Bayley was responsible for significant contributions to the measurement of infant intelligence and human development. (Institute of Human Development, University of California, Berkeley)

one factor, genetic or environmental, as possessing the greatest importance.

Bayley was an outstanding developmental psychologist distinguished by her contributions and her early anticipation of current topics. Although she spent most of her professional life at the University of California, Berkeley, she also spent ten years at the National Institute of Mental Health in Maryland beginning in 1954 as chief of the Section on Early Development, Laboratory of Psychology. Bayley was a leader in her field who left a legacy of work and contributions worthy of further study.

See also: INFANCY; INTELLIGENCE; MILESTONES OF DEVELOPMENT

Bibliography

Lipsitt, Lewis P., and Dorothy H. Eichorn. "Nancy Bayley." In Agnes N. O'Connell and Nancy Felipe Russo, eds., *Women in Psychology: A Bio-Bibliographic Sourcebook.* New York: Greenwood Press, 1990.

Rosenblith, Judy F. "A Singular Career: Nancy Bayley." *Developmental Psychology* 28 (1992):747–758.

Publications by Bayley

"Mental Growth during the First Three Years: A Developmental Study of Sixty-One Children by Repeated Tests." *Genetic Psychology Monographs* 38 (1933):1–38.

Studies in the Development of Young Children. Berkeley: University of California Press, 1940.

"On the Growth of Intelligence." *American Psychologist* 10 (1955):805–818.

"Implicit and Explicit Values in Science as Related to Human Growth and Development." *Merrill-Palmer Quarterly* 2 (1956):121–126.

"Value and Limitations of Infant Testing." *Children* 5 (1958):129–133.

"The Accurate Prediction of Growth and Adult Height." *Modern Problems in Paediatrics* 7 (1962):234–255.

"Research in Child Development: A Longitudinal Perspective." *Merrill-Palmer Quarterly* 11 (1965):183–208.

"Behavioral Correlates of Mental Growth: Birth to Thirty-Six Years." *American Psychologist* 23 (1968):1–17.

Tracy L. Smith

BEHAVIOR ANALYSIS

Behavior analysis is the scientific study of how a specific observable (and therefore measurable) behavior is related to specific observable events in the environment of that behavior—events (changes in the environment) that are antecedent (prior) to and those that are consequent to the behavior in question. The behavior of all living organisms is continuously and lawfully influenced (changed) by its consequences: Some increase and others decrease the probability of every response. Hence, the unique physical and social environment of an infant develops a unique person by selecting (strengthening) some behaviors (motor, verbal, and emotional) in certain situations and ignoring or punishing (weakening) others. In this continuous process of selection by consequences, every new skill encounters new features of the environment. Consequently, every person has some behaviors similar to those of everyone else and some that are different from anyone else. Behavior analysis is used to improve behavior by altering the environment.

See also: SKINNER, B. F.; THEORIES OF DEVELOPMENT

Bibliography

Bijou, Sidney W., and Donald M. Baer. *Child Development*, Vol. 1: *A Systematic and Empirical Theory.* New York: Appleton-Century-Crofts, 1961.

Skinner, B. F. "Selection by Consequences." *Science* 213 (1981):501–504.

Don Bushell Jr.

BELL CURVE

In 1835 Belgian statistician and astronomer Lambert Quételet suggested applying statistical probabilities to quantitative trait differences between individuals. The resulting Bell Curve, a bilateral graphic with tails resembling a bell's rim, served to compare individual characteristics against those of a group. In 1869 Francis Galton (supporter of Darwin's evolutionary theory) extended the meaning of the graph to include the measurement of natural ability in addition to other traits. It reflects distributions of most normally developed human physical, intellectual, and personality traits, designating a probable frequency for each value of the trait. The average of a set of values becomes the distribution mean, located midpoint in this graphic. Valuable in psychological testing, comparing individuals' abilities relative to others may suggest relevant outcomes such as need for special educational treatment. Some genetics-oriented researchers have generated controversy by applying Bell Curves to intelligence data collected on racial groups. Questionable assumptions about intellectual inferiority among some races leads to flawed educational treatments, impeding ability development for specific groups.

See also: DEVELOPMENTAL NORMS; INTELLIGENCE

Bibliography

Anastasi, Anne. *Psychological Testing*, 5th edition. New York: Macmillan, 1982.

Herrnstein, Richard J., and Charles Murray. *The Bell Curve: Intelligence and Class Structure in American Life.* New York: Free Press, 1994.

Patricia A. Haensly

BILINGUAL EDUCATION

Bilingual education programs in schools aim to teach students to listen, comprehend, speak, read, and write in a language other than their native tongue. This is done most effectively when use of their primary language is encouraged as well. Students in bilingual classes acquire greater skills and acquire them more quickly when they continue to practice both languages. This also increases their effectiveness in the other core classroom subjects and helps them to develop social competencies. A language may be acquired by being in the environment where the language is spoken and participating in that cultural setting, or it may be learned in a classroom with field techniques that allow practice in the new language. Therefore, one goal of bilingual education is to create an environment where students and their cultures are fully supported.

See also: LANGUAGE ACQUISITION DEVICE;
LANGUAGE DEVELOPMENT

Bibliography

Baker, Colin. *A Parents' and Teachers' Guide to Bilingualism.* Clevedon, Eng.: Multilingual Matters, 2000.

Baker, Colin. *Foundations of Bilingual Education and Bilingualism.* Clevedon, Eng.: Multilingual Matters, 1997.

Baker, Colin, and Sylvia Prys Jones. *Encyclopedia of Bilingualism and Bilingual Education.* Clevedon, Eng.: Multilingual Matters, 1998.

Valdes, Guadalupe, and Richard Figueroa. *Bilingualism and Testing: A Special Case of Bias.* Norwood, NJ: Ablex Publishing Corporation, 1994.

Deana Reimer
David Nelson

BINET, ALFRED (1857–1911)

Alfred Binet's most significant contribution to the field of child psychology was the development of the first intelligence test.

Binet was born in Nice, France, in 1857. He received a law degree in 1878 but became interested in the field of psychology in 1880. Binet did not receive any formal graduate training in psychology. His first appointment was in a French laboratory, the Salêptrière, conducting research on hypnosis under the supervision of Jean Charcot. In 1890 Binet rejected Charcot's theories and began research on cognition at the Sorbonne's Laboratory of Physiological Psychology. In 1894 Binet became the director of the laboratory, where he worked until his death in 1911.

The unifying theme of Binet's research was the examination of individual differences and similarities in cognition. Binet studied a range of populations, including children, mental hospital patients, and professional artists. His research topics were also wide-ranging, including studies of consciousness, sensation, creativity, language development, memory development, and mental fatigue.

Binet's most influential contributions to the field of psychology were in the area of intelligence testing. In contrast to his contemporaries who supported the measurement of physical features or a single factor as an assessment of intelligence, Binet supported a functional, multidimensional view of intelligence that emphasized reasoning and comprehension. Because of his unique approach to studying intelligence, the Paris school system asked Binet to develop a test that could be used to identify children who would benefit from special education classes. In 1905 Binet and his collaborator, Theophile Simon, responded to this request by creating the first intelligence test, the Binet-Simon Scale. Binet revised the scale in 1908 and again in 1911.

The first intelligence test was developed by Alfred Binet in 1905. (Psychology Archives, The University of Akron)

A second focus of Binet's research was the cognitive development of his two daughters, Alice and Madeleine. His extensive observations and experimental studies of his daughters allowed him to develop several theories about cognitive development. Binet believed that the purpose of cognitive development is to allow children to adapt to the physical and social demands of their environment, emphasizing the fact that children learn by assimilating new experiences into their existing ways of thinking.

An important milestone in Binet's career was the creation of the first laboratory based in a European school for young children, the Laboratory of Experimental Pedagogy. The purpose of this laboratory was to develop a systematic line of experimental research with children and to provide training for teachers on how to educate mentally retarded children. The establishment of this laboratory was a major event in the formation of the field of child psychology.

In addition to Binet's considerable direct contributions to the field of psychology, his work has also influenced the research of subsequent generations of child psychologists.

See also: DEVELOPMENTAL NORMS; INTELLIGENCE

Bibliography

Wolf, Theta. *Alfred Binet.* Chicago: University of Chicago Press, 1973.

Publications by Binet

Binet, Alfred, and Theophile Simon. *A Method of Measuring the Development of the Intelligence of Young Children,* 3rd edition. Chicago: Chicago Medical Book, 1915.

Jennifer D. Wishner

BIRTH

Throughout the animal kingdom, birth is universally recognized as a miracle of renewal where, once again, a life begins. While humans are better than ever at saving the lives of even the smallest newborn, the whole process of birth is one of amazing change and brings finality to nine months of preparation.

Labor

Labor is the beginning of the active birth process. Many expectant mothers ask themselves the important question "Is this it?" more than once in the late weeks of pregnancy. Sometimes they feel a slight contraction and then nothing more. Such contractions, known as Braxton-Hicks contractions, are relatively painless and begin as early as the sixth month and may continue throughout the pregnancy. Real labor contractions cause more discomfort, occur with greater regularity, and are intensified by walking.

Other signs may or may not indicate that labor is beginning, such as an ache in the small of the back, abdominal cramps, diarrhea, indigestion, "show" (a small amount of blood-tinged mucus emerging from the vagina), and the "water breaking" (a discharge of fluid from the vagina). The discharge of fluid, which is caused by the rupture of membranes, can occur some time before actual labor begins. The only certain signs of labor are the appearance of the show and the onset of regular, rhythmic contractions that increase in frequency and strength. When the fluid from the amniotic sac is discharged, the first line of defense against infection is broken. Often, if labor does not begin after the water breaks, the physician may induce labor.

Stages of Labor

Labor progresses through three stages: dilation, or "the opening," expulsion, and placental. The first stage, dilation, can last anywhere from two hours to sixteen hours or more. At first, each contraction is thirty to forty-five seconds in duration and occurs about every fifteen to twenty minutes. The contractions are involuntary and the woman cannot start them or stop them at will or make them come faster or slower. Their function is to dilate the cervix until it is wide enough to let the baby through—usually about four inches (ten centimeters). In the course of the first stage of labor the contractions increase in frequency until they are only a minute or two apart. Each contraction itself also becomes longer and, toward the end of the first stage, may last ninety seconds.

At the end of the first stage there may be a series of very intense contractions; during this time the cervix has been stretched around the baby's head. The woman may feel ready to give up, but this phase, known as transition, is soon over. It rarely lasts more than half an hour and is often much shorter. In expulsion, the second stage of labor, the involuntary contractions continue to be long in duration and closely spaced, but now the woman has a strong urge to bear down with her abdominal muscles. At each new contraction she pushes down with all her strength as the baby's scalp comes into view, only to disappear again when the contraction ends. This is known as crowning. With each contraction more and more of the baby's head can be seen. At this point in labor, some obstetricians may perform an episiotomy (making a small slit in the skin outside the vagina toward the anus) to prevent this tissue from tearing. When the baby's head comes out as far as its widest diameter, it stays out, and in a short time it is free. The head may be molded (elongated in shape as a result of its passage through the cervix), but the soft skull bones that have been squeezed together soon recover their normal shape.

Some babies will give their first cry at this point. With the next contractions the shoulders emerge, and the rest of the body slips out easily. The feelings of both parents at this time are almost impossible to put into words: elation, exhaustion, and great feelings of tenderness and caring.

It was once the practice for the doctor to hold the baby up by the feet immediately following delivery to allow fluid and mucus to escape from the baby's mouth and nose, so that the infant could start breathing, usually with a gasp and a cry. Today it is more usual to aspirate the mucus from the baby's mouth and nose by suction as soon as the head is delivered. This gives the baby a slight head start on independent breathing.

As soon as delivery is complete, the umbilical cord is clamped and cut. The baby is then wrapped in a receiving blanket, and someone performs a variety of procedures that vary from hospital to hospital. Typically, drops of silver nitrate are placed in the baby's eyes to prevent infection, both mother and baby are given plastic identification bracelets, and fingerprints of the mother and sometimes footprints of the baby are taken.

At this time the neonate's general state of health is evaluated using the APGAR scoring system. At one, five, and ten minutes after birth the baby is given a score of 0, 1, or 2 on Activity (muscle), Pulse (or heart rate), Grimace (or reflex action), Appearance (color), and Respiration (breathing). This test provides very general information on whether the baby's life-sustaining functions appear normal and what kinds of potentially dangerous problems may be present. The majority of children score between 5 and 10, and 90 percent have a score of 7 or better; there is no reason for concern unless the score is below 5.

During the third or placental stage, the afterbirth (the placenta and cord) is expelled from the uterus. Labor is now completed.

The length of the entire process varies greatly, as does the actual experience of labor. Fifteen hours is an average figure for the duration of birth from the first contraction to the expulsion of the afterbirth for a first birth. But this average covers a spectrum of labor as long as twenty-four hours and as short as three hours or less. Labor is usually longer for first babies than for later ones, and longer for boys than girls. Two reasons for a longer first labor might be the easier adaptation of the woman's body to the process and the reduced amount of anxiety present in subsequent births.

"Gentle Birth" Techniques

One way that the process of labor can be made easier for the expectant mother is the use of certain techniques often referred to as gentle births, such as the Lamaze and Dick-Read methods of childbirth. Both of these became very popular in the early 1970s. Grantly Dick-Read believed that pain during childbirth is not inevitable but is the result of fear passed on from mother to daughter over the generations. Dick-Read stressed that by educating the woman about the birth experience, the fear of the unknown can be removed. In its place a more positive view about delivery can be substituted. In 1967 a French obstetrician, Fernand Lamaze, developed a method for childbirth he called "childbirth without pain." This popular technique usually begins in the third trimester of pregnancy when the woman practices breathing and other exercises with her "coach" (usually the father). These exercises are used during labor to help a woman control her anxiety and be able to relax and push at the appropriate time. By practicing the exercises in advance, the command or suggestion of the coach is quick in coming and easy to maintain at the time of childbirth.

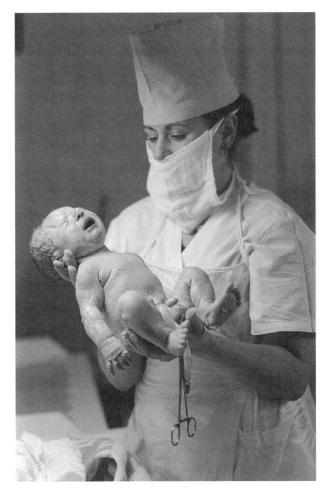

A doctor holding a newborn baby boy at a hospital in Moscow. The birth was complicated because the infant's umbilical cord was wrapped around his neck. Doctors had to push on the mother's belly and use forceps to get him out. (David & Peter Turnley/Corbis)

There are a substantial number of studies showing that prepared childbirth enhances feelings of self-esteem, increases the husband's degree of participation, and even strengthens the marital relationship. Whereas in the 1970s fathers were still marginally included in the birth of their children, it is almost the exception in the early twenty-first century when they are not.

What are the baby's first impressions of the world he or she is being thrust into? One French obstetrician, Frederick Leboyer, believes that the very act of being born can be a terrifying experience. In Leboyer's view, the violence of modern delivery techniques contributes a good deal to this "hell and white hot" experience.

The Leboyer technique involves a number of radical changes in the delivery procedure. As soon as the infant begins to emerge, the physicians and nurses attending the birth lower their voices, and the lights in the delivery room are turned down. Everyone handles the baby with the greatest possible tenderness. Immediately after delivery the baby is placed on the mother's abdomen, where the baby can start breathing before the umbilical cord is cut. After a few minutes the obstetrician places the baby in a lukewarm bath, an environment very much like the amniotic fluid. In this way the difference between the fetal environment and the world is minimized.

Is Leboyer's method better? Safe? Of the few studies that have been done, the results seem to indicate that babies delivered this way are similar to others delivered in a more conventional fashion. Whether or not there are any long-lasting effects will have to be judged after sufficient information is available about these "gentle birth" babies as they grow.

Alternate Birth Centers

Hospitals operate as bustling, crisis-oriented places. Such institutions are for sick people, and pregnancy is not considered an illness by supporters of a new kind of environment for giving birth—the alternate birth center. Alternate birth centers were developed because many parents objected to what they felt to be the impersonal, needlessly technological, and increasingly expensive childbirth procedures available in the conventional hospital setting. As a growing number of women chose to give birth at home, the risks involved became a concern. Alternate birth centers, then, are a response to both the dissatisfaction with hospitals and the hazards of home births.

These centers were all but unheard of in 1969. Within a few decades, at least 1,000 had been established, and the trend continued into the early twenty-first century. In 1978 the medical establishment officially endorsed many elements of this alternate care, recommending that it be included in conventional maternity services. Out-of-hospital facilities for the management of low-risk deliveries were also established.

Alternate birth centers provide a relaxed, home-like atmosphere for the pregnant woman, her family, and the newborn. The most dramatic aspect of an alternate birth center compared with a conventional hospital is the room where the deliveries take place. Unlike the operating-room atmosphere to which laboring women are generally sent at the most uncomfortable, critical moment, the birthing room—the location of the woman's predelivery hours—is a cheerfully decorated suite resembling a bedroom. Women in labor move about freely. They rest as they choose and may be accompanied by their husbands, families, and friends. An attending nurse, midwife, or doctor delivers the baby into this low-key, family-oriented environment. It is dimly lit, quiet, and peaceful.

The new mothers, and those with them, report a sense of control and contentment in contrast to the anxiety and isolation experienced by many in the traditional delivery room. Many of these centers also encourage the participation of other siblings in various stages of the pregnancy and birth.

Following the birth, the new family remains in the birthing room, in close physical contact. The newborn is placed on the mother's bare skin (which can act almost like a "natural incubator") and has the first opportunity to suckle and enjoy eye contact. A soothing warm bath may be administered. In these first hours, bonding between the parents and child has a unique quality. In some birthing rooms, siblings may also share these special experiences. The entire family leaves the alternate birth center together, usually earlier than from the traditional setting.

For safety, birthing-room facilities keep a significant amount of emergency equipment hidden within the suite itself and deliver only low-risk births. Nonetheless, of these births, approximately 10 percent develop problems best handled in a more conventional setting. When located in a hospital, birthing rooms are usually adjacent to traditional delivery and operating rooms.

Midwives

At one time the use of a midwife conjured up visions of birth-attending barbarians in a dimly lit, unsanitary room. Today, nothing could be further from the truth. Midwifery as a profession has the status it deserves as an integral and indispensable component of prenatal care and childbirth. Popular in Europe for many years, it is becoming more so in the United States.

Midwives are increasingly associated with physicians, where they can handle the majority of the prenatal care that needs to be done and up to 90 percent of the actual births. The remaining births that are of high risk are usually under the physician's care.

A woman might choose to have a child delivered by a midwife for several reasons. One of the most important is that the traditional medical community continues to treat pregnancy as an illness and the pregnant woman as a sick person. This kind of thinking is slowly being rejected, in part as the result of a U.S. Supreme Court action ruling that pregnancy is a disability and not a disease. There are several other reasons why midwives are becoming more popular:

- New changes in the law allow the licensing of midwives.
- There is, as a result of the women's movement, a sharp increase in the demand for women practitioners to assist in deliveries.

- Midwives are better trained today than ever and often go through intensive university-based classes in physiology and obstetrics.
- The role of technology in childbirth has been questioned in that it tends to be dehumanizing. Midwives are less likely to resort to such techniques, which in some cases may present more dangers to the woman and the infant than not.
- The federal government endorses the use of midwives and encourages institutions to employ them.

Perhaps the best combination is a midwife working directly with a physician so there is adequate technical backup if necessary.

Complications

Most "complications" can usually be dealt with successfully by the obstetrician and the hospital staff. The baby may, for example, come out bottom first in what is called a breech presentation. Sometimes one foot is first to appear, and sometimes the umbilical cord comes out alongside the head. The doctor must manage these variations and often actually turn the baby before birth with great skill to avoid any further complications.

Babies, for the most part, deliver themselves. It is when complications develop that the training and expertise of the health-care provider are needed. The fetal heartbeat is monitored during labor, and when there is cause for concern, a cesarean delivery may need to be performed.

A cesarean birth is one in which the baby is delivered through a surgical incision made into the woman's abdomen and uterus. Although it is generally considered a safe operation for both mother and baby, it is still major surgery. Babies delivered by cesarean do not have molded heads and look better in general than babies born vaginally. A cesarean delivery might be performed for reasons such as difficult and perhaps dangerous labor, fetal distress, breech presentation, and previous cesareans. These reasons explain some 50 percent of all cesareans being performed. As a rule, a cesarean delivery is planned ahead of time and performed before labor has a chance to begin. Today it can be performed even after the uterine contractions have started if the child cannot be delivered otherwise.

Another means of helping nature during birth is through a tonglike instrument, known as forceps. These concave, elongated tools are inserted as two separate units into the vagina. Each is placed on the baby's head. When the handles are joined, the baby be rotated and pulled.

A forceps delivery may be required if the mother's contractions slow down or stop. Today, hormones are usually given to make the contractions continue. But danger signs from either fetus or expectant mother could call for delivery with forceps.

The use of forceps either in the first stage of delivery or early second stage can cause brain damage to the child. At these stages it is important to place the forceps accurately on the child's head. It is also necessary to use considerable force to pull the baby's head out. This is called high forceps delivery and is almost never used today because of the danger involved. Low forceps delivery, that is, the use of forceps in the actual delivery stage, is rarely damaging to the child and is still commonly used in many hospitals.

See also: CESAREAN DELIVERY; PREGNANCY; PRENATAL DEVELOPMENT

Bibliography
Goer, Henci. *The Thinking Woman's Guide to a Better Birth.* New York: Berkley, 1999.
Leiter, Gila, and Rachel Kranz. *Everything You Need to Know to Have a Healthy Twin Pregnancy.* New York: Dell, 2000.
Mahler, Margaret S., Fred Pine, and Anni Bergman. *The Psychological Birth of the Human Infant: Symbiosis and Individuation.* New York: Basic Books, 2000.
Simkin, Penny. *The Birth Partner* Cambridge, MA: Harvard Common Press, 2001.
Stoppard, Miriam. *Conception, Pregnancy, and Birth.* New York: Dorling Kindersley, 2000.

Neil J. Salkind

BIRTH DEFECTS

A birth defect is an abnormality, present at birth, of the structure, function, or metabolism of a part of the body. Almost 150,000 babies are born each year with a birth defect. There are more than 4,000 known birth defects, which, when taken together, are the leading cause of infant death in the United States.

Causes of Birth Defects

Although the causes of most birth defects are unknown, many are attributable to a combination of factors. Some birth defects are the result of genetic determinants, such as an abnormality due to an inherited trait or a problem with a gene or chromosome. For instance, researchers have linked various physical malformations, metabolic abnormalities, certain vision and hearing losses, and other birth defects to specific genes that are inherited from one (or in rare cases, both) parent. Problems may also arise from defects in a gene or chromosome structure or number. Down syndrome, which may lead to mental retardation, cardiac difficulties, and other problems, is caused by an extra copy of chromosome 21. As one of the most common serious birth defects, Down syndrome affects 1 in 900 births, and there is a substantially increased risk of giving birth to a child with Down syndrome if the mother is over thirty-five years of age.

Myriad environmental, or nongenetic, factors have also been linked to birth defects. Prescription and nonprescription medications, illicit drugs, and other harmful chemicals can cause newborn abnormalities. Alcohol use during pregnancy has been linked to fetal alcohol syndrome, which occurs about once in every 1,000 births. Infants with fetal alcohol syndrome are born with a range of preventable physical and mental abnormalities.

Several birth defects can be traced to a mutation in a single gene or chromosome (e.g., neurofibromatosis type 1 and cystic fibrosis) or environmental influence (e.g., thalidomide, rubella virus, and ionizing irradiation), but most are due to a combination of these factors. This is referred to as multifactorial inheritance. Neural tube defects and orofacial clefts (cleft lip and cleft palate) are two types of anomalies that are thought to have a multifactorial cause in most instances. Cleft lip, which results from an incomplete development of the lip, and cleft palate, which is an incomplete development of the roof of the mouth, may occur singly or in combination with each other. Cleft lip with or without cleft palate occurs more often than cleft palate alone, but infants with cleft palate alone are much more likely to have birth defects that involve other organ systems and are more likely to have chromosomal anomalies. Although these conditions can be remedied through surgery, speech and hearing difficulty may be associated with cleft palate. The complexity of the causes of these birth defects are apparent in that they are associated with environmental factors such as maternal alcohol consumption, which has been observed at higher rates among Native Americans and Caucasians and relatively low rates in African Americans, and that there is increased risk for infants born to a parent with a cleft lip and/or palate.

Heart defects, the most common type of birth defect, affect about 25,000 infants each year and are considered to have a multifactorial genesis. Because of improvements in diagnostic techniques such as echocardiography, the number of infants diagnosed with heart defects has increased dramatically in the 1980s and 1990s. Heart defects vary greatly in severity and can occur in isolation or can be one component of a complex syndrome (such as Down syndrome). Malformations of the heart, such as atrial septal defects or ventricular enlargement, may be a result of using alcohol or certain medications during pregnancy. Mutations in certain genes have also been reported to cause some of the defects. Some malformations can be repaired with surgery. Although these types of birth defects are not completely preventable, a pregnant woman can reduce risk by discussing medications she is using with her doctor and by avoiding alcohol.

Prevention of Birth Defects

In the past ten years, there have been significant strides in understanding ways to prevent some birth defects. For example, a daily supplement to the diet of 500 micrograms of folic acid, a B vitamin, has been shown to prevent up to 70 percent of cases of neural tube defects. Neural tube defects, which include anencephaly, spina bifida, and encephalocele, are serious and often lethal birth defects of the spine and central nervous system. The recognition that many of these birth defects can be prevented with folic acid has led to initiatives at the state and national levels aimed at educating women about the importance of consuming the appropriate amount of this vitamin on a daily basis. In 1996 the U.S. Food and Drug Administration issued a rule (effective January 1, 1998) requiring that all enriched grain products sold in the United States be fortified with 140 micrograms of folic acid per 100 grams of product. As a result of these public health initiatives, the rate of spina bifida and anencephaly has declined substantially since the early 1990s.

Because several birth defects are caused by infections, prevention initiatives also emphasize immunization and information. For example, because of widespread vaccination for rubella (German measles), the birth defects caused by this infection rarely occur in the United States. Information about the risk of birth defects resulting from maternal infection with syphilis or other sexually transmitted diseases may stimulate the development of services to help women at greatest risk. Cytomegalovirus, the most common of the congenital viral infections, affects almost 40,000 infants each year. It can be passed through bodily fluids, such as saliva, blood, and breast milk. It is often passed to a pregnant woman from a child who is infected but is not showing symptoms; for example, an infected child may sneeze and then touch a pregnant woman, thus infecting her. An infant born to a mother who has contracted cytomegalovirus is at an increased risk for mental retardation and vision or hearing loss.

Although many types of birth defects are preventable, prevention is complicated by the fact that most serious birth defects occur during the early weeks of

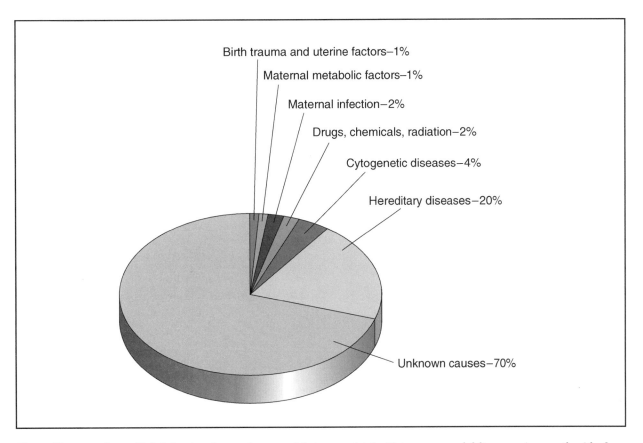

Birth trauma and uterine factors–1%

Maternal metabolic factors–1%

Maternal infection–2%

Drugs, chemicals, radiation–2%

Cytogenetic diseases–4%

Hereditary diseases–20%

Unknown causes–70%

The specific cause of many birth defects is unknown, but several factors associated with pregnancy and delivery can increase the risk of birth defects. Nongenetic factors such as a variety of medications and drugs are known to cause abnormalities in newborns. (Electronic Illustrators Group)

pregnancy, often before a woman even knows she is pregnant. This is why strategies aimed at preventing birth defects must focus on improving the health of women prior to pregnancy. Screening and diagnostic tests, such as ultrasound, maternal serum a-fetoprotein screening, amniocentesis, and chorionic villus sampling, are used to monitor the health of the fetus and to identify certain fetal malformations and chromosomal disorders; they cannot, however, be used to prevent these conditions from occurring. Decisions about whether to use prenatal testing, which tests are appropriate, and how to use the results must be made by the mother in conjunction with her physician.

Consequences of Birth Defects

An infant with a birth defect presents many challenges both for the child and the family. Children with sensory abnormalities, such as hearing or sight loss, have been shown to experience the greatest difficulty in psychosocial adjustment, whereas children with cardiac malformations experience maladjustment to a lesser extent. There have not been many studies addressing either the type of psychological

problems or the long-term effects experienced by children with birth defects. A study of over 3,000 children in Canada reported that most children with cystic fibrosis (an inherited gene mutation that causes problems with the lungs, pancreas, and other organs) have some type of major psychiatric diagnosis, with anxiety disorder being the most common. Long-term research is needed, however, to assess any lasting effects of a child's condition on his or her mental and emotional well-being.

One component of a child's psychosocial development is related to social pressure. Studies have found that individuals with spina bifida and Down syndrome do not perceive themselves as sick. Many of the social difficulties experienced by children with birth defects are not caused directly by the anomaly but by the expectations of what is normal and expected in their communities.

Studies of the families of children with birth defects have focused on psychological stresses experienced by mothers. Mothers of infants with very low birthweights (which is a factor closely related to birth defects) experience greater psychological stress than mothers of normal weight infants. Overall, studies have shown that families of children with birth defects may experience more distress, as measured by higher levels of mental health treatment, than families of children without birth defects. These families, however, are no more prone to divorce, social isolation, or alcohol problems than families without a child affected by a birth defect.

There are a growing number of web-based resources for information about birth defects. The March of Dimes and the Centers for Disease Control and Prevention provide information and links to other web sites for information about specific conditions. Additionally, there are state and national birth defect monitoring programs. The purpose of these projects is to conduct surveillance about birth defects to target information dissemination, track changes in prevalence, and identify trends. This information stimulates research about prevention and affects program development. Several states use information from their birth defects registries to refer infants and their families to appropriate services.

See also: TERATOGENS

Bibliography

Asch, Adrienne. "Prenatal Diagnosis and Selective Abortion: A Challenge to Practice and Policy." *American Journal of Public Health* 89 (1999):1649–1657.

Cadman, David, Micheal Boyle, Peter Szatmari, and David R. Offord. "Chronic Illness, Disability, and Mental and Social Well-Being: Findings of the Ontario Child Health Study." *Pediatrics* 79 (1987):805–813.

Centers for Disease Control and Prevention. "Recommendations for the Use of Folic Acid to Reduce the Number of Cases of Spina Bifida and Other Neural Tube Defects." *Morbidity and Mortality Weekly Report* 41, no. RR-14 (1992).

Gedaly-Duff, Vivian, Susan Stoeger, and Kathleen Shelton. "Working with Families." In Robert E. Nickel and Larry W. Desch eds., *The Physician's Guide to Caring for Children with Disabilities and Chronic Conditions*. Baltimore: Brookes, 2000.

Heller, Anita, Sandra Rafman, Inta Svagluis, and Ivan Barry Pless. "Birth Defects and Psychosocial Adjustment." *American Journal of Diseases of Children* 139 (1985):257–263.

Kalter, Harold, and Josef Warkany. "Congenital Malformations: Etiologic Factors and Their Role in Prevention." *New England Journal of Medicine* 308 (1983):424–431.

Lynberg, Michele C., and Larry D. Edmonds. "Surveillance of Birth Defects." In William Halpern and Edward Baker eds., *Public Health Surveillance*. New York: Van Nostrand Reinhold, 1992.

National Center for Health Statistics. "Trends in Spina Bifida and Anencephalus in the United States, 1991–1999." *Health E-Stats*, December 2000.

Nickel, Robert E. "Prenatal Drug Exposure." In Robert E. Nickel and Larry W. Desch eds., *The Physician's Guide to Caring for Children with Disabilities and Chronic Conditions*, 4th edition. Baltimore: Brookes, 2000.

Nickel, Robert E., and Larry W. Desch, eds. *The Physician's Guide to Caring for Children with Disabilities and Chronic Conditions*, 4th edition. Baltimore: Brookes, 2000.

Schott, Jean-Jacques, D. Woodrow Benson, Craig T. Basson, William Pease, G. Michael Silberbach, Jeffrey P. Moak, Barry J. Maron, Christine E. Seidman, and Jonathan G. Seidman. "Congenital Heart Disease Caused by Mutations in the Transcription Factor NKX2-5." *Science* 281 (July 1998):108–111.

Singer, Lynn T., Ann Salvator, Shenyang Guo, Marc Collin, Lawrence Lilien, and Jill Baley. "Maternal Psychological Distress and Parenting Stress after the Birth of a Very Low-Birthweight Infant." *Journal of the American Medical Association* 281 (1999):799–805.

Anita Farel
Robert Meyer
Maggie Hicken

BIRTH ORDER AND SPACING

Birth order is defined as the science or method of understanding the dynamics of an individual's place in the family. A large amount of research has been conducted on birth order, also known as ordinal birth position. Birth order has fascinated parents, physicians, and others for over one hundred years, in part because everyone is a participant. Everyone is born into a family and thus are affected, one way or another, by birth order position. In fact, the dynamics and persuasive influences brought on by birth order between family members are often unmistakable.

Effects of Birth Order Discovered

Alfred Adler, one of the first psychologists to examine birth order, used the term "family constellation" to help explain some of the personality differences that tend to develop within families. This research into family dynamics evolved from the study of genetics. Scientists found that the influence of genetics alone did not explain the extreme differences in children from the same family.

Although Adler frequently is mentioned as one of the fathers of birth order research, much of what he hypothesized has been refuted. For example, Adler claimed that second-born children were the highest achievers because of their relatively relaxed style. After numerous subsequent studies on birth order, however, it is now generally accepted that firstborns typically achieve the most and are often more intelligent than other siblings. Interestingly, of the first twenty-three American astronauts sent into outer space, twenty-one were firstborns and the other two were only children.

Since Adler, social scientists have spent a considerable amount of time asking the basic question of whether birth order makes any difference in how we develop as individuals. Generally, the answer is yes. A person's birth order position in the family has been linked to differences in achievement, intelligence, attitudes, and behaviors, including the presence of juvenile delinquency, mental illness, and success or failure in marriage. Clearly, however, many people are most interested in the various personality traits or tendencies that accompany the different birth order positions. Moreover, the literature is rather consistent when it comes to identifying these characteristics, one of the few areas where there is general agreement.

Birth Order Characteristics

In what order a child is born into a family is not the only determinant of behavioral characteristics or of future success or failure, but there is little doubt that birth order may influence certain personality traits. Listed below are various characteristics that correspond to the main three birth order positions: oldest/only, middle, and youngest. It is important to remember that these are only tendencies and that environment, genetics, and parenting styles all play a significant role in how children develop as individuals.

Characteristics of Firstborn and Only Children

Firstborn and only children typically get a lot of attention from their parents. Much of what they do is recorded in baby books and little achievements are celebrated as major events, so it is no wonder that these children often develop an appreciation for success and seek ways to acquire new skills. These children are seldom allowed to be just kids. Parents tend to be demanding of firstborn and only children, which leads to high expectations and undue pressure. Typical characteristics of firstborn and only children include:

- Self-confidence
- Perfectionism
- Good organizational skills
- High achievement goals
- Scholarliness
- Conservatism
- A tendency to make lists
- Good communication skills with adults

Characteristics of Middle Children

Research indicates that middle children seem to be more relaxed and impartial than their older and younger siblings. They sometimes feel "squeezed" and accordingly develop characteristics that help them negotiate—and sometimes manipulate—their place in the family environment. Because of their ability to play diplomat and peacemaker, they appear to have balanced personalities. Middle children tend to be:

- Flexible

- Diplomatic
- Independent
- Balanced
- Resourceful
- Generous
- The opposite of their oldest sibling

Characteristics of Youngest Children

As the "babies" of their families, youngest children often do not get enough credit for their accomplishments. Consequently, they may rebel or simply stop trying to please authority figures. Youngest children typically acquire wonderful social skills because of their interactions with older siblings. They are generally charming, playful, and sometimes a little absent-minded. Research seems to indicate that youngest children tend to be attracted to vocations that are people-oriented, such as sales and teaching. Youngest children are inclined to be:

- Risk takers
- Outgoing
- Creative
- Funny and charming
- Rebellious
- Persistent
- Lacking in self-discipline

The Importance of Spacing

While researchers do not always agree on how spacing (the years between each birth) between siblings influences personality and behavior, there is a general belief that children have an easier adjustment if siblings are not extremely close in age. Sibling rivalry does have a tendency to decrease as the age spread increases, which may result in better-adjusted children. Research indicates that this rivalry is at a peak when there is two year's difference between children. Other variables such as parenting styles, gender, and physical/mental characteristics of the child seem to have more influence on behavioral outcomes than spacing.

Criticisms

While much of the research on birth order is considered useful, many psychologists are quick to point out that it lacks strong scientific merit. One social psychologist has even likened birth order theory to astrology because of its rather liberal and far-reaching implementation. Another mentions that it is often a way for people to deny responsibility for their behavior. Judith Blake, author of *Family Size and Achievement*

(1989), believes the size of the family into which a child is born is more important than the order of births in the family. She argues that the fewer the siblings there are, the more attention each child gets from the parents. And the more attention the child receives, the greater the chances of achievement in school verbal and behavioral skills are used more often through interaction with parents.

Probably the biggest setback to birth order research came from the writings of two Swiss psychologists, Cecile Ernst and Jules Angst. In a noteworthy 1983 critique of over a thousand studies on birth order, Ernst and Angst openly criticized the method by which many of these studies were conducted. Background variables, they argued, were inadequately controlled within the research, thereby rendering much of the significance of birth order useless. They further argued that the differences between families and number of siblings might be the cause for particular trends. A similar critique by Carmi Schooler in the early 1970s also called into question the validity of much of the birth order literature, citing most often poor research design as the culprit in the misrepresentation of the effects of birth order.

Birth Order Today

In spite of these criticisms, research into birth order and its effects on personality, behavior, achievement, and intellect continue. In fact, a comprehensive research project on birth order by Frank Sulloway, called *Born to Rebel* (1996), seems to refute much of what Ernst and Angst questioned in regard to the significance of birth order on personality and development. Sulloway does this through the use of a sophisticated scientific method called meta-analysis, in which pooled studies are used to increase the statistical significance. In other words, the more data that are examined, the less likely there is for error to occur. It is important to note that as Sulloway reviewed the criticism of Ernst and Angst, he was able to find 196 birth order studies that did meet the standards for what these two researchers called "properly controlled research." Sulloway subsequently examined the five main personality traits and how these relate to human development: openness to experience, conscientiousness, agreeableness, neurosis (emotional instability), and extroversion. Out of 196 studies, 72 of them substantiated the following components:

- Openness to experience: Firstborns are more conforming, traditional, and closely identified with parents.
- Conscientiousness: Firstborns are more responsible, achievement-oriented, and organized.
- Agreeableness: Latterborns are more easygoing, cooperative, and popular.

- Neurosis (emotional instability): Firstborns are more jealous, anxious, neurotic, and fearful.
- Extroversion: Firstborns are more outgoing, assertive, and likely to exhibit leadership qualities.

In addition to contradicting much of the criticism aimed at birth order research, Sulloway's research details his efforts to gather data on thousands of people who were involved in historic controversies. He wanted to know what set apart the rebels from the reactionaries throughout history. His conclusion is one that suggests family structure, not necessarily church, state, or economy, as the impetus to historical change. He makes a case that firstborns, whatever their age, sex, class, or nationality, specialize in defending the status quo while latterborns specialize in toppling it.

Conclusion

Whether or not birth order is accepted as a legitimate means of understanding people, it is difficult to ignore many of the general characteristics and tendencies that seem to attach themselves to the three common ordinal positions. However, it is important to remember that, in the end, it really is up to the individual to shape his or her own tendencies. Each child is unique. Likewise, each family situation is unique. A variety of factors will impact birth order dynamics, including spacing, gender, physical differences, disabilities, birth order position of parents, divorce, and sibling death. Most social scientists will, at the minimum, agree that birth order is simply one of numerous ways to probe the enigma known as the human personality.

See also: FAMILY SIZE; PARENTING; SIBLINGS AND SIBLING RELATIONSHIPS

Bibliography

Adler, Alfred. *Understanding Human Nature.* New York: Faucett World Library, 1927.

Blake, Judith. *Family Size and Achievement.* Berkeley: University of California Press, 1989.

Ernst, Cecile, and Jules Angst. *Birth Order: Its Influence on Personality.* New York: Springer-Verlag, 1983.

Leman, K. *The New Birth Order Book: Why We Are the Way We Are.* Grand Rapids, MI: Fleming H. Revell, 1998.

Schooler, Carmi. "Birth Order Effects: Not Here, Not Now!" *Psychological Bulletin* 78:161–175.

Sulloway, Frank. J. *Born to Rebel: Birth Order Family Dynamics and Creative Lives.* New York: Pantheon, 1996.

Sutton-Smith, B., and B. G. Rosenberg. *The Sibling.* New York: Holt, Rhinehart, and Winston, 1970.

Toman, W. *Family Constellation.* New York: Springer, 1976.

James A. Troha

BIRTHWEIGHT

Birthweight is an important indicator of the approximate maturity of a newborn infant and the ability of that newborn infant to survive. The birthweight of an infant is dependent on the duration of the pregnancy and its rate of fetal growth. Infants who are delivered earlier than normal are expected to be of smaller birthweight than average. Additionally, infants who had slower or faster fetal growth can also have lower or higher than usual birthweights. Figure 1 portrays the birthweight distribution of singleton live births (babies born singly) to U.S. resident mothers from 1995 to 1997. The graph reveals a somewhat bell-shaped distribution with most births (about 80%) concentrated between 2,750 and 4,250 grams (between 6 pounds and 9 pounds, 4 ounces). The median birthweight for U.S. singleton, full-term (forty weeks of gestation) births is nearly 3,500 grams (7 pounds, 11 ounces).

The close relationship between an infant's birthweight and the risk of dying within the first year of life has long been recognized, and birthweight is often used by researchers as a measure of mortality risk. At light and heavy birthweights, an infant's risk of mortality soars (see Figure 1), although in recent decades, heavier infant births have become less associated with high mortality risks, probably because of medical intervention. Nevertheless, very light infants continue to be at grave risk of mortality, morbidity (disease), and long-term developmental problems.

Populations with more infants born at very high or very low birthweights predictably have higher infant mortality rates. Therefore, it is an established procedure to take birthweight into account when making comparisons of mortality among newborn populations. Whether the comparison involves temporal, geographic, socioeconomic, hospital, or other contrasts, infant mortality differences are typically examined within birthweight categories. Investigations of improving trends in infant mortality rates often start with an examination of the extent to which any changes are related to improvements in the distribution of birthweights within categories (e.g., fewer births at extreme birthweights), as opposed to reductions in birthweight-specific mortality rates (e.g., infants in specific birthweight categories having better survival).

Nearly all of the decline in infant mortality rates in the United States in the last quarter of the twentieth century was due to improvements in survival rather than any improvement in the birthweight distribution. Better survival within birthweight groups has been attributed to advances in obstetric and newborn medical care. The increasing medical care costs that have accompanied these advances, however, raise concerns about overly relying on medical technology to reduce infant death rates. Accordingly, research attention has been directed at finding the determinants of low birthweight in order to develop more cost-effective, population-wide programs to further diminish infant mortality.

Variations of average birthweight have been associated with infant gender, multiple birth factors, and maternal factors, such as race and ethnicity, size, nutrition, and current and previous pregnancy medical risk characteristics. One of the unresolved questions among researchers is whether there is a single common average human birthweight or whether there are normal variations in average birthweight among population subgroups. This question entails important medical care, public health policy, and political aspects as it engenders debate about what is a "normal" birthweight, what is a "high-risk" birthweight, and whether a single "one-size-fits-all" criteria for high-risk birthweights is equally valid for all infants.

Low Birthweight

The term "low birthweight" is used to describe infants who are born at the lower extreme of the birthweight distribution. In 1948 the World Health Assembly recommended that a single definition of low birthweight (LBW) be established for consistent vital statistics and other public policy purposes. The current definition, a weight of less than 2,500 grams (approximately 5 pounds, 8 ounces), was derived from earlier recommendations by Ethel Dunham and Arvo Ylppo. Marked advances in medical technology and practice have occurred since the 2,500-gram criteria for LBW was established, resulting in vastly improved survival rates for LBW infants. The improvements in survival led to the need for further classifications of LBW to better identify high risk infants. Very small infants are now further categorized as very low birthweight (VLBW; less than 1,500 grams (3 pounds, 5 ounces)) and extremely low birthweight (ELBW; less than 1,000 grams (2 pounds, 3 ounces)).

The increased risk of poor outcome for LBW is illustrated by Figure 1. Of the single live births to U.S. resident mothers from 1995 to 1997, 6.1 percent were LBW and 1.1 percent were VLBW. Low birthweight and VLBW infants, however, made up 60 percent and 45 percent, respectively, of the infant deaths. The infant mortality rate for LBW infants was 63 deaths per 1,000 live-born LBW infants and was 259 deaths per 1,000 for VLBW infants.

Low birthweight includes both preterm delivery and fetal growth restriction, but these two categories have very different determinants. Despite extensive

FIGURE 1

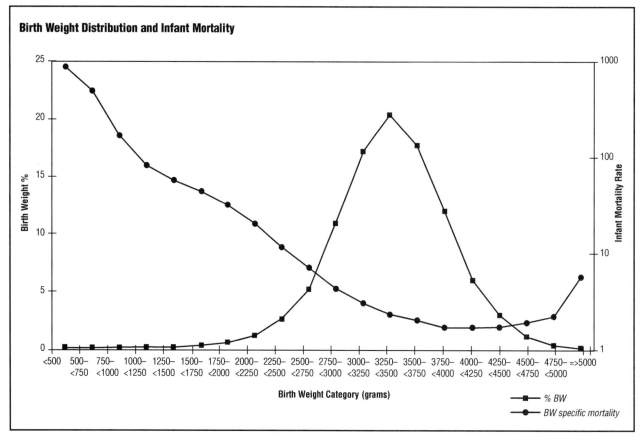

Birth Weight Distribution and Infant Mortality

SOURCE: *Martha Slay, Greg R. Alexander, and Mary Ann Pass.*

research, current knowledge is limited about the causes of preterm delivery. Risk factors associated with preterm birth include cigarette smoking during pregnancy, prior preterm birth, low prepregnancy weight, and maternal chronic diseases; but known risk factors account for less than one-fourth of preterm births. The factors associated with fetal growth restriction are more readily understood than those of preterm delivery. Cigarette smoking during pregnancy, low maternal weight gain, and low prepregnancy weight account for nearly two-thirds of all fetal growth restriction and seem to be the most promising areas for possible interventions. Other associated factors include multiple births (e.g., twins), infant gender, and several factors relating to the mother, including: birthweight, racial or ethnic origin, age, height, infections, history of prior low birthweight delivery, work/physical activity, substance use/abuse, cigarette smoking, alcohol consumption, and socioeconomic status. While prenatal care was once touted as a highly effective means to prevent low birthweight, more recent assessments have raised serious challenges to this assumption, leaving the matter now in doubt.

Poverty, given its association with reduced access to health care, poor nutrition, lower education, and inadequate housing, may be an appreciable factor underlying the risk of delivering a LBW infant. Socioeconomic status is linked to individual behaviors, such as cigarette smoking and alcohol consumption, and varies markedly by race and ethnicity. While socioeconomic status and race/ethnicity cannot be termed "causes" of low birthweight, they serve as indicators of complex links between environmental, psychological, and physiological factors that may result in higher risks of low birthweight.

The percentage of LBW infants in the United States rose during the last two decades of the twentieth century. This increase, coupled with the improved survival of LBW infants, has heightened the need to further understand the long-term outcomes of LBW infants in regard to growth, development, and disease, as well as the impact these children have on the health care system. When compared to normal birthweight children, LBW children have higher rates of mental retardation, cerebral palsy, blindness, deafness, psychomotor problems, school failure, subnormal growth, and health problems, which are compounded by poverty and related adverse socio-economic factors.

High Birthweight

High birthweight (HBW), or macrosomia (large body), in an infant also increases the risk to the infant and mother. A widely agreed upon definition of macrosomia has yet to be established but often-used definitions include a birthweight equal to or exceeding 4,000 grams (8 pounds, 12 ounces), 4,250 grams (9 pounds, 4 ounces), or 4,500 grams (9 pounds, 14 ounces), as well as a birth weighing at or above the ninetieth percentile of birthweights for the infant's gestational age. While one-third of macrosomic births are still unexplained, several factors are known to contribute to excessive fetal size, including large size of parents (especially the mother), multiparity diabetes in the mother, and prolonged gestation. Older maternal age, male infants, and previous delivery of a high birthweight infant also seem to be indicative of macrosomic births. Babies of diabetic women are usually large at birth, but they behave clinically as if they are immature. These infants are not longer in average length but have increased fetal weight. Because glucose, a substance necessary for fetal growth, is elevated in both diabetic and obese women, these mothers are more likely to have macrosomic births.

Risks for birth injuries rise rapidly for heavier babies, with vaginal deliveries being related to higher morbidity and mortality for both the infant and the mother. Lacerations of the birth canal and hemorrhaging may occur to the mother, fetal death may occur due to asphyxia (lack of oxygen), and infants may suffer broken clavicles and neurological damage. While cesarean delivery has been prescribed as the best delivery method to prevent fetal death or injury, others suggest that vaginal birth is still possible for some macrosomic infants.

See also: INFANT MORTALITY; PREMATURE INFANTS

Bibliography

Alexander, Greg. "Preterm Birth: Etiologies, Mechanisms, and Prevention." *Prenatal and Neonatal Medicine* 3, no. 1 (1998):3–9.

Alexander, Greg, and Carol Korenbrot. "The Role of Prenatal Care in Preventing Low Birth Weight." *Future of Children* 5, no. 1 (1995):103–120.

Alexander, Greg, John Himes, Rajni Kaufman, Joanne Mor, and Michael Kogan. "A U.S. National Reference for Fetal Growth." *Obstetrics and Gynecology* 87, no. 2 (1996):163–168.

Alexander, Greg, Mark Tompkins, Marilee Allen, and Thomas Hulsey. "Trends and Racial Differences in Birth Weight and Related Survival." *Maternal and Child Health Journal* 3, no. 1 (1999):71–79.

Alexander, Greg, and Michael Kogan. "Ethnic Differences in Birth Outcomes: The Search for Answers Continues." *Birth* 23, no. 3 (1998):210–213.

Alexander, Greg, Michael Kogan, John Himes, Joanne Mor, and Robert Goldenberg. "Racial Differences in Birth Weight for Gestational Age and Infant Mortality in Extremely-Low-Risk U.S. Populations." *Paediatric and Perinatal Epidemiology* 13 (1999):205–217.

Alexander, Greg, Michael Kogan, Joyce Martin, and Emile Papiernik. "What Are the Fetal Growth Patterns of Singletons, Twins, and Triplets in the United States?" *Clinical Obstetrics and Gynecology* 41, no. 1 (1998):115–125.

Bérard, J., P. Dufour, D. Vinatier, D. Subtil, S. Vanderstichele, J. C. Monnier, and F. Puech. "Fetal Macrosomia: Risk Factors and Outcome." *European Journal of Obstetrics and Gynecology and Reproductive Biology* 77, no. 1 (1998):51–59.

Berkowitz, G. S., and Emile Papiernik. "Epidemiology of Preterm Birth." *Epidemiologic Review* 15 (1993):414–444.

Dunham, Ethel, and Paul McAlenney. "A Study of 244 Prematurely Born Infants." *Journal of Pediatrics* 9 (1936):717–727.

Gregory, Kimberly, Olivia Henry, Emily Ramicone, Linda Chan, and Lawrence Platt. "Maternal and Infant Complications in High and Normal Weight Infants by Method of Delivery." *Obstetrics and Gynecology* 92 (1998):507–513.

Guyer, Bernard, Marian MacDorman, Joyce Martin, Kimberely Peters, and Donna Strobino. "Annual Summary of Vital Statistics, 1997." *Pediatrics* 102 (1998):1333–1349.

Hack, Maureen, Nancy Klein, and H. Gerry Taylor. "Long-Term Developmental Outcomes of Low Birth Weight Infants." *Future of Children* 5, no. 1 (1995):176–196.

Hughes, Dana, and Lisa Simpson. "The Role of Social Change in Preventing Low Birth Weight." *Future of Children* 5, no. 1 (1995):87–103.

Institute of Medicine, Committee to Study the Prevention of Low Birth Weight. *Preventing Low Birth Weight*. Washington, DC: National Academy Press, 1985.

Kolderup, Lindsey, Russell Laros, and Thomas Musci. "Incidence of Persistent Birth Injury in Macrosomic Infants: Association with Mode of Delivery." *American Journal of Obstetrics and Gynecology* 177, no. 1 (1997):37–41.

Kramer, Michael. "Determinants of Low Birth Weight: Methodological Assessment and Meta-analysis." *Bulletin of the World Health Organization* 65 (1987):663–737.

Kramer, Michael, Louise Séguin, John Lydon, and Lise Goulet. "Socio-Economic Disparities in Pregnancy Outcome: Why Do the Poor Fare So Poorly?" *Paediatric and Perinatal Epidemiology* 14 (2000):194–210.

Paneth, Nigel. "The Problem of Low Birth Weight." *Future of Children* 5, no. 1 (1995):19–34.

Sacks, David, and Wansu Chen. "Estimating Fetal Weight in the Management of Macrosomia." *Obstetrical and Gynecological Survey* 55 (2000):229–239.

Shiono, Patricia, Virginia Rauh, Mikyung Park, Sally Lederman, and Deborah Zuskar. "Ethnic Differences in Birthweight: The Role of Lifestyle and Other Factors." *American Journal of Public Health* 87 (1997):787–793.

Thomson, A. M., and Soloman Leonard Barron, eds. "Perinatal Mortality." *Obstetrical Epidemiology*. London: Academic Press, 1983.

Tompkins, Mark, Greg Alexander, Kirby Jackson, Carlton Hornung, and Joan Altekruse. "The Risk of Low Birth Weight: Alternative Models of Neonatal Mortality." *American Journal of Epidemiology* 122 (1985):1067–1079.

World Health Organization. *Manual of the International Statistical Classification of Diseases, Injuries, and Causes of Death, Sixth Revision, Adopted 1948.* Geneva: World Health Organization, 1948.

Martha Slay
Greg R. Alexander
Mary Ann Pass

BLACK ENGLISH

African American Vernacular English (AAVE), also referred to as Black English, African American English, and Ebonics, is a rule-governed variety of English spoken by some African Americans in the United States. Most linguists agree that the dialect has its roots in the Creole language developed as a result of contact between West Coast Africans and European traders. Creole, brought by slaves to North America, went through further transformation as a result of contact with southern white varieties of English. Social isolation and segregation of African Americans further increased the divergence of the dialect from other dialects of English spoken in the United States.

The dialect differs from Standard American English (SAE) in phonology (e.g., "bafroom" for "bathroom"), morphology (e.g., nonobligatory plural with numerical quantifier; "two dog" for "two dogs"), and syntax (e.g., habitual or general state marked with uninflected "be"; "she be fussing" for "she is fussing now"). The features are optional and the frequency of their use varies as a function of the speaker, interlocutor, and context.

Controversies surrounding AAVE center on its legitimacy as a distinct dialect of English, the extent to which its linguistic features differ sufficiently from SAE to be considered a distinct language, and the extent to which its linguistic features result in mutual unintelligibility between speakers of the AAVE and SAE. Some critics of AAVE view it as being "broken English" and its use as a deficit to be corrected. Others have argued that AAVE is a unique language just as French and Russian are unique languages. AAVE is neither; it is a rule-governed variety of English. The differences between the two dialects has the potential of penalizing AAVE speakers who are assessed with test instruments that do not take into consideration the features of their dialect. Further, the sociopolitical reality dictates that educators facilitate the acquisition of SAE while respecting the legitimacy of AAVE.

See also: LANGUAGE ACQUISITION DEVICE; LANGUAGE DEVELOPMENT

Bibliography
Baugh, John. *Beyond Ebonics: Linguistic Pride and Racial Prejudice.* New York: Oxford University Press, 2000.

Mufwene, Salikoko, John Rickford, Guy Bailey, and John Baugh, eds. *African American English.* New York: Routledge, 1998.

Wolfram, W., C. T. Adger, and D. Christian. *Dialects in Schools and Communities.* Mahwah, NJ: Erlbaum, 1999.

Aquiles Iglesias

BLENDED FAMILIES

Although approximately 50 percent of marriages end in divorce in the United States, living in a family headed by a single parent is usually only a temporary situation for most parents and children. The majority of divorced men and women will eventually remarry. In fact, roughly one-third of divorced people will remarry within the first year after their divorce. As a result of these multiple marriages, families may take a variety of forms. One form, the blended family, consists of unrelated siblings (i.e., stepsiblings) from either the mother's or father's previous marriages or romantic relationships, who are brought into a new family when parents cohabitate or remarry. Family members' adaptations to the new relationships in their stepfamily evolve over time and are influenced by a variety of factors.

See also: CHILD CUSTODY AND SUPPORT; DIVORCE; STEPFAMILIES

Bibliography
Hetherington, E. Mavis, Sandra Henderson, and David Reiss. *Adolescent Siblings in Stepfamilies: Family Functioning and Adolescent Adjustment.* Monographs of the Society for Research in Child Development 64, no.4, serial no. 259 (1999).

Wilson, B. F., and S. C. Clarke. "Remarriages: A Demographic Profile." *Journal of Family Issues* 13 (1992):123–141.

Glendessa M. Insabella

BOWLBY, JOHN (1907–1990)

John Bowlby was an English psychiatrist who developed attachment theory, one of the century's most influential theories of personality development and social relationships. Born in London, England, Bowlby graduated from Cambridge University in 1928 and began his professional training at the British Psychoanalytic Institute as a child psychiatrist. He was trained in the neo-Freudian object-relations approach to psychoanalysis, which taught that children's emotional disturbances were primarily a function of their fantasies generated by internal conflict. While embracing the psychoanalytic emphasis on the importance of the early years for children's healthy emotional development, Bowlby felt that this approach neglected the importance of their actual early experiences with their parents.

After World War II, Bowlby became the head of the Children's Department at the Tavistock Clinic, where he focused his clinical studies on the effects of mother-child separation. He completed a monograph for the World Health Organization on the sad fate of homeless children in postwar Europe and collaborated with James Robertson on a film, *A Two-Year-Old Goes to the Hospital*. These works drew the attention of child clinicians to the potentially devastating effects of maternal separation, and led to the liberalization of family visiting privileges for hospitalized children.

Unsatisfied with the psychoanalytic view that the child's love of mother derived from oral gratification, Bowlby embraced the ethological theories of Konrad Lorenz and Niko Tinbergen, which stress the evolutionary foundations of behavior as a source of explanation for mother-child attachment relationships. He presented his first formal statements of ethologically based attachment theory to the British Psychoanalytic Society in 1957. Bowlby argued that mother-child attachment has an evolutionary basis, promoting the child's survival by increasing mother-child proximity, particularly when the child is stressed or fearful. The mother thus serves as a secure base for the young child's exploration of the world. Bowlby expanded his theory of attachment in his *Attachment and Loss* trilogy (volume 1: *Attachment*, volume 2: *Separation*, and volume 3: *Loss*). Bowlby's theory was supported by the empirical work of his collaborator, Mary Dinsmore Salter Ainsworth, who examined the normative development of attachment relationships across cultures as well as the maternal care-giving patterns that predict individual differences in the quality of mother-infant attachment security.

Controversial at first, attachment theory became a dominant principle of social and personality development by the 1980s, generating thousands of research papers and serving as a theoretical basis for clinical intervention programs. After his retirement in 1972, Bowlby continued to develop the clinical application of attachment theory. He completed a biography of Charles Darwin shortly before his death in 1990.

Bibliography

Bretheron, Inge. "The Origins of Attachment Theory: John Bowlby and Mary Ainsworth." *Developmental Psychology* 28 (1992):759–775.

Holmes, Jeremy. *John Bowlby and Attachment Theory*. London: Routledge, 1993.

Publications by Bowlby

Maternal Care and Mental Health. Geneva: World Health Organization, 1946.

"The Nature of the Child's Tie to His Mother." *International Journal of Psychoanalysis* 39 (1958):1–23.

Attachment and Loss, Vol. 1: *Attachment*. New York: Basic Books, 1968.

Attachment and Loss, Vol. 2: *Separation, Anxiety, and Anger*. London: Penguin Books, 1973.

English psychiatrist John Bowlby argued that mother-child attachment has an evolutionary basis. (Bill Varie)

Attachment and Loss, Vol. 3: *Loss: Sadness and Depression*. New York: Basic Books, 1980.

Bowlby, John, James Robertson, and Dina Rosenbluth. "A Two-Year-Old Goes to the Hospital." *Psychoanalytic Study of the Child* 7 (1952):82–74.

Nancy Hazen

BRAIN DEVELOPMENT

The development of the human brain occurs rapidly in the first years of life and continues at a slower pace into adolescence. The major steps involved in brain development, both before and after birth, play important roles in psychological development.

The Cerebral Cortex

The cerebral cortex is a thin, flat sheet of cells at the outer surface of the brain. Understanding the development of this part of the brain is important for understanding psychological development, as it is

FIGURE 1

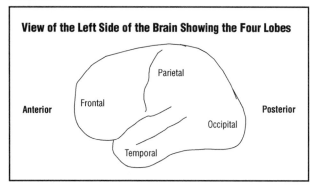

View of the Left Side of the Brain Showing the Four Lobes

SOURCE: *Mark H. Johnson and Michelle de Haan.*

thought that the cortex underlies humans' complex intellectual abilities. The cortex is divided into four lobes: the occipital, parietal, temporal, and frontal lobes, as illustrated in Figure 1. In all of these lobes the cortex consists of six layers of cells, and each of the six layers is made up of particular types of cells and connections to and from other cells. In adults, the cortical lobes can be divided even further into areas that specialize in different functions, such as language and movement.

Development of the Cerebral Cortex

Neurons (the cells of the cortex that are involved in processing information) are formed before birth during the sixth to eighteenth weeks after conception. In the cerebral cortex, neurons find their way to the correct position by moving along the long fibers of radial glia cells, which are like ropes extending from the inner to the outer surface of the brain. The length that neurons must travel is especially long for those that will end up in the frontal lobes, and this may increase the likelihood that they will end up in the incorrect position and disrupt information processing. Schahram Akbarian and his colleagues suggested in a 1993 paper that such errors might contribute to schizophrenia.

Once neurons have traveled to their final positions, they begin to differentiate or take on their mature characteristics. One aspect of differentiation is the growth and branching of dendrites. The dendrites of a neuron are like antennae that pick up signals from many other neurons and, if the circumstances are right, pass the signal down the axon and on to other neurons. The pattern of branching of dendrites is important because it affects the amount and type of signals the neuron receives. During development one change that occurs is an increase in size and complexity of neurons' dendritic trees. For example, by adulthood the length of the

dendrites of neurons in the frontal cortex can increase to more than thirty times their length at birth. A second aspect of differentiation that occurs in most neurons is myelination. Myelin is a fatty sheath that forms around neurons and helps them transmit signals more quickly. Myelin begins to form around neurons before birth and continues to do so even into adulthood in some areas of the cortex.

The points of communication between neurons are called synapses, and these begin to form in the brain in the early weeks of gestation. The generation of synapses occurs at different times in different cortical areas. For example, the maximum density of synapses is reached at about four months in the visual cortex but not until about twenty-four months after birth in the prefrontal cortex. This pattern parallels behavioral development, where functions of the visual cortex (such as 3-D vision) develop earlier than some functions of the prefrontal cortex (such as planning for the future).

Regressive Events

At the same time that the brain is growing and increasing in size and complexity, regressive events are also occurring. One example is the elimination of synapses. During the process of synapse formation, the number of synapses increases above the level observed in the adult and remains at this level for some time. Then, synapses are eliminated until the adult number is reached. For example, in certain parts of the visual cortex the density of synapses per neuron reaches a peak of about 150 percent of the adult level at about age four months then starts to decrease at the end of the first year of life to reach the adult level by about age four. The timing of this process is different for different areas of cortex. In the frontal cortex, the peak level is reached at about one year of age, and it then slowly declines to reach adult levels sometime in adolescence. This loss of synapses does not reduce the range of behaviors but may be related to the stabilization of important networks of neurons in the brain.

Neuronal Activity

The adult brain has a very large number of dendritic branches and synapses between cells that are organized in a very specific way. There simply is not enough space in the human genome to specifically encode all of this information. Instead of being only a passive "readout" of genetic information, normal development of the brain depends in part on the activity of the neurons themselves. Even while the baby is still in the womb, neuronal activity (the electrical firing of cells) is very important. For example, it has been discovered that the rhythmical waves of firing of groups of receptor cells in the eyes play an important role in helping to structure some parts of the brain involved in vision. This activity cannot be a response to visual input, since the eyes are closed at this age. Instead, it appears that one part of the nervous system can create a kind of "virtual environment" specifically to aid the formation of other, later developing, parts.

The Effect of Experience on Brain Development

Once a baby is born, the external world can begin to influence the activity of neurons and thereby the pattern of brain development. According to Mark Johnson and his colleagues, for example, newborns less than one hour old tend to orient their heads and eyes to look at faces more often than many other complex patterns. This reaction is like a reflex and may well be controlled not by the cortex but by evolutionarily older, subcortical parts of the brain. All of this staring at faces serves a critical purpose in providing the necessary input for training some of the slower-developing "higher" brain areas within the cerebral cortex. Thus, infants themselves play an important and active role in determining the subsequent organization of the cerebral cortex.

One way that experience affects brain development is by determining which synapses are retained during the process of synapse elimination. Useful synapses are kept, while surplus ones are lost. This type of learning through selective synapse elimination is thought to happen only at certain points in development. This means that there are some types of learning that may only occur during certain points in development, sometimes called sensitive or critical periods. If certain synaptic connections are not laid down early in life, they are less likely to become established later in life. For example, some children are born with cataracts (a clouding of the lens that prevents patterned light from reaching the eye's receptor cells) and experience visual deprivation during the first months of life until the cataracts are treated. These children, even when tested years after vision has been restored, show some difficulties in face recognition, according to a study by Daphne Maurer and her colleagues. Thus, visual experience in the first months of life appears critical for the ability to recognize faces and cannot be replaced even by years of later experience.

The sensitivity of the young brain to the inputs it receives means that different patterns of brain organization can occur in infants with different types of experience. One example is individuals who are deaf from birth and thus do not receive typical auditory inputs. While some aspects of their visual processing re-

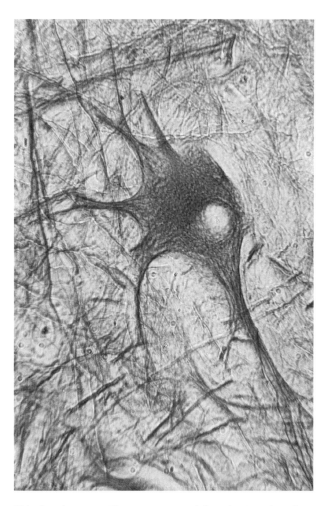

Spinal cord neurons. Neurons must travel from the spot where they are born to arrive at the particular region where they will be used in the mature brain. (Frank Lane Picture Agency/Corbis)

main unchanged, their processing of visual motion and information in the visual periphery are enhanced and reorganized. One interpretation is that there are surplus visual connections that are normally eliminated during development but that, in the absence of auditory input, remain and take over what would normally be auditory cortex.

Of all the cortical areas, the frontal areas appear to develop the slowest, as many functions attributed to the frontal lobe, such as planning for the future, do not mature until adolescence. This does not mean, however, that the frontal lobes are not working early in life and suddenly are "switched on" in adolescence. For example, if a seven-month-old baby watches an object being hidden in one of two locations she can remember a few seconds later where it is hidden. In contrast, a monkey with an injury to the frontal lobe has difficulty with this task. That human infants can perform a task that monkeys with damage to the frontal lobes cannot suggests that the frontal lobe is beginning to work already in young infants. The development of the ability to keep things in mind even when they are not observable may be related to the emergence of infants' objection to separation from the caregiver that often occurs around age seven to nine months. Thus, areas of the cortex that appear to develop late may be functioning in simpler ways earlier in life rather than remaining completely "silent."

Summary and Conclusions

Initially the young brain contains more components and connections than it will in adulthood, and the inputs it receives shape the elimination of this surplus. This provides a way in which individuals can develop in similar ways even if the plan of development is not encoded specifically in the human genome. Different areas of the brain develop at different times, and this is related to the development of their behavioral functions. The infant plays an active role in her own brain development by selectively attending to stimuli, such as faces and speech, that are important for subsequent development.

See also: LANGUAGE DEVELOPMENT

Bibliography

Akbarian, Schahram S., William E. Bunney Jr., Stephen G. Potkin, Sharon B. Wigal, Jennifer O. Hagman, Curt A. Sandman, and Edward G. Jones. "Altered Distribution of Nicotinamide-Adenine Dinucleotide Phospate-Diaphorase Cells in Frontal Lobe of Schizophrenics Implies Disturbances of Cortical Development." *Archives of General Psychiatry* 50 (1993):169–177.

Diamond, Adele. "The Development and Neural Bases of Memory Functions as Indexed by the AB and Delayed Response Tasks in Human Infants and Infant Monkeys." In Adele Diamond ed., *The Development and Neural Bases of Higher Cognitive Functions.* New York: New York Academy of Sciences, 1990.

Huttenlocher, Peter R. "Synaptogenesis, Synapse Elimination, and Neural Plasticity in Human Cerebral Cortex." In Charles A. Nelson ed., *Threats to Optimal Development.* Hillsdale, NJ: Erlbaum, 1994.

Johnson, Mark H., Suzanne Dziurawiec, Hayden D. Ellis, and John Morton. "Newborns' Preferential Tracking of Face-Like Stimuli and Its Subsequent Decline." *Cognition* 40, no. 1, (1991):1–19.

Katz, Larry C., and Carla J. Shatz. "Synaptic Activity and the Construction of Cortical Circuits." *Science* 274 (1996):1133–1138.

Le Grand, Richard, Catherine H. Mondloch, Daphne Maurer, and Henry P. Brent. "Early Visual Experience and Face Processing." *Nature* 410 (2001):890.

Neville, Helen. "Developmental Specificity in Neurocognitive Development in Humans." In Michael S. Gazzaniga ed., *The Cognitive Neurosciences.* Cambridge, MA: MIT Press, 1997.

Rakic, Pasko. "Specification of Cerebral Cortical Areas." *Science* 241 (1988):170–176.

Rakic, Pasko. "The Development of the Frontal Lobe: A View from the Rear of the Brain." In Herbert H. Jasper, Silvano Riggio, and Patricia S. Goldman-Rakic eds., *Epilepsy and the Functional Anatomy of the Frontal Lobe.* New York: Raven Press, 1995.

Zecevic, Nada. "Synaptogenesis in Layer 1 of the Human Cerebral Cortex in the First Half of Gestation." *Cerebral Cortex* 8 (1998):245–252.

Mark H. Johnson
Michelle de Haan

BRAZELTON, T. BERRY (1918–)

Born in Waco, Texas, T. Berry Brazelton is among the most prominent and trusted pediatricians of the twentieth century. Following his graduation from Columbia University's College of Physicians and Surgeons in 1943, Brazelton trained in pediatrics, with five additional years of training in child psychiatry. After extensive study in the paradigm of pathological development, Brazelton completed a fellowship with experimental psychologist Jerome Bruner to learn about the healthy stages of child development.

With this diverse training, Brazelton was able to narrow and refine his views of the importance of creating strong family support and encouraging the individuality of every child. The belief that an infant's behavior provides clues for parents that can strengthen the bond between child and parent can be seen throughout much of Brazelton's work. This approach of viewing families as cohesive units and promoting positive self images for children at all developmental stages is among the many reasons for his success as a pediatrician.

Brazelton is Clinical Professor of Pediatrics Emeritus at Harvard Medical School and Professor of Psychiatry and Human Development at Brown University. He is also active in many national organizations. Brazelton is a past president of the Society for Research in Child Development (1987–1989) and the National Center for Clinical Infant Programs (1988–1991). At Children's Hospital in Boston, he is founder and codirector of the Touchpoints Center, as well as the Brazelton Institute, both of which further his philosophy and commitment to children and families. It was at Children's Hospital in the early 1970s that Brazelton developed the Brazelton Neonatal Behavioral Assessment Scale (BNAS), an evaluation tool to assess physical and neurological responses of newborns as well as emotional well-being and individual differences. In addition, as cofounder of a grassroots advocacy group for parents, Parent Action, he has made several appearances before the United States Congress to speak on behalf of underprivileged families and children.

Brazelton's name and face are familiar in many households as a contributing editor to *Family Circle* magazine, as a syndicated newspaper columnist to the *New York Times,* as a guest on National Public Radio,

As part of his research, pediatrician T. Berry Brazelton proposed that an infant's behavior provides clues for parents that can strengthen the bond between child and parent. (AP/Wide World Photos)

and as host of the television program *What Every Baby Knows*. He is also the author and/or coauthor of a number of books, including *Touchpoints*, and more than 200 scientific articles.

See also: BRAZELTON NEONATAL ASSESSMENT SCALE; MILESTONES OF DEVELOPMENT

Bibliography

"Neonatal Behavior Assessment Scale." The Brazelton Institute of Children's Hospital [web site]. Boston, Massachusetts, 2000. Available from http://www.childrenshospital.org/brazelton; INTERNET.

"Touchpoints." The Brazelton Touchpoints Center of Children's Hospital [web site]. Boston, Massachusetts, 2000. Available from http://www.childrenshospital.org/touchpoint; INTERNET.

Publications by Brazelton

Touchpoints—The Essential Reference: Your Child's Emotional and Behavioral Development. Reading, MA: Addison-Wesley-Longman, 1994.

Vicki Diane Peyton

BRAZELTON NEONATAL ASSESSMENT SCALE

T. Berry Brazelton, a pediatrician and researcher, published the Brazelton Neonatal Assessment Scale

(BNAS) in the early 1970s. The scale enables parents, health care professionals, and researchers to understand a newborn's language, as well as individual strengths and needs in depth. The BNAS assesses various behaviors of infants until two months of age and takes about thirty minutes to administer. This assessment evaluates four main areas, including the infants' ability to monitor their own breathing, temperature, and other bodily systems; control their motor movements; maintain an appropriate level of consciousness, which ranges from quiet sleep to a full cry; and interact socially with parents and other caregivers. The purpose of the BNAS is to help professionals assess the infant's pattern of response to the environment and then assist parents with strategies to build a positive relationship with their infant.

See also: BIRTH; BRAZELTON, T. BERRY; REFLEXES

Bibliography

Brazelton, T. Berry, and Bertrand G. Cramer, eds. "The Assessment of the Newborn." *The Earliest Relationship.* Reading, MA: Perseus Books, 1990.

Tedder, Janice L. "Using the Brazelton Neonatal Assessment Scale to Facilitate the Parent-Infant Relationship in Primary Care Settings." *Nurse Practitioner* 16 (1991):27–36.

Joan Ziegler Delahunt

Urie Bronfenbrenner worked to develop theory and research methods that looked at patterns of development across time. (Urie Bronfenbrenner)

BRONFENBRENNER, URIE (1917–)

Urie Bronfenbrenner was born in 1917 in Moscow. At the age of six he arrived in the United States with his family. His father, a physician and neuropathologist, worked at a state institution in New York. He can recall his father's concern with the overreliance on a single IQ testing to place children in institutions for the mentally retarded. Russian immigrant psychologists also visited his home and discussed outstanding psychologists, such as Kurt Lewin and Lev Vygotsky. In 1934 he won a scholarship to Cornell University where he majored in psychology. From Cornell, he went on to receive his master's degree in developmental psychology from Harvard University, and in 1942 he received his doctorate from the University of Michigan. Immediately after his graduation from Michigan, he entered the U.S. Army, serving as a psychologist from 1942 to 1946. After teaching briefly at Michigan for two years, he moved to Cornell University in 1948. His father, confined to a sanatorium for tuberculosis, continued to influence Bronfenbrenner's thinking in psychology through letter writing.

Bronfenbrenner's highly productive contributions to developmental psychology contain several connected themes. He worked to develop theory and research methods that looked at patterns of development across time. He also became interested in social and political policies and practices affecting children and families. In addition, he has always sought to communicate his ideas about development to the widest possible audience.

His lifelong interest as a psychologist in the interactions between the developing child and the environment have led him to develop his social ecology of human development. Here, he considers the development to take place within nested systems. He calls these the microsystem (such as the family or classroom), the mesosytem (which is two microsystems in interaction), the exosystem (which is a system influencing development, such as a parental workplace), and the macrosystem (the larger cultural context). Each system contains roles, norms, and rules that can powerfully shape development.

In addition to being a founder of Head Start, Bronfenbrenner has won numerous awards, honors, and honorary degrees for his many significant contributions to developmental psychology. In 1996 the American Psychological Association awarded him the Lifetime Contribution to Developmental Psychology in the Service of Science and Society Award. Bronfenbrenner holds the position of Jacob Gould Shurman Emeritus Professor of Human Development and Family Studies of Psychology at Cornell University.

See also: THEORIES OF DEVELOPMENT

Bibliography

Publications by Bronfenbrenner

The Ecology of Human Development: Experiments by Nature and Design. Cambridge, MA: Harvard University Press, 1979.

"Ecology of the Family as a Context for Human Development." *Developmental Psychology* 22 (1986):723–742.

Bronfenbrenner, Urie, Peter McCelland, Elaine Wethington, Phyllis Moen, and Stephen J. Ceci. *The State of Americans: This Generation and the Next.* New York: Free Press, 1996.

Thomas J. Russo

BRUNER, JEROME (1915–)

Jerome Bruner was born October 15, 1915 in New York, the youngest of four children in a "nominally observant" Jewish family. He was a leading voice in the cognitive revolution that overtook psychology in the 1960s, ending a half-century of domination by behaviorism. As a professor of psychology at Harvard and as Director, with George Miller, of the Center for Cognitive Studies, he was a major force in redirecting psychology toward the study of cognitive processes involved in language and thought and their development. As Watts Professor of Psychology at Oxford University he extended his work increasingly into issues of children's cognitive and linguistic development and the role of education in this process. Because Bruner has applied this perspective to a number of problems (including perception, thinking, language development, and education), he is widely regarded as the world's greatest living psychologist. He is the author of some twenty books, one of which, *The Process of Education* (1960), has been translated into twenty-one languages.

Bruner's view of mind was shaped by his encounters as an undergraduate at Duke University with William McDougall's contrarian views: nativism versus empiricism and mentalism versus materialism. His ideas were further extended by the conflicts he encountered at Harvard as a graduate student between the whole-person theorists Gordon Willard Allport and Henry Murray, and the experimentalists Edwin Garrigues Boring and Karl Spencer Lashley. The eventual product was an experimental approach to the higher mental processes of the language and thinking of whole persons best represented in the landmark volume authored with Jacqueline Goodnow and George Austin, *A Study of Thinking* (1956).

Bruner's contributions to developmental psychology are no less distinctive. He introduced the work of

Jerome Seymour Bruner was a leading voice in the cognitive revolution that overtook psychology in the 1960s. (Archives of the History of American Psychology)

Jean Piaget and Lev Vygotsky to the attention of North Americans, extending and adding a cognitive process perspective to intellectual development, work well represented by the volume produced with his students Patricia Greenfield and Rose Olver, *Studies in Cognitive Growth* (1966). Along with Colwyn Trevarthyn and T. Berry Brazelton, Bruner pioneered the study of infant perception and their predispositions to language, work culminating in the book *Child's Talk* (1983).

Bruner has been a strong proponent of the importance of culture in human development, including education as an aspect of that culture. Minds, he argues, have the properties they do not just because we are all humans, but because of the rules and rituals of child-rearing and formal education. Cultural rules and routines and the narrative forms people learn to use to interpret their own and others' lives are the themes of *The Culture of Education* (1996).

An insightful accounting of his development as a psychologist through his first sixty years is to be found in his autobiography, *In Search of Mind: Essays in Autobiography* (1983). The fact that he continues to be devoted to the problem of the cultural uses of narrative and interpretation is exemplified by his books, with

Anthony Amsterdam, *Minding the Law* (2000) and *The Uses of Narrative: Law, Literature, and Life* (forthcoming).

Bruner's contributions to psychology and to scholarship generally have been acknowledged through two Festschrifts dedicated to him: *The Social Foundations of Language and Thought: Essays in Honor of Jerome S. Bruner* (Olson, 1980) and *Language, Culture, Self: The Philosophy of Jerome Bruner* (Bakhurst and Shanker, 2001); the International Balzan Prize (1987); and the awarding of twenty-four honorary degrees from around the world, including Geneva, Harvard University, and University of California, Berkeley.

Bibliography

Publications by Bruner

Beyond the Information Given: Studies in the Psychology of Knowing. New York: Norton, 1973.

Child's Talk: Learning to Use Language. New York: Norton, 1983.

In Search of Mind: Essays in Autobiography. New York: Harper and Row, 1983.

The Culture of Education. Cambridge, MA: Harvard University Press, 1996.

Bruner, Jerome S., and Anthony Amsterdam. *Minding the Law.* Cambridge, MA: Harvard University Press, 2000.

David R. Olson

BULLYING

Bullying involves teasing, insulting, tormenting, intimidating, or being verbally or physically aggressive toward a victim. Bullying behavior may also be indirect, taking the form of rumors, social exclusion, nasty notes, and other insidious means. Bullying is typically repetitive in nature, with bullies targeting victims repeatedly. This behavior tends to be sustained over a long period of time—it frequently persists over a year or more. Bullying can be carried out by a single child or groups of children. This behavior is more common among children with psychological disturbances and tends to be more frequently seen in boys than in girls. The behavior often creates an atmosphere of fear and intimidation among those affected. The bully-victim interaction is characterized by an imbalance of power; that is, the victim is or feels incapable of defending him- or herself, and the bully is or is perceived to be more powerful than the victim.

See also: FRIENDSHIP; VIOLENCE

Bibliography

Boulton, Michael. "Concurrent and Longitudinal Relations between Children's Playground Behavior and Social Preference, Victimization, and Bullying." *Child Development* 70 (1999):944–954.

Kumpulainen, Kirsti, Eila Rasanen, Irmeli Henttonen, et al. "Bullying and Psychiatric Symptoms among Elementary School-Age Children." *Child Abuse and Neglect* 22 (1998):705–717.

Olweus, Dan. *Bullying in School: What We Know and What We Can Do.* Oxford: Blackwell, 1993.

Smith, Peter, and Paul Brain. "Bullying in Schools: Lessons from Two Decades of Research." *Aggressive Behavior* 26 (2000):1–9.

Michele Knox

C

CATTELL, JAMES (1860–1944)

Born in Harrisburg, Pennsylvania, in 1860, J. McKeen Cattell was the fourth president of the American Psychological Association (1896) and the first psychologist elected as a member of the National Academy of Sciences in 1901. He was the founder of the related areas of differential psychology and psychometrics.

Cattell was the son of the president of Lafayette College in Easton, Pennsylvania. As a young man he was educated at home, and then in the college classroom by the faculty members of that university, eventually receiving his undergraduate degree in 1880. In 1881 he traveled to Germany to pursue a degree in philosophy with Rudolph Lotze. Lotze died shortly after Cattell's arrival so he completed the year with Wilhelm Wundt in Leipzig. Cattell returned to the United States for a year at Johns Hopkins University, then continued with his work in Wundt's laboratory, receiving his Ph.D. with Wundt in 1886. Cattell then traveled to Cambridge University in England to pursue a degree in medicine (a pursuit which he shortly abandoned). While studying in England, he became acquainted with Francis Galton, the cousin of Charles Darwin. Galton was gathering anthropometric data (measurements of the human body) in an attempt to verify Darwin's evolutionary propositions. Since Cattell was known for his methods of measuring "psychological" attributes, Galton felt that such measures would be a valuable addition to his arsenal of human attributes and persuaded Cattell to develop some psychological "tests." These tests included most of the standard assessments of Wundt's lab, including reaction time and various sensory tasks. Early in his development, Cattell became fascinated with the differences between and among individuals in psychological traits, including intelligence. He devoted his life to measuring those differences. It is fair to say that Cattell founded the fields of differential psychology and psychometrics.

Cattell returned to the United States in 1889 and took a position with the University of Pennsylvania as its first professor of psychology, moving to a similar position at Columbia University in 1891. At Columbia he began a program of testing directed toward more effective placement of incoming students into curricula. He was convinced that by measuring various mental and physical attributes of these students, an analysis might be done that would reveal the nature and structure of intelligence. In 1892 he joined with other prominent philosopher/psychologists (e.g., William James, Hugo Munsterberg, and G. Stanley Hall) to found the American Psychological Association, becoming its fourth president in 1896. He continued his student-testing project at Columbia but when the results were finally analyzed, the disappointing conclusion was that none of his "mental tests" showed any relationship to measures of student success.

From a period beginning in 1900 until he left Columbia in 1917, he devoted most of his scientific efforts to the ranking of scientists, including psychologists, according to their judged "eminence" by their colleagues. While at Columbia he was a vocal

James Cattell's contribution to the discipline of child development can be seen through his early appreciation of individual differences and their measurement. (Psychology Archives, University of Akron)

critic of university governance and individual university administrators. Cattell was a pacifist and vigorously opposed the entry of the United States into World War I (this made him even more unpopular). As a result of accumulated tensions, he was dismissed from Columbia in 1917. Four years later he founded the Psychological Corporation, which was intended to be a nonprofit psychological consulting firm that would provide testing services to clients through the cooperative efforts of applied psychologists throughout the country. Virtually every big name in applied psychology at the time bought "shares" in the Psychological Corporation or agreed to join the external consulting staff of the corporation. The "profits" from the endeavor were to be returned to psychology in the form of research support. Cattell believed firmly that research support should be centered in scientific organizations and not in government agencies or universities. Until his death in 1944, Cattell remained active in applied psychology both in the United States and abroad.

Cattell's contribution to the discipline of child development can be seen through his early appreciation of individual differences (differential psychology) and

the measurement of those differences (psychometrics).

See also: INTELLIGENCE; LEARNING

Bibliography

Landy, Frank. "Development of I/O Psychology." In Thomas K. Fagan and Gary R. VandenBos eds., *Exploring Applied Psychology: Origins and Critical Analyses.* Washington, DC: American Psychological Association, 1993.

Landy, Frank. "Early Influences on the Development of Industrial and Organizational Psychology." *Journal of Applied Psychology* 82 (1997):467–477.

Sokal, Michael M. "James McKeen Cattell and the Failure of Anthropometric Mental Testing, 1890–1901." In William R. Woodward and M. G. Ash eds., *The Problematic Science: Psychology in Nineteenth Century Thought.* Westport, CT: Greenwood, 1982.

Publications by Cattell

"Mental Measurement." *Philosophical Review* 2, no. 3 (1893):316–332.

"On Errors of Observation." *American Journal of Psychology* 5 (1893):285–293.

"A Statistical Study of Eminent Men." *Popular Science Monthly* 53 (1903):357.

Cattell, James McKeen, and L. Farrand. "Physical and Mental Measurements of Students at Columbia University." *Psychological Review* 3 (1896):618–648.

Frank J. Landy

CESAREAN DELIVERY

There are two ways that a baby can be born. The most common way is through the mother's birth canal. This is known as vaginal birth. The other way is by means of incisions made in the mother's abdominal wall and her uterus (womb). This method is called cesarean delivery, or cesarean birth. In the United States, about one out of every five births is by the cesarean method, although this proportion varies depending upon the year, the region of the country, and some other factors. In some South American countries the cesarean delivery rate is as high as 50 percent or more.

Historical Overview

The origin of the term "cesarean birth" or "cesarean section," as it is often called, is disputed. Clearly, the name does not come from the Roman emperor Julius Caesar having been born by such an operation. In his day this operation was fatal to the mother, and it is known that Caesar's mother survived his birth. There are references to abdominal birth in Roman documents dating to as early as 715 B.C.E. when it was mentioned as the *Lex Regis,* or Law of the King: If a pregnant woman died, the baby was to be delivered as quickly as possible through an abdominal incision to save its life. In the time of the Caesars this law became the *Lex Cesare,* from which the modern name for cesarean birth may have been derived. Also "cesarean" may have been derived from the Latin word *cadere,* which means "to cut." Furthermore, in Rome children born by abdominal delivery were referred to as *caesones.* Because of the high maternal death rate from cesarean births, the operation was rarely performed until the twentieth century, when modern surgery was improved with the development of anesthesia and the means to control hemorrhage and to prevent and treat infection. By 1950 it was possible for a hospital in New York City to report that 1,000 consecutive cesarean deliveries had been performed without a single maternal death.

Shifting Reasons for Cesarean Delivery

Until 1970 cesarean births accounted for fewer than one in twenty births in the United States. The reason cesarean births were performed was largely for conditions that threatened the life of the mother. These conditions included uterine hemorrhage, hypertension of pregnancy, tuberculosis, diabetes, heart disease, and prolonged labor caused by disproportion between the size of the infant and the size of the birth canal. A small proportion of the cesarean births were performed because the baby (fetus) was in danger of hypoxia (lack of oxygen) as when the umbilical cord slips out of its normal position. Also, some cesarean deliveries were performed as repeat cesarean births for women who had a previous baby by cesarean, because it was believed that once a cesarean had been performed, all subsequent births should be by cesarean delivery.

In the early 1970s, electronic means of continuously monitoring a baby's heart rate during labor became available, and intensive care for newborns was beginning to result in dramatic improvements in the survival of seriously ill infants. In addition, the frequency of serious maternal complications of cesarean birth had continued to decline. As a result of these improvements in the care of mothers and infants, doctors became more inclined to recommend cesarean delivery in situations where either the mother or infant were at any increased risk of illness or long-term developmental abnormality that might be caused by vaginal birth. For example, before 1970 almost all breech births (in which the buttocks or feet of a baby rather than its head are the first to be born) were by vaginal delivery, but by 1988 almost all such births were by cesarean delivery. The increase in the use of cesarean delivery to prevent harm to the fetus from labor and vaginal delivery accounted for the increase in the cesarean birthrate from 5 percent of live births

in 1970 to 25 percent in 1988. After 1988 the rate of cesarean birth began to decline somewhat so that by 1996 it was 21 percent.

One of the common reasons for cesarean birth is repeat cesarean delivery, which accounts for approximately 25 percent of all cesarean births. Women who have had a cesarean delivery are at risk of the uterine incision rupturing during labor. This can result in the death of or the serious injury to the infant and life-threatening hemorrhage and possible need for a hysterectomy for the mother. The risk of uterine rupture depends upon the type of uterine incision. A vertical incision in the uppermost portion of the uterus has a 12 percent risk of rupturing during labor. This type of incision was used commonly in the early part of the twentieth century but now is used only on rare occasions. A woman who has had a cesarean birth by this method should have all subsequent births by cesarean delivery before the onset of labor to avoid a catastrophic rupture of the uterus. A transverse incision in the lower portion of the uterus, which is now the most common method of performing a cesarean delivery, is associated with a 0.5 percent risk of rupture during labor. Most women who had this type of cesarean delivery can safely attempt a trial of labor and vaginal delivery provided that labor occurs where there are facilities for and personnel who can perform an immediate cesarean delivery if signs of uterine rupture occur. The increase in the incidence of vaginal birth after a previous cesarean birth accounted for the gradual decline in the cesarean delivery rate after 1988.

The Cesarean Operation

The cesarean operation, which usually takes from thirty to sixty minutes, begins with the administration of anesthesia by use of intravenous and inhaled anesthetic agents (general anesthesia) or the injection of anesthetic medications into the spinal canal (spinal anesthesia) or just outside of the spinal canal (epidural anesthesia). The skin of the abdomen is cleansed with antiseptic solution and surgical drapes are placed to maintain a sterile operating field during the procedure. An incision is made in the abdomen, after which a second incision is made in the uterus (womb) that is large enough to permit removal of the baby. The umbilical cord is clamped and cut, and the infant is handed to a nurse or doctor assigned specifically to care for the infant. The placenta (afterbirth) is then delivered through the same incisions. The incisions are closed with sutures (stitches) or other types of wound-closure devices. The expense of a cesarean birth is about two to three times that of a vaginal birth because of the additional personnel, equipment, and time required for performing the operation and the somewhat longer hospital stay following the birth.

Complications Related to Cesarean Delivery

Complications of the birth process may affect either the mother or the infant. Whereas the risk of complications for the mother is somewhat greater in a cesarean birth than in a vaginal birth, the risk of complications for the infant is greater from vaginal birth than from cesarean birth. Moreover, the type and severity of complications from each method of birth differs for both the mother and the infant. Complications of cesarean birth for the mother during the operative procedure include adverse reactions to anesthetic agents, injury of abdominal organs and hemorrhage from the surgical incisions; and after the procedure, pneumonia, urinary or wound infections, and blood clots in the legs, abdomen, or lungs. The most common long-term complication of cesarean birth is the risk of rupture of the uterine incision in a subsequent pregnancy, and the consequent increase in risk of future pregnancies having to be delivered by cesarean.

Complications of vaginal birth for the mother include many of the complications that occur in cesarean birth, but they occur much less often and are usually less severe. The long-term complication of vaginal birth is the increased risk of pelvic muscle dysfunction that manifest as urinary or rectal incontinence.

Overall, the risk of maternal death from a cesarean birth (4 per 10,000 births) is four times greater than from a vaginal birth (1 per 10,000 births). Cesarean births, however, are often performed for medical or obstetrical complications that, by their nature, increase the risk of death for mothers. If one excludes pregnancies with such complications, there still remains a one and one-half times greater risk of the mother dying as a result of cesarean birth as compared to vaginal birth.

Complications of vaginal birth for an infant include birth trauma (fractured limbs or injured nerves resulting in paralysis of an arm), asphyxia (lack of oxygen) causing brain damage, and acquiring an infection from the mother's birth canal (herpes simplex virus or group-B *streptococcus*). Complications of cesarean birth for infants include lacerations from the surgeon's knife and a respiratory illness caused by the failure of excess fluid to be cleared from the infant's lungs.

Balancing the benefits and risks of vaginal birth as compared to cesarean birth for both the mother and the infant in a wide variety of birthing situations is the complex problem faced by doctors and midwives, who care for women during their pregnancies. Increasingly, women are becoming more involved in the decisions about the way in which they will give birth. During her pregnancy, a woman should be provided with accurate and updated information about the benefits and risks of the alternative methods of delivery for her situation so that together with her physician or midwife she can make an informed decision about the method of birth.

See also: BIRTH; MIDWIVES

Bibliography

Bowes, Watson, Jr. "Clinical Aspects of Normal and Abnormal Labor." In Robert Creasy and Robert Resnik eds., *Maternal-Fetal Medicine,* 4th edition. Philadelphia: Saunders, 1999.

Hankins, Gary, Steven Clark, F. Gary Cunningham, and Larry Gilstrap. "Cesarean Section." In *Operative Obstetrics.* Norwalk, CT: Appleton and Lange, 1995.

Phelan, Jeffrey, and Steven Clark, eds. *Cesarean Delivery.* New York: Elsevier, 1988.

Watson A. Bowes Jr.

CHILD ABUSE

The world in which many children live is punctuated by violent act after violent act. In many situations children become victims of this violence. Some children have been the direct targets of an act of violence, while other children have been indirectly affected through witnessing such acts; it is often difficult to distinguish between these two cases based on outward appearance alone. There are yet other children living in situations just as egregious where violence does not play a significant role. Theirs is merely an existence where their needs are not adequately met, including basic necessities of food and shelter, protection, structure, and supervision. Society labels these children as victims, when in fact they are the truest of survivors. What greater challenge can there be than having caretakers who cannot be trusted to provide adequate care? The common denominator of maltreatment is that those responsible for the child's well-being are either unable or unwilling to care for the child properly. Intervention from others is warranted to ensure that the needs and welfare of the child are fully considered.

Definitions of Child Maltreatment

The phrase "child abuse" often immediately brings to mind the image of a child beaten black and blue by an angry parent or caregiver. This is merely one scenario and perhaps the easiest to contrive because one can see what has been done to the child. It sparks people's emotions and a desire to take action against the offending adult. In reality there are many faces of child abuse and many more acts that leave scars "invisible" to the naked eye. There is a tendency to ignore children who display no physical or outward signs of abuse. A large number of these children go unrecognized, living in environments that hinder their potential and their development as secure, healthy individuals.

"Child maltreatment" is a term designed to draw attention away from the purely abuse-related acts or injuries that children suffer. It is an all-inclusive term to describe, in essence, when a caregiver does something or fails to do something that has harmed or threatens to harm a child in his or her care. Child abuse refers to acts of commission, which are done to a child and cause harm (or the threat of harm), whereas child neglect refers to acts of omission, acts that are not done to or for a child, which result in harm (or the threat of harm). In using the separate categories of child abuse and child neglect there are further distinctions that can be made. Abuse is often categorized into physical, sexual, psychological, and emotional abuse. Neglect is often categorized into physical, emotional, medical, and educational neglect. The most commonly reported statistics are those for physical abuse, sexual abuse, and overall child neglect.

How are child abuse and neglect manifested? Physical abuse involves harming the physical body with such acts as kicking, punching, stabbing, or beating a child with an object; whereas physical neglect involves not taking care of the needs of the physical body with food or shelter. A child's exposure to a harmful environment (such as one in which drug use is occurring) could also be construed as physical neglect because of the threat of harm to the child (i.e., if the child were capable of getting to the drugs himself, or if the drugs impaired the ability of the caretaker to adequately supervise the child). Similarly, emotional abuse might involve harming a child emotionally by yelling, threatening the child, or calling the child demeaning names, such as "stupid." Emotional neglect would be failing to provide emotional support for a child such as happens when a caretaker abandons a child or lacks any affection for a child. For many children, different forms of maltreatment occur at the same time.

While these definitions seem self-explanatory, there is much debate about what constitutes abuse and neglect in the United States. In other words, the practical application of these terms is not always easy. At the broad ends of the spectrum, there is usually little argument about whether abuse or neglect has occurred. If a parent takes an iron and intentionally burns his two-year-old child just because the child wet the bed at night, few would argue that this was child abuse. Yet, if a single parent working two jobs to support the family has no time at the end of the day to interact with his children, is this neglect? The larger issue is that having such definitions implies that there are certain standards for parenting or caring for children. With such a diverse and multicultural population, clear differences in parenting styles and standards exist. The task of deciding where abuse and neglect fall in that spectrum is challenging.

Another issue of debate in defining child maltreatment involves the societal response to child maltreatment. Social workers, medical professionals, and law enforcement personnel are most often involved in cases of child maltreatment. Each profession has its own criteria for identifying abuse and neglect. Law enforcement, for example, is concerned with proof of abuse or neglect and assigning culpability; in other words, who is to blame? The law requires respondents to look for and present "evidence" of maltreatment, when evidence may not be readily apparent. In many sexual abuse cases, for example, a child has made statements that indicate abuse, but the physical exam of the child is normal. Despite what the child has disclosed, it is rare for these cases to be brought to trial without physical evidence of abuse being present.

Incidence of Child Maltreatment

Annual data on the occurrence of child maltreatment in the United States are collected and analyzed by the National Child Abuse and Neglect Data System (NCANDS). This is a systematic, nationwide effort that was launched to collect data from state child protective service agencies, the primary state agency responsible for responding to child maltreatment. Each state reports the numbers of children reported for suspected maltreatment, investigated, and subsequently determined to be abused or neglected.

The NCANDS report for 1998 states that the estimated number of children reported for suspected maltreatment was more than 2.8 million. The estimated number of children abused or neglected in the United States during that year was 903,000. Of this number, more than half were victims of neglect, nearly one-quarter were physically abused, and approximately 12 percent were sexually abused. Approximately 25 percent of the children experienced multiple forms of abuse. These percentages are typical of the breakdown from year to year.

The rate of abuse and neglect for 1998 was 12.9 per 1,000 children less than eighteen years of age. This is actually a slight decrease from the previous year. Since records have been maintained by NCANDS, however, there has been an upward trend in the number of maltreated children. In 1974 the number of reports for suspected maltreatment was merely 60,000; in 1980, the number increased to greater than one million. Several factors contribute to this dramatic increase, including changes in child abuse reporting laws and an increased recognition of abuse and neglect as real societal problems. Early laws governing reporting of suspected child maltreatment required only professionals to report to the state child protective service agencies. By the late twentieth century, most states required anyone with a suspicion of maltreatment to make a report. There is also evidence that the level of violence in society has increased such that it has been declared a public health epidemic. Violence toward children and violence involving children (as witnesses) are both on the rise.

The numbers of maltreated children are impressive, but it is commonly accepted that these numbers are inaccurate. The cases reported to social services represent only the "tip of the iceberg" of all maltreated children. There are several ways researchers know this to be true. One indication that some children are missed comes from studies of child fatalities. Many children are killed as a result of abuse or neglect, but not all are identified as victims of abuse or neglect at the time of their death. Second, parent surveys and other periodic national surveys obtain higher rates of abuse and neglect than that counted by social services. In some cases the difference in rates is not trivial. For example, a nationwide telephone survey of parents found a nearly tenfold increase in rates of physical maltreatment compared to rates reported by social services.

Obtaining accurate numbers of maltreated children is difficult for other reasons. A fundamental reason is that simply defining what constitutes child maltreatment, as previously mentioned, is problematic. Maltreatment definitions also vary from state to state. The potential for missing abuse clearly exists when only two-thirds of reported cases are investigated, in part because of an overburdened social services system.

Consider also the process by which children are identified as being maltreated—someone has to make a report. This process relies on individuals recognizing abuse and taking action. Several studies have identified resilient kids—where abuse or neglect is occurring at home but the children find ways to cope. These children are less likely to be identified, as are very young children who cannot relate what has happened to them. Then there are biases (based on race, gender, and socioeconomic status) that make individuals more likely to suspect and report maltreatment. Poor families are notoriously suspect because of presumably higher financial stress and the frequently associated lack of education and resources. The opposite also happens: there are biases that prevent suspicion of abuse, leading to many maltreated children being missed. Girls are traditionally viewed as the only victims of sexual abuse, and young boys who act out are labeled as hyperactive but the question of sexual abuse is never entertained. Even if abuse is recognized and suspected, someone must take action, which is a well-known barrier to intervention. People are reluctant to become involved in family matters even if it means helping a child.

Developmental Perspectives of Child Maltreatment

It is very important to have an understanding of the relationship between child development and child maltreatment. Childhood is typically a time of rapid change and growth. Each stage of development brings new challenges and changes in the physical, cognitive, and behavioral makeup of a child. These changes are reflected in the epidemiology of maltreatment, which is the pattern of abuse and neglect that is commonly seen. Child development affects all of the following: the precipitating factors that lead to maltreatment; the susceptibility of a child to different types of maltreatment at different ages; the physical findings of abuse or neglect; the treatment options following maltreatment; and the likelihood of long-term sequelae (secondary effects) from abuse or neglect.

Infants are at the greatest risk for all types of maltreatment, including fatal maltreatment. This is relatively easy to understand from a developmental standpoint. Child neglect occurs commonly as infants are the most dependent on their caregivers to provide the basic necessities of life in a stable, secure environment. Parents who are overwhelmed by life stressors and have personal limitations, or have certain cognitive or medical conditions (such as mental retardation or depression) may become caregivers who cannot pick up on infant cues. In these situations there is a risk of poor attachment and emotional neglect. Parents can also be easily frustrated by an infant whose crying or temperament makes them difficult to handle, leading to the potential for physical abuse. This risk is dangerously high given that infants are already at higher risk for physical abuse because of their physical attributes, such as softer bones, small size, and the inability to resist physical harm or verbalize what happens to them. The "shaken baby syndrome" illustrates this principle. An infant has limited muscle tone, particularly in the neck, and an infant's head size is proportionally larger than other parts of its body. An infant that is forcibly shaken can get a form of whiplash, which creates forces that shear the delicate and developing brain. These infants suffer significant neurological damage and often die as a result of the brain injury and swelling.

The toddler and preschool years provide new challenges as children are growing and developing new physical skills. These physical skills enable children to run, climb, and openly explore in areas they previously could not, so caregiver supervision becomes increasingly important. A neglectful caregiver will not make the environment safe or provide appropriate boundaries. Verbal skills increase and children vocalize their emerging independence. A parent unprepared for the typical use of the word "no" may interpret this as defiant behavior and resort to harsh physical punishment that becomes abusive, not recognizing the appropriateness of the child's behavior for this developmental stage. Toilet training during these years is one of the more common parental stressors and precipitant of abuse.

School-age children and adolescents have a lower overall risk of maltreatment. They spend less time in the presence of caregivers because of school, after-school activities, and peer interactions. They are also less dependent as their physical and cognitive development allows them to do many things for themselves. Physically they are larger in size, stature, and strength, and it takes more force to cause injury. Sexual abuse, however, is more prevalent among school-age children and teens, particularly girls. The reason for this increase is related in part to the physical developmental changes that occur in both boys and girls as they enter puberty.

Treatment and System Responses

When it is determined that a child has been abused or neglected, the system will intervene. The primary state agency responsible for children is social services, but children are first identified in any number of ways: by neighbors, relatives, day-care staff, teachers, or medical professionals. Medical professionals and day-care staff often identify young children, because the doctor's office and the day-care center are common places for children to be seen on a regular basis. School personnel frequently identify older children when changes in behavior, attendance, or school performance are noticed. Suspicions of abuse or neglect are then referred to the appropriate social services agency for a more thorough investigation.

One of the first concerns for social services is the safety of the child. The agency's primary purpose is to ensure that no further harm comes to the child. If the perpetrator of maltreatment (the person suspected of abusing or neglecting the child) is to continue to have access to the child, this can be handled in

In August 1954 eleven-year-old Joe Roach was found chained to his bed in his home in Houston, Texas. Rather than going into the house to sleep and be mistreated by his parents the night before, the boy spent the night in a doghouse in the backyard of his home. (Bettmann/Corbis)

several ways. What happens next will depend on the type and severity of abuse or neglect and the mandates of the state. The perpetrator will often contract with social services and agree not to maltreat the child. The person can agree to leave the home temporarily. The child can also be removed from the unsafe environment and placed in the care of a relative or foster family.

Many times children will require a medical evaluation to determine what harm has been done, document the extent of harm, and treat any new or existing medical conditions. The needs of the whole child should be addressed during a medical evaluation, although emergent needs are prioritized. In the case of shaken baby syndrome, for example, the majority of these children are brought in on an emergency basis when they stop breathing at home. Obviously these children require intensive care even before the determination of abuse is made. For other children, the medical evaluation may entail treating a broken bone, tending to lacerations, evaluating bruises, or examining for sexually transmitted diseases. It can also involve recommending a developmental evaluation for a child who is developmentally delayed or recommending medical and behavioral treatment for depression.

Further treatment usually involves obtaining mental health services or additional services for the family. The goals of these services are to assist the child and family in coping with the maltreatment and to restore family functioning. Mental health services can be directed to the child or to the child's caretakers, if the child is too young or unable to participate actively in treatment sessions on her own. Play therapy is very commonly employed in this setting. For the family, evaluating the home environment and the circumstances surrounding the abuse or neglect is critical to assisting the family and preventing maltreatment from reoccurring. There may be social services such as food stamps or parenting education that can assist the family and reduce family stressors. Parents and caregivers may also be prior victims of child maltreatment and/or violence in other forms and benefit from mental health, substance abuse, or domestic violence resources themselves.

Consequences of Maltreatment

The consequences of maltreatment for children who are abused or neglected vary a great deal. There are many factors that affect what happens after maltreatment, including: the developmental stage of the child at the time of the abuse or neglect, the type and chronicity of abuse or neglect, the relationship of the perpetrator to the child, and the child's temperament and natural ability (intelligence). There are also several different categories of consequences, including: medical or physical consequences; emotional, behavioral, or cognitive consequences; short-term versus long-term consequences; and consequences with or without intervention by social services or others.

One significant principle that appears in the child maltreatment literature repeatedly is that children suffering multiple types of abuse or neglect tend to have a poorer outcome than children who suffer only one type or incident of abuse or neglect. Studies that document the long-term effects of child abuse and neglect mirror these findings. These studies show that lifestyle choices and responses to stress may be altered, leading to greater risk for adult criminal behavior and significant health problems (such as heart disease) in adulthood.

Prevention of Maltreatment

Unfortunately, there is little data on how to prevent child maltreatment. Home visiting programs have shown the most promise in the primary prevention of maltreatment, which is preventing abuse or neglect before it occurs. Home visiting programs involve pairing new parents with someone trained or experienced in child development so that the new parents can learn how to care for and respond to the needs of their infants. The most widely modeled programs, when studied, have been successful in reducing the incidence of but have not entirely eliminated child maltreatment in the study populations. Issues of funding in many geographic regions have limited the availability of such services to those families considered at higher risk for maltreatment.

Efforts in the prevention of maltreatment primarily function on the level of secondary prevention. Intervention by social services or other professionals occurs when maltreatment has already taken place or when children are considered already at risk for abuse or neglect. In these situations the focus is on preventing further abuse or neglect, as well as treating and minimizing complications of the maltreatment that has occurred.

There is no doubt that prevention of child maltreatment is a complex issue. There are multiple factors involved when a child is abused or neglected, factors related to the individual child, the family structure, and other environmental stressors (such as poverty). The cycle of violence is a well-known phenomenon, where today's victims become tomorrow's perpetrators. In order to prevent child maltreatment, prevention itself must become a priority. This will require commitment and collaboration from many sources, including individuals, professionals, community groups, and government agencies. All of these sources must be willing to work together to make a difference for children.

See also: DOMESTIC VIOLENCE

Bibliography

Center for the Future of Children. "The Future of Children: Protecting Children from Abuse and Neglect." Los Altos, CA: David and Lucille Packard Foundation, 1998.

Elliott, Barbara A. "Prevention of Violence." *Primary Care* 20 (1993):277 288.

Felitti, Vincent J., Robert F. Anda, Dale Nordenberg, David F. Williamson, Alison M. Spitz, Valerie Edwards, Mary P. Koss, and James S. Marks. "Relationship of Childhood Abuse and Household Dysfunction to Many of the Leading Causes of Death in Adults: The Adverse Childhood Experiences (ACE) Study." *American Journal of Preventive Medicine* 14 (1998):245–258.

Garbarino, James. "Psychological Child Maltreatment." *Primary Care* (1993):307–315.

Goldson, Edward. "The Affective and Cognitive Sequelae of Child Maltreatment." *Pediatric Clinics of North America* (1991):1481–1496.

Kendall-Tackett, Kathleen A. "The Effects of Neglect on Academic Achievement and Disciplinary Problems: A Developmental Perspective." *Child Abuse and Neglect* (1996):161–169.

Mackner, Laura M., Raymond H. Starr, and Maureen M. Black. "The Cumulative Effect of Neglect and Failure to Thrive on Cognitive Functioning." *Child Abuse and Neglect* (1997):691–700.

Maxfield, Michael G., and Cathy Spatz Widom. "The Cycle of Violence: Revisited Six Years Later." *Archives of Pediatrics and Adolescent Medicine* 150 (1996):390–395.

Newberger, Eli H., Robert L. Hampton, Thomas J. Marx, and Kathleen M. White. "Child Abuse and Pediatric Social Illness: An Epidemiological Analysis and Ecological Reformulation." *American Journal of Orthopsychiatry* (1986):589–601.

O'Hagan, Kieran P. "Emotional and Psychological Abuse: Problems of Definition." *Child Abuse and Neglect* (1995):449–461.

Olds, David L., John Eckenrode, Charles R. Henderson Jr., Harriet Kitzman, Jane Powers, Robert Cole, Kimberly Sidora, Pamela Morris, Lisa M. Pettitt, and Dennis Luckey. "Long-Term Effects of Home Visitation on Maternal Life Course and Child Abuse and Neglect: Fifteen-Year Follow-Up of a Randomized Trial." *Journal of the American Medical Association* (1997):637–643.

Sirotnak, Andrew P., and Richard D. Krugman. "Physical Abuse of Children: An Update." *Pediatrics in Review* 15 (1994):394–399.

Theodore, Adrea D., and Desmond K. Runyan. "A Medical Research Agenda for Child Maltreatment: Negotiating the Next Steps." *Pediatrics* (1999):168–177.

Thompson, Ross A., and Brian L. Wilcox. "Child Maltreatment Research: Federal Support and Policy Issues." *American Psychologist* 50 (1995):789–793.

Wissow, Lawrence S. "Child Abuse and Neglect." *New England Journal of Medicine* 21 (1995):1425–1431.

Wolock, Isabel, and Bernard Horowitz. "Child Maltreatment as a Social Problem: The Neglect of Neglect." *American Journal of Orthopsychiatry* (1984):530–543.

Adrea D. Theodore

CHILD CUSTODY AND SUPPORT

Child custody refers to the legal and physical rights and responsibilities parents have with respect to their child. Legal child custody refers to the right to make all major decisions regarding the child's health, welfare, education, and religious training. Physical custody is the right to the daily care and control of the child. The parents' marital status in relation to each other has no bearing on the determination of custody. There are different types of child custody that connote various combinations of legal and physical rights.

Sole legal custody gives one parent the right to legal custody, independent of the other parent. This parent is called the "custodial" parent and the other parent is referred to as the "noncustodial" parent. Noncustodial parents typically have visitation rights, including overnight visits and vacations.

Sole physical custody grants exclusive physical custody to one parent. Granting one parent both sole legal and physical custody is typically done only when the other parent has neglected or abused the child.

Joint legal custody grants legal custody rights to both parents equally. This means that each parent needs to inform and achieve agreement with the other parent before making major decisions for the child.

Joint physical custody grants physical custody rights to both parents, although the actual amount of time each parent spends with the child may not be equal. Parents with joint physical custody usually have a parenting plan that specifies the actual times the child will spend with each parent.

Split custody refers to "splitting" siblings between parents and may entail any combination of physical and legal custody.

If parents cannot agree on a custody arrangement, the court will impose an arrangement that is based on the "child's best interests."

Historical Overview of Custody Law

What constitutes the "child's best interests" has been marked by great ideological shifts. Until the mid-nineteenth century, fathers were unequivocally favored in custody decisions and mothers had virtually no rights. Under English law, upon which U.S. law is based, children and their mothers were viewed as a man's property or "chattel." Over the next hundred years, psychologists increasingly emphasized that mothers were biologically predisposed to be the better parent because they were more nurturing. The role of the father was viewed as an indirect one, as the provider for the mother-child relationship. As a result, the allocation of custody shifted from a complete right of fathers to a sweeping preference for mothers. This maternal preference was fortified by the "tender years doctrine," which held that children of tender years should be raised by their mothers.

In the 1970s and 1980s, significant changes occurred. The courts moved away from the presumption that mothers are always the best parents and discarded the tender years doctrine because it was based solely on gender and was therefore unconstitutional. Perhaps the most prominent change was the shift to a preference for joint custody, a shift based on the presumption that it is important for children to have a continuing relationship with both parents.

States differ in the extent to which they endorse joint custody. Some express a presumption in favor of joint custody. Under the Uniform Child Custody Jurisdiction Act, judges are required to give "full faith and credit" to custody orders issued in other states and to enforce these decrees.

Factors in Determining the Child's Best Interest

The majority (an estimated 90%) of custody cases are settled according to parents' wishes. The court will accept whatever parents agree on. This process has been criticized because it does not necessarily ensure the child's best interest. Critics point out that this procedure may be especially harmful to children if violence exists in the family; the terms of the agreement may not necessarily be fair but may be coerced and may prolong the child's exposure to violence. When parents cannot agree, the court tries to evaluate the best interests of the child, considering the following factors:

- The parent-child relationship. It has been recommended that young children be placed with their "primary caregiver" to minimize disruption for the child. Fathers have protested that this standard favors mothers. In response, supporters of this standard have suggested that it provides an incentive for fathers to be involved in their children's upbringing from the beginning.

- The wishes of the child. Whether to consider the wishes of the child is controversial and varies from state to state. There is a concern that children may not know what is in their best interests and may even pick the worst parent just because he or she is more permissive. A further concern is that letting the child choose will induce guilt feelings in the child later on.

- Parents' mental and physical health. These should be relevant only if they affect child rearing. Courts may also consider the child's age and gender and any special needs the child may have.

- Lifestyle and conduct of parents. These factors are considered only if they affect the child (e.g., parents' substance abuse, child's exposure to secondhand smoke). Courts have moved away from considering parents' sexual behavior, unless it can be shown that a parent's activities have a negative impact on the child. If neither parent is fit to have custody of the child the court may award custody to a third party (e.g., relatives or foster parents).

- Parents' ability to provide adequately for the child. Courts take into account each parent's ability to provide such necessities as food, clothing, and medical care.

- Continuity with the primary caregiver, the other parent, and with home, schools, and community. To promote continuity, courts may favor the parent who is more likely to allow the nonresidential parent access to the child.

Critics point out that the best interests of the child standard is so imprecise that it promotes conflict between divorcing parents and judicial bias and arbitrariness in decision making. "Judicial discretion" entitles judges to consider all, some, or none of the factors, or they may weigh them according to their own personal values and views.

The Number of Children in Custody Allocations

The exact number of children involved in custody allocations is not known. Reporting is not uniform, consistent, or comprehensive within and across states. Based on figures from the National Center for Health Statistics, at a divorce rate of 4.1 per 1,000 population in the United States in 1999 (amounting to 1.1 million divorces) and an average rate of 0.9 children per divorce decree, approximately one million children were affected by divorce. It should be noted, however, that divorce data do not provide complete estimates of the total number of children involved in custody allocations, because one out of three children in the United States is born to unmarried parents. More informative estimates stem from the reports of household living arrangements compiled by the U.S. Bureau of the Census. The majority (85%) of children who lived with a single parent in 1998 lived with their mother. About 40 percent of these children lived with mothers who had never been married.

Evaluation of Various Custody Arrangements

Because of the great diversity of individual and family characteristics it is not possible to make a generalization that one custody type is better for all children or all parents. Nevertheless, when examining research on child custody certain trends emerge.

Joint custody has the advantage of assuring the child of continuing contact with both parents. It alleviates some of the burdens of parenting as parents get time off for their own interests. The disadvantages of joint custody include less stability for children, as they must be shuttled between the parents, and problems for parents who want to move to a different area. Perhaps the most crucial consideration in deciding custody is that ongoing parental conflict is a primary predictor of children's maladjustment. Children who continue to feel "caught in the middle" when parents fight face particularly negative outcomes.

Joint custody has been linked to higher satisfaction with the custody arrangement in parents and better adjustment in children if it is self-selected and parents are cooperative. (Bob Daemmrich, Stock Boston, Inc.)

Child Support

All states require that parents support their children financially until they reach the age of majority (age eighteen) and in some instances even longer if the child has special needs. Noncustodial parents are typically required to pay child support, whereas custodial parents are presumed to fulfill their financial obligation through their daily care of the child. If parents share physical custody, child support is based on the percentage of time the child lives with each parent and each parent's income in relation to their combined incomes.

The Office of Child Support Enforcement reported that nearly ten million child support orders, involving approximately twenty million children, existed in 1999. Enforcement of child support has become a national concern, and many new enforcement mechanisms exist to compel so-called deadbeat parents to pay child support. Enforcement may include seizure of property and tax refunds, the reporting of nonpayment to credit bureaus, suspension of driver's and professional licenses, and imprisonment, fines, or both. The most widely used and effective enforcement tool is wage withholding by employers, a tool used in 60 percent of such cases.

The receipt of child support has been linked positively to greater attainment of educational goals and reductions in children's behavioral problems. The likelihood that fathers pay child support increases with the amount of contact with the child. This does not mean, however, that more contact causes higher and more stable child support payments. A more likely explanation is that greater parental commitment causes both of these occurrences—regular and higher child support payments as well as higher levels of contact.

See also: DIVORCE; MEDIATION

Bibliography

Arditti, J. A., and T. Z. Keith. "Visitation Frequency, Child Support Payment, and the Father-Child Relationship Postdivorce." *Journal of Marriage and the Family* 55 (1993):699–712.

Kelly, Joan B. "Current Research on Children's Postdivorce Adjustment: No Simple Answers." *Family and Conciliation Courts Review* 31, no. 1 (1993):29–49.

Maccoby, Eleanor E. "The Custody of Children of Divorcing Families: Weighing the Alternatives." In Ross A. Thompson, Paul R. Amato eds., *The Postdivorce Family: Children, Parenting, and Society.* Thousand Oaks, CA: Sage, 1999.

Maccoby, Eleanor E., Robert H. Mnookin, Charlene E. Depner, and H. Elizabeth Peters. *Dividing the Child: Social and Legal*

Dilemmas of Custody. Cambridge, MA: Harvard University Press, 1992.

U.S. Bureau of the Census. *Current Population Reports: Marital Status and Living Arrangements, March 1998.* Washington, DC: U.S. Government Printing Office, 1998.

U.S. Department of Health and Human Services, Administration for Children and Families, Office of Child Support Enforcement. *Child Support Enforcement FY 1999 Preliminary Data Report.* Washington, DC: U.S. Department of Health and Human Services, 2000.

U.S. Department of Health and Human Services, National Center for Health Statistics. *First Marriage Dissolution, Divorce, and Remarriage: United States.* Washington, DC: U.S. Government Printing Office, 2001.

Veum, J. R. "The Relationship between Child Support and Visitation: Evidence from Longitudinal Data." *Social Science Research* 22 (1993):229–244.

Cornelia Brentano

CHILDREN WITH SPECIAL HEALTH CARE NEEDS

Children with special health care needs include those with chronic illnesses (i.e., asthma, sickle cell anemia, diabetes), physical disabilities (i.e., cerebral palsy, spina bifida), and developmental/emotional disabilities (i.e., autism, Down syndrome). As advances in health care have allowed medically fragile and/or disabled children to live longer, attention has focused on understanding their unique "developmental" needs. The impact of an illness or disability on a child's cognitive, social, and emotional development varies over time as the child's developmental level changes. In addition, the implications of the illness/disability are different depending upon the child's developmental level at its onset and the limitations of the disorder at each level of development. Professionals who work with children with special health needs must keep the above in mind, and must also understand the effects (both negative and positive) of the illness/disability on the family system, and how these in turn can affect the child's development.

See also: DEVELOPMENTAL DISABILITIES; DOWN SYNDROME

Bibliography

McPherson, Merle, Polly Arango, Harriette Fox, et al. "A New Definition of Children with Special Health Care Needs" (commentary). *Pediatrics* 102 (1998):137–140.

Thompson, Robert, Jr., and Kathryn Gustafson. *Adaptation to Chronic Childhood Illness.* Washington, DC: American Psychological Association, 1996.

Janeen C. Manuel
Elizabeth C. Allen

CHILDREN'S RIGHTS

The United Nations Convention on the Rights of the Child (UNCRC) is the clearest and most comprehensive expression of what the world community wants for its children. It arose in the 1970s as a reaction to the weakening global humanitarian response to children. The United Nations unanimously endorsed the convention on November 20, 1989 and it became international law in 1990.

The UNCRC is an international human rights treaty, which focuses on the rights of the child from a developmental-ecological perspective. It assumes that the child's overall development is a function of a number of factors (psychological, social, educational, and cultural) and contexts (home, school, community, and country). The convention's developmental framework represents the latest thinking in international child-related policies.

The UNCRC is comprised of fifty-four articles that seek to safeguard and uphold children's minimal health, civil, humanitarian, and family rights. It can be divided into three main parts: key principles, specific rights, and ways in which the convention should be monitored. Protection of children against discrimination, abuse and neglect, and armed conflict are issues outlined in Articles 2, 19, and 38, respectively. Parent-child relationships are defined in several articles, including Articles 5, 9, and 10. The treaty also calls on states and countries to ensure survival of children to the maximum extent (health care, food, and clean water in Article 24; education in Articles, 28 and 29).

The UNCRC uses the principle of "a child's best interest" as a standard measuring tool for policy, thereby defining children not as objects, but as individuals with human rights. Consequently, the UNCRC is an important advocacy tool for children worldwide.

See also: DOMESTIC VIOLENCE

Bibliography

Detrick, S. *A Commentary on the United Nations Convention on the Rights of the Child.* The Hague: Kluwer Law International, 1999.

Muscroft, S., ed. *Children's Rights: Reality or Rhetoric?* London: International Save the Children Alliance, 1999.

Rebello, Pia, L. Cummings, and M. Gardinier. "The United Nations Convention on the Rights of the Child: A Call to Child Development Professionals around the World." Paper presented at the Biennial meeting of the Society for Research in Child Development, Indianapolis, IN, April 1995.

United Nations Children's Fund (UNICEF) in the United Nations Convention on the Rights of the Child [web site]. Available from http://www.unicef.org/crc; INTERNET.

Pia Rebello Britto

CHRONIC ILLNESS

Chronic illnesses among children traditionally have been defined based on a specific diagnosis. More recently, chronic conditions are being defined along several dimensions: they have a biological, psychological, or cognitive basis; have lasted or are likely to last at least one year; and result in limitations of function, activities, or social roles, and/or dependence on medications, special diets, medical technology, assistive devices, or personal assistance to compensate for functional limitations, and/or require medical care or related services. The impact of childhood chronic health conditions on the child and the family vary, even among children with the same diagnosis, depending for example, on age of onset, whether the condition is stable, whether it affects a child's ability to participate in normal childhood activities, whether normal life expectancy is threatened. Major conditions—asthma, spina bifida, craniofacial anomalies, congenital heart disease, and sickle cell anemia—require diverse medical, allied health, educational, and supportive interventions.

See also: DEVELOPMENTAL DISABILITIES

Bibliography

Perrin, James. "Introduction." In Nicholas Hobbs and James Perrin eds., *Issues in the Care of Children with Chronic Illness*. San Francisco: Jossey-Bass, 1985.

Stein, Ruth, Laurie Bauman, Lauren Westbrook, Susan Coupey, and Henry Ireys. "Framework for Identifying Children Who Have Chronic Conditions: The Case for a New Definition." *The Journal of Pediatrics* 122, no. 3 (1993):342–347.

Anita Farel

CHRONOLOGICAL AGE

Chronological age refers to the period that has elapsed beginning with an individual's birth and extending to any given point in time. Chronological age is used in research and in test norm development as a measure to group individuals. Developmental research looks for age-related differences or behavior changes as a function of age.

Using chronological age provides a means to roughly assure the equivalence of such factors as physical experience, social interaction, learning, and acculturation among others. Chronological age is not necessarily a predictor of an individual's stages of development, as the rate at which individual's progress through stages may not be identical. Problems in using chronological age include such issues as school readiness and the evaluation of premature infants. As medical technology has advanced in the treatment of premature infants, chronological age has been challenged as an appropriate measure for this group with gestational age or durational pregnancy being proposed as a means of adjusting chronological age.

See also: DEVELOPMENTAL NORMS; STAGES OF DEVELOPMENT

Bibliography

du Toit, M. K. "A Life-Span Developmental Orientation: The Relevance of Chronological Age in Life-Span Developmental Psychology: A Theoretical Observation." *South African Journal of Psychology* 22 (1992):21–26

Kraemer, Helena, Anneliese Korner, and Shelley Horwitz. "A Model for Assessing the Development of Preterm Infants as a Function of Gestational, Conceptual, or Chronological Age." *Developmental Psychology* 21 (1985):806–812.

Kenneth F. McPherson

CIRCUMCISION

Circumcision in the United States refers to the removal of foreskin from the glans (head) of the penis. This is a surgical procedure, primarily performed in neonates. Developmentally, the foreskin becomes retractable by three years of age. Neonatal circumcision is safe, requiring only locally applied anesthesia. Commonly used devices are the Gomco and Mogen clamps or Plastibell. These methods involve estimation of the amount of foreskin to be removed, freeing the inner layer of the foreskin from its attachment to the glans, and control of bleeding. Circumcision is considered an elective procedure, requiring parental request and written consent. The decision regarding circumcision includes consideration of cultural, religious, and ethnic traditions as well as the medical risks and benefits. Controversy exists as to the relative medical benefits of circumcision because of issues involving urinary tract infections in infants under twelve months old, sexually transmitted diseases (STDs), HIV transmission, and penile cancer.

See also: MILESTONES OF DEVELOPMENT

Bibliography

American Academy of Pediatrics, Task Force on Circumcision. "Circumcision Policy Statement." *Pediatrics* 103 (1999):686–693.

Stang, Howard, Megan Gunnar, Leonard Snellman, et al. "Local Anesthesia for Neonatal Circumcision." *Journal of the American Medical Association* 259 (1988):1507–1511.

Carol A. Miller

CLASS SIZE

Many studies have linked smaller class sizes in schools to increased student achievement, yet this finding remains controversial. Other researchers have found no such link, or have noted small and largely meaningless effects. When increases in achievement are found, however, they tend to be centered on the early primary grades and students who are disabled or high-risk. In one example, Project STAR (Student-Teacher Achievement Ratio) in Tennessee, students were randomly assigned to either large or small classes during the early primary grades. It was found that students from smaller classes reported higher achievement, which persisted through seventh grade. Increased achievement is attributed to the teacher's increased ability to respond to students, fewer classroom discipline problems, and reduced likelihood of teacher burnout. Teachers universally report their belief that they teach more effectively and with less frustration in smaller classrooms, although sometimes this is not supported by independent observations. It appears that some training for teachers in how to make the most of smaller class sizes is beneficial.

See also: HOME SCHOOLING; SCHOOL VOUCHERS

Bibliography

Achilles, Charles. "Students Achieve More in Smaller Classes." *Educational Leadership* 53, no. 5 (1996):76–77.

Bennett, Neville. "Annotations: Class Size and the Quality of Educational Outcomes." *Journal of Child Psychology and Psychiatry* 39, no. 6 (1998):797–804.

Susan L. O'Donnell

CLASSICAL CONDITIONING

Classical conditioning is a basic behavioral process in which stimuli come to evoke responses: When an object or event (such as food) that already evokes a behavior (such as salivation) is associated with one that does not (such as a bell), the latter may evoke a reaction similar to that of the first object or event. When the stimuli are no longer associated, the conditioning weakens (called extinction); when stimuli resemble the conditioned stimulus, they evoke similar reactions (called generalization). First systematically studied by Ivan P. Pavlov (1849–1936), classical conditioning became a model for all behavioral development. B. F. Skinner's (1904–1990) research, for a while, on the conditioning of voluntary (operant) behavior through reinforcement restricted its scope. Classical conditioning occurs only in the involuntary (respondent) behavior of reflexes, glands, and internal organs (e.g., orienting reactions, intestinal functions, insulin secretion, heart rate), especially as they participate in emotional behavior (e.g., anxiety, elation). Today, classical conditioning and extinction are widely used in the treatment of emotional disorders (e.g., phobias) and the side-effects of medical treatments (e.g., nausea caused by chemotherapy).

See also: LEARNING; SKINNER, B. F.

Bibliography

Catania, A. Charles. *Learning,* 4th edition. Upper Saddle River, NJ: Prentice-Hall, 1998.

Kehoe, E. J., and M. Macrae. "Classical Conditioning." In William O'Donohue ed., *Learning and Behavior Therapy.* Boston: Allyn and Bacon, 1998.

Rescorla, R. A. "Pavlovian Conditioning: It's Not What You Think It Is." *American Psychologist* 43 (1988):151–160.

Edward K. Morris

CLEFT LIP/CLEFT PALATE

A cleft lip is a birth defect that occurs when the lip and the front part of the dental arch fail to form and fuse correctly. Cleft palate is the failure of the back part of the hard or soft palate to form. Approximately 1 in 800 newborns has a cleft lip or palate. Every day in the United States, fourteen babies are born with cleft lip (with or without cleft palate) and seven babies are born with cleft palate alone. There are 150 U.S. and Canadian interdisciplinary cleft and craniofacial teams that help coordinate care with multiple health professionals (including medical, surgical, dental, orthodontic, speech pathology, and psychosocial workers). Issues faced by families may include feeding difficulties, speech and articulation problems, dental development, ear infections and hearing concerns, teasing and stigmatization, multiple surgical treatments, and sometimes learning problems. Treatment results are generally excellent and most children born with cleft lip and/or palate grow up to be well-adjusted and successful adults.

See also: BIRTH DEFECTS

Bibliography

Bzoch, Kenneth R. *Communicative Disorders Related to Cleft Lip and Palate,* 4th edition. Austin, TX: Pro-Ed, 1997.

"Oral Health in America—Executive Summary: A Report of the Surgeon General." In the U.S. Department of Health and Human Services, U.S. Public Health Service [web site]. Washington, DC, 2000. Available from http://www.nidcr.nih.gov/sgr/execsumm.htm; INTERNET.

Strauss, Ronald P. "The Organization and Delivery of Craniofacial Health Services: The State of the Art." *Cleft Palate-Craniofacial Journal* 36, no. 3 (1999):189–195.

Ronald P. Strauss

CLIQUES

The term cliques refers to clusters of children and adolescents whose mutual friendships form a cohesive network. By middle childhood, clique boundaries can be defined by identifying groups of children who all reciprocally and mutually nominate one another as close friends. Cliques can play an important role in psychological adjustment. The presence of reciprocal friendships is associated with adaptive social development and healthy psychological functioning. Similarly, the quality of children's friendships within a clique, including the level of companionship, intimacy, reliable alliance, instrumental aid, and conflict with a friend, for example, is associated with concurrent and future psychological health. Children's engagement in specific prosocial or risk-taking/deviant behaviors is also strongly associated with the behavior of their closest friends. Not only do children and adolescents appear to select their friends based in part on these similar attributes and behavioral styles, but the relationships can then lead to increases in the frequency of each child's specific behaviors during the course of the friendship.

See also: FRIENDSHIP

Bibliography

Brown, B. Bradford. "The Role of Peer Groups in Adolescents' Adjustment to Secondary School." In Thomas J. Berndt and Gary W. Ladd eds., *Peer Relationships in Child Development.* New York: John Wiley, 1989.

Bukowski, William, Andrew Newcomb, and William Hartup, eds. *The Company They Keep: Friendship in Childhood and Adolescence.* New York: Cambridge University Press, 1996.

Laursen, Brett, ed. "Close Friendships in Adolescence." *New Directions for Child Development,* vol. 60. San Francisco, CA: Jossey Bass, 1993.

Mitchell J. Prinstein

COGNITIVE DEVELOPMENT

It does not take an expert to observe the many magnificent changes that take place in a human being from the time of birth through early childhood and beyond. Parents lovingly mark these changes in baby books and with photographs. Other relatives remark at the new abilities that babies seem to acquire daily. While parents may have just one or a few children to observe, developmental psychologists study many more. By studying many children over time, experts can chart the changes, and then begin to explain how they occur.

Overview of Cognitive Development

There are many different types of changes that occur over the course of a child's development. In general, cognitive development refers to the changes over time in children's thinking, reasoning, use of language, problem solving, and learning. The field is vast and researchers across the world study many different aspects of children's thinking at different points in development. For example, some researchers are interested in changes during infancy, such as when a baby recognizes her caregivers, remembers simple events, and understands the language spoken around her. Some researchers examine toddlers to learn how young children progress in their use of language and their understanding of the perspectives of the people around them. The early school years are studied to learn how children become more sophisticated in their ability to solve problems and use their memories. Yet others are interested in the possible changes in academic performance of school-age children and adolescents when they transition from grade school to middle school or from middle school to high school.

Although developmental psychologists begin their work by charting the changes they see in the developing human, their ultimate goal is to explain how those changes came about. This is challenging because humans are dynamic, complex beings who are shaped by different people and events. It is often difficult to draw conclusions about exactly which influences and experiences are most important for particular aspects of cognitive development. Thus, psychologists examine a variety of influences including changes in the brain, the influence of parents, the effect of a child's interaction with siblings and peers, and the role of culture. Typically, in order to accurately characterize aspects of development, psychologists must consider interactions between physiological changes in the brain and the child's social environment. For example, people often use child-directed speech when talking with young children. This type of language accentuates word boundaries and is spoken more slowly compared to adult-directed speech. This aspect of the child's environment may interact with changes in the baby's brain to help the baby comprehend the language spoken around her.

Three theories have had a substantial influence on research in cognitive development. It is important to examine these theories, and a subset of the key experimental demonstrations that support them, to understand how each perspective emphasizes different influences as critical to a child's development. Interestingly, historical trends in the field can often be explained by understanding which theory was most influential during various periods over the last half of the twentieth century.

The first major theory of cognitive development emerged during the 1950s when the work of Swiss psychologist Jean Piaget was discovered and translated. A second major theory of cognitive development, known as the sociocultural theory, can be attributed to translations of work done by Russian psychologist

Lev Vygotsky, who was a contemporary of Piaget. A final important class of theories, information-processing theories, has focused on the child's ability to process information and emerges from an interaction between environmental influences and physiological changes in the child's brain. These three theoretical perspectives have been influential for more than half a century and continue to inform developmental research that is conducted in the early twenty-first century.

Piaget's Theory of Cognitive Development

Piaget is considered the father of cognitive development because his studies were the first to examine children's thinking and because he offered a comprehensive theory of how cognition changed over time. His theory of cognitive development was based on data from a series of experiments and interviews of children (including his own) that explored their thinking in a variety of contexts. Piaget's theory consisted of four stages of development from birth to adolescence: sensorimotor, preoperational, concrete operational, and formal operational.

Piaget's Four Stages

The sensorimotor stage describes the years from birth to about age two. During this time the infant learns to coordinate the visual and tactile information she receives from the world around her with her emerging motor skills. For example, the child learns that by moving her eyes she can see a different part of her world and monitor how her arms or legs are interacting with various objects. Throughout these first two years of life the infant becomes increasingly aware of the world outside of herself and develops her ability to act on it.

The preoperational stage lasts from about two years of age until about six years of age. Piaget described preoperational children as egocentric; they have difficulty seeing the world from a perspective that is different from their own. A classic illustration of this was children's performance on Piaget and Bärbel Inhelder's three mountain task. Children viewed a three-dimensional display of three mountains from a particular perspective. Each mountain was slightly different in shape and had a small distinguishing reference object on top (e.g., a church steeple). The child was asked to select a two-dimensional picture that represented what another person would see from a different vantage point. Not surprisingly, the children were unsuccessful at seeing the display from another person's perspective. They often chose the picture of the mountains as they saw them from their own perspective.

FIGURE 1

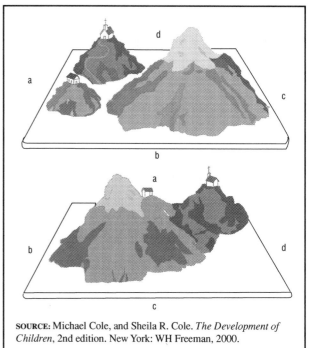

SOURCE: Michael Cole, and Sheila R. Cole. *The Development of Children*, 2nd edition. New York: WH Freeman, 2000.

Preschool children shown this diorama of three mountains with a distinctive landmark on each mountain were unable to say how the scene might look from perspectives other than the one they had adopted at the moment. (From Piaget & Inhelder, 1956.)

The third stage, concrete operations, lasts from about six years of age until about twelve years of age. In this stage, children become more flexible in their thinking and more able to perform concrete mental operations, such as conservation, which requires the simultaneous consideration of multiple pieces of information. In a typical task involving the conservation of liquid, water from a short, fat glass is poured into an empty glass that is tall and skinny. In order to understand that the volume of water does not change even though the level of the water does, the child must account for change in two different aspects at once: the circumference of the glass and the height of the liquid in that glass.

Piaget argued that in the formal operations stage children become even more flexible in their thinking and are able to think about the world more abstractly. During this final stage, from about twelve years of age through adolescence, children can think about hypothetical problems and give hypothetical solutions to those problems, such as how a society would maintain peace if there were no laws.

Critiques of Piaget's Theory

Piaget is widely recognized for his substantial contribution to the study of cognitive development.

His experiments laid the foundation for much of the early work that examined cognitive development. During the 1970s and 1980s, however, much research questioned the timing of Piaget's stages. Because children vary widely as to when a particular stage starts or ends, it is unclear whether cognitive development occurs in stages, as Piaget's theory suggests, or whether it is a continuous process. Specifically, many researchers believe that Piaget underestimated the timing of some of children's abilities and that sometimes children understand a concept before they are able to demonstrate their understanding of it. This "competence performance gap" can occur when a child's motor skills are not advanced enough or their language skills are not sophisticated enough to indicate their knowledge and mental processes.

One example of a cognitive deficit inappropriately attributed to the preoperational stage of development involves object permanence. A child who understands object permanence realizes that an object continues to exist when it is moved out of sight. Some researchers suggest that a competence performance gap accounts for Piaget not finding evidence of object permanence in the sensorimotor stage. Piaget conducted the following experiment to examine an infant's understanding of object permanence. He showed an object such as a stuffed animal to an infant and then placed it behind an opaque screen that was in front of the infant. Piaget noticed that as soon as the object "disappeared" behind the screen the infant acted as if it had never existed and did not try to look behind the screen. Contrary to Piaget's suggestion that the infants in this study were unaware that the object still existed when it was out of view, some researchers have argued that these infants did indeed realize that the object existed, but that it was difficult for them to coordinate reaching around the screen with their memory for the object.

Researchers tested whether it was truly the difficulty of coordinating the motor skills or whether the children thought that out of sight was out of mind as Piaget had argued. Renee Baillargeon and her colleagues used a method different from Piaget's and were able to show that infants as young as four months old seemed to understand that an object that was out of sight still existed. Baillargeon used a methodology known as habituation, which exploits the tendency of infants to look at interesting displays until they become bored and look away. Thus, this method provides information about which objects in the environment capture an infant's attention without relying on their ability to coordinate motor movements. Subsequently, researchers can change a display in certain ways to examine whether the infant is sensitive to the change. Typically, a researcher records the length of time that an infant looks at the subsequent changed display. If the infant does not look at the second display for a longer amount of time than he looked at the first display, then the researcher concludes that the infant does not see this display as different from the original. If the infant does look for a longer amount of time, then it is assumed that he sees the subsequent display as novel and distinct from the first display.

To test this prediction, Baillargeon and Julie DeVos created a display that showed two events. In one display, a short carrot moved from one side of a screen to the other by passing behind an opaque screen. In the other scenario, a tall carrot passed behind the identical opaque screen. Once the infant habituated to the display, one of two different subsequent displays was shown: an "impossible" event in which the tall carrot passed behind a new screen containing a translucent window that should show the top of the carrot but did not, or a "possible" event showing the short carrot moving behind the screen where it just passed underneath the translucent window and was not seen until it came out on the other side. Because infants as young as four months looked longer at the "impossible" event than the "possible" event, Baillargeon suggested that the infants did remember the characteristics of the carrots and had expectations about whether they should appear in the window. Based on findings such as this, some researchers have argued that Piaget underestimated infants' understanding because he did not take into account the gap between the child's understanding and her ability to demonstrate that understanding. Piaget had contended that infants appear to understand object permanence at nine months old, which is when infants can coordinate their motor skills to successfully reach for a hidden object.

Piaget also seemed to underestimate children's ability to see the world from another person's viewpoint. Piaget used the three mountain task as evidence that children had difficulty taking another's perspective. The three mountain task, however, is not easy. Although the mountains are slightly different in size and have small distinguishing marks on the top, they are still quite similar in appearance. According to Helen Borke, when this task has been modified using a town scene that contains familiar animals and a number of different-shaped landmarks, children in the preoperational stage are successful at taking another person's perspective despite Piaget's contrary prediction.

During the 1980s and 1990s an area of research concerned with children's perspective-taking abilities engaged the field of cognitive development. This area focused on a child's "theory of mind," suggesting that children have theories for the way their minds work, as well as the way other people's minds work. Heinz Wimmer and Josef Perner developed a classic demonstration of children's "theory of mind." Using a task called the Maxi Chocolate Task, Wimmer and Perner told children a story about a child named "Maxi," who places a piece of chocolate in the kitchen cabinet and then goes out to play. While he is out to play, his mother moves the chocolate to another location. Later, Maxi comes home and he wants his chocolate. The test question to the child participant is, "Where will Maxi look for his chocolate?" Three-year-olds typically respond that Maxi will look for the chocolate in the second location, because they themselves know it is there and it is difficult for them to understand that their perspective is different from Maxi's. Alternatively, most four-year-olds and nearly all five-year-olds take the perspective of Maxi and answer that he will look for the chocolate in the kitchen cabinet where he left it because he does not know that his mother has moved it. Thus, contrary to Piaget's suggestion that only children between six and eight years of age will have developed a "theory of mind," this task has shown that four- and five-year-olds can take the perspective of another person.

Beyond Piaget

The work examining children's "theory of mind" is one example of how cognitive development research at the end of the twentieth century and the beginning of the twenty-first century has moved away from experiments designed to test Piaget's theory. Many researchers are no longer focused on showing which Piagetian tasks can be done earlier and instead focus on providing theoretical explanations for why and when children might be successful on certain tasks. Some of these studies employ modern neuro-imaging techniques (such as positron emission tomography, functional magnetic resonance imaging, and electrical encephalographic techniques) to examine the effects of cognitive development in the brain. For example, if psychologists using these techniques can map out when the various brain structures develop during childhood, it may become possible to predict when various skills and capabilities that rely on those structures will emerge. Another burgeoning area of research in cognitive development examines the influence of culture on cognition in order to test for the universality or uniqueness of development across cultures. For example, the study of culture is critical for investigating how language and thought may affect each other, understanding why some people believe intelligence is primarily innate and others believe it is primarily the product of effort, and determining how people may solve problems differently based on their cultural norms and ideals.

Vygotsky's Sociocultural Theory

Vygotsky's theory emphasized the influence of culture, peers, and adults on the developing child. To understand this influence, Vygotsky proposed the "zone of proximal development." This zone refers to the difference in a child's performance when she attempts a problem on her own compared with when an adult or older child provides assistance. Imagine that a child is having difficulty with writing letters, and with the help of an adult who writes out sample letters or helps the child trace over letters, this same child is able to make progress. The help from the adult is called scaffolding. Just as the scaffolding of a building helps to support it, assistance from adults and peers in a child's environment helps support the child's development.

Vygotsky also discussed the importance of cultural tools to the sociocultural approach. These are items in the culture such as computers, books, and traditions that teach children about the expectations of the group. By participating in the cultural events and using the tools of the society, the child learns what is important in his culture. For example, in the United States a child attends school from about six years of age until eighteen years of age, and thus it is in school that children learn important skills such as mathematics. In some countries, such as in Brazil, however, children learn mathematics via buying and selling candy in the streets of the city.

Information-Processing Theories

Vygotsky believed the influence of the environment was crucial for development, whereas Piaget believed that the child's ability to independently explore her world was important. Although neither researcher emphasized the role of physiological changes in the brain and their contribution to a child's increasing ability to process information, neither would deny the significance of those changes for development. Information-processing theories attempt to account for changes in a child's cognitive ability via interactions between the developing brain and the child's increasing knowledge of the world. For example, researchers interested in these interactions may examine changes in working memory and how a child's world knowledge affects it.

Working memory (sometimes called short-term memory) is the memory that allows a person to remember a phone number that he has just looked up in the phone book. It involves mental rehearsal processes that maintain the information in memory. The capacity of young children's working memory is under debate. Early on, researchers measured the number of digits children could remember. Results

FIGURE 2

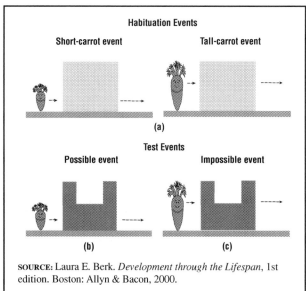

Habituation Events

Short-carrot event | Tall-carrot event

(a)

Test Events

Possible event | Impossible event

(b) | (c)

SOURCE: Laura E. Berk. *Development through the Lifespan*, 1st edition. Boston: Allyn & Bacon, 2000.

Study in which infants were tested for object permanence using the habituation-dishabituation response. (a). First, infants were habituated to two events: a short carrot and a tall carrot moving behind a yellow screen, on alternate trials. Then two test events were presented, in which the color of the screen was changed to blue to help the infant notice that now it had a window. (b). In the possible event, the short carrot (which was shorter than the window's lower edge) moved behind the blue screen and reappeared on the other side. (c). In the impossible event, the tall carrot (which was taller than the window's lower edge) moved behind the screen, did not appear in the window, but then miraculously emerged intact on the other side. Infants as young as three-and-one-half months dishabituated to the impossible event. This suggests that young babies must have some notion of object permanence—that an object continues to exist where it is hidden from view. (Adapted from R. Baillargeon and J. DeVos, 1991, "Object Permanence in Young Infants: Further Evidence." Child Development, 62, p. 1230. © The Society for Research in Child Development. Reprinted by permission.)

from this work suggested that children had a smaller working memory capacity compared to adults. For example, participants were asked to listen to a list of single digits and repeat them back in the order they had heard them. Researchers found that adults could typically remember between five and nine digits and children typically remembered about three or four.

Despite this clear result, other researchers, such as Robbie Case, argue that the overall capacity of working memory does not change over the course of development. What changes is the child's ability to efficiently process information. For example, in order to perform well on a digit span task one has to represent the numbers in some way. Adults and older chil-

dren can quickly repeat the numbers aloud or in their mind. Case, D. Midian Kurland, and Jill Goldberg found that young children take longer to repeat a number. Therefore more of the young child's resources are taken up with saying the numbers than with efficiently remembering them.

Implications of Cognitive Development for Schooling and Parenting

Research in cognitive development prompted by information-processing theories, Piaget's stage theory, and Vygotsky's sociocultural theory have not only informed the work of developmental psychologists but also proved useful in schools and to parents. For example, teacher and student understanding of the workings of memory can affect student performance in school, and teachers can use developmental research to help students become more aware of strategies that may help them improve their memory. In turn, students can enhance their "meta-memory" skills by becoming more aware of the limitations of their memory and the activities that may enhance it. For example, students can learn that repeatedly reading over their class notes does not ensure later recall of that material. Instead, mental strategies called "mnemonics" may be used to successfully learn information in a manner that promotes later recall. For example, one technique, called elaboration, involves relating the material to be learned to already known information in memory. This process, by associating new information with old information, not only helps prevent forgetting, but also increases the number of cues that may lead to later retrieval of that information.

Parents can also benefit from the knowledge gained from current and past research in cognitive development. For example, Vygotsky described parental roles as being critical in a child's development. Early on parents can provide the help that children need to develop certain culturally relevant skills. Parents' sensitivity to their child's skill level and their ability to allow the child to gradually take on more and more responsibility in a task provides an excellent way for children to learn.

Researchers in the field of cognitive development strive to describe and understand changes in children's thinking over the course of development. The work of Piaget and his stage theory of cognitive development guided much of the early work in that field. More recent investigations, however, attempt to understand the continuity of development. Researchers investigate interactions between biological and environmental variables, and thus focus on the ways in which culture, the family, the peer group, and the developing brain make complex contributions to a child's development.

See also: ABSTRACT REASONING; PIAGET, JEAN; THEORIES OF DEVELOPMENT; THREE MOUNTAIN TASK; VYGOTSKY, LEV

Bibliography

Baillargeon, Renee. "Object Permanence in 3 1/2- and 4 1/2- Month Old Infants." *Developmental Psychology* 23 (1987):655–664.

Baillargeon, Renee, and Julie DeVos. "Object Permanence in Young Infants: Further Evidence." *Child Development* 62 (1991):1227–1246.

Borke, Helen. "Piaget's Mountains Revisited: Changes in the Egocentric Landscape." *Developmental Psychology* 11 (1975):240–243.

Case, Robbie. *The Mind's Staircase.* Hillsdale, NJ: Lawrence Erlbaum, 1991.

Case, Robbie, D. Midian Kurland, and Jill Goldberg. "Operational Efficiency and Growth of Short-Term Memory Span." *Journal of Experimental Child Psychology* 33 (1982):386–404.

Pascual-Leone, Juan. "Organismic Processes for Neo-Piagetian Theories: A Dialectical Causal Account of Cognitive Development." In A. Demetriou ed., *The Neo-Piagetian Theories of Cognitive Development: Toward an Integration.* Amsterdam: Elsevier, 1988.

Piaget, Jean, and Bärbel Inhelder. *The Child's Conception of Space.* London: Routledge and Kegan Paul, 1956.

Saxe, Geoffrey B. *Culture and Cognitive Development: Studies in Mathematical Understanding.* Hillsdale, NJ: Lawrence Erlbaum, 1991.

Vygotsky, Lev. *Mind in Society.* Cambridge, MA: Harvard University Press, 1978.

White, Sheldon H., and David B. Pillemer. "Childhood Amnesia and the Development of a Socially Accessible Memory System." In J. F. Kihlstrom and F. J. Evans eds., *Functional Disorders of Memory.* Hillsdale, NJ: Lawrence Erlbaum, 1979.

Wimmer, Heinz, and Josef Perner. "Beliefs about Beliefs: Representation and Constraining Function of Wrong Beliefs in Young Children's Understanding of Deception." *Cognition* 13, no. 1 (1983):103–128.

Jennifer R. Dyer

COGNITIVE STYLE

How can several people look at one common object and describe it correctly, yet in so many different ways? Why is it that people exhibit the same variability when experiencing identical events? Psychologists believe that individual biological and psychological differences affect the ways in which people perceive events, objects, sights, sounds, and feelings. Thus, when several people encounter an identical object or event, each might experience a different perception of that object or event. There is no question that the exposure of infants and children to different experiences shapes their personalities and influences who they are and how they interpret things. And many ed-

ucators and researchers are now focusing their attention on these differences to further understand how individuals in the classroom perceive information and learn in different ways.

Cognitive style is the manner by which individuals perceive information in the environment and the patterns of thought that they use to develop a knowledge base about the world around them. The concept of styles of cognition, an area under continuing investigation, has been discussed and researched in the psychological community as early as the late 1930s. Knowledge gained concerning cognitive styles provides the opportunity to learn more about individual differences. This knowledge can then be applied to assist teachers, counselors, and all professionals who are involved in children's learning experiences.

There are three very important cognitive styles: leveling-sharpening, field-dependence/field-independence, and reflectivity-impulsivity. Cognitive styles are distinct from individual intelligence, but they may affect personality development and how individuals learn and apply information. And while research has shown that these differences precede environmental shaping, the effects of cognitive styles can be accented or mitigated by many outside factors, such as classroom setting, social experiences, and vocational choices. It is for this reason that research in this area is so important and that it is critical to train educational professionals in methods to address these differences in the classroom.

Leveling and Sharpening

Leveling and sharpening is a cognitive style that represents the way in which an individual uses previous memories when attempting to assimilate new information with prior knowledge. This cognitive style was described in the mid-1950s and was studied by Philip Holzman and George Klein, among others. Prior to the 1990s, the Squares Test, which was developed by the Menninger Foundation, was one of the methods of identifying levelers and sharpeners.

People who are levelers tend to select many memories from the past in an attempt to clarify and categorize newly acquired information. Sharpeners, on the other hand, seem to select fewer memories when processing new knowledge. In his 1997 book *Cognitive Styles and Classroom Learning*, Harry Morgan contended that, overall,sharpeners tend to have more accurate identifications of new knowledge and can relate recently acquired material to old material with more specificity. This may be due to an ability to selectively sort and store pieces of memories and to carefully differentiate associations between past experiences. By contrast, levelers inaccurately blend features of memories together and then oversimplify the new material or miscategorize it altogether. They can miss distinguishing features among similar, yet not identical, objects. This could result in definitions of later knowledge that are ambiguous.

Field-Dependence and Field-Independence

Another area where individuals show differences in their abilities to discriminate events or visual, auditory, or tactile cues from their surrounding environments is known as field-dependence/field-independence. Herman Witkin conducted much of the original research in this area in the 1950s. A field-dependent person has difficulty finding a geometric shape that is embedded or "hidden" in a background with similar (but not identical) lines and shapes. The conflicting patterns distract the person from identifying the given figure. A person who is field-independent can readily identify the geometric shape, regardless of the background in which it is set. This manner of interpretation, however, is not limited to visual cues. Many researchers are studying auditory and other sensory perception abilities that may vary from person to person.

There is also a strong connection between this cognitive style and social interactions. People who are field-dependent are frequently described as being very interpersonal and having a well-developed ability to read social cues and to openly convey their own feelings. Others describe them as being very warm, friendly, and personable. Interestingly, Witkin and Donald Goodenough, in their 1981 book *Cognitive Styles*, explained that this may be due to a lack of separation between the self and the environment (or "field") on some level. Field-dependent people notice a lack of structure in the environment (if it exists) and are more affected by it than other people.

By contrast, individuals who are field-independent use an "internal" frame of reference and can easily impose their own sense of order in a situation that is lacking structure. They are also observed to function autonomously in social settings. They are sometimes described as impersonal and task-oriented. These people, however, do have the ability to discern their own identity of self from the field. In addition, a strong correlation has been discovered between gender and field orientation. Women are more likely to be field-dependent, whereas men are frequently field-independent. Career tasks and job descriptions are also closely aligned with field-dependence/field-independence.

Specifically of concern to educators is the discovery that field-dependent children do not do as well in large group settings or class activities where the lessons are not highly structured. There are also indications that these same individuals do not perform as well on open-ended questions as compared to students who are field-independent.

Reflectivity and Impulsivity

Reflectivity and impulsivity are polar ends of a spectrum in a third and very substantial cognitive style. Studies in this domain began in the early 1960s with several researchers, such as Jerome Kagan. One of the methods for testing this cognitive style involves administration of the Matching Familiar Figures Test, which requires subjects to view a picture of an object and then attempt to match the object when presented with the same object in a group of similar objects. The test is then scored according to the time required to identify the objects and the accuracy of identification.

Neil Salkind and John Wright have studied scoring measures for this cognitive style. People who are slower than the median, but score more accurately than the median, are considered to be "reflective." In a classroom, these would typically be the students who take extended time on a task and produce very accurate work. Those who test faster than the median but score below the median of accuracy are "impulsive." These individuals are frequently described as students who rush through assignments, frequently missing the correct answers. In addition, impulsive students do not consider as many alternative answers when presented with open-ended questions as compared to reflective students. These same students also have a more global approach to information processing and do not identify the parts of a whole as readily as their peers. They also have difficulty with delayed gratification on tasks. Reflective students are more analytical in their problem-solving approach and do not have the same level of difficulty with delayed gratification.

Given that these differences in reflectivity-impulsivity are apparent as early as preschool, it is fascinating to consider developing classrooms that provide equal opportunities for learning and demonstration of application to students at both ends of this spectrum. Several studies indicate, however, that the traditional classroom favors the reflective students over the impulsive ones. Specific to education, studies have found that students who are placed with a reflective teacher tend to score more reflectivity at the end of the year than at the beginning, while students placed with an impulsive teacher score higher levels of impulsivity at the end of the year. This indicates that there is some environmental influence on the level of reflectivity-impulsivity and its expression in student behavior.

It is important to note that correlational studies have been conducted on any relationship between intelligence and each of the three cognitive styles. There is consistent data indicating no direct relationship exists between cognitive styles and intelligence. Nevertheless, an individual's ability to acquire knowledge on an equal plane with peers, or to demonstrate his or her knowledge in specific social or academic settings, may be affected by cognitive styles. Through early childhood development, continued success or frequent difficulties in these abilities could affect personality and social interactions.

Because of the potential influence of cognitive styles, additional educational research is necessary to assess the full effect that cognitive style has on a child's perception, analysis, and application of information presented in the classroom setting. There is also an implication that some assessment techniques used by educators may, by the nature of presentation, solicit different responses from students with differing cognitive styles. These testing methods should also be studied in terms of their interactions with individual cognitive styles.

See also: COGNITIVE DEVELOPMENT

Bibliography

Bransford, John, Ann Brown, and Rodney Cocking, eds. *How People Learn: Brain, Mind, Experience, and School.* Washington, DC: National Academy Press, 2000.

Brumby, Margaret N. "Consistent Differences in Cognitive Styles for Qualitative Biological Problem-Solving." *British Journal of Educational Psychology* 52 (1982):244–257.

Greene, L. R. "Psychological Differentiation and Social Structure." *Journal of Social Psychology* 109 (1972):79–85.

Morgan, Harry. *Cognitive Styles and Classroom Learning.* Westport, CT: Praeger, 1997.

Nummendal, S. G., and F. P. Collea. "Field Independence, Task Ambiguity, and Performance on a Proportional Reasoning Task." *Journal of Research in Science Teaching* 18, no. 3 (1981):255–260.

Salkind, Neil J., and John P. Poggio. "Sex Differences in Impulsivity and Intellectual Ability." *Sex Roles* 4, no. 1 (1978):91–96.

Salkind, Neil J., and John Wright. "The Development of Reflection-Impulsivity and Cognitive Efficiency." *Human Development* 20 (1977):377–387.

Witkin, Herman A. "Individual Differences in Ease of Perception of Embedded Figures." *Journal of Personality* 19 (1950):1–15.

Witkin, Herman A., C. A. Moore, Donald R. Goodenough, and P. W. Cox. "Field-Dependent and Field-Independent Cognitive Styles and Their Educational Implications." *Review of Educational Research* 47 (1977):1–64.

Witkin, Herman A., and Donald Goodenough. *Cognitive Styles: Essence and Origins.* New York: International Universities Press, 1981.

L. R. S. Martens

COHORT

A cohort refers to a group of people that were born at the same period of time. They are likely to share some common experiences such as social, cultural, and historical influences that are unique to them. Examples of well-known cohorts include "baby boomers" and "Generation Xers." Cohort effects arise when changes in performance are due circumstances specific to a particular time and place, rather than age. Thus, if looking at physical development, children born during times of conflict or war may have retarded physical growth due to stress and food deprivation. Therefore, growth pattern norms might be inaccurate if based on this cohort. Another example would be gender differences in vocational aspirations for adolescents. Career choices by males and females could depend on whether fifteen-year-olds born in 1985 participated in the study versus fifteen-year-olds born in 1935. Both cross-sectional and longitudinal research designs are susceptible to cohort effects. A cross-sequential design may be used when cohort effects are suspected.

See also: DEVELOPMENTAL NORMS; STAGES OF DEVELOPMENT

Bibliography

Miller, Scott. *Developmental Research Methods,* 2nd edition. Englewood Cliffs, NJ: Prentice-Hall, 1998.

Katherine M. Robinson

COMORBIDITY

Comorbidity is a medical term derived from the root word "morbidity." According to the *Oxford English Dictionary,* morbidity refers to "the quality or condition of being diseased or ill; a pathological state or symptom; a morbid characteristic or idea" as well as "prevalence of disease; the extent or degree of prevalence of disease in a district." In reference to child development, comorbidity is a term used when a child is identified to have two or more simultaneous mental health or physical disorders or diseases. The study of comorbidity is the study of conditions that tend to occur together. For example, there is a high comorbidity of attention deficit disorder and learning disabilities in children, meaning that the prevalence of learning disabilities is significantly higher than expected by chance among those with attention deficit disorder, and vice versa.

See also: LEARNING DISABILITIES; MENTAL DISORDERS

Bibliography

Gabbard, G. O. *Treatment of Psychiatric Disorders*, 3rd edition. Washington, DC: American Psychiatric Association, 2001.

Bryna Siegel

COMPUTER LITERACY

The term "computer literacy" refers to the ability to use the tools associated with a personal computer appropriate to one's age. Because technology is an ever-evolving field, definitions of computer literacy vary with time; what was considered literate in the 1980s became obsolete by the 1990s, and in the future expectations will change and expand even further. It is not useful, therefore, to list current tools as defining computer literacy. Rather, it is generally better to view computer literacy in terms of the amount of assistance required for use. Young children should be able to use developmentally appropriate programs with assistance. Elementary and middle school children are expected to be able to operate computers and applications independently, relying on adults to help with problem solving. Older adolescents should be mostly independent in their ability to manipulate data, applications, and machines.

See also: COMPUTERS; LEARNING

Bibliography

Casey, Jean. *Early Literacy: The Empowerment of Technology.* Englewood, CO: Libraries Unlimited, 2000.

Hoot, James, and Steven Silvern. *Writing with Computers in the Early Grades.* New York: Teachers College Press, 1988.

Wepner, Shelley, William Valmont, and Richard Thurlow, eds. *Linking Literacy and Technology: A Guide for K–8 Classrooms.* Newark, DE: International Reading Association, 2000.

Steven B. Silvern

COMPUTERS

Computers are ubiquitous. As computers have become less expensive they have been purchased by more and more families for their homes. Because of this, many children begin to use computers at an early age. Even if computers are not available in their home, children almost certainly will begin to come into contact with computers in school.

Some adults are amazed by how readily young children use computers. Many children find that using computers gives them a sense of power and accomplishment. And, unlike many adults whose first or primary contact with computers is work related, most children first use computers for entertainment purposes and games. This is by no means the only use that children have for computers. Children also use computers for accessing information, as well as for writing stories and research papers.

In addition, children use a variety of learning programs, which either seek to teach or reinforce basic skills in math, language, reading, and other subjects. Other software allows children to draw pictures or create visual works of art and self-expression. Communication with others is growing as an application of computers by children, particularly as more homes and schools gain access to the Internet. As computers continue to become more powerful, increasing numbers of children are using computers to create multimedia presentations and even web sites that include pictures, text, audio, and even video.

Because computer use is promoted in schools, and because computers are so ubiquitous, children have a great deal of exposure to them. Not everyone, however, is comfortable with the use of computers by young children. Some, including the Alliance for Childhood, have called for a halt to the use of computers by young children. Such groups cite the costs as well as possible health effects that using computers may have on children. The true impact that early computer use has on children is uncertain. Even though there is not enough information to state authoritatively that computers have any negative effects on children, the possible adverse effects that have been cited are serious enough to warrant consideration.

Possible Negative Effects of Computer Use

One of the most compelling arguments made against the use of computers by children is the risk of repetitive motion injury such as carpal tunnel syndrome. This problem may be greater for children than for adults because their musculature and skeletal systems are not fully formed and may be at greater risk for injury. Children's risk of suffering repetitive motion injuries may be further increased because they tend to use computers that are sized for adults, placed on adult-sized furniture, and positioned for an adult user.

Another possible risk of using computers is eyestrain, which may include dryness due to not blinking enough, headaches, and blurry vision. To reduce this risk, it is important to limit the time spent staring at the screen; take frequent breaks, making sure to focus the eyes on distant objects; and blink frequently. It is also important to position the monitor sixteen to twenty-seven inches away and in a way that ensures that the user views it at a slightly downward angle.

Following some highly publicized events in Japan, it has been suggested that there may be a risk of seizure for children playing video games containing bright flashing lights. Many video games include

An elementary school student uses a computer in the school library while another students looks on. The ease and facility with which children use computers comes from the ability children have for assimilating tools in their environment for their personal use. (O'Brien Productions/Corbis)

a warning to this effect in their documentation. Fortunately, very few children are susceptible to this condition. For those who are, however, this is potentially a very serious situation.

There also has been some attention given to the possible risk of exposure to electromagnetic radiation from the computer's monitor. Some people note that such radiation exposure may be greatest at the back and sides of the monitor, which may be important because computer labs in schools are often arranged in such a way as to put a child's head next to or directly in front of another computer's monitor. Once again there is insufficient proof that this is a real threat. According to the Occupational Safety and Health Administration, the risk of exposure to electromagnetic radiation is very low when the user is positioned correctly in relationship to the monitor.

Some people caution that there may be a link between computer use and obesity in children. This opinion is often based on studies that find links between television viewing, reduced activity, and childhood obesity. It is not clear, however, that sedentary activities cause obesity. It may be that children who are sedentary and therefore at a greater risk of obesity may choose sedentary activities such as television viewing and computer use over more physical activities.

Some studies show that there is a correlation between a child's preference for violent video games and measures of aggression. This is an area that will receive more attention as realism and violence levels in video games continue to increase.

Possible Positive Effects of Computer Use

As with studies that reveal potential risks of using computers, many studies that show potential benefits from the use of computers are correlational and cannot demonstrate cause and effect. Others are complicated by having factors other than computer use as potentially being partially responsible for the findings.

There seems to be a correlation between the presence of a computer in a child's home and achievement in school. This evidence is still not strong enough to state categorically that having a computer makes children smarter. Computer use by children can result in gains on a number of developmental stages. For instance appropriate computer use can be related to improvements in nonverbal skills, long-term memory, mathematical skills, language skills, and problem-solving skills. It should be noted that computer use alone does not ensure gains in any of these areas.

Developmentally Appropriate Uses of Computers

Children under the age of three are, in most cases, not developmentally ready to begin using computers. While some software has been developed for children at very early ages, it is believed by many that the use of such software does not tap into the child's innate desire to experience things through kinesthetic or whole-body exploration. While use of computers by children at very early ages may not be harmful, the benefits of such use seem to be small. There are those, however, who believe that early computer use with a parent or other adult can be a bonding experience.

At about three to five years of age children are developmentally ready to explore computers. At this young age, it is best for children to be given the opportunity to control their exploration of the computer and software. Early use should be limited in duration, and frustration should be avoided. Children at this stage enjoy interacting with active links and areas on the screen, discovering the effects of clicking different choices. Some research indicates that this kind of computer use gives children an increased sense of their impact on their environment, which leads to a greater sense of self-efficacy.

Children ages five to about seven are ready to begin using computers for more directed purposes, which may include communication, information gathering, and skills development. Appropriate software selection is important and children should have several to choose from. It is a good idea for children at this age to have some control over how they use the computer including some choice about software. Another appropriate use for children in this age range is for cooperative activities. Working with others on computers can reinforce language skills and help build cooperative work skills.

At ages seven and beyond, children are ready to continue using computers for a variety of purposes. In addition to skills development, children may use computers to create presentations that exercise or demonstrate their mastery of concepts or processes. As use of the computer as a communications tool expands, the computer can become increasingly important as a tool that the child can use to accomplish other tasks. Such use should expand as appropriate for the child. At these ages, however, some children begin to spend too much time using computers and other technologies, especially video games.

Conclusion

Children can use computers in effective and positive ways. Positive uses of computers by children are developmentally appropriate and can reinforce the attainment of desirable skills and traits such as math mastery, verbal language use, and cooperation skills. Computers, however, can also be used in ways that may be harmful to the child. Possible harmful effects from computers, such as repetitive motion injuries and eyestrain, most often stem from overuse of computers and use of computers that are positioned inappropriately for children. If children are to use computers, they should be taught to limit their computer use to reasonable lengths of time. They should be supervised appropriately while using computers in ways that might expose them to inappropriate material or practices.

See also: COMPUTER LITERACY; INTERNET

Bibliography

Armstrong, Alison, and Charles Casement. *The Child and the Machine.* Beltsville, MD: Robins Lane Press, 2000.

"Children and Computer Technology." *Future of Children* 10, no. 2 (2000). Available from http://www.futureofchildren.org/cct/; INTERNET.

Cuban, Larry. *Teachers and Machines.* New York: Teachers College Press, 1985.

"Fool's Gold: A Critical Look at Computers in Childhood." In the Alliance for Childhood [web site]. College Park, Maryland, 2000. Available from http://www.allianceforchildhood.net/projects/computers/computers_reports.htm; INTERNET.

McCain, Ted, and Ian Jukes. *Windows of the Future.* Thousand Oaks, CA: Corwin Press, 2001.

Papert, Seymour. *Mindstorms.* New York: Basic, 1980.

Papert, Seymour. *The Children's Machine.* New York: Basic, 1993.

Papert, Seymour. *The Connected Family.* Atlanta, GA: Longstreet Press, 1996.

Van Scoter, Judy, Debbie Ellis, and Jennifer Railsback. "How Technology Can Enhance Early Childhood Learning." In the Early Connections [web site]. Portland, Oregon, 2001. Available from http://www.netc.org/earlyconnections/byrequest.html; INTERNET.

Brian Newberry

CONCRETE OPERATIONAL THINKING

Concrete operational thinking is the third stage in French psychologist Jean Piaget's theory of cognitive development. Children typically reach this stage, which is characterized by logical reasoning about real situations without being influenced by changes in appearances, at the age of seven or eight. Whereas three-year-olds believe a ball of dough becomes larger if it is flattened, eight-year-olds understand that flattening the ball does not change the total amount of dough. Older children generally are able to understand three concepts that help them to realize that the amount of dough is unchanged. First, an item's appearance can change without changing its identity; the total amount of the dough does not change when it changes shape. Second, the effects of actions can be reversed; flattened dough can be rolled again. Third, a change in one dimension can be compensated for by an opposite change in another dimension; flattened dough covers a wider area but is also thinner than rolled dough.

See also: COGNITIVE DEVELOPMENT; PIAGET, JEAN

Bibliography

Furth, Hans. *Piaget for Teachers.* Englewood Cliffs, NJ: Prentice-Hall, 1970.

Piaget, Jean, and Bärbel Inhelder. *The Psychology of the Child.* New York: Basic Books, 1969.

Karen E. Singer-Freeman

CONDUCT DISORDER

Conduct disorder is a pattern of behavior in which individuals consistently disregard and violate the rights of others. The specific types of behaviors are varied and can include physical violence, repeated lying, damaging property, and stealing. Conduct disorder is believed to have roots in family interaction early in development, although its full expression may not occur until adolescence. For example, many studies show that family members train each other to engage in conflictive and coercive behavior that may lead to later conduct problems. This can be seen especially among siblings, as they can observe each other interacting with their parents and "practice" aggressive and bullying behavior with each other. During adolescence, however, individuals with conduct problems may form social networks with others, both friends and siblings, who are also trained in coercive behavior, and thus reinforce and encourage each other's antisocial tendencies.

See also: FRIENDSHIP; JUVENILE DELINQUENCY

Bibliography

Dishion, Thomas J., K. M. Spracklen, D. W. Andrews, and G. R. Patterson. "Deviancy Training in Male Adolescent Friendships." *Behavior Therapy* 27 (1996):373–390.

Patterson, G., Thomas J. Dishion, and L. Bank. "Family Interaction: A Process Model of Deviancy Training." *Aggressive Behavior* 10 (1984):253–267.

Rowe, D.C., and B. Gulley. "Sibling Effects on Substance Abuse and Delinquency." *Criminology* 30 (1992):217–233.

Slomkowski, Cheryl, Richard Rende, Katherine Conger, R. Simons, and Rand Conger. "Sisters, Brothers, and Delinquency: Evaluating Social Influence During Early and Middle Adolescence." *Child Development* 72 (2001):271–283.

Cheryl Slomkowski
Richard Rende

CONFORMITY

Conformity is a change in beliefs or behaviors when youth yield to real or imagined social pressure. Conformity is affected by developmental level, situations, and persons involved. Young children tend to conform to their parents' rules and expectations. As children become older, they become more autonomous from their parents, and also become more peer-oriented. Conformance to parents in neutral or prosocial situations (i.e., helping, volunteering) decreases gradually as a child ages. However, peer conformity, especially to antisocial behaviors (i.e., alcohol use, criminal acts) increases with age. Youth may engage in misconduct to avoid rejection, to stay in peers' good graces, or to gain approval. Children from families that are permissive and neglectful are likely to be more susceptible to peer influence and may join gangs to feel a sense of belonging. During middle and late adolescence, youth strike a balance between conformity to parents, peers, and their own individual identity.

See also: FRIENDSHIP

Bibliography

Berndt, Thomas J. "Developmental Changes in Conformity to Peers and Parents." *Developmental Psychology* 15 (1979):608–616.

Fulingi, Andrew J., and Jacquelynne S. Eccles. "Perceived Parent-Child Relationships and Early Adolescents' Orientation Towards Peers." *Developmental Psychology* 29 (1993):622–632.

Rhonda Cherie Boyd

CONGENITAL DEFORMITIES

Congenital deformities include a broad range of physical abnormalities existing from birth, although some, such as scoliosis, may not manifest until later in life. The most common are craniofacial deformities, such as cleft lip or palate, and skeletal deformities, such as clubfoot or spina bifida. Certain chromosomal disorders such as Fragile X syndrome and Down syndrome also have associated physical abnormalities, as have substance-induced problems such as fetal alcohol syndrome. The impacts of congenital deformities can be primary, such as delays in the development of motor and language skills, or secondary, such as social ostracism and low self-esteem. Surgical procedures may help with many of the physical abnormalities, although these can involve multiple surgeries and may cause more stress for the child and family members. Congenital abnormalities are best thought of as chronic illnesses; multidisciplinary, as well as psychosocial, interventions at the individual, family, and community levels are usually recommended.

See also: DEVELOPMENTAL DISABILITIES

Bibliography

Brewer, E. J., M. McPherson, P. R. Magrab, and V. L. Hutchins. "Family-Centered, Community-Based Coordinated Care for Children with Special Health Care Needs." *Pediatrics* 83 (1989):1055–1060.

Smith, D. W. *Smith's Recognizable Patterns of Human Malformation,* 4th edition, edited by K. L. Jones. Philadelphia: Saunders, 1988.

William E. Sobesky

CONSERVATION

Conservation refers to an understanding that a quantity (i.e., liquid, number, mass) remains constant despite arbitrary transformations. In the classic Piagetian conservation of liquid task, children are presented with two identical containers holding equal amounts of liquid. Liquid from one of the containers changes in appearance by being poured into a taller, narrower container. The children are asked to judge the equivalence of the transformed liquid and the liquid that remained in its original container, and to justify their answer. A child who grasps conservation is able to take two dimensions into account simultaneously and therefore understands that the change in the height of the transformed liquid is compensated for by the narrower width. That is, despite changes in appearance, the quantity of liquid remains the same. An understanding of conservation marks the presence of Piaget's concrete operational stage of cognitive development, usually reached between five and seven years of age.

See also: PIAGET, JEAN

Bibliography

Diamond, Nina. "Cognitive Theory." In Benjamin Wolman ed., *Handbook of Developmental Psychology*. Englewood Cliffs, NJ: Prentice-Hall, 1982.

Donaldson, Margaret. "Conservation: What Is the Question?" *British Journal of Psychology* 73 (1982):199–207.

Rebecca M. Starr

CONTRACEPTION

Contraception refers to the use of hormones, surgery, physical devices, chemicals, fertility awareness, or breast-feeding to prevent pregnancy. Contraceptive methods and the prevalence of use vary substantially around the world. Modern methods predominate in North America, led by female sterilization (34% of all use), oral contraceptive pills (21%), male sterilization (20%), and condoms (14%). Female sterilization involves surgically removing part of the fallopian tubes or blocking them with clips, rings, or heat destruction. Similar techniques on the vas deferentia (spermatic ducts) sterilize men. Oral methods combine estrogen with progestogen, normal female hormones, to prevent ovulation, or use progestogen alone to make cervical mucus hostile to sperm penetration. Barrier methods create a barrier between ovum and sperm and are often combined with chemicals that kill sperm (spermicides) to increase effectiveness. Male condoms cover the penis, female condoms line the vagina, and diaphragms or caps cover the cervix. Other methods include hormonal injections or implants; intrauterine devices that block implantation of a fertilized egg; periodic abstinence during the time of the menstrual cycle when a woman is most likely to be fertile; and withdrawal of the penis, prior to the release of sperm.

See also: ARTIFICIAL INSEMINATION; BIRTH; PREGNANCY

Bibliography

United Nations, Department of Economic and Social Affairs, Population Division. "World Contraceptive Use in 1998." In the United Nations [web site]. Available from http://www.undp.org/popin/wdtrends/wcu/fwcu.htm; INTERNET.

Philip Hannaford

COOPERATIVE LEARNING

Cooperative learning refers to a variety of instructional strategies in which students work in small, usually mixed-ability, groups and are expected to help one another learn academic material or complete projects together. There are many forms of cooperative learning that are often used in elementary schools. Students may simply be asked to work together, without any particular structure or goal. But cooperative learning research finds greater success when groups have reward interdependence, task interdependence, or both. Reward interdependence means that group members can achieve success only if the whole group accomplishes some objective. For example, groups may be evaluated based on the sum or average of individual quiz scores or average ratings of individual products, or based on an evaluation of a common product, such as a report, a mural, or a project to which all group members contributed. The group's success may be recognized by the teacher using praise, certificates, or other symbolic rewards, or it may count toward a portion of children's grades. Task interdependence exists when each group member is responsible for a unique portion of a group task, and the group cannot meet its goal unless all students do their parts.

Cooperative learning can be used in every subject and at every age level. Research has found that cooperative learning can increase academic achievement, especially if there are group goals or rewards and if the only way groups can achieve their goals is if all group members have learned the material being studied (as demonstrated on individual quizzes, compositions, or other products). This structure causes students to teach each other, to assess each other's understanding, and to encourage each other to excel. Peer teaching, which is beneficial both to the child who teaches and to the child being taught, and peer encouragement are the main explanations research has identified for the achievement effects of cooperative learning. Research has also identified positive effects on outcomes such as intergroup relations, attitudes toward mainstreamed classmates, self-esteem, and general attitudes toward school.

See also: LEARNING

Bibliography

Johnson, David, and Roger Johnson. *Learning Together and Alone: Cooperative, Competitive, and Individualistic Learning*, 4th edition. Boston: Allyn and Bacon, 1994.

Kagan, Spencer. *Cooperative Learning*. Boston: Charlesbridge, 1995.

Sharan, Yael, and Shlomo Sharan. *Expanding Cooperative Learning through Group Investigation*. New York: Teachers College Press, 1992.

Slavin, Robert. *Cooperative Learning: Theory, Research, and Practice*, 2nd edition. Boston: Allyn and Bacon, 1995.

Webb, Noreen, and Annemarie Palincsar. "Group Processes in the Classroom." In David Berliner and Robert Calfee eds., *Handbook of Educational Psychology*. New York: Simon and Schuster-Macmillan, 1996.

Robert E. Slavin

CO-PARENTING

Co-parenting includes the ways parents support or undermine their partner's parenting and how parents manage their relationship in the presence of their children, whether in intact or divorced families. The study of co-parenting addresses the question of how interactions between family members affect children's development. Focus is on the mutual investment and engagement of parents in child rearing. Co-parenting is somewhat, but not completely, influenced by the quality of the parents' relationship with each other. Through methods including observations of family interactions and parental self-report, researchers study different aspects of co-parenting, including hostility-competition; warmth between parents, responsiveness, and cooperation; communication, conflict, help, and support. Research demonstrates that co-parenting affects children's development during the toddler, preschool, middle childhood, and adolescent years. For example, parents' hostility and competition around child rearing when children are infants is related to children's aggression in preschool. Researchers are studying how co-parenting during children's early years sets up patterns of family interactions that affect children's social and emotional functioning over time.

See also: PARENTING; WORKING FAMILIES

Bibliography

Brody, Gene, Zolinda Stoneman, Trellis Smith, and Nicole Morgan Gibson. "Sibling Relationships in Rural African-American Families." *Journal of Marriage and the Family* 61 (1999):1046–1057.

McHale, James, and Jeffrey Rasumussen. "Coparental and Family Group-Level Dynamics during Infancy: Early Family Precursors of Child and Family Functioning during Preschool." *Development and Psychopathology* 10 (1998):39–59.

McHale, James, and P. A. Cowan, eds. *Understanding How Family-Level Dynamics Affect Children's Development: Studies of Two-Parent Families*. San Francisco: Jossey-Bass, 1996.

Amy R. Susman-Stillman

CORPORAL PUNISHMENT

Corporal punishment is the application of physical force to the body for the purposes of discipline. Corporal punishment of children, especially in schools, is declining in acceptability and use. Advocates, such as the Family Research Council, make careful distinctions between physical punishment and physical violence or abuse, and often cite the Bible in support of corporal punishment. Recommended forms of corporal punishment include spanking of the buttocks with the open hand and light slaps to the hand of the child. Opponents of corporal punishment cite studies indicating that corporal punishment can cause physical harm, is ineffective for changing behavior, leads to abuse, and may lower the intelligence of the child. Changing social attitudes toward corporal punishment have led to the prosecution of some parents and lawsuits against school personnel using corporal punishment. Many groups, including the American Academy of Pediatrics, recommend against corporal punishment and advocate its elimination from schools.

See also: DISCIPLINE

Bibliography

"Corporal Punishment in Schools (RE9754)." In the American Academy of Pediatrics [web site]. Elk Grove Village, Illinois, 2000. Available from http://www.aap.org/policy/re9754.html; INTERNET.

Robinson, B. A. "Child Corporal Punishment: Spanking." In the Ontario Consultants on Religious Tolerance [web site]. Kingston, Ontario, 2000. Available from http://www.religioustolerance.org/spanking.htm; INTERNET.

Brian Newberry

COURT APPOINTED SPECIAL ADVOCATE ASSOCIATE PROGRAM

The Court Appointed Special Advocate (CASA) program is a nationwide program that trains adults to be advocates for children who are in the judicial system. After a training period, which includes an overview of topics such as juvenile law, child development, and social work, adults interact with their children in and out of court and work with the children to ensure that their rights are being protected and their needs are being met. CASA started through the actions of a Seattle judge who conceived the idea of using trained community volunteers to speak in court for the best interests of abused and neglected children. This first program was very successful and soon judges across the country began using citizen advocates. In 1990 U.S. Congress encouraged the expansion of CASA with passage of the Victims of Child Abuse Act. By the beginning of the twenty-first century, more than 900 CASA programs were in operation, with more than 42 million women and men serving as CASA volunteers.

See also: DELINQUENCY

Bibliography

Child Welfare League of America [web site]. 2001. Available from http://www.cwla.org; INTERNET.

Children's Defense Fund [web site]. 2001. Available from http://www.childrensdefense.org; INTERNET.

National CASA Association. Available from http://www.casanet.org; INTERNET.

National Office of Juvenile Justice and Delinquency Prevention [web site]. 2001. Available from http://www.ncjrs.org/jjhome.htm; INTERNET.

Neil J. Salkind

CRITICAL/SENSITIVE PERIODS

The concept of critical/sensitive periods is of interest in discussions of the influence of biological and experiential factors during periods of developmental change. A critical or sensitive period is defined as a period when certain experiences are particularly important because they have a significant influence on later development. Let us begin our consideration of this concept with a case example that illustrates some of the significant developmental changes that occur during the period of infancy and early childhood.

Eve is a typical, healthy newborn human infant. She is raised by parents who are sensitive to her unique needs and characteristics, and who regularly provide her with appropriate stimulation and parenting. The first five years of Eve's life will be witness to rapid, significant changes in her behavior and abilities.

Language development provides one example of these changes. As a newborn, Eve prefers the sound of human voices to other sounds and can discriminate between the language of her culture and other languages. She cries, usually when she has some physical needs, such as hunger. By five to six months of age, she will coo when contented and may be babbling or producing simple combinations of consonants and vowels. By twelve to eighteen months of age, she will be speaking in single word sentences and will understand more than fifty words. By twenty-four months of age her vocabulary will have expanded to approxi-

mately 200 words and she will be producing hundreds of different two- and three-word sentences. By the age of five, Eve will have a vocabulary of about 2,000 words and will use many of the grammatical structures of her native language, without ever taking part in a formal language lesson.

The period from birth to five years of age will also include significant changes in Eve's social relationships. As a newborn, she can discriminate her mother's face, voice, and smell from all others. By three months of age, she will smile at her parents and will react positively to most strangers. Between seven and twelve months of age she will begin to demonstrate specific attachments to her parents, will display anxiety when strangers approach, and will be distressed by separation from her parents. By three to four years of age, Eve will continue to be securely attached to her parents, but her distress at separation from them will diminish, and she will be able to confidently participate in a nursery school program.

The study of human development is the study of change. As the case of Eve illustrates, the changes that occur during infancy and childhood are happening at a pace that is more rapid and impressive than at any other period in the lifespan. Although psychologists agree that these developmental changes during infancy and childhood are impressive and extraordinary, they often disagree on the best way to understand and explain these changes.

One area of disagreement is the discussion of whether developmental changes are the result of biological, genetic factors or of the kinds of experiences that the child has had. Another area of disagreement is the discussion of whether developmental changes occur in a series of unique stages or periods.

The concept of a critical/sensitive period is related to both of these areas of discussion. The critical/sensitive period is determined by biological maturation and characterized by increased vulnerability or responsivity to specific experiences. If these specific experiences occur during this period, then development will continue on its typical course. If these specific experiences do not occur, there may be a significant disruption or difficulty in subsequent development.

What evidence is there supporting this notion of a critical period in development? Is there a difference between a critical period and a sensitive period?

Language Development: Critical or Sensitive Period?

Language development provides one example that can illustrate the concept of a critical/sensitive period. Although language development is a process that psychologists have long debated, there is agreement that a strong biological basis for language acquisition exists. In 1967, Eric Lenneberg first proposed the notion of a critical period for language acquisition. He suggested that the period between infancy and puberty (the beginning of adolescence) was a critical period for language acquisition. This critical period was thought to end at puberty because of important maturational changes in the brain that occur at this time. Language must be acquired during the critical period if it is to be acquired at all. Alternatively, if the period from infancy to puberty is viewed as a sensitive period, rather than a critical period, language will be learned most easily during this period. After the sensitive period, language can be learned, but with greater difficulty and less efficiency.

What evidence is there supporting this concept of a critical period for language acquisition? How could a researcher ever test this idea? Information about this issue comes from different sources. These sources include a few unfortunate and extreme cases of childhood deprivation—children who were deprived of typical social experiences and stimulation.

Perhaps the most well-known of these was the case of Genie, who was described in a series of publications in the 1970s. Genie was essentially kept in isolation by a maltreating parent, with no exposure to language and normal social experiences for the time between toddlerhood and early adolescence. When she was discovered, she had some understanding of language but did not speak. After nearly one year of intensive training and instruction, she had a vocabulary of about 200 words and was speaking in two-word sentences. Six years later, she had made much progress, but she was still much less advanced in her language than other people her age who had normal experiences growing up.

Since Genie was able to acquire language following the onset of adolescence, the notion that language learning is impossible after the critical period cannot be supported. Rather, language learning can occur after the onset of adolescence but may be incomplete. The period between infancy and adolescence, therefore, may be a sensitive period for language learning—language can be acquired more easily during this time—rather than an absolutely critical period.

Infant-Parent Attachment: A Critical/Sensitive Period for Social Development

Illustrative examples of the concept of a critical/sensitive period can also be found in the domain of social development. One particularly interesting example is the formation of the infant-parent attachment relationship.

Attachment is the strong emotional ties between the infant and the caregiver. This reciprocal relationship develops over the first year of the child's life, and especially during the second six months of the first year. During this time, the infant's social behavior becomes increasingly organized around the principal caregiver.

John Bowlby, a twentieth-century English psychiatrist who was strongly influenced by evolutionary theory, formulated and presented a comprehensive theory of attachment. In the late 1950s and early 1960s, he first proposed that there is a strong biological basis for the development of this relationship. According to Bowlby, the infant-parent attachment relationship develops because it is important to the survival of the infant and also provides a secure base from which the infant can feel safe exploring their environment.

Bowlby suggested that there was a sensitive period for the formation of the attachment relationship. This period is from approximately six months to twenty-four months of age and coincides with the infant's increasing tendency to approach familiar caregivers and to be wary of unfamiliar adults. In addition, according to Bowlby and his colleague Mary Ainsworth, the quality of this attachment relationship is strongly influenced by experiences and repeated interactions between the infant and the caregiver. In particular, Ainsworth's research, that was first published in the late 1960s, demonstrated that a secure attachment relationship is associated with the quality of caregiving that the infant receives. More specifically, consistent and responsive caregiving is associated with the formation of a secure attachment relationship.

If the period from six months to twenty-four months is viewed as a critical period for the development of the attachment relationship, the relationship must be formed during this specific period in early development. Alternatively, if this period is viewed as a sensitive period, the infant-parent attachment relationship will develop more readily during this period. After the sensitive period, this first attachment relationship can develop, but with greater difficulty. As in the case of language development, information about whether there is a critical or sensitive period for the formation of a secure attachment relationship comes from different sources. These sources include cases of infants who did not experience consistent caregiving because they were raised in institutions prior to being adopted.

The early research documenting such cases was published in the 1940s. This research consistently reported that children reared in orphanages for the first years of life subsequently exhibited unusual and maladaptive patterns of social behavior, difficulty in forming close relationships, and indiscriminately friendly behavior toward unfamiliar adults. The results of this early research contributed to the decline of such forms of institutional care. Furthermore, these results supported the notion of a critical period for the formation of the attachment relationship.

Research published in the 1990s has contributed to a modification of this notion of a critical period. These research results have come from studies of infants in Eastern Europe who were abandoned or orphaned and, therefore, raised in institutions prior to adoption by families in North America and the United Kingdom. These results have indicated that these adoptees were able to form attachment relationships after the first year of life and also made notable developmental progress following adoption. As a group, however, these children appeared to be at an increased risk for insecure or maladaptive attachment relationships with their adopted parents. This evidence, then, is consistent with the notion of a sensitive period, rather than a critical period, for the development of the first attachment relationship, rather than a critical one.

See also: AINSWORTH, MARY DINSMORE SALTER; BOWLBY, JOHN; STAGES OF DEVELOPMENT

Bibliography

Curtiss, Susan. *Genie: A Psycholinguistic Study of a Modern Day "Wild Child."* New York: Academic Press, 1977.

Goldberg, Susan. *Attachment and Development.* New York: Oxford University Press, 2000.

Marvin, Robert S., and Preston A. Britner. "Normative Development: The Ontogeny of Attachment." In Jude Cassidy and Phillip R. Shaver eds., *Handbook of Attachment: Theory, Research, and Clinical Applications.* New York: Guilford Press, 1999.

Newport, Elissa L. "Contrasting Conceptions of the Critical Period for Language." In Susan Carey and Rochel Gelman eds., *The Epigenesis of Mind: Essays on Biology and Cognition.* Hillsdale, NJ: Erlbaum, 1991.

Rutter, Michael. "A Fresh Look at 'Maternal Deprivation.'" In Patrick Bateson ed., *The Development and Integration of Behaviour: Essays in Honor of Robert Hinde.* New York: Cambridge University Press, 1991.

Ann L. Robson

CRYING

Crying is a phenomenon that has puzzled people throughout the ages. People cry when they are sad, afraid, angry, in pain, or depressed, and yet people also cry when they are happy. Crying occurs in all emotions—it even contributes to the physiological well-being of an individual from birth to death. It is this versatility that makes crying so difficult to understand. Furthermore, tears are not always a function of emotion. Crying is a very important aspect of infant development that acts as a tool for communication.

The Physiology of Crying

There are three types of tears. The first type is basal tears. Because the eyeball's surface is riddled with irregularities, basal tears create a thin coat over the eye which smoothes out the surface. This helps to protect and lubricate the eye. Without this lubrication, a person would see a very distorted picture, and it would be painful when the eyeball moves. The eye needs this coating all the time so the body must constantly replace these tears due to the loss caused by evaporation. A typical person will produce five to ten ounces a day. In addition, basal tears contain antibacterial chemicals.

The second type is irritant tears. Irritant tears occur when a person is exposed to freshly cut onions or has a foreign object in his or her eye. They are called irritant tears because they are produced when a foreign object, foreign chemical, or a simple poke irritates the eye. The body will also produce more irritant tears if the basal tears evaporate too rapidly and the eye is left with an insufficient amount to properly lubricate the eye. Ironically, a person with excessively watery eyes suffers from having dry eyes. It is the irritant tears that cause the watery eyes because the body is compensating for the lack of basal tears.

The third type of tear is psychic or emotional. These are the tears that well up inside and spill over the eyelid because of specific emotional states. They are definitely more voluminous than the two types of tears previously mentioned, and they have been found to have a different chemical make-up. William Frey has shown that these chemicals are linked to depression and stress. Frey believes that crying is the body's attempt of ridding itself of these pollutants, thus reducing stress and avoiding depression.

The Crying of Newborns

Newborn babies are not capable of crying for emotional reasons, but they share the same physiological properties of tears as mentioned above. For newborns, crying is a fundamental means of communication. Crying is not a matter of frustration caused by the baby's inability to express itself verbally—that would imply that the baby is aware of formal language but doesn't have the ability to use it. On the contrary, for the first few weeks crying is a reflexive property and is thought to have no emotional reasons. Newborns do not have the psychological capacity to hold an emotion such as fear or anger, so their cries are not a result of emotional imbalances. They are an

A crying toddler may depend more on internal feelings and moods rather than physiological needs. (Anna Palma/Corbis)

involuntary reaction to pain, hunger, and tiredness. Therefore, crying is the means by which the infant communicates these physiological imbalances to the caretaker.

Other physical imbalances may include excessive energy or tension in the muscles. Since newborn babies do not have a way to relieve stress, it is thought that crying is also a way for them to discharge the energy or tension.

The cries of a young newborn are short, high in pitch, and repetitive. They are short in duration due to the infant's underdeveloped lungs and muscles. The loudness and intensity of the cry can vary according to the newborn's needs. For example, crying due to hunger can be differentiable from crying due to pain. A hunger cry is rhythmic in nature which starts with a whimper and becomes louder and more sustained while a cry from pain starts with a shriek followed by a second of silence, as the baby gets a breath, and continues with more rigorous, high intensity cries. Studies have shown that mothers can identify the baby's need just by hearing the cry.

The Crying of Infants

Over the first few months psychological development allows the infants to move from involuntary cries, which speak exclusively of physiological de-

mands, to voluntary cries that now become an integral part of the infant's expressive and emotional development. The infant begins to show these psychological advancements by smiling and engaging with the mother. As a result, the infant now holds the capacity to cry because of anger and because of a need for attention.

During this time, the infant also undergoes physiological changes, which allows the infant more voluntary control over vocalization. The cries now become more sustained, and the pitch increases with a melancholy undertone. An anger cry is similar to a hunger cry in that it is rhythmic, but it is much more intense.

Between seven and nine months, the infant experiences a cognitive development that results in additional reasons for crying. For example, the baby now cries because of fear, whether it is due to strangers or a strange place. Separation from the parent can also elicit fear, which is commonly illustrated by a crying baby at bedtime. Furthermore, an infant's more active memory can lead to uncertainty of a situation. Crying ensues as the infant attempts to make sense of the unfamiliar events or surroundings.

The Crying of Toddlers

At seventeen to twenty-four months of age, the infant's self-awareness increases. Fear of failure, understanding of rules, and consequences if those rules are broken all become part of the child's psychological make-up. The child now cries because of an unfair situation such as wanting a toy that they cannot have. Henceforth, the source of crying depends more on internal feelings and moods rather than physiological needs, although they still retain the ability to unleash cries of pain in emergency situations.

Finally, the toddler becomes more mobile at this stage of development, therefore becoming more active and inquisitive of his or her surroundings. Frustration often sets in when he or she cannot perform a certain task correctly such as fitting a square peg into a round hole. Crying could be the toddler's method of reducing the stress and frustration of the situation.

The Duration of Crying

Infants typically cry between thirty minutes and two hours a day. Over two hours a day is too much and may be an indication of a physical ailment. It has been estimated that an infant will experience 4,000 crying episodes before the age of two. Many studies have been conducted around the world in an effort to determine whether or not different circumstances can affect the amount of crying by an infant. Surprisingly, the results were inconclusive and in some areas contradictory. Despite the fact that these studies were conducted in different cultures, it was found that on average, extra handling, on-demand feeding, and other nurturing from the mother made little difference to the amount of crying or even to the specific times the babies cried. In fact, evening time proved to be the peak time for infant crying across the board, and gender was shown to have no impact on the amount or duration.

It has been shown through a longitudinal study of twenty-six infant-mother pairs in 1972 by Bell and Ainsworth that there does exist a relationship between crying and maternal response. Mothers who responded quickly to a crying baby over the first nine months actually yielded a baby that cried less after the nine-month period. It is thought that because of the prompt attention of the mother, the infant becomes more secure and less demanding of the mother's contact. Although other studies have substantiated these findings, it is not possible to generalize for all infants because amount of crying depends on the mother's responsiveness, personality, individual needs for love and closeness to mother, and a tolerance for boredom, jealousy, hunger, pain, and fatigue.

The Psychology of Crying

There are several different theories that attest to the psychology behind crying. As a child develops from adolescence through adulthood, the causes of crying encompass all aspects of the human emotional scale. Now a person can cry for a multitude of reasons that range from anger, pain, misery, grief, sorrow, joy, and intense pleasure. One can break down crying into three different levels that differ in psychological magnitude.

Level one consists of physiological conditions such as a broken arm or skinned knee. This is the same type of crying that infants utilize in the first few months of life. Even though infants develop out of this basic level and cry for other reasons, this type of crying still remains throughout the life of the person.

For example, a five-year-old child will be quick to shed tears due to a hurt knee or a twenty-five-year-old person may cry because of intense pain caused by an injury.

Level two entails moods and emotions. It begins when an infant cries from anger and develops further as more feelings are added to their emotional scale. As the child matures and an increase in self-awareness ensues, a sense of pride settles in and becomes a sensitive area. So, a fifteen-year-old may not cry as readily over a hurt knee, but he or she may shed tears due to humiliation.

Level three consists of deeper emotion usually associated with intense prayer, or a deep appreciation. For example, a thirty-year-old person could weep because of a powerful poem or due to a selfless display of humanity. Not all people can reach this level of crying. It demands a higher level of awareness of the world, self, and relationship between the two.

Conclusion

No other study has given conclusive proof that other species cry. Crying is unique only to humans. Perhaps that is the reason for the complexity of this phenomenon. Complex beings bring forth complex issues that may prove impossible to sufficiently understand. Because of its versatility and unbiased relation to age, gender, and culture, crying will continue to puzzle people for years to come.

See also: LANGUAGE DEVELOPMENT; PARENTING

Bibliography

Abell, Ellen. "Infant Crying: I'm Trying to Tell You Something." Available from http://www.humsci.auburn.edu/parent/crying/index.html; INTERNET.

Lester, Barry, and Zachariah Boukydis C. F. *Infant Crying: Theoretical and Research Perspectives.* New York: Plenum Press, 1985.

Lutz, Tom. *Crying.* New York: W. W. Norton and Company, 1999.

Murry, Thomas, and Joan Murry. *Infant Communication: Cry and Early Speech.* Houston, TX: College Hill Press, 1980.

Sammons, W. A. H. *The Self-Calmed Baby.* Boston: Little Brown, 1989.

Timothy K. Loper

D

DATING

Dating works to meet the needs of both identity achievement and the development of intimacy (both of which are chief tasks of adolescence), in that as one gradually becomes closer to another, one becomes more self-aware. In coming to know the self, adolescents begin to move away from the known world of family relationships and toward the world of peers. In doing so, adolescents become aware of differences between self and others as they work to develop a system of personal values and beliefs, honing a sense of who they are and who they wish to be. In this search for self, dating can have a positive impact on self-esteem and self-image.

This exploration also includes coming to know the sexual self, by exploring aspects of sexuality in terms of both dress and behavior. As adolescents work to find their place in the adult world, they develop a more distinct sense of ownership of their bodies and how that body functions. In addition, they become more aware of those to whom they are attracted, what they find sexually pleasing, and how it feels to be involved both physically and emotionally with one person.

The capacity for intimacy is initially developed in same-sex friendships and then extended into opposite-sex relationships. For females, dating typically provides a context for further expression of intimacy, while the experience provides for males a context for further development of intimacy. In general, intimacy skills of the average young adolescent are poorly

developed; consequently, the art of managing close relationships tends to develop through a process of trial and error. As the individual matures and acquires more dating experience, she becomes more comfortable with aspects of self-disclosure, emotional closeness, and the experience of being cared for by a member of the opposite sex.

Who Dates When?

Children develop crushes early on, and report "going together" as early as fifth grade. However, middle school seems to be the more typical time when adolescents begin developing an interest in members of the opposite sex.

Even while chaperoned dating has virtually disappeared, the median age at which dating begins decreased from sixteen in 1924 to thirteen in 1990. Most females begin dating by fourteen years of age, while males begin between fourteen and fifteen. Initially, dating takes the form of mixed-gender groups involved in common activities, with dating as a couple delayed until approximately fifteen or sixteen years of age. By sixteen, more than 90 percent of all adolescents report having had at least one date, and by their senior year in high school, 50 percent of adolescents report dating more than once a week. The majority of teens report having had at least one exclusive relationship during middle adolescence, lasting several months to perhaps a year. And even though females tend to be more assertive, males continue to initiate most dating encounters.

107

Steady versus Multiple Dating

Dating relationships range from informal casual dating to involved, steady relationships. Steady dating is more common among older adolescents, with 30 percent of males and 40 percent of females between the ages of sixteen and eighteen indicating that they are going steady. Many argue it is not advisable to allow adolescents younger than fifteen to date intensively, as it appears to have a negative effect on interpersonal development; dating may limit their interactions with others and lead to social immaturity. Debra Haffner, in her book *From Diapers to Dating*, argues that middle-school children should not be permitted to date someone more than two years older than themselves, as research indicates young teens who date older teens are more likely to become involved in high-risk behaviors. In addition, involvement in dating too early and too intensely may impede opportunities for same-sex relationships and casual opposite-sex relationships, both of which enhance the development of intimacy at later ages.

There are advantages and disadvantages to both steady and multiple dating (going out with more than one person). While the most serious long-term disadvantage of going steady appears to be early marriage, dating a single person on a steady basis can provide a sense of security for the adolescent and meet emotional and social needs. In addition to feeling popular, adolescents who date steadily tend to be those who report the highest self-esteem. Nevertheless, adolescents who have clear educational and/or vocational goals tend to go steady less often, and females who have higher levels of self-esteem tend to date frequently, but are less likely to go steady. Finally, multiple dating often involves the adolescent in more superficial relationships and provides fewer opportunities to develop the interpersonal skills that are involved in getting to know one person well.

Consequently, a moderate degree of dating with more serious involvement delayed until late adolescence may be the optimal balance. Haffner recommended that parents set limits for children regarding dating by deciding when, if, and under what circumstances the child may date and then supervising and monitoring dating behavior. She advised parents to talk with their children when they come home from group or single dates, ask open-ended questions, and listen without judging. Most importantly, she argued, parents must take their children's feelings seriously.

Dating and Sex

Dating is a major arena for exploring sexual activity, and studies indicate that sexual behavior among adolescents has increased. Jane Brooks reported in *The Process of Parenting* that approximately three-fourths of teens believe sex before marriage is acceptable if two people love each other, although females more so than males link intercourse to feelings of love. The genders agreed, however, that having a reputation for being sexually active and going to the male's home when his parents are not there clearly implies the expectation of intercourse.

According to Brooks, about one million girls between the ages of fifteen and nineteen become pregnant annually. Haffner reported that among teens in grades seven to twelve, strong parental and family connections and perceived parental disapproval were related to the decision not to have intercourse. More specifically, adolescents who felt close to their parents were more likely to postpone intercourse, had fewer sexual partners, and used contraception more reliably when they did have intercourse than were teens that were not close to their parents. Haffner encouraged parents to talk with their children about abstinence, as well as birth control and sexually transmitted diseases, to better inform them about which behaviors the parents feel are age-appropriate and which are not. She cautioned against being too restrictive, however, citing evidence that teens with very strict parents are more likely to become pregnant. Most importantly, she contended, the child needs to know the parents want him to come to them, or another trusted adult, if he is beginning to think about the possibility of sexual activity.

Avoiding unwanted sex is also an issue for this age group in that dating may lead to sexual activity that is coerced or forced. Larry Bennett and Susan Fineran found that 43 percent of high school students reported having been victimized by sexual or physical violence within a one-year period; frequency estimates indicate that between 15 and 25 percent of high-school-aged females have been the victims of date rape. These forms of violence among high school peers tend to be influenced by relationship, gender, effects on the victim, and apparent beliefs about male role power and personal power. Since many adolescents do not report their victimization, those closely involved with adolescents should be attentive to behavioral indicators of sexual abuse: depression, psychosomatic illnesses, irritability, avoidance of men, loss of confidence, nightmares, fears of going outside/inside, and anxiety.

Not Dating

Although romantic relationships are an integral part of adolescence, approximately 10 percent of male and female high school seniors report having never dated. Adolescents who do not begin dating at

Dating relationships range from informal casual dating to involved, steady relationships, with steady dating being more common among older adolescents. (Wartenberg/Picture Press/Corbis)

a time similar to their friends may be dropped from peer groups, and adolescent females who do not date demonstrate delayed social development, increased dependence on their parents, and feelings of insecurity.

Similar issues exist for gay and lesbian teens. While it is common for the preadolescent teen to be attracted to or develop a crush on someone of the same sex, research indicates that sexual orientation typically emerges by eighteen years of age and that homosexual youth report feeling different at an early age. With far fewer opportunities for dating and minimal support for developing same-sex romantic relationships, teens in this group may be deprived of the opportunity to date those to whom they feel most attracted. This social disapproval may interfere with the development of intimacy, and lack of participation in satisfying relationships may lead to feelings of inadequacy, which could in turn impair development of friendships as well as other relationships later in adulthood. Parents of homosexual teens need to let their children know their love is unconditional as they demonstrate their support and acceptance.

Conclusions

Dating during the years of child development clearly affects both personal and social growth as the individual works to acquire skills related to interacting with others. While not without its challenges, the dating experience can provide positive feedback to adolescents as well as a sense of interpersonal attachment with their peers. Relationships gained through dating then prepare adolescents for continued emotional growth into adulthood.

See also: ADOLESCENCE; SEXUAL ACTIVITY; SOCIAL DEVELOPMENT

Bibliography

Adams, Gerald, Thomas Gullotta, and Carol Markstrom-Adams. *Adolescent Life Experiences,* 3rd edition. Pacific Grove, CA: Brooks/Cole, 1994.

Bennett, Larry, and Susan Fineran. "Sexual and Severe Physical Violence among High School Students: Power Beliefs, Gender, and Relationships." *American Journal of Orthopsychiatry* 68 (1998):645–652.

Brooks, Jane. *The Process of Parenting,* 4th edition. Mountain View, CA: Mayfield, 1996.

Conger, John, and Anne Petersen. *Adolescence and Youth,* 3rd edition. New York: Harper and Row, 1984.

Dacey, John, and Maureen Kenny. *Adolescent Development,* 2nd edition. Boston: McGraw-Hill, 1997.

Dusek, Jerome. *Adolescent Development and Behavior,* 2nd edition. Englewood Cliffs, NJ: Prentice Hall, 1991.

Furman, Wyndol, and Elizabeth Wehner. "Romantic Views: Toward a Theory of Adolescent Romantic Relationships." In Raymond Montemayor, Gerald Adams, and Thomas Gullotta eds., *Personal Relationships during Adolescence.* Thousand Oaks, CA: Sage, 1994.

Haffner, Debra. *From Diapers to Dating: A Parent's Guide to Raising Sexually Healthy Children.* New York: Newmarket Press, 1999.

Jaffe, Michael. *Adolescence.* New York: Wiley, 1998.

Levy-Warren, Marcia. *The Adolescent Journey: Development, Identity Formation, and Psychotherapy.* Northvale, NJ: Jason Aronson, 1996.

Miller, Kristelle. "Adolescents' Same-Sex and Opposite-Sex Peer Relations: Sex Differences in Popularity, Perceived Social Competence, and Social Cognitive Skills." *Journal of Adolescent Research* 4 (1990):173–189.

Rice, F. Phillip. *The Adolescent: Development, Relationships, and Culture,* 9th edition. Boston: Allyn and Bacon, 1999.

Savin-Williams, Ritch. "Dating Those You Can't Love and Loving Those You Can't Date." In Raymond Montemayor, Gerald Adams, and Thomas Gullotta eds., *Personal Relationships during Adolescence.* Thousand Oaks, CA: Sage, 1994.

Seifert, Kevin, and Robert Hoffnung. *Child and Adolescent Development,* 5th edition. Boston: Houghton Mifflin, 2000.

Sorenson, Susan, and Patricia Bowie. "Vulnerable Populations: Girls and Young Women." In Leonard Eron and Jacquelyn Gentry eds., *Papers of the American Psychological Association on Violence and Youth,* Vol. II: *Violence and Youth: Psychology's Response.* Washington, DC: American Psychological Association, 1994.

Steinberg, Laurence. *Adolescence,* 2nd edition. New York: McGraw-Hill, 1989.

Thornton, Arland. "The Courtship Process of Adolescent Sexuality." *Journal of Family Issues* 11 (1990):239–273.

Vicary, Judith, Linda Klingaman, and William Harkness. "Risk Factors Associated with Date Rape and Sexual Assault of Adolescent Girls." *Journal of Adolescence* 18 (1995):289–306.

Youniss, James, and Denise Haynie. "Friendship in Adolescence." *Development and Behavioral Pediatrics* 13, no. 1 (1992):59–66.

Rebecca J. Glover

DAY CARE

According to the U.S. Census Bureau, in 1998, a record 59 percent of the 3.7 million mothers of infants were in the labor force (36% were working full-time); a total of 73 percent of the 31.3 million mothers of children older than one year were in the labor force (52% were working full-time). Although some working mothers cared for their children while they worked, most relied on some type of nonmaternal care, commonly known as child care or day care. The following information focuses on day care for children under five years old in three main sections: types of day care and demographic information; the effects of day care on children's development, including concerns about health as well as cognitive and social development; and day care as a social phenomenon.

Types of Day Care and Demographic Information

According to the U.S. Census Bureau, in 1995, 75 percent of the 19.3 million children under age five were in some form of regular day-care arrangement. Multiple care arrangements were common; 44 percent regularly spent time in more than one arrangement per week (the average was two). Many types of day care were used. Whereas 50 percent of these children were cared for by relatives (such as a grandparent at 30% or the other parent at 18%), 49 percent were cared for by nonrelatives. Some children were cared for in their homes by a nonrelative such as a babysitter, nanny, or au pair (9%), while others were left with a nonrelative such as a friend or neighbor in the caregiver's home (9%).

Other types of nonrelative care include day-care centers (15%) and family day care (13%). A day-care center is an organized facility that is licensed to provide care for many children. Caregivers in centers can change often, and high turnover is frequently a problem. Family day cares are operated in a home environment and may or may not be licensed. States regulate licensed family day cares and day-care centers, and the standards among states vary (e.g., larger versus smaller adult to child ratios required). Some centers surpass state regulations to meet special accreditation standards (such as the National Association for the Education of Young Children, NAEYC).

Other types of care in organized facilities include nursery or preschools (14%), Head Start (3%), and school programs (2%). Nurseries and preschools are schools for young children that focus on specific learning activities and educational goals (for more information, see the Nursery/Preschool section). Head Start is a federally funded program that serves low-income families and children, typically ages three to four years, with the goal of increasing school readiness. Elementary schools may also offer care, either in preschool programs or through early kindergarten admittance.

The Census found that the use of day care was related to parental employment. Of the 25 percent of children under age five not in any regular day-care arrangement, 96 percent had a parent who was not working or in school. In contrast, of the 75 percent who were in a regular arrangement, 98 percent had a parent that was working or in school. On average, these children spent 35 hours per week in day care. Parents who were not working or in school also used day care; 43 percent of their children were in a regular arrangement, possibly for enrichment purposes or educational development.

The Census also found that the use of day care was related to certain family characteristics, including marital status, ethnicity, parental education, and child age. Children of never-married parents were more likely to be in relative (55%) than nonrelative care (40%); children with married parents were equally likely to be in either type (49% each). Concerning ethnicity, there were no large differences in use of relative or nonrelative care between European-American or African-American parents (about 50% of children in both groups were cared for in each type), but children of Hispanic parents were more likely to be in relative (43%) than nonrelative care (34%). For parental education, children of parents with at most a high school diploma were more likely to be in relative (48%) than nonrelative care (38%); those with parents with at least some college education were more likely to be in nonrelative (59%) than relative care (52%). Concerning child's age, only 19 percent of children under one year of age attended an organized facility, while 50 percent of children ages three or four years attended organized facilities.

Family income was also related to type of care used. Children of parents in poverty were more likely to be in relative (41%) than nonrelative care (32%). One factor that may contribute to this difference is that relatives are often not paid while nonrelatives are usually paid for their services. Children not in poverty were equally likely to be cared for in both types (about 53% each). In addition, poor families spent on average 35 percent of their annual income on day care; nonpoor spent only 7 percent on average. In 1997, the National Institute of Child Health and Human Development (NICHD) Study of Early Child Care found that mother's income, in particular, was associated with use of day care. Families that relied more on the mother's income placed their infants in day care at an earlier age and used it for more hours per week than families less dependant on the mother's income.

Effects of Day Care

The effect of day care on children's development is related to the quality of the care the children receive. The Cost, Quality, and Outcomes Study of Child Care (CQO) investigated this issue and identified three levels of quality: low, mediocre, and high. Table 1 provides characteristics of each level. Higher quality was related to higher caregiver wages, higher caregiver education and training, and lower adult to child ratios.

This study examined the prevalence of each quality level. For preschool-aged children, only 24 percent of the day-care center classrooms were of high quality, 66 percent were mediocre quality, and 10 percent were low quality. For infants and toddlers, only 8 percent of the classrooms were of high quality, 52 percent were mediocre quality, and a full 40 percent were low quality. In a separate study of family day cares, only 9 percent provided good quality care, and a full 35 percent provided care that was potentially harmful to children's development.

Health and Safety

The effects of day care on children's health and safety vary by the quality of the setting and the attention paid to these issues. Because their immune systems are not yet fully functional, infants and toddlers are more susceptible to illnesses than older children. Infectious diseases (mainly upper respiratory and gastrointestinal) are higher among children in family day care and day-care centers than among children cared for in their own homes. However, scrupulous attention to hand washing and hygiene can cut the rate of infectious disease transmission substantially. Children in day-care centers may also be prone to injuries if the playground equipment is unsafe. This risk can be reduced by paying attention to the height of playground structures and the resilience of the surface under the equipment. The American Association of Public Health and the American Academy of Pediatrics developed a document entitled "Caring for Our Children" that provides comprehensive health and safety guidelines for day-care facilities.

Cognitive Development

The effects of day care on cognitive development are also related to the quality of the setting. The CQO study found that children in higher quality day care demonstrated more advanced cognitive skills than children in lower quality care. Specifically, their language development was more advanced, and they had better premath skills. In addition, compared to children who received low quality care, children who received high quality care in their preschool years continued to show heightened cognitive skills into the early school years.

The NICHD study researched this issue further by examining both day care quality and family characteristics. This study also found care quality to be related to language development as well as school readiness. However, family characteristics (such as family income, mother's vocabulary, and the home environment) were more strongly associated with children's cognitive development than day-care experience. This study also compared children who were and were not in day care and found that when family

TABLE 1

Characteristics of Low, Mediocre, and High Quality Day Care

Low	Mediocre	High
Atmosphere is either chaotic or overly strict	Children spend most of their time in large groups rather than in small groups or individual activities	Atmosphere is friendly and respectful
Adults are inattentive, unresponsive, or overly harsh	Adults provide little or no educational guidance	Adults have close relationships with the children and provide educational guidance to support learning
Materials and activities are scarce, completely lacking, or developmentally inappropriate	There may be enough materials for all the children or some may be damaged	Rooms are well organized with a variety and good amount of age appropriate materials and activities that are changed frequently to keep up with the children's interests and abilities
Insufficient attention is paid to the individual needs of the children	Little attention is paid to individual children	Children's individual needs are attended to
Basic nutritional, health, and safety needs are not met and play spaces indoors and out may be dangerous	Basic nutritional needs are met and the children's safety needs are generally attended to	Safety, nutritional needs, and personal care are attended to and met while encouraging the development of self-help skills

SOURCE: Table adapted from Ellen Peisner-Feinberg, Margaret R. Burchinal, Richard M. Clifford, Noreen Yazejian, Mary L. Culkin, J. Zelazo, Carolee Howes, Patricia Byler, Sharon Lynn Kagan, and Jean Rustici. *The Children of the Cost, Quality, and Outcomes Study Go to School Technical Report.* Chapel Hill: Frank Porter Graham Child Development Center, 2000.

factors were controlled for, few differences between the groups existed. Comparisons showed that children in high quality care sometimes scored higher than children in exclusive maternal care, and children in low quality care sometimes scored lower. More frequently than not, however, children in exclusive maternal care and children in day care scored similarly on cognitive measures.

Effects on Social Development

The effects of day care on social development are also associated with care quality. The CQO study found that children in higher quality day care had more positive attitudes about themselves, their relationships with peers were more positive, and their social skills were more advanced than were those in lower quality care. Further, the quality of the day care they had attended continued to be related to their social development in the early school years. Children who had close relationships with their day-care providers were rated as more sociable through kindergarten and as having fewer problem behaviors through second grade than children whose relationships with their day-care providers were not close. Also, children who had more positive classroom climates in day care were found to have better relationships with their peers in second grade. The NICHD study similarly found that care quality was associated with children's social development. However, they also noted that family characteristics, especially mother's sensitivity, were more strongly associated with children's behavior than their day-care experience (e.g., age of entry into care and care type).

One specific concern that the NICHD study addressed was whether using nonmaternal care affects the emotional attachment formed between infants and their mothers. The study found that the use of day care was not in and of itself associated with the quality of the attachment relationship. However, if mothers were low in sensitivity and the infants were either in poor quality care, in day care for more than ten hours per week, or experienced multiple settings before age fifteen months, then the infants were more likely to be insecurely attached to their mothers. Thus, the results suggest that the quality of mother-infant attachment is related to a combination of day care and home characteristics.

Day Care as a Social Phenomenon

The use of day care has increased dramatically as increasing numbers of mothers have chosen to work outside of the home. According to the U.S. Census, only 31 percent of mothers of infants were working in 1976. This percentage climbed to 47 percent in 1984 and to 59 percent in 1998. As mentioned in a review by Kathleen McCartney and Deborah Phillips, societal views of day care have also changed over time. When day care was first formally established in the United States, a stigma was attached to its use. In the late 1800s through the early 1900s, day nurseries were established to make up for the "poor home environments" of working immigrants. Societal views changed during the Great Depression and World War II, when the need for day care was seen as temporary; the expectation was that mothers would later return home to their children, and federal funds for day-care programs were immediately withdrawn after these crises were over. In the 1960s, educational day-care programs, such as Head Start (which began in 1965), were established to compensate for disadvantaged home environments. In contrast to day nurseries, which were established to make up for home environments that were viewed as poor because of deficiencies on behalf of the parents, the home environments were seen as disadvantaged due to factors beyond the parent's control such as poverty and discrimination in the 1960s. The focus of the programs in this later era was on educational intervention and increasing school readiness to overcome these factors. In the 1980s and 1990s, mothers who used day care were conflicted and felt pressured to stay home and work. As maternal employment becomes more normative, societal views may continue to shift.

Conclusion

In conclusion, day care is an important issue in the United States given the increasing numbers of working mothers. Given the low prevalence of high quality care and the potential effects of low quality care, an important task for workers in early childhood is to increase the availability of high quality care. In addition, parents who choose to use day care must carefully search for and select high quality care for their children.

See also: AFTER-SCHOOL PROGRAMS; PRESCHOOL

Bibliography

Helburn, Suzanne, Mary L. Culkin, John Morris, et al. *Cost, Quality, and Child Outcomes in Child Care Centers* Public Report. Denver: University of Colorado, 1995.

Kontos, Susan, Carollee Howes, Marybeth Shinn, and Ellen Galinsky. *Quality in Family Child Care and Relative Care.* New York: Teachers College Press, 1995.

Kotch, Jonathan B., and Donna Bryant. "Effects of Day Care on the Health and Development of Children." *Current Opinion in Pediatrics* 2 (1990):883–894.

McCartney, Kathleen, and Deborah Phillips. "Motherhood and Child Care." In Beverly Birns and Dale F. Hay eds., *The Different Faces of Motherhood.* New York: Plenum, 1988.

National Institute of Child Health and Human Development Early Child Care Network. "Infant Child Care and Attachment Security: Results of the NICHD Study of Early Child Care." *Child Development* 68 (1997):860–879.

National Institute of Child Health and Human Development Early Child Care Network. "The Relation of Child Care to Cognitive and Language Development." *Child Development* 71 (2000):960–980.

Peisner-Feinberg, Ellen, Margaret R. Burchinal, Richard M. Clifford, et al. *The Children of the Cost, Quality, and Outcomes Study Go to School* Technical Report. Chapel Hill, NC: Frank Porter Graham Child Development Center, 2000.

Pungello, Elizabeth P., and Beth Kurtz-Costes. "Why and How Working Women Choose Child Care: A Review with a Focus on Infancy." *Developmental Review* 19 (1999):31–96.

Smith, Kristin. *Who's Minding the Kids? Child Care Arrangements: Fall 1995.* Current Population Reports, P70-70. Washington, DC: U.S. Census Bureau, 2000.

U.S. Census Bureau. *Record Share of New Mothers in Labor Force, Census Bureau Reports.* Press Release, October 24, 2000. Washington, DC: U.S. Census Bureau, 2000.

Elizabeth P. Pungello
Daniel J. Bauer

DEATH

The American poet Edna St. Vincent Millay once said, "Childhood is the kingdom where no one ever dies." This can be read in two ways: either children never encounter death or they never die. Many Americans rigidly adhere to such mythologies, as childhood death is now a relatively rare event, so that the probability of an infant surviving to age fifteen is close to 99 percent and life expectancy at birth is seventy-nine years. By contrast, in 1900, a couple faced a fifty-fifty chance that one of their three children would die before they grew up.

Because of the strong desire to spare children unnecessary anguish, many adults avoid discussing dying and death with them. "Why take away their innocence?" and "They'll find out soon enough, when they are older," are typical justifications for this. Because of such denial of death, many adults assume that children do not think about death, should not attend funerals, and are not capable of grieving over loss. When a child is unexpectedly thrown into an encounter with death, such as when a pet or grandparent dies, frequently no explanation accompanies the experience, or euphemisms and metaphors (e.g., "Grandma is having a long sleep") are invoked that may promote even more confusion and anxiety for the child. Fortunately, recognition of the importance of learning and educating about dying and death has begun to open up meaningful dialogues and has led to significant research findings.

The Development of a Concept of Death

When one looks and listens carefully, one learns that children are very interested and curious about death. It is one of their first intellectual puzzles that is played out whenever they see a dead bug on the windshield; when they engage in the game of "here" and "not here" in peekaboo; or when they shoot a target dead with the shotgun blast of their finger. Yet, a mature understanding of death, involving a number of components, is accomplished only along with an overall conceptual development about how things in the world work. Most adults and older children understand that death is universal and inevitable; all living things die. Death is irreversible (the dead do not come back), and the body becomes nonfunctional (all functions and activities associated with the physical being cease). The causes of death, ranging from the deterioration of old age, illness, accidents, and homicides, to perhaps extreme psychological distress, are also fairly well known. In contemporary Western societies, it is rare to find widespread belief that magic, bad thoughts, or evil spirits are the sources of death. Finally, a foundation of most Western (and Eastern) belief systems is that some intangible dimension of persons—their soul or spirit—continues beyond the death of their physical bodies, a concept known as noncorporeal continuation.

A classic 1948 study by Maria Nagy of almost 400 Hungarian children aged three to ten revealed that arriving at a mature concept of death requires development through three stages. "Auntie Death," as Nagy was called, learned through interviews and pictures drawn by the children that between the ages of three and five years (Stage 1), children believed that death involved a continuation of life, but at a reduced level of activity and experiences. The dead do not do much, their condition resembles sleep, and they can return to the world of the living. Of greatest concern to the youngest children was the fear of separation, not necessarily the fear of dying or being dead. During Stage 2, identified by Nagy as from five to nine years of age, children progressed to an understanding that death is final and irreversible. Death takes on concrete imagery and a personality, in the guise of skeletons, or the "boogeyman." Such personification leads to another interesting belief of this period: Death can be evaded, if you can only outsmart or outrun that nasty boogeyman! Thus, universality in death is a concept yet to be achieved. Final, the achievements of Stage 3 (age nine and older) reflected the mature components of death.

Although this research was done in the mid-twentieth century, Nagy's findings continue to be applicable. Subsequent research has suggested that children arrive at a mature concept of death at an earlier age than suggested by Nagy, that children do not personify death to the extent that Nagy found, and that modern technology has found its way into their descriptions (death is like a hard drive crash). Furthermore, there is a strong connection between death concepts and overall cognitive development, so that children's understanding of what causes death changes from magical ("I wished he was dead and now he is"), naive ("You die from eating a dirty bug"), and moral ("My Daddy died because I was a bad child") to a more scientific, rational approach ("You die when your body wears out or when you get an incurable disease"). Researchers have also learned that

it is too simplistic to view just age as the determining factor with regard to death concepts. Children who have experienced a parent's death, who are dying themselves, or who have witnessed violent, traumatic death will perceive death in an adultlike manner at much earlier ages than children who have not had such experiences.

Children Who Are Dying

As difficult as it is to acknowledge that children think about death, it is even harder for adults to conceive of children dying. The significant accomplishments of modern medicine have certainly made this a relatively rare event. However, there still are many children and families who must cope with the realities of terminal illnesses such as cancer, AIDS, or cystic fibrosis.

In the 1970s and 1980s Myra Bluebond-Langner spent countless hours listening to the stories of dying children and their families. What she learned has offered an important window to the experiences of the dying child, and those of their healthy siblings. According to Bluebond-Langner, children who are dying become very sophisticated about the nature of their illness and hospital procedures. As they enter repetitive cycles of sickness, treatments, and remission, and as they observe children with similar illnesses dying, their self-perceptions gradually change from "I am sick but I will get better" to "I am sick and eventually I will die from this illness." These children know about death at much earlier ages than do healthy children. These children also quickly learn that it causes great pain for their parents and other adults if they bring up the possibility of their dying. In their efforts to protect their elders and to ensure their continued visits and care, many terminally ill children engage in a game of "mutual pretense" wherein everyone knows they are dying but they are reluctant to talk about it in an open and meaningful way.

Bluebond-Langner also found that the well siblings of dying children were in significant need of care and nurturance. As the demands and psychological stress of the illness took its toll on their parents, the healthy siblings were frequently neglected and living in "a house of chronic sorrow." Furthermore, siblings' roles in their families were ambivalent and undefined. "Should I parent my parents?"; "Should I take the place of my dead brother (sister)?"; "Why do I feel both happy and sad that she died?"; "Should I just disappear?"—these were some of the concerns of the siblings.

The knowledge gained from these trying circumstances is important. Children who are dying need

Adolescents grieve very deeply and with prolonged intensity. They often find solace with their peers, as is the case with these students from Columbine High School in Littleton, Colorado. The students were reacting to several fatal shootings that took place at the school in 1999. (David Zalubowski)

open communication, assurances that they will not be abandoned, and a sense of normalcy to the extent to which they are capable. Older children and adolescents also need to feel that they have some control over their situation, and they need to be treated as unique individuals. Many of these concerns are applicable to their well siblings. And, of course, their parents need an incredible amount of social and emotional support as they encounter their ultimate nightmare.

Childhood Grief

Many people encounter death during their childhood. When George Dickinson asked college students to write about their first experiences with death, he found the average age of this first loss to be 7.95 years. Most of these deaths involved the death of a grandparent or a pet.

Grief is an individual affair, no matter if the griever is an adult or a child. Although there are aspects of grief that are common to all people, it is important to recognize that children do not express their sadness over loss in the same manner as do adults. Further, it is necessary to take into consideration the child's developmental concept of death and who has died. A child younger than five, for example, may have a difficult time understanding why grandma is not coming back. Regardless of who it is, death involves not only the loss of a person who was meaningful to the child but also a relationship that would have evolved over time as the child changes into an adolescent and adult. Thus, grieving and understanding the nature of the loss may be a lifelong process for children, especially when they lose a parent.

Children do not typically hold onto their grief over a sustained period as do adolescents and adults. Upon learning the news of a death, they may cry, especially if others around them are doing so, but then return to other activities (e.g., watching television or riding a bicycle). They also may refuse to talk about the person who has died, or show a lack of interest in what is going on around them. Cycling in and out of grief, however, may be a very adaptable way of handling the intense emotions that will overwhelm children. As they have no road map from prior experience, the situations involving death may be especially frightening, especiallyif distressed adults emotionally abandon them. Some children may hide their grief in order to protect their loved ones. Even with a limited concept of death, very young children understand loss when their routines are disrupted and when the person who has died is no longer there. Thus, very young children may play out their grief by insisting on enacting the familiar behavioral patterns they had engaged in with the deceased, such as a daily walk around the street. It also is not unusual for children to regress (as in toilet training), show aggression toward others, have difficulty sleeping, show fear of the dark, or show a lack of interest in activities that formerly were very appealing. In contrast to children, adolescents grieve very deeply and with prolonged intensity. Adolescents appear to find solace with their peers and may reject the well-intended help of adults.

Bereaved children do not necessarily have long-term problems. One of the most important lessons learned from the Child Bereavement Study undertaken by Phyllis Silverman and William Worden of Harvard University is that many children who have lost a parent show positive psychological adjustment a year or two after their loss. These researchers found that it was important for children to maintain the connection to the deceased person through mementos, dreams, or visits to the cemetery. These children also reconstruct their relationship throughout their development, with the aid of their memories and feelings, and in an open environment where it is possible to talk about who was lost.

Helping Children with Death Experiences

When children feel that it is all right to talk about death, they will do so. Frequently their questions occur when there is a "teachable moment," for instance, when the class pet hamster or the relative of a friend has died. This is the time for parents or other adults to be open and honest, and to be aware of the developmental level of the children's understanding. Honesty involves avoiding euphemisms such as "death is like sleep or a long vacation"; clearly stating the facts about death as in "Grandma's body doesn't work anymore and she won't be coming back"; and even admitting ignorance as to what happens after death. Caring adults should also be aware that the questions might be frequently repeated, as the child tries to incorporate the death into his or her understanding of how life works. There also are a number of books that have been written for children about dying and death, and these too may open a dialogue about this topic.

In addition to open and honest discussion, bereaved children need emotional support, as much consistency and continuity with their past lives as possible, opportunities to remain connected to the person who has died, and to not be avoided by the other significant people in their lives. From teachers, other adults, and friends, they need to feel that they are not weird or different from other children. Most importantly, what all children need when it comes to death is to feel that they are on the "same side of the wall, rather than alone on the other side" (Schaeffer 1988, p. 141).

See also: MILESTONES OF DEVELOPMENT

Bibliography

Barrett, Ronald K. "Children and Traumatic Loss." In Kenneth J. Doka ed., *Children Mourning, Mourning Children*. Washington, DC: Hospice Foundation of America, 1995.

Bluebond-Langner, Myra. "Meanings of Death to Children." In Herman Feifel ed., *New Meanings of Death*. New York: McGraw-Hill, 1977.

Bluebond-Langner, Myra. "Worlds of Dying Children and Their Well Siblings." *Death Studies* 13, no. 1 (1988):1–16.

Corr, Charles A. "Children's Understandings of Death." In Kenneth J. Doka ed., *Children Mourning, Mourning Children*. Washington, DC: Hospice Foundation of America, 1995.

Dickinson, George. "First Childhood Death Experiences." *Omega* 25 (1992):169–182.

Edmondson, Brad. "The Facts of Death." *American Demographics* 73 (April 1997):46–53.

Kastenbaum, Robert J. *Death, Society, and Human Experience*, 7th edition. Needham Heights, MA: Allyn and Bacon, 2001.

Koocher, Gerald P. "Children, Death, and Cognitive Development." *Developmental Psychology* 9 (1973):369–375.

Marwit, Samuel J., and Sandra S. Carusa. "Communicated Support Following Loss: Examining the Experiences of Parental Death and Parental Divorce in Adolescence." *Death Studies* 22 (1998):237–255.

Nagy, Maria H. "The Child's Theories Concerning Death." *Journal of Genetic Psychology* 73 (1948):3–27.

Schaeffer, Daniel J. *Loss, Grief, and Care*. Binghamton, NY: Haworth Press, 1988.

Silverman, Phyllis R. *Never Too Young to Know: Death in Children's Lives*. New York: Oxford University Press, 2000.

Worden, William, and Phyllis R. Silverman. "Parental Death and the Adjustment of School-Age Children." *Omega* 32 (1996):91–102.

Illene C. Noppe

DEFENSE MECHANISMS

Defense mechanisms are unconscious strategies used to cope with conflict, anxiety, and disturbing emotions, as well as to maintain social and emotional well-being. The theory of defense mechanisms originated from Sigmund Freud's psychoanalytical work. Children can adaptively employ these defenses to help resolve conflicts that arise at the stages of psychosexual development—the oral, anal, phallic, and genital stages. As children reach milestones in their development, they also learn to master their environment. In this process they are likely to experience anxiety and other negative feelings at various developmental stages. Defense mechanisms are means to manage the anxious, depressive, and angry emotions that can be both normal and abnormal reactions to family, community, school, and peer environments. There are numerous defense mechanisms, including withdrawal, repression, regression, denial, identification, projection, reaction formation, fantasy, and displacement. For example, a child who is having difficulty learning fractions may employ withdrawal and not participate in math class to cope with the frustration and avoid failure. Children commonly use defense mechanisms so that they can competently cope with emotional conflict, fears, stressful environments, abuse, and negative affect.

See also: THEORIES OF DEVELOPMENT

Bibliography

Burland, J. Alexis. "Current Perspectives on the Treatment of Neuroses in Children and Adolescents." In M. Hossein Etezady ed., *The Neurotic Child and Adolescent.* Northvale, NJ: Jason Aronson, 1990.

Mordock, John. "Teaching Children Self-control through Counseling." In Judah Ronch, William Van Ornum, and Nicholas Stillwell eds., *The Counseling Sourcebook: A Practical Reference on Contemporary Issues.* New York: Crossroad Publishing, 1994.

Rhonda Cherie Boyd

DELINQUENCY

Delinquent behavior, according to legal definitions, includes such acts as robbery, assault, property damage, drug possession, and other similar crimes committed by youth. Delinquency also includes what are known as status offenses, which are acts considered to be rule violations because individuals who commit them are not of legal age. Examples of typical status offenses include drinking alcohol, smoking, and truancy. Although delinquency is technically defined as a single law-breaking act, researchers have found that some youths' delinquent behavior is of sufficient frequency and severity to represent an identifiable pattern of behavior that becomes apparent at an early age. Indeed, as early as the 1950s, important research by experts such as William McCord and Joan McCord began to identify factors that helped explain an early onset pattern of antisocial and delinquent behavior. This research cited harsh parenting as a leading contributor to the development of this pattern.

The Early Onset/Persistent Pattern

Many experts have studied the early onset/persistent (EOP) pattern because such youth are observed to enter a "developmental pathway" to adolescent antisocial and delinquent behavior by showing aggression and other problem behaviors as early as the preschool period and continuing a pattern of antisocial behavior into adulthood. Children progress on this pathway by displaying a progression of behaviors, including: having tantrums in preschool; fighting with peers and defying adults during elementary school; being truant, using drugs, smoking, and shoplifting in junior high; and committing crimes in adolescence and young adulthood. This group constitutes between 5 percent and 7 percent of delinquent adolescents but tends to be responsible for the majority of recorded delinquent acts. There are two other important distinguishing features of EOP youth: Their delinquent acts tend to be of high severity, and they are likely to be antisocial in all arenas of their lives.

Current knowledge about the origins of delinquency is not complete, but a substantial amount of information has been amassed over the last century. In addition to identifying distinct patterns of delinquent behavior, investigators have made significant discoveries about the factors that may place a child on a pathway toward delinquent behavior. What follows is a discussion of the types of factors that have been reliably associated with delinquency at various developmental periods. These are factors that, when present, increase the risk for involvement in delinquency but should never be considered causal. This is an important point to grasp because, while strong statements can be made about which factors increase the risk for becoming delinquent, the present state of knowledge does not allow experts to make definitive statements about the precise "causes" of delinquency.

Studies frequently find that EOP delinquent youth come from environments of poverty marked by high levels of instability and life stress. Importantly, experts have been careful to point out that these factors do not alone account for the development of delinquency. Rather, it is the effects that poverty and life stress tend to have on parenting that make them powerful risk factors. Parents in these environments tend to have fewer resources and less social support than

A reform school workroom, circa 1854. In the past, delinquent youths were sent to reform schools for punishment, not rehabilitation, with little attempt made to understand the source of the delinquent behavior. (Library of Congress)

what is required for optimally raising their children. Consequently, they are more likely to be emotionally unavailable and to use inconsistent, harsh, and sometimes abusive disciplinary strategies. Because of their limited resources, parents in these situations tend to provide inadequate monitoring of their children, thus allowing them ample opportunities for an active life of delinquent behavior. These are all factors that are frequently found in the backgrounds of EOP delinquent youth.

Experts have turned to emotion regulation processes to explain why early parenting factors are associated with EOP delinquent behavior. They have observed that, starting in the first year of life, children depend exclusively on caregivers to help them regulate their emotions and to stay organized in the face of arousing situations. In optimal caregiving contexts, children are free to explore their environments and to experience a wide range of emotions because they are confident that their caregivers will be available in times of distress. When parents experience high levels of life stress, mental health problems such as depression, and low amounts of social support, they have fewer resources to devote to their parenting.

Without adequate parental support, children in such environments are likely to develop maladaptive coping skills for dealing with disorganizing emotions (such as anger and sadness) and are likely to behave aggressively and impulsively instead. This is especially true of maltreated children because their caregivers are frequently the source of their distress and are likely to be emotionally unavailable and unsupportive.

Research shows that once a pattern of aggressive, defiant, and impulsive behavior has been established, it is highly resistant to change. This is true in large part because the environments that help give rise to this pattern are themselves highly stable. Because of countless repetitions over time, maladaptive patterns of emotion regulation become deeply ingrained by the elementary school years to the extent that they become core components of a child's personality structure. Moreover, certain "vicious cycle" processes begin to take over. For example, children who show high levels of aggression and other antisocial behavior are more likely to be rejected by their peers and to receive negative attention from teachers, which in turn leads to more aggression. As these children progress through school, they are frequently suspended and/or expelled, begin to fail academically, and eventually develop adversarial relationships with the school system. By the time they enter high school, these children have had a lifetime of training and preparation for delinquent behavior in adolescence and quickly find peers who reinforce their patterns of behavior. In fact, one of the strongest findings is that delinquent children associate with and commit many of their offenses in the company of delinquent peers. Other vicious cycles can be found in the homes of most EOP youth. Power-assertive discipline strategies are more likely to be used, which in turn reinforce aggressive habits. Moreover, groundbreaking work by Gerald Patterson in 1982 showed that parents of EOP youth tend to use parenting strategies marked by an escalation of conflict, which also reinforces aggressive behaviors.

The Adolescence-Limited Pattern

In 1993, Terrie Moffitt showed that youth follow not one but at least two distinct developmental pathways to adolescent delinquency and antisocial behavior. Contrasting with the EOP group is what Moffitt termed the adolescence-limited (AL) pattern. As the name implies, these youth show no notable signs of problem behavior until adolescence, when they begin to engage in high levels of delinquent and other antisocial behavior similar to the EOP group. AL youth, however, begin to cease their delinquent behavior toward the end of adolescence, and many of these youth cease to engage in such behavior entirely by their mid-twenties. Although the behavior patterns of AL youth are often indistinguishable from those of the EOP group, AL delinquent acts are more likely to be status offenses rather than violent crimes, and the delinquent behavior of AL youth tends to be limited to certain contexts such as the peer social arena.

Adolescence-limited delinquent behavior is an interesting phenomenon because it follows a very different developmental pathway. These youth tend to (1) come from relatively stable backgrounds; (2) show normal levels of academic achievement and social competence; and (3) not have experienced maltreatment. Experts have discovered that these are reasonably well-adjusted youth who are motivated to assert their independence by engaging in what they perceive as "mature" behavior such as alcohol use and smoking. Because AL delinquent behavior is likely to cease by young adulthood, some experts have wondered whether it may be appropriately considered a normal part of adolescent "experimentation." Nevertheless, because of its risky nature, this pattern should not be dismissed as harmless given the consequences it may entail, such as pregnancy, criminal prosecution, and substance addiction.

Future Research into Delinquency

Gaps in scientists' knowledge about the development of delinquency continue to stimulate vigorous research activity. For example, a large research effort has focused on the exploration of other patterns of delinquent behavior given that some studies have identified some children who begin a pattern of antisocial behavior at early ages but stop by adolescence. Because these children are exceptions, however, most of the research on the development of delinquency has focused on more typically observed patterns such as the EOP and AL types. Nevertheless, researchers continue to work on pinpointing what helps to remove children from a delinquent pathway, especially because efforts to curb and prevent delinquency have consistently met with disappointing results. Other researchers in this field have turned their lens to female delinquency. This new emphasis is important because the preponderance of the research has focused on male delinquency because of its staggeringly higher incidence; this has left many questions unanswered regarding how delinquency develops in females. Studies addressing these and other important issues promise new insights into delinquency in the future.

See also: SOCIAL DEVELOPMENT; TRUANCY; VIOLENCE

Bibliography

McCord, William, and Joan McCord. *Origins of Crime: A New Evaluation of the Cambridge-Somerville Youth Study.* New York: Cambridge University Press, 1959.

Moffitt, Terrie E. "Adolescence-Limited and Life-Course-Persistent Antisocial Behavior: A Developmental Taxonomy." *Psychological Review* 100 (1993):674–701.

Patterson, Gerald R. *A Social Learning Approach to Family Intervention: Coercive Family Processes.* Eugene, OR: Castalia, 1982.

Benjamin Aguilar
Byron Egeland

DEVELOPMENT

Development is the process of change over time as a result of the interaction between environmental and genetic forces. It involves progressive, cumulative changes in structure, function, behavior, or organization. For example, development can refer to change in physical size or shape, mental function, perceptual capacity, or behavior.

Development involves changes that persist over time, rather that those that are temporary or situation-specific. It commonly refers to progressive change toward more complex levels of functioning. For humans, the term often refers to children's growing physical and mental capacities that allow them to participate in their social, intellectual, and cultural worlds. However, the term "development" is properly applied across the entire lifespan and can also refer to changes that are regressive rather than progressive. For example, the reduction in visual acuity that results from aging of the structures of the eye can also be considered a developmental change.

Development can occur gradually and incrementally (quantitative change) or involve stagelike transitions (qualitative change). The term itself is neutral in reference to whether the root cause is environmental or genetic, although different theories of development ascribe different roles to these interacting forces.

See also: MILESTONES OF DEVELOPMENT; THEORIES OF DEVELOPMENT

Bibliography

Bronfenbrenner, Urie. *The Ecology of Human Development: Experiments by Nature and Design.* Cambridge, MA: Harvard University Press, 1979.

Reber, Arthur S. *The Penguin Dictionary of Psychology.* New York: Penguin Books, 1985.

Liesette Brunson

DEVELOPMENTAL DISABILITIES

The term "developmental disabilities" includes all mental and physical impairments or combination of mental and physical impairments that (1) occur before a person is twenty-two years old; (2) are expected to continue indefinitely; (3) result in limitations in one or more areas of development such as physical, cognitive, behavioral, emotional, or social development; and (4) reflect a child's need for individualized services or treatment in school or community-based settings. Developmental disabilities is a generic term that includes medical or diagnosed conditions such as Down syndrome and cerebral palsy that have a known biological, genetic, or neurological cause. In addition, children with developmental disabilities may be delayed in attaining developmental milestones such as walking and talking for reasons that are unknown or thought to be related to environmental conditions such as poverty. Examples of common broad categories of developmental disabilities include mental retardation, autism, and learning disabilities.

See also: DEVELOPMENTAL NORMS; MILESTONES OF DEVELOPMENT

Bibliography

Batshaw, Mark, and Yvonne Perret. *Children with Disabilities: A Medical Primer,* 3rd edition. Baltimore: Brookes, 1992.

Gallimore, Ronald, Lucinda Bernheimer, Donald MacMillan, Deborah Speece, and Sharon Vaughn, eds. *Developmental Perspectives on Children with High-incidence Disabilities.* Mahwah, NJ: Erlbaum, 1999.

Levine, Melvin, William Carey, and Allen Crocker, eds. *Developmental-Behavioral Pediatrics,* 3rd edition. Philadelphia: Saunders, 1999.

Thurman, S. Kenneth, and Anne Widerstrom. *Infants and Young Children with Special Needs: A Developmental and Ecological Approach,* 2nd edition. Baltimore: Brookes, 1990.

Marjorie Erickson Warfield

DEVELOPMENTAL NORMS

Developmental norms are defined as standards by which the progress of a child's development can be measured. For example, the average age at which a child walks, learns to talk, or reaches puberty would be such a standard and would be used to judge whether the child is progressing normally. Norms have also been used as a basis for the "ages and stages" approach to understanding child development, made famous most notably by Yale University pediatrician and educator Arnold Gessell and University of Chicago educator Robert Havighurst. In using the idea of norms, Havighurst presented a set of developmental tasks tied closely to what behavior one might observe at what age. These sets of developmental tasks became a tool for teachers to use to help judge the appropriateness of certain types of curriculum for children of certain ages or developmental levels. While norms are usually thought of as being age-related, norms can also be tied to other developmental variables such as race, ethnicity, and sex.

See also: MILESTONES OF DEVELOPMENT; STAGES OF DEVELOPMENT

Bibliography

Leach, Penelope. *Your Baby and Child: From Birth to Age Five.* New York: Knopf, 1997.

Schaefer, Charles E., and Theresa Foy Digeronimo. *Ages and Stages: A Parent's Guide to Normal Childhood Development.* New York: Wiley, 2000.

Neil J. Salkind

DEWEY, JOHN (1859–1952)

John Dewey was born in Burlington, Vermont, to Archibald Sprague and Lucina Rich Dewey. He graduated from the University of Vermont in 1879 and then worked for three years as a high school teacher, focusing primarily in the areas of the classics, the sciences, and algebra. Dewey was also an assistant principal and principal before becoming a graduate student in philosophy at Johns Hopkins University in 1882. He earned his Ph.D. in 1884.

Dewey taught philosophy at the University of Michigan for ten years (1884–1894) before moving to the University of Chicago, where he was chairman of the Department of Philosophy. He also chaired the Department of Pedagogy and directed the Laboratory School. Dewey left Chicago in 1904 to teach at Columbia University in New York City from 1905 to 1930, serving in an emeritus capacity until 1939. He continued to write and lecture on a wide variety of topics until his death in 1952.

During his long teaching career, Dewey wrote many important works on a variety of subjects, including inquiry, social justice, ethics, education, and democracy. Indeed, Dewey sought to examine the bases of these themes as a means to provide individuals with the capacity to experience intellectual freedom—a prerequisite for a democratic society. Some of these works include *My Pedagogic Creed* (1897), *How We Think* (1910), *Democracy and Education* (1916), *Experience and Nature* (1925), *The Public and Its Problems* (1927), and *Logic: The Theory of Inquiry* (1938).

Dewey was genuinely concerned about social problems and believed that educational processes could be used to eliminate many of society's ills. Toward that end, Dewey sought to provide educators with strategies for reaching students that would honor each child's individual strengths and interests. Dewey believed, in particular, that schools and school systems should not be factorylike in nature, where all students were expected to master content in a predetermined and uniform way. On the contrary, Dewey recommended restructuring schools so that children could think and learn in their own ways and teachers would be guides to students' learning.

Dewey remains a significant influence in the fields of education and child development. By suggesting that authentic educational experiences were those that sprang from a child's natural inclinations and were reinforced through innovative teaching and supportive surroundings, Dewey's philosophy provides a basis for individualized instruction, multiculturalism, and special education, as well as general education.

See also: LEARNING

Bibliography

Campbell, James. *Understanding John Dewey*. Peru, IL: Open Court Publishing, 1995.

"Chronology of Dewey's Life and Work." The Center for Dewey Studies. In the Southern Illinois University at Carbondale [web site]. 2001. Available from http://www.siu.edu/üdeweyctr/; INTERNET.

"A Short, Annotated Reading List." The Center for Dewey Studies. In the Southern Illinois University at Carbondale [web site]. 2001. Available from http://www.siu.edu/üdeweyctr/; INTERNET.

Donna M. Davis

John Dewey sought to provide educators with strategies for reaching students that would honor each child's individual strengths and interests. (Columbiana Collection, Columbia University Libraries)

DIALECTICAL PERSPECTIVES

Dialectical analysis originated with the theories of the philosopher Georg Hegel (1770–1831), who posited that conflict and change are the fundamentals of human life. Hegel's theories influenced modern dialectical perspectives, which are concerned with action and change occurring during cognitive development rather than development in universal stages. The foremost proponent of dialectical psychology was Lev Semanovich Vygotsky (1896–1934). He theorized that children's development always takes place in a social context and that the social environment always plays a significant role in all aspects of development. According to Vygotsky, development is organized and regulated by adults through interactions between the developing child and the adult. Higher mental functions first occur on a social level through social interactions and are then internalized by the child. This process is called the zone of proximal development, which is a bidirectional interaction where a child performs beyond his or her skills with the support and direction of an adult.

See Also: COGNITIVE DEVELOPMENT

Bibliography

Clarke-Stewart, Alison, Susan Friedman, and Joanne Koch. *Child Development: A Topical Approach.* New York: John Wiley and Sons, 1985.

Damon, William, ed. *The Handbook of Child Psychology,* Vol.1: *Theoretical Models of Human Development.* New York: John Wiley and Sons, 1998.

Raymond Buriel
Terri De Ment

DISCIPLINE

Discipline is the practice of guiding children's behavior toward an acceptable direction as judged by parents, teachers, and society. Discipline can take many different forms, including corporal punishment, which is characterized by physical contact between the parent (or teacher or some other adult) and the child; time-out, where the child is removed from the setting in which the misbehavior occurred; and nonphysical punishment, where an unpleasant, but not physical, consequence follows the behavior. While discipline can take many forms, the results of many studies indicate that nonphysical punishment, accompanied by an explanation, is most effective in changing a child's behavior. Physical punishment sets a poor role model to resolve conflicts and deal with problems, and suppresses but does not replace misbehavior.

See also: CORPORAL PUNISHMENT; PARENTING

Bibliography

"Alternatives to Discipline." Available from http://childparenting.about.com/parenting/childparenting/gi/dynamic/offsite.htm?site=http//www.awareparenting.comtwenty.htm; INTERNET.

"How to Discipline Children." Available from http://childparenting.about.com/parenting/childparenting/library/blhowto.htm; INTERNET.

Kennedy, Rodney Wallace. *The Encouraging Parent: How to Stop Yelling at Your Kids and Start Teaching Them Confidence, Self-Discipline, and Joy.* New York: Three Rivers Press, 2001.

Neil J. Salkind

DIVORCE

Changing economic and social conditions at the beginning of the twentieth century created public concern about family breakdown and ushered in the scientific study of marriage and the family. Central to this emerging science was the identification of the causes, correlates, and consequences of marital dissolution. Increased divorce rates over the course of the century ensured continued focus on this topic and resulted in a large body of research on the impact of divorce on children.

Divorce Rates and Demographics

Divorce rates in the United States showed an upward trend from the late nineteenth century to the late twentieth century, rising from 0.3 divorces per 1,000 people in 1867, the first year for which national data are available, to a peak of 5.3 per 1,000 people during the period from 1979 to 1981. In the 1980s the divorce rate stabilized and began trending downward, with a figure of 4.4 divorces per 1,000 people recorded for 1995. It is projected that approximately one-half of the first marriages of the baby boom generation will end in divorce but that the rate will decline to 40 percent for the generations that followed the baby boomers. The median length of a first marriage that ends in divorce is eight years, and three out of four men and two out of three women remarry. Divorce is a more likely outcome for second marriages; approximately 60 percent end in divorce after a median length of five to six years.

Several factors increase the probability of divorce. Briefly, divorce rates are almost twice as high for black as for white families, two to four times higher for individuals who marry while in their teens, about 50 percent higher for couples who lived together prior to marriage, and about 25 percent higher for individuals whose own parents were unmarried at their birth or whose parents were separated prior to the individual turning sixteen. Higher education levels are related to lower divorce rates, which is due in part to the tendency for more highly educated individuals to marry later and to have been raised in intact families. Families with one or two children are less likely to divorce than those without children or those with more than two children. Divorce rates in families with a preschool child are about half of those for childless families and lower than those for families with school-age children; however, this protective effect may be limited to firstborns. Thus, the likelihood that a child will experience a divorce depends on a number of social and demographic factors.

Impact of Divorce on Children

Researchers have consistently found that children from divorced families score significantly lower on a variety of indexes of well-being compared to children from two-parent families. An analysis of ninety-two studies involving 13,000 children found, however, that the differences are small, ranging from .08 of a standard deviation for psychological adjustment (e.g., depression, anxiety) to .23 for conduct problems (e.g., aggression, delinquency). Intermediate-sized differences were found for academic achievement (.16), social adjustment (.12), and self-concept (.09). Similar differences emerged across thirty studies conducted in the 1990s.

These findings may not appear to justify the strong public concern expressed about the harmful effects of divorce on children. But despite these small differences, some children experience serious problems following parental divorce. For example, in large nationally representative samples, researchers have found that children whose parents divorce are twice as likely to see a mental health professional compared to children from two-parent families. But receipt of mental health services may over- or underestimate psychological problems. It is therefore worth noting that on a widely used measure of child adjustment, approximately 20 percent of boys and 25 percent to 30 percent of girls who had experienced parental divorce showed clinically significant problems compared to approximately 10 percent of children from two-parent families. These data show that children from divorced families are at risk for serious problems but that resilience is the most common outcome. In fact a handful of studies even document positive outcomes for children when their parents divorce.

How a Child's Age Affects Divorce's Impact

Various theories of child development suggest that children younger than age five or six are particularly vulnerable to the effects of parental separation. The disruption of attachment relations, combined with the child's limited cognitive abilities to understand divorce, is central to this vulnerability. Although most children are young when their parents separate because divorce risk is greater earlier in marriage (of all children who experience divorce by age twelve, 66% experience it by age six), preschoolers and infants are the least studied groups in the divorce literature. In fact, data on developmental differences in response to parental separation are surprisingly limited.

The ninety-two-study analysis described earlier found roughly equal differences among children in preschool, elementary school, and high school for most outcome measures. But analyzing studies that assess children of different ages at a single point in time confounds children's age at the time of divorce with the amount of time elapsed since the divorce, both of which could account for the results. Data from a large, nationally representative sample of children have been used to avoid this problem. These data demonstrated that children showed greater adjustment with increasing age (e.g., birth to age five, age six to ten, age eleven to sixteen), with the youngest age group being the most severely affected by divorce. Importantly, however, age differences were statistically significant on only one of the nineteen measures used. In sum, robust age-at-separation effects, such as gender effects, have not been empirically demonstrated. Clinical observations, however, show that children's concerns resulting from parental separation and how they express their concerns do vary with age.

Although on average, children from divorced and continuously married homes differ, more striking is the considerable overlap in the distribution of functioning in these two groups. Perhaps the most salient feature found through research is the individual variability in the impact of divorce on children. To gain a deeper understanding, one therefore must go beyond group comparisons to investigate the time course, moderators, and mediators of children's adaptation after divorce and clearly recognize that divorce is a process that begins prior to the physical separation of parents and may continue long after. Although the separation may be the single most salient event in the divorce process for children, it represents just one of a long series of events that may challenge their adaptation; the nature and number of events as well as what children bring to them is likely to account, in part, for the variability in child outcome.

Time Course of Children's Adaptation to Divorce

It is common for children to experience sadness, anxiety, anger, sleep disturbances, and other symptoms in the months following a parental separation. Indeed, for the first one to two years after divorce both boys and girls tend to show subclinical behavioral and emotional distress and are likely to be more oppositional, do more poorly in school, and have difficulties getting along with peers. After this "crisis" period abates, however, adjustment problems tend to decline but the gap in psychological well-being between offspring in divorced and continuously married families remains and may increase over time. Indeed, parental divorce continues to affect individuals into adulthood and is associated with multiple problems, including marital distress, low socioeconomic attainment, and poor subjective well-being. Individuals whose parents divorce are also more likely to get divorced themselves, which may reflect difficulties in developing satisfying interpersonal relationships or simply a greater tendency to see divorce as a viable option when marital difficulties arise. It is possible that divorce shapes children's attitudes and expectations about close relationships, which in turn influence their behavior in these relationships.

Variables That Moderate and Mediate the Impact of Divorce on Children

Many variables mediate or moderate the impact of divorce on children, including a conflicted relationship with a parent (especially the custodial parent), inept parenting, postdivorce economic hardship, interparental conflict, inadequate social support, and the number of negative life events experienced (e.g., moving, changing schools). Children who use active coping (e.g., seeking social support) and who do not blame themselves for the separation adjust better than those who cope via distraction or avoidance or who engage in self-blame. An analysis of sixty-three studies suggested that contact with noncustodial fathers who exhibit authoritative parenting is related to beneficial child outcomes. There is mixed evidence on whether parental remarriage benefits children.

Ameliorating the Impact of Divorce on Children

Access to therapeutic interventions, especially school-based support programs, is associated with improved postdivorce adjustment. Perhaps the greatest effort to help children has occurred through programs targeted at parents. A growing number of states are offering (or mandating) education or mediation programs for divorcing parents. Divorce mediation leads to speedier dispute resolution, greater compliance in payment of child support, and greater involvement of the father in the children's lives. Although parties who participate in mediation and in education programs tend to be satisfied with them, there is little evidence to suggest that they benefit children. But absence of evidence is not equivalent to evidence of absence. Evaluation research is acutely needed to improve the efforts to help children whose parents separate.

See also: CHILD CUSTODY AND SUPPORT; MEDIATION

Bibliography

Allison, Paul, and Frank Furstenberg. "How Marital Dissolution Affects Children: Variations by Age and Sex." *Developmental Psychology* 25 (1989):540–549.

Amato, Paul. "The Consequences of Divorce for Adults and Children." *Journal of Marriage and the Family* 62 (2000):1269–1287.

Amato, Paul, and Bruce Keith. "Consequences of Parental Divorce for the Well-Being of Children: A Meta-Analysis." *Psychological Bulletin* 110 (1991):26–46.

Cherlin, Andrew, P. Lindsay Chase-Lansdale, and Christine McRae. "Effects of Divorce on Mental Health throughout the Life Course." *American Sociological Review* 63 (1998):239–249.

Emery, Robert. "Divorce Mediation: Negotiating Agreements and Renegotiating Relationships." *Family Relations* 44 (1995):377–383.

Emery, Robert. *Marriage, Divorce, and Children's Adjustment,* 2nd edition. Thousand Oaks, CA: Sage, 1999.

Grych, John, and Frank D. Fincham. "Interventions for Children of Divorce: Toward Greater Integration of Research and Action." *Psychological Bulletin* 110 (1992):434–454.

Hetherington, E. Mavis, and W. Glen Clingempeel. *Coping with Marital Transitions: A Family Systems Perspective* 57 (1992):1–242.

Sweet, James, and Larry Bumpass. "Disruption of Marital and Cohabitation Relationships: A Social Demographic Perspective." In T. Orbuch ed., *Close Relationship Loss: Theoretical Perspectives.* New York: Springer-Verlag, 1992.

Wallerstein, Judith, and Joan Kelley. *Surviving the Breakup: How Children Actually Cope with Divorce.* New York: Basic, 1980.

Frank D. Fincham

DOMESTIC VIOLENCE

In general, the term "domestic violence" refers to violence that occurs in the home. Although violence in the home can be directed toward children, the elderly, or other household members, most often this term is used to represent violence between adolescents and/or adults who are currently or were previously involved in a romantic or intimate relationship. Domestic violence occurs between spouses, ex-spouses, and couples who are dating or who dated previously. The violence between these individuals is not limited to the home setting and may occur in locations outside the home as well.

Types of Violence

Domestic violence can involve physical, sexual, emotional, and psychological forms of abuse. Physical violence can include but is not limited to pushing, kicking, slapping, punching, and choking, and the use of objects to inflict pain upon the other person. Individuals may inflict sexual violence upon their partners by forcing them to have sex against their will, using sexual acts to degrade them, inflicting physical pain during sexual intercourse, calling their partners sexually degrading names, and requiring them to engage in sex with other individuals. Violence can also be enacted in the form of emotional and psychological abuse with the use of tactics such as intimidation, insults, threat of harm, isolation, and control of financial resources by the abuser.

Incidence

Violence between intimate partners occurs among people at all socioeconomic and education levels and within all ethnic, racial, religious, age, and sexual identity groups. The U.S. Department of Justice estimated that in 1998 about one million violent crimes were committed against persons by their current or former intimate partners. The majority of these crimes (85%) were committed against women, with women aged sixteen to twenty-four experiencing the highest rate of violence. The Federal Bureau of

Investigation reported that 32 percent of female murder victims in 1999 were murdered by a husband or boyfriend, while 3 percent of male victims were murdered by a wife or girlfriend. In 2001 the U.S. Department of Health and Human Services estimated that approximately one-fourth of all hospital emergency room visits by women resulted from domestic assault.

Although estimates are available as to the incidence of violent crimes occurring between intimate partners, many consider the figures to underrepresent the actual rates of occurrence. Victims of domestic violence may refrain from reporting abuse for a variety of reasons including a belief that it is a "private matter," fear of retaliation by the abuser, a desire to avoid feelings of shame, or a belief that the police could not effectively intervene. It has been suggested that individuals at higher socioeconomic status levels may be especially underrepresented in rates of occurrence because they have access to additional resources and do not need to rely as heavily on assistance from the police.

Impact on Victims and Children

The impact of domestic violence on victims varies according to the intensity and the type of violence inflicted. Victims may need to seek medical attention for injuries; may experience psychological problems such as depression and anxiety; and may even die as a result of the abuse. The children of victims may also be negatively affected through exposure to such violence. Children who witness domestic violence may experience feelings of depression and anxiety, have difficulty interacting with other children, and display increased rates of aggression. Some research suggests that children exposed to domestic violence may have an increased risk of becoming a victim or victimizer in future relationships. Children in violent families are also at greater risk for being abused themselves. Nevertheless, even though domestic violence can have serious consequences on the physical and emotional well-being of children, not all children exposed to violence will be affected to the same extent. Researchers have been limited in their ability to study the range of effects on children because the researchers often focus their studies on children in shelters, who may display more severe problems than other children. Additionally, it is difficult to determine the number of children who witness violence because the rates of occurrence available are only estimates that may underrepresent certain populations.

Causes of Domestic Violence

Not only is it challenging to determine the impact of violence on children, but determining the cause of

domestic violence is also complex. Nevertheless, three general approaches attempt to examine possible reasons for violent behavior between individuals who are or have been intimately involved.

Individual Characteristics

One approach focuses on the characteristics of the individuals in the relationship. This approach studies psychological characteristics associated with the violent individual and the victim. Although one attribute by itself will not necessarily explain the characteristics of an abuser or a victim, it is thought that the examination of all attributes combined will help to predict which individuals may be predisposed to be violent or to become a victim of violence.

According to the first theoretical approach, characteristics associated with individuals who abuse their partners include low self-esteem, isolation from social support, a manipulative nature, and a desire for power and control (Kakar 1998). These individuals are likely to be unable to cope with stress, be unwilling to take responsibility for their own actions, have extreme feelings of jealousy and possessiveness, be overly dependent on the victim, and/or have certain mental or psychological disorders. Additionally, some studies have indicated that violent individuals are more likely to abuse drugs or alcohol. The use of controlled substances, however, has not been shown to necessarily cause violence.

The characteristics that have been associated with the victims of violence are used to explain why individuals would become involved with and/or remain in a relationship with an abusive person. Attributes associated with the victim include low self-esteem; isolation from social support; feelings of shame, guilt, and self-blame; and mental illness such as depression. Some researchers suggest that victims experience feelings of helplessness that prevent them from leaving the relationship. After repeated failures of escape, victims believe that they cannot escape the relationship and resign themselves to remain in the violent atmosphere.

Another theory used to explain why victims remain in abusive relationships proposes that violence occurs in a cycle. This theory, first introduced by Lenore Walker in 1979, contains three main phases: (1) tension-building, (2) acute battering incident, and (3) calm, loving respite. The first phase includes minor incidents of abuse such as verbal attacks. During this stage the victim submits to the wishes of the violent individual in order to appease the attacker. The second phase contains more severe abuse and is followed by the third phase or the "honeymoon period." In the last phase, the abuser becomes loving and attentive and apologizes profusely for the attack. The victim

Women and children living together in a shelter for victims of domestic violence. Many cases of domestic violence and abuse go unreported for fear of retaliation by the victimizer. (Hulton-Deutsch Collection/Corbis)

believes that the violent behavior will stop and remains in the relationship. The tension-building occurs again, however, and the cycle repeats itself, leaving the victim to feel trapped and helpless.

Family Structure

Another approach to understanding domestic violence moves attention away from the individual and focuses on the structure of the family. In this approach, it is believed that certain characteristics put a family or a couple at risk for violence. Individuals who have witnessed violence within their own family as a child may be more likely to imitate similar behavior in their relationships as adults. At the same time, conditions exist that produce stress and conflict on the family. Factors such as low socioeconomic status; low-income occupations, which may result in frequent unemployment; and little to no social support from family, friends, or the community create high levels of stress. It is hypothesized that individuals who have learned to resolve conflict with violence use violence as a method of coping with these types of stressors (Flowers 2000).

Societal Perspective

A third approach takes a broader perspective than the previous two and examines domestic violence in the context of society and societal values. Violence against women is considered to be accepted by society as it has been supported through law and religion since the beginning of recorded time. This approach examines the traditional dominance of men

in society, which has condoned and even encouraged men to act violently toward women to maintain dominance and control over them. An unequal distribution of power in the relationships between men and women assigns women a lower status. From this position of subordination, women become dependent upon their spouses or partners and are subjected to the demands and abuse of their mates.

The societal perspective may help to explain the lack of public attention to problems of domestic violence and prosecution of abusers until the 1970s. Permission for violence by men against their wives has been reinforced through Western religion and law for centuries. Examples of spousal abuse can be found in the Bible and serve to justify a husband's right to control the behavior of his wife. During the Middle Ages, English common law allowed a husband to chastise his wife as long as he used a stick no larger than the width of his thumb, a concept commonly known as the "rule of thumb." Although legislation was enacted in the American colonies to outlaw domestic violence in 1641, with later laws originating in the late 1800s, the laws were not usually enforced and served only to curtail extreme cases of violence. It is purported that American society's apparent acceptance of domestic violence resulted from long-held beliefs in Western society that supported a husband's control of his wife and that discouraged intervention by the law.

Legislation and Support Services

Parallel to the women's movement in the 1970s, Americans began to demand tougher legislation and greater police intervention in cases of domestic violence. Since then, laws have been passed that allow police to make arrests without a warrant when probable cause is evident, require police to inform victims of their rights and provide assistance, and require mandatory arrests of offenders under certain conditions. Additional legislation allows victims to receive financial compensation for attacks, prohibits stalking, and also provides for easier prosecution of rape of a spouse (Flowers 2000).

Not only have laws been enacted to arrest and prosecute violent partners, but services for victims have also arisen in response to public concern. Victims of abuse may receive support through social service agencies that assist them in accessing medical care and mental health services. Shelters are available that allow victims to stay temporarily in a safe environment while they recover from abuse and search for new living arrangements. Some shelters have also extended their services to include counseling and educational programs for clients. In addition, victims may access hot lines manned by crisis counselors who can offer advice to the individual about the abusive situation and provide referrals to other support agencies. Attendance to victim support groups and meetings with clergy members also provide individuals with opportunities to analyze their current situation and examine means of escaping the abuse.

Although support services for victims have increased and tougher legislation against violent offenders has been enacted, domestic violence remains a significant problem in society. It affects not only the victims of the violence, but also the children who witness it and the community that must decide if and how to intervene. Determining the cause of domestic violence is complex, thereby making it difficult to find viable solutions. Nevertheless, the struggle continues to control and prevent a serious problem that pervades all levels of U.S. society.

See also: CHILD ABUSE; DIVORCE; VIOLENCE

Bibliography

Buzawa, Eve S., and Carl G. Buzawa. *Domestic Violence: The Criminal Justice Response,* 2nd edition. Thousand Oaks, CA: Sage, 1996.

Federal Bureau of Investigation. *Uniform Crime Report, 1999.* Washington, DC, 2001. Available from http://www.fbi.gov/ucr/99cius.htm; INTERNET.

Flowers, Ronald Barri. *Domestic Crimes, Family Violence, and Child Abuse: A Study of Contemporary American Society.* Jefferson, NC: McFarland, 2000.

Gordon, Judith S. *Helping Survivors of Domestic Violence: The Effectiveness of Medical, Mental Health, and Community Services.* New York: Garland, 1998.

Kakar, Suman. *Domestic Abuse: Public Policy/Criminal Justice Approaches towards Child, Spousal, and Elderly Abuse.* San Francisco: Austin and Winfield, 1998.

Kashani, Javad H., and Wesley D. Allan. *The Impact of Family Violence on Children and Adolescents.* Thousand Oaks, CA: Sage, 1998.

U.S. Department of Health and Human Services. "Administration for Children and Families Press Room Fact Sheet: Domestic Violence." Washington, DC, 2001. Available from http://www.acf.dhhs.gov/programs/opa/facts/domsvio.htm; INTERNET.

U.S. Department of Justice. "Bureau of Justice Statistics Special Report: Intimate Partner Violence." Washington, DC, 2000. Available from http://www.ojp.usdoj.gov/bjs/abstract/ipv.htm; INTERNET.

Walker, Lenore E. *The Battered Woman.* New York: Harper and Row, 1979.

Tracey R. Bainter

DOWN SYNDROME

Down syndrome, named after the physician Langdon Down, is the most common genetic form of mental retardation, occurring in 1 to 1.5 of every 1,000 live births. In approximately 95 percent of cases, Down syndrome results from an extra chromosome on the twenty-first of the twenty-three pairs of human chromosomes. Exactly what causes the addition of the extra chromosomal material associated with Down syndrome is not clear, although risk factors include maternal age and possibly paternal age. People with Down syndrome usually function in the moderate range of mental retardation, with IQs generally ranging from 40 to 55 on average, though IQs can sometimes be higher or lower. People with Down syndrome experience particular deficits in certain aspects of language development, particularly expressive language, articulation, and grammar. Despite these deficits, many individuals with Down syndrome have relatively good social skills.

See also: DEVELOPMENTAL DISABILITIES;
   MILESTONES OF DEVELOPMENT

Bibliography

Burack, Jake, Robert Hodapp, and Edward Zigler, eds. *Handbook of Mental Retardation and Development.* New York: Cambridge University Press, 1998.

Rondal, Jean, Juan Perera, Lynn Nadel, and A. Comblain. *Down Syndrome: Psychological, Psychobiological, and Socio-Educational Perspectives.* London: Whurr Publishers, 1996.

Sigman, Marian. "Developmental Deficits in Children with Down Syndrome." In Helen Tager Flusberg ed., *Neurodevelopmental Disorders: Developmental Cognitive Neuroscience.* Cambridge, MA: MIT Press, 1999.

Simonoff, E., P. Bolton, and M. Rutter. "Mental Retardation: Genetic Findings, Clinical Implications and Research Agenda." In M. Hertzig and E. Farber eds., *Annual Progress in Child Psychiatry and Child Development: 1997.* Philadelphia, PA: Brunner/Mazel, 1998.

David W. Evans

E

EAR INFECTIONS/OTITIS MEDIA

Otitis media, commonly called an ear infection, is the most frequent illness of early childhood except for the common cold. Otitis media is an inflammation of the middle ear. There are two types: (1) acute otitis media, an infection of the middle ear with accompanying fluid; and (2) otitis media with effusion, in which the middle ear fluid is not infected. Fluid in the middle ear can persist for several weeks or months after an infection is gone. Otitis media is more common in boys, children from low-income families, those exposed to tobacco smoke, bottle-fed children (compared to breast-fed children), and children who are under two years of age and attend child care. In most cases, otitis media is accompanied by mild to moderate hearing loss (equivalent to plugging one's ears with a finger), which goes away once the fluid resolves. Some studies have shown that frequent hearing loss in children with otitis media may lead to speech, language, and school difficulties. Other studies, however, have failed to find these associations. Researchers are still studying the otitis media developmental linkage. Special attention should be paid to the hearing and language development of children who have frequent otitis media.

See also: LANGUAGE ACQUISITION DEVICE

Bibliography

Paradise, Jack. L., Christine A. Dollaghan, Thomas F. Campbell, Heidi M. Feldman, Beverly S. Bernard, Kathleen Colborn, Howard E. Rockette, Janine E. Janoky, Dayna L. Pitcairn, Diane L. Sabo, Marcia Kurs-Lasky, and Clyde G. Smith. "Language, Speech Sound Production, and Cognition in Three-Year-Old Children in Relation to Otitis Media in Their First Three Years of Life." *Pediatrics* 105 (2000):1119–1130.

Roberts, Joanne E., Margaret R. Burchinal, Sandra C. Jackson, Stephen R. Hooper, Jack Roush, Martha Mundy, Eloise Neebe, and Susan A. Zeisel. "Otitis Media in Early Childhood in Relation to Preschool Language and School Readiness Skills among African-American Children." *Pediatrics* 106 (2000):1–11.

Stool, Sylvan E., Alfred O. Berg, Stephen Berman, Cynthia J. Carney, James R. Cooley, Larry Culpepper, Roland Eavey, Lynne Feagans, Terese Finitzo, Ellen Friedman, et al. *Otitis Media with Effusion in Young Children: Clinical Practice Guideline, Number 12.* Rockville, MD: Agency for Health Care Policy and Research, Public Health Service, U.S. Department of Health and Human Services, 1994.

Joanne E. Roberts

EARLY INTERVENTION PROGRAMS

Early intervention programs provide special services to children from birth through age five who are at-risk or have special needs. The scope of these programs may also include the child's family. Early intervention services and programs focus on the areas of cognition (thinking skills), speech/language, motor skills, self-help skills, and social-emotional development. It is not uncommon to find programs that also include services such as nursing, social work, nutrition, and counseling. For example, the Head Start early intervention program offers two meals a day to children as part of its nutritional services.

Professionals, including early intervention teachers, occupational therapists, physical therapists, and speech-language pathologists, usually provide these services. A governing agency generally oversees the running of these programs, their services, and the service providers.

How Children Qualify for Early Intervention

There are several ways children can participate in an early intervention program. The most common way is by having their level of development assessed using a formal, standardized assessment. Individual states have regulations regarding the use of these assessments and their role in qualifying children for early intervention services. Children are also eligible to receive early intervention services if they have a known disability, such as Down syndrome, which carries the likelihood that a delay in later development will occur. Finally, in most states, professionals who work with children may recommend that a child receive early intervention services based on their professional judgment.

With the passage of Public Law 94-142 in 1977, now called the Individuals with Disabilities Education Act (IDEA), the federal government requires that states provide early intervention services for children from birth through age five. In most circumstances, these services are provided free of charge to families.

In addition to focusing on children with special needs, the federal government in the 1990s began increasing its early intervention focus on programs for children who are at-risk because of their socioeconomic status as well as other risk factors such as an unstable home environment, including the presence of violence and drug abuse. For children who are at-risk, the most common way to qualify for an early intervention program is for the family's income to be below a certain dollar threshold.

How Early Intervention Programs Work

Early intervention services and programs take many forms. The philosophy behind the delivery of these services is to serve the child and the family in the most natural setting. Many children are provided early intervention services in their home, a home child-care setting, a preschool setting, or a combination of these. Services can be provided on an individual basis or in a group, and good early intervention programs include a strong parental component that supports the family while giving the family information about issues the family views as important.

The Foundation of Early Intervention

A growing awareness of the importance of the early years and their long-lasting impact on future development began in the early twentieth century and continued into the early twenty-first century. Building upon that awareness, the idea took hold that providing children with a solid, stimulating foundation in the early years can greatly affect their development. The results of brain research captured the attention of child development specialists in the 1990s. The extent to which a child develops is no longer thought to be due only to the child's genetic makeup. Professionals now believe that how a person's brain, and consequently the rest of the person, develops is based on the interaction between the person's environment and the genes the person was born with. The classic study conducted by two psychologists H. H. Skeels and H. B. Dye in Iowa orphanages in 1939 supports the knowledge scientists have in the early twenty-first century. The results of this study revealed that children in the orphanages who interacted with women with mental retardation improved their IQ scores dramatically, while those who did not receive any interaction or stimulation did not gain any IQ points. In fact, the latter children lost IQ points when given the same standardized test.

In addition to understanding the importance of the environment and early experiences, scientists know that the brain's capacity for learning is not fixed in the early years but can actually increase as a result of early intervention. For example, if an at-risk child with a language delay receives early intervention services, she can often overcome this delay and do just as well as her peers in school. By contrast, if a child has a language delay and does not receive any early intervention services, not only will she fail to close this gap, but the gap will also often widen, leading to further learning difficulties throughout her life. Scientists also believe there are certain times in a child's development that are critical periods for learning certain skills. Although children and adults can acquire new skills throughout their lives, windows of opportunity in the early years open and then close, thus affecting development.

A Successful Early Intervention Program: Head Start

As early intervention programs have grown in popularity and number over the years, several stand out as exceptional programs. Probably the best-known early intervention program for children is Head Start. The Head Start program was developed in 1965 by the federal government as an effort to combat poverty in the United States. Head Start con-

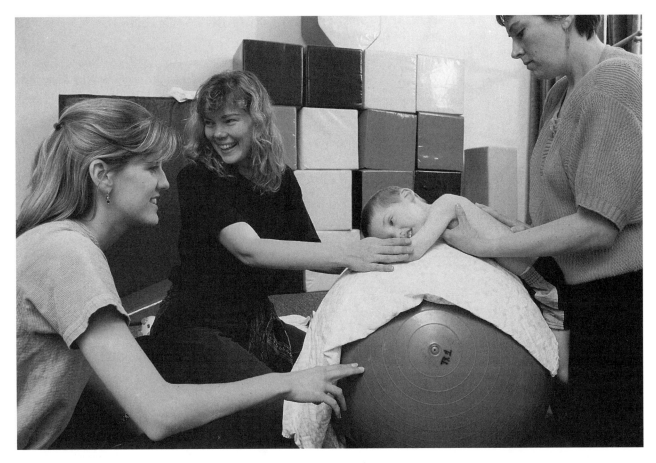

A physical therapist massages a young boy by rolling him on an inflatable ball while another physical therapist steadies it. Early intervention strategies, such as physical therapy, can help children overcome developmental disabilities. (Owen Franken/Corbis)

tains four basic principles: (1) the provision of a high-quality early childhood education; (2) the promotion of good health through the treatment of health problems and by providing children with good health care; (3) the active participation of parents in the programs in which their children participate; and (4) the use by families of social services in the community when needed. Head Start has expanded over the years and at the beginning of the twenty-first century included the Early Start Program, which serves infants and toddlers, and the American Indian Head Start and Migrant Head Start Programs.

The Effectiveness of Early Intervention Programs

Another well-known early intervention program is the High/Scope Perry Preschool Study conducted in Ypsilanti, Michigan, from 1962 to 1967. Few early intervention programs have tracked the outcomes of its participants as well as this study has. This program divided African-American children born into poverty and at-risk for failing in school into two groups. One group participated in a high quality early interven-

tion program, one that had well-trained teachers and a curriculum focusing on developmentally appropriate activities; the other group received no early intervention services. The immediate results and the results over time have shown that the children receiving early intervention services were far more successful than the children who did not. At age twenty-seven, participants in the study who received early intervention services were found to have a higher level of income earned per month, a higher level of education completed, a lower arrest rate, and a higher home ownership rate than the children who did not receive early intervention services. Over the lifetime of the participants, project researchers estimate that society has received more than $7 for every $1 invested.

The Effectiveness of Early Intervention Services for Children with Special Needs

The effectiveness of early intervention services for children with special needs has been remarkable. People with disabilities and the members of their families report that early intervention services increased their quality of life. In addition, the results of research have demonstrated that when children with special needs receive early intervention services, they tend to live more productive lives, score higher on standardized assessments, and contribute more to society. Often, the effects of their disability are lessened while new skills are learned. Children with disabilities who receive early intervention are less likely to develop a secondary disability as a result of not attending to the primary disability. For example, a child with a visual impairment is often delayed in cognitive and motor skills because he does not use the environment as a learning tool. Early intervention services can minimize these secondary delays by teaching the child to explore the environment and learn.

Public Support for Early Intervention Programs

While the level of public support for early intervention programs is sometimes in dispute, primarily because of their cost, the effectiveness of such programs is not. Children who have participated in an early intervention program tend to spend less time in special education, tend to be retained a grade less often, and tend to stay in school and graduate. Although U.S. society was not funding early intervention programs for children at-risk to the extent that would make them commonplace in communities, early intervention programs and the effectiveness of them were beginning at the dawn of the twenty-first century to gain recognition in the public's eye.

Politicians often place increased funding of these programs on their political agendas. In addition, some states are now moving toward offering state-funded preschool programs to all four-year-olds in an effort to follow the national trend of getting children ready to learn. Early intervention programs such as the one included in the High/Scope Perry Preschool study illustrate that the cost factor over time appears to outweigh the cost of funding these programs. Early intervention programs have, over time, proven to make a difference in the lives of children and their families.

See also: HEAD START

Bibliography
"Children Champions." In the National Association for the Education of Young Children [web site]. Washington, DC, 2000. Available from http://www.naeyc.org/default.htm; INTERNET.

Peterson, Nancy L. *Early Intervention for Handicapped and At-Risk Children.* Denver: Love Publishing, 1987.

Shonkoff, Jack P., and Samuel J. Meisels. *Handbook of Early Intervention.* Cambridge, Eng.: Cambridge University Press, 2000.

Erin L. Smith-Bird

EGOCENTRISM

According to Swiss developmental psychologist Jean Piaget, egocentrism is the tendency of children to cognize their environment only in terms of their own point of view. Piaget theorized that the degree of egocentrism is directly related to the child's level of cognitive development. In the infant stage (birth to age two) children are just learning to recognize and interact with the environment and are thus completely egocentric. In the toddler and preschool stages (ages two to six) children are able to represent the world to themselves in symbols and images but are unable to distinguish their point of view from that of others. In the middle childhood stage (ages six to twelve) children develop greater cognitive abilities and therefore have declining levels of egocentrism and are able to visualize a situation from another's point of view. In the adolescent stage (ages twelve to nineteen) egocentrism further declines as individuals develop the ability for fully abstract thought and are thus able to analyze a situation from many perspectives.

See also: COGNITIVE DEVELOPMENT; PIAGET, JEAN

Bibliography
Piaget, Jean. *The Construction of Reality in the Child.* New York: Basic Books, 1954.

Richard J. Castillo

EMOTIONAL DEVELOPMENT

When you're drawing up your list of life's miracles, you might place near the top the first moment your baby smiles at you . . . Today, she looked right at me. And she smiled . . . Her toothless mouth opened, and she scrunched her face up and it really was a grin . . . The sleepless nights, the worries, the crying—all of a sudden it was all worth it . . . She is no longer just something we are nursing and carrying along—somewhere inside, part of her knows what's going on, and that part of her is telling us that she's with us (Greene 1985, pp. 33–34).

In his journal of the early years of his daughter's life, reporter Bob Greene depicted the important roles that emotions play in children's development. He noted the impact that his daughter's first smile had on him, washing away the worry and fatigue of early parenting. He also revealed the belief that emotions make us human and contribute significantly to the meaning of relationships. His daughter's smile was interpreted to mean that she was gaining awareness of her environment. Moreover, her smile meant that she was no longer merely a creature who needed feeding and cleaning, but that she was telling him that "she's with us"—becoming an active contributor to family relationships.

Although the diary entry points out the importance of emotions in everyday life, a national survey released by the organization Zero to Three revealed that parents have relatively little knowledge and information about their children's emotional development. Although parents believed that what they did as parents had the greatest influence on their children's emotional development, they also said that they had the least information in this area.

This lack of information about children's emotional development may stem in part from emotions being internal processes that are difficult to study. Because of this, for many decades researchers ignored the study of emotions. More recently, the study of emotions and emotional development has seen a resurgence of interest as developmental scientists agree that the study of emotions is central to an understanding of child development. Additionally, more sophisticated methods have been developed to study emotions.

Historically, emotions have proved remarkably difficult to define. This might seem surprising given that emotions are such a common human phenomenon. Emotions have been considered to be synonymous with certain patterns of facial expression, physiological reactions, muscular feedback, or brain activity. None of these definitions has proved adequate, and emotions are now considered to be closely linked with what a person is trying to do: They reflect a person's attempt or readiness to establish, maintain, or change the relation between the person and his or her environment. For example, a child who overcomes obstacles to a goal is likely to experience happiness. In contrast, a child who has a goal blocked is likely to experience anger. A child who gives up a goal is likely to experience sadness. These are not the only ways that emotions can be generated, but this functional definition of emotion helps us understand that emotions organize and coordinate both intrapsychic (e.g., thoughts and motivations) and interpersonal (e.g., social interactions) processes.

Emotional Development in Infancy and Toddlerhood

There is a fair amount of consensus that distress, pleasure, anger, fear, and interest are among the earliest emotions experienced by infants, although exactly when these emotions appear is still debated. As infants develop, emotions become more differentiated. For example, the earliest smiles are reflexive and

often occur during sleep. By six months, smiling is more sophisticated and social. It increasingly results from the interactions between infants and their caregivers. Crying is another powerful emotional behavior that is present in early development and is an effective tool for communicating with the social world. Children cry more during infancy than at any other period and their cries differ in their patterns depending on whether they are in pain, hungry, or angry.

Infants also have strategies for regulating their emotions. Research by Sarah Mangelsdorf and her colleagues indicates that from six to eighteen months, infants' emotional regulation strategies change. Although gaze aversion and sucking characterize younger infants' responses to a distressing situation, older infants are better able to engage in self-soothing or distract themselves.

Emotions and Early Relationships

It is clear that parents play an important role in children's emotional development. Through relationships with caregivers, children develop a sense of themselves and of others, and get clues about the way that the world works. For example, an infant who has fallen down and is unsure of whether he is hurt may look to his parent for information. Social referencing provides an infant with an opportunity to get feedback from a caregiver about how to feel in an uncertain situation.

Joseph Campos and his colleagues studied young children's fear of heights using a clever apparatus known as the "visual cliff" (which has a pane of glass over a visible drop-off). Fear or wariness of heights does not emerge until after some experience with crawling—it is not inborn. New crawlers will crawl over what appears to be a cliff, whereas infants with a month or two of crawling experience will not. Importantly, parents' facial expressions can also encourage infants to cross the cliff or stay in place. An infant who sees her mother display a fear expression will not cross, whereas a happy expression will encourage movement across the cliff. Thus, children can learn how to feel in emotional situations by observing their parents' reactions, and many of the common fears (such as fear of spiders) are thought to be learned in this way.

Stanley Greenspan detailed a series of emotional stages during infancy and toddlerhood that span the course of development from self-regulation to emotional understanding. He believes that the key to healthy emotional development is based on the "fit" between the parent's style of interaction and the interactive style and needs of the child. Take the case of a highly irritable infant and a highly negative and demanding parent. This may be a more challenging relationship than one between the same highly irritable infant and a more positive and flexible parent. The fit between parent and child may also contribute to the security of the attachment between infants and their parents. By working with parents to help them overcome difficulties in their parenting styles, parents can discover how to better meet the emotional needs of their young children.

Self-Conscious Emotions

Around eighteen months of age, toddlers develop a more sophisticated sense of self that is marked by self-recognition and the emergence of self-conscious emotions, such as shame, pride, and embarrassment. Michael Lewis developed a poignant method to study this development. A toddler is placed in front of a mirror and then the parent wipes some rouge on the child's nose before moving the child back to the mirror. Although children under eighteen months are unlikely to show signs of embarrassment at the rouge on their nose, children between eighteen and twenty-four months do. Self-recognition makes possible a more sophisticated understanding of the self and brings about new levels of emotional development.

Emotional Development during Childhood

During childhood, children's emotionality becomes more advanced. Their emotionality is focused less on themselves, and their advanced cognitive skills allow for more sophisticated responses when emotions are experienced.

Vicarious Emotional Responding

As noted earlier, emotions are viewed as important determinants and consequences of interactions with others. Thus, emotions can be caused by observing and recognizing what is happening to others. For example, when five-year-old Rachel became sad when her infant sister cried because she was sick, Rachel's feeling of sadness was the result of the condition of her sister rather than what was happening directly to herself. This type of emotional responding is known as vicarious emotional responding—responses that occur because of exposure to someone else's emotional state.

Janet Strayer and Nancy Eisenberg identified different types of vicarious emotional responses. For example, empathy is an emotional state that matches another person's emotional state—feeling bad because someone else is feeling bad. In contrast, sympathy refers to feeling sorry or concerned for others because of their emotional states or conditions. When Rachel felt sad when her sister cried, she was display-

ing sympathy. Sympathy frequently, but not always, results from empathy.

Martin Hoffman found that empathy appears fairly early and increases across childhood. Although infants cannot distinguish their own feelings from those of others, they occasionally respond to others' emotions. For example, infants often cry when they hear another infant crying. During early childhood, children tend to act and think in ways that focus on their own needs and desires. They are likely to respond to another's emotional distress in ways that they themselves find comforting. When three-year-old Ben saw his mother crying, he became sad and brought her his favorite stuffed animal to cheer her up. In this situation, Ben projected his own needs onto his mother.

As children develop the capacity to take the perspective of others, they increasingly become aware of other people's feelings. Until later childhood, however, children's empathic and sympathetic responses are limited to the feelings of familiar persons in familiar situations. Preschoolers, for example, are likely to be emotionally responsive to everyday events (such as getting hurt or being made fun of) that cause distress to familiar people or animals. During later childhood, the scope of children's concerns generalizes to conditions of unknown others who are less fortunate than themselves (such as the poor).

Childhood Anger

Anger is a common emotion at any developmental period. The causes of anger, however, change across childhood. For instance, at age five months, Carlos may become angry because he is hungry, with the anger occurring out of Carlos's basic needs not being met. At five years of age, however, Carlos may become angry because his sister took away his toy, with this anger resulting from Carlos's lack of control over the situation. Most of young children's anger occurs as a result of conflicts over materials, resources, and space. With age, anger is more likely to result from how one is treated. Thus, the causes of anger become increasingly social.

How children express anger also changes with age. For instance, when his sister took his toy away when he was age three, Carlos expressed his anger in the form of a tantrum. His mother, however, helped him find better ways to express his feelings, and by age six Carlos is able to tell his sister he is angry and request that she give him back his toy. As a result, the temper tantrums of the "terrible twos and threes" diminish as children find better ways to express their anger and make adjustments.

Language and Emotion

Before the age of two or three, children's expression of emotion occurs nonverbally, through facial, vocal, and gestural expressions. Once children develop the ability to use their words to express how they are feeling, they become better able to express, regulate, or explain their own (and others') emotions. The increased understanding that comes from the use of emotion language promotes, maintains, and regulates social interactions.

Emotion language has been found to emerge around twenty months and increases rapidly during the third year. By two years of age, children refer to a range of feeling states in themselves and others. Lois Bloom and her colleagues found that once children acquire the words for naming the emotions they are feeling, they begin to integrate these into their conversations. Because emotions are relevant and important, young children's talk often focuses on their emotional experiences.

Parents' use of emotion language has important consequences for children's emotional development. For example, when Kaneesha's mother saw her crying and asked her why she was sad, her mother had defined Kaneesha's emotional state. Repeated exposure to these labels can lead to differences in how children experience and express emotions. Parents, for instance, are more likely to talk about sadness and less likely to discuss anger with their daughters than their sons. After repeated exposure to these emotional labels, it is not be surprising that boys may be more likely to experience or express anger than girls, whereas girls are more likely to experience or express sadness. This pattern is consistent with common gender-emotion stereotypes in many Western countries.

Understanding Emotions

As cognitive development becomes more advanced, young children become increasingly aware of their own and others' emotions. As a result, children begin to develop a more complex understanding of the causes and consequences of emotions, how to control emotions, and the nature of emotional experiences. For example, although infants as young as one year of age can express ambivalence, a child's understanding of mixed emotions does not emerge until later in childhood. The work of Susan Harter and her colleagues has shown that children are first able to understand that people can experience two different, consecutive emotions (e.g., feeling scared and then feeling sad) at age six. Soon thereafter, children are capable of understanding that two related emotions of can co-occur (i.e., being both sad and afraid at the same time). By age ten, they are able to understand that mixed and unrelated emotions can occur simultaneously (e.g., feeling both happy and sad at the same time). This type of enhanced understanding gives children a better grasp of how emotions are tied to their social lives.

Two children leave flowers at London's Kensington Palace following the death of Princess Diana. As children develop the capacity to take the perspective of others, they increasingly become aware of other people's feelings, such as grief and sadness. (David & Peter Turnley/Corbis)

Emotional Development during Adolescence

Emotional development continues once children reach adolescence. In fact, emotions have often been used to define the period of adolescence. For some people, the changes associated with adolescence conjure up pictures of strong emotions—a developmental period characterized as a time when teens become moody and negative. These images, however, are accurate for only a minority of adolescents. Most adolescents cope with the changes in emotionally positive ways.

When emotional stress does arise, it often is the result of adolescents' conflicts with their parents. These conflicts frequently occur because adolescents are striving to make independent choices and do not agree with parents' requests and opinions as readily as they did when they were younger. Conversations about general household tasks and curfews can be potentially volatile—for instance, when a young person's desire to stay out late with his friends conflicts with the parents' needs to make sure their child is safe and home at a reasonable hour.

Although adolescents' conflicts over family issues can have an emotional impact, emotional extremes more often center on interactions with peers, particularly romantic partners. These extreme feelings are tied to the adolescent's self-perceptions, sometimes producing feelings of worthlessness and sometimes eliciting strong joy and desire. Depending on the unique characteristics of the young person, the availability of parental support, and the amount and kind of stress in an adolescent's life, some teens are able to surmount difficult emotional situations, whereas others may despair.

Emotion and Autonomy/Identify Formation

During this transition period, adolescents confront the challenge of developing autonomy—the capacity to think, feel, and act on their own. The quest for autonomy not only involves separation from parents and the development of self-reliance but also raises issues related to emotionality. One aspect of autonomy involves the need for the adolescent to realize that her emotions are independent from those of her parents, a process referred to as "emotional autonomy." During this period, adolescents may feel pulled between the need for close emotional ties with their parents and the need to develop their own emotional responses. For parents, the difficulty arises as to how to encourage emotional autonomy and independence while avoiding tension and conflict. If parents and teens can compromise and adapt during this period of change, it can be a positive time of exploration for both.

Anxiety and Depression

When emotional development becomes distorted, outcomes for children and teens can be put at risk. If not effectively dealt with, unresolved issues of emotional development can lead to more serious emotional disorders. At least one in five children and adolescents displays symptoms of emotional disorders, with anxiety and depression as the most common types.

Anxiety disorders include, among others, panic disorder, obsessive-compulsive disorder, and phobias (excessive fears). Although most children encounter feelings of anxiety or fear, these usually do not become debilitating. Anxiety disorders generally have an onset early in childhood and persist into adulthood. Additionally, anxiety disorders may become exacerbated over time and sometimes lead to other disorders, such as depression.

Depression is generally characterized by hopelessness, low self-esteem, and sadness, and not only affects children's emotionality but also their physical well-being. Beginning in the 1970s, the age of onset of depression started decreasing, and by the early twenty-first century, depression commonly begins during adolescence. Estimates of clinical depression range from 4 percent to 12 percent of adolescents, with older adolescents having higher rates. Before puberty, rates of depression are low and occur equally in boys and girls. After puberty, girls report increased depression, with rates about twice those of boys.

Evidence is growing that problems with hormonal activity in the brain and nervous system often result in depression. The onset of puberty and associated hormonal changes may influence adolescents' emotional states. Also, some teens seem more prone to depression because they have cognitive styles in which they define their circumstances in terms of hopelessness and self-blame.

Summary

Beginning in infancy and spanning the course of childhood and adolescence, emotionality represents a critical aspect of development. Although the precise factors that affect emotional development vary from individual to individual, emotions influence how children relate to others, how they feel about themselves, and the direction in which development proceeds. The study of emotional development in children and adolescents is incomplete, however. Researchers are only beginning to better understand the interplay between children's life experiences and the complex developmental and emotional tasks they face.

See also: MILESTONES OF DEVELOPMENT; STAGES OF DEVELOPMENT

Bibliography

Bloom, Lois, and J. Capatides. "Expression of Affect and the Emergence of Language." *Child Development* 58 (1987):1513–1522.

Campos, Joseph J., B. I. Bertenthal, and R. Kermoian. "Early Experience and Emotional Development: The Emergence of Wariness of Heights." *Psychological Science* 3 (1992):61–64.

Greene, Bob. *Good Morning, Merry Sunshine.* New York: Penguin, 1985.

Greenspan, Stanley I., and N. T. Greenspan. *First Feelings: Milestones in the Emotional Development of Your Baby and Child.* New York: Viking Penguin, 1985.

Harter, Susan, and B. J. Buddin. "Children's Understanding of the Simultaneity of Two Emotions: A Five-Stage Developmental Acquisition Sequence." *Developmental Psychology* 23 (1987):388–399.

Hoffman, Martin L. "Empathy, Its Development and Prosocial Implications." In C. B. Keasey ed., *Nebraska Symposium on Motivation*, Vol. 25. Lincoln: University of Nebraska Press, 1978.

Lewis, Michael. "Self-Conscious Emotions: Embarrassment, Pride, Shame, and Guilt." In Michael Lewis and J. M. Haviland eds., *Handbook of Emotions.* New York: Guilford Press, 1993.

Mangelsdorf, Sarah C., J. R. Shapiro, and D. Marzolf. "Developmental and Temperamental Differences in Emotion Regulation in Infancy." *Child Development* 66 (1995):1817–1828.

Strayer, Janet, and Nancy Eisenberg. "Empathy Viewed in Context." In Nancy Eisenberg and Janet Strayer eds., *Empathy and Its Development*. New York: Cambridge University Press, 1987.

Zero to Three. *What Parents Understand about Child Development*. Washington, DC: Zero to Three, 1997.

Richard A. Fabes
Cynthia A. Frosch
Amy Buchanan

Sroufe, L. Alan, Robert G. Cooper, and Ganie B. De Hart. *Child Development: Its Nature and Course*. New York: McGraw-Hill, 1996.

Strayer, J., and Schroeder, M. "Children's Helping Strategies: Influences of Emotion, Empathy, and Age." In Nancy Eisenberg ed., *Empathy and Related Emotional Responses*. San Francisco: Jossey-Bass, 1989.

Zahn-Waxler, Carolyn, Marian Radke-Yarrow, and R. King. "Child-Rearing and Children's Prosocial Initiations toward Victims of Distress." *Child Development* 50 (1979):319–330.

Joanne Bitetti
Jane Brown-O'Gorman

EMPATHY

Empathy is the ability to share another's emotional experience. It is a prosocial behavior that underlies altruism. Empathy, along with affection, gratitude, sympathy, and compassion, are complex social emotions that contribute to the moral behavior that cements society. Since empathy is an internal affective reaction, it has been inferred through various behaviors including emotional expression, social referencing, helping behavior, and self-report.

M. L. Hoffman has proposed a developmental theory of empathy that has at least four stages. In the first stage, emotional contagion, an infant will cry upon hearing the cries of another. At this stage, it is not clear whether the infant can distinguish who is in distress. The next stage emerges in the second year when a toddler, who can differentiate between self and other, will express egocentric empathy. Upon hearing the cry of another, the toddler will provide help that he himself would find comforting, such as offering his own favorite toy. The third stage appears in the third year as the child begins to take the perspective of another and can offer help that the other might need. Finally, in middle childhood, the fourth stage is achieved; the child realizes that he and others are independent persons whose emotions may be tied to their unique history of past events.

The development of empathy is influenced by cognitive development, the increasing ability to differentiate self and other and to take another's perspective. Children who receive nurturing from parents who model empathy and who explain the reasons behind moral behavior are more likely to demonstrate empathy.

See also: ALTRUISM; PERSONALITY DEVELOPMENT

Bibliography

Eisenberg, Nancy, ed. *Empathy and Related Emotional Responses*. San Francisco: Jossey-Bass, 1989.

Hoffman, M. L. "Development of Moral Thought, Feeling, and Behavior." *American Psychologist* 34 (1979):958–966.

Oatley, Keith, and Jennifer M. Jenkins. *Understanding Emotions*. Cambridge, MA: Blackwell, 1996.

EMPLOYMENT IN ADOLESCENCE

Youth employment is worthy of notice because the number of young workers is increasing in both developed and developing countries. Youth employment encompasses youths between the ages of fifteen and twenty-four working part-time or full-time for money, outside their family. Youths younger than fifteen working for money are regarded as child laborers; such labor is prohibited in many regions.

Youth laborers are, obviously, at the age of secondary schooling. Most of them take a part-time job to earn some pocket money after school. Some of them, mostly academic underachievers, discontinue formal schooling and take up a full-time job. According to Catherine Loughlin and Julian Barling, half of the youths between the ages of seventeen and nineteen in the United States have part-time or full-time jobs. In addition, many senior secondary students work around twenty hours a week, and about 10 percent of senior secondary students work more than thirty-five hours a week, just like full-time workers. Julian Barling and E. Kevin Kelloway found that 25 percent of Canadian youths in the seventeen to nineteen age group work more than twenty hours a week. Similar results were found for a developed city in Asia, Hong Kong. The labor participation rate for Hong Kong youths was 25 percent for those fifteen to nineteen and 78 percent for those nineteen to twenty-four.

Young people who work go through a growing process that is influenced by their working experiences. The impacts of youth employment are quite controversial.

Job Nature

Generally, job nature is an important subject of youth employment. The most popular jobs for school-age youths include private tutoring, baby-sitting, and jobs that require few skills and offer low wages and little opportunity for further career development.

These jobs include food services, manual work, retail sales, building construction, office work, and grocery stores. In food services, youth may serve as cleaners, waiters/waitresses, and cashiers. Youths involved in manual work mostly operate simple machines that require no licenses (e.g., copying machine, paper shredder, lawn mower). Duties in retail sales are very simple, such as selling clothes or accessories and checking stocks.

Negative Impacts

Although the duties arranged for young employees are straightforward and simple, there are still some hidden dangers. The dangers might cause bodily as well as psychological harm. In particular, there are serious concerns about the impacts of working experiences on the youths' development. James R. Stone and Jeylan T. Mortimer emphasized in a 1998 article for the *Journal of Vocational Behavior* that early working experiences affect adolescents' mental health development in terms of adaptability. Many researchers have obtained both positive and negative outcomes of young employment. The most noteworthy result was that long working hours was particularly likely to cause negative impact on a youth's development. Adolescents who worked more than twenty hours a week were found to be more likely to have low academic standing, to abuse substances, and to be delinquent. Ellen Greenberger and Laurence Steinberg pointed out in their 1986 book *When Teenagers Work* that working adolescents engage in more deviant behaviors and school tardiness than adolescents who are not employed.

With reference to working adolescents' academic performance, M. R. Frone reviewed many articles and concluded that senior secondary students who spend more time working have poor results in their studies. The reason for this is that many of them cut down the time they spend on homework and study, as well as time spent participating in extracurricular activities. In essence, their school attachment declines, and the likelihood that they will pursue further education also declines, particularly for boys. The results of a 1995 study conducted by Linda P. Worley found that students working about three hours a week had good school results (an average grade point average [GPA] of 3.08). Those working ten to twenty hours a week achieved average grades (average GPA of 2.77). Students who worked more than twenty hours a week, however, had poor school results (average GPA of less than 2.5). Nevertheless, the students tended to deny the negative consequences. Out of 248 twelfth-graders, 62 percent said that working had no negative influence on their school results. Greenberger and Steinberg also found that the rate of school dropout

was comparatively low for students who worked fewer than twenty hours a week. Twenty working hours a week, therefore, seems to be the threshold for the negative impact of employment on school adaptability.

Positive Impacts

Although there are clear negative impacts of youth employment, working also entails some positive effects, especially for academic underachievers. Observers increasingly accept the notion that working contributes to the personality development of young people. Working enriches young people's life experiences, thereby enhancing self-confidence, self-responsibility, self-discipline, self-initiation, self-esteem, and independence. Greenberger and Steinberg also noted that young workers acquire some skills that are not provided in school. Workplaces offer young people a real-life environment to examine and practice the knowledge and skills that they learned in school. Moreover, young people have the opportunity to experience adult society, which contributes to their social development in such areas as organizing skills and socializing techniques. Working might also encourage them to keep up with their studies, particularly when an employer suggests that the young worker improve his grades. Above all, working experiences help young people think about their possible career trajectories. Frequently, young people are influenced by their early working experiences and sometimes choose a similar or relevant job in the future. For both boys and girls, youth employment results in definite rewards, such as income, employment opportunities, and career prestige.

Money from Working

Among the practical rewards of employment, income is the most important matter to youths. Young workers realize that money relates to most things in their daily life and that the relationship between time and money is very significant. When young people earn money through their labor, they learn that working is the right way to use up their time. Moreover, an issue related to money that should not be overlooked is how young people spend their money. In Greenberger and Steinberg's study, the researchers found that half of the senior secondary students spent most of their income on their own needs, such as clothes, accessories, audio entertainment, and social activities. The researchers also found that about 82 percent of the students did not use their incomes for family expenditures. Hence, young workers are free to use their income, and this provides opportunities to learn about: spending money, saving money, per-

A young waiter serves hamburgers and french fries at a diner in Japan. Jobs in the food service industry are very popular for adolescents. (Michael S. Yamashita/Corbis)

sonal finance arrangement, and the consequences of expenditures. All these areas help develop the person's character and individuality.

Parental Perspectives

Although employment offers many learning opportunities, the most difficult task for young workers is managing the pressure. The pressure might be caused by tight job schedules, poor working environments, boring tasks, conflicts with other roles, and autocratic supervisors. All are great challenges to young people whose abilities and mentalities are still immature. Some parents want to protect their children from such pressures so they will not allow their children to work. Other parents do not allow their children to work because they believe that early employment and drug abuse are interrelated. Some might also be threatened by the reduction in parental authority that occurs when their children claim independence because of their ability to make money. In fact, when young people are free to work and use their incomes voluntarily, they also desire to have more independence in other areas. Clearly, working means independence. If parents believe their chil-

dren working is better than them staying at home, they are willing to accept this growing process of independence. The hardships of work are perceived to be positive mediators of the growing process.

Young workers in the stage of learning and working need guidance and assistance from their parents to resist the negative impacts of work. Parents should also monitor the problems their children face at work. Discussing with children their working abilities and attitudes and their personal finance arrangements could strengthen their outlook on work. Youths definitely need their parents to provide emotional support and suggestions of ways to handle the work experience during the adolescent years. In sum, parental supervision and limited working hours might be the best ways to prevent the negative impacts of youth employment.

See also: WORKING FAMILIES

Bibliography

Barling, Julian, and E. Kevin Kelloway. "Introduction." In Julian Barling and E. Kevin Kelloway eds., *Young Workers: Varieties of Experience.* Washington, DC: American Psychological Association, 1999.

Erik Erikson extended psychoanalytic theory in several significant and important ways. (Psychology Archives, University of Akron)

Frone, Michael R. "Developmental Consequences of Youth Employment." In Julian Barling and E. Kevin Kelloway eds., *Young Workers: Varieties of Experience.* Washington, DC: American Psychological Association, 1999.

Greenberger, Ellen, and Laurence Steinberg. *When Teenagers Work: The Psychological and Social Costs of Adolescent Employment.* New York: Basic, 1986.

Hong Kong Census and Statistics Department. *1996 Population By-Census.* Hong Kong: Government Printer, 1996.

Loughlin, Catherine, and Julian Barling. "The Nature of Youth Employment." In Julian Barling and E. Kevin Kelloway eds., *Young Workers: Varieties of Experience.* Washington, DC: American Psychological Association, 1999.

Stone, James R., and Jeylan T. Mortimer. "The Effect of Adolescent Employment on Vocational Development: Public and Education Policy Implications." *Journal of Vocational Behavior* 53 (1998):184–214.

Worley, Linda P. "Working Adolescents: Implications for Counselors." *School Counselor* 42 (1995):218–223.

Wing Ling Li

ERIKSON, ERIK (1902–1994)

Erik Erikson was born in Frankfurt, Germany, on June 15, 1902. At the age of twenty-five he accepted an invitation to educate children whose parents were studying with Sigmund Freud in Vienna. While in Vi-

enna Erikson underwent psychoanalysis with Freud's daughter Anna Freud and was trained in the psychoanalytic tradition. Because of the rise of fascism in Europe, he immigrated to the United States in 1933 and became the first child psychoanalyst in Boston. Erikson held positions at Harvard University, Yale University, the University of California–Berkeley, and several other eminent institutions over the course of his career, despite the fact that he had no formal academic training beyond high school.

Erikson was trained as an orthodox psychoanalyst, but he extended psychoanalytic theory in several significant and important ways. In contrast to Freud's approach, in which personality was formed and relatively fixed at the age of five, Erikson took a lifespan approach to personality development, assigning importance to individuals' lives after early childhood. Erikson divided the development of personality into eight stages over the lifespan, with each stage characterized by its own crisis and two possible outcomes: (1) trust vs. mistrust; (2) autonomy vs. shame and doubt; (3) initiative vs. guilt; (4) industry vs. inferiority; (5) identity vs. role confusion; (6) intimacy vs. isolation; (7) generativity vs. stagnation; and (8) integrity vs. despair. According to Erikson, the conflicts in each stage arise because societal and maturational factors make new demands on an individual, and each conflict or crisis must be resolved before an individual is prepared to proceed to the next stage.

Erikson referred to the eight crises enumerated above as psychosocial stages of development, thereby emphasizing the important role that social and cultural factors play in personality development. This emphasis contrasted with Freud, who emphasized psychosexual development. Drawing upon his anthropological work with the Sioux and Yurok Indians as well as other groups, Erikson stressed that the sequence of the psychosocial stages was the same invariant across cultures, but the ways in which individuals from different cultures met each of the conflicts varied. Furthermore, Erikson highlighted the fact that the unique time and historical factors of the larger society also affected personality formation across the lifespan.

Further, Erikson argued that the main task for individuals in life was the quest for identity and not, as Freud believed, the defense against unpleasant tensions. Erikson placed the crisis of identity formation in the adolescent period, in which individuals must achieve an integrated understanding and acceptance of themselves in society. The achievement of identity formation was thought to be central to all subsequent stages of development.

In sum, Erikson's work has had a major impact on the field of developmental psychology. Despite the fact that many of his ideas have been difficult to test empirically, Erikson has influenced developmentalists in several areas, particularly those interested in adolescent development.

See also: SOCIAL DEVELOPMENT; THEORIES OF DEVELOPMENT

Bibliography

Publications by Erikson
Childhood and Society. New York: Norton, 1950.
Identity: Youth and Crisis. New York: Norton, 1968.

Matthew J. Hertenstein

ETHICAL GUIDELINES FOR RESEARCH

Both the American Psychological Association and the Society for Research in Child Development have outlined standards for performing ethical research with children. The most important principle for both organizations is that children must be protected from harm during research investigations. Researchers must use the least stressful procedures possible; minimize deception about the goals of the research; ensure that potential stress is outweighed by the benefits, such as financial compensation or treatment; and correct unforeseen negative consequences of the research. The child's participation must be based on informed and voluntary consent. Parents or legal guardians must be informed of all aspects of the research that could affect their willingness to let their child participate, including study procedures, risks and benefits, protection of the child's privacy, and the child's freedom to discontinue participation. They must be allowed to ask questions and to make a voluntary decision about their child's participation. Children also should be informed about the study, in age-appropriate language, and given the chance to agree or disagree to participate. Researchers should share findings responsibly with parents and the scientific community in a way that protects participants' identities and minimizes misinterpretation.

See also: METHODS OF STUDYING CHILDREN

Bibliography

American Psychological Association. "Ethical Principles of Psychologists and Code of Conduct." *American Psychologist* 47 (1992):1597–1611.
Society for Research in Child Development. *Ethical Standards for Research with Children.* Chicago: SRCD, 1990.

Debora Bell-Dolan

EXERCISE

From the time of such theorists as French philosopher and writer Jean-Jacques Rousseau (1712–1778), it has been believed that the child's health plays an important role in development. Some theorists have recognized the importance of regular physical activity in promoting healthy children. It was not until the twentieth century, however, that researchers began examining the importance of regular exercise in the development of children.

Exercise and Fitness

Children seem to have an endless supply of energy. They are often highly active and are almost constantly playing. Play is any spontaneous activity used for the child's amusement. Exercise is more planned and structured. The allure of amusement for children can be a motivating tool to direct children's activities for the purpose of exercise.

Exercise is used for the development of fitness, which comes in two primary forms, motor fitness and physical fitness. Motor fitness includes balance, coordination, motion, and speed and is developed in the first few years of a child's life through play exercises. Physical fitness includes aerobic fitness, muscular strength and endurance, flexibility, and body composition. Physical fitness can be addressed in children as young as five years of age and continues to affect health through adulthood.

Aerobic fitness involves the efficiency of the heart and lungs. An exercise program that consists of continuous activity for twenty to thirty minutes four to six times a week produces an improvement in aerobic fitness. Any improvement in aerobic fitness leads to a decreased risk of cardiovascular disease and a measurable decrease in stress. Children with high levels of aerobic fitness grow up to be healthier adults.

Muscle strength and endurance measure how strong muscles are and how long they are able to do work. Children improve muscle strength and endurance when they exercise. A typical program would have various exercises for each area of the body. Each exercise is usually repeated eight to ten times. The benefits of increased strength and endurance include more efficient muscles and a decreased risk of injuries. By strengthening muscles around joints, joints become stronger, thus avoiding many hyperflexibility injuries.

Flexibility is the range of motion in joints. The range of motion a joint has is determined by the tightness of muscles and other connective tissue surrounding a joint. Joints can have too much range of motion (known as hyperflexibility), or they can have a limited

To make sure they receive enough balance in their exercise program, children should be encouraged to take part in a variety of activities. Regular exercise—such as ballet class or sports—affects not only motor and physical fitness but also such developmental areas as cognitive ability, social development, and self-esteem. (Barry Lewis/Corbis)

range of motion. Stretching should be done regularly to prevent overtightness. Each stretching exercise, such as touching one's toes, should be held for at least thirty seconds without bouncing. This should be done three times for each exercise.

Body composition is a major area of concern in physical fitness. Studies have shown that children are getting fatter. The body mass index (BMI) is a weight-to-height comparison (weight divided by height squared). Children who are above the 85th percentile on the BMI are considered overweight. Studies have shown that overweight children tend to remain overweight as adults. Early intervention appears to be the key to maintaining normal weight throughout life. Children are able to lose excess weight by combining an intense exercise program with dietary monitoring and counseling. For these children, normal weight can be maintained into adulthood only if these exercise and eating habits become a permanent lifestyle change.

Sources of Exercise

Children get exercise from their play activities. Children who are highly active typically do not carry excess weight. While this regular activity is rarely long enough or intense enough to provide other immediate health benefits, active children tend to become active adults, and active adults are generally healthier than sedentary adults.

School physical education (PE) programs tend to be the primary source of exercise for children. PE programs provide opportunities for activity and to teach children about the principles of exercise. The limited time allotted for PE programs in most schools provides little benefit to children's health. Children typically spend two to four hours a week in PE programs. This is not enough time to adequately cover physical health education as well as give children time to exercise in class to improve their own fitness levels.

Athletic programs tend to provide children with the most exercise, but of a limited nature. Each sport has different demands and exercises the body in specific ways. For example, football is good for developing motor skills and strength but does very little for aerobic fitness. Swimming, on the other hand, is very good for aerobic fitness but can hinder flexibility. Children should be encouraged to take part in a variety of complementary sports in order to increase all areas of fitness.

Community programs provided by local recreation departments, YMCAs, or Boys and Girls Clubs exist in many areas. These programs are often not as strenuous as athletic programs but provide more time for improving children's fitness.

Exercise affects not only motor and physical fitness but also such developmental areas as cognitive ability, social development, and self-esteem. These benefits should also be considered when involving children in exercise activities.

Cognitive Development and Exercise

Although there has not been much evidence to show a direct impact of exercise on cognition, exercise has been theorized to help in the development of cognitive ability. Some studies have shown the use of small muscle exercises to increase brain growth, although whether this leads to improved cognitive ability has not been determined.

One study compared children who exercised with children who did not exercise. Children who exercised performed better on a standardized test than children who were not in the exercise group. This study suggests that children who regularly exercise may perform better in school.

Social Development and Exercise

Exercise can be used as a tool to achieve socialization. Many different exercises play a role in socialization: partnered exercise such as dancing help children learn to cooperate; games and dances passed on from older generations help to inculturate children; and group sports teach teamwork as well as sportsmanship.

Self-esteem is directly influenced by exercise by providing the opportunity for children to explore their bodies' abilities. This exploration molds children's self-concept. When exercise is based on individual performance levels and improvements are made, increased self-esteem often results. By using tools such as self-talk, goal-setting, and self-assessment, exercise can help children gain a more positive self-concept and better self-esteem. Positive self-esteem leads to improved cognitive and social development.

The Right Amount of Exercise

In normally active children, exercise-related injuries and problems are few and far between. Physical education teachers, coaches, and doctors can typically provide the supervision necessary to prevent harm from occurring. Teachers and coaches are educated specifically about exercise in children. Professionals who work closely with children can help each child determine his or her own limits.

The primary risk associated with exercise is overuse injuries such as muscle strains, tendonitis, stress fractures, and other soft tissue damage. These are typically caused by doing too much too soon and are usually repaired by resting the injured area.

Two areas of concern specific to children are injuries to the growth plate and increased risk of heat ex-haustion/heat stroke. Children's bones have weak areas near each end where growth takes place. These are called growth plates and are susceptible to breakage. Also, for children competing at an elite level in high-impact sports such as gymnastics there is an increased risk of a premature closing of this growth plate, which could result in stunted growth. By increasing exercise intensities gradually over time, these types of injuries can be avoided.

Children's body temperature regulation has not yet matured so there is increased risk of temperature misregulation during exercise. Children are more susceptible than adults to heat exhaustion and heat stroke in extreme heat conditions and to hypothermia in chilly water. These extreme temperature conditions should be avoided whenever possible or children should be closely monitored while exercising at these times.

Parents of preteen girls are often concerned about exercise's impact on the menstrual cycle. Endurance sports such as running and swimming promote lean body mass, yet a certain amount of body fat is necessary for proper menstrual function. Late onset of menstruation or the cessation of menstruation can be caused by extreme lean body composition. This does not, however, appear to lead to long-term reproductive health problems.

All children, even those with chronic illnesses such as asthma and diabetes and those with motor dysfunction, must include exercise as part of a total fitness program. All children can engage in exercise that will increase their overall heath. In special cases, professionals such as doctors, teachers, and coaches can work together to create an exercise program that will benefit the health and self-esteem of a child.

Regular exercise is important to the development of healthy children. With proper use of exercise principles and good professional supervision, exercise can help all children develop into healthy adults.

See also: MOTOR DEVELOPMENT

Bibliography

Armstrong, Neil, and Joanne Welsman. *Young People and Physical Activity.* New York: Oxford University Press, 1997.

"Exercise (Physical Activity) and Children." In the American Heart Association [web site]. Dallas, Texas, 2000. Available from http://www.americanheart.org/Heart_and_Stroke_A_Z_Guide/exercisek.html; INTERNET.

Pařízková, Jana. *Nutrition, Physical Activity, and Health in Early Life.* Boca Raton, FL: CRC Press, 1996.

Rowland, Thomas W. *Exercise and Children's Health.* Champaign, IL: Human Kinetics Books, 1990.

Shawn R. A. Svoboda-Barber

F

FACILITATED COMMUNICATION

Facilitated communication is a controversial technique for assisting individuals with autism and related language impairments to communicate. It typically involves an adult facilitator who physically guides the individual's hand to select letters or symbols from a communication device, such as an alphabet board. When facilitated, many individuals with autism have supposedly shown unexpectedly advanced language skills, including the ability to spell and compose highly sophisticated messages. The technique is controversial because the facilitator may intentionally or unintentionally influence the selection of letters or symbols. Indeed, considerable experimental evidence has shown that, more often than not, it is the facilitator, rather than the individual being facilitated, who is responsible for the content of the resulting messages. In light of this evidence, numerous professional groups have issued position statements highlighting the lack of empirical support for facilitated communication and the need to verify that facilitated communications are free from facilitator influence.

See also: AUTISM

Bibliography

Jacobson, J. W., J. A. Mulick, and A. A. Schwartz. "A History of Facilitated Communication: Science, Pseudoscience, and Antiscience Science Working Group on Facilitated Communication." *American Psychologist* 50 (1995):750–765.

Konstantareas, M., and G. Gravelle. "Facilitated Communication." *Autism* 2 (1998):389–414.

Jeffrey Sigafoos

FAILURE TO THRIVE

Children who fail to grow properly have always existed. In earlier times when many children did not survive the first few years, small or sickly children were a fact of life. More recently, medicine has increasingly turned its attention to the unique problems of children, among them the problems of growth failure and most interestingly to the problem of malnutrition and growth failure in children without obvious organic illness. The case of so-called nonorganic failure to thrive, growth failure without apparent medical cause, is the main focus of this discussion.

The medical concept of "failure to thrive" in infants and young children dates back about a century. L. Emmett Holt's 1897 edition of *Diseases of Infancy and Childhood* included a discussion of a child who "ceased to thrive." Chapin correctly recognized in 1908 that growth failure was primarily caused by malnutrition, but that temporarily correcting caloric intake and improving growth often proved futile after the child returned to her (often impoverished) environment. By 1933 the term "failure to thrive" formally entered the medical literature in the tenth edition of Holt's text.

Failure to thrive is not a discreet diagnosis or a single medical condition (such as chicken pox), but rather a sign of illness or abnormal function (as a rash or fever may be a sign of chicken pox virus infection). In infants and young children, the term "failure to thrive" is most broadly defined as physical growth that for whatever reason falls short of what is expected of a normal, healthy child. Statistical norms have been published for the growth patterns of normal children. Plotting a child's height, weight, and head circumference on such charts yields valuable diagnostic information. In children younger than age two, inadequate growth may be defined as falling below the third or fifth percentile for the age, where weight is less than 80 percent of the ideal weight for the age, or where weight crosses two major percentiles sequentially downward on a standardized growth chart.

The concept of failure to thrive, however, encompasses not just disturbances of the more obvious aspects of physical development but the more subtle aspects of psychosocial development in infancy and early childhood. "Thriving" is a concept that implies that a child not only grows physically in accordance with published norms for age and sex, but also exhibits the characteristics of normal progress of developmental milestones in all spheres—neurological, psychosocial, and emotional.

Early observations that an organic illness could not be found in many cases of failure to thrive led to the categorization of failure to thrive into the subclasses of organic and nonorganic causal factors. This classification ultimately proved too simplistic, both organic and environmental factors acting together may cause poor growth, but it served to sharpen thinking about the nonorganic causes.

Organic versus Nonorganic Failure to Thrive

Organic failure to thrive is that caused by the harmful effects on growth of organic disease. Growth failure can be an extremely sensitive marker for unsuspected systemic disease, revealing illness long before it would normally be detected. Likewise, the progress of therapy is often dramatically mirrored by improvement in growth. Any significant illness in an infant or young child can cause growth failure. Thus growth failure alone alerts the physician to search for possible medical causes. Nevertheless, the search for organic disease in young children with an initial diagnosis of failure to thrive most often finds no physical (organic) condition to explain the growth failure; the failure is therefore termed nonorganic.

The modern understanding of this disorder views it as a fundamental failure of maternal-infant attachment. In fact, it is referred to in psychiatric literature as feeding disorder of attachment, as well as maternal deprivation, deprivation dwarfism, and psychosocial deprivation. Nonorganic failure to thrive reflects a failed relationship between a mother and her infant during the first year of life. Its chief characteristic is a lack of engagement or bonding between mother and infant in the daily routine of care, most dramatically with respect to feeding.

Diagnosis

Nonorganic failure to thrive can be understood in terms of both physical and emotional deprivation of the child, and has both physical and behavioral signs. Caloric deprivation of an infant may be caused more or less innocently by lactation failure, extreme poverty, parental ignorance of proper infant feeding, or strange nutritional beliefs. Parents of children with nonorganic failure to thrive, however, typically give a history of adequate or often exaggerated amounts of nutritional intake belied by the child's obvious malnourished state.

By interviewing and observing the mother, it is noted that feedings are marked by a lack of the mutual pleasurable relationship of giving and receiving that is the hallmark of normal feedings. In contrast, the mother may admit that she props the bottle or even sometimes forgets regular feedings.

There may be other evidence of poor caregiving and physical neglect, such as unwashed skin, diaper rash, skin infections, and dirty clothing. The back of the baby's head may be flat with a bald patch over the flattened area, implying that the child is left unattended for long periods of time lying on his back in the crib. The baby may exhibit a lack of appropriate social responsiveness, with an expressionless face and classic avoidance of eye contact. Normal vocal responses, such as cooing and blowing raspberries, may be absent. In children older than five months, there may be no anticipatory reaching for interesting objects. Motor milestones may be delayed. When held, instead of cuddling normally, the baby characteristically arches his back and scissors his legs, or lies limp as a rag doll in the examiner's arms. By contrast, babies with organic failure to thrive typically do not show the characteristic withdrawal behaviors of nonorganic failure to thrive infants, and respond best to their mothers.

Prominent features in the mother's history may include symptoms of acute or chronic depression, personality disorder, substance abuse, and a generally high level of psychosocial stress related to poverty, social isolation, or spousal abuse. Often the mother was abused or neglected as a child, producing an apparently transgenerational pattern of insecure attachment. Parents of infants with nonorganic failure to thrive are often initially evasive. They usually take the baby to an emergency room for another illness, whereupon the baby's malnutrition attracts attention. Upon the child's admission to the hospital, the parents may disappear for several days.

Treatment

Inpatient investigation and initial treatment is warranted for infants under a year in the following cases: when the infant is suffering from more severe growth failure; when there are signs of emotional deprivation; when the parents have not sought medical intervention; when the infant shows signs of physical abuse; when the infant's hygiene has been seriously neglected; when the mother appears severely disturbed or is abusing drugs or alcohol or is living a chaotic lifestyle overwhelmed with stresses; or when the mother-infant interaction appears uncaring and includes feelings of anger.

During hospitalization, a primary-care nurse is assigned to establish a warm and nurturing relationship with the baby. The baby typically begins to blossom in its social interactions and rapidly gains weight. As the baby begins to improve both in terms of weight gain and psychosocially, hospital personnel can help the mother engage with her baby, teaching her to receive and express the mutual signals of mother-infant bonding. Understanding and addressing the mother's needs for emotional support and encouragement is essential to rehabilitating the mother-infant relationship. The degree to which parents are aware of the cause of the problem and actively cooperate in their baby's reattachment has been found to be predictive of the long-term outcome. Appropriate referrals to child protective services agencies must be made both to ensure the child's continued safety and to monitor the efforts to help the parents learn needed skills.

Long-Term Prognosis for Recovery

Severe nonorganic failure to thrive is a potentially fatal illness. Nutritional deprivation can lead to death from starvation or overwhelming infection due to a weakened immune system. With detection and intervention, infants can in some cases recover from the effects of their condition. Brain size as measured by head circumference may be permanently reduced, especially if the failure to thrive occurred in the first six months of life. During this time of its most rapid growth, the brain is very susceptible to permanent damage from the effects of poor nutrition.

Later emotional and learning problems are common in these children. A 1988 Case Western Reserve University study found that the mean IQ score for three-year-old children with a prior history of failure to thrive was 85. A follow-up study of children from this group showed that even those who subsequently participated in early intervention programs had problems of personality development, deficient problem-solving skills, and more behavioral problems in general as compared to the controls. These problems included impulse control, gratification delay, and the ability to adapt behaviorally to new situations. An Israeli study found that at age five, about 11.5 percent of children with a history of failure to thrive had some manifestations of developmental delay, compared with no delays in the control children. They likewise found an 18 percent incidence of poor school performance compared with a 3.3 percent rate in the control group. Another follow-up study of children diagnosed with nonorganic failure to thrive found that at age six, half of the children in the study sample of twenty-one had abnormal personalities and two-thirds learned to read at a later-than-normal age. Two of the twenty-one had died under suspicious circumstances, pointing up the vulnerability of children with psychosocial failure to thrive. Another study determined that out of fifteen children initially diagnosed with growth failure caused by emotional deprivation, only two were functioning well three to eleven years after diagnosis. Infants hospitalized with failure to thrive prior to six months of age exhibited decreased cognitive development, despite long-term outreach intervention programs. Earlier age of onset of growth failure, lower maternal education level, and lower family income all predicted lower cognitive level.

Summary

Failure to thrive in young children represents significantly suboptimal growth due to intrinsic medical (organic) or environmental (nonorganic) factors. Nonorganic failure to thrive in particular represents a recognizable syndrome of poor growth in infants and young children with specific diagnostic features. Nonorganic failure to thrive in early infancy poses a significant risk of adverse long-term developmental effects.

See also: MILESTONES OF DEVELOPMENT; RESILIENCY

Bibliography

Berwick, D. "Nonorganic Failure to Thrive." *Pediatrics in Review* 1 (1980):265–270.

Berwick, D., J. C. Levy, and R. Kleinerman. "Failure to Thrive: Diagnostic Yield of Hospitalization." *Archives of Disease in Childhood* 57 (1982):347–351.

Bithoney, William, Howard Dubowitz, and H. Egan. "Failure to Thrive/Growth Deficiency." *Pediatrics in Review* 13 (1992):453–459.

Casey, P. "Failure to Thrive." In M. Levine, W. Carey, and A. Crocker eds., *Developmental-Behavioral Pediatrics*. Philadelphia: Saunders, 1992.

Drotar, D., and L. Sturm. "Prediction of Intellectual Development in Young Children with Early Histories of Nonorganic Failure to Thrive." *Journal of Pediatric Psychiatry* 13 (1988):281–296.

Frank, D. A., and Susan H. Zeisel. "Failure to Thrive." *Pediatric Clinics of North America* 35 (1988):1187–1206.

Gahagan, S., and R. Holmes. "A Stepwise Approach to Evaluation of Undernutrition and Failure to Thrive." *Pediatric Clinics of North America* 45 (1998):169–187.

Ramsay, M., E. Gisel, and M. Boutry. "Nonorganic Failure to Thrive: Growth Failure Secondary to Feeding Skills Disorder." *Developmental Medicine and Child Neurology* 35 (1993):285–297.

Schwatrz, I. David. "Failure to Thrive: An Old Nemesis in the New Millennium." *Pediatrics in Review* 21 (2000):257–264.

Skuse, D., A. Pickles, D. Wolke, and S. Reilly. "Postnatal Growth and Mental Development: Evidence for a 'Sensitive Period.'" *Journal of Child Psychology and Psychiatry* 35 (1994):521–545.

Zenel, Joseph. "Failure to Thrive: A General Pediatrician's Perspective." *Pediatrics in Review* 18 (1997):371–378.

Jeffrey W. Hull

FAMILY SIZE

Family size is a variable of great interest to those who study children. Empirical studies consistently have found a negative association between family size and children's mental ability, intelligence, and educational attainment. Two theoretical explanations have been posited to explain these negative relationships. Dilution theory suggests that as the number of siblings increases, fewer resources (e.g., parental love and attention, finances) are available to facilitate the development of each child. The confluence model offers a more complex explanation that considers the interrelationships among the number of siblings, child spacing, birth order, and parent-child interactions. Although larger families include positive characteristics such as increased family socialization and father involvement, increased family size also is associated with more authoritarian parenting, which, in turn, can negatively impact a child's self-esteem, self-differentiation, and ego identity. Empirical studies have supported certain aspects of these perspectives. Much of this research, however, has been criticized for drawing conclusions based on "between family comparisons" that do not take family-specific variables (e.g., family resources, parents' intelligence, sibling interactions) into account.

See also: PARENT-CHILD RELATIONSHIPS; SIBLINGS AND SIBLING RELATIONSHIPS

Bibliography

Blake, Judith. *Family Size and Achievement.* Berkeley: University of California Press, 1989.

Hoffman, L. W. "The Influence of the Family Environment on Personality: Accounting for Sibling Differences." *Psychological Bulletin* 110 (1991):187–203.

Kuo, H., and R. M. Hauser. "How Does Size of Sibship Matter? Family Configuration and Family Effects on Educational Attainment." *Social Science Research* 26 (1997):69–94.

Rodgers, J. L., H. H. Cleveland, E. van den Oord, and D. C. Rowe. "Resolving the Debate over Birth Order, Family Size, and Intelligence." *American Psychologist* 55 (2000):599–612.

Debbie Madden-Derdich

FATHERS

In the 1990s, researchers and social commentators began to document recent social and cultural shifts in how men see themselves in their role as fathers and how families, policies, and others conceptualize them in these roles. For example, increased women's labor force participation has reconfigured child-care environments for children, giving fathers the opportunity to play a more active role in the care of their children. In cases in which the mother and father of a child do not reside in the same household, men's groups have argued that while men accept their responsibilities for the economic and psychological well-being of their children, they also demand legal rights and access to their children. Moreover, according to the U.S. Bureau of the Census, the number of single fathers living with their children increased by 25 percent during the late 1990s, reflecting an increased acceptance by courts and society of paternal custody, an increased tendency on the part of men to seek custody, and a greater willingness on the part of mothers and judges to agree to paternal custody.

These social shifts parallel changes in the cultural ideals of good fathering and have important implications for child well-being. In general, children who grow up with involved, caring, and nurturing fathers tend to experience academic success and good peer relationships, and take less risky behaviors. In contrast, father absence is consistently associated with poor school achievement, early childbearing, and high risk-taking behavior. Although the mechanism by which positive father involvement affects children's outcomes is unclear, there is enough evidence to assert that fathers matter to the social, economic, and psychological development of their children, themselves, and their families.

History and Background of Father Involvement

Interest in fathers and their role in their children's development have sustained researchers' attention off and on since the 1970s. Sociodemographic, cultural, economic, and historical changes—women's increasing labor force participation; increased nonparental care for children; increases in nonmarital childbearing and cohabitation; and father absence in some families and increased father presence in others—have greatly affected how families organize themselves. These changes have led to different family structures and different expectations and beliefs about the roles of fathers and mothers. The "ideal" father had undergone an evolution from the colonial father, to the distant breadwinner, to the modern involved dad, to the father as co-parent. For example, in the second half of the nineteenth century, fathers in the United States left their small farms and businesses to seek employment away from home in an emerging industrial economy. While fathers were away from home, mothers were solely responsible for rearing their children. This breadwinning and nurturing dichotomy of parental roles defined parental involvement and was associated with fathers' absence and mothers' caretaking. Thus, father-child interactions were considered unimportant for children's development.

These changes in parental roles and expectations can be linked to four trends: women's increasing labor force participation, the absence of many men from some families, the increased involvement of other fathers in their children's lives, and the increased cultural diversity of American families. At the dawn of the twenty-first century, a new ideal of "co-parent" is emerging in which the gender division of labor in domestic and breadwinning responsibilities is less clear. Co-parents must share financial and caregiving tasks and responsibilities equally, and their roles are gender-free.

Father Involvement: What Is It and How Is It Measured?

Attempts to broaden the conceptualization of fatherhood have stimulated considerable debate among researchers, theorists, policymakers, and the public at large regarding the diversity of family types and parental roles. The ecology of family life is continuing to change and thus many children will grow up in the twenty-first century without their biological fathers and/or with stepfathers. It is estimated that one-third of children will spend some time in a nonmarital or stepfamily before they reach the age of eighteen. Dissolutions of stepfamilies are also increasing. This complicated family structuring will expose children to situations that demand adjustment to novel and complex relationships with sets of parents and siblings. Different father types—biological, "social," stepfather—will increasingly shape children's attachments, social-emotional competencies, linguistic and cognitive attainments, and orientation to family and work. Theoretical models of parenting must be reformulated to accommodate new family structures as well as culturally diverse conceptions of fatherhood.

Investigators of father involvement have struggled with definitions of what it means to be an "involved father." Father involvement is a multidimensional, continually evolving concept—both at the level of scholarship and at the level of cultural awareness. Although cultural ideals of fatherhood have evolved over time, much of what is understood about parenting (and particularly what is thought of as good parenting) stems from research and theory developed on mothers—the maternal template. In effect, it is a struggle against generational, gender, class, and ethnic biases.

The unidimensional focus of father involvement research (i.e., on the amount of fathering) in the 1970s and 1980s yielded to broader and more inclusive definitions. For example, Michael Lamb and his colleagues, in a 1987 article, distinguished among *accessibility*—a father's presence and availability to the child, regardless of the actual interactions between father and child; *engagement*—a father's experience of direct contact, caregiving, and shared interactions with his child; and *responsibility*—a father's participation in such tasks as selecting a pediatrician and making appointments, selecting child-care settings or babysitters, arranging after-school care and the care of sick children, talking with teachers, and monitoring children's whereabouts and activities. Others have distinguished among the types of activities in which fathers and their children engage (e.g., play, direct care) or between the quantity and quality of care.

Multidimensional constructions of father involvement, however, have not yet been integrated into a comprehensive conceptual framework. The challenge for researchers is to strike a balance between sensitivity to multiple dimensions of father involvement and explanatory parsimony. Questions need to be asked about relations among dimensions of father involvement and how changes to one dimension (e.g., responsibility) affect others (e.g., availability). In addition, it is unclear whether these models capture variation across types of family structure and ethnic/cultural groups. Likewise, researchers must consider father involvement as it operates within a family system that gives it a particular meaning and significance.

What Does Research Say about Father Involvement?

Much of the previous research on fatherhood was motivated by the notion that fatherless families were becoming the norm in the United States. By 1999, almost a quarter of children lived with only their mothers, 4 percent lived with only their fathers, and 4 percent lived with neither of their parents, according to the Federal Interagency Forum on Child and Family Statistics. Hence the literature on "absent" fathers has focused mainly on the physically absent (i.e., nonresident father), rather than on the psychologically absent father. This body of research characterizes the father's role as unidimensional—either physically present or not. When one accounts for the distinction between physical versus psychological absence, both the patterns of involvement and the consequences of physical absence are less straightforward. For example, there are little data on the variation of father involvement in intact families. It is also not clear how "absent" men have been from their families. In 1999 Lerman and Sorensen reported that two-thirds of fathers of children born out of wedlock had a substantial amount of contact with at least one nonmarital child. There is also little understanding of the nonfinancial ways that some fathers—especially nonresidential fathers—contribute to their families. Green and Moore reported in 2000 that nonresident low-income fathers often provided financial support informally, rather than through the formal child support enforcement system. Fathers may prefer these less formal systems, because they feel they have more control over how money for the child is spent.

Nevertheless, research consistently shows that children growing up without their father face more difficulties—even when studies control for family income—and are at risk for low school achievement, low involvement in the labor force, early childbearing, and delinquency. Boys growing up without fathers seem especially prone to exhibit problems in the areas of sex-role and gender-identity development, school performance, psychosocial adjustment, and control of aggression. Girls are affected by father-absence too, although the effects on girls may be less enduring, dramatic, and consistent than the effects on boys. Holding race, income, parent's education, and urban residence constant, Harper and McLanahan in 1998 found that boys with nonresident fathers had double the odds of being incarcerated; boys who grew up with a stepfather in the home were at an even higher risk of incarceration, roughly three times that of children who remained with both their natural parents.

Fathers' emotional investment in, attachment to, and provision of resources for their children are associated with the well-being, cognitive development, and social competence of young children even after the effects of such potentially significant confounds as family income, neonatal health, maternal involvement, and paternal age are taken into account. Fathers play an important role in their children's socialization and there are many ways in which fathers influence their children's relationships with peers. In a 2001 publication, Ross and colleagues proposed three different paths that lead to variations in children's peer relationships. These paths include lessons learned in the context of the father-child relationship, fathers' direct advice concerning peer relationships, and fathers' regulation of access to peers and peer-related activity.

In addition, fathers have been found to be important players in the development of children's emotional regulation and control. During middle childhood, paternal involvement in children's schooling in both single-father and two-parent families is associated with greater academic achievement and enjoyment of school by children. For both resident and nonresident fathers, active participation in their children's lives, rather than simply the amount of contact, appears to be formatively important. In adolescence too, stronger and closer attachments to resident biological fathers or stepfathers are associated with more desirable educational, behavioral, and emotional outcomes. High involvement and closeness between fathers and adolescents, rather than temporal involvement per se, protect adolescents from engaging in delinquent behavior and experiencing emotional distress. Thus, both quantity and quality of father involvement combined into the concept of "positive paternal involvement" result in positive child outcomes.

Antecedents of Father Involvement

There is an emerging body of research on the factors that predict positive father involvement. Father involvement is likely affected by multiple interacting systems operating over the life course, including a father's mental health, expectations, family relations, support networks, community and culture, the child's own characteristics, and even public policies.

Paternal depression and aspects of personality have been found to predict the quality of father-infant attachment and interaction. Parenting stress has also been found to be negatively associated with security of father-child relationships, quality of father-infant interactions at four months of age, and father nurturance toward an ill infant.

Related to expectations is the notion of intendedness, that is, the extent to which a father intended or welcomed the birth of his child. There is some evidence that a father's positive parenting may be strongly associated with whether the pregnancy was intended. Unwanted and mistimed childbearing has been linked to negative children's self-esteem.

Mother-father relationships are very important. A father who has a positive relationship with the mother of his child is likely to be more involved in his child's life. Fathers in positive marriages are more likely to have secure infants, positive attitudes toward their children and their role as a parent, and low levels of parenting stress. The father's relationship with other family members, friends, his partner's family, and with members of his own family of origin are also important. In one study, men who received more emotional support from their work and family relations had more secure infants.

A father's economic status clearly affects his ability to provide adequate child support and may ultimately affect his relationship with both his partner and child. More-educated fathers play with and teach their children more than do less-educated fathers, and fathers' academic achievement is associated with the amount of time spent as primary caregivers. A father's job loss is associated with negative outcomes for the child, and fathers in poor and welfare families, particularly those facing chronic poverty, are less involved in their adolescent children's lives.

Little is known, however, about how child characteristics affect a father's reactions to his child and his investment in the father role. A father's involvement may vary with the child's temperament or gender, for instance. Some fathers may find it trying to engage in responsive and reciprocal interactions with babies who have difficult temperaments; others may interact differently with their sons and daughters.

Public policies have an impact on the amount, frequency, and type of father involvement. For some fathers, child support laws, which are not linked to visitation rights, are a deterrent to child contact. Similarly, parental leave policies make it difficult for a father to take time away from work to take care of his child. Most employers do not offer parental leave, and when it is offered, it is unpaid. This lack of support may create a disincentive for men to be more involved in the care of their children.

Research and Good Fathering

Since the 1990s, a new body of research on fatherhood has emerged that goes beyond the simple dichotomy of presence versus absence to a deeper understanding of the multidimensional levels of parental involvement that make a difference in children's development. There is enough evidence to suggest that positive and nurturing parental involvement can make an important contribution to the healthy development of children. In addition to providing economic resources for their children, positively involved fathers can make a difference in their children's lives by providing options, being a good role model, and helping them to negotiate complex social interactions. Children who grow up with in-

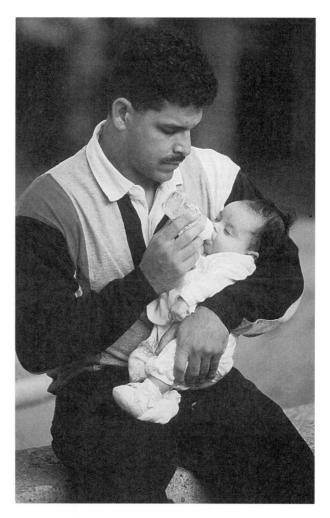

A father in San Antonio, Texas, feeds his infant son. Fathers' attitudes and reports about their infants and their role as fathers have been found to predict a secure father-infant attachment at twelve months. (Sandy Felsenthal/Corbis)

volved, caring fathers tend to be psychologically better adjusted, engage in less risky behavior, and have healthy relationships with others.

Given that almost a quarter of American children live without a father and that most of these children live in poverty, policymakers and others have placed fathers, especially low-income fathers, on the national spotlight. There is, however, little research on how low-income men interact with their children, how parental involvement alters their own developmental trajectories, and what barriers they need to overcome to become positive influences in their children's lives. This type of information will be crucial for researchers who study antecedents of father involvement and impacts on children, but also for policymakers and educators who promote positive father involvement.

See also: PARENT-CHILD RELATIONSHIPS; PARENTING; SINGLE-PARENT FAMILIES

Bibliography

Amato, P. R., and F. Rivera. "Paternal Involvement and Children's Behavior Problems." *Journal of Marriage and Family* 61 (1999):375–384.

Axinn, W. G., J. S. Barber, and A. Thornton. "The Long-Term Impact of Parents' Childbearing Decisions on Children's Self-Esteem." *Demography* 35 (1998):435–443.

Belsky, J. "Parent, Infant, and Social-Contextual Antecedents of Father-Son Attachment Security." *Developmental Psychology* 32 (1996):905–913.

Brown, S. S., and L. Eisenberg. *The Best Intentions.* Washington, DC: National Academy Press, 1995.

Bumpass, Larry L., J. A. Sweet, and T. C. Castro-Martin. "Changing Pattern of Marriage." *Journal of Marriage and Family* 52 (1990):747–756.

Cox, M. J., M. T. Owen, V. K. Henderson, and N. A. Margand. "Prediction of Infant-Father and Infant-Mother Attachment." *Child Development* 28 (1992):474–483.

Gottman, J. M., L. Katz, and C. Hoover. *Meta-emotion.* Mahwah, NJ: Lawrence Erlbaum, 1997.

Harper, C. C., and S. S. McLanahan. "Father Absence and Youth Incarceration." Paper presented at the annual meetings of the American Sociological Association, San Francisco, CA, 1998.

Hetherington, E. M., and S. H. Henderson. "Fathers in Stepfamilies." In Michael E. Lamb ed., *The Role of the Father in Child Development,* 3rd edition. New York: Wiley, 1997.

Hetherington, E. M., and M. Stanley-Hagan. "Divorced Fathers: Stress, Coping, and Adjustment." In Michael E. Lamb ed., *The Father's Role: Applied Perspectives.* New York: Wiley, 1986.

Lamb, Michael E., J. Pleck, E. L. Charnov, and J. A. Levine. "A Biosocial Perspective on Paternal Behavior and Involvement." In J. B. Lancaster, J. Altmann, A. Rossi, and L. R. Sherood eds., *Parenting across the Life Span: Biosocial Perspectives.* Chicago: Aldine, 1987.

McBride, B. A. "The Effects of a Parent Education/Play Group Program on Father Involvement in Child Rearing." *Family Relations* 39 (1990):250–256.

Noppe, Illene C., L. D. Noppe, and F. P. Hughes. "Stress as a Predictor of the Quality of Parent-Infant Interactions." *Journal of Genetic Psychology* 152 (1991):17–28.

Nord, C., D. A. Brimhall, and J. West. *Fathers' Involvement in Their Children's Schools.* Washington, DC: Office of Educational Research and Improvement, U.S. Department of Education, 1997.

Palkovitz, R. "Reconstructing 'Involvement': Expanding Conceptualizations of Men's Caring in Contemporary Families." In Alan J. Hawkins and David C. Dollahite eds., *Generative Fathering: Beyond Deficit Perspectives.* Thousands Oaks, CA: Sage, 1997.

Parke, Ross D. *Fatherhood.* Cambridge, MA: Harvard University Press, 1996.

Parke, Ross D. "Father Involvement: A Developmental Psychological Perspective." *Marriage and Family Review* 29, no. 4 (2000):43–58.

Parke, Ross D., and Armin A. Brott. *Throwaway Dads.* Boston: Houghton Mifflin, 1999.

Perloff, Janet D., and J. Buckner. "Fathers of Children on Welfare: Their Impact on Child Well-Being." *American Journal of Orthopsychiatry* 66 (1996):557–571.

Pleck, E. H. "Paternal Involvement: Levels, Sources, and Consequences." In Michael E. Lamb ed., *The Role of the Father in Child Development,* 3rd edition. New York: Wiley, 1997.

Radin, N. "Primary-Caregiving Fathers in Intact Families." In Adele Eskeles Gottfried and Allen W. Gottfried eds., *Redefining Families: Implications for Children's Development.* New York: Plenum Press, 1994.

Seltzer, J. A. "Father by Law: Effects of Joint Legal Custody on Nonresident Fathers' Involvement with Children." *Demography* 35, no. 2 (1998):135–146.

U.S. Bureau of the Census. *Current Population Reports: Growth in Single Fathers Outpaces Growth in Single Mothers* (Series P-20 No. 1344). Washington, DC: U.S. Government Printing Office, 1999.

Yongman, M. W., D. Kindlon, and F. Earls. "Father Involvement and Cognitive Behavioral Outcomes of Preterm Infants." *Journal of the American Academy of Child and Adolescent Psychiatry* 343 (1995):58–66.

Natasha J. Cabrera

FETAL ALCOHOL SYNDROME

Fetal alcohol syndrome (FAS), caused by exposure of the fetus to alcohol, is diagnosed on the basis of three types of birth defects: growth retardation, physical anomalies, and central nervous system dysfunction. The amount of alcohol necessary to cause FAS is unknown, but is thought to be related to timing and duration of exposure. The best intervention is prevention. Encouraging women to abstain from alcohol use during pregnancy is the best way to prevent FAS.

There is no cure for FAS, only treatment for the associated complications such as attention deficit disorder. Children diagnosed with FAS are at risk for long-term effects. Facial characteristics, frequently associated with FAS, may change with age. However, growth problems persist throughout adulthood. The most serious birth defects relate to the central nervous system, and these also continue into adulthood. Affected children may have decreased IQ scores and behavioral disorders. The incidence of FAS is 1 to 2 infants per 1,000 live births.

See also: BIRTH DEFECTS; SUBSTANCE ABUSE

Bibliography

Bauer, Charles. "Perinatal Effects of Perinatal Drug Exposure Neonatal Aspects." *Clinics in Perinatology* 26 (1999):87–106.

Jones, K. L. "Fetal Alcohol Syndrome." *Pediatrics in Review* 8(1996):122–126.

Kenner, Carole, and Karen D'Apolito. "Outcomes for Children Exposed to Drugs In Utero." *Journal of Obstetric, Gynecologic, and Neonatal Nursing* 26 (1997):595–603.

Martinez, Alma, J. Colin Partridge, Xylina Bean, and H. William Taeusch. "Perinatal Substance Abuse." In H. William Taeusch and Roberta Ballard eds., *Avery's Diseases of the Newborn.* Philadelphia: W. B. Saunders, 1998.

Meica M. Efird

FIRSTBORN CHILDREN

Many people believe that firstborn children, because of their privileged position in the family, behave differently than later-born children. Although parents, siblings, and nonparents probably overemphasize the influence of birth order, evidence suggests that the experiences of individuals are related to their ordinal position in the family.

Psychologists have studied the distinctive personality of firstborn children for more than a century. Alfred Adler, the father of individual psychology, postulated that the child's position in the family has a monumental effect on the child's personality. He believed that the firstborn child is dethroned by the birth of a sibling and the firstborn must now share parental attention with a rival. In order to cope with this traumatic betrayal, firstborns become problem children or they strongly emulate their parents. Because of their identification with their parents and their perceived loss of status, power and authority become extremely important to firstborn children. Although Adler's theory was not based on empirical research, it spurred thousands of studies that related birth order to everything from extrasensory perception to juvenile delinquency.

Many of the commonly held ideas about firstborns originate from inferences about their interactions with parents and siblings. The extant literature suggests that parents harbor expectations of how firstborns should behave and parents act in accordance with those beliefs. During infancy, mothers attend to firstborns by responding to and stimulating them more than latterborns. Mothers also tend to rate their firstborn infants as more difficult than later-born children. This finding may reflect that mothers feel more comfortable in their parenting role by the time a subsequent child enters the family. The relative amount of attention that firstborn preschoolers receive tends to decline with the birth of siblings. Nevertheless, firstborn children continue to experience distinctive relationships with their parents. Investigators have found that parents expect higher achievement, are more controlling, and make added demands on their firstborn young children. Moreover, throughout childhood, fathers tend to be more involved with their firstborns relative to later-born children.

Firstborns also seem to initiate more interactions, both positive and negative, with their younger siblings than vice versa. They are more likely to engage their younger siblings in conversation, but they are also more likely to be verbally disapproving. As compared to older peers, firstborn children tend to instruct younger siblings by providing appropriate feedback and guidance. The opportunity to be a "teacher" may help explain why firstborn children, on average, have higher IQs than only or youngest children.

Speech and Intelligence

Firstborn children are temporarily only children and thus are exposed to one-to-one speech with their parents. When a new child is born, firstborns and their siblings receive less child-directed speech and are privy to multiparty speech. Specifically, mothers appear to provide more linguistic support and more complex grammatical statements to their firstborns even when their firstborns and latterborns are observed at the same age. Concordantly, firstborn toddlers have larger vocabularies, reach language milestones earlier, and demonstrate more sophisticated grammar than their siblings. The early language competence of firstborns may partially explain the proclivity of firstborns to achieve in school. In contrast, later-born children's skill in conversational speech and their expertise in understanding the mental states of others potentially contribute to their renowned social acumen.

On average, firstborn children have been cited as having higher intelligence levels than later-born children. For example, one study examined scores on the 1965 National Merit Scholarship Qualifying Test and, regardless of family size, the scores tended to be higher for firstborns. The confluence model has been proposed to explain the superior intellectual rankings of firstborns. In this paradigm, a child's intellectual level depends on the average intellectual level of all the family members. When a new child is born into the family, the intellectual environment declines. This model states that, in general, large families have impoverished intellectual climates, as there are many immature minds for several years. Also, age spacing between siblings is an important variable in this theory. Small age differences are beneficial to the firstborn in that the firstborn is not exposed to very young siblings for too long. In addition, the firstborn has the opportunity to teach siblings, which facilitates the crystallization of knowledge of the firstborn. Applying the confluence model, if one could choose an ordinal position, one would prefer to be a firstborn with a younger sibling close in age. With its emphasis on average intellectual atmosphere, the confluence model has created much debate.

Some of the implications of the theory have not received support in the literature. For example, additional adults in the household, such as grandparents, do not seem to increase children's IQ as would seem to be predicted by the confluence model. Further-

Literature suggests that parents harbor expectations of how firstborns should behave, then act in accordance with those beliefs. During infancy, for example, mothers attend to firstborns by responding to and stimulating them more than latterborns. (Tim Pannell/Corbis)

more, differences found in IQ among firstborns, latterborns, and only children are typically small and unstable.

Birth Order and Personality

The results of research regarding the associations between birth order and personality are varied. In general, meta-analyses of systematic studies indicate that firstborn children are achievement-oriented, ambitious, conforming, anxious, assertive, and less empathetic than latterborns. Frank J. Sulloway, using a Darwinian perspective, argued that children assume different personalities or niches within the family to gain favor with parents. Firstborns do this by identifying with their parents and by conforming to parental standards. Because firstborn children are older, wiser, and more powerful, latterborns become diverse in their interests and they become more open to experience. Sulloway's treatise stemmed from his study of 3,890 career histories of scientists. Even though many firstborns were scientists (e.g., Isaac Newton, Albert Einstein, Sigmund Freud), supporters of the scientists were predominantly latterborns. Sulloway interpreted this finding as indicative of the personality differences between firstborn and later-born children.

Firstborns tend to reject new theories, especially when the innovation upsets the status quo, while latterborns are more receptive to revolutionary thinking. As an example, Sulloway found that for every 12.8 firstborns who supported evolution, there were 124 latterborns who welcomed the theory. This personality trait, openness to experience, and the concomitant defensiveness and conservatism of firstborns holds true even when size of the family, socioeconomic status, and culture are taken into account.

Some researchers have concluded that the effect of birth order on children's behavior is overrated. Many studies have not systematically controlled for intercorrelated family variables such as age spacing between siblings, size of family, and ages of siblings. Thus, certain child behaviors associated with birth order may actually be due to family size. Beyond birth order, other predictors such as gender, temperament, parenting styles, and socioeconomic status influence children's development and must be considered. For example, the literature has indicated that in families with two sisters, second-born daughters are more conforming than firstborn daughters.

Are all firstborn children power-hungry conservatives as suggested by Adler, or "goody-goodies" as proclaimed by Sulloway? Intuitively, the experiences of firstborns are affected by their ordinal position in the family. The literature has shown that parents have disparate expectations for firstborn children, although these expectations vary within and among cultures. Studies have also demonstrated that parents are more involved with their firstborn children. Moreover, evidence exists that there are behavioral, intellectual, and personality differences between firstborns and latterborns. Although it is important to acknowledge that birth-order investigators face methodological challenges, the status of being the first child in a family clearly plays some role in a child's development.

See also: BIRTH ORDER AND SPACING; SIBLINGS AND SIBLING RELATIONSHIPS

Bibliography

Adler, Alfred. *The Individual Psychology of Alfred Adler: A Systematic Presentation in Selections from His Writings,* edited and annotated by Heinz L. Ansbacher and Rowena R. Ansbacher. New York: Basic, 1956.

Hoff-Ginsberg, Erika. "The Relation of Birth Order and Socioeconomic Status to Children's Language Experience and Language Development." *Applied Psycholinguistics* 19 (1998):603–629.

Sulloway, Frank J. *Born to Rebel: Birth Order, Family Dynamics, and Creative Lives.* New York: Pantheon, 1996.

Zajonc, R. B., and Gregory B. Markus. "Birth Order and Intellectual Development." *Psychological Review* 82, no. 1 (1975):74–88.

Lisa Baumwell

FRAGILE X SYNDROME

Fragile X syndrome is an inherited disorder caused by a trinucleotide repeat expansion of DNA on the X chromosome. This expansion results in the absence or severe deficiency of the FMR1 protein (FMRP), which is known to be essential for normal brain function. FMRP appears to have an RNA-binding activity and may play an important role in synaptic maturation. Approximately 1 per 4,000 males and 1 per 6,000 females are affected. Males with Fragile X syndrome typically have moderate to severe mental retardation, which may be accompanied by hyperarousal or autisticlike behavior. Physical features include large ears, large testicles, and loose connective tissue. Females are more mildly affected; about one-third develop normally, one-third exhibit mild learning disabilities, and one-third have mild mental retardation. Carriers, approximately 1 per 260 women, are typically unaffected, and the risk of expansion to the full disorder increases with successive generations. Identification using DNA analysis of blood is highly accurate but must be specifically requested, and thus many cases go undiagnosed.

See also: BIRTH DEFECTS; DEVELOPMENTAL DISABILITIES; GENOTYPE; PHENOTYPE

Bibliography

Bailey, Donald B., and David Nelson. "The Nature and Consequences of Fragile X Syndrome." *Mental Retardation and Developmental Disabilities Research Reviews* 1 (1995):238–244.

Hagerman, Randi J., and Amy Cronister. *Fragile X Syndrome: Diagnosis, Treatment, and Research,* 2nd edition. Baltimore: Johns Hopkins University Press, 1996.

Mazzacco, Michelle M. "Advances in Research on the Fragile X Syndrome." *Mental Retardation and Developmental Disabilities Research Reviews* 6 (2000):96–106.

Don Bailey

FREUD, SIGMUND (1856–1939)

Sigmund Freud was born Sigismund Schlomo Freud on May 6, 1856, in Freiburg, Moravia, which later became the Czech Republic. As the founder of modern psychoanalysis, Freud was to change the conceptions of human mental life by showing that many seemingly illogical, unconscious psychological processes ignored by contemporary conventional science are powerful influences shaping human beings across the lifespan, including day-to-day actions, attractions, and avoidances.

Freud entered the University of Vienna in 1873 at age seventeen to study medicine. He studied the humanities for his first year and read philosophy widely (admiring Ludwig Feuerbach), which validated his reservations about the specialized study of medicine. Freud worked in Carl Claus's laboratory in Vienna (a propagandist of Darwin) and saw himself as an "intellectual researcher into nature" (Gay 1998). Freud completed his education at the University of Vienna in 1881 at the age of twenty-five. His education continued when, as a trained neurologist, he studied under the tutelage of eminent mentors such as Ernst Brucke, a famous physiologist, and Theodore Meynert, a brain anatomist and psychiatrist.

Freud's innovation in the field of human mental health was to give a developmental account of a dynamic, embodied mind in which unconscious processes played a determining role. Freud was an evolutionary naturalist. He saw humans as Oedipal apes, driven to survive and reproduce; and as cultural creatures, born more dependent than most animals into nuclear families, capable of identifying with those we love and of internalizing parental sanctions and ideals. This legacy has informed child development's concerns with the quality of parent-child interactions and the acquisition of abilities and morality alike.

Freud used clinical methods and observation since his theory suggests bias may arise in self-report due to defensiveness where impulses or thoughts conflict with morals. His case study method privileged the unique in-depth study of an individual; his theory development on this basis showed his equal commitment to generality, to discovering lawlike patterns. Privileging the early years as formative of personality (even where individuals may consciously recollect very little of them), his clinical work revealed the active contribution of the child to development. His essays on infantile sexuality in 1905 (which posited an active infantile sexuality that could scarcely be countenanced in his late-nineteenth-century culture) suggested personality was shaped by the pattern and quality of parental attendance to a child's bodily and affectional needs. He never renounced his conviction that drives—the most prominent of which in his early thought was the sex drive—were the impetus for much of our mental life.

Having studied hysteria with Jean Charcot at the Salpêtrière, a pathological laboratory in Paris (1885–1886), Freud went on to reveal how some bodily symptoms were psychological in origin (i.e., psychogenic). Wishes, losses, conflicts, of which humans may consciously know very little, may be expressed as dreams, physical symptoms, inhibitions, wordless anxieties, slips of the tongue, and bungled actions. His work with Josef Breuer in 1895 displaced hypnosis with the use of the "talking cure," where unconscious conflicts were traced via free association, whereby the patient said anything that came to mind without self-censorship. The talking cure was supple-

Sigmund Freud changed the conception of human mental life by showing that many seemingly illogical, unconscious psychological processes are powerful influences shaping human beings across the lifespan. (Hulton-Deutsch Collection Limited/Corbis)

mented after 1900 by the analysis of dreams. Symptoms could be relieved when conflicts were emotionally recontextualized, in part through the relationship to the analyst where past issues came alive again in the present (a technique called transference).

As a Jewish scholar in bourgeois Vienna, Freud was influenced by and an observer of a civilized sexual morality that he felt required of us a surplus repression (where urges and associated longings are pushed from awareness and denied expression), which damaged health and hindered contributions to culture. Financial problems had delayed his marriage to Martha Bernays (they were engaged in 1882 and married in 1886), and the realities of marriage were not equal to his expectations. Freud believed that World War I confirmed his theories about aggression and the regression to more primitive behavior that collectivities made possible. Freud suffered much loss in his life and wrote poignantly about the links between mourn-

ing and depression. In 1923 he discovered a cancerous growth on his palate, but, cherishing his cigars, sought neither specialists nor oral surgeons, going instead to general practitioners. His daughter Anna, who was to be his professional successor, tended the father who had analyzed her until his death in 1939.

See also: THEORIES OF DEVELOPMENT

Bibliography

Appignanesi, Lisa, and John Forrester. *Freud's Women.* London: Virago Press, 1993.

Gay, Peter. *Freud: A Life for Our Times.* London: J. M. Dent and Sons, 1998.

Wollheim, Richard. *Freud.* London: Fontana, 1971.

Publications by Freud

The Standard Edition of the Complete Psychological Works of Sigmund Freud, translated by James Strachey, in collaboration with Anna Freud, assisted by Alix Strachey and Alan Tyson. London: Hogarth, 1953.

Doris McIlwain

FRIENDSHIP

Friends are people who feel affection for one another and enjoy spending time together. Reciprocity characterizes the nature of most friendships. Friends typically have mutual regard for one another, exhibit give-and-take in their behaviors, and benefit in comparable ways from their social interaction. The formation, nature, and effects of friendship all change as children develop. Despite these changes, having friends is important to children's overall development, and friendship has an impact on children's social, emotional, and cognitive growth.

Friend Selection

Who is friends with whom? For young children, proximity is a key factor in friend selection. Preschoolers tend to become friends with peers who are nearby physically as neighbors or playgroup members. Similarity in age is a major factor in friendship selection, and children tend to make friends with age-mates, particularly in Western societies, where schools are segregated by age. Another powerful factor in friend selection is gender: girls tend to be friends with girls, and boys tend to be friends with boys. The preference for same-sex friends emerges in preschool and continues through childhood. To a lesser degree, children tend to be friends with peers of the same race.

Beyond these basic factors, a key determinant of friendship is similarity of interests and behaviors. During the preschool and elementary years, children prefer peers who have a similar style of play. As children grow older, they tend to have friends who have similar temperaments, prosocial and antisocial behaviors, and levels of acceptance by peers. Adolescent friends tend to be similar in their interests and attitudes, and in the degree to which they have explored options in regard to issues such as dating, education, and future occupations.

Changes in the Nature of Friendship

The quality and nature of friendship vary as a function of age. Children as young as two can have friends, and even twelve- to eighteen-month-olds select and prefer some children to others. Toddlers laugh, smile at, touch, and engage in more positive interactions with some peers more than others. In the preschool years cooperation and coordination in children's interactions with friends increases, and friends are more likely to engage in shared pretend play. Friends also have higher rates of conflict than nonfriends, likely due to the greater amount of time they spend together. However, friends are more likely than nonfriends to resolve conflicts in ways that result in equal outcomes rather than one child winning and another losing.

In the elementary school years, interactions among friends and nonfriends show the same patterns as in the preschool years but become more sharply defined. Closeness, loyalty, and equality become important features of friendship. Friends, as opposed to acquaintances (or nonfriends), talk more to each other, cooperate, and work together more effectively. In conflicts, friends are more likely to negotiate, compromise, take responsibility for the conflict, and give reasons for their arguments.

During adolescence peers become increasingly important. Friendships evolve into more intimate, supportive, communicative relationships. Many teens become intimate friends with members of the opposite sex, usually around the time that they start dating. Social competencies such as initiating interactions, self-disclosure, and provision of support increase as preadolescents mature into early adolescents, and are related to quality of friendship. In general, during early adolescence friends begin to value loyalty and intimacy more, becoming more trusting and self-disclosing. Tolerance of individuality between close friends also increases with age, and friends' emphasis on control and conformity decreases.

Changes in the Conception of Friendship

Children's conception of friendship changes with age. Young children define friendship primarily on the basis of interactions in the here-and-now and actual activities with their peers. At age seven or eight, friends tend to be viewed in terms of rewards and costs (e.g., certain friends are fun to be with or have interesting toys). When children are about ten years old, issues such as loyalty, making an active attempt to understand one another, and openly discussing personal thoughts and feelings become important components of friendship. Preadolescents and adolescents emphasize cooperative reciprocity (doing the same for one another), equality, trust, and mutual understanding between friends. It is unclear how much the age differences in children's conceptions of friends reflect real differences in their thinking about friendships or reflect differences in how well young children can express their ideas.

Influence of Parenting on Friendship

As children develop, they spend increasing amounts of time alone and with friends. Particularly during adolescence, there is a dramatic drop in the amount of time teens spend with their parents. Despite these changes in time allocation, research indicates that parents influence interactions with peers. Children and adolescents bring many qualities to their friendships that develop early in life as a result of socialization experiences in the family. Researchers find that children and adolescents from warm, supportive families are more socially competent and report more positive friendships. Further, there is evidence that parental responsiveness lessens the effects of negative peer influences. For example, an adolescent with a close friend who uses drugs is at risk primarily if the adolescent's parents are cold, detached, and disinclined to monitor and supervise the adolescent's activities. Research also suggests that adolescents without close friends are more influenced by families than peers, and that adolescents in less cohesive and less adaptive families are more influenced by peers than family members.

Influence of Friends on One Another

Friends can have negative effects on children if they engage in problematic behaviors. For example, aggressive children tend to have aggressive friends. Similarly, adolescents who smoke or abuse alcohol or drugs tend to have friends who do so. However, because children tend to chose friends who are similar to themselves in behaviors, attitudes, and identities, it is difficult to determine whether friends actually affect one another's behavior or if children simply seek out peers who think, act, and feel as they do. Some research suggests that friends do influence one another's behavior, at least to some degree or for some people. For example, some investigators have

As children grow older, their conception of friendship may change. Younger children tend to view friends in terms of rewards and costs; older children begin to look at friends using emotional terms, such as loyalty and trust. (O'Brien Productions/Corbis)

found that peer contact predicts problem behavior primarily among children who have a history of problem behavior.

Friends likely influence children and adolescents in positive as well as negative ways. Friends influence academic achievement and prosocial behaviors. Particularly during adolescence, individuals are influenced by friends because they admire their peers and respect the opinions of their friends, not typically because of coercive pressures. Teens are most influenced by peers in middle adolescence, compared to early and late adolescence.

Friendship and Healthy Development

As suggested by important developmental theorists like Jean Piaget, Lev Vygotsky, and Harry Stack Sullivan, friends provide emotional support, validation and confirmation of the legitimacy of one's own thoughts and feelings, and opportunities for the development of important social and cognitive skills. Children with friends are less likely to feel lonely, and friendships provide a context for the development of social skills and knowledge that children need to form positive relationships with other people.

In general, having friends is associated with positive developmental outcomes, such as social competence and adjustment. For example, young children's initial attitudes toward school are more positive if they begin school with a large number of prior friends as classmates. Exchanges with friends also promote cognitive development. This is because children are more likely to criticize each other's ideas and to elaborate and clarify their own thoughts with friends than nonfriends or adults. Children also benefit from talking and working together, and older friends often act as mentors for younger children. Friendships serve as a buffer against unpleasant experiences, like peer victimization and teasing from other children. Because friendships fill important needs for children, it might be expected that having friends enhances children's long-term social and emotional health. In fact, having a close, reciprocated best friend in elementary school has been linked to a variety of positive psychological and behavioral outcomes for children, not only during the school years but also years later in early adulthood. This is especially true if children's friendships are positive and do not have many negative features.

In summary, the nature of friendship changes as children grow, and friendship plays an important role in development. As children mature, friends rely on each other and increasingly provide a context for self-disclosure and intimacy. Adolescent friends, more than younger friends, use friendships as a context for self-exploration, problem solving, and a source of honest feedback. Friendship is important in healthy growth and development, and children with close friendships reap the benefits of these relationships well into adulthood.

See also: SOCIAL DEVELOPMENT

Bibliography

Bukowski, William, Andrew Newcomb, and Willard Hartup, eds. *The Company They Keep: Friendship in Childhood and Adolescence.* New York: Cambridge University Press, 1996.

Piaget, Jean. *The Moral Judgment of the Child.* New York: Free Press, 1965.

Rubin, Kenneth, William Bukowski, and Jeffrey Parker. "Peer Interactions, Relationships, and Groups." In William Damon ed. *Handbook of Child Psychology,* Vol. 3: *Social, Emotional, and Personality Development,* 5th edition, edited by Nancy Eisenberg. New York: Wiley, 1998.

Savin-Williams, Ritch, and Thomas Berndt. "Friendship and Peer Relations." In Shirley Feldman and Glen Elliot eds., *At the Threshold: The Developing Adolescent.* Cambridge, MA: Harvard University Press, 1990.

Sullivan, Harry. *The Interpersonal Theory of Psychiatry.* New York: Norton, 1953.

Vygotsky, Lev. *Mind in Society: The Development of Higher Psychological Processes.* Cambridge, MA: Harvard University Press, 1978.

Youniss, James, and Jacqueline Smollar. *Adolescent Relations with Mothers, Fathers, and Friends.* Chicago: University of Chicago Press, 1985.

Amanda Sheffield Morris
Nancy Eisenberg

G

GAY- AND LESBIAN-HEADED FAMILIES

Openly gay and lesbian people are choosing to have children in increasing numbers, although the largest group of lesbian- and gay-headed families is still comprised of those parenting children from prior heterosexual relationships. Methods for creating "intentional" families include adoption, foster parenting, alternative insemination, and surrogacy. Laws regarding adoption and foster parenting vary by state as well as by country (in the case of international adoption). The exact number of lesbian- and gay-headed families is difficult to ascertain. Secrecy is still a fairly common practice because of the risk of losing children and employment as a result of sexual orientation. One study reported that in 1999, 3.9 million children age nineteen and under had gay or lesbian parents. Gay- and lesbian-headed families experience a variety of forms of discrimination, including underrepresentation in governmental policy, legal protection, educational environments, communities of faith, access to medical treatment and reproductive technology, insurance coverage, and the media. Several research studies have shown that children raised in lesbian- and gay-headed households score on par with other children in measures of socio-emotional well-being. Some studies have found that children of lesbian and gay parents display a higher degree of empathy and awareness and respect for diversity than children of heterosexual parents.

See also: PARENT-CHILD RELATIONSHIPS; PARENTING

Bibliography

Buxton, Amity. *The Other Side of the Closet: The Coming-Out Crisis for Straight Spouses.* Santa Monica, CA: IBS Press, 1991.

Kaeser, Gigi. *Love Makes a Family: Portraits of Lesbian, Gay, Bisexual, and Transgender Parents and Their Families,* edited by Peggy Gillespie. Amherst, MA: University of Massachusetts Press, 1999.

Aimee Gelnaw

GENDER-ROLE DEVELOPMENT

Gender-role development is one of the most important areas of human development. In fact, the sex of a newborn sets the agenda for a whole array of developmental experiences that will influence the person throughout his or her life.

The often controversial study of the development of gender is a topic that is inherently interesting to parents, students, researchers, and scholars for several reasons. First and foremost, one's sex is one of the most salient characteristics that is presented to other people. Second, who one is as a male or a female becomes a significant part of one's overall identity; it is one of the first descriptors people use about themselves. Labeling oneself as a "boy" or "girl" can begin as early as age eighteen months. Third, gender is an important mediator of human experiences and the way in which individuals interact with each other and the physical environment. Individuals' choices of friends, toys, classes taken in middle school, and vocation all are influenced by sex. Finally, the study of sex, gender development, and sex differences becomes the focal point of an age-old controversy that has influenced the field of developmental psychology: the nature-nurture controversy. Are gender roles and sex differences biologically determined? What are the effects of society and culture on gender and sex? How do biology (nature) and environment (nurture) interact and mutually influence each other in this significant dimension of human development?

When discussing gender-role development, the definitions of the terms "sex" and "gender" need to be understood. Referring to the nature-nurture controversy, scholars have found it important to distinguish those aspects of males and females that can be attributed to biology and those that can be attributed to social influences. The term "sex" denotes the actual physical makeup of individuals that define them as male or female. Sex is determined by genetic makeup, internal reproductive organs, the organization of the brain (such as in the control of hormone production), and external genitalia. By contrast, the behavior of individuals as males or females, the types of roles they assume, and their personality characteristics, may be as much a function of social expectations and interactions as their biological makeup. For example, in American culture, females are expected to be nurturing, and males aggressive. These behaviors and characteristics are dependent upon the social context. In order to differentiate social roles and behaviors from biological features, scholars refer to these as "gender" and "gender roles." Obviously, sex and gender are intertwined. Social expectations usually are enacted once body parts reveal the biological makeup of the individual.

The Development of Sex and Gender

Both sex and gender have a developmental story to tell that begins before birth (prenatal) and continues throughout the lifespan. Important developmental changes occur from conception through the adolescence years, and there are important theoretical perspectives and research studies that have tried to shed light on these developmental accomplishments.

Prenatal Development

Gender-role development begins at conception. If the fertilized cell has an XY chromosomal pattern, the baby will become a genetic male; an XX chromosomal pattern will lead to a genetic female. There cannot be a genetic male without that Y chromosome. Sometimes there are aberrations to these patterns, which can ultimately lead to a number of syndromes

such as females with only one X chromosome (Turner's syndrome) or males with two Xs and one Y (Klinefelter's syndrome). Frequently these syndromes result in some form of cognitive and physical impairment.

At around week six of gestation, the hormone testosterone will stimulate the tissues into developing into the male internal organs; otherwise, the organs will become part of the female reproductive system. Then, by around three or four months, the external genitalia are formed. It is also during early prenatal development that the brain, bathed by the male and female hormones, may differentiate into a "female" or "male" brain (for example, female brains may be more symmetrically organized), but most of this research is still inconclusive.

Prenatal sex differentiation culminates at birth. When the proclamation of "It's a boy!" or "It's a girl!" is made, the complex process of socialization begins. It is important to recognize that the path of prenatal development may take significant deviations. Aside from the chromosomal abnormalities already mentioned, there are instances during prenatal development when females are bathed by the male hormones (androgens), and situations where male genital tissues are insensitive to the differentiating function of the male hormones. Both situations can lead to a baby born with ambiguous genitalia. In such situations, parents face agonizing decisions: whether to surgically "correct" the condition and whether to raise the baby as a female or as a male.

Infancy

Overall, the sex differences between boys and girls in the first year of life are minimal. Boys may be a bit more active or fussier and girls more physically mature and less prone to physical problems, but that may be the extent of the significant differences. Yet, baby boys are bounced and roughhoused, whereas girls are talked to more. Mothers tend to ignore the emotional expressions of their infant sons, while fathers spend more time with their boys than with their girls. Even during infancy, their names, their clothing, the "sugar and spice" messages in baby congratulation cards, and their room furnishings shape girls and boys. According to Marilyn Stern and Katherine H. Karraker, adults will characterize the same baby as strong and hardy if they think it is a male, and delicate and soft if they think it is a female. In these and other ways, gender-role socialization has already begun in earnest.

Early Childhood

The years from about age two to age six are crucial years in the development of gender roles. It is during these years that children become aware of

The years from about age two to age six are crucial in the development of gender roles. During these years, children become aware of their gender, where play styles and behaviors begin to crystallize around that core identity of "I am a girl" or "I am a boy." (Reflection Photolibrary/Corbis)

their gender, where play styles and behaviors begin to crystallize around that core identity of "I am a girl" or "I am a boy," and that the social context of family, school, the peer group, and the media exert potent messages in stereotyped ways. Because of the centrality of gender-role development during these years, most theories of social and personality development highlight the early childhood years. For example, in the psychoanalytic theory of Sigmund Freud, in the third stage of psychosexual development a male child encounters the Oedipal Crisis, a time when the only way in which he can cope with his desire for his mother and fear of his father is to completely identify and incorporate his father's characteristics within himself. Freud posited a similar process for girls' desires for their fathers (the Electra complex). Although many contemporary psychologists do not agree with this theory in general, Freud is credited with highlighting the development of gender and gender-role behav-

iors very early in childhood and their link to identification with parents.

Social learning theory, developed by Albert Bandura, emphasizes the importance of children's imitation of the behavior of others (models). The theory posits that boys learn how to behave as boys from observing and imitating masculine behaviors, especially from their fathers, and girls learn from imitating females, especially their mothers. When children imitate same-sex behaviors, they are rewarded, but imitating the other sex may carry the threat of punishment. Although the research indicates that most parents value the same behaviors for their sons and daughters, some rewards or punishments are given on the basis of gender typing, particularly during play. This is even more true for boys than for girls, with fathers being the most punitive if, for example, they observe their sons playing with Barbie dolls or sporting red fingernail polish.

Finally, cognitive developmental theory underscores the importance of understanding what it means to be a boy or girl in the development of gender roles. In 1966 Lawrence Kohlberg conceived of gender development as a three-stage process in which children first learn their identity ("I am a boy"), then gender stability ("I will always be a boy and grow up to be a man"), and finally gender constancy ("Even if I wore a dress, I would still be a boy"), all by about six years of age. A newer version of this approach, formulated by Carol Martin and Charles Halverson in 1981, emphasized the development of gender schemas—children's ideas of gender that help them categorize experiences as relevant to one sex or the other.

Regardless of which theoretical explanation of gender roles is used, the early acquisitions of such ideas and behaviors make for very stereotyped youngsters. Because young children see the world in black-and-white terms, they may go as far as to insist that only men could be physicians, even when their own pediatrician is a woman!

Middle Childhood

Whereas parents play a significant role in gender socialization when their children are very young, when most Western boys and girls enter school they separate into gender-segregated groups that seem to operate by their own set of peer-driven rules. Gender segregation is such a widespread phenomenon that boys and girls seem to work and play together only when there is a coercive adult present. During unstructured free time, the lapse into the "two cultures of childhood" (Maccoby 1998, p. 32) is quite obvious—the other sex becomes "toxic." A typical boys' group is large, competitive, hierarchical, with one or two boys at the top of the pecking order, and organized around large group outdoor activities such as sports. Rough-and-tumble play and displays of strength and toughness frequently occur. In contrast, girls' groups tend to be smaller and dependent on intense, intimate conversations where the emphasis is upon maintaining group cohesion. Girls try very hard to be "nice" to one another, even as they attempt to covertly promote their own agenda. In her 1998 book The Two Sexes, Eleanor Maccoby stated her belief that this segregation, hints of which may be seen as early as age four or five, begins when girls shy away from their exuberant, active male playmates, who do not rely as much upon language for persuasion and influence. The boys' groups ultimately evolve into a strict order that avoids anything perceived as feminine. Girls have much greater latitude in American society to cross that sacred border. Maccoby contended that these interaction styles, to some extent, continue throughout adolescence and adulthood.

Adolescence

Erik H. Erikson believed that adolescence represented a crucial turning point in the development of a sense of identity. All of the physical, social, and cognitive changes of these years lead to frequent soul-searching about "Who am I?" Such uncertainty and insecurity also can further promote conformity into one's gender role, or "gender intensification." During early adolescence, boys may emulate "macho" role models and be quite homophobic; girls may adhere to strict dress codes (e.g., that which is "in") and play down their intellectual talents and abilities. The timing of puberty may also have significant implications for adolescent gender development. Girls are more likely to encounter social difficulties when they mature early, but for boys the opposite is true.

For many adolescents, the uncertainties, conflicting demands, and withdrawal of adult and community support are predictors of significant problems. Much has been written about how difficult the adolescent years are for girls, as they are more likely than boys to experience depression, eating disorders, and low self-esteem. This may vary, however, according to the ethnicity of the girl, as African-American teenagers do not seem to express such negative views about themselves. In his 1998 book Real Boys, William Pollack emphasized the realization that gender-role socialization makes life hard for boys. Because Western culture provides boys little opportunity for self-expression and close emotional relationships, the suicide rate and rate of violence in teenage boys is far greater than for girls.

By the end of adolescence, both sexes usually become more tolerant of themselves and others in terms of their consideration of gender-related behaviors. Individuals' evolution as men and women continues throughout the lifespan, however, as each person encounters major life transitions such as marriage, parenthood, middle age, and old age. It is important to recognize that although humans emphasize the differential paths of boys and girls in the development of gender roles, the fundamental dimensions of humanity—male and female—are more similar than different.

See also: ERIKSON, ERIK; PERSONALITY DEVELOPMENT

Bibliography

American Association of University Women. *Shortchanging Girls, Shortchanging America: A Call to Action.* Washington, DC: American Association of University Women, 1991.

Bandura, Albert. *Social Learning Theory.* Englewood Cliffs, NJ: Prentice-Hall, 1977.

Beal, Carole R. *Boys and Girls: The Development of Gender Roles.* New York: McGraw-Hill, 1994.

Bridges, Judith S. "Pink or Blue: Gender-Stereotypic Perceptions of Infants as Conveyed by Birth Congratulations Cards." *Psychology of Women Quarterly* 17 (1993):193–205.

Denmark, Florence, Vita Rabinowitz, and Jeri Sechzer. *Engendering Psychology*. Boston: Allyn and Bacon, 2000.

Erikson, Erik H. *Identity, Youth, and Crisis*. New York: Norton, 1968.

Fagot, Beverly I., and Mary D. Leinbach. "The Young Child's Gender Schema: Environmental Input, Internal Organization." *Child Development* 60 (1989):663–672.

Halpern, Diane F. *Sex Differences in Cognitive Abilities*, 3rd edition. Mahwah, NJ: Lawrence Erlbaum, 2000.

Kohlberg, Lawrence. "A Cognitive-Developmental Analysis of Children's Sex Role Concepts and Attitudes." In Eleanor E. Maccoby ed., *The Development of Sex Differences*. Stanford, CA: Stanford University Press, 1966.

Maccoby, Eleanor E. *The Two Sexes: Growing Up Apart, Coming Together*. Cambridge, MA: Harvard University Press, Belknap Press, 1998.

Martin, Carol L., and Charles F. Halverson. "A Schematic Processing Model of Sex Typing and Stereotyping in Children." *Child Development* 52 (1981):1119–1134.

Pollack, William. *Real Boys*. New York: Henry Holt, 1998.

Rheingold, Harriet L., and Kaye V. Cook. "The Content of Boys' and Girls' Rooms as an Index of Parents' Behavior." *Child Development* 46 (1975):445–463.

Stern, Marilyn, and Katherine H. Karraker. "Sex Stereotyping of Infants: A Review of Gender Labeling Studies." *Sex Roles* 20 (1989):501–522.

Vasques, Melba J. T., and Cynthia de las Fuentes. "American-Born Asian, African, Latina, and American Indian Adolescent Girls: Challenges and Strengths." In Norine G. Johnson and Michael C. Roberts ed., *Beyond Appearance: A New Look at Adolescent Girls*. Washington, DC: American Psychological Association, 1999.

Illene C. Noppe

GENERATION GAP

The term "generation gap," which came into popular and scholarly use during the late 1960s and early 1970s, refers to differences in values of older and younger generations. Initially, it was thought that adolescents needed to express opinions and internalize value systems that were distinct from their parents' to individuate successfully and create separate identities. But parents often do not perceive striking dissimilarities between their own values and those of their offspring, in part because of their need to feel connected to their children. Although it is possible to contrast the political ideology and consumer behaviors of cohorts of parents and adolescents in a society, typically few differences exist when comparing the values of older and younger generations within a family line. Contrary to the prediction that the generation gap promotes identity achievement, adolescents report a weaker sense of personal identity when they view family life differently from their parents.

See also: ERIKSON, ERIK; GRANDPARENTS

Bibliography

Bengston, V. L. "The Generation Gap." *Youth and Society* Vol. 2 (1970):7–32.

Fiese, Barbara H. "Dimensions of Family Rituals across Two Generations: Relation to Adolescent Identity." *Family Process* Vol. 31 (1992):151–162.

Lynott, P. P., and R. Roberts. "The Developmental Stake Hypothesis and Changing Perceptions of Intergenerational Relations, 1971–1985." *The Gerontologist* Vol. 37 (1997):394–405.

Mead, Margaret. *Culture and Commitment: A Study of the Generation Gap*. New York: Basic Books, 1970.

Barbara H. Fiese
Julie Poehlmann

GENETIC COUNSELING

Genetic counseling is the professional guidance and education of individuals, families, or potential parents in matters concerning diseases with a genetic component. The process involves a trained genetic counselor who reviews medical records, collects a family history of genetic disorders in relatives, and investigates the scientific literature for known genetic causes. The Human Genome Project has supported the identification of the causes and the development of diagnostic tests for many birth defects. Parents at risk of having children with particular birth defects are those who have previously had affected children or those with affected relatives. For birth defects with a known genetic etiology a genetic counselor may suggest prenatal genetic testing, which can identify affected offspring prenatally from parents at risk of having children with particular birth defects. The genetic counselor will analyze the results of genetic testing and advise the potential parents of the probability of having affected children. The counselor will also explain the alternatives for dealing with the risk of occurrence and provide options for alternative courses of action. Genetic counseling can aid in decreasing the number of children with genetic disorders by providing at-risk parents alternatives that will allow them to have children without particular birth defects. Counseling also helps parents cope with the emotional, social, and economic consequences of genetic disease.

See also: BIRTH DEFECTS; HUMAN GENOME PROJECT

Bibliography

National Human Genome Research Institute. "Information for Patients and Families." Available from http://www.nhgri.nih.gov/Policy_and_public_affairs/Communications/Patients_and_families/; INTERNET.

Oak Ridge National Laboratory. "Genetic Counseling." Available from http://www.ornl.gov/hgmis/medicine/genecounseling.html; INTERNET.

David W. Threadgill
Robert E. Boykin

GENOTYPE

The term "genotype" refers to the specific genetic makeup of an individual and is often used with reference to allelic or mutant differences between individuals at one or more genes. The genotype of an individual is the genetic information within an individual's specific DNA sequence that sets the limits upon which nongenetic parameters like environment modulate normal and abnormal phenotypes. Genotypes at specific genes known to cause birth defects are used as diagnostics in genetic counseling to identify parents carrying specific disease genes and in prenatal genetic testing for offspring that will have birth defects. For example, a description of a mutation within the gene that causes cystic fibrosis is a genotype, while manifestation of the disease is the phenotype. The results of the Human Genome Project are being used to identify DNA sequences that cause birth defects. The genotypes associated with birth defects are then available for development of more accurate diagnostic tests.

See also: GENETIC COUNSELING; HUMAN GENOME
   PROJECT

Bibliography

Oak Ridge National Laboratory. "The Science behind the Human Genome Project." Available from http://www.ornl.gov/hgmis/project/info.html; INTERNET

David W. Threadgill
Robert E. Boykin

Arnold Gesell was one of the first psychologists to systematically describe children's achievements in terms of physical and psychological development. (UPI/Corbis-Bettmann)

GESELL, ARNOLD (1880–1961)

Prior to the early twentieth century, scientific observations of children were not common. Arnold Gesell was one of the first psychologists to systematically describe children's physical, social, and emotional achievements, particularly in the first five years of life. In fact, the developmental norms established by Gesell and his colleagues are still used by pediatricians and psychologists today.

Gesell was born and raised in Alma, Wisconsin, and received a doctorate in psychology in 1906 from Clark University. In 1911 he began a faculty position in education at Yale University. While fulfilling the requirements of his teaching and research position, he also worked toward a doctorate in medicine, which he earned in 1915. While at Yale, Gesell established and directed the Clinic of Child Development, where children's achievements in terms of physical and psychological development were observed and measured. Gesell's observations of children allowed him to describe developmental milestones in ten major areas: motor characteristics, personal hygiene, emo-

tional expression, fears and dreams, self and sex, interpersonal relations, play and pastimes, school life, ethical sense, and philosophic outlook. His training in physiology and his focus on developmental milestones led Gesell to be a strong proponent of the "maturational" perspective of child development. That is, he believed that child development occurs according to a predetermined, naturally unfolding plan of growth.

Gesell's most notable achievement was his contribution to the "normative" approach to studying children. In this approach, psychologists observed large numbers of children of various ages and determined the typical age, or "norms," for which most children achieved various developmental milestones.

When Gesell retired from Yale in 1948, his colleagues established a private institution in his name in New Haven, Connecticut, called the Gesell Institute of Child Development. During the 1970s and 1980s Gesell's research prompted many books and articles to be published by researchers associated with the institute. These writings became popular with parents and teachers because they described the typical behaviors to be expected of children at each age; however, Gesell's writings have been criticized by other psychologists because he did not readily acknowledge that there are individual differences in child development, and his focus on developmental norms implied that what is typical for each age is also what is desirable. Nevertheless, his practice of carefully observing, measuring, and describing child development created a foundation for subsequent research that described both average developmental trends and individual differences in development.

See also: DEVELOPMENTAL NORMS; THEORIES OF DEVELOPMENT

Bibliography

Crain, William. *Theories of Development: Concepts and Applications,* 4th edition. Upper Saddle River, NJ: Prentice Hall, 2000.

Thelen, Esther, and Karen Adolph. "Arnold Gesell: The Paradox of Nature and Nurture." In Ross Parke, Peter Ornstein, John Rieser, and Carolyn Zahn-Waxler eds., *A Century of Developmental Psychology.* Washington, DC: American Psychological Association, 1994.

Thomas, R. Murray. *Comparing Theories of Child Development,* 5th edition. Belmont, CA: Wadsworth, 2000.

Publications by Gesell

Gesell, Arnold, Francis Ilg, Louis Bates Ames, and Glenna Bullis. *The Child from Five to Ten.* New York: Harper and Row, 1977.

Sherry L. Beaumont

GIFTED CHILDREN

Little consensus exists among professionals as to what defines a gifted child. According to the results of the Intelligence Quotient (IQ) Test, a child can be gifted intellectually (where the most frequently used defining score is an IQ of 130) or academically (a ninety-fifth percentile ranking). But a gifted child may also show exceptional talent in creativity, the performing arts, or athletics. Most definitions of giftedness include multiple categories, incorporating social or creative talents as well as intellectual and academic abilities. Selection of children for gifted programs depends on the definitions schools employ. Thus, a creative, poor, or underachieving genius may not be discovered if a school's definition relies solely on IQ scores. Intellectually gifted children are usually intrinsically motivated and demonstrate exceptional abilities in math, language, or art at early ages. They sometimes suffer socially, mostly in relating to peers, but not always. Because profiles of gifted children are quite diverse, understanding and identifying giftedness should take this complexity into account.

See also: INTELLIGENCE; SOCIAL DEVELOPMENT

Bibliography

Davis, Gary, and Sylvia Rimm. *Education of the Gifted and Talented,* 4th edition. Boston: Allyn and Bacon, 1998.

Winner, Ellen. *Gifted Children.* New York: Basic Books, 1996.

Vanessa C. Gallo

GINOTT, HAIM G. (1922–1973)

Haim Ginott was a clinical psychologist, child therapist, parent educator, and author whose work has had a substantial impact on the way adults relate to children. He began his career as an elementary school teacher in Israel in 1947 before immigrating to the United States. There he attended Columbia University in New York City, earning a doctoral degree in clinical psychology in 1952.

Ginott's work with troubled children at the Jacksonville, Florida, Guidance Clinic helped him refine his unique combination of compassion and boundary setting. While many of his contemporaries favored one or the other, Ginott wove the two into a seamless whole that showed respect for children's feelings while setting limits on their behavior. Ginott said that he was strict with unacceptable behavior but permissive with feelings. His aim was to help parents socialize their children while simultaneously cultivating their emotional well being. Ginott's books, *Between Parent and Child, Between Parent and Teenager,* and *Teacher and Child,* were popular for many years and were translated into thirty languages. Rather than accuse, cajole, or correct parents in his parenting groups, he showed compassion for their struggle even as he encouraged them to listen with understanding and empathy to their children. His method for working with parents is described by Arthur R. Orgel (1980).

At the heart of Ginott's method is the recognition that denying feelings makes them more intense and confused. By contrast, the acknowledgment of feelings allows people to heal and consequently become better problem solvers. For example, Ginott wrote of a twelve-year-old girl who was tense and tearful when her cousin left after spending the summer with her. Ginott recommended that parents acknowledge their children's feelings in situations like this with responses such as "You miss her already" and "The house must seem kind of empty to you without Susie around."

Ginott's continuing impact is underscored in the influential book by John Gottman on raising emotionally intelligent children: "Ginott's theories had never been proven using empirically sound, scientific methods. But . . . I can provide the first quantifiable evidence to suggest that Ginott's ideas were essentially correct. Empathy not only matters; it is the foundation of effective parenting" (p. 35). Following Ginott's example, Gottman encourages parents to be "emo-

Haim Ginott's work had a profound effect on the way adults and children relate to one another. (Alice Ginott)

tion coaches" rather than being dismissive, disapproving, or laissez-faire.

While Ginott's influence is evident in works by Gottman and also by his students Adele Faber and Elaine Mazlish, his greatest contribution and continuing legacy may be teaching the communication skills that help parents relate to their children in a caring and understanding way without diminishing parental authority.

Bibliography

Gottman, John M. *Raising an Emotionally Intelligent Child: The Heart of Parenting*. New York: Simon and Schuster, 1996.

Orgel, Arthur R. "Haim Ginott's Approach to Parent Education." In M. J. Fine ed., *Handbook on Parent Education*. New York: Academic Press, 1980.

Publications by Ginott

Teacher and Child. New York: Macmillan, 1972.

Between Parent and Teenager. New York: Macmillan, 1969.

Between Parent and Child. New York: Macmillan, 1965.

H. Wallace Goddard
Alice Ginott

GRANDPARENTS

A grandparent is the parent of a parent who traditionally has served as a comforting presence in a child's life. In contemporary society children's relationships with grandparents vary greatly depending on the stability of a child's nuclear family, physical distance, the frequency and type of contact, and the degree of emotional attachment. In some cases the ties are strictly symbolic. At the other end of the spectrum are grandparents who are highly significant to the emotional or financial well-being of a child. The number of children in the United States with grandparents as primary caregivers is on the rise, and this increase is attributed to factors such as increasing drug use, teenage pregnancy, and divorce among parents. Grandmothers are more likely to play a central role in child rearing in African-American families than in any other ethnic group. Due to an increase in life expectancy in the United States, older children and young adults are more likely to have a living grandparent than in past generations.

See also: GENERATION GAP; PARENT-CHILD RELATIONSHIPS

Bibliography

Hagestad, G. "Continuity and Connectedness." In Vern L. Bengston and Joan F. Roberston eds., *Grandparenthood*. Beverly Hills, CA: Sage, 1985.

Kornhaber, Arthur. *Contemporary Grandparenting*. Thousand Oaks, CA: Sage, 1996.

Marianne Scholl

GROWTH RATE

Infancy is a time of rapid growth. Generally, children double their birth weight by five months of age, triple it by twelve months, and quadruple it by twenty-four months. During the toddler years growth stabilizes by around five years, and children grow in height faster than in weight. Steady growth continues from seven to ten years of age. Gains in the thickness of fat tissue are greater in girls during this time because girls tend to reach puberty before boys. Adolescence and the onset of puberty bring another rapid growth spurt. In girls puberty typically occurs between eleven and fourteen years of age. In boys the growth spurt may begin at age twelve or thirteen, peak at fourteen, and end at age eighteen or nineteen. Generally, growth in boys is more rapid and lasts longer, and more muscle mass is gained. Growth potential is strongly influenced by genetics and through maintenance of proper health and nutrition.

See also: DEVELOPMENTAL NORMS; MATURATION; MILESTONES OF DEVELOPMENT

Bibliography

Chumlea, William Cameron. "Growth and Development." In Patricia M. Queen and Carol E. Land eds., *Handbook of Pediatric Nutrition,* Gaithersburg, MD: Aspen Publishers, 1993.

Satter, Ellyn. *Child of Mine: Feeding with Love and Good Sense.* Palo Alto, CA: Bull Publishing, 1991.

Jennifer E. N. Fedie

H

HALL, GRANVILLE STANLEY (1844–1924)

Granville Stanley Hall, the first president of the American Psychological Association, was born in Ashfield, Massachusetts. Hall was enrolled in Williston Seminary, and then went to Williams College, where he graduated in 1867.

Around 1870 Hall traveled to Germany, where he was influenced by Nature-philosophy, especially by its genetic (i.e., developmental) approach. After obtaining his doctorate at Harvard University under the supervision of William James in 1878, he visited Germany again to study experimental psychology (with Wilhelm Wundt and others) and physiology. In 1883 he founded the first psychology laboratory in the United States at Johns Hopkins University, and became president of Clark University in 1889. There he began to develop a systematic theory of child development. By that time he had been involved in educational theory and practices that were based on progressivism and ancestral recapitulation theory proposed by German biologist Ernst Haeckel.

Hall believed that curricula should be attuned to sequentially emerging children's needs that reflect the evolutional history of humankind. In addition, by studying the natural, normative course of child development, one could construct an evolutionary history of human behavior, mind, and culture, which is the chief concern of present-day evolutionary psychology. Hall encouraged the collection of anecdotal descriptions of individual children's behavior by psychologists as well as by educators and parents. He also introduced a questionnaire method to understand the content of children's minds. These methods, which have been criticized as methodologically weak, have been reappraised by contemporary psychologists like Sheldon White. Hall's most influential work is *Adolescence* (1904). In it he explained psychological development up to adolescence mainly in terms of the biological theory of recapitulation. Hall believed in the perfectibility of humankind; thus adolescents' adaptability might provide the jumping-off point for the fulfillment of human potential and evolutionary advancement.

Hall's influence as a developmentalist and promoter of child study movement was seen in non-Western countries like Japan, especially around the 1900s. That was the period when Japanese educators and psychologists began their effort to collect child development data in Japan as a necessary provision for establishing education suited to the nation. Hall also set a meeting ground for Freudian psychoanalysis and American psychiatry and psychology in 1909, leading to acceptance of psychoanalysis in the United States and stimulating later studies. Toward the end of his life Hall published a book, *Senescence* (1922), which dealt with various aspects of changes and their problems. Though the biological theories Hall adopted had long been discredited, the last decade of the twentieth century witnessed a reappraisal of Hall's contribution to the developmental sciences.

See also: DEVELOPMENTAL NORMS; THEORIES OF DEVELOPMENT

171

Granville Stanley Hall (sitting center) was the first president of American Psychological Association. (Corbis-Bettmann)

Bibliography

Appley, Mortimer Herbert. "G. Stanley Hall: Vow on Mount Owen." In Stewart H. Hulse and Bert F. Green, Jr. eds., *One Hundred Years of Psychological Research in America: G. Stanley Hall and the Johns Hopkins Tradition.* Baltimore: Johns Hopkins University Press, 1986.

Cairns, Robert B. "The Making of Developmental Psychology." In *Handbook of Child Psychology,* Vol. 1, 5th edition, edited by Richard M. Lerner. New York: Wiley, 1998.

Dixon, Roger A., and Richard M. Lerner. "A History of Systems in Developmental Psychology." In *Developmental Psychology: An Advanced Textbook,* 3rd edition, edited by Marc H. Bornstein and Michael E. Lamb. Hillsdale, NJ: Lawrence Erlbaum, 1992.

Morss, John R. *The Biologizing of Childhood: Developmental Psychology and the Darwinian Myth.* Hove, United Kingdom: Lawrence Erlbaum, 1990.

Ross, Dorothy G. *Stanley Hall: The Psychologist as Prophet.* Chicago: University of Chicago Press, 1972.

White, Sheldon H. "G. Stanley Hall: From Philosophy to Developmental Psychology." *Developmental Psychology* 28 (1992):25–34.

Publications by Hall

"The Contents of Children's Minds on Entering School." *Pedagogical Seminary* 1 (1891):139–173.

Adolescence: Its Psychology and Its Relations to Physiology, Anthropology, Sociology, Sex, Crime, Religion, and Education. New York: Appleton, 1904.

Senescence, the Last Half of the Life. New York: Appleton, 1922.

Hideo Kojima

HANDEDNESS

The term "handedness" typically refers to a person's preference for the use of a particular hand in familiar, unimanual tasks such as handwriting and throwing a ball. Depending on the criteria used, 65 to 90 percent of adults are right-handed, about 4 percent are left-handed, and the rest are mixed-handed, preferring the right hand for some tasks and the left for others. The tendency to prefer the right hand exists across cultures, and fossil evidence suggests that this preference dates to prehistoric times. Some bias toward the use of the right hand is evident even before birth, but within individual infants, hand preference often varies across time and tasks. It is not until sometime in the second year after birth that handedness becomes clearly established for the majority of children. Because the preferred hand is controlled by the opposite cerebral hemisphere, handedness brings up important questions about how functional differences develop between the two sides of the brain.

See also: DEVELOPMENTAL NORMS; MOTOR DEVELOPMENT

Bibliography

Young, Gerald, Sidney Segalowitz, Carl Corter, and Sandra Trehub, eds. *Manual Specialization and the Developing Brain.* New York: Academic Press, 1983.

Gwen E. Gustafson
Xin Chen

HARLOW, HARRY (1905–1981)

Harry Harlow received his B.A. and Ph.D. in psychology from Stanford University and then joined the faculty at the University of Wisconsin, where he established the Psychology Primate Laboratory. When Harlow's lab joined the Wisconsin Regional Primate Laboratory in 1964, Harlow became the director of the merged research center. He is most famous for his scientific study of love. Starting in 1957, Harlow systematically manipulated the rearing conditions of baby rhesus monkeys. Some were reared with mothers, others without. Harlow provided "surrogate mothers" either of terry cloth wrapped around a sloped wooden block or of wire mesh. Nippled bottles that fed milk on schedule were attached to the upper thoracic section of the surrogates.

Harlow's findings disproved predictions by reinforcement theorists that love is a secondary or derived drive associated with the reduction of hunger/thirst. Whether they received milk exclusively from a wire mother or a cloth mother, babies clung to the cloth mother up to eighteen hours a day. Nursing seemed primarily to ensure frequent and intimate body contact of infant with mother. At 250 days, monkeys reared alone initially showed fear and disturbance when presented with a cloth mother, but gradually learned to play on her and use her for comfort when frightened. Harlow's primate findings provided early confirmation of later attachment research. When frightened or upset, securely attached human infants demand and obtain comfort from proximity to their mothers. The cloth mother served as a comfort in open field tests. Scary toys such as a wind-up, drumming teddy bear frightened the infant monkeys. They screamed and cowered while crouching immobilized. But when the cloth surrogate mother was present, the baby would climb on and clutch her, then relax enough to explore the room and toys adventurously. Total emotionality scores were cut in half when the cloth mother was present, but not when a cloth diaper was present.

Harlow demonstrated the staying power of infant monkey "love" by removing some infants from their cloth surrogates for five months. Reunion episodes revealed that deprivation had intensified the tie to the "mother." Reunited monkeys clung to the cloth mother and would not descend for exploration during three-minute test sessions.

Baby monkeys without playmates or real mothers behaved in socially incompetent ways. Six months of social isolation rendered the animals permanently inadequate socially. Infant-infant play was slower for cloth-mother-reared infants, who caught up in about a year. Sexual behaviors were abnormal for the surro-

Harry Harlow's primate studies offered important insights into issues such as human maltreatment of infants and familial love. (Harlow Primate Laboratory, University of Wisconsin)

gate reared monkeys. If impregnated, mothers behaved quite abnormally. Infants of motherless mothers showed extremes of sexuality and aggressiveness. This primate research contributed clinical insights to issues of human maltreatment of infants.

Harlow's work won him election to the National Academy of Sciences. He received the National Medal of Science in 1967 and the Gold Medal Award of the American Psychological Association in 1973.

See also: ATTACHMENT

Bibliography

Publications by Harlow

"The Nature of Love." *American Psychologist* 13 (1958):673–85.

"The Development of Affectional Patterns in Infant Monkeys." In B. M. Foss ed., *Determinants of Infant Behaviour*. London: Methuen, 1959.

Harlow, Harry F., and M. K. Harlow. "Social Deprivation in Monkeys." In M. L. Haimowitz and N. R. Haimowitz eds., *Human Development*. New York: Thomas Y. Crowell, 1966.

Alice Sterling Honig

HEAD START

Head Start was launched in 1965 as part of the Lyndon Johnson administration's "war on poverty," with the goal of bridging the school-readiness gap that exists between disadvantaged and more privileged preschool children. The program calls for extensive involvement of parents, and it attempts to provide the children with better preschool skills. Since its inception, Head Start has been extensively researched, and studies have shown mixed results. The immediate positive effects on children's school performance declined in subsequent years. But Head Start "graduates" are more likely to complete high school and less likely to repeat a grade or be placed in special education classes. Their families are also more likely to benefit from measures such as mental health services, nutrition education, and social services for the child and family.

See Also: EARLY INTERVENTION PROGRAMS

Bibliography

Conger, John J. "Hostages to Fortune: Youth, Values and the Public Interest." *American Psychologist* 43 (1988):291–300.

Lee, V. E., Jeanne Brooks-Gunn, E. Schnur, and F. Liaw. "Are Head Start Effects Sustained? A Longitudinal Follow-Up Comparison of Disadvantaged Children Attending Head Start, No Preschool, and Other Preschool Programs." *Child Development* 61 (1990):495–507.

Zigler, Edward F., and Sally J. Styfco. "Head Start: Criticisms in a Constructive Context." *American Psychologist* 49 (1994):127–132.

Zigler, Edward F., and Jeanette Valentine, eds. *Project Head Start: A Legacy of the War on Poverty.* New York: Free Press, 1979.

Sarit Guttmann-Steinmetz

HEALTH INSURANCE

Health insurance is a prepayment plan that provides services or monetary reimbursements for medical care needed because of illness or disability. Health insurance is provided to individuals either through voluntary plans that are commercial or nonprofit or through obligatory national insurance plans that are usually connected with a Social Security program.

Medical Coverage for America: Past and Present

Health insurance in the United States originated around 1850 as voluntary programs through cooperative mutual benefit and fraternal beneficiary associations, as well as through some commercial companies, industries, and labor unions that offered limited coverage. President Theodore Roosevelt instigated the idea for government health insurance in the early 1900s, but his concept never materialized because of the public's fear of socialized medicine.

Over time, many plans were developed by societies of practicing physicians, but it was the community-sponsored, nonprofit service plans based on contracts with hospitals and subscribers that drew the greatest enrollment. Under the name "Blue Cross and Blue Shield," these plans extended coverage to dependents while excluding coverage of accidents and diseases covered by workers' compensation laws, but their limitations—such as excluding those who could not afford the coverage and senior citizens—led to their downfall and subsequent restructuring in the mid-1990s.

In 1965 the federal government created two national health insurance programs: Medicare for the elderly and Medicaid for the poor. The Health Maintenance Organization (HMO) Act was passed by Congress in 1973 to provide low-cost alternatives to hospitals and private doctors through employer-based plans.

While there are many health insurance options available in the country, the United States remains the only Western industrial nation without some form of comprehensive national health insurance. According to the U.S. Bureau of the Census, 15.5 percent of the population was without health insurance coverage in 1999, and 13.9 percent of the uninsured were children (under age eighteen). Even though the uninsured rate for children decreased between 1998 and 1999, poor children continued to represent the highest number without health insurance coverage, making up 28.2 percent of all uninsured children in 1999.

Providing Children with Health Insurance

Health insurance plays a critical role in ensuring that children access the health care they need—and without it, the health status of children and the well-being of families is jeopardized. Studies have shown that lack of health insurance affects children in all aspects of their lives, not just their health. Those without primary or preventive care generally use inappropriate, more expensive services and have more serious medical problems. Their neglected health problems cause them to miss school and fall behind in their studies, possibly affecting future educational and employment opportunities, and may prevent them from achieving their full potential.

Because of the serious consequences of the lack of health insurance, providing children with medical care is a constant area of concern for the U.S. government. There are three major sources of health insurance for children in the United States: employment-based or privately purchased; Medicaid; and the State Children's Health Insurance Program.

According to the Census Bureau, 68.9 percent of children were covered by an employment-based or privately purchased health insurance plan in 1999. Privately purchased plans can be bought through numerous health insurance companies. While full-time employees may receive the option of health-care coverage for themselves and their families through pay-deduction contributions, this coverage is often not guaranteed.

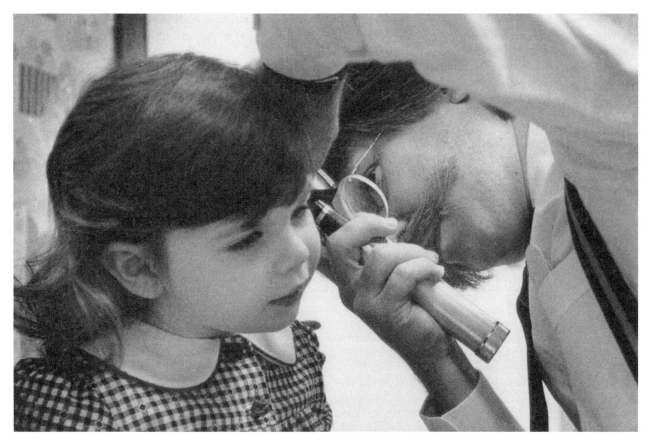

If their health problems are neglected, children may lose out on important developmental activities. Over time, this loss can prevent children from achieving their full potential. (American Academy of Pediatrics)

In 1999, 20 percent of children were covered by Medicaid. Since its beginning in 1965, Medicaid has been instrumental in financing health-care costs for the poor. Medicaid is a jointly funded, federal-state health insurance program for certain low-income and needy people and is administered by the Health Care Financing Administration. It covers approximately 36 million individuals including children, the aged, people who are blind or disabled, and people who are eligible to receive federally assisted income maintenance.

While Medicaid offers a great deal of health insurance coverage to children, the Balanced Budget Act of 1997 took the government's efforts one step further by allowing states to expand Medicaid eligibility with an enhanced federal match. Once passed, the Balanced Budget Act of 1997 restored Medicaid to those who previously lost the entitlement after passage of the Personal Responsibility and Work Opportunity Act of 1996. It also granted states greater flexibility when determining eligibility.

A major provision of the Balanced Budget Act of 1997 was the State Children's Health Insurance Program (SCHIP), also known as Title XXI, which allowed for more than $40 billion to be given to states over a ten-year period. This stipulation allowed states to implement Medicaid eligibility expansions and provisions to ensure enrollment of all children qualified for Medicaid under federal legislation. The passage of Title XXI helped form health insurance programs in each state for infants, children, and teens. For little or no cost, these state insurance programs pay for doctor visits, prescription medicines, hospitalizations, and much more. Although each state has different eligibility rules, most states insure children who are eighteen years or younger and whose families earn up to $34,100 a year (for a family of four).

SCHIP has been widely supported, and in 1999 the American Academy of Pediatrics (AAP) recommended that states implement the following to ensure that all children who are eligible for Medicaid are enrolled in the program:

- immediately extend Medicaid coverage to all children at or below the federal poverty level who are younger than nineteen years old to take advantage of the enhanced federal match offered under Title XXI;
- ensure that Medicaid-eligible children who lose cash benefits under the Supplement Security In-

come program as a result of welfare reform remain enrolled in Medicaid;

- eliminate asset testing to determine Medicaid eligibility;
- guarantee twelve months of continuous Medicaid eligibility for children younger than nineteen years;
- adopt presumptive Medicaid eligibility options for children younger than nineteen years, similar to the option available for pregnant women;
- ensure that a redetermination of eligibility be made before disenrolling any children from Medicaid because of changes in their eligibility for cash assistance under the Temporary Assistance for Needy Families program; and
- ensure that children who are removed from their homes by the state are immediately enrolled in Medicaid.

The AAP and other national organizations strongly support the expansion of Medicaid because of the countless children who have yet to benefit from it. The AAP estimated that in 1997, approximately 4.5 million uninsured children were eligible for Medicaid but were not enrolled. Another 4.6 million children who were privately insured were also eligible for Medicaid as a supplement to their private insurance but were not enrolled.

The Children Left Behind

While Medicaid's benefits seem endless, many may question why so many children do not have the health insurance that they so desperately need. When Medicaid was separated from welfare during the mid-1980s the hope was that children would benefit from major eligibility expansions. But state eligibility procedures have been shaped over time by federal rules that penalize states for enrolling ineligible beneficiaries, and the AAP indicates that there has been silence about the millions of eligible beneficiaries who are not enrolled. Beginning with the passage of Title XXI, the AAP has put a call out to pediatricians, other health-care professionals, and child advocates to assist state Medicaid agencies in providing outreach to families whose children are uninsured or underinsured.

In the United States there are specific groups of children that are at an especially high risk for being without health insurance. A national survey in 1998 found that teens, children of color, and children in single-parent families were at a particularly high risk for being uninsured. Other research also indicated that the educational status of adult family members is a good predictor of a child's insurance status. For instance, parents who have not completed high school are likely to work in unskilled jobs lacking health insurance benefits, and therefore their children are most likely to be without health coverage. The Census Bureau reported that black children had a higher rate of Medicaid coverage in 1999 than children of any other racial or ethnic group. The rate for black children was 36.2 percent, compared with 30.8 percent for Hispanic children, 16.7 percent for Asian and Pacific Islander children, and 13.2 percent for white non-Hispanic children.

In order to increase enrollment in Medicaid, President Clinton in 1998 launched the Children's Health Insurance Outreach Initiative, which gave the states additional funds and flexibility to find and enroll hard-to-reach children. President Clinton's initiative also challenged the public and private sectors to educate families about Medicaid and SCHIP. An additional step taken by the Clinton administration was the nationwide "Insure Kids Now" campaign in 1999 to enroll eligible children in Medicaid and SCHIP.

While Title XXI is a significant progression for U.S. social policy by offering a way to reduce the number of children who are uninsured, there are many variables that must coincide for the program to be successful. The biggest issues that remain are: reaching those who are eligible for Medicaid and educating families about the importance of health insurance for their children.

See also: STATE CHILDREN'S HEALTH INSURANCE PROGRAM

Bibliography

American Academy of Pediatrics. "Implementation Principles and Strategies for the State Children's Health Insurance Program." *Pediatrics* 107 (2001):1214–1220.

American Academy of Pediatrics, Committee on Child Health Financing. "Medicaid Policy Statement." *Pediatrics* 104 (1999):344–347.

Health Care Financing Administration [web site]. Boston, 2001. Available from http://www.hcfa.gov; INTERNET.

Perloff, Janet D. "Insuring the Children: Obstacles and Opportunities." *Families in Society: The Journal of Contemporary Human Services* (September 1999):516.

U.S. Bureau of the Census. "Health Insurance Coverage: Consumer Income." Washington, DC: U.S. Bureau of the Census, 1999.

Beth A. Kapes

HEALTHY START

The Healthy Start Initiative, a community-driven demonstration project begun in 1991, is the largest federal public health program dedicated to improving the health of mothers and infants in high-risk communities in the United States. Its original goal was to reduce infant mortality by 50 percent through community-driven strategies that provided direct, innovative prenatal services and health system service changes. Permanently authorized through the Children's Health Act of 2000 (PL 106-310), the Healthy Start Initiative is involved in over ninety communities and focuses on three programs:

1. Assuring access to and use of comprehensive services for Healthy Start participants through direct safety net services involving outreach, case management, and health education.

2. Strengthening local health systems through development and implementation of a biannual system development plan.

3. Bringing a consumer/community voice to improve maternal and infant health through the use of local consortia.

In addition, the Healthy Start Initiative has now broadened its developmental focus to address the health of mothers and infants from conception through two years postpartum, including attention to maternal depression and interconceptional health. This newer focus should help better integrate public health pregnancy and birth outcome oriented programs with child and parent development programs, which often serve the same families.

See also: EARLY INTERVENTION PROGRAMS

Bibliography
Healthy Start National Resource Center (HSNRC). In the National Center for Education in Maternal and Child Health (NCEMCH) [web site]. Arlington, Virginia, 2001. Available from http://www.healthystart.net; INTERNET.

Milton Kotelchuck

HEARING LOSS AND DEAFNESS

About 1 in 1,000 children demonstrates hearing loss to a level considered deaf or partially hearing and in need of special educational support. Severity of hearing loss may differ in one ear compared to the other and will vary greatly for different children.

Levels of Hearing Loss

Hearing loss is measured in decibels (dB) and is generally subdivided into three major groups. A loss greater than 55 dB is considered severe to moderate. Hearing loss is termed severe if it averages between 70 and 90 dB. Averaged across all frequencies, a hearing loss in the better ear of 90 dB or greater is considered profound. A child with mild loss of less than 40 dB may still be able to hear speech and have only moderate difficulties. With a loss between 40 and 55 dB some children can still hear some speech sounds, and these children may get a boost from a hearing aid.

In addition to the degree of hearing loss, the frequency range that is affected profoundly influences hearing ability. A child with mild hearing loss across the frequencies used for producing speech may have more difficulties. Speech will sound quite distorted and less intelligible for a child with 55 dB loss, who will hear more vowels than consonants, since vowels are transmitted at higher frequencies. A complete audiometric assessment of a child's hearing loss must, therefore, provide information for each ear, across a range of frequencies.

Additional problems suffered by hearing impaired children are: brain damaged (8%), cerebral palsy (7%), heart disorder (6%), perceptual-motor difficulties (10%), emotional and behavioral problems (19%), and visual deficits (18%)" (Harris 1990, p. 208).

Sign Languages

In the mid-1700s, Charles-Michel de l'Epée, a French cleric, observed that twin girls who had grown up together used fluent gestures to communicate with each other, and it occurred to him that this gestural language might already be equipped with syntax. He proposed to extend the native sign language of the deaf with supplementary methodical signs until this sign language became the intellectual equivalent of any spoken language. Today there are many sign languages based on hand signs and they differ widely in different countries and are not mutually intelligible for a deaf person. American Sign Language (AMSLAN or ASL) is a true language with syntactic and morphological rules different from those of spoken English. ASL signs are distinguished from one another by hand shape, movement, location in space, orientation of the hands during signing, and facial expression. In a book published in 1979, Edward Klima and Ursula Bellugi provided specific descriptions of ASL grammar and rules.

Some signing systems have added artificial signs for English morphemes such as verb tense markers and "is." Signed English, Seeing Essential English (SEE), and Cued Speech are a few of the manual forms developed. SEE was developed to represent spoken English literally, so that a signed sentence would be as complete as the spoken one. When the syntactic language skills of deaf children of deaf parents who used either ASL or SEE were analyzed, children in the SEE group achieved higher scores. The performance of the SEE children was closer to the English scores of hearing children. Nevertheless, some researchers, while observing teachers who employed a signed English system, found that many of the declarative statements and questions signed were grammatically incorrect. This may occur when teacher training is not rigorous and may also occur simply because of the increased number of signs required by SEE compared with ASL. Some specialists reason that it is not necessary to sign each and every morpheme of oral English, because a child can infer the missing elements from predictable structure and semantics, as well as through lipreading and use of residual hearing. A potential problem when SEE is used is that some children may not have the necessary reasoning and thinking skills to deduce from context the deleted segments of a manual message. Young children may be bombarded with too much information; they can misinterpret a message because of stress.

Deafness in Relation to Language and Social Development

Language deficits are the most serious consequence of hearing impairment. The effects of deafness on language development are complex. Hearing loss may vary across the range of frequencies. Children with severe or profound hearing loss generally have greater difficulty learning language. Children "who are born deaf, or who become deaf in the first year of life, have considerably more difficulty in developing language than do children whose deafness is acquired later in life" (Harris 1992, p. 96). Their opportunities as infants for turn-taking talk with significant caregivers are limited. Hearing parents use far fewer signs with them than the number of words used by hearing parents of hearing infants. Deaf toddlers of hearing parents cannot carry on extended conversations nor can they ask for clarifications, repetitions, or confirmations to repair frustrating communication breakdowns.

Whether a child has hearing or deaf parents is an important influence on the effect of hearing loss. Children born to deaf parents may be familiar with sign language from birth. Often on developmental tests they outperform their deaf peers born to hearing parents (about 95% of deaf children), who may experience sign language only when they go to school. Some studies show that deaf preschoolers lag about two years behind on language development tests, but they have similar categorization skills and similar scores on tests of nonverbal cognitive ability as their hearing peers.

The timing of diagnosis and intervention differs quite widely for infants born deaf, and this timing af-

fects social and language development. Only about 10 percent of deaf infants are diagnosed in the first year, and accurate diagnosis may not occur until three years of age for up to 44 percent of deaf babies. Many children do not have a chance at early intervention because identifying hearing loss is not a regular part of an early detection system in infancy. Yet, current technology makes it possible in the earliest months of life to confirm that infants with normal hearing respond clearly to changes in phonemes, even when these phonemes are confounded later in their culture's language system (such as "l" and "r" in Japanese); for example, by about ten months of age, hearing Japanese infants no longer respond differently to the "l" and "r." Thus, early diagnosis of hearing can be accomplished and needs to become a mandatory procedure included in pediatric care for young infants. Legislation is beginning to mandate screening for hearing in newborns.

Social skills and intimate interactions of deaf children suffer when diagnosis is delayed. Adults may not be sensitive to orienting the infant to watch for facial expressions or to alert the child to visually relevant and interesting events. Peers in nursery school may shout at the deaf child who seems to be able to move about the playroom with ease to get a preferred toy, but who does not respond to invitations to play or to cues for assuming a role in a pretend play scenario. Sensitive teachers in inclusive preschool classrooms help deaf children so they, too, can participate in the world of imaginative play so typical of and so important for preschoolers. The deaf child without a friend in such a situation may shadow an adult teacher or act lonely and withdrawn. Teachers can actively encourage play group entry skills and teach all the children how to sustain sessions of play activity.

Training of early childhood educators should include ideas for activities and interactions that will increase chances for deaf children to be included in social play. In some inclusive classrooms, all the children learn some signs in order to communicate with children with hearing deficits. Finger plays and singing games that involve a lot of hand and body motions are one way to promote inclusion in play.

Language Assessment

Reasons for language assessment vary and become particularly crucial if a child has reached school age and has difficulties with lessons. Tests for measuring receptive and expressive language in childhood depend mainly on a tester using oral language. Thus, even a receptive language test such as the Peabody Picture Vocabulary Test (PPVT), which requires only that a child listen to the examiner ("Show me bed") and then point to one of four pictured items on a page, depends on a child's hearing ability. The Grammatical Analysis of Elicited Language-Preschool Sentence Level (GAEL-P) (is a test that specifically analyzes the English skills of deaf and hard-of-hearing preschoolers. In the single-word vocabulary part of this test, children are asked to identify objects either by signs or by speech. Children are also asked to select objects that the tester names with signed and spoken words. The number of words the preschoolers produce and understand is a measure of their expressive and receptive vocabularies.

Testing requires decisions about why, how, and what tests to use. Marie Thompson and her colleagues suggested that reasons for assessment of deaf school-age children are: "To provide numerical scores to school districts; to identify a developmental language level and specific language targets for remediation; to measure efficacy of intervention based upon change in language behavior" (Thompson, Biro, Vethivelu, Pious, and Hatfield 1987, p. 30). These authors provide an extensive array of tests from which to choose when creating a custom-tailored battery of tests for a particular hearing-impaired school-age child.

Education of Deaf Children: Research Findings

The majority of deaf youngsters do not receive infant intervention and early exposure to ASL. When they do, the language patterns of children learning ASL from early infancy closely parallel the developmental progression of hearing children acquiring oral language. Infants learning ASL as a first language generally develop their first signed words at about the same age and sometimes even earlier than children learning an oral language. The two-word stage in ASL learning has some semantic features similar to the production of telegraphic speech among toddlers learning oral language. Overregularization of grammatical features ("I falled down") and overextension of word meanings (for example, calling all men "daddy") occur among toddlers whether they are using manual signs or oral speech.

Research suggests that knowing ASL early as a first language aids deaf children in developing better skills with the English language. Orally educated deaf children of hearing parents have been found to outperform manually educated children of hearing parents. This may mean that parental mastery of the language used in the earliest transactions with a child is most important for a young child's developing language skills.

Some drawbacks to education for deaf infants occur when hearing parents have not learned to use ASL or they use it infrequently and provide only sim-

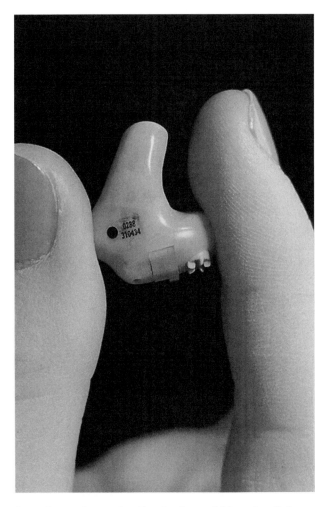

Depending on the severity of hearing loss, a child may benefit from using a hearing aid. (L. Steinmark, Custom Medical Stock Photo)

ple signs. In addition, the variety of existing signing systems can be a serious source of frustration and inconsistency for children. Support for and educational opportunities for parents and caring family members to learn sign language should be an important goal of intervention programs for deaf infants.

Families and educators have differed historically in promoting different educational approaches to help deaf children develop language. Oralist programs emphasize that deaf children are best served by learning to read lips, by auditory training to use residual hearing as much as possible, and by articulation training to improve spoken enunciation.

Manual systems are urged by those who believe that some deaf children will have a poor educational prognosis with only oral methods. Use of manually coded English (such as finger spelling and ASL) in combination with speech is called *total communication.* Quigley and King provided an overview in 1982 of the half-dozen most commonly used sign systems.

Most of these systems share the common feature of adapting some ASL signs for vocabulary items. They invent new signs, for example, for plurals and as affixes for expressing verb tense and number agreement. ASL has fewer such elements. Reduplicated movement in ASL signals the progressive aspect, whereas some sign systems prefer to invent more movements to get closer to standard English, as in signing "The dog is barking" (in ASL this would be signed as "Dog bark, bark, bark").

Although sign systems are now an integral part of the curriculum for most deaf children, educational opportunities for the very young deaf child may be severely limited if a child is not participating in an educational program and if the parents themselves have limited knowledge of or use of sign systems.

Writing and Reading

Essays of deaf students frequently reveal patterns of ungrammatical English usage. Discrepancies that are similar to those of very young children developing normally include failure to invert subject and auxiliary when using a question, or omission of the verb "to be" (the copula) in a sentence. But deaf children often show other difficulties in mastering English syntax in their writing. For example, a ten-year-old wrote: "We perttey fun camp after home. The will week fun camp after car." An eighteen-year-old wrote: "A boy give to a dog eat the bread" (Quigley and King 1982, pp. 444–445).

Some of the distinct syntactic structures that deaf children generate involve a confusion between "have" and "be" ("Mama have sick") and an incorrect pairing of auxiliary with verb markers ("Mary has washing the dishes"). In using the passive voice, deaf children are likely to delete the word "by." They are also likely to delete conjunctions ("Eddie carried, dumped trash"). Question formation is difficult ("Who a girl bought you a doll?"). Relative pronouns may be deleted and substitutions made ("I patted the girl's arm was hurt").

In writing, deaf children's essays often overuse simple sentence structure. This may result from classroom drills to encourage the development of syntactic skills as well as spelling and punctuation rules. Reading materials, however, more commonly have advanced sentence structure; they require more mastery of complex sentences than are used in spoken conversations.

Effectiveness of Oral and Manual Educational Systems

Controversy still exists as to the relative effectiveness of oral and manual educational systems. Some intensive oral programs do report good English proficiency. Some total communication programs likewise report positive outcomes in English proficiency for their graduates. Studies suggest that the academic and social benefits of total communication are increased and sustained when total communication is used both in the school and in the home.

There is some agreement that the nature of the child's hearing loss and the degree of the child's cognitive ability may have a greater effect on successful educational outcome than other intervention program variables that are measured. At present, "unequivocal statements about the value of particular approaches or the consequences of not following one approach or another are unwarranted" (Musselman, Lindsay, and Wilson 1988, p. 88).

Specialists agree that early interventions with deaf infants and young children must emphasize communication exchanges during activities. When adults exchange signs in play contexts (such as "peekaboo" and pretend driving a toy car on a track) and during daily routines, such as getting ready for bed or going shopping for a toy, then young deaf children begin to organize knowledge of events into mental representations and cognitive categories. The more generous the provision of such intimate and motivating interactions, the more a child has an opportunity to attempt to express cognitive structures in ASL or in oral language. Thus, organized, interpretable, and rich experiences within naturally occurring social routines are necessary for language development. Early interveners, often parents, need to provide abundant opportunities for signing. They need to maintain eye contact and show vigorous interest in the deaf baby's attempts to communicate gesturally. When the infant is playing with a toy, adults need to compose their hands in front of the baby and provide the sign for that toy. In contrast, toddlers will be delayed in learning signs if the parent takes a toy away first and waits for the child to look up and see the parent making the sign while holding the toy. Parents can receive much help from written materials.

Teachers need to seat a deaf child so there is good visibility. They must learn the optimal distance (under one foot) to stand when trying to communicate with a child using a hearing aid; and they must learn to change a hearing aid battery and/or cord. When a child with profound hearing loss wears two hearing aids connected to a cassette-player-like box suspended by straps at the waist, this apparatus is sometimes called a "phonic ear." Teachers may wear a microphone that amplifies their voice for a hearing-impaired child with poor lipreading and sign language skills.

Teachers need to use a child's name and articulate clearly and slowly when directing speech to a hearing-impaired child. They should kneel at a desk and focus on cuing. Cued speech, developed by Dr. Cornett at Gallaudet University in Washington, D.C., is a system of teacher hand cues that enhances lipreading by children. The hand cues, used near the lips, match what is being said to clarify ambiguities. Cued speech used by a trained adult helps the hearing-impaired school-age child increase reading skills.

Multimedia technology has been used to develop materials and activities for Mexican-American deaf children, the fastest-growing minority group in the U.S. school-age population of deaf children. Video dictionaries of sign language can be built directly into stories onscreen. CD-ROM reading software is now becoming available for hearing-impaired children.

Teachers and parents working together create opportunities for deaf children so that they can use total language communication to achieve interpersonal goals. Enthusiasm and acceptance help hearing-impaired children experiment with their language systems so that they can learn well and have a positive social effect on others, as well as engage in peer friendships.

See also: AMERICAN SIGN LANGUAGE; LANGUAGE DEVELOPMENT

Bibliography

Andrews, J. F., and D. L. Jordan. "Multimedia Stories for Deaf Children." *Teaching Exceptional Children* (May/June 1998):28–33.

Blasi, M. J., and L. Priestley. "A Child with Severe Hearing Loss Joins Our Learning Community." *Young Children* 53, no. 2 (March 1998):44–49.

Gregory, S., and S. Barlow. "Interactions between Deaf Babies and Their Deaf and Hearing Mothers." In Bencie Woll ed., *Language Development and Sign Language*. Bristol, Eng.: International Sign Linguistics Association, 1988.

Harris, John. *Early Language Development: Implications for Clinical and Educational Practice*. London: Rutledge, 1990.

Harris, Margaret. *Language Experience and Early Language Development: From Input to Uptake*. Hillsdale, NJ: Lawrence Erlbaum, 1992.

Kampfe, C. M., and A. G. Turecheck. "Reading Achievement of Prelingually Deaf Students and Its Relationship to Parental Method of Communication." *American Annals of the Deaf* 132 (1987):11–15.

Klima, Edward S., and Ursula Bellugi. *The Signs of Language*. Cambridge, MA: Harvard University Press, 1979.

Kovalik, Gail, Melanie Norton, and Susan Meck. *Deafness: An Annotated Bibliography and Guide to Basic Materials*. Chicago: American Library Association, 1992.

Lederberg, A. R., and V. S. Everhart. "Conversations between Deaf Children and Their Hearing Mothers: Pragmatic and Dialogic Characteristics." *Journal of Deaf Studies and Deaf Education* 5 (2000):303–322.

Marschark, Marc. *Raising and Educating a Deaf Child*. New York: Oxford University Press, 1997.

Mayne, A., C. Yoshinaga-Itano, A. L. Sedey, and A. Carey. "Expressive Vocabulary Development of Infants and Toddlers Who Are Deaf or Hard of Hearing." *Volta Review* 100 (2000):1–28.

McArthur, Shirley H. *Raising Your Hearing-Impaired Child: A Guideline for Parents*. Washington, DC: Alexander Graham Bell Association for the Deaf, 1982.

Musselman, C., P. Lindsay, and A. Wilson. "An Evaluation of Trends in Preschool Programming for Hearing-Impaired Children." *Journal of Speech and Hearing Disorders* 53 (1988):71–88.

Quigley, Stephen P., and Cynthia M. King. "The Language Development of Deaf Children and Youth." In Sheldon Rosenberg ed., *Handbook of Applied Psycholinguistics: Major Thrusts of Research and Theory*. Hillsdale, NJ: Lawrence Erlbaum, 1982.

Quigley, S. P., and Peter V. Paul. *Language and Deafness*. London: Croom Helm, 1984.

Thompson, Marie, P. Biro, S. Vethivelu, C. Pious, and N. Hatfield. *Language Assessment of Hearing Impaired School Age Children*. Seattle: University of Washington Press, 1987.

Alice Sterling Honig

HEREDITY VERSUS ENVIRONMENT

Many aspects of human characteristics (such as height and eye color) are largely genetically determined. Psychology researchers, however, tend to be interested in dimensions that are relatively less determined by genetics—traits that subject more to environmental influences, such as how a person feels, acts, and thinks. Given that the degree of genetic determination appears to vary from one dimension to another (e.g., spatial skills versus language acquisition), how can one determine the relative influences of heredity and environment for various human characteristics, and how can one understand the complex relationship between them?

For example, Javier has two biological daughters who share the same biological mother. Both are tall, well mannered, and musically inclined. Despite these similarities, the older child appears socially reserved and quiet, while the younger one, who was born into the same family environment, seems more outgoing. In addition, one of his children has been diagnosed with a learning disability while the other seems exceptionally well-functioning cognitively. How can these similarities and differences between the two children be explained? One may think, "Well, Javier is tall and he is also a talented musician himself, so these girls must have gotten these 'good genes' from Javier. And he is quite strict when it comes to disciplining his children, so that explains their good manners. But why is the younger one so sociable—and what about her learning disability? Maybe she hasn't been read to as much as the older one has." In essence, hereditary influences and various environmental factors in these children's lives are being weighed and analyzed in explaining the characteristics of these children.

The field of behavioral genetics aims at understanding the observable differences in a wide variety of human characteristics, typically by analyzing the contributions made by heredity and environment in the development of the characteristics in question. Although the research in behavioral genetics is ideologically and methodologically diverse, it is fair to state that it often helps one theorize how much heredity and environment contribute to an observed outcome, and how various factors may interact with each other to create a particular outcome. At the root of such research endeavors lies what is called the nature-nurture controversy.

The Nature-Nurture Controversy

What are the roles of heredity and environment in the development of various human characteristics? The nature-nurture controversy deals with this perennial question. The works by several early philosophers are often viewed as marking the beginning of this controversy. As early as the seventeenth and the eighteenth centuries, philosophers such as René Descartes and Immanuel Kant argued that human cognition is largely reflective of genetically determined predispositions, since environmental factors do not adequately explain the variations in our cognitive capabilities. They therefore took the nativist perspective that humans are born with certain cognitive tendencies. By contrast, the clean slate view, proposed in 1690 by the British philosopher John Locke, focuses instead on the role of the surrounding environment in describing human thoughts. Locke compared the human mind to a piece of blank paper without any ideas written on it, and he suggested that only from experience do humans draw reason and knowledge. Following these diametrically opposed ideas, scientists have since extensively explored the roles of heredity and environment. Before describing such efforts in detail, it is useful to define relevant concepts.

Nature and Nurture Defined

Nature refers to heredity: the genetic makeup or "genotypes" (i.e., information encoded in DNA) an individual carries from the time of conception to the time of death. Heredity may range from genetic predispositions that are specific to each individual and that therefore potentially explain differences in individual characteristics (e.g., temperament), to those supposedly specific to certain groups and that therefore account for group differences in related characteristics (e.g., gender and height), and to those that are theorized to be shared by all humans and are generally thought to set humans apart from other species (e.g., the language acquisition device in humans).

The notion of nature, therefore, refers to the biologically prescribed tendencies and capabilities individuals possess, which may unfold themselves throughout the course of life.

Nurture, by contrast, refers to various external or environmental factors to which an individual is exposed from conception to death. These environmental factors involve several dimensions. For example, they include both physical environments (e.g., secondhand smoking and prenatal nutrition) and social environments (e.g., the media and peer pressure). Also, environmental factors vary in their immediacy to the individual; they involve multiple layers of forces, ranging from most immediate (e.g., families, friends, and neighborhoods) to larger contexts (e.g., school systems and local governments) to macro factors (e.g., international politics and global warming). To complicate matters even further, the factors in each of these layers influence and are influenced by elements within and outside of these layers. For example, the kind of peers a child is exposed to may depend on his or her parents' view of what ideal playmates are like, the local government's housing policies, and the history of race relations.

What Is the Controversy?

Despite its nomenclature, the nature-nurture controversy in its current state is less dichotomous than commonly believed. In other words, the term "nature-nurture controversy" suggests a polarization of nature and nurture; continuity and interaction, however, more aptly describe the central processes involved in this controversy. Therefore, it is not about whether either heredity or environment is solely responsible for observed outcomes. Rather, it is more about the extent to which these factors influence human development and the ways in which various factors influence each other.

For example, following the fifteen-person massacre committed by two boys at Columbine High School in Colorado in April 1999, the media were flooded with people offering their interpretations of what drove these high school students to commit this heinous and violent act. Some were quick to attribute the boys' actions to such environmental factors as inadequate parenting practices in their families and the violence prevalent and even glorified in the American media. Others, by contrast, were convinced that these boys were mentally ill as defined in the American Psychiatric Association's *Diagnostic and Statistical Manual of Mental Disorders* and that their ability to make responsible judgments had been impaired, perhaps due to a chemical imbalance to which they were genetically predisposed. Which argument is "correct," according to most researchers? Probably neither. Most theorists agree that both nature and nurture are intertwined and influence most aspects of human emotion, behavior, and cognition in some ways. Given the prevailing views in current psychology, most researchers would agree that the violent acts committed by these boys probably stemmed from an unfortunate interaction among various hereditary and environmental factors. Researchers, however, may disagree on (1) the extent to which heredity and environment each influences particular developmental outcomes and (2) the way in which a mixture of hereditary and environmental factors relate to each other. In other words, the controversy involves the extent of contribution as well as the nature of interaction among a variety of genetic and environmental forces. How do researchers address these issues?

Exploring Heredity and Environment: Research Methods

Since as early as the 1930s, researchers have attempted to estimate the contribution of hereditary and environmental factors to various aspects of human cognition, by comparing pairs of individuals varying in genetic relatedness. These studies are often called kinship studies, and twin studies and adoption studies represent two of the most common types of such studies. They have been extensively conducted to estimate the heritability of a wide variety of human characteristics.

Twin Studies

In traditional twin studies, monozygotic (identical) twins and dizygotic (fraternal) twins are compared in terms of their emotional, behavioral, and cognitive similarities. In the process of cell divisions upon formation of a zygote, sometimes the resulting cells fully multiply and produce two identical babies; they are called monozygotic twins, since they come from a single zygote and are genetic "carbon copies." In other words, any genetic information concerning physical and psychological predispositions should be exactly the same for these twins.

By contrast, dizygotic twins develop from two separate zygotes, as a result of two eggs being fertilized by two sperms independently. Consequently, the genetic profiles of the resultant babies are similar only to the extent that they share the same set of biological parents. By comparing the correlations of a particular dimension, such as intelligence test scores, between identical twins and those between fraternal twins, researchers can theoretically compute the relative influences of nature and nurture on the dimension. For example, Sandra Scarr reported an interesting finding in the book *Intelligence, Heredity, and Environment*. She found a correlation for IQ test scores of .86 for identical twins and .55 for fraternal twins, indicating

These children—slumdwellers in 18th-century London—faced few positive prospects as they grew to adulthood. Scientists and philosophers have long struggled with the debate as to how much environmental conditions, both positive and negative, influence individual development. (Archive/Hulton Getty Picture Library)

that identical twins' scores are more like one another than those of fraternal twins. Some influence of heredity, therefore, is evident. If IQ scores were 100 percent genetically determined, however, the correlation for identical twins would have been 1.00. In this example, therefore, heredity appears to play an important, but not definitive, role in explaining the determinants of what is measured through IQ tests.

In addition to these heritability estimates, researchers also study concordance rates: the rates at which both twins develop the same, specific characteristics. The absence or presence of a particular mental illness would be a good example. If both twins had clinical depression in all pairs examined in a study, then the concordance rate would be 100 percent for this sample. On the other hand, if all twins in a study had one individual with clinical depression and another with no depression, then the concordance rate is 0 percent. Reportedly, concordance rate for clinical depression is reportedly about 70 percent for identical twins and about 25 percent for fraternal twins. This appears to demonstrate a sizable genetic contribution involved in the development of depression.

Despite scholars' consensus that genetic contributions are not to be ignored, these correlational data are often believed to be exaggerated. Identical twins are genetically predisposed to a great deal of similarities, and, through a process known as reactive correlation, people around them tend to treat them similarly, which may help lead the twins to be similar beyond what their genetic profiles may warrant. The correlation of .86 between the IQ scores of identical twins, for example, may be contaminated with this reactive correlation. Identical twins encounter environmental experiences that are extremely similar to each other's, as the environment tends to react similarly to those who are genetically similar. As a result, for instance, adults and peers may treat identical twins similarly, and teachers may also develop similar expectations about these twins in terms of their emotional, behavioral, and cognitive functions. This similarity in environmental influences and expectations, therefore, may cause heritability estimates and concordance rates to be exaggerated.

Furthermore, the process of active correlation (or niche-picking) suggests the possibility that children's genetic predispositions cause them to seek particular environments, causing the differences in hereditary predispositions to be enhanced by the subsequent environmental exposure. If a child has the genetic predisposition to enjoy cognitive challenges, for example, that may prompt the child to seek situations, friends, and activities that suit this particular predisposition—provided that such choices are offered to the child. This child, therefore, may start out with a small genetically prompted inclination to want to use his or her "brains," but such a tendency would subsequently be magnified through environmental influences.

Given the varying degrees of genetic similarities between identical and fraternal twins, these sources of confusion may theoretically become more consequential when twins grow up in the same family. This is because twins reared in the same family are typically subject to the same resources, parenting philosophy, living environments, and so on. Their genetic predispositions, therefore, are most likely promoted—or inhibited—in similar ways. For example, if a pair of twins share the hereditary predispositions for musicality and their upper-middle-class parents own a piano and are interested in fostering musicality in these children, their musical potential will perhaps be cultivated in very similar ways. Specifically, their parents will probably get the same or similar piano teacher(s) for them, and they will probably be encouraged to practice equally. Therefore, the genetic similarities between the twins are magnified by virtue of them growing up in the same household. How does one address these concerns? Adoption studies provide some answers.

Adoption Studies

Compared to traditional twin studies, adoption studies are theorized to offer better alternatives for separating hereditary influences from genetic ones. There are typically two variations in adoption studies: ones involving comparisons of identical twins reared apart and ones comparing the degree of similarity between adopted children and their biological and adoptive parents. Identical twins reared apart share genetic patterns with each other, yet they do not share the same environmental experiences. Adopted children, by contrast, typically share with the rest of the adoptive family similar environmental experiences but do not share any genes with them. The advantage of adoption studies is that researchers can reasonably estimate the heritability by comparing the heritability estimates and concordance rates of pairs of individuals varying in genetic relatedness and in environmental distance. A typical adoption study may involve, for instance, comparing the concordance rates for the following two pairs: a child and her biological parent (shared genes but not environments) versus the same child and her adoptive parents (shared environments but not genes). Though the estimates of hereditary influences are generally lower in adoption studies than in twin studies, adoption studies provide results that are largely consistent with twin studies. In a 1983 study, Sandra Scarr and Richard Weinberg found that the IQ scores of adopted children showed higher correlations with the IQ scores of their biological parents than with those of their adopted parents. Similarly, John Loehlin, Lee Willlerman, and Joseph Horn demonstrated through a 1988 study that in the area of clinical depression, adopted children tended to have much higher concordance rates with their biological relatives than with their adoptive relatives.

Still, many scholars argue that heritability may be overestimated in these studies. First, the reactive and active correlations discussed earlier would occur, to a degree, even if the twins were reared separately, as the twins share all of the hereditary predispositions. Second, one must also examine the possibility that parents may systematically treat their adoptive children differently than they do their biological children, which may explain the less-than-expected resemblance between children and their adoptive parents. Given that biologically related individuals tend to share greater hereditary similarities, it is fair to state that heritability estimates may be thrown off by environmental effects induced by particular genetic predispositions.

Beyond Heritability

As illustrated so far, most psychology researchers are in agreement that heredity and environment both play significant roles in the development of various human traits. Researchers may disagree, however, on the extent to which heredity and environment contribute to the development of a particular dimension, and on how various factors may affect each other to create a certain human characteristic. Neither heritability estimates nor concordance rates provide useful information on the latter type of disagreement: how various hereditary and environmental factors interact with each other to result in a particular characteristic. Mental health, education, and applied psychology researchers are especially concerned about optimizing the developmental outcomes among people from all backgrounds. To this end, knowing that there is a .86 heritability estimate for IQ scores among identical twins, for example, is not particularly helpful in terms of establishing ways of maximizing the life choices and opportunities for individuals. In attaining such goals, it is crucial to understand how various factors relate to each other. Naturally, in order to do so, one must first identify which factors are involved in the development of a given trait. Unfortunately, researchers have had very limited success in identifying specific genetic patterns that influence particular psychological and behavioral characteristics.

Nevertheless, this is not to suggest that one should ignore the role of heredity as reflected in heritability estimates altogether and focus on optimizing the environmental factors for every child. Heredity, as has been examined, undoubtedly contributes to the development of various human traits. Also, researchers exploring environmental influences have found that contrary to what most theorists expected, environmental factors that are shared by reared-together twins do not appear to be relevant in explaining the development of particular traits. It is therefore unlikely that exposing every child to a "one size fits all" environment designed to foster a particular trait, would benefit everyone equally. Some may react favorably to such an environment, while others may not react to it at all; there may be yet others who react negatively to the same environment. The notion of "range of reaction" helps us conceptualize the complex relationship between heredity and environment; people with varying genetically influenced predispositions respond differently to environments. As suggested by Douglas Wahlsten in a 1994 article in *Canadian Psychology,* an identical environment can elicit different reactions in different individuals, due to variations in their genetic predispositions. In a hypothetical scenario, Wahlsten suggested that increasing intellectual stimulation should help increase cognitive performances of some children. Moderate, rather than high, levels of intellectual stimulation may, however, induce optimal cognitive performances in others. By contrast, the same moderate levels of stimulation may actually cause some children to display cognitive performances that are even worse than how they performed in a minimally stimulating environment. In addition, the "optimal" or "minimal" performance levels may be different for various individuals, depending on their genetic makeup and other factors in their lives. This example illustrates the individual differences in ranges of reaction; there is no "recipe" for creating environments that facilitate the development of particular characteristics in everyone. Heredity *via* environment, rather than heredity *versus* environment, therefore, may better characterize this perspective.

These views are consistent with the 1990s' backlash against the view that was prevalent in the mid- to late twentieth century among many clinical psychologists, social workers, and educators, who focused solely on environmental factors while discounting the contributions of hereditary factors. Among the theories they advocated were that gay males decidedly come from families with domineering mothers and no prominent masculine figures, that poor academic performances result from lack of intellectual stimulation in early childhood, and that autism stems from poor parenting practices. Not surprisingly, empirical data do not support these theories. Still, people often continue to believe, to some extent, that proper environments can prevent and "cure" these nonnormative characteristics, not realizing that heredity may play significant roles in the development of these traits.

Some scholars believe that this "radical environmentalist" view found its popularity in the 1950s as a reaction to racist Nazi thinking, which held that some groups of individuals are genetically inferior to others and that the undesirable traits they are perceived to possess cannot be prevented or modified. These assumptions are harmful, as they limit the opportunities for advancement of some people, strictly because of their membership in a stigmatized group. It is nevertheless important to reiterate that individual differences, as opposed to group differences, in genetic predispositions are evident in the development of most emotional, behavioral, and cognitive traits. With this in mind, it is also important to realize that focusing on optimizing environmental influences while ignoring hereditary influences may lead to the neglect of the developmental needs of some individuals, and it may be just as harmful in some cases as focusing exclusively on hereditary influences.

See also: PHENOTYPE

Bibliography

American Psychiatric Association. *The Diagnostic and Statistical Manual of Mental Disorders: DSM-IV.* Washington, DC: American Psychiatric Association, 1994.

Bronfenbrenner, Urie. *The Ecology of Human Development: Experiments by Nature and Design.* Cambridge, MA: Harvard University Press, 1979.

Efran, Jay, Mitchell Greene, and Robert Gordon. "Lessons of the New Genetics." *Family Therapy Networker* 22 (1998):26–41.

Locke, John. "Some Thoughts concerning Education." In R. H. Quick ed., *Locke on Education.* Cambridge, Eng.: Cambridge University Press, 1892.

Loehlin, John, Lee Willerman, and Joseph Horn. "Human Behavior Genetics." *Annual Review of Psychology* 38 (1988):101–133.

Lykken, David. *The Antisocial Personality.* Hillsdale, NJ: Lawrence Erlbaum, 1995.

McGee, Mark, and Thomas Bouchard. "Genetics and Environmental Influences on Human Behavioral Differences." *Annual Review of Neuroscience* 21 (1998):1–24.

McGuffin, Peter, and Michael Pargeant. "Major Affective Disorder." In Peter McGuffin and Robin Murray eds., *The New Genetics of Mental Illness.* London: Butterworth-Heinemann, 1991.

Newman, H. H., F. N. Freeman, and K. J. Holzinger. *Twins: A Study of Heredity and Environment.* Chicago: University of Chicago Press, 1937.

Plomin, R. *Genetics and Experience: The Interplay between Nature and Nurture.* Thousand Oaks, CA: Sage, 1994.

Plomin, Robert, J. C. DeFries, and John Loehlin. "Genotype-Environment Interaction and Correlation in the Analysis of Human Behavior." *Psychological Bulletin* 84 (1977):309–322.

Scarr, Sandra. "Behavior-Genetic and Socialization Theories of Intelligence: Truce and Reconciliation." In R. J. Sternberg and E. L. Grigorenko eds., *Intelligence, Heredity, and Environment.* New York: Cambridge University Press, 1997.

Scarr, Sandra, and Richard Weinberg. "The Minnesota Adoption Studies: Genetic Differences and Malleability." *Child Development* 54 (1983):260–267.

Waddington, C. H. *The Strategy of the Genes.* London: Allen and Unwin, 1957.

Wahlstein, Douglas. "The Intelligence of Heritability." *Canadian Psychology* 35 (1994):244–259.

Daisuke Akiba

HIGH RISK INFANTS

A developmental delay is diagnosed when a child does not reach a developmental milestone (for example, sitting, walking, or combining words) at the expected age, despite allowing for individual variation in the rate of development. Each year, many children are born at increased risk of a developmental disability or delay. Infant and preschooler development is a complex, dynamic process that begins at birth and evolves as infants interact with their caregivers and environment. Approximately 10 percent of infants will reflect developmental delay.

The key to intervention and rehabilitation lies in identifying those infants at significant risk of develop-

mental disability. However, early identification remains difficult. The normal variation in development among children is broad. Also, development must be monitored in several areas (motor, cognitive, psychosocial) simultaneously, and it can be easy to overlook a small delay in only one area. Parents and pediatricians may be reluctant to discuss their fears that a child may have a developmental delay. Lastly, the age at which developmental difficulties manifest, often depends on the developmental stage of the child. It is common for hyperactivity, language delays, and emotional disorders to be diagnosed at about three to four years of age. However, learning disabilities and mild mental retardation are frequently not diagnosed until a child enters school. Assessment of developmental risk includes medical and social history, physical examination, and developmental observation of the child. Often developmental surveillance tools, such as standardized tests that screen several or all areas of development, are used to help identify the child with delay.

Not all children with developmental disability have known risk factors at birth and many times the cause of delay is not known. An infant with an established risk typically has a diagnosed medical condition known to be associated with a high probability of developmental disability. Examples of conditions with established risk are chromosomal abnormalities (such as Trisomy 21), sensory impairments (such as visual or hearing impairment), and neurological defects.

Risk Factors

There are many influences that can affect development. These influences are termed risk factors and are often divided into biological risk and environmental risk. However, it is recognized that there is often significant overlap and influence between the two categories. Biological and environmental stresses are interactive and together have an additive effect on developmental outcome. Therefore, infants with multiple risk factors typically have a greater risk of disability than infants with single risk factors.

Biological risk factors tend to be associated with more severe developmental disability, mental retardation, and multiple handicaps. Included in this category are prenatal influences such as chromosomal disorders, congenital infections, congenital malformations (both of the brain or other organs), and intrauterine growth retardation. Maternal substance abuse during the pregnancy is also a significant prenatal, and often ongoing, risk factor. Then there are the perinatal (around birth) influences on development. Infants born prematurely are at increased risk of developmental disability. They are also at risk for chronic lung disease, deafness, and brain hemorrhages, which add to their developmental risk. Infants with severe lung disease or neonatal seizures are at increased risk. Some infants have metabolic or endocrine disorders such as hypothyroidism or phenylketonuria, which place them at increased risk without appropriate intervention. Lastly, acquired infections in infancy, particularly involving the brain, can result in compromised development. Children with developmental delay due to biological risk factors are often diagnosed in infancy.

Compromised developmental outcome is due to both biologic and environmental risk factors. Over time, environmental influences affect the development of biologically at-risk children. The environment has the potential to maximize or minimize early developmental delays. Environmental risk factors are cumulative, with each having a small incremental effect on cognitive abilities. The adverse effects of a poor environment become increasingly more evident from about two years of age onward. This influence is most strongly seen in the areas of verbal and general cognitive development. As children age, the tests used to measure intelligence place more and more emphasis on language, and therefore the environmental influences assume greater importance. The reverse is also true: A good environment can have a temporizing effect on the degree of developmental disability, but it does not determine whether the disability occurred. Environmental influence seems to be minimized when the biologic risk is severe.

Environmental risk factors are legion and varied. First, consider that the environment includes caregiver-child interactions, family resources, physical properties, and organization. Within the area of caregiver-child interaction is parenting ability. Limited parenting ability, whether due to youth, inexperience, mental retardation, illicit drug abuse, or mental illness, is a risk factor for developmental disability. Inadequate supervision can lead to accident and injury. Child neglect or abuse increases the risk of developmental compromise. Additionally, parenting ability can be limited due to physical separation because of divorce or incarceration. Caregiver-child interactions also include disciplinary techniques and the family's beliefs and attitudes. All of these can affect development.

Many children at risk of developmental disability often live in families with limited resources, frequently referred to as low socioeconomic status. Housing, financial statuses, maternal education, availability of medical insurance, and availability of appropriate play materials are all part of family resources. Homelessness, poverty, low maternal education, single parent families, and lack of medical insurance have all been associated with increased risk of developmental compromise. Unavailability of medical insurance usually means that preventative medical care, when most developmental surveillance takes place, and prenatal care are not obtained. Additionally, a family's ability to cope when suffering from stressful life events, such as divorce, loss of a job, or death, depends on their own resources and access to external sources of support.

Additional environmental influences impacting development are the physical properties of the environment, such as personal space, crowding, and excessive noise. The level of organization is also an influence. This includes the predictability, structure, and regularity of the home. Over many years, children who live in poor or disorganized families are at increased risk of slower cognitive development and diminished school performance when compared to their peers from more advantaged families.

Intervention and Rehabilitation

The prevention of developmental disabilities starts before conception. Good nutrition and adequate prenatal care are essential components of a healthy pregnancy, assuring the best outcome for an infant, regardless of additional risk factors or disabilities. With improvements in neonatal intensive care and the care of premature infants, there is hope that the risks associated with prematurity will diminish.

Influencing development in children's lives requires a societal commitment to the prevention and rehabilitation of developmental disabilities. In 1997, the Individuals with Disabilities Education Act (IDEA) amendments (PL 105-17) re-established the right to a free and appropriate education for all school-age children, regardless of their disability. Additionally, the federal government provides financial assistance to states for the development of early intervention programs for infants and toddlers with known developmental delays or disabilities and their families. At each state's discretion, infants and toddlers considered at risk for developmental disabilities may be enrolled in early intervention programs.

Early intervention programs are a system of therapeutic and educational programs that work with an infant or young child, from birth to age three, and their family to prevent or minimize adverse developmental outcomes for that child. An infant-toddler specialist typically assists families. Therapeutic approaches could include physical therapy, occupational therapy, or speech and language therapy for the child. These services can be provided through a center-based or home-based model and include en-

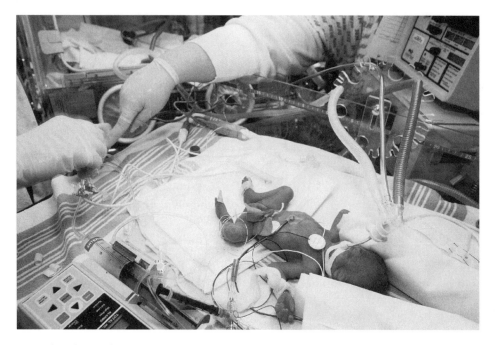

Hospital workers tend to a premature infant in a neonatal unit. High risk infants can include babies who are born prematurely or with a disease such as phenylketonuria (PKU). (Annie Griffiths Belt/Corbis)

couragement of active parental participation. No single intervention model meets the needs of all children at risk; therefore, an individualized approach to providing services is necessary. Early intervention programs also work in conjunction with other services that assist families in functioning. These other services could include drug counseling programs, home health aides, transportation to medical evaluations, parenting classes, and support groups. At age three, children transition to preschool programs that continue to provide intervention and therapeutic services until age five, when the child transitions into the public school system.

Only a small proportion of at-risk infants go on to have developmental delay. Early intervention services are expensive and time-consuming. Generally, these services are reserved for children with known developmental delay, while a tracking system monitors high-risk infants and identifies developmental delays. Each state determines if at-risk infants will be automatically eligible or monitored for developmental delays and then referred for services.

Early identification of infants at high risk permits parent counseling and planning for the child's future. Early intervention with quality, long-term services can significantly improve the quality of life, minimize secondary complications, and improve cognitive function. But frequently early intervention does not prevent a developmental disability from occurring if the biological risk is high. Additionally, intervention

services often help parents through a particularly difficult time.

See also: BIRTH DEFECTS; BIRTHWEIGHT; PREMATURE INFANTS

Bibliography

Allen, Marilee C. "The High-Risk Infant," *Pediatric Clinics of North America* 40 (1993):479–490.

Aylward, Glen P. "The Relationship between Environmental Risk and Developmental Outcome," *Developmental and Behavioral Pediatrics* 13 (1992):222–229.

"Individuals with Disabilities Education Act." In the U. S. Department of Education, Office of Special Education and Rehabilitative Services [web site]. Available from http://www.ed.gov/offices/OSERS/IDEA; INTERNET.

Kruskal, Maureen, Michael C. Thomasgard, and Jack P. Shonkoff. "Early Intervention for Vulnerable Infants and Their Families: An Emerging Agenda," *Seminars in Perinatology* 13 (1989):506–512.

Ostrosky, Michaelene M. "Early Education for Children with Special Needs." In the National Parent Information Network—Parent News [web site]. University of Illinois at Urbana-Champaign, Champaign, Illinois, 1997. Available from http://npin.org/pnews/1997/pnew997/pnew997b.html; INTERNET.

Kristi L. Milowic

HISPANIC CHILDREN

The term "Hispanic" incorporates a diverse group of people comprised of individuals from a variety of countries and representing great diversity in socioeconomic status, age, history, and ethnicity. According to U.S. Bureau of the Census estimates for the year 2000, about 12 percent of the total population in the United States was Hispanic. While Hispanic people share a common language, they still represent a heterogeneous group of adults, children, and families living in various cities within the United States.

The diversity of Hispanic people underscores the difficulty in making generalizations about individuals. Because Hispanic children may differ in their attitudes and beliefs as a result of their families and their interaction with North American culture, it is important to not assume that all Hispanic children are the same. With this recognition, there are many cultural beliefs and practices, as well as elements of family structure and family roles, that are common to many Hispanic children and that can provide a better understanding of Hispanic children and their lives.

Definitions and Terms

Much controversy exists over how to describe the heterogeneity of individuals from Latin America. The most frequently used term in the United States is "Hispanic," which is derived from Hispania, the ancient name for the Iberian Peninsula. Nevertheless, because this name emphasizes Spanish origins, many prefer the term "Latino" or "Latina," descriptors that acknowledge the African-American and Indian ancestry of many individuals as well. Indeed, many individuals from Latin America are descendants of Indian nations, including the Olmecs, Mayans, Aztecs, and Incas. "Latino" and "Latina" are terms that are gaining in popularity, but Hispanic is still the most commonly used name and is the term that appeared in the 2000 U.S. Census.

Demographic Characteristics

Hispanic children include those children who are born to Hispanic parents in the United States, as well as those individuals who recently immigrated to the United States from Hispanic countries. Within the United States, the majority of Hispanic youth are Mexican, Cuban, and Puerto Rican, with some children and families from the Dominican Republic and from Central and South America. Of those from Central and South America, the countries of origin for the majority are Colombia, Ecuador, El Salvador, Guatemala, Nicaragua, and Peru.

As a result of immigration patterns and historical events, Hispanic families live in communities in various cities and states within the United States, primarily in metropolitan areas. Some Hispanics have come to America as a result of extremely poor economic conditions in their countries, as well as civil wars and political strife. With the goal of escaping problems and acquiring a better life, individuals and families have immigrated, both legally and illegally, to the United States. The United States has had a history of opening and closing borders with Latin American countries, and it is this ever-changing relationship that has contributed to some of the difficulties facing Hispanic immigrants, as well as the large presence of Hispanics within the United States.

According to U.S. Census estimates for 2000, Mexicans, who primarily live in California, Texas, Arizona, and New Mexico, comprised 65 percent of the Hispanic population in the United States. After Puerto Rico became a territory of the United States in 1917, large groups of Puerto Ricans came from the island to settle, mostly in New York and New Jersey. A large wave of Hispanics from Cuba, who fled the political leadership of Fidel Castro, immigrated to states such as Florida.

Language

Spanish is the common language uniting Hispanic people, though there are some Hispanics whose native language is French or Portuguese. Spanish is considered a Romance language, with similarities to other Latin-derived languages such as French and Italian. While most Hispanic individuals speak Spanish, there are a variety of Spanish dialects and linguistic characteristics that distinguish speakers from various Hispanic groups. Differences in daily expressions, vocabulary, and accents can be found in the Spanish spoken by different individuals of Hispanic descent.

Many Hispanic children who are raised in the United States are bilingual, able to speak both Spanish and English. Most Hispanic children speak Spanish at home and learn English at school. Hispanic children, however, also have very different degrees of Spanish and English language proficiency, depending on levels of acculturation and family and community environments.

Acculturation and Biculturalism

Hispanic children living in the United States generally experience some form of acculturation, the process whereby an individual incorporates cultural traits of another group. For Hispanic immigrants, acculturation occurs as they live in the United States and their behaviors begin to resemble those of North Americans. While living in predominantly Hispanic communities may slow acculturation in some individuals, children who attend school in the United States are usually exposed to North American cultural traits and then face the challenges of incorporating these new values and characteristics into already existing family beliefs.

For children born in the United States to Hispanic parents, acculturation may still occur as individuals live and grow in the United States. Furthermore, these children are often living bicultural lives, having the experience of living within two cultures. While many suggest that this experience can be wrought with difficulties as Hispanic children try to balance and incorporate these often disparate cultures, others believe that it can ultimately be enriching.

Cultural Values

Each Hispanic family and individual is unique, but there are many cultural values shared by Hispanic children living in the United States. Beyond the common language of Spanish, many Hispanic families also share religious beliefs and practices. These beliefs, along with family structure, food and dietary customs, and certain traditional holidays and celebrations, form the cornerstone of Hispanic communities.

Religion and Spirituality

Hispanic families and individuals engage in various practices of spirituality, including formal religion and different folk religions. Historically, the common religion of Hispanic people was that of the Roman Catholic Church, and a large number of Hispanic children are still baptized as Catholics. Nevertheless, Hispanic children today represent a variety of denominations, such as Baptist and Methodist, as well as other religions, such as Judaism. Members of some Hispanic groups also practice folk religions, such as Santeria, Espiritismo, and Curanderismo. While the belief in spirits of deceased persons differs across Hispanic cultures, many children learn about beliefs by observing family or community practices, and often see the frequency with which saints, angels, and God are invoked by adults.

Celebrations

Hispanic families celebrate a variety of cultural holidays and events, and children often play a large role in these events. As religion is a foundation for many Hispanic families, a number of celebrations and festivities emerge from Catholicism, such as Christmas and Easter. In addition, many Hispanic families also celebrate *bautismos* (baptisms), *confirmaciones* (confirmations), *cumpleaños* (birthdays), and *quinceañeras* (a rite of passage into adulthood for girls at age fifteen).

Families

Just as there is a great diversity in Hispanic children, there is also a variety of Hispanic family types. Traditionally, Hispanic families are two-parent households with fathers as economic and legal leaders of the family. Within the United States, however, Hispanic children are also likely to grow up in a home with a single parent, usually a mother. U.S. Census estimates in 2000 suggested that single mothers led 24 percent of Hispanic households. In general, Hispanic families are relatively young, partly as a result of the high fertility rates for Hispanics, as well as migration rates (individuals who migrate tend to be younger, thus more likely to have children). The U.S. Census Bureau estimated that the median age for Hispanic individuals in 2000 was twenty-seven.

Hispanic families are also likely to be larger than those of the general population. Indeed, in many Hispanic families, relatives such as aunts, uncles, grandparents, and cousins, and also neighbors and friends, are often considered family and play a role in child rearing and care. It is through these extended families that Hispanic children often learn about family traditions and values and become part of communities of other Hispanics. The importance of family, both extended and immediate, is a value shared by most Hispanic individuals.

Education and Schools

Hispanic children, with the general exception of Cuban Americans, face major challenges in education as they have low rates of educational achievement and high rates of poverty. These difficulties, along with language barriers, are a key factor in Hispanic families having individuals who are less educated and more likely to be underemployed and unemployed. According to U.S. Census estimates for 2000, 44 percent of Hispanics age twenty-five and older do not have a high school diploma.

Debates over the value of bilingual education for Spanish-speaking students continue to be prominent in the United States, with proponents arguing that students learning in English as well as their native language do better academically. Opponents disagree, stating that children living in the United States should be taught in English. The issue of bilingual education is still a well-debated topic and will likely remain a controversial issue for years to come.

Several factors account for some of the challenges faced by Hispanic children and adults in the United States, including discrimination, economic conditions, and language barriers. As the fastest-growing minority population, however, Hispanics are becoming more prominent in political arenas and are making great strides toward increasing employment and educational opportunities. As society addresses the difficulties faced by continued discrimination and poverty, Hispanic children will continue to have

Hispanic families celebrate a variety of cultural holidays and events, and children often play a large role in these events. These children are taking part in the Calle Ocho Parade in Miami, Florida. (Steven Ferry)

greater opportunities to prosper within the United States.

See also: RACIAL DIFFERENCES

Bibliography

Carrasquillo, Angela. *Hispanic Children and Youth in the United States: A Resource Guide.* New York: Garland, 1991.

Koss-Chioino, Joan, and Luis Vargas. *Working with Latino Youth.* San Francisco: Jossey-Bass, 1999.

Rodriguez, Gloria. *Raising Nuestros Niños: Bringing up Latino Children in a Bicultural World.* New York: Fireside, 1999.

U.S. Bureau of the Census. "Census Bureau Facts for Features: Hispanic Heritage Month 2000." In the U.S. Bureau of the Census [web site]. Washington, DC, 2000. Available from http://www.census.gov/Press-Release/www/2000/cb00ff11.html; INTERNET.

Lisa M. Edwards

HOME SCHOOLING

In the simplest terms, home schooling can be defined as the education of school-aged children in the home setting. Home schooling has become an increasingly popular way of educating children for a number of reasons. These reasons include, but are not limited to, religious beliefs, living in a dangerous neighborhood, a poor public education system, and the belief that parents themselves can provide their son or daughter with a good education.

Origins and Development

Origins of home schooling in the United States can be traced back to the seventeenth century—prior to public education and compulsory attendance laws. Although some town schools existed, home schooling was often the only option available to colonial children and the early pioneers. Because of nationwide compulsory attendance laws and the beginning of public education in the early twentieth century, however, the need for home schooling significantly decreased. This decrease did not last long, though, as expression of religious beliefs and dissatisfaction with public education increased throughout the twentieth century. By 1980 it was estimated that 15,000 students were being home schooled, a much smaller number in comparison to the early twenty-first century, but also much larger when compared to the previous eighty years.

It is estimated that between 700,000 and 1.3 million children in the United States are home schooled. In 2001 this represented approximately 3 to 5 percent of all students from kindergarten through grade twelve. Numerous studies have shown that the majority of home-schooled students come from a two-parent, middle-class household. Though more single mothers without college education are beginning to home school their children, most parents have some college education and a higher income than the national norm. Other typical characteristics of home school families include the following: (1) Equal numbers of boys and girls are home schooled with children ranging in age from three to seventeen; (2) though the mother is usually the primary teacher, both parents play an active role in the process; (3) there are generally three or more children in the family; (4) more than 70 percent regularly attend religious services, representing a variety of backgrounds; (5) children are usually home schooled a minimum of three years; and (6) though students usually study all traditional school subjects, home school parents generally place an emphasis on reading, mathematics, and science.

Reasons for Home Schooling

As mentioned before, parents choose to home school their children for many different reasons. The two most popular are called ideological and pedagogical, with those home schooling for ideological reasons called ideologues and those doing so for pedagogical reasons called pedagogues. Ideologues are generally motivated by religious beliefs and choose instructional methods focused on religious teachings, moral values, and patriotism, mixed with basic skills. The majority of ideologues, though not all, are fundamentalist Christians who have a strong desire to connect their religious beliefs to their instructional curricula.

Parents who choose to home school their children for pedagogical reasons can be separated into two groups. The first group, originating in the late 1960s, includes parents who want their children to develop individual awareness and fulfill their potential. Because of this motivation, they typically use loosely defined curricula where their children are placed in unstructured, exploration-seeking environments. The second group of pedagogues has chosen to home school their children because of dissatisfaction with the climate or quality of the education provided in the public school setting. Contrary to the first group, these parents usually teach their children in structured environments, focusing on the learning of basic skills, discipline, and patriotism.

How, When, and How Much

Because parents choose to home school their children for different reasons, every home school looks a little different. Studies have shown, however, that ideologues usually teach a more traditional curriculum, and many include biblical training and the teaching of religious history. Out of their desire for their children to become self-aware and develop their potential, the first group of pedagogues discussed above believes that education should consider all aspects of the human experience—rational, emotional, spiritual, aesthetic, and creative. Unfortunately, very few studies have examined how the second group of pedagogues educates their children. This is a reflection of the wide variety of reasons why this particular group of parents decides to home school their children.

Each home school also looks different in terms of when parents begin to home school their children, how many hours are spent "in school," and how much parents spend to home school their children. Similar to how parents choose to educate their children, these decisions are also a reflection of why parents have chosen to home school. For example, while most parents begin educating their children around the age of six, there are some who begin as young as age three or four and others who wait until the child is between ten and twelve. One reason for such variability is that parents are the ones who determine when their child is ready for school. Though there is still much variety, most studies have shown that the average home-schooled child spends three to four hours per day being educated. Additional time is also spent on special projects such as field trips, reading for pleasure, cooking, playing, gardening, and so forth. Finally, most studies have found that the national average spent on home schooling is $500 a year per child.

Academic and Social Outcomes

Despite concerns that home-schooled children will have poorly developed social skills and will not learn at a similar rate as their same-age peers, most studies have revealed the opposite. In fact, most studies have shown that home schools produce superior social and academic results. For example, one study found that 50 percent of 224 home-schooled children in Michigan scored as well as or better than 90 percent of their same-age peers and only 10.3 percent scored below the national average on a measure of self-concept and self-esteem. Another study revealed that home-schooled students generally participate in at least five extracurricular activities outside the home, with 98 percent participating in at least two or more activities.

Academic and achievement results are similar. For example, almost 25 percent of home-schooled students are enrolled one or more grades above their same-age peers in public and private schools. Achievement test scores for home-schooled students are also exceptionally high, with students in grades one to four performing one grade level above their same-age public and private school peers. Finally, students who have been home schooled their entire academic life have higher scholastic achievement test scores than students enrolled in public or private schools. Because of these results, colleges and universities have begun to accept larger numbers of home-schooled students. For example, Harvard, Dartmouth, Oxford, UCLA, and Yale, among others, have accepted and enrolled home-schooled students.

Legal Requirements

Though home-schooled students have succeeded and continue to succeed, their parents' fight to be able to home school has not proceeded without court involvement. For example, in the late 1970s and throughout the 1980s, compulsory attendance laws of various states were challenged in court. By 1986, however, all states had adopted some form of legislation recognizing home schooling as an education option. Now, only ten states require parents to have specific qualifications to home school their children, and these include a high school diploma, GED, or some college. Fifteen states require simply that home schooling parents be "competent" and instruction be "thorough." Thirty states require testing or other evaluation of home-schooled students. Finally, nearly all states require parents to file basic information with either the state or local education agency, and many states have additional requirements, such as the submission of a curricular plan or the testing of parents.

Cooperation between Public and Home Schools

Although the National Parent Teacher Association and the National Education Association oppose home schooling, there are numerous examples of cooperation between public and home schools today. In 1991, for example, Iowa passed legislation giving home-schooled students dual enrollment and granting them the opportunity to take part in academic and instructional programs in the school district, participate in extracurricular activities, and use the services and assistance of the local educational agencies. Another example is Michigan, where school districts are required to open "nonessential elective courses" to home-schooled students.

Because of this increasing nationwide cooperation, greater freedom to home school in all states, and

Home schooling has become an increasingly popular way of educating children for a number of reasons, including—but not limited to—religious beliefs, a poor local public education system, and the belief that parents themselves can provide their son or daughter with a good education. (Laura Dwight/Corbis)

strong academic results, home schooling is becoming an increasingly popular option for parents who are either dissatisfied with public education or desire to teach their children what they consider important. Further, home school families have created their own home schooling organizations and co-ops, and curricular companies have been formed that exclusively cater to their needs. In connection with this support and greater public acceptance of home schooling as a viable educational alternative, it is expected that the popularity of home schooling will continue to increase well into the twenty-first century.

Bibliography

Mayberry, Maralee, J. Gary Knowles, Brian Ray, and Stacey Marlow. *Home Schooling: Parents as Educators.* Thousand Oaks, CA: Corwin Press, 1995.

Rudner, Lawrence. "Scholastic Achievement and Demographic Characteristics of Home School Students in 1998." *Education*

Policy Analysis Archives [web site]. Available from http://epaa.asu.edu/epaa/v7n8/; INTERNET.

Russo, Charles, and William Gordon. "Home Schooling: The In-House Alternative." *School Business Affairs* (December 1996):16–20.

Jason D. Rehfeldt

HOMELESS CHILDREN

Children who do not have a consistent, adequate nighttime residence are considered to be homeless. There are as many as 250,000 homeless children (birth to sixteen years of age) in the United States, including children who are living in shelters or "doubled up" with friends and relatives. Common causes of homelessness for families with children include poverty, lack of affordable housing, and domestic violence. The lack of a stable place to live can have severe effects: Compared to housed children, homeless children are more likely to experience poor health, developmental delays, behavioral and mental health problems, and low educational achievement. Although the Education of Homeless Children and Youth Program established by Congress in 1987 has dramatically improved school attendance by homeless children, their families still frequently face barriers to receiving needed services because of their lack of a permanent address.

See also: LATCHKEY CHILDREN; RESILIENCY

Bibliography

Shinn, Marybeth, and Beth Weitzman. "Homeless Families Are Different." In J. Baumohl ed., *Homelessness in America*. Washington, DC: National Coalition for the Homeless, 1996.

Theresa Lawton Hawley

HOMEWORK

Homework is a tool for reinforcing and expanding on concepts introduced in the classroom. It can help foster independence, self-discipline, and a love of learning in younger children and can improve an older child's performance on standardized tests. Critics of homework say that it overburdens children and can adversely affect a child's development by cutting in on leisure time and creating tension in the home. In addition, some children may be at a disadvantage if their parents are ill prepared to assist with homework because of their work schedules or their inability to comprehend the subject matter. Some education experts have also pointed out that studies have never conclusively proven that homework improves overall academic performance among grade-school children.

Despite these criticisms, many believe that homework has a place in a child's education. Homework is most effective when assignments are meaningful, have a clear purpose and instructions, and are well matched to a student's abilities.

See also: HOME SCHOOLING

Bibliography

"Helping with Homework: A Parent's Guide to Information Problem-Solving." *ERIC Digest* (November 1996).

Kralovec, Etta, and John Buell. *The End of Homework*. Boston: Beacon Press, 2000.

National Institute of Child Health and Human Development. "How Do Children Spend Their Time? Children's Activities, School Achievement, and Well-Being." *Research on Today's Issues* 11 (August 2000).

Patricia Ohlenroth

HUMAN GENOME PROJECT

The Human Genome Project began in earnest in 1990 as an international, publicly funded effort to determine the sequence of the three billion base pairs of human DNA. The major goals of the project are to identify and functionally characterize the estimated 30,000 to 40,000 genes in human genome and to address the ethical, legal, and social issues that will arise from the use of the project's results in medical practice. The initial sequencing phase of the project was complete in 2000. Biomedical researchers are building upon the knowledge, resources, and technologies emanating from the Human Genome Project by identifying specific genotypes that contribute to human health and disease phenotypes. The ultimate goal is to use this information to develop new ways to treat, cure, or even prevent diseases that afflict humankind. The identification of genes and genotypes that cause birth defects and other diseases is being made possible by the project. The introduction of this information into medical practice, in particular through genetic counseling, will have a major impact on improving child health and development by providing more accurate diagnostic tests for disease carriers and prenatal testing for birth defects.

See also: GENETIC COUNSELING; GENOTYPE; PHENOTYPE

Bibliography

Department of Energy. "Human Genome Research." Available from http://www.er.doe.gov/production/ober/hug_top.html; INTERNET.

National Human Genome Research Institute. "The Human Genome Project." Available from http://www.nhgri.nih.gov/HGP/; INTERNET.

David W. Threadgill
Robert E. Boykin

HYPERACTIVITY

See: ATTENTION DEFICIT HYPERACTIVITY DISORDER

HYPOTHESIS

A hypothesis may be thought of as a well-informed guess that is drawn from a theory or collection of ideas. It provides the basis from which a reasoned prediction about the relationship between two or more factors is made (e.g., early attachment and the child's later educational attainment). The prediction should define clearly the factors and the group of people within which the relationship can be observed. After planning how best to control for the effect of the factors and assembling participants who reflect the defined group, scientific testing can proceed. The data gathered are then checked to see whether the hypothesis is supported or not.

Supporting data, however, cannot be taken as conclusive proof of the theory. Logically it is more persuasive to predict no relationship between two factors and then find through testing that there is a relationship. This is called the null hypothesis and is the theoretical basis for statistical examination of the data to test whether the relationship between the factors is greater than chance.

See also: METHODS OF STUDYING CHILDREN

Bibliography

Popper, Karl R. *Conjectures and Refutations: The Growth of Scientific Knowledge.* London: Routledge and Kegan Paul, 1963.

Anthony Lee

I

IDENTITY DEVELOPMENT

The process of developing an identity begins with the infant's discovery of self, continues throughout childhood, and becomes the focus of adolescence. Erik Erikson, a pioneer in the field of personality development, identified the goal of adolescence as achieving a coherent identity and avoiding identity confusion. Identity is multidimensional and may include physical and sexual identity, occupational goals, religious beliefs, and ethnic background. Adolescents explore these dimensions, and usually make commitments to aspects of their identity as they move into early adulthood. Periodically, adults may reevaluate and alter certain aspects of their identity as life circumstances change.

Identity development begins with children's awareness that they are separate and unique individuals. First indications of this awareness are evident in infancy when children begin to recognize themselves. For example, when researchers place a dot of rouge on a child's nose, two-year-olds who see themselves in a mirror will touch their noses (Bullock and Lutkenhaus 1990). That is, they recognize the reflected image as themselves. Also, the words "me," "I," and "mine" emerge very early in children's language. These findings are consistent with Erikson's psychosocial stage of *autonomy versus shame and doubt,* when infants establish their identity as independent persons.

During childhood, self-awareness grows and changes. Preschoolers describe themselves in terms of observable characteristics and behaviors, including physical attributes ("I have brown eyes"), preferences ("I like to ride my bike"), and competencies ("I can sing 'Itsy, Bitsy Spider'"). Between ages six and twelve, children begin to include less concrete aspects of the self in their descriptions. School-aged children talk about their feelings ("I love my dog") and how they fit into their social world ("I'm the best fielder on my team"). During Erikson's stage of *initiative versus guilt* children explore their skills, abilities, and attitudes and incorporate the information into their view of self.

The physical, cognitive, and social changes of adolescence allow the teenager to develop the identity that will serve as a basis for their adult lives. During Erikson's stage of *identity versus role confusion,* adolescents' description of self expands to include personality traits ("I'm outgoing") and attitudes ("I don't like stuck-up people"). The emergence of abstract reasoning abilities allows adolescents to think about the future and experiment with different identities.

James Marcia (1991) hypothesized that identity development involves two steps. First, the adolescent must break away from childhood beliefs to explore alternatives for identity in a particular area. Second, the adolescent makes a commitment as to their individual identity in that area. Marcia identified four "Identity Statuses" to describe the process of identity development. Some aspects of identity, especially among young adolescents, may be foreclosed. The *foreclosure status* is when a commitment is made without exploring alternatives. Often these commitments are based

The act of playing "dress-up" is common during the childhood years. Girls may wear their mother's dresses, jewelry, and high-heel shoes to identify themselves as "grown-up women." (Françoise Gervais/Corbis)

foster identity achievement. Identity achievement is important because it is associated with higher self-esteem, increased critical thinking, and advanced moral reasoning.

Aspects of Identity

The physical changes associated with puberty initiate adolescents' exploration of their physical and sexual identity. For females, an important component of their identity and worth is related to their physical appearance. The changes in the male body may not be as important as their timing. Early maturing males have advantages in athletics, hold more leadership roles in school, and are viewed more positively by peers and adults. The effects of timing for females are not as clear and may be less important in their development.

The exploration of a sexual identity occurs within the context of the "presumption of heterosexuality" (Herdt 1989) that exists in American culture. Heterosexual adolescents spend little or no time considering their sexual identity as anything but heterosexual. However, the same is not true for homosexual adolescents. In American culture the homosexual is often degraded and stigmatized. This cultural context makes forming a sexual identity for the homosexual adolescent more challenging than for the heterosexual adolescent. Following the pattern of identity development in general, homosexual adolescents may experience a period of confusion and exploration before accepting and committing to their homosexual identity. Adolescents who do not complete this process may feel isolated and guilty. This can lead to increased drug and alcohol abuse or even suicidal thoughts (Mondimore 1996). Regardless of orientation, the development of a clear sexual identity is important for the transition to Erikson's early adulthood stage of *intimacy versus isolation.*

The emergence of abstract thought in adolescence also permits the exploration of religious and spiritual beliefs. Sixty percent of adolescents report that religion is very or pretty important in their lives (Youth Indicators 1993). The development of a religious identity follows the same pattern as other aspects of the individual's identity. Even though the adolescent may eventually adopt beliefs that were similar to their childhood beliefs, the process of exploration is important in achieving a religious identity and avoiding foreclosure or diffusion.

When asked to introduce themselves, most adults will begin talking about their occupation or career. Three phases of career development have been described (crystallization, specification, and implementation) that are closely tied to the development of

on parental ideas and beliefs that are accepted without question. However, adolescents often begin to question their ideas and beliefs and enter what Marcia called a "moratorium." The *moratorium status* is characterized by the active exploration of alternatives. This may be reflected in attending different churches, changing college majors, or trying out different social roles. Such exploration may be followed by *identity achievement.* Identity achievement occurs when the adolescent has explored and committed to important aspects of their identity. Although adolescents explore multiple aspects of their identities, commitments to occupational, religious, or ethnic identity may occur at different times. Some adolescents become overwhelmed by the task of identity development and neither explore nor make commitments. This describes Marcia's *diffusion status,* in which adolescents may become socially isolated and withdrawn. Supportive parents, schools, and communities that encourage exploration in communities and schools identity (Kail and Cavanaugh 2000). Although young children often say things like "I want to be a doctor," it is not until adolescence that career goals are clarified in the context of identity development. Young adolescents explore career goals that fit with their personality and interests. A thirteen-year-old who enjoys and excels at science may express interest in being a science teacher or a doctor. During this crystallization phase choices are tentative, and teens may explore a number of career options. By late adolescence, many teenagers make choices that limit career options by choosing a job or additional education and/or training (specification). With this the career path begins to be incorporated into their identity. Once individuals enter their chosen job or career (implementation), it becomes a part of how they see themselves.

Unlike most Caucasian adolescents, minority adolescents must decide the degree to which their racial or cultural background will be part of their identity (Phinney and Kohatsu 1997). Painful issues surrounding identification with a minority subculture, such as racism and inequality, can lead some minority adolescents to avoid the issue through foreclosure or diffusion. In particular, during early adolescence minority teenagers may deny any interest in their racial or cultural background. However, as they become more aware of the conflicts between their subculture and the dominant culture, minority adolescents often begin to explore their heritage. Interactions with other members of the same culture, and attendance at religious services or cultural celebrations, can increase the adolescents' knowledge and encourage a sense of pride in their ethnic background. Achieving a positive ethnic identity is associated with higher self-esteem and better grades, as well as better relations with family and friends. The most positive outcome appears to be achievement of a bicultural identity that allows the adolescent to function effectively in either setting (Phinney and Kohatsu 1997).

Identity achievement during adolescence serves as a basis for our adult expectations and goals for ourselves (Whitbourne 1987). As individuals enter early adulthood they use their current understanding of who they are to develop a *lifespan construct* which serves as the link between the identity developed in adolescence and the adult self (Kail and Cavanaugh 2000). The lifespan construct is an integration of an individual's past, present, and culture. This construct includes a *scenario* and a *social clock*. The scenario is the individual's expectation of what they will do in the future (e.g., go to medical school and establish a practice in family medicine), and the social clock links these events to the age when they will happen (e.g., get married by age thirty). The experience people acquire throughout life leads to continuous modifications in the life construct. Nevertheless, adults who feel they have (to some degree) met their life goals are more likely to experience the sense of fulfillment that Erikson called *generativity* in middle adulthood and *ego integrity* in old age.

Identity development is ultimately the result of a lifelong journey. The person that people ultimately become is unique, however the process by which identity develops is similar among individuals. Although identity development is most often associated with adolescence, each developmental stage offers opportunities for reevaluation and modification.

See also: PERSONALITY DEVELOPMENT; SELF-CONCEPT

Bibliography

Bullock, Merry, and Paul Lukenhaus. "Who Am I? The Development of Self-Understanding in Toddlers." *Merrill-Palmer Quarterly* 36 (1990):217–238.

Herdt, Gilbert, ed. "Introduction: Gay and Lesbian Youth, Emergent Identities, and Cultural Scenes at Home and Abroad." In *Gay and Lesbian Youth*. New York: Harrington Park Press, 1989.

Kail, Robert V., and John C. Cavanaugh. *Human Development: A Lifespan View*, 2nd edition. Belmont, CA: Wadsworth, 2000.

Marcia, James. "Identity and Self-Development." In Richard Lerner, Anne Peterson, and Jeanne Brooks-Gunn eds., *Encyclopedia of Adolescence* (Vol. 1). New York: Garland, 1991.

Mondimore, Francis M. *A Natural History of Homosexuality*. Baltimore: John Hopkins University Press, 1996.

Phinney, Jean, and E. L. Kohatsu. "Ethnic and Racial Identity Development and Mental Health." In John Schulenberg, Jennifer Maggs, and Klaus Hurrelmann eds., *Health Risks and Developmental Transitions during Adolescence*. Cambridge, Eng.: Cambridge University Press, 1997.

Whitbourne, Susan. "Personality Development in Adulthood and Old Age: Relationships among Identity Style, Health, and Well-being." In K. W. Schaie ed., *Annual Review of Gerontology and Geriatrics* (Vol. 7). New York: Springer, 1987.

Youth Indicators. "Trends in the Well-being of American Youth." Washington, DC: U.S. Government Printing Office, 1993.

Eva G. Clarke
Elaine M. Justice

IMAGINARY AUDIENCE

The term "imaginary audience" was introduced by David Elkind to refer to the tendency of adolescents to falsely assume that their appearance or behavior is the focus of other people's attention. Having an imaginary audience is believed to result in the self-consciousness that is characteristic of adolescence and is often linked conceptually with *personal fable*, which involves having a strong belief in one's own uniqueness. Researchers have assessed imaginary audience by asking adolescents questions about what they would do in social situations that are potentially embarrassing (e.g., you arrive at what you thought was a costume party but you are the only person in a costume). More recently, Daniel Lapsley and his colleagues described imaginary audience as reflecting the developmental process of separation-individuation and measured it by assessing the frequency of adolescents' daydreams about themselves and others.

See also: ADOLESCENCE

Bibliography

Elkind, David. "Egocentrism in Adolescence." *Child Development* 38 (1967):1025–1034.

Elkind, David, and Robert Bowen. "Imaginary Audience Behavior in Children and Adolescents." *Developmental Psychology* 15, no. 1 (1979):38–44.

Lapsley, Daniel K., David P. Fitzgerald, Kenneth G. Rice, and Sara Jackson. "Separation-Individuation and the 'New Look' at the Imaginary Audience and Personal Fable: A Test of an Integrative Model." *Journal of Adolescent Research* 4, no. 4 (1989):483–505.

Vartanian, Lesa Rae. "Separation-Individuation, Social Support, and Adolescent Egocentrism: An Exploratory Study." *Journal of Early Adolescence* 17 (1997):245–270.

Marjorie Taylor

IMAGINARY PLAYMATES

Imaginary playmates have fascinated psychologists, parents, and teachers for many years. Although psychologists have been writing about imaginary playmates since the late 1800s, only a handful of articles and book chapters exist on this topic, with only a few of those empirically based. Some experts think that children with imaginary playmates are likely to be between the ages of three and six, be of at least average intelligence, possess good verbal skills, be characterized as creative and cooperative with adults, and be an only child. They also tend to come from families that value active rather than passive behavior and who watch less television than their peers. Imaginary playmates are drawn from television, stories, or real people, or can also be original characters developed by the child.

Having an imaginary playmate is typically assumed to have a positive effect on children's social and cognitive development. Contributions to social development are thought to include increased opportunities for practicing positive social skills, taking another's perspective, and experimenting with relationships. The assumed cognitive benefits associated with having an imaginary playmate include the ability to engage in creative and original thought, as well as to use abstract reasoning skills. In a 1992 article, however, S. Harter and Christine Chao reported that children with imaginary playmates were rated as less competent in cognitive, physical, and social skills than their peers who did not have imaginary playmates, though the researchers cautioned that these findings had to be replicated before they could be viewed with confidence.

There are significant differences in reported prevalence rates. Older studies found that about 15 percent to 30 percent of preschool children had an imaginary friend, whereas Dorothy Singer and Jerome Singer found in 1990 that 65 percent of the young children had an imaginary playmate.

Regarding gender differences, in one study boys tended to have imaginary friends who were more competent than they were and girls tended to have imaginary friends that were less competent (Harter and Chao 1992). Another study found that while the majority of both boys and girls had same-sex imaginary friends, more girls than boys had friends of the opposite gender, and boys had more nonhuman imaginary friends than girls did (Manosevitz, Prentice, and Wilson 1973).

Clearly more research is needed in order to understand the characteristics of the children who develop an imaginary playmate, the benefits associated with having an imaginary playmate both long- and short-term, and the role of adults in supporting social and cognitive development through interactions related to the imaginary playmate.

See also: FRIENDSHIP

Bibliography

Gilbertson, S. A. "Play Behavior in Preschool Children: Relations to Imaginary Companions." Paper presented at the meeting of the Rocky Mountain Psychological Association, Denver, CO, 1981.

Harter, S., and Christine Chao. "The Role of Competence in Children's Creation of Imaginary Friends." *Merrill-Palmer Quarterly* 38 (1992):350–363.

Hurlock, E. B., and W. Burstein. "The Imaginary Playmate." *Journal of Genetic Psychology* (1932):390–392.

Manosevitz, Martin, Norman M. Prentice, and Frances Wilson. "Individual and Family Correlates of Imaginary Companions in Preschool Children." *Developmental Psychology* 8 (1973):72–79.

Singer, Dorothy G., and Jerome L. Singer. "Imaginary Playmates and Imaginary Worlds." In *The House of Make-Believe.* Cambridge, MA: Harvard University Press, 1990.

Somers, Jana U., and Thomas D. Yawkey. "Imaginary Play Companions: Contributions of Creative and Intellectual Abilities of Young Children." *Journal of Creative Behavior* 181 (1984):77–89.

Svendsen, Margaret. "Children's Imaginary Companions." *Archives of Neurological Psychology* 32 (1934):985–999.

Vostrosky, C. "A Study of Imaginary Play Companions." *Education* 15 (1895):383–397.

Rebecca B. McCathren
M. Gutierrez
G. Holliday

IMMUNIZATION

Immunization is recognized as one of the greatest public health achievements of the twentieth century. The widespread use of immunization is responsible for dramatic reductions in, and in some cases the elimination of, specific infectious diseases.

Goals of Immunization

Immunizations can partially or completely prevent illness by a specific microorganism. By preventing illness, immunizations avert the acute effects of disease, complications of disease, and long-term disability related to disease. When immunizations are widely used, the spread of disease within the population can also be prevented. By preventing outbreaks of disease, immunizations reduce health-care expenditures, including the costs of: (1) prescription and over-the-counter medications, (2) health-care provider visits (including office and emergency room visits), (3) hospitalization, and (4) long-term disability or long-term care. Immunizations also save money by reducing the number of days of work loss by employees because of personal illness or illness in a dependent family member.

Immunizations can provide active or passive protection against an infectious disease. In active immunization, entire organisms (e.g., inactivated bacteria; live, weakened virus) or their parts (e.g., bacterial toxoid; inactivated, viral antigen) are administered. The immune system responds to the vaccine by producing a long-lasting, protective immune response in the recipient. Examples of active immunization include all of the vaccines used in the standard childhood immunization schedule (see Table 1). In passive immunization, preformed antibodies against specific microorganisms are administered. Protection lasts only months because of the relatively short half-life of the antibodies. Passive immunization is used before or immediately after an exposure to an infectious agent to prevent infection. Passive immunization is used for a number of infectious agents, including hepatitis B, rabies, respiratory syncitial virus, tetanus, and varicella-zoster. The remainder of this discussion will be directed toward active immunizations used during childhood.

Immunizations can be recommended on either a universal or a selective basis. Universal immunizations are directed at all members of a population. The eventual goal of immunizing all susceptible individuals is the complete eradication of a disease, as in the case of smallpox. Selective immunizations are directed at individuals who are considered at high risk of a disease, or at high risk of complications of a disease.

In the United States, the choice and timing of immunizations are made jointly by three national organizations—the Advisory Committee on Immunization Practices branch of the federal government's Centers for Disease Control and Prevention, the Committee on Infectious Diseases of the American Academy of Pediatrics, and the American Academy of Family Physicians. The complete schedule for universal immunizations is updated and published annually (see Table 1). Alterations to the schedule (e.g., addition of newly approved vaccines and changes in the timing of vaccines) can nevertheless be made throughout the year.

Immunization Success

Immunization against smallpox is an example of the success possible through universal vaccination programs. Accounts of immunization against smallpox were reported as long ago as the 1600s. At that time, uninfected individuals were exposed to material (e.g., pus) from patients suffering from mild disease in the hopes of preventing more serious or fatal disease. In the late 1700s, Edward Jenner, a physician in England, promoted the widespread use of the cowpox virus to prevent smallpox. Two centuries later, on October 26, 1979, the World Health Organization declared that smallpox had been eradicated from the entire world.

The success of other immunization campaigns in the United States is shown in Table 2. The incidence of vaccine-preventable disease has been reduced between 97.6 and 100 percent through the use of universal immunization.

This success could not have been achieved without the combined efforts of researchers, health-care providers, and families. Researchers are responsible for the development of a wide variety of safe, effective vaccines against common childhood diseases. Health-care providers are responsible for ensuring that children receive the appropriate and required immunizations. And families are responsible for bringing their children in for routine child-health supervision visits. At the beginning of the twenty-first century in the United States, record numbers of children were being immunized. This is an essential part of the success of immunizations in this country.

TABLE 1

Recommended Childhood Immunization Schedule United States, January–December 2001

Vaccines[1] are listed under routinely recommended ages. ☐Bars☐ indicate range of recommended ages for immunization. Any dose not given at the recommended age should be given as a "catch-up" immunization at any subsequent visit when indicated and feasible. ⬭Ovals⬭ indicate vaccines to be given if previously recommended doses were missed or given earlier than the recommended minimum age.

Age ▶ Vaccine ▼	Birth	1 mo	2 mos	4 mos	6 mos	12 mos	15 mos	18 mos	24 mos	4-6 yrs	11-12 yrs	14-18 yrs
Hepatitis B[2]		Hep B #1									Hep B[2]	
			Hep B #2			Hep B #3						
Diphtheria, Tetanus, Pertussis[3]			DTaP	DTaP	DTaP		DTaP[3]			DTaP	Td	
H. inuenzae type b[4]			Hib	Hib	Hib	Hib						
Inactivated Polio[5]			IPV	IPV		IPV[5]				IPV[5]		
Pneumococcal Conjugate[6]			PCV	PCV	PCV	PCV						
Measles, Mumps, Rubella[7]						MMR				MMR[7]	MMR[7]	
Varicella[8]						Var					Var[8]	
Hepatitis A[9]										Hep A-in selected areas[9]		

Approved by the Advisory Committee on Immunization Practices (ACIP), the American Academy of Pediatrics (AAP), and the American Academy of Family Physicians (AAFP).

1. This schedule indicates the recommended ages for routine administration of currently licensed childhood vaccines, as of 11/1/00, for children through 18 years of age. Additional vaccines may be licensed and recommended during the year. Licensed combination vaccines may be used whenever any components of the combination are indicated and its other components are not contraindicated. Providers should consult the manufacturers' package inserts for detailed recommendations.

Universal Immunizations

A combination vaccine against diphtheria, tetanus, and pertussis (DTP) was first licensed in the 1940s. The initial vaccine consisted of diphtheria and tetanus toxoids (a weakened form of the toxin that actually does the damage in the infections), and inactivated, whole pertussis bacteria. As seen in Table 2, tremendous reductions have been achieved in all three diseases. Use of the original whole-cell pertussis vaccine was marred in the past by concerns that the vaccine could cause brain injury (specifically, an encephalopathy). While this was largely disproven, the concerns were enough to lead many people to refuse the vaccine in the 1970s. In both Great Britain and Japan, the decline in immunization coverage resulted in epidemics of pertussis. In Great Britain alone, more than 100,000 cases of pertussis occurred between 1977 and 1979. In both countries, vaccination programs were restarted after the consequences of low immunization rates were seen. In the United States, a switch from the whole-cell pertussis vaccine to an acellular preparation with significantly less fever and local reactions was made in 1991.

The first polio vaccine was the injectable, inactivated polio vaccine (IPV) introduced in 1955. The live-attenuated oral polio vaccine (OPV) was licensed in 1960. Since the polio virus attacks the nerve cells that control muscle movement, vaccines against polio are responsible for enormous reductions in paralytic poliomyelitis throughout the world, and for the eradication of natural polio infection from the entire western hemisphere. In the United States, the OPV was used principally from the 1960s until 1997. Since 1997, a transition has been made to the IPV in order to eliminate any chance of vaccine-associated paralytic poliomyelitis caused by OPV. IPV has no risk of

TABLE 2

Declines in Vaccine–Preventable Childhood Diseases in the United States

Disease	Maximum # of Cases	Year	1998	Percent Change
Diphtheria	206,939	(1921)	1	99.9-
Haemophilus influenza	20,000*	(pre-1985)	54	99.7-
Measles	894,134	(1941)	89	99.9-
Mumps	152,209	(1968)	606	99.6-
Pertussis	265,269	(1934)	6,279	97.6-
Poliomyelitis (paralytic)	21,269	(1952)	0**	100.0-
Rubella	57,686	(1969)	345	-99.4
Congenital Rubella Syndrome	20,000*	(1964-1965)	5	-99.9
Smallpox	48,164	(1900-1904)	0	100.0-
Tetanus	1,560	(1923)	34	-97.8

*Estimated number

**Excludes one case of vaccine-associated polio reported in 1998

SOURCE: Alan Uba.

causing paralytic poliomyelitis. A complete switch to IPV occurred in the United States in January 2000.

The first live, attenuated measles vaccine was licensed in 1963, followed by mumps and rubella (German measles) vaccines in 1967 and 1969. The combined measles, mumps, and rubella (MMR) vaccine has been available since 1971. In the 1980s, epidemics of measles in the United States demonstrated the importance of immunizing and reimmunizing against measles. Concerns have been expressed over a possible link between autism and the measles vaccine, and this issue is discussed below under "Controversy over Vaccination."

The first hepatitis B vaccine was licensed in 1981. In the United States, an attempt at selective immunization of individuals (e.g., those having contact with blood or blood products, including health-care workers) with the hepatitis B vaccine did not control the number of new cases. Universal immunization of infants against hepatitis B with a vaccine began in 1990.

The *Haemophilus influenzae* type b (HIB) vaccine was first licensed in 1985. The initial vaccine could only be used in older children because it did not evoke protective immunity in younger infants. Unfortunately, most HIB disease occurs in the first two years of life. Subsequently, a new vaccine was introduced in 1990 that proved extremely effective in early infancy. By 1998, rates of serious bacterial infection due to HIB had declined by 99.7 percent since the introduction of the newer HIB vaccine in 1985.

A chicken pox (varicella) vaccine was licensed in 1995. Before the vaccine was available, an estimated four million cases of chicken pox infection occurred in the United States each year. While most cases of natural infection were uncomplicated, chicken pox was responsible for an estimated eleven thousand hospitalizations and one hundred deaths per year. Once the vaccine was available, chicken pox became the most common vaccine-preventable cause of death in the United States. Universal immunization with the chicken pox vaccine began the same year that the vaccine was licensed.

The pneumococcal-conjugate vaccine was licensed in 2000. *Streptococcus pneumoniae* (pneumococcus) is a leading cause of serious bacterial infection in childhood, including pneumonia, bacteremia (bacteria in the blood), and meningitis. Pneumococcus is also the most common cause of ear infections in children.

Selected Immunizations

Selected immunizations are directed at high-risk populations. These populations include: (1) individuals with underlying immune system disorders, (2) individuals with chronic underlying medical conditions that make them more susceptible to severe infection, and (3) individuals with increased risk of contracting infection.

Impediments to Vaccination

The success of universal immunization campaigns requires high rates of immunization. Factors that interfere with the delivery of immunizations include: (1) lack of access to health care, (2) lack of knowledge about appropriate immunizations for children, (3) misconceptions about contraindications to vaccination (reasons that vaccination may be inadvisable), and (4) missed opportunities for immunizations.

Controversy over Vaccination

Public fears about the possibility of adverse central nervous system effects of immunizations have followed several routine childhood vaccines. In the 1970s there were concerns over neurologic side effects (primarily, encephalopathy) of pertussis vaccination. In the mid-1990s there were concerns over central nervous system demyelinating disease (e.g., Guillain-Barré syndrome, multiple sclerosis) and the hepatitis B vaccine. While concerns over pertussis and hepatitis B vaccines have largely diminished in the United States, fear increased in the late 1990s over a possible association between autism and the MMR vaccine.

Controversy over the MMR vaccine followed publication of an article in the journal Lancet in early 1998 written by Andrew Wakefield. Based on observations and investigations made in twelve children, the authors suggested a link among the MMR vaccine, chronic intestinal inflammation, and autism.

Two subsequent epidemiologic studies, by B. Taylor and L. Dales, failed to identify an association between the MMR vaccine and autism. The Taylor study, from the United Kingdom, demonstrated increasing rates of autism, but a comparison of rates before and after the MMR vaccine was introduced in the United Kingdom in 1988 failed to uncover a link between the two. The Dales study, from California, demonstrated an almost fourfold relative increase (373%) in autism between 1980 and 1994. Immunization rates, however, increased by only 14 percent during the same period.

Until the cause or causes of autism are better defined, controversy will continue in this area. Currently, there is little, if any, scientific evidence linking the MMR vaccine and autism. Meanwhile, the global eradication of measles is still a possibility through widespread use of measles-containing vaccines. Eradication of measles would eliminate the estimated 880,000 deaths that occur worldwide as a result of measles infection.

The Future

The immunization schedule is constantly evolving. Future changes include vaccines against additional diseases, new vaccine combinations, and novel approaches to immunization. New routes for vaccine administration (e.g., nasal vaccines, vaccines incorporated into foods) are also being evaluated.

See also: BIRTH DEFECTS; RUBELLA

Bibliography

American Academy of Pediatrics. Committee on Infectious Diseases. *Red Book, 2000: Report of the Committee on Infectious Diseases,* 25th edition. Elk Grove Village, IL: American Academy of Pediatrics, 2000.

American Academy of Pediatrics. Committee on Infectious Diseases. "Recommended Childhood Immunization Schedule: United States, January–December 2001." *Pediatrics* 107, no. 1 (2001):202–204.

Centers for Disease Control and Prevention. "Achievements in Public Health, 1900–1999: Impact of Vaccines Universally Recommended for Children—United States, 1990–1998." *Morbidity and Mortality Weekly Report* 48, no. 12 (1999):243–248.

Centers for Disease Control and Prevention [web site]. Atlanta, GA, 2001. Available from http://www.cdc.gov; INTERNET.

Dales, L., S. J. Hammer, and N. J. Smith. "Time Trends in Autism and in MMR Immunization Coverage in California." *Journal of the American Medical Association* 285, no. 9 (2000):1183–1185.

Radetsky, Michael. "Smallpox: A History of Its Rise and Fall." *Pediatric Infectious Disease Journal* 18, no. 2 (1999):85–93.

Taylor, Brent, Elizabeth Miller, C. Paddy Farrington, Maria-Christina Petropoulos, Isabelle Favot-Mayaud, Jun Li, and Pauline A. Waight. "Autism and Measles, Mumps, and Rubella Vaccine: No Epidemiologic Evidence for a Causal Association." *Lancet* 353 (June 12, 1999):2026–2029.

Wakefield, A.J., S. H. Murch, A. Anthony, J. Linnell, D. M. Casson, M. Malik, M. Berelowitz, A. P. Dhillon, M. A. Thomson, P. Harvey, A. Valentine, S. E. Davies, and J. A. Walker-Smith. "Ileal-Lymphoid-Nodular Hyperplasia, Non-specific Colitis, and Pervasive Developmental Disorder in Children." *Lancet* 351 (February 28, 1998):637–641.

Alan Uba

IN VITRO FERTILIZATION

In vitro fertilization is the term for a process whereby a mature egg from the female and a sperm from the male are placed in culture media where fertilization can occur. For humans, the first clinically successful in vitro fertilization occurred in 1978. If accomplished, cell division results in six to eight cells in about forty-eight hours, or a blastocyst of 100 cells in about 120 hours. One or more can then be transferred into the uterus with a 20 percent to 60 percent expectation of pregnancy depending on many variables, including age, cause of infertility, and number of fertilized eggs, or pre-embryos, transferred.

Pregnancy rates increase with number of pre-embryos transferred, as do the multiple pregnancy rates. In the United States (1998), 360 clinics conducted 80,634 treatment cycles; 31 percent of deliveries were multiple, compared to 3 percent in the general population.

In vitro fertilization has expanded to include the use of donor eggs, donor sperm, cryopreservation, intracytoplasmic sperm injection (ICSI), and the use of surrogate uteri.

See also: ARTIFICIAL INSEMINATION; REPRODUCTIVE TECHNOLOGIES

Bibliography
Rabe, Thomas, Klaus Diedrich, and T. Strowitzki. *Manual on Assisted Reproduction.* Berlin: Springer-Verlag, 2000.

Howard W. Jones Jr.

INDIVIDUALS WITH DISABILITIES EDUCATION ACT

With bipartisan support, the 105th U.S. Congress and President Clinton signed into law on June 4, 1997, P.L. 105-76, the latest amendments to the IDEA. This reauthorized federal legislation is an education, early intervention, and civil rights law with the goal of ensuring an opportunity for all children and youth to learn and develop regardless of disability, from birth through age twenty-one.

The law, which provides various types of financial assistance, consists of four parts:

- Part A, "General Provisions," describes general purposes, provisions, and definitions.
- Part B, "Assistance for Education of All Children with Disabilities," describes federal assistance to states and local schools in implementing the law's provisions—notably the provision of a free appropriate public education (FAPE) for children ages three through twenty-one years old.
- Part C, "Early Intervention Program for Infants and Toddlers with Disabilities," describes federal support to states and communities to implement the provisions—focusing on family centered collaborative services—for children from birth to three years old.
- Part D, "National Activities to Improve Education of Children with Disabilities," describes how the federal government supports states and communities in implementing Parts B and C of the law through various activities and grants covering training, research, program improvement, technical assistance, parent support, and information dissemination.

IDEA, now twenty-five years old, calls for federal-state-local partnerships, including sharing the financial support for the Parts B and C programs. Nationwide over six million eligible children receive a free appropriate public education (FAPE), and almost 200,000 infants and toddlers are served. The U.S. Department to Education and its Office of Special Education and Rehabilitative Services administers this $7.4 billion program that aims to produce positive results for children across the nation.

See also: DEVELOPMENTAL DISABILITIES

Bibliography
Council for Exceptional Children (CEC) for the IDEA Partnership Projects. Available from http://www.ideapractices.org/lawandregs.htm; INTERNET.

Pascal Louis Trohanis

INDUCTIVE REASONING

Inductive reasoning is logical thinking that operates from specific cases to general principles. For example, a preschooler might conclude that dolphins are fish because they live in water and swim as fish do. As children develop more sophisticated thinking, they are able to employ deductive reasoning, in which they use general principles to form hypotheses. Adolescents, for example, might have heard that dolphins are mammals. They could test this hypothesis by identifying the definition of mammal and testing whether it applies to dolphins.

Inductive reasoning as applied to child development has an additional meaning that is very different from the one described above. Inductive reasoning, also called induction, is the kind of reasoning used by parents to help children understand the effect of their behavior on others. For example, a parent might say to a preschool-aged child, "When you throw sand on your friend he feels very sad and doesn't want to play with you anymore." Research demonstrates that this parental control technique, induction, is associated with higher levels of social competence in children than when parents use coercion or "love withdrawal" (Rollins and Thomas 1979).

See also: LEARNING

Bibliography
Berger, Kathleen. *The Developing Person through the Life Span,* 5th edition. New York: Worth Publishers, 2000.

Hoffman, Martin. "Affective and Cognitive Processes in Moral Internalization." In E. T. Higgins, D. N. Ruble, and W. W. Hartup eds., *Social Cognition and Social Development: A Sociocultural Perspective.* New York: Cambridge University Press, 1983.

Rollins, Boyd, and Darwin Thomas. "Parental Support, Power, and Control Techniques in the Socialization of Children." In Wesley Burr, Reuben Hill, F. Ivan Nye, and Ira Reiss eds., *Contemporary Theories about the Family.* New York: Free Press, 1979.

H. Wallace Goddard

INFANCY

Infancy, the period between birth and eighteen to twenty-four months, has fascinated parents, philosophers, and developmental scientists perhaps more than any other period of the lifespan. The study of infants allows us to understand the origins of physical and psychological life. Furthermore, during no other period of life are physical and psychological changes more pervasive and rapid than in infancy.

Around the turn of the twentieth century, William James, an influential philosopher, psychologist, and parent, remarked that the world of the infant is a "blooming, buzzing, confusion." Throughout the twentieth century, researchers devised ingenious methods to study the infant and found that James severely underestimated the infant. We know now that infants' capacities are quite sophisticated in several domains, including perception, cognition, and emotion. Furthermore, infants' capacities in these domains and others continue to develop in infancy and beyond. Below are summaries of some of the key findings that scientists have uncovered about infants in several domains. The boundaries between these domains are somewhat artificial and arbitrary, but they nevertheless allow for an orderly arrangement of some of what is known about the human infant.

Physical Development

The infant's physical structure and central nervous system undergo dramatic and rapid change during the first two years of life. The infant's weight doubles by five months of age, triples by twelve months of age, and quadruples by the age of twenty-four months. The infant's length does not change as rapidly as its weight, for the infant's length at birth is already 75 percent of what it will be at two years of age. Changes in length and weight are accompanied by transformations in the infant's body proportions. The head grows the fastest and matures the earliest, followed by the rest of the body downward (e.g., the neck, torso, legs). In addition, those parts that are closest to the center of the infant's body (e.g., the trunk) grow faster and mature earlier than do parts that are farther from the center (e.g., the hands). The rapid changes in infants' body proportions affect other domains of development, including perceptual, motor, cognitive, and emotional.

The physical structure of the brain develops rapidly as well. Although a human is born with almost all of the neurons that he or she will ever have, the human brain triples in weight by age three and quadruples in weight by age fourteen. Two primary reasons account for this dramatic change in the brain's weight and size. First, a fatty substance called myelin forms around a part of the neuron, causing substantial growth of the brain and increasing its neural conduction. Second, a part of the neuron called the dendrite branches multiple times, creating numerous synapses or connections with other neurons. It is for these reasons that a brain that weighs 370 grams (13 ounces) at birth will weigh 1,080 grams (38 ounces) by the age of three.

At one time, scientists assumed that the newborn's brain was "hard-wired" and that the environment played little, if any, role in its development. Researchers studying human and nonhuman species have provided overwhelming evidence that experience does, in fact, play a powerful and enduring role in the infant's brain development. The infant's experiences "mold" the brain by preserving active synapses and pruning less active or inactive ones. Interestingly, researchers have found sensitive periods in which the brain is affected by experience more so than at other times.

Perceptual and Motor Development

At birth, infants' sensory systems are available for processing perceptual information from the world and from their own bodies, but each system operates, for the most part, within a more limited range than later in infancy. Newborns' senses of taste and smell are particularly well established; in the first two weeks of life, infants can discriminate among sweet, sour, and bitter tastes, and can recognize the smell of their mother's milk. Infants' hearing is also relatively mature at birth, although the loudness threshold for detecting sound is ten to twenty decibels higher in newborns than in adults. Young infants are highly attuned to human voices, especially their mother's. In addition, infants localize sounds, and by the end of their first month, if not sooner, they differentiate speech sounds in a manner comparable to adults. In fact, one-month-olds across cultures differentiate speech sounds not evident in their particular native languages. Thus, young infants demonstrate a wider range of speech sound sensitivity than adults; by ten to twelve months, however, infants' sensitivity to speech sounds narrows and conforms to their native language.

From birth, infants demonstrate distinct preferences for the human face and are especially attuned to moving rather than static stimuli. By two months, infants' color vision is well established. At the same time, infants can process depth information by some cues, a capacity that continues to develop into the middle of the first year. Infants' overall visual acuity, however, is much more limited than that of adults. In the first two to three months, infants cannot discrimi-

In a visual acuity test, an infant sits on his mother's lap and looks at gray and striped circles. Of all the sensory systems, infants' visual capabilities have been the most thoroughly investigated. (Laura Dwight/Corbis)

nate fine visual detail and tend to focus on areas of a stimulus where the contrast between light and dark is greatest, such as the hairline or the eyes of a face. By six to eight months, however, visual acuity nears adultlike maturity.

Infants' perceptual development is inextricably linked to their motor, or action, development. Like adults, infants' action in the world guides their perception of the world, just as their perception of the world guides their action in it. For example, the ability to perceive through touch the size, texture, and hardness of objects develops over the first six to nine months of life in parallel with changes in how infants manually explore objects. At birth, infant action is limited, rather inflexible, and reflexive, largely because they lack control of their heads and trunks. When provided with postural support, however, newborns demonstrate rudimentary reaching abilities, directing their arms in the general direction of objects. Within the first weeks of life, infants are able to support their own heads, facilitating gaze and the scanning of the environment. By three to four months, infants begin using vision to guide their reaching efforts, resulting in successful contact with objects. With experience in visually guided reaching, infants increasingly coordinate their grasping of an object with the movement of their arm toward the object. Between five and seven months, infants develop sufficient trunk control to support their independent

sitting, which in turn provides a solid position for head and arm activity.

Infants around seven to nine months begin to move themselves in the environment by means of crawling, which opens up a whole new world of exploration for them. Between eight and twelve months, infants begin to stand, first by using furniture or other objects to support themselves and then by establishing postural control to support independent standing. Walking soon follows as infants move into their second year. With each new motor transition, infants gain new means of perceptually apprehending the world. At the same time, infants rely on their perceptual development to establish more efficient means of acting on the world. For example, infants must rely on what they see and feel when crawling or walking over surfaces in order to continuously update their action and make their action fit the ever-changing demands of the environment.

Enormous individual differences mark the timing of developmental changes in both perceptual and motor development. Increasingly, developmental psychologists have shifted their focus away from simply documenting infants' perceptual and motor milestones toward understanding how these changes occur and how the domains of perception and action constantly and seamlessly interact to produce unique, individual pathways of development.

Cognitive Development

Cognition, comprised of mental processes such as conceiving, reasoning, memory, and symbolization, organizes humans' action in and perception of the world and is the foundation of humans' status as psychological beings. Speculation over the developmental origin of cognition has fueled philosophical inquiry for millennia. The modern study of infant cognitive development takes its own origin from the theory and research of Swiss psychologist Jean Piaget.

According to Piaget, infants are born with no mental framework in place and only gradually construct a conceptualization of the world through their experience with it. The experience of the infant is initially bound by the immediacy of perception and action, a "sensorimotor intelligence." Piaget argued that newborns have no concept of self or object and simply experience a wash of sensations. Only rudimentary schemas for interacting with the world are available to them. They will, for example, grasp objects placed in their hands, suck on objects that contact their mouths, and visually track moving objects. As infants apply these and other basic perception-action schemas to different objects and situations, they gradually adjust their action to the vast complexity of the world, increasingly accounting for specific objects and events. In the process, a more generalized and abstract sense of the world and infants' place in it emerges. By the end of infancy, the child has built a primitive understanding of objects and events as independently existing in time and space. For Piaget, a consequence of the infant period is an emerging representational ability, captured in the consolidation by eighteen to twenty-four months of an "object concept," which allows the child to conceive of an object's existence even when it is no longer available to the senses (e.g., out of view).

The study of representation in general—and the object concept in particular—has remained at the forefront of research in infant cognition. Examining infant search behavior, Piaget established six developmental stages through which infants pass before establishing a mature object concept. For example, during the third stage, around four to eight months, infants will search out a partially covered toy. But if the toy is completely hidden, infants will not search for it, as if it no longer exists. By the fourth stage, around eight to twelve months, infants will search for a completely covered toy, but when the toy is then hidden in another location, infants search exclusively at the initial hiding site, as if the toy's existence coincided with that particular location in space. More recent studies, using infant looking behavior, suggest that even younger infants have formed certain expectations about objects and their physical properties.

For example, infants expect an object to stop moving when it contacts a solid barrier and expect that two inanimate objects must come in contact with one another for one object to set the other in motion. Young infants seem to apply these expectations even to events that occur out of view. When three-month-olds see a ball roll behind a screen, and then the screen is lifted to reveal a barrier to the ball's path, they look much longer, as if surprised, at the event when the ball is revealed resting at the other end of the barrier, having seemingly moved through the solid barrier. Whether these expectations constitute conceptual understanding of objects has been a source of debate.

Studies of infant imitation and memory have further contributed to the understanding of infant representational ability. Newborns will imitate the action of an adult sticking out his tongue, even though they cannot see themselves imitate the action. Some psychologists have argued that newborns must possess an abstract representational system for linking their unseen facial movements with what they see the adult doing. Around nine months, representation is clearly in place as infants, having only observed an adult play with a toy in a particular way, will imitate the adult when given a chance twenty-four hours later to play with the toy. In this deferred imitation, infants must represent what they have seen twenty-four hours earlier and must recall from memory the representation. Prior to nine months, infants can retain memories for weeks or even months, but they retrieve those memories only if sufficient cues are present to allow them to recognize the familiarity of an event.

Socioemotional Development

Emotions pervade infants' daily lives in that they are the means by which infants accomplish their goals, as well as the primary medium through which communication occurs. Newborns display general patterns of distress and excitement. Later in the first year, other emotional expressions develop such as joy, surprise, sadness, disgust, anger, and fear. For example, infants begin to smile at others around six to eight weeks of age and begin to show wariness of strangers, as well as separation distress, between seven to nine months of age. More complex emotions, including embarrassment, pride, shame, and guilt, become evident in the last half of the second year.

Emotional expressions are displayed not only by the infant but also by the caregiver. Developmentalists have found that infants begin to detect adults' emotional displays (vocal and facial) by the age of two months. For example, young infants are able to distinguish between a smiling face and one that appears to be frowning. It is not until the middle of the first year that infants begin to understand the meaning of facial displays (i.e., understanding that the displays are emotional). Beginning around ten months of age, infants use the emotional displays of others to regulate their own behavior toward events they encounter in the world, a phenomenon called social referencing. For example, infants at the end of the first year will avoid ambiguous objects toward which their caregivers act disgusted, while they will approach and touch objects toward which their caregivers smile.

Individual differences in infants' socioemotional development have fascinated developmentalists for decades, particularly infants' attachment styles and temperamental differences. Attachment refers to an enduring emotional tie that one person forms to another. It is a tie in which the infant takes another (typically the caregiver) as a protective figure, finding increased security in their presence, missing them in their absence, seeking them in times of stress or alarm, and using them as a secure base from which to explore. According to John Bowlby, the tendency for infants to form attachments is evolutionarily based, being evident across cultures and in other mammalian species. All human infants, even those who have been mistreated and abused, form attachments to others.

The attachment behaviors that infants display change with development. The very young infant can only cry when distressed, look to the caregiver if he or she is nearby, and be attractive to adults. In time, however, infants take on an increasingly active role. Older infants can deliberately signal to the attachment figure by, perhaps, calling for the caregiver. Furthermore, infants acquire the ability to remain in close proximity to their attachment figure with the onset of crawling between seven and nine months.

While all infants form attachments, there are individual differences in infants' attachments that have enduring socioemotional consequences. Mary Ainsworth devised a laboratory procedure (called "strange situation") consisting of a series of maternal separations and reunions designed to categorize twelve-month-old infants' attachment styles to their caregivers. According to this research, infants can be categorized into three groups depending on the attachment behaviors they display: (1) "securely attached" infants seek comfort from the caregiver during reunions and, once comforted, play with toys; (2) "insecurely attached-avoidant" infants avoid their mothers during reunion and focus their attention on their play; and (3) "insecurely attached-resistant" infants are ambivalent during reunion, first approaching the caregiver and then pushing her away. Through subsequent research a fourth category of infants was identified in which infants in the Strange Situation display "disorganized-disorganizing" attachment behavior, characterized by contradictory behavior toward their mothers during reunion (e.g., walking to the mother and then abruptly falling to the floor and rocking).

Attachment researchers have found a consistent relation between infants' attachment behaviors in the Strange Situation and infants' history of interaction with their primary caregivers. Mothers of "securely" attached infants tend to be sensitive and responsive to their infants' emotional signals, whereas mothers of "insecure" infants tend to ignore or to respond inconsistently to their infants' emotional signals. Infants who are classified as "disorganized-disoriented" tend to have caregivers who are frightening to, or frightened of, their infants. In sum, infants' history of interaction influences their quality of attachment, which, in turn, is related to their socioemotional development later in life.

In contrast to the individual differences in attachment thought to arise because of varying interactional histories, temperament researchers study enduring differences in emotionality, and behavioral responses to stimuli, that are due to constitutional factors. Various researchers have identified various temperamental attributes, but most researchers agree that the following are important components of temperament:

- Activity level—the typical pace or vigor of one's activities
- Irritability/negative emotionality—how easily or intensely upset one becomes over negative events
- Soothability—the ease with which one calms after becoming upset
- Fearfulness—one's wariness of intense or highly unusual stimulation
- Sociability—one's receptiveness to social stimulation

Behavioral genetic studies comparing identical twins to fraternal twins indicate that the components of temperament are moderately heritable. In addition, infants' temperament, particularly activity level, irritability, sociability, and shyness, endures to some extent into childhood and adulthood. One important point, however, is that temperament does not determine personality in later life. The study of temperament thus highlights a significant principle that cuts across all developmental phenomena; biology dynamically interacts with environment in the development of humans.

When taken together, some of the key findings in infants' physical, perceptual, motor, cognitive, and socioemotional development indicate that infants are qualitatively different from adults; infants are not simply miniature adults. Furthermore, development is characterized by several reorganizations both within and between domains, thereby precipitating changes in infants' perceptions of the world, as well as the way in which they act upon it. The period of infancy is likely to continue to generate fundamental and important questions that challenge scientists.

See also: STAGES OF DEVELOPMENT

Bibliography

Ainsworth, Mary S., M. C. Blehar, E. Waters, and S. Wall. *Patterns of Attachment.* Hillsdale, NJ: Lawrence Erlbaum, 1978.

Bowlby, John. *Attachment and Loss,* Vol. 1: *Attachment.* New York: Basic, 1969.

Fogel, Alan. *Infancy: Infant, Family, and Society.* Belmont, CA: Wadsworth, 2001.

Muir, Darwin, and Alan Slater, eds. *Infant Development: The Essential Readings.* Malden, MA: Blackwell, 2000.

Piaget, Jean. *The Construction of Reality in the Child.* New York: Basic, 1954.

Stern, Daniel N. *The Interpersonal World of the Infant.* New York: Basic Books, 1985.

Matthew J. Hertenstein
David C. Witherington

INFANT MORTALITY

Infant mortality is defined as the death of a live-born infant within the first year of life. As an indicator of a nation's health status, infant mortality can serve as a reflection of a society's available resources and technology (including social distribution, access, and use), the status of women in society, and the health care provided to the most vulnerable segments of the population. Common causes of infant death include birth defects, complications related to prematurity, sudden infant death syndrome (SIDS), and respiratory distress syndrome. In 1996 these accounted for more than half of all infant deaths in the United States. Other causes include maternal and placental complications, infections, and unintentional injuries.

While the yearly infant mortality rate (the annual number of infant deaths/annual number of live-born infants per thousand) in the United States has been declining steadily from 100 in 1915 to 7.2 in 1998, its ranking among other developed countries continues to worsen, leaving the United States ranked behind most Western European countries. This poor ranking internationally can be attributed in part to global variations in live birth definitions and recording practices, but it also reflects racial and ethnic disparities in health status, access to health care, and socioeconomic conditions.

See also: BIRTH DEFECTS; BIRTHWEIGHT; PREMATURE INFANTS; PRENATAL CARE

Bibliography

Kleinman, Joel. "Infant Mortality." *Healthy People 2000: Statistical Notes* 1, no. 2 (1991):1–8.

Peters, Kimberly, Kenneth Kochanek, and Sherry Murphy. "Deaths: Final Data for 1996." *National Vital Statistics Reports* 47, no. 9 (1998):85.

Singh, Gopal, and Stella Yu. "Infant Mortality in the United States: Trends, Differentials, and Projections, 1950 through 2010." *American Journal of Public Health* 85 (1995):957–964.

Guyer, Bernard, Marian MacDorman, Joyce Martin, Stephanie Ventura, and Donna Strobino. "Annual Summary of Vital Statistics: 1998" *Pediatrics* 104, no. 6 (1999):1229–1247.

Guyer, Bernard, Mary Anne Freedman, Donna Strobino, and Edward Sondik. "Annual Summary of Vital Statistics: Trends in the Health of Americans during the Twentieth Century." *Pediatrics* 106 (2000):1307–1317.

Mary Ann Pass
Martha Slay
Greg R. Alexander

INJURIES

Accidents, according to dictionary definitions, are events that happen by chance and are not predictable and therefore are not preventable. In contrast, from a public health perspective, injuries were first clearly conceptualized by William Haddon (1964) as damage done to the body as a result of often predictable and therefore preventable energy exchange. This energy exchange may be kinetic, thermal, or chemical. For example, kinetic energy can result in injury when someone falls, hits the dashboard in a car crash, is penetrated by a bullet, or is hit on the head with a baseball bat. Injuries associated with thermal energy result in burns. Chemical energy can create injury through contact with caustics or via ingestion of a wide assortment of poisonous substances. Injuries can also occur when there is a lack of energy (e.g. frostbite) or an essential agent such as oxygen (e.g. drowning). Consequently, because of the connotation that accidents happen by chance, and therefore aren't preventable, injury control specialists no longer use the term "accident," preferring to refer to injury occurrences in terms of the specific circumstances—"crashes," "falls," "fires"—or as "events" or "incidents."

The literature on traumatic injury includes both unintentional injuries (known in common parlance as "accidents") and intentional injury (i.e. violence). Some types of injury are not so easily categorized in this way—for example, traumatic brain injury resulting from having been a shaken baby. While this type of injury is inflicted, it does not usually result from a typical violent act, which involves intent to do harm. Rather, it often results from attempts to quiet a cranky baby by an individual unaware of the risks. Yet the physiological results are often devastating.

Injuries occur as part of a process that can be understood within the social-ecological framework as described by Urie Bronfenbrenner in 1979. This framework can be extended in a public health context to conceptualize behaviors or health outcomes such as injury as a result of interactions among individual characteristics (intrapersonal level) and interactions among individuals (interpersonal), as well as with the physical and social environment, including institutional and cultural elements. Developmental characteristics enhance or reduce the possibilities that a child will experience an injury. For example, young children are not developmentally prepared cognitively to assess and avoid risk. Toddlers are curious and developmentally eager to explore. They also have relatively large heads that can throw off their balance and contribute to their risk of falling headfirst (e.g., into a toilet or bucket) while exploring their surroundings. Similarly, characteristics of young children learning to pull themselves up may create problems as they may pull objects down on themselves (e.g. a hot cup of coffee or books).

Injuries often occur when there is a mismatch in the performance of the person and demands of a task. For example, if a task demands that a certain level of judgment of risk avoidance is required to prevent an injury, a person unable to exert that level of judgment or avoidance behavior will be more likely to experience an injury. A child's developmental status may mitigate against being able to judge risks appropriately, identify preventive measures, and/or perform proper avoidance behaviors. Consequently, interventions must be designed that are sensitive to the performance capacities of the individual to be protected and that do not place the burden of protection on the exposed individual. Rather, interventions are generally most successful if they are devised to address features of the environment common to all individuals and that do not rely exclusively on individual actions. Such approaches typically employ engineering or design changes as opposed to efforts designed only to change knowledge, attitude, or behavior.

Incidence of Injuries to Children

To fully understand the problem of childhood injuries, it is important to examine how many cases of injury are occurring, in which population groups, for example, distributions by age, race, and gender. Data across sources are not always comparable due to differences in measurement, definitions, or data compilation practices. Hence, understanding of the incidence of any public health problem necessitates careful review of the data sources and consideration of what they can and can't reveal about the problem.

Measurement Issues

As with any public health problem, it is important to have data available from routine surveillance—the systematic, ongoing collection of information about illnesses, injuries, or events. To fully understand the magnitude of the problem, one must consider both the mortality (fatalities) and morbidity (nonfatalities) associated with injury. Mortality is readily assessed using data available from death certificates. Data are coded as to the underlying causes of death and can yield valuable information about factors contributing to the injury. In states having medical examiner systems, these records can provide more detail about the circumstances of death.

The Centers for Disease Control and Prevention report that for every child who dies as a result of an injury, there are an estimated 34 who are injured seriously enough to require hospitalization, and another 1,000 who receive medical care in an outpatient setting. Even more children experience injuries that result in limitations of their activities or cause discomfort but that do not require medical attention. Hospitalized injuries can be examined using hospital discharge data compiled in each state as well as nationally. The standards of reporting, however, are not as stringent as with death statistics. Underlying causes are not uniformly coded in all states, some requiring that this information be included and others reporting on a voluntary basis.

Data about nonhospitalized cases are even less uniformly compiled. There are few statewide and no national reporting systems for emergency department cases. Injuries treated in private doctor's offices, urgent care centers, or by school nurses may or may not be routinely documented, but there are no national record-keeping systems to monitor these events systematically. Consequently, information about injury morbidity is of variable quality.

Types of Injuries

Causes of injury death differ by age and by type of injury, as demonstrated in Table 1. The data presented in these figures reflect only mortality.

In 1998, 18,292 U.S. children died as a result of injuries, for an overall death rate of 23.55 per 100,000 population. Of these fatalities, 12,416 were classified as unintentional, 3,461 as homicide, and 2,061 as suicide. Rates varied by race and gender, with boys (aged zero to nineteen) experiencing an overall death rate of 32.04 per 100,000, compared to 14.63 for girls. As shown in Table 2, racial differences

TABLE 1

Injury Death Rates (per 100,000) by Age Group, United States, 1998

Ages	<1	1–4	5–9	10–14	15–19
Transportation Related:					
Occupant	3.31	2.17	1.92	2.63	17.28
Pedestrian	0.18	1.58	1.15	1.02	1.80
Pedal cyclist	0	0.04	0.35	0.64	0.34
Other Cause Related:					
Fires/burns	1.27	1.91	1.11	0.63	0.51
Ingestions	0.47	0.35	0.08	0.17	2.15
Drowning	2.12	3.40	1.28	1.08	2.32
Suffocation	11.76	1.19	0.44	1.34	2.76
Falls	0.58	0.32	0.13	0.16	0.69
Intentional Injury Related:					
Homicide	8.53	2.63	0.85	1.49	11.68
Suicide	0	0	0	1.65	8.89
Firearm Related Deaths:					
All intents	0.13	0.51	0.48	2.25	16.27
Unintentional	0	0.10	0.17	0.35	0.72
Homicide	0.13	0.38	0.30	0.99	9.57
Suicide	0	0	0	0.80	5.56

SOURCE: *Kristen Kucera.*

reveal higher rates for minority youth, with Native Americans experiencing the highest rates of unintentional injury and suicide while African Americans' rates for homicide exceed those of other ethnic groups. Some of this difference is attributable to environmental conditions associated with poverty (African Americans and Native Americans) and/or living in rural areas (Native Americans) where risks are high and rapid access to medical care is less readily available.

Injury patterns differ by both age and type of event, as demonstrated in Tables 1 and 3. For all age groups, motor vehicle crashes were a significant cause of fatalities in 1998. The youngest children (infants) are most likely to be fatally injured as a result of suffocation, motor vehicle traffic, and drowning/submersion. For toddlers, the leading causes of injury death are motor vehicle traffic, drowning/submersion, and homicide, while for those in the five to fourteen age group (elementary and middle-school age), most fatal injuries result from motor vehicle traffic, homicide, and drowning/submersion. In contrast, teenagers are fatally injured as a result of motor vehicle crashes, homicide, and suicide.

As shown in Table 3, various causes of injury fatality exhibit differing patterns depending on age. In part, this is a function of different developmental factors that impinge on children's abilities to avoid injury events (e.g., being able to walk without falling, being able to make judgments about avoiding risks, testing authority, having transient depression, acting impulsively). In addition, children have greater or lesser exposures to different risky situations (e.g., crossing streets without a parent, playing sports, riding a tricycle near traffic, being a teenage driver, owning or carrying firearms, working on a construction crew) based on the practices of their parents (e.g., level of supervision provided, drinking and smoking behaviors, disciplinary practices); or because of social, economic, or cultural factors (e.g., access to affordable, high-quality child care; well-constructed homes that are equipped with fire safety devices such as smoke detectors; practices of riding in the back of pickup trucks; use of hazardous products such as firearms, baby walkers, in-line skates, or trampolines.

Morbidity

Morbidity (i.e., nonfatal injury) is both much more common than mortality and presents different patterns of injury. In 1997, 213,000 hospitalizations of children ages zero to fifteen in the United States resulted from injuries, while in 1996 alone an estimated 8.71 million in this age group were treated and released from emergency care. Using 1990s data from North Carolina on unintentional injury for children under age fifteen, Table 4 lists the differences in injury patterns by age group for the leading causes of death, of nonfatal, hospitalized injuries, and estimated incidence of injuries treated in outpatient settings. This demonstrates the importance of considering the range of injury outcomes in establishing priorities and devising preventive strategies.

Furthermore, several child and adolescent injury problems are not easily recognized in the health care system at all, yet have profound effects on injury occurrence and developmental outcomes. One type of event is child abuse and neglect. Reporting through social services systems and national surveys indicates that as many as 1.5 million children a year experience physical or sexual abuse at the hands of an adult caretaker. Likewise, children and adolescents may be sexually assaulted or raped by strangers or experience injuries in dating relationships, similar to domestic violence experienced by adults. National estimates indicate that as many as 1.4 million persons under age eighteen experience sexual assault or rape each year. In addition, it is estimated that 8.8 percent of adolescents may experience violence in their dating relationships, including incidents of hitting, slapping, or being physically hurt.

Other types of circumstances that put teenagers at risk of nonfatal injuries are sports participation and employment. Together, these two categories of injury result in more emergency care for teenagers than any other categories. Sports and occupational injury are the two most common categories. National data suggest that as many as 3.5 million youth under age 14 are injured in sports and recreational activities annu-

TABLE 2

Injury Death Frequency and Rate per 100,000 by Racial Group, Ages 0–19, United States, 1998								
	Unintentional		Sucide		Homicide		TOTAL	
	n	Rate	*n*	Rate	*n*	Rate	*n*	Rate
African American	2194	18.26	222	1.85	1693	14.09	4203	34.98
Native American	221	24.67	60	6.7	42	4.69	329	36.73
White	9733	15.84	1722	2.8	1639	2.67	13342	21.72
All Others	268	18.06	57	1.71	87	2.62	418	12.57
TOTAL	12416	15.99	2061	2.65	3461	4.46	18,292	23.55

SOURCE: *Kristen Kucera.*

ally, 775,000 of them requiring emergency care. Seventy-five percent are boys. Similarly, youth who are employed are exposed to a variety of hazards, with as many as half experiencing injuries at work.

Developmental Delays as a Result of Injury

Just as development affects whether a child is at risk of experiencing an injury-producing event, so is development affected by being injured. Injuries with the greatest impact in the behavioral and emotional development of the child are head injuries, specifically traumatic brain injuries, and severe burns. Little research has been done on the outcome of other types of injuries in children and adolescents.

Brain Injury

As reported in 1996, more than 100,000 children and adolescents are hospitalized each year with traumatic brain injury (TBI), of which about 88 percent are classified as mild, 7 percent moderate, and 5 percent severe. Although children under five years of age have the lowest rate of TBI, the severity of injury is disproportionately high. Evaluations of neurological and psychological outcomes following pediatric TBI, however, have been focused almost exclusively on school-age children and adolescents. The few studies that have assessed the consequences of mild TBI for infants and/or preschoolers identified lower IQ scores in infants and young children than in older children who suffered a mild TBI. Philip Wrightson, Valerie McGinn, and Dorothy Gronwall (1995) studied preschoolers who sustained mild head injuries and reported that deficits in cognitive development, identified at twelve months after injury, were significantly associated with reading ability at age six and a half. It is not clear if mild TBI and concussion result in long-term problems in children given the difficulty in differentiating effects that may be a direct consequence of mild TBI or of learning disabilities or at-

tention deficits in the TBI group, which do not manifest themselves until later in development.

Follow-up studies of severe TBI in school-age children and adolescents identified physical, cognitive (e.g., lower IQ scores), language, and psychological deficits that may be temporary or permanent. The most common language problems are word retrieval difficulties and decreased speed of information processing. Follow-up studies for as long as three years after the TBI reveal persistent neurobehavioral deficits. Acute behavioral problems include emotional outbursts, restlessness, and low tolerance to stimulation.

Cognitive delays have significant effects on social, educational, and vocational prognosis of children following TBI. For example, in a study in which TBI children were compared with age, gender, and grade-matched peers, Kenneth Jaffe and his colleagues found that more severe head injury was associated with lowered neurobehavioral functioning. Developmental deficits include lack of attention and long, heightened distractibility, short-term memory impairment, difficulty with logical thinking and reasoning, slowed reaction time, and impaired spatial or visual motor skills. The duration of post-traumatic amnesia was reported to be the best predictor of these deficits. Severe TBI results in significant neurobehavioral deficits that are persistent after the first year and that are related to the severity of the head injury.

The effects of age at injury on subsequent cognitive development are unclear. In studies examining cognitive, social, academic, and vocational outcomes following severe TBI, some have reported that age at injury was not predictive of long-term outcome. Others identified more severe consequences in children ages zero to six than in older children. Several studies of outcomes following TBI failed to find associations between age at injury and either severity of cognitive consequences and the rate of recovery of neuropsychological, or behavioral disturbance. Several other

TABLE 3

Frequencies of Leading Causes of Injury Death by Age Group, United States, 1998			
Infants (age <1)	**Preschoolers (age 1 – 4)**	**Elementary/Middle School Age (age 5 – 14)**	**Teenagers (age 15 – 19)**
Suffocation 376	MV Traffic 627	MV Traffic 1781	MV Traffic 5060
MV Traffic 158	Drowning/submersion 496	Homicide 460	Homicide 2311
Drowning/Submersion 63	Homicide 399	Drowning/submersion 444	Suicide 737
Fire/burn 43	Fire/burn 264	Suicide 317	Drowning/submersion 439
Injury as a proportion of all deaths: 5%	64%	68%	88%

SOURCE: *Kristen Kucera.*

studies, however, suggest that trauma to the brain may have more severe outcomes and more significant long-term consequences for infants and preschoolers than for older children. A number of findings regarding the language and memory effects of TBI in infants, school-age children, and adolescents are also consistent with the hypothesis that skills in a rapid stage of development at the time of TBI were more adversely affected than already well-established skills.

A study that determined the long-term outcome of severe brain injury in preschoolers revealed that none of the children who were younger than four years old at the time of the severe brain injury were able to live independently or work full-time in adulthood. Other studies also reported abnormalities following TBI in 40 percent of children with minimal or no loss of consciousness.

Injury can have important consequences for family functioning, which in turn adversely affects the family's ability to assist the child in achieving her full potential. Most of these adverse effects are seen in families with children who sustained severe head injury. Several studies have revealed that the level of family functioning before the injury was a better predictor of family functioning at one year after the injury than the severity of the TBI. The researchers inferred that family dysfunction prior to the injury event was likely to continue following the injury. Parental overreaction and family dysfunction were likely to exacerbate the child's emotional reaction to the injury. Poverty can exacerbate these problems and further decrease the level of functioning of children following TBI.

Burns

Burns also produce devastating results for child development. The effects of the injury on the psycho-

logical and emotional health of children and the family demonstrate inconsistent findings.

Studies conducted in the 1970s revealed that 50 percent of children showed signs of emotional disturbance several years after their injury. Studies in the 1980s indicated that the prevalence of these symptoms might be much lower and that the level of family and child functioning prior to the injury were the most important predictors of postburn adjustment and coping. A survey of burned children in 1985 found psychosocial maladjustment in 15 percent of the children. For some of the children and families, however, psychological disturbance existed before the injury and might have hindered emotional and even physical recovery afterward. The premise that visible scarring is more damaging than hidden burn scars has not been studied well. Adaptation takes place over a period of years. In the first couple of years after the burn, children have developmental regression, phobias, and various other symptoms. These symptoms progressively resolve in the subsequent years.

Parents are frequently stressed by the child's behavior, depressed over the burn and the child's future, and have feelings of guilt regarding the circumstances leading to the injury. Some research has shown that parental stress clearly differentiated parents of burned children from other parents; children with better psychological adjustment come from families that have higher levels of cohesion, independence, and more open expressiveness. This has important implications for interventions as mothers and burned children can be identified and given special support at the time of the initial care for the child's injury.

TABLE 4

Leading Causes of Unintentional Deaths (1996–98), Hospitalizations (1996–98), and Estimated Cases of Non-Admitted Cases of Unintentional Injury (1998), North Carolina *(Source: Golden & Runyan, 2000)*

Leading Causes of Unintentional Injury Deaths (Age 0–14), NC, 1996–98	Leading Causes of Unintentional Injury Hospitalization (Age 0–14), NC, 1996–98	Estimated Leading Causes of Unintentional Injury Receiving Outpatient Care (Age 0–14), NC, 1998
MV Occupant	Falls	Falls
Pedestrian	MV Occupant	Bicycle
Drowning	Poisons	Cut/Piercing injury
Fire	Struck by person/object	MV Occupant
Suffocation	Bicycle	Struck by person/object
Bicycle	Natural Environment	Natural Environment
Firearm	Pedestrian	Poisons
Other transportation	Burns/Scalds	Burns/scalds
Poisons	Cut/Piercing injury	Pedestrian

Strategies to Ameliorate Injuries

Drawing on the same social-ecologic principles that help describe the factors affecting the occurrence of injuries, William Haddon developed two frameworks for conceptualizing injury interventions. The first outlined injury interventions aimed at different phases in the energy transfer process. The ten countermeasures were directed at reducing the potential for damage to the body from an energy source. Table 5 shows examples pertaining to reducing childhood bicycle crash injuries.

Later, Haddon proposed a different, but similar, model to help stimulate intervention development: the Haddon Matrix. This model is widely used to identify potential interventions, and has two dimensions. The first depicts the target of change, including the person at risk (or the person's caretaker); the source of energy (e.g., products to which children are exposed—toys, motor vehicles, household poisons); the physical environment (e.g., playgrounds, roadways, homes, schools, day-care facilities); or the social environment (e.g., norms about behaviors such as drinking or child discipline; regulatory policies governing drinking ages, playground safety, or use of bicycle helmets). The second dimension depicts the phase at which the intervention has its effect—whether at the time of the injury event (e.g., a seat belt that deploys during a crash); at a time prior to the event, helping to prevent the event (e.g., antilock brakes); or after the event to reduce the effects of the event (e.g., gas tanks engineered to prevent explosions). Putting these two dimensions together creates a four by three matrix. Using the matrix as a brainstorming tool, one can fill in the twelve cells with ideas of potential interventions (see example in Table 5 pertaining to bicycle safety).

Choosing among the multiple alternative intervention ideas can be complex but several principles can help sort out the types of intervention ideas. Interventions may be voluntary or mandatory. And they might be active or passive. Active interventions require that the person to be protected takes protective action (e.g., putting on a bike helmet, testing water temperature in the baby's bathtub). In contrast, passive interventions are those that do not require action on the part of the individual being protected or deliberate action by a caretaker. Rather, they are engineered or set up such that protection is automatic (e.g., installation of airbags in cars, setting the temperature for hot water heaters at a safe level; automatic shutoffs on appliances). In general, interventions that require less individual effort result in more success. That is, passive interventions tend to be more successful than ones that require individual action. There are significant trade-offs, however, in making choices among the different options.

A third dimension added to the Haddon Matrix by Carol Runyan addresses the kinds of trade-offs that frequently occur in public health decision making. By considering alternative interventions derived from the two-dimensional matrix, a planner can examine the value issues involved in each choice and compare various options. As a result, decisions can be made more logically and the rationale for a given decision can be explained to others. For example, an intervention requiring restrictions on the purchase of firearms limits the freedom of gun enthusiasts, while at the same time affording greater freedom for children to live in environments with fewer guns and thus increasing child safety. Likewise, some interventions are more costly than others, requiring design changes in products (e.g., improvements in car design to reduce rollovers in crashes) or in the design of physical

TABLE 5

Haddon Matrix Applied to Prevention of Bicycle Crash Injuries in Children

Phases at Which Interventions Have Their Effects	Host (children)	Agent/ Vehicle (bicycle or helmet)	Physical Environment (roadway)	Social Environment (community norms, policies, rules)
			Factors to Be Changed by Intervention	
Pre-event (before crash)	•Teach children to abide by traffic safety rules	•Ensure that bicycles have reflectors	•Ensure that grates on streets are positioned so as not to trap bike wheels	•Pass legislation requiring building of bicycle paths
Event (during crash)	•Teach children to use bicycle helmets correctly	•Design helmet to be crash resistant	•Install roadway signs that are less likely to injure cyclist who hits them	•Require helmet use by all riders
Postevent (after child is injured in crash)	•Provide first aid and CPR	•Design bicycles with fewer sharp edges to injure cyclist who has crashed	•Ensure installation of emergency call boxes near bike paths	•Increase availability of emergency and rehabilitation care facilities

SOURCE: *Kristen Kucera.*

space (e.g., changing the equipment on a playground at a child-care facility). Other strategies require that funds be made available to make special provisions for protecting children without personal resources (e.g., car seat or smoke detector give-away programs for low-income families), while limiting higher-income families' access to the funds.

Summary

Injury is a major public health problem for children. Data to assess the magnitude of the problem are of variable quality and in need of continuous improvement, but it is clear that special risks exist for certain subgroups of the population, including different risks by ethnic group, age, and gender. It is important to examine data from multiple sources to understand the problem, including information about deaths as well as injuries resulting in hospitalization or outpatient (e.g., emergency department) care. Other types of injuries are not as easily captured in these data systems and require efforts to estimate risks through other means—for example, collecting data from social services or through research surveys about child abuse, from schools about sports injury, or from youth about employment-related injuries.

Research tracking the long-term effects of different types of injury suggests that the developmental outcomes of more severe injuries may be profound.

Injuries are not accidents. Causes can be identified and preventive strategies developed. There are numerous interventions to choose from in addressing prevention of traumatic injuries, each with its own advantages and disadvantages.

See also: MOTOR DEVELOPMENT

Bibliography

Bronfenbrenner, Urie. *The Ecology of Human Development.* Cambridge, MA: Harvard University Press, 1979.

Dunn, Kathleen, Carol Runyan, Lisa Cohen, and Michael Schulman. "Teens at Work: A Statewide Study of Jobs, Hazards, and Injuries." *Journal of Adolescent Health* 22, no. 1 (1998):19–25.

Finkelhor, David, Gerald Hotaling, I. A. Lewis, and Christine Smith. "Sexual Abuse in a National Survey of Adult Men and Women: Prevalence, Characteristics, and Risk Factors." *Child Abuse and Neglect* 14, no. 1 (1990):19–28.

Haddon, William, Edward Suchman, and David Klein. *Accident Research: Methods and Approaches.* New York: Harper and Row, 1964.

Hennes, Halim, Martha Lee, Douglas Smith, John R. Sty, and Joseph Losek. "Clinical Predictors of Severe Head Trauma in Children." *American Journal of Diseases of Children* 142 (1988):1045–1047.

Jaffe, Kenneth, M., Gayle C. Fay, Nayak Lincoln Polissar, Kathleen M. Martin, Hillary A. Shurtleff, J'May B. Rivara, and Richard Winn. "Severity of Pediatric Traumatic Brain Injury and Neurobehavioral Recovery at One Year: A Cohort Study." *Archives of Physical Medicine and Rehabilitation* 74 (1993):587–595.

Koskiniemi, Marjaleena, Timo Kyykka, Taina Nybo, and Leo Jarho. "Long Term Outcome after Severe Burn Injury in Preschoolers Is Worse than Expected." *Archives of Pediatric Adolescent Medicine* 149 (1995):249–254.

Runyan, Carol. "Using the Haddon Matrix: Introducing the Third Dimension." *Injury Prevention* 4 (1998):302–307.

System YRBS. "Youth Risk Behavior Surveillance: United States, 1999." *Mortality and Morbidity Weekly Report* 49 (2000):1–96.

Theodore, Andrea, and Desmond Runyan. "A Medical Research Agenda for Child Maltreatment: Negotiating the Next Steps." *Pediatrics* 104 (1999):168–177.

Wrightson, Philip, Valerie McGinn, and Dorothy Gronwall. "Mild Head Injury in Preschool Children: Evidence That It Can Be

Associated with a Persisting Cognitive Defect." *Journal of Neurology, Neurosurgery, and Psychiatry* 59 (1995):375–380.

Carol W. Runyan
Janet Abboud Dal Santo
Kristen L. Kucera

INTELLIGENCE

Intelligence is the ability to solve problems. It is also commonly referred to as practical sense or the ability to get along well in all sorts of situations. People cannot see, hear, touch, smell, or taste intelligence. On the other hand, the more they have, the better able they are to respond to things around them. Anyone interested in understanding intelligence will find many theories, definitions, and opinions available.

During the late nineteenth century, scientists were interested in the differences in human thinking abilities. Out of these interests evolved the need to distinguish between children who could learn in a school environment and those who could not. At the turn of the nineteenth century, Alfred Binet and Theodore Simon developed a set of questions that helped identify children who were having difficulty learning. This set of questions was later used in the United States by Lewis Terman of Stanford University and eventually became the Stanford-Binet Intelligence Test. The main purpose for looking at intelligence is to be able to measure it; measuring thinking ability helps psychologists predict future learning of children and, if necessary, develop educational programs that will enhance learning.

In addition to general thinking ability, other definitions of intelligence describe the specific ways a child responds to problems. For example, Howard Gardner is interested in how children use different abilities to display intelligence. In particular, he says that children have mathematical, musical, interpersonal, linguistic, spatial, bodily-kinesthetic, intrapersonal, and naturalistic intelligences. He theorizes that children have all these types of intelligence, but have more ability in one than the others. Theorist Daniel Goleman argues that general intelligence, measured by the traditional test, is not as useful in predicting success in life as the measurement of emotional intelligence. He suggests that abilities such as initiative, trustworthiness, self-confidence, and empathy are more important to consider than general intelligence. Therefore, until specific tests of these types of intelligence are developed, determining how much a child has of one type of intelligence is not possible.

Measuring Intelligence as a Comprehensive Process

Although people cannot see intelligence, it can be measured. Psychologists measure intelligence using several methods such as the Stanford-Binet scale, the Wechsler Intelligence scales, and the Kaufman Assessment Battery for Children. These tests measure abilities such as information processing, memory, reasoning, and problem solving. Tasks that measure these abilities include identifying the missing part in a picture, repeating numbers, or defining vocabulary words. These tests also measure a child's ability to respond in an acceptable way to different social situations. The important factor in all established intelligence tests is that the child must be able to see, hear, or speak in order to pass the test. A child who is able to hear and answer questions will score the best.

For children who cannot speak or hear, there are tasks for measuring nonverbal intelligence within each of the tests. Some of these include items such as completing puzzles or reproducing a design using blocks. However, instructions are given verbally, so a child will need to hear and understand questions in order to respond. There are other less frequently administered tests of performance, such as the Test of Non-verbal Intelligence where instructions are given in pantomime. In cases where a child does not speak English, translated intelligence tests that measure the same abilities can be used. In cases where no translation exists, the use of a qualified translator is acceptable.

The method of measuring intelligence of infants and toddlers not old enough to speak is a little different. For example, instead of identifying children who cannot learn, psychologists measure whether the infants or toddlers have developed a common ability by a certain age. One test used with this age group is the Bayley Scales of Infant Development. This test includes tasks such as rolling over, smiling, and imitating sounds. Specifically, psychologists want to know how an infant is developing compared to other infants of the same age.

After psychologists give intelligence tests they can begin to determine a child's level of intelligence by looking at the amount of items the child answered correctly compared to other children of the same age. Correct responses are tallied and referred to as intelligence quotients, or IQ. The scores of the children in the original group are distributed around an average score of 100. Most children have average intelligence and score between 85 and 115. Very few children score in the low range of mental retardation or the high range of gifted.

Several important factors should be considered when discussing an IQ score. If the child was having a bad day or if the examiner made an error in scoring, the results would not be typical. Psychologists must consider these factors in addition to how the child performs on other tests that measure the child's academic achievement and typical behavior at home. In other words, intelligence is not based on one score from one test. In fact, levels of intelligence cannot be determined unless all of these factors are considered.

Typically, psychologists who are highly trained and professionally qualified in giving intelligence tests will determine intelligence. For the most part, intelligence tests are administered to elementary school children because learning difficulties are easier to notice when children begin school. In most cases a teacher will suspect something different about the performance of a child and will ask the school psychologist about this occurrence. In other cases, parents may want to know if their child is ready for school and will ask about testing services in their community. Nevertheless, assessing a child's level of intelligence helps identify the strengths and weaknesses in the child's learning abilities. This leads to individual learning programs for the child and more useful tasks at school.

Certainly, it is important to consider how individuals think about information in order to predict learning performance. For this reason, intelligence tests are necessary, and in some states required by law. However, it is equally important that educators do not place children in less demanding classrooms only because they think a child may not be able to learn at a faster pace. As previously discussed, intelligence may be increased. Limiting the type of learning opportunities a child should get will prevent learning new problem-solving skills; educators do not want to frustrate a child who needs a different type of program, and will change learning tasks as needed.

Environmental and Genetic Influences on Intelligence

Typically, the way a child thinks and solves problems stays the same from age six on. After beginning school, a child's ability to think appears to develop at a normal rate through grade levels that match the child's age. If a child is given problem-solving tasks, then the child will learn how to solve problems and vice versa. Fortunately, children who are not given the chance to learn how to think about problems before attending school will ultimately catch up. Because of this, psychologists are careful when interpreting low intelligence scores in children younger than age six. This also means that while low intelligence cannot be cured, it can be changed. In fact, educational programs are specifically planned to improve environments in order to increase educational and life skills.

In addition to a child's environment, the intelligence of the child's parents has some influence on the amount of intelligence the child is born with. Questions about the influence of genetics are explained by looking at characteristics children inherit from parents. While studying twins, some scientists have shown that intelligence is largely inherited. Researchers also found that the higher the parents' IQs, the higher their child's IQ tended to be. At the same time, there was less consistency between the IQs of adoptive parents and their adoptive children. Many other factors are related to the development of intelligence. These include parent education, family financial status, family size, and early schooling. Parents who provide a rich learning environment and foster good learning behaviors will have children with better than average IQ scores, barring any medical causes of mental retardation.

Low Intelligence Scores

Psychologists who identify low levels of thinking ability will describe the child as having below average intelligence. A score of sixty-nine or less results in this classification. Unfortunately, this description has potentially negative effects. A child may think the meaning of the low score is a definite sign that they cannot learn and will fail to learn in order to verify the classification. Historically, there is a negative meaning attached to low IQ scores. Therefore, the suggestion that a child has mental retardation can be devastating to the child's family. Due to the nature of errors in testing and the fact that intelligence can be changed, scores that fall at or around seventy, should be interpreted very carefully. Finally, teachers and parents may expect that children with this classification cannot learn, therefore giving them challenging tasks is not necessary. If children are not expected to learn, given a low IQ score or classification, then no one may demand higher performances from them.

It is very difficult to predict outcomes based on the score of an intelligence test, because these tests do not measure other important factors, such as motivation. In addition, intelligence tests are sometimes used inappropriately with minority children who may not understand certain items because of cultural differences. Therefore, any intelligence test score must be fully understood and interpreted with great care.

See also: DEVELOPMENTAL NORMS

Bibliography

Kamphaus, Randy. *Clinical Assessment of Children's Intelligence.* Boston: Allyn and Bacon, 1993.

Mackintosh, N. J. *IQ and Human Intelligence.* New York: Oxford University Press, 1998.

Nuthall, Ena, Ivonne Romero, and Joanne Kalesnik. *Assessing and Screening Preschoolers: Psychological and Educational Dimensions,* 2nd edition. Boston: Allyn and Bacon, 1999.

Laura A. Webber

INTERNET

The Internet—also called the World Wide Web, or web—is a vast system of connections among individual computers and computer networks, allowing information and programmed activities to be easily shared by individuals around the world. According to the National Center for Education Statistics (NCES), over 90 percent of primary school students in the United States report using the Internet at home, at school, or in both settings. Educational uses emphasize searching for information about classroom projects or topics. As with printed media, it is necessary to assist children in determining the source and reliability of web-based information.

For entertainment, "kids only" sites provide links to topics of interest to children, often emphasizing popular culture heroes. For example, the cable television channel "Cartoon Network" maintains a web site that allows children to "interact" with favorite animated figures and play games based on these characters. Chat and e-mail features of these sites encourage communication among geographically distant peers.

Because of the risk that children will be exposed to developmentally inappropriate content, most parents and schools discourage children from unsupervised Internet exploration. Anxiety about adult themes and predatory contact led to the Children's Online Privacy Protection Act (COPPA) of 1998, which requires web sites to seek parental permission before collecting personal or identifiable information from children, and the Recreational Software Advisory Council on the Internet (RSACi), which supervises a voluntary four-category rating system for Internet sites.

See also: COMPUTER LITERACY; HOME SCHOOLING

Bibliography

Kids Interacting with Developmental Software (KIDS) [web site]. Available from http://www.childrenandcomputers.com/Default.asp; INTERNET.

National Associate for the Education of Young Children (NAEYC) Technology Caucus [web site]. Available from http://www.techandyoungchildren.org/index.shtml; INTERNET

Northwest Educational Technology Consortium [web site]. Available from http://www.netc.org/index.html; INTERNET.

Sharon Seidman Milburn

J

JUVENILE DELINQUENCY

Juvenile delinquency refers to the violation of a criminal law by a juvenile. In most states a juvenile is anyone under age eighteen, but in some states a person is considered an adult at age sixteen or seventeen. If a juvenile has committed an act that would be a crime if committed by an adult, then the juvenile has committed juvenile delinquency. Moreover, juvenile delinquency includes acts that are legal for adults. These acts are called status offenses because they are illegal only for people with the status of being a juvenile. Whereas crimes consist of such acts as murder and rape (which are illegal for both juveniles and adults), examples of status offenses are running away from home and truancy (which are illegal only for juveniles). Juvenile courts, as opposed to criminal courts, generally have jurisdiction over the crimes and status offenses committed by juveniles.

See also: ADOLESCENCE; VIOLENCE

Bibliography

Empey, LaMar T., Mark C. Stafford, and Carter H. Hay. *American Delinquency: Its Meaning and Construction*. Belmont, CA: Wadsworth, 1999.

Jensen, Gary F., and Dean G. Rojek. *Delinquency and Youth Crime*. Prospect Heights, IL: Waveland Press, 1998.

Mark C. Stafford

K

KESSEN, WILLIAM (1925–1999)

William Kessen was born in Key West, Florida, in 1925. Kessen's many honors included memberships in the Society of Experimental Psychologists and the American Academy of Arts of Sciences. The only child of a ship's engineer and a homemaker, his journey toward Yale began as a bespectacled youth who declared himself a Roosevelt liberal. The first in his family to attend college, Kessen entered the University of Florida in 1941 to study history and acting. Drafted into the war when he was eighteen, Kessen served as a clerk-typist and read voraciously during his thirty-four months of service. After the war, and supported by the GI Bill, Kessen completed his undergraduate degree in psychology at the University of Florida. On his shifting interests toward psychology, Kessen wrote that he "became convinced that the ills of the world were not to be tackled by legal or historical strategies, but by empirical and psychological ones" (1991, p. 287). Kessen went on to Brown University to pursue masters and doctoral degrees with Gregory Kimble, who remains a leading expert on classical conditioning. At Brown, Kessen met his "best and truest friend," Marion Lord. They fell in love and married in 1950. Following Kimble to Yale, Kessen's 1952 fifteen-page dissertation entitled "Response Strength and Conditioned Stimulus Intensity" was carried out in the tradition of the eminent behavioral psychologist Clark Hull.

During his graduate tenure at Yale, many prominent social scientists, including Neal Miller, John Dollard, and Robert Sears, joined in an effort to integrate Ivan Pavlov and Sigmund Freud by transforming Freudian concepts into a behaviorist framework. At the same time, psychoanalyst Kaethe Maria Wolf came to the Yale Child Study Center after having worked with developmental psychologists Charlotte Buehler and Jean Piaget. Large and powerful ideas surrounded Kessen when he chose to do postdoctoral work with Wolf. She introduced Kessen to the complexities of Freud and Piaget during the heyday of behaviorism before her untimely death in 1957. In the years to come, Kessen would pursue at least three distinct paths in psychology—all broke new ground and generated young colleagues. Immediately after his doctorate and with the first stirrings from the cognitive revolution, Kessen turned from rats to babies, first probing their earliest sensory and perceptual development, and later their changing place in culture and history. Kessen created and maintained a prestigious infant laboratory from the 1950s through the 1970s. He and many widely recognized students did pioneering studies of the visual development of human babies, focusing much on infant eye movements in response to different shapes, colors, and sizes. Studies of olfactory and taste preferences of young babies also left their marks in the literature. As time passed, questions of structure and context of child development grew more pressing. His "historico-conceptual" line was never far from sight.

In 1959 Kessen, together with his other lifelong friend, George Mandler, published a philosophical treatise *The Language of Psychology*. It was a deep and

223

In 1965 William Kessen published The Child, *in which he commented on primary works from many of the medical, religious, philosophical, psychological, and pedagogical roots of contemporary developmental psychology.* (Michael Marsland, Yale University)

incisive treatment of logical positivism, the reigning philosophy of science at the time. Shortly after the book's publication and with the end of the "Age of Theory," Kessen and others abandoned the logical positivistic vision of psychology as a science. In June 1959 the Social Science Research Council invited Kessen and other distinguished developmental psychologists to form the Committee on Intellective Processes Research. Included in the several conference reports of the Committee were five *Monographs of the Society for Research in Child Development* (SRCD), including one edited by Kessen and Clementina Kuhlman entitled *The Thought of the Young Child.* These were groundbreaking conferences that helped American psychologists become familiar with the still unfamiliar work of Jean Piaget. In his own report, "Stage and Structure in the Study of Children," Kessen incisively explored the many and sometimes ambiguous meanings of "stage" and "structure" in developmental psychology, focusing on the works of Piaget and Freud.

In 1970 Kessen was lead author on the definitive guide to infancy research published in *Carmichael's Manual of Child Psychology.* Five years later, he published *Childhood in China,* in which he gathered together observations made while leading a state department delegation to study early education in China.

Kessen's decisive turn toward exploring the historical and cultural context of both children and child psychology may be marked by his 1979 article "The American Child and Other Cultural Inventions" in *American Psychologist.* Based upon his presidential address to Division 7 (Developmental Psychology) of the American Psychological Association, Kessen argued that both children and child psychology emerge from and are defined by the contours of social change, intellectual currents, and institutional arrangements. The child, having been redefined as culturally and historically variable, was not a stable object of study; neither was the concept of development (beyond certain kinds of biologically driven growth) a source of scientific certainty. Thus child psychology could not and should not attempt to attain the older positivistic ideal of stable and universal truths. Kessen continued to publish a string of historical and philosophical essays, including the 1990 Heinz Werner lectures, published by Clark University Press, in which he challenged some of the most basic assumptions of developmental psychology. The essays leave the reader with vexing questions about the meaning of development itself.

Kessen traveled widely inside and outside academe. In addition to his travels in China, he joined delegations to the Soviet Union, Norway, and Czechoslovakia. With his family he spent two glorious years in Tuscany (their "second home"), studying early education in Italy. Kessen held numerous administrative positions, including chair of the Department of Psychology as well as Secretary for Yale University. He was a charming, lively, and insightful conversationalist who moved easily between the policy world in Washington and the philanthropic worlds centered in New York and Chicago. Although not one to easily shed his scholastic circumspection, Kessen retained a quiet but wise stance on political issues related to children, families, and government. Kessen taught generations of students; he was a great and magnanimous teacher, beloved by both undergraduate and graduate students. Without seeming to meddle, Kessen nurtured generations of students with his grace, insight, wisdom, compassion, and good humor.

Kessen died on February 13, 1999, in New Haven, Connecticut. At the time of his death he held the Eugene Higgins Chair of Psychology and Pediatrics at Yale University. He is survived by his wife, their three daughters, triplet sons ("six spectacular children"), and numerous grandchildren.

Bibliography

Publications by Kessen

Mandler, George, and William Kessen. *The Language of Psychology.* New York: Wiley, 1959.

Kessen, William, and Clementina Kuhlman, eds. *Thought in the Young Child: Report of a Conference with Particular Attention to the Work of Jean Piaget,* vol. 27 (2, Serial no. 83): Monographs of the Society for Research in Child Development, *1962.*

The Child. New York: Wiley, 1965.

Kessen, William, Marshall Haith, and Phillip H. Salapatek. "Human Infancy: A Bibliography and Guide." In Paul H. Mussen ed., *Carmichael's Manual of Child Psychology,* 3rd edition. New York: Wiley, 1970.

Kessen, William, ed. *Childhood in China: The American Delegation on Early Childhood Development in the People's Republic of China.* New Haven: Yale University Press, 1975.

"Rousseau's Children." *Daedalus* 107, no. 3 (1978):155–166.

"The American Child and Other Cultural Inventions." *American Psychologist* 34 (1979):815–820.

Bronfenbrenner, Urie, Frank S. Kessel, William Kessen, and Sheldon H. White. "Towards a Critical Social History of Developmental Psychology." *American Psychologist* 41 (1986):1218–1230.

Kessen, William, and Emily D. Cahan. "A Century of Psychology: From Subject to Object to Agent." *American Scientist* 74 (1986):640–649.

The Rise and Fall of Development. Worcester, MA: Clark University Press, 1990.

"Nearing the End: A Lifetime of Being 17." In Frank S. Kessel, Marc H. Bornstein, and Arnold J. Sameroff eds., *Contemporary Constructions of the Child: Essays in Honor of William Kessen.* Hillsdale, NJ: Lawrence Erlbaum, 1991.

"Avoiding the Emptiness: The Full Infant." *Theory and Psychology* 3, no. 4 (1993).

Emily D. Cahan

KLINEFELTER'S SYNDROME

Klinefelter's syndrome (genotype 47, XXY) is a chromosomal anomaly in which affected males have an extra X chromosome. It occurs in 1:1,000 to 1:2,000 newborn males and has been detected in .003 percent of spontaneous abortions. This condition generally arises from failure of chromosomes to separate properly during meiosis. Specifically, an egg cell bearing an additional X chromosome (or a sperm bearing both an X and a Y chromosome) unites with a normal sex cell. Approximately one-third of affected individuals show multiple Xs (48, XXXY or 49, XXXXY) or both normal and abnormal cell lines (46, XY/47, XXY).

Klinefelter's syndrome is generally not apparent until puberty, at which time secondary sexual devel-

opment does not proceed. Clinical features include small testes, tall stature, breast development, reduced hormonal levels, and sterility. Mosaics, or individuals with mixed cell lines, may be fertile. Behavioral features include depressed verbal intelligence, reduced activity, increased stress, and feelings of reduced masculinity. Families may be advised to seek hormonal therapy and counseling for these children.

See also: BIRTH DEFECTS; DEVELOPMENTAL DISABILITIES; GENOTYPE

Bibliography

"Klinefelter Syndrome." In the On-line Medical Dictionary, 1995–1998. Available from http://www.graylab.ac.uk/omd/index.html; INTERNET.

Plomin, Robert, John DeFries, Gerald McClearn, and Peter McGuffin. *Behavioral Genetics,* 4th edition. New York: Worth Publishers, 2001.

Nancy L. Segal

KOHLBERG, LAWRENCE (1927–1987)

Born in Broxville, N.Y., Lawrence Kohlberg was a professor of Education and Social Psychology at Harvard University and is best known for his influential work in moral development and moral education.

As a young man, Kohlberg served in the U.S. Merchant Marine after World War II. He then volunteered to help smuggle Jewish refugees out of Europe and through a British blockade into British-controlled Palestine. He was captured and held in a detention center on Cyprus, finally being rescued by the Haganah, a Jewish fighting force.

Kohlberg's interest in morality developed from these experiences and from the theories of Jean Piaget, who studied the cognitive development of children. In his doctoral dissertation, Kohlberg examined the ways that children reason about what is right and wrong. He presented boys, ages ten to sixteen, with a series of moral dilemmas—stories about people in situations who had to make difficult decisions. The most famous dilemma asks whether a man whose wife is dying from a rare form of cancer should steal the only medicine that might save her life from a scientist who refuses to sell the drug at a price the man can afford.

Based on this research, Kohlberg developed his theory of moral development. He proposed three levels of moral reasoning. At the first level (preconventional), children's decisions are based on avoiding punishment and receiving rewards. At the second level (conventional), upholding the rules of society is the highest value. At the highest level (postconventional), individuals follow universal moral

Lawrence Kohlberg (1927–1987) studied the moral development of children and devised three stages of moral reasoning. (Barry Donahue, Harvard Office of News and Public Affairs)

principles that may be more important than the rules of a particular country or group. Clearly Kohlberg was influenced by his own experiences when he broke England's law in order to carry out what he believed was a higher moral imperative: to aid refugees of the Holocaust.

Kohlberg extended his theory into practice with applications to moral education in classrooms. Following criticism that his work dealt with moral reasoning, but not moral action, he developed a program in which participatory democracy in the classroom served as the basis for moral development.

A major debate about Kohlberg's theories was sparked by Carol Gilligan, a professor at Harvard, whose research reflected the view that women's morality differs from that of men's, on whom most of Kohlberg's research was based.

Kohlberg also applied the cognitive-developmental approach to the development of gender identity. His research showed that children's understanding of gender is linked to their level of cognitive development.

See also: MORAL DEVELOPMENT; STAGES OF
DEVELOPMENT

Bibliography

Publications by Kohlberg

"A Cognitive-Developmental Analysis of Children's Sex-Role Concepts and Attitudes." In E. E. Maccoby ed., *The Development of Sex Differences.* Stanford, CA: Stanford University Press, 1966.

The Psychology of Moral Development: The Nature and Validity of Moral Stages. San Francisco: Harper and Row, 1984.

Child Psychology and Childhood Education: A Cognitive Developmental View. New York: Longman, 1987.

Laura E. Levine

L

LAISSEZ-FAIRE PARENTS

Laissez-faire is a French term meaning "to let people do as they please." Applied to parenting, the term refers to a permissive style in which parents avoid providing guidance and discipline, make no demands for maturity, and impose few controls on their child's behavior. Permissive parents allow their children to make their own decisions regarding matters such as mealtimes, bedtimes, and watching television. Research published in 1989 by Diana Baumrind found that children of permissive parents tend to be impulsive, disobedient, rebellious, demanding, and dependent on adults. As teens, many of these children had poor self-control, poor school performance, and a high rate of drug use. Baumrind found that the best adjusted and most academically competent children had authoritative parents who were neither too lenient nor too strict; these parents set reasonable limits for their children, were warm and responsive, and did not use harsh methods of punishment.

See also: PARENT-CHILD RELATIONSHIPS; PARENTING

Bibliography
Baumrind, Diana. "Rearing Competent Children." In William Damon ed., *Child Development Today and Tomorrow.* San Francisco: Jossey-Bass, 1989.

Ann D. Murray

LANGUAGE ACQUISITION DEVICE

The Language Acquisition Device (LAD) is a hypothetical brain mechanism that Noam Chomsky postulated to explain human acquisition of the syntactic structure of language. This mechanism endows children with the capacity to derive the syntactic structure and rules of their native language rapidly and accurately from the impoverished input provided by adult language users. The device is comprised of a finite set of dimensions along which languages vary, which are set at different levels for different languages on the basis of language exposure. The LAD reflects Chomsky's underlying assumption that many aspects of language are universal (common to all languages and cultures) and constrained by innate core knowledge about language called Universal Grammar. This theoretical account of syntax acquisition contrasts sharply with the views of B. F. Skinner, Jean Piaget, and other cognitive and social-learning theorists who emphasize the role of experience and general knowledge and abilities in language acquisition.

See also: LANGUAGE DEVELOPMENT

Bibliography
Chomsky, Noam. *Aspects of the Theory of Syntax.* Cambridge, MA: MIT Press, 1965.

Laura L. Namy

LANGUAGE DEVELOPMENT

Mike (age five years, discussing the game of baseball): *Mom, did you know that baseball games need a vampire?*

Mom: *A vampire?*

Mike: *Yes, the vampire stands in back of the catcher and catches any of the balls that the catcher misses.*

Joshua (age three, picking up the book *Sleeping Beauty*): *Let's read Sleeping Buddha.*

Child (age four): *Nobody doesn't likes me.*

Parent: *You mean, "Nobody likes me."*

Child: *OK. Nobody doesn't likes you.*

These excerpts are not mere anecdotes from three- and four-year-olds' everyday conversations. Rather, they are glimpses into the inner workings of the human mind. Language is a uniquely human behavior and is one of the most complicated behaviors in which humans engage as a species. Neither birds nor have language, and though people have spent countless hours trying to train chimps and gorillas, even they have not mastered the system. Yet, by the time children can walk, they have spoken their first words and can comprehend about fifty words. By the time children can run, they speak in full sentences and use language to control their environment and their parents. The average three-year-old has the computational power and symbolic sophistication to do what our most advanced computers cannot do—to use human language to communicate with others, and to represent things in the past, the present, and the future. The average four-year-old has mastered the complex system we call language and is fully conversant with adults and peers.

Languages as an Orchestral Work in Progress

For centuries, philosophers and psychologists have tried to understand how it is that children learn their first language. Are humans simply endowed with language? Are humans carefully taught? To address these questions one must first ask, "What is language?" One way of thinking about the problem is to assume that language is like an orchestra. It is composed of many parts that intricately work together to provide a unified sound. Just as there are sections in the orchestra (the strings, the brass, the wind instruments, and the percussion), there are components of language in sounds, meanings, words, grammar, and rules for how one uses each of these parts in culturally appropriate ways. Language acquisition, then, is really the development of many pieces of a language system that must evolve and work in tandem to perform the "score" of human talk.

The First Year: Sounds and Meanings

The journey into language begins with the sound component of the orchestra. The first piece that parents notice occurs at around three or four months when children begin to gurgle and coo. Cooing consists of series of vowel sounds that babies tend to make and that—at least American parents—respond to. Just a couple of months later, at about seven months, these same infants start to babble. The first consonant sounds (e.g., "ba," "ga") enter into the language, and the product sounds much more like speech. In this period, children seem to carry on conversations with consonant-vowel sounds that only they can understand (e.g., "ba ga ga ga ba ba?").

The beginning of language, then, starts with a strong appearance from the "sound" component of the language orchestra. The exact role of the sound component in the development of later language, however, has been hotly debated. Is babbling, for example, a form of prespeech? Is it merely an avenue for young children to practice using their vocal chords and to imitate sounds that they hear with mouth movements that they can make? Scientists still are not sure. Yet it is interesting that even deaf children babble with sounds and that this babbling does not wane until about the point when canonical babbling comes in. Deaf children of deaf parents babble with their hands and show the same progression toward canonical babbling as do hearing children.

Even though sounds are the most dominant components of early language, the second half of the first year also represents enormous progress in how children learn to express new meanings—even before they have mastered language. Notably, by eight months of age children are quite adept at using eye gaze and grunts to indicate what they are looking at and to request an action from a parent. This prelinguistic stage is heightened further when the child learns to point. Pointing is a specifically human gesture that dramatically increases the child's ability to communicate. At around ten months, the forefinger is used to make what some have called "proto-declaratives" and "proto-imperatives"—otherwise known as statements and commands. As any parent will attest, these commands are quite direct and clear, even though the child is still technically "prelinguistic."

The Second Year: From First Words to the Fifty-Word Watershed to Grammar

Pointing opens the way toward language. Yet most parents find that true language emerges with the first words at around thirteen months. There is a fuzzy line between recognizable sounds and first words. By way of example, "mama" and "papa" will be among the early sounds interpreted as words by parents. With no intention of bursting bubbles, the sounds used to make these "words" are easy for babies to produce. Whether they really function as words is another story. To qualify as *real*, a word must sound like a known word and be used consistently—even in different contexts—to mean the same thing. So, for example, a child who uses the word "flower" to refer only to a flower on the front porch and not to the flower in the dining room vase is not credited with having spoken a word.

First words are often body parts or proper names (such as the name of the family pet), and they seem to be learned laboriously during the first few months. By sixteen months, most children say fifty words, most of which are names for objects and people in their environment (e.g., dog, daddy, ear, apple, juice, bottle). After children reach this critical mass of fifty words, something seems to happen inside that leads to a "naming explosion." Typical eighteen- to twenty-month-olds can learn as many as nine new words a day. Children need to hear a word used only once to use it in a reasonably appropriate way.

This fifty-word watershed is also important for another reason. After children achieve this critical mass of words, they combine words for the first time. Thus, at about eighteen months, grammar bursts onto the productive scene. The first word combinations that children produce omit articles (e.g., "the," "an"), prepositions (e.g., "to," "from") and inflections (e.g., plural "s," "-ing"), making the language sound "telegraphic," or as if children were sending a telegram where words and particles cost money. These children can now say "That kitty" to mean "That is a kitty" or "Daddy ball" to mean "Daddy has a ball." Everywhere in the world, children's first word combinations are expressing the same thoughts. Children ask for more of something (e.g., "More milk"), reject things (e.g., "No bottle"), notice things (e.g., "Look kitty"), or comment on the fact that something disappeared (e.g., "Allgone milk"). These children express entire paragraphs in their short utterances and talk about the "here and now" rather than about the past or future.

The Third Year: Refining Grammar

When children are two to three, their grammatical development becomes refined. Children may put together an actor and a verb, "Mommy go," or a verb and an object, "eat lunch." They are still limited by how much they can produce at a given time. If, for example, they wanted to say that they would not eat lunch, they could not utter "No eat lunch" in the early stages, but rather would have to limit their output to

"No eat" or "No lunch." Shortly, however, this window expands and the number of words they can use in a sentence increases.

During the middle of the third year, children become sophisticated grammar users who can speak in longer sentences and who begin to include the small grammatical elements that they omitted before. For the first time, they use "ing" on their verbs, saying "running" whereas before they could only say "run." They begin to add tense to their verbs (e.g., "walked") and parents can even see evidence of grammatical "rules." For example, the child who said "went" earlier may now know the past tense rule (add "-ed") and may now say "goed"—much to parents' surprise. In such cases, however, "went" eventually reemerges and is used correctly.

The Fourth Year: Language Use in Social Situations

Having mastered the sound system of language, learned the meanings of words, and learned how to structure sentences, children turn their attention to mastering the ways to use language in social situations at around three or four years of age. The child who says "More milk" is cajoled by parents to "use the magic word—*please*." Children now struggle to understand what people really mean to say. This is no mean feat, as is shown by the four-year-old who took the phone caller's sentence literally when asked, "Is your mother home?" This child answered "yes" and then hung up on the caller! Children need to learn that not all language can be taken literally.

Deeper Understandings of Language Development

As has been seen, children have a lot to learn in their first three or four years, and they constantly show what they know by what they say and how they say it. In fact, what they say has been the universal metric of language development. It is what the pediatrician records during routine office visits. And it is what a parent quickly jots down in the child's baby book. Yet, to pay attention only to what is on the surface would obscure most of what is going on in early language development. There is so much more going on behind the scenes.

In the late twentieth century and into the twenty-first century, the headline news in infant psychology has come from the ability to peer in on language development during the first year of life. Indeed, there has been a virtual explosion in understanding what children can understand even before they can speak. It has been learned, for example, that language learning starts in the womb. Newborns actually respond differently to a poem that was read to them constantly in the last months of pregnancy than to a new poem. They even show some recognition of their own mother's voice. Further, it is now known that even two-day-old infants can distinguish between their own language and a foreign language. Four-month-old infants recognize their own names. Six-month-olds understand the names "mommy" and "daddy" and can accurately indicate which label goes with which person. Research shows that eight-month-olds are sophisticated statisticians, finding patterns of syllables in the speech that they hear. They quickly learn that they had heard some patterns in the speech they heard and not others. And nine-month-olds already know that in English most words start with heavy stress as in "KITCHen" and "STAple" and not with weak stress as is found in such words as "enJOY" and "reGARD."

Advancements in science and new methodologies have also shown that ten-month-olds are no slouches. They comprehend about ten to twenty words, and by sixteen months they understand around one hundred words. By sixteen months these babies, who are one-word speakers, are five- or six-word listeners. They know that the sentence "Big Bird is tickling Cookie Monster" means something different than the sentence "Cookie Monster is tickling Big Bird." Together these new findings indicate that babies who are only babbling and pointing are really working very hard—on the inside—to master the many components of language and to use them in an organized way. Before they utter their first word, babies have cracked the sound code, learned a lot about what words refer to, and have started noting the patterns of grammar. A complete account of language development will have to include what babies know, not just what they say.

Whether a person is French or American, lives in a castle or a tent, and is deaf or hearing, the course of language development appears to be the roughly the same. To be sure, there is some individual variation. For example, some children use mostly object names (e.g., "book," "dog"), while others collect and use more social language, such as "please" and "thank you." The overwhelming impression gained from the study of language, however, is that despite the minor variations, children assemble their language orchestra in roughly the same way. This is even true for children who are lucky enough to grow up in a family in which more than one language is spoken. These children will learn both languages with ease. Young children are incredibly skilled at learning multiple languages at the same time.

Language Development When Things Go Awry: Everyday Problems

Though problems in language acquisition are relatively rare, there are a number of circumstances that can contribute to atypical patterns of development in which language might develop more slowly than is typical. Perhaps the biggest challenge is knowing when the problems are real enough to merit expert attention. The problems that have garnered the most attention are ear infections, speech/articulation problems, language delay, and stuttering.

Ear Infections

The most common cause for language problems are ear infections, more specifically, "otitis media." Otitis media involves an accrual of fluid in the ear that results in temporary hearing loss. As one might expect, the condition has more severe consequences if it occurs in both ears than if it occurs in just one ear. About one-third of children suffer from extensive bouts of otitis media (greater than three bouts in the first year), and children who are in alternate care environments or who are around other children are reported to have higher incidents of the condition. On average, two-year-olds will have had six infections, each of which will have lasted for an average of four weeks.

Given the frequency of ear infections, it is no wonder that researchers have asked whether otitis media causes short-term or lasting effects on language development. The results of their studies, however, are mixed. Children with greater than three bouts of otitis media in the first year do tend to talk later than their peers. By the age of four years, however, these children have caught up in most areas. The research is somewhat mixed regarding long-term effects. Recent evidence suggests that there may be mild long-term effects of otitis media in two areas. First, children who have had many ear infections tend to have poorer attention spans in early elementary school. Second, they tend to be poorer at storytelling at seven years of age. While language does not seem to be affected then, there are some signs that children with early ear infections might have small but more lasting effects that could infringe on later school abilities.

Speech/Articulation Problems

Anecdotally, the cause for most concern comes from claims of immature or poorly articulated speech. While parents often worry about the four-year-old child who uses "baby talk," saying "Dat is not de way dat you sould do dis," most of these errors are well within the normal range of development. Children show remarkably consistent patterns as they attempt to pronounce common adult words. For example, a child might pronounce the word "pot" as "bot. "Notice that the "p" and the "b" are both sounds made with closed lips. Thus, they are easily confused. Or children might simplify the word "bread" into "bed" and "spill" into "pill." Sometimes they also get the stresses and accents correct but fail to accurately reproduce the adult target. Words such as "Sleeping Buddha" for "Sleeping Beauty "and "vampire" for "umpire" in the opening examples of this article provide some sense of these errors of "assimilation."

Language Delay

As with speech/articulation problems, language delay represents another cause for concern for some parents. Many have heard the story of the child who says nothing until his third birthday and then, when sitting at dinner, asks for a fork in perfect English. When asked why he hadn't said anything before, the child said, "Up to now, everything has been perfect!" This joke is not far off the mark.

There are two forms of language delay. Some children understand everything but just do not talk. These children are not of real concern to parents. On the other hand, for some children, language development is not merely hidden from view but may not be progressing on course. Since the late 1990s there have been major developments in distinguishing between these two types of language delay. Parents seem to know the difference. They can often tell when children understand language and when they do not. If the child has not said even a few words by eighteen months or has not put two words together by twenty-four months, the parents should consider taking the child to a speech therapist. The child's hearing is the first thing that should be tested.

Stuttering

As with language delay and articulation, stuttering has both a common form and a more clinical form. Many parents find that at around age two, their children seem to stutter. They have a great deal to say and are not yet proficient at getting their message out. The result is a kind of verbal logjam. Children start a sentence, stop, flounder for a bit, and then start again. This is all quite normal and usually passes over the course of the next couple of months. By three years of age, speech therapists take stuttering more seriously. Stuttering runs in families and is more prevalent among boys than girls. Several cautionary notes are raised by speech therapists with regard to stuttering. First, if the child is stuttering at age two or two-and-a-half, it is important to not make a point of it. One should just slow down the rate of the conversation and proceed as if nothing has gone wrong. Bringing stuttering to the child's attention can often exacerbate the condition. Second, if the child of around age three is stuttering and the parent sees the child trying to inhibit the stuttering by making jerky motions with the hands or blinking the eyes while speaking, a speech therapist should be consulted.

Explaining Language Development

As noted earlier, language proceeds on a common course for most children. In fact, the weight of the scientific evidence supports the view that children are prewired to learn language. This strong view, however, leaves one pondering the role of input—the language that children are exposed to. Does parental input make no difference in the language development of the child? Can therapists make any difference in correcting language problems if things go awry? A brief review of the role of input in language will help set the record straight and will also provide some feel for the theoretical landscape that guides research in the field of language acquisition at the beginning of the twenty-first century.

First and foremost, it is known that language input must make some difference because all children do not speak the same language. French children will learn French, and Chinese children will learn Chinese. Thus, whatever is built in must be "just enough" to allow children to learn any language and not so much to determine the particular language a child will learn. That input makes some difference is therefore a given. What has been debated, however, is whether this input serves as a trigger for language development or as a mold. On the side of the trigger theories, researchers find that parents do not actively "teach" their children grammar. No parent would ever utter the sentence "I goed to the potty." Yet most parents are overjoyed when they hear this from the child. They do not stop to suggest that the sentence should be "You WENT to the potty."

There is also mounting evidence for those who believe that parents mold language in children. Though parents do not teach children grammar, they do teach children when to say their "pleases" and "thank yous." Further, it is widely accepted that parents who talk more with their children have children who learn more words and use grammar earlier. Input becomes apparent in the limited, but real, individual differences in language development between children.

Language development is the product of an interactive and dynamic system that has components of instinct and of input—of nature and of nurture. The human mind must be built so that young learners selectively attend to certain parts of the input and not to others. With respect to sounds, infants must recognize that the sounds of language are different than the many other sounds that come out of the mouth—sneezes, coughs, and burps do not name objects. In word learning, children must assume that words generally refer to categories of objects, actions, and events. This means that there is not a different name for every table or chair that one encounters in the environment. To learn a grammar, young minds must detect patterns of words but not pay attention, for example, to the syllable structure of every fifth word. Nature provides the starting points for language development, and nurture (the environment) drives the course of that development over time.

Given this interactive view of language, the job for the language scientist of the future is both to identify the selective tendencies of the mind and to see how, in concert with particular inputs, these built-in tendencies allow the child to construct a system that is capable of creating language performances over and over again throughout the course of a human life. The language orchestra, then, is a product of membership in the human species. Humans are given the instruments and the starting points. The language that a person hears around her everyday fine-tunes her sound and helps her build her repertoire. And each child becomes the conductor who pulls all of the components together in a flawless performance that is virtually completed by the time she is three years of age.

See also: LANGUAGE ACQUISITION DEVICE

Bibliography

Golinkoff, Roberta Michnick, and Kathy Hirsh-Pasek. *How Babies Talk.* New York: Dutton/Penguin, 2000.

Kathy Hirsh-Pasek
Roberta Michnick Golinkoff

LATCHKEY CHILDREN

Latchkey children are defined by the authors of *The Facts on File Dictionary of Education* as: "School-aged children who are typically unsupervised after school hours because of working parents and, therefore, who carry a house key to let themselves in after school." This straightforward definition overlooks children who have a parent at home, but the parent offers little or no appropriate adult supervision. Children and young teenagers who have access to some type of after-school care but fail to attend that care on some days and so are unsupervised are also overlooked by this definition. Siblings not much older than those they supervise may also inadequately care for young children. The term "latchkey children" also promotes a number of stereotypes not yet clearly born out in empirical studies. Examples of such stereotypes in-clude *all* latchkey children: are more likely to abuse tobacco, alcohol, and other drugs; are more sexually active; are poorer students academically; have inadequate self-concepts; are more self-reliant; are more fearful, apprehensive, and insecure; have little inner control; and are more likely to be involved in criminal activity compared to adult-supervised peers. Given the stereotypes attached to the term "latchkey children," it might better be replaced with a term such as "unsupervised children" or "self-care children."

Prevalence

There is evidence that the number of children needing before- and after-school care is growing. Two factors are of particular importance in this growth. First, the number of single-parent families has grown at an astounding rate since the 1970s. According to the U.S. Bureau of the Census, the number of family groups maintained by one parent grew from 3.8 million in 1970 to 11.8 million in 1998. Second, there are more mothers of school-age children in two-parent families choosing to enter the out-of-home workforce. From 1986 to 1998, the number of husband and wife couples in the workforce grew from 25.4 million to 30.6 million.

Estimates of the number of unsupervised or inadequately supervised children range from 3.5 million to 17.5 million for children between the ages of five and fourteen. The large discrepancy in estimates is mainly due to the variety of definitions. Some estimates include only children who have no supervision; others include those with no adult supervision. Still other estimates include those who are inadequately supervised, periodically unsupervised, or supervised by a parent or other adult who is emotionally or psychologically unavailable. No matter which estimate is used, it is clear that too many children do not receive the supervision that would maximize their physical, social, emotional, psychological, and spiritual development.

Dilemmas for Parents

Parents work outside the home because they desire to be in the workforce or because they feel that they have financial needs. Lois Hoffman, in a 1974 study, found that children did better when parents were in their preferred situation (working outside the home or being home with the children) than when they were in their nonpreferred situation. Parents with the greatest financial needs but limited financial resources are often surprised to find that it actually costs more for the second person to work outside the home than that person earns. Thus, such parents are less able to meet their financial obligations when both

After school, many children come home to an unsupervised environment while their parents are still at work. Studies have shown that these children are most likely to use drugs and engage in behavior that is inappropriate for their age group. (Kelly/Mooney Photography/Corbis)

persons work. Solutions for providing appropriate care for children must also examine the needs and resources of the parents.

Children have varying characteristics that affect their need for supervision and the type of supervision that will be adequate. Among these factors are age, developmental level, maturity, and physical, social, and emotional problems. Environmental resources such as the neighborhood, the home itself, and the quantity and quality of available community programs are also important.

It is a mistake to lump all children together and fail to recognize the wide variation among them and also the variation in situations and resources. For example, one situation might involve a mature twelve-year-old child who follows an agreed-upon routine while at home, has a secure home, can communicate via telephone or computer with at least one parent, and has a neighbor who checks in once or twice and watches the house. Quite another situation might involve a thirteen-year-old child who is beginning to ex-

plore drugs and sexuality, cannot be depended upon to follow an agreed-upon routine, has little contact with parents after school, and lives in an unsafe neighborhood. The range of individual and situational variables must be taken into account when attempting to understand both problems and solutions for children in need of supervision.

Mixed Empirical Findings

Numerous studies have been conducted since the 1970s investigating unsupervised children from psychological, sociological, and educational perspectives. The findings have been quite mixed, with some researchers finding clear differences between supervised and self-care children and some failing to do so. Among the former, Ruth C. Reynolds found that unsupervised children were at greater risk than supervised children for negative feeling, insecurity, accidents, abuse, neglect, and fear. Thomas J. Long and Lynette Long found that 30 percent of the unsupervised African-American children in their study reported high levels of fear. Peter Mulhall reported that middle school and junior high school students who were home alone after school two or more days per week were four times more likely to have gotten drunk in the previous month than those who had parental supervision five or more times a week. Merilyn B. Woods reported that low-income urban fifth graders who were unsupervised had more academic and social problems than similar children of higher income who were in after-school supervision. Lynne Steinberg found that fifth to ninth graders who were more removed from adult supervision were more susceptible to peer pressure to commit antisocial acts than were their supervised peers. Lorene C. Quay found that latchkey children revealed more loneliness than did children who went home to their mother. John M. Diamond and his colleagues found that unsupervised boys in the fifth and sixth grades scored lower on achievement tests than supervised boys. Javaid Kaiser found similar results.

Other studies found no differences between self-care and supervised children on a number of variables. Nancy L. Galambos and James Garbarino found that supervised and unsupervised fifth and seventh graders in rural settings did not differ on school adjustment, school orientation, achievement, and levels of fear. Stephen C. Messer and his colleagues reported no differences in personality tests and SAT scores between college students who had previously been in self-care and those who had been in supervised care. J. L. Richardson and colleagues found that stress levels of unsupervised students did not predict substance use. Hyman Rodman, David J. Pratto, and Rosemary S. Nelson found no differences among supervised and unsupervised children on measures of self-esteem, internal or external locus of control, and a behavior rating scale for urban and rural children of racial diversity. Deborah Lowe Vandell and Janaki Ramanan reported that children in the care of single mothers after school had lower scores on Peabody Picture Vocabulary Tests and higher ratings for antisocial behaviors than children in other types of adult after-school supervision.

The type of after-school activities in which children are engaged also plays an important role in their adjustment. Jill K. Posner and Deborah Lowe Vandell found that children involved in coached sports and after-school academic activities were better adjusted in the fifth grade than children who spent their time after school watching television and hanging out.

Programs

A wide variety of after-school programs have been lauded in the literature. These programs vary on several dimensions. Some programs focus on contact with working parents by telephone or computer. Some child-care facilities provide video monitoring of children, with the video stream transmitted to the parent's work computer. This technology could certainly be adapted to the home. Other programs stress after-school sitters in the home or neighbors who regularly look in on older children and youth. Many programs emphasize adult-supervised activities in the community such as sports, drama, dance, music, academics, and recreation. It appears that these programs vary in quality, cost, and availability in any given community. Too often parents with sufficient resources can provide high-quality and varied adult-supervised activities after school, whereas those with limited resources do not have these same possibilities.

Conclusions

Most communities have before- and after-school supervised programs, but these opportunities may not be financially available for those who need them most, namely children who have single mothers and dual-worker low-income families. Parents must not only be aware of and have access to quality adult-supervised programs, but also know the particular strengths and needs of their child. Such strengths and needs change as the child matures. Children under age twelve should not be left alone in self-care or in the care of those who cannot adequately provide for their needs and safety. For mature adolescents, partial care and periodic supervision may be sufficient. Reevaluation should occur regularly. It is much less expensive to provide these programs for children than to deal with the consequences in adulthood.

See also: STREET CHILDREN; WORKING FAMILIES

Bibliography

Berns, Roberta M. *Child, Family, School, Community: Socialization and Support,* 4th edition. Fort Worth, TX: Harcourt Brace, 1997.

Diamond, John M., Sudesh Kataria, and Stephen C. Messer. "Latchkey Children: A Pilot Study Investigating Behavior and Academic Achievement." *Child and Youth Care Quarterly* 18 (1989):131–140.

Galambos, Nancy L., and James Garbarino. "Adjustment of Unsupervised Children in a Rural Ecology." *Journal of Genetic Psychology* 14 (1985):227–231.

Hoffman, Lois W. "Effects of Maternal Employment on the Child: Review of the Research." *Developmental Psychology* 10 (1974):204–228.

Kaiser, Javaid. "The Role of Family Configuration, Income, and Gender in the Academic Achievement of Young Self-Care Children." *Early Child Development and Care* 97 (1994):91–105.

Lamorey, Suzanne, Bryan E. Robinson, Bobbie H. Rowland, and Mick Coleman. *Latchkey Kids: Unlocking Doors for Children and Their Families,* 2nd edition. Thousand Oaks, CA: Sage, 1999.

Long, Thomas J., and Lynette Long. "Latchkey Children: The Child's View of Self Care." ERIC Database no. ED211229 (1981).

Messer, Stephen C., Karl L. Wuensch, and John M. Diamond. "Former Latchkey Children: Personality and Academic Correlates." *Journal of Genetic Psychology* 150 (1988):301–309.

Mulhall, Peter F. "Home Alone: Is It a Risk Factor for Middle School Youth and Drug Use?" *Journal of Drug Education* 26, no. 1 (1996):39–48.

Posner, Jill K., and Deborah Lowe Vandell. "After-School Activities and the Development of Low-Income Urban Children: A Longitudinal Study." *Developmental Psychology* 35 (1999):868–879.

Quay, Lorene C. "Personal and Family Effects on Loneliness." *Journal of Applied Developmental Psychology* 13, no. 1 (1992):97–110.

Reynolds, Ruth C. "What Research Has to Say about Latchkey Programs." ERIC Database no. ED267922 (1985).

Richardson, J. L., K. Dwyer, K. McGuigan, W. B. Hansen, C. Dent, C. A. Johnson, S. Y. Sussman, B. Brannon, and B. Flay. "Substance Use among Eighth-Grade Students Who Take Care of Themselves after School." *Pediatrics* 84 (1989):556–565.

Rodman, Hyman, David J. Pratto, and Rosemary S. Nelson. "Child Care Arrangements and Children's Functioning: A Comparison of Self-Care and Adult-Care Children." *Developmental Psychology* 21 (1985):413–418.

Shafritz, Jay M., Richard P. Koeppe, and Elizabeth W. Soper. *The Facts on File Dictionary of Education*. New York: Facts on File, 1988.

Steinberg, Lynne. "Latchkey Children and Susceptibility to Peer Pressure: An Ecological Analysis." *Developmental Psychology* 22 (1986):433–439.

U.S. Bureau of the Census. "All Parent/Child Situations, by Type, Race, and Hispanic Origin of Householder or Reference Person, 1970 to Present." Washington, DC: U.S. Bureau of the Census, 1998.

U.S. Bureau of the Census. "Married Couples by Labor for Status of Spouse, 1986 to Present." Washington, DC: U.S. Bureau of the Census, 1998.

Vandell, Deborah Lowe, and Jill K. Posner. "Conceptualization and Measurement of Children's After-School Environments." In Sarah L. Friedman and Theodore D. Wachs eds., *Assessment of the Environment across the Lifespan*. Washington, DC: American Psychological Association Press, 1999.

Vandell, Deborah Lowe, and Janaki Ramanan. "Children of the National Longitudinal Survey of Youth Choices in After-School Care and Child Development." *Developmental Psychology* 27 (1991):637–643.

Woods, Merilyn B. "The Unsupervised Child of the Working Mother." *Developmental Psychology* 6 (1972):14–25.

Dennis H. Karpowitz

LEAD POISONING

Lead is an environmental toxin that can cause mental retardation, brain damage, or death in children. Young children are particularly at risk because they can accidentally eat leaded paint chips or breathe lead-contaminated dust. Although lead-based paint for household use has been banned in the United States since 1977, deteriorated older houses remain important sources. Once inside the body, lead affects the brain, heart, liver, kidney, and blood. Initially only high measurable blood lead levels (<60 micrograms/deciliter or µg/dL) associated with seizures, coma, or death were recognized as lead poisoning; learning and behavior problems have been shown at lower levels (10–20 µg/dL). Although national surveys have shown decreases in blood lead levels in children one to five years of age from 88 percent during 1976–1980 to 4 percent during 1991–1994, poor young minority children in inner cities remain at risk for significant exposure. Treatment consists of eliminating lead from the home environment, adding iron to the diet, and, if necessary, providing medications to remove lead from the body.

See also: DEVELOPMENTAL DISABILITIES

Bibliography

American Academy of Pediatrics, Committee on Environmental Health. "Screening for Elevated Blood Levels." *Pediatrics* 101 (1998):1072–1078.

"Blood Lead Levels in Young Children—United States and Selected States, 1996–1999." *Morbidity and Mortality Weekly Report* 49 (2000):1133–1137.

Hwang, Mi Young, Richard Glass, and Jeff Molter. "*JAMA* Patient Page: Protect Your Child Against Lead Poisoning." *Journal of the American Medical Association* 281 (1999):2406.

Markowitz, Morri. "Lead Poisoning." *Pediatrics in Review* 21 (2000):327–335.

John I. Takayama

LEARNING

Learning can occur in a variety of manners. An organism can learn associations between events in their environment (classical or respondent conditioning), learn based upon the reinforcements or punishments that follow their behaviors (operant or instrumental conditioning), and can also learn through observation of those around them (observational learning). Learning principles are of particular importance for school performance.

Classical or Respondent Conditioning

In the early twentieth century, Ivan Pavlov, a Russian scientist, unwittingly stumbled upon an important discovery for the field of behavioral psychology. While studying digestion in dogs, he discovered that after being fed a few times, the animals would salivate before actually receiving food. The dogs were associating external cues such as the sound of the food cabinet being opened with being fed, so they would salivate upon hearing these sounds before they saw the food.

This phenomenon is called classical conditioning or respondent conditioning. Pavlov found that by pairing a previously neutral stimulus, such as the sound of a cabinet being opened, with a stimulus that generates an automatic response, such as presenting meat, which automatically causes dogs to salivate, a dog will come to associate the neutral stimulus with the automatic response. After many pairings of the neutral stimulus (sound) with the automatic stimulus (meat), the response to the neutral stimulus, without the presence of the automatic or unconditional stimulus, produced salivation on its own. So, eventually, just hearing the cabinet being opened was sufficient for Pavlov's dogs to begin salivating.

Under natural circumstances, food causes a dog to salivate. This response is not learned or conditioned so the food is called an unconditioned stimulus while salivation is called an unconditioned response because it occurs without any prior conditioning or learning. After multiple pairings of the sound with food, however, the sound alone would cause the dogs to salivate. The sound has now become a conditioned stimulus and the salivation is the conditioned response because the dogs have been conditioned to salivate to the sound.

Pavlov later found that he did not even need to pair the conditioned stimulus (sound) directly with the unconditioned stimulus (food) in order to cause a conditioned response. He found that if he first conditioned the dogs to salivate at the sound, and then paired the sound with a wooden block, the dogs would eventually salivate at the sight of the block alone even though the block itself was never paired with the food. This is called second-order conditioning; a second neutral stimulus is paired with the conditioned stimulus and eventually becomes a conditioned stimulus as well.

In the 1920s John Watson, an American psychologist, applied the principles of classical conditioning to human beings. He conducted an experiment on an eleven-month-old baby, "Little Albert," in which a startling noise occurred as Albert was presented with a white rat. Startling noises are unconditionally upsetting to infants, causing them to cry and crawl away, while young children are not afraid of white rats. After multiple pairings of the rat and the startling noise, however, Little Albert developed a fear of the rat, crying and crawling away even if the loud noise did not occur. Watson thus showed that classical conditioning also works with humans and that it works for spontaneous emotional responses as well as physiological ones.

Manipulating Classical Conditioning

Researchers have found many phenomena associated with classical conditioning. In some cases a neutral stimulus very similar to the conditioned stimulus will elicit the conditioned response even if it has never been paired with the unconditioned stimulus before; this phenomenon is known as generalization. An example of generalization in Pavlov's dogs would be the dogs salivating to a sound of a different pitch than the one that was paired with food. Discrimination training can eliminate generalization by presenting the generalized stimulus without the unconditioned stimulus (food).

It is possible to erase the effects of conditioning by presenting the conditioned stimulus without the unconditioned stimulus. In other words, after successfully conditioning a dog to salivate to a sound, experimenters can eliminate the effects of the conditioning by presenting the sound many times without presenting the food. This process is called extinction. After a period following extinction, the original conditioned response might return again; this phenomenon is called spontaneous recovery, and it can be eliminated through a new series of extinction trials.

Classical Conditioning and Psychopathology

Behavioral theorists believe that certain psychological disorders are a result of a form of classical conditioning. Watson's experiment on Little Albert suggests that phobias might be learned through pairing a neutral or harmless stimulus with an unconditionally frightening event, thus causing the person to associate fear with the harmless stimulus. Treatment for phobias involves extinguishing the association between fear and the neutral stimulus through so-called systematic desensitization and flooding.

In systematic desensitization, patients are slowly presented with the feared object in stages, beginning with the least-feared situation and ending with a situation that provokes the most fear. The therapist teaches the patient to remain relaxed as the feared object approaches so eventually the patient associates it not with fear but with calmness and relaxation. One example is the case of Little Albert, in which Watson attempted to extinguish the baby's fear of the white rat by giving him food (a stimulus that elicited pleasure) while showing the white rat. In this case, the white rat ceases to be paired with a fear-inducing stimulus and instead becomes linked to a pleasure-inducing stimulus.

In flooding, the therapist attempts to alter the pair that has been classically conditioned. In this case, however, the patient agrees to be surrounded by the fear-inducing stimulus and not attempt to escape the situation. Flooding functions like extinction because the stimulus is present without the aversive response, so association weakens between the neutral stimulus and the fear response. After a long period, the patient ceases to be afraid of the stimulus.

Thus, classical or respondent conditioning is a purely behavioral type of learning. Animals or people conditioned in this manner do not consciously learn the associations between the stimuli and the responses. Instead, because the pairings occur repeatedly, the conditioned stimulus elicits the conditioned response unconsciously. In some instances, however, these responses are not automatic; instead, certain outcomes will induce the animals or humans to repeat the behavior while other outcomes cause them not to repeat the behavior.

Operant or Instrumental Conditioning

Operant conditioning, also known as instrumental conditioning, is based on the consequences that follow an organism's behavior. Behaviors that are followed by a reward, or reinforcement, usually increase in frequency, while behaviors that are followed by punishments usually decrease in frequency. The context in which the rewards or punishments are received has an effect on how the association between the behavior and the consequence following the behavior are learned. In addition, how often reinforcement follows any particular behavior has an effect on how well the association is learned.

The Effect of Reward or Punishment on Behavior

American psychologist Edward Thorndike's Law of Effect states that depending on the outcome, some responses get weakened while other responses get strengthened, and this process eventually leads to learning. Thorndike noted that when an animal was rewarded for a certain behavior, that behavior became progressively more frequent while behaviors that did not elicit a reward weakened and became sporadic, finally disappearing altogether. In other words, unlike classical conditioning, what follows a behavior or response is what is primarily important.

In his mid-twentieth-century experiments with rats and pigeons, American psychologist B. F. Skinner found that animals use their behaviors to shape their environment, acting on the environment in order to bring about a reward or to avoid a punishment. Skinner called this type of learning operant or instrumental conditioning. A reward or reinforcement is an outcome that increases the likelihood that an animal will repeat the behavior. There are two types of reinforcement: positive and negative. Positive reinforcement is something given that increases the chance that the animal or person will repeat the behavior; for example, smiling or praise whenever a student raises her hand is a form of positive reinforcement if it results in increased hand-raising. Negative reinforcement occurs when something is taken away;

stopping an electric shock to elicit a behavior from a rat is an example, because whatever behavior the rat exhibited to terminate the shock will increase.

A punishment, on the other hand, is an outcome for which the likelihood of a future behavior decreases. For example, spanking or slapping a child is an example of punishment, as is grounding, because all three can be expected to reduce the occurrence of the behavior that preceded them.

There are a number of ways in which someone can manipulate an animal's or a person's behavior using operant or instrumental conditioning. One of these methods is called shaping and involves reinforcing behaviors as they approach the desired goal. Suppose a person wants to train a dog to jump through a hoop. He would first reward the dog for turning toward the hoop, then perhaps for approaching the hoop. Eventually he might reward the dog only for walking through the hoop if it is low to the ground. Finally, he would raise the hoop off the ground and reward the dog only for jumping through the hoop.

The Role of Context

Context is extremely important for operant conditioning to occur. Both animals and people must learn that certain behaviors are appropriate in some contexts but not in others. For instance, a young child might learn that it is acceptable to scribble with a crayon on paper but not on the wall. Similarly, Skinner found that animals can discriminate between different stimuli in order to receive a reward. A pigeon can discriminate between two different colored lights and thereby learn that if it pecks a lever when a green light is on it will receive food, but if it pecks when the red light is on it will not receive food.

What is more, animals can discriminate between different behaviors elicited by different contexts. For example, a rat can learn that turning around clockwise in its cage will result in getting food but that in a different cage turning counterclockwise will bring a reward. Animals will also generalize to other stimuli, performing the desired behavior when a slightly different stimulus occurs. For instance, a pigeon that knows that pecking a lever when a green light is on will bring food might also peck the lever when a different-colored light is on. Both generalization and discrimination help animals and people learn which behaviors are appropriate in which contexts.

Reinforcement Schedules

The rate of reinforcement can also affect the frequency of the desired response. Delaying reinforcement slows learning down, although research shows that humans can learn from delayed reinforcements, and that it is often difficult to forfeit immediately positive outcomes in order to avoid adverse ones later.

The schedule of reinforcement also plays a critical role in affecting response rates. There are two types of reinforcement schedules: interval schedules and ratio schedules. Interval schedules are reinforcement schedules in which rewards are given after a certain period of time. Ratio schedules are schedules in which rewards are given after a specific number of correct responses. As seen below, the time interval or response ratio can either be fixed or variable.

The schedule that elicits the most rapid frequency of responses is the fixed ratio schedule. In this case, the animal knows it will receive a reward after a fixed number of responses so it produces that number as quickly and frequently as possible. This phenomenon also occurs with people; if craftspeople are paid for each object they make, they will try to produce as many objects as possible in order to maximize their rewards.

Generating nearly as rapid a frequency of responses as the fixed ratio schedule is the variable ratio schedule. In this case, the number of responses needed to produce a reward varies so the animal or person will emit the desired behavior frequently on the chance that the next time might bring the reward. Lotteries and slot machines function on a variable ratio schedule, thus inducing people to want to play again.

Interval schedules tend to produce slower frequencies of response. A fixed interval schedule will produce fewer responses early in the interval with an increase as the time for the reward approaches. One example in human behavior is the passing of bills in Congress. As elections approach, the number of bills passed increases dramatically, with a swift decline after the election. A variable interval schedule, on the other hand, produces a slow but steady frequency of response; for instance, a teacher giving "pop" quizzes at irregular intervals encourages her students to maintain a consistent level of studying throughout the semester.

Although classical or respondent conditioning involves automatic responses to behavior, operant or instrumental conditioning is a result of the decision to produce a certain behavior in order to receive a reward or avoid a punishment.

Observational Learning

Learning does not always occur directly as a result of punishment or reinforcement, but can occur through the process of watching others. Children can learn from observing rewards or punishments given to someone else, and do not need to be the recipients themselves. This form of social learning is called observational learning. The terms "imitation" and "modeling" are often used interchangeably and are types of observational learning.

Imitation and Modeling

Imitation may be a powerful means through which infants can learn from those around them. Andrew Meltzoff and M. Keith Moore's classic 1977 study illustrated imitation of tongue protrusion, lip protrusion, and mouth opening by two- to three-week-old infants. For this behavior to occur, infants must match what they see the model doing with what they feel themselves doing, and it has been demonstrated in infants three days old. Thus, it seems that imitation occurs from birth onward and that infants may learn many new behaviors in this way.

As children grow, they imitate more complex behaviors than simple mouth movements. A researcher who has performed much research in the area of observational learning in children is Albert Bandura. His best-known study of modeling in children involved aggressive behavior. While children observed, models either physically attacked or nonaggressively interacted with a large inflatable doll called Bobo. The children were then given the opportunity to play with Bobo. Those who had observed the aggressive model displayed twice as much aggressive behavior as those who had observed the nonaggressive model. In addition, the children who had observed the aggressive model performed aggressive acts that had not been modeled, illustrating that generalization had occurred. These findings indicate that children can indeed learn what behavior is appropriate in a given situation through observation alone.

Observational learning can have other effects as well. The opposite of the Bobo findings can occur in which inhibition of a class of behaviors becomes less likely after observation. Often inhibition occurs after observing another person being punished for performing a certain type of behavior, such as aggressive behavior in general.

Through his studies on observational learning, Bandura developed his cognitive theory of observational learning. He posited that four mental processes need to be present in order for observational learning to occur. One mental process is that of attention; that is, a child must find the model interesting enough to hold the child's attention. The child must also be able to hold the model's behavior in memory in order to imitate the behavior later. In addition, without sufficient motor control, the child would be unable to mimic the model's behaviors. Finally, motivation is integral in that the child must have a reason to perform the behavior that was modeled.

Bandura's cognitive theory of observational learning is helpful for understanding why children

Developmental toys and games such as "Memory" are invaluable to a child's learning process. (Robert J. Huffman, Field Mark Publications)

imitate behavior in some cases and not others. In particular, children are more likely to imitate a model when they see the model's behavior rewarded rather than punished. In addition, self-efficacy beliefs play into a child's choice of imitation. If the child believes that she does not have the talent necessary to imitate a particular behavior, she will not attempt to do so. Thus it seems that both cognitive and social factors come into play in observational learning, and that is why Bandura's theory is also called a social cognitive theory of learning.

Observational Learning in Practice

Observational learning can be seen in practice in many settings. First, it seems that children can imitate behaviors they have seen on television—behaviors that are often aggressive behaviors. There are many factors that determine whether a child will imitate an aggressive model on television. The observing child must first identify with the model in order to consider imitating the model. The consequences of the aggres-

sive behavior are also a factor. In addition, if the child is old enough to realize that aggression on television does not represent reality, he is less likely to imitate the behavior. Finally, what the parents tell the child about the aggressive behavior he is viewing also plays a role in whether or not the child will imitate the behavior.

Observational learning is also important in the learning of sex roles. It has been found that children can learn appropriate behaviors for each sex by reading, watching television, or observing real models.

Another type of behavior that has been found to be learned through observation is prosocial behavior (positive or helpful behavior). Children increase their giving and helping behaviors after observing a peer or adult doing the same and even after viewing such behavior on a television program. In addition, it has been found that modeling of prosocial behavior results in more prosocial behavior in the learner than simple statements that prosocial behavior is good.

Observational learning is often used in therapeutic settings. People can be trained in assertiveness through observation of an assertive therapist. In addition, people can learn to overcome phobias through observation of others interacting calmly with the object of their fear.

In sum, imitation and modeling, both of which are forms of observational learning, begin with simple behaviors in infancy and continue on to complex behaviors in childhood and adulthood. Bandura has theorized that cognitive and social factors interact in observational learning and affect whether an observer will imitate a behavior or not. Observational learning occurs in many settings and has also been used in therapy.

Relationship of Learning to School Performance

The concepts discussed above (such as conditioning, imitation, and modeling) would seem to have little role to play in modern education. Teachers, especially in the later grades, favor so-called constructive approaches to learning, which means that they arrange the environment in such a way that children are allowed to discover relationships on their own. This approach stands in contrast to the concept of conditioning, where the child can be seen as a passive receptacle who absorbs what the teacher presents, without regard to how it fits with the child's preexisting knowledge. Educators continue to debate these two extreme approaches, and some forms of conditioning and imitation, such as drilling multiplication tables, continue to be popular in U.S. schools. Furthermore, in classes for children with special needs, it is still common for classical and operant principles to shape children's behavior. In such classrooms, teachers award points for acceptable behavior and take away points for unacceptable behavior. Children can redeem these points for perks such as extra recess. So, notwithstanding the debate between learning theorists and constructivists, learning principles are still common in classrooms although the application is sometimes not a conscious result of the teacher's planning.

See also: MEMORY

Bibliography

Bandura, Albert. *Social Foundations of Thought and Action: A Social Cognitive Theory.* Englewood Cliffs, NJ: Prentice-Hall, 1986.

Bandura, Albert, Dorothea Ross, and Sheila Ross. "Transmission of Aggression through Imitation of Aggressive Models." *Journal of Abnormal and Social Psychology* 63 (1961):575–582.

Domjan, Michael. *The Essentials of Conditioning and Learning.* Pacific Grove, CA: Brooks/Cole, 1996.

Freidrich, Lynette, and Aletha Stein. "Prosocial Television and Young Children: The Effects of Verbal Labeling and Role Playing on Learning and Behavior." *Child Development* 16 (1975):27–36.

Hay, Dale, and Patricia Murray. "Giving and Requesting: Social Facilitation of Infants' Offers to Adults." *Infant Behavior and Development* 5 (1982):301–310.

Meltzoff, Andrew, and M. Keith Moore. "Newborn Infants Imitate Adult Facial Gestures." *Child Development* 54 (1983):702–709.

Parke, Ross, and Ronald Slaby. "The Development of Aggression." In Paul Mussen ed., *Handbook of Child Psychology*, 4th edition. New York: Wiley, 1983.

Schiamberg, Lawrence. *Child and Adolescent Development.* New York: Macmillan, 1988.

Spiegler, Michael D., and David Guevremont. *Contemporary Behavior Therapy*, 4th edition. Elmsford, NY: Pergamon, 1990.

Stephen J. Ceci
Rebecca L. Fraser
Maria Gabriela Pereira

LEARNING DISABILITIES

It is estimated that 5 percent to 10 percent of school-age children and adolescents have learning disabilities (LDs), with some estimates approaching 17 percent. LDs fall on a continuum and range in severity from subtle to marked impairment. A substantial number of learning-disabled students receive special education services. In 1975 the U.S. Congress enacted the Education for All Handicapped Children Act (PL 94-142), which was an educational bill of rights assuring children with disabilities a free and appropriate education in the least restrictive environment. Disabilities that qualified for services under this law included mental retardation, hearing deficiencies, speech and language impairments, visual impairments, emotional disturbances, orthopedic impairments, a variety of medical conditions (categorized as "other health-impaired"), and specific learning disabilities. This law was reauthorized under the Education of the Handicapped Act amendments and, subsequently, the Individuals with Disabilities Education Act (IDEA). Children with learning disabilities also may receive services under Section 504 of the Rehabilitation Act of 1973 (a civil rights law that protects individuals with disabilities from discrimination by recipients of federal financial assistance). The latter law is designed to provide modifications and accommodations to minimize the negative effect on "major life activities"; all IDEA children qualify under Section 504, but the reverse is not true. As many as 50 percent of children with LDs have concomitant disorders such as attention deficit hyperactivity disorder, anxiety problems, school refusal, depression, Tourette's syndrome, or behavior problems. It is estimated that 35 percent to 50 percent of students seen in mental health clinics have language and/or learning disorders.

Definition of Learning Disabilities

Despite federal regulations, the definition of learning disabilities is controversial. The U.S. government defines a specific learning disability as a disorder in one or more of the basic psychological processes involved in understanding or use of spoken or written language, which may be manifest as an inability to listen, think, speak, read, write, spell, or do mathematic calculations. While the definition could include the conditions of perceptual handicaps, brain injury, minimal brain dysfunction, dyslexia, and developmental aphasia, it is not applicable to students whose learning problems are the result of visual, hearing, or motor handicaps, mental retardation, emotional disturbance, or environmental/cultural disadvantage. The major premise is that a significant discrepancy exists between the child's potential and her actual level of academic or language skills.

Each state, however, may determine cutoffs for discrepancies or definitions of processing disorders, leading to variability among states and even differences among districts within a given state. The definition and diagnosis of an LD vary, depending on whether the purpose is to qualify for services or to clinically identify the reason for a child's poor academic performance. In the former, measurement of intelligence and levels of achievement is employed; in the latter, administration of IQ and achievement is extended to include evaluation of attention, memory, and neuropsychological function. Moreover, the age of identification varies, depending on the type of LD; some may not be apparent early because academic skills in areas affected by the LD have not yet been challenged.

The psychiatric definition of LDs (as found in the American Psychiatric Association's *Diagnostic and Statistical Manual of Mental Disorders: DSM-IV*) differs considerably from both federal and state classification systems, adding further to the ambiguity. Learning disabilities are presumed to be due to central nervous system dysfunction, and occur across the lifespan. They reportedly occur more in males, although research in the late 1990s by Sally Shaywitz has disputed this contention.

The Discrepancy Issue

The "discrepancy issue" has been established as the primary criterion for identifying children with LDs. Unfortunately, discrepancy formulae are controversial, potentially inaccurate, and inappropriate for detecting cognitive deficits. There are three types of discrepancy formulae.

With an aptitude-achievement discrepancy, a disparity exists between a child's intellectual ability (as measured by an intelligence test) and his actual level of academic achievement (measured by an achievement test). Certain LDs (e.g., a short-term memory problem or central processing dysfunction), however, may also affect a child's performance on IQ tests, thereby reducing the discrepancy between aptitude and achievement. This discrepancy model is useful from third grade onward, and certain disabilities (such as fine motor dyspraxia, retrieval memory dysfunction, and organization problems) often are not detected. Children with the most severe LDs frequently have the smallest discrepancy.

An intracognitive discrepancy (a disturbance in basic psychologic processes) occurs in children who have a specific type of cognitive dysfunction such as a deficit in auditory processing, short-term memory, or visual processing. This type of LD is difficult to operationalize, but is useful in identifying preschool and primary-age children who have learning problems.

An intra-achievement discrepancy reflects divergence or inconsistency in educational achievement performances. This could occur between academic areas (such as reading versus mathematics) or within an academic area (such as a marked difference between reading decoding and reading comprehension).

Regression models, which attempt to correct the problems inherent in discrepancy comparisons, are used in many states. Here a statistical relationship between IQ and achievement is considered, allowing for equal probability of identification of an LD across IQ levels, thereby potentially enhancing identification rates. Research in the 1990s, however, failed to demonstrate valid differences on school-related measures between poorly achieving groups of students with an IQ/achievement discrepancy and those with poor school performance and no discrepancy.

Learning Disability Subtypes

There are many different subtypes of learning disabilities. Byron Rourke, writing in 1993, reported three major groupings: (1) reading/spelling, (2) arithmetic, and (3) reading/spelling/arithmetic. Larry Silver, also writing in 1993, suggested a model that includes input disabilities (visual/perceptual, auditory/perceptual, and sensory integrative), integrative disabilities (sequencing, abstraction, and organization), memory disabilities, and output disabilities (language and motor). Reading/spelling disabilities are by far the most prevalent form, with such disabilities estimated to comprise from 5 percent up to 17 percent of the child and adolescent population. Estimates for the occurrence of disorders of written expression range from 2 percent to 8 percent. Although

Learning disabilities, such as dyslexia, can be caused by premature birth or asphyxia at a younger age. In other cases, the direct cause of a learning disability is not known. (Ellen B. Senisi/Photo Researchers, Inc.)

the prevalence of arithmetic LDs ranges from 1 percent to 6 percent, it is not clear whether weak mathematics performance is due to the quality of instruction or an actual LD.

Nonverbal LDs are often overlooked, occur less frequently than reading disorders, and are characterized by problems in arithmetic computation, graphomotor skills, reading comprehension, math reasoning, science, complex concept formation, visual memory, and social-behavioral skills; these are often found in children with white-matter disorders, and are assumed to be more right-hemisphere-based. As of the late 1990s, a classification schema (based on reading disability/dyslexia research) was applied to all achievement domains included in federal and state definitions of LD. Three major types of LDs were identified: specific language impairment, specific reading disability/dyslexia, and specific math disability.

The area of greatest knowledge is reading disorders. These fall into two main groupings: phonological (dysphonetic) and orthographic (dyseidetic). The former is more prevalent and is characterized by deficits in decoding and word analysis, with guesses made based on the initial letter of the word and misspellings being phonetically inaccurate. Shaywitz wrote in 1998 that a deficit in basic phonemic awareness (inability to segment phonemes [the smallest unit of sound] into phonological units) is the underlying cause in virtually all cases of dyslexia. The ortho-

graphic reading disability subtype involves an inability to develop a memory for the whole word (gestalt), with visuospatial reversals occurring (e.g., "was" read as "saw") and misspellings being phonetically accurate. There also is a mixed reading disorder, which consists of characteristics found in both types of deficit. The major new finding is that reading disabilities are more strongly associated with auditory rather than visual deficits.

Causes and Diagnosis

With regard to causes, research extends to family, genetic, and neuroanatomic bases, with most work being done in language and reading disabilities. There appears to be heritability in language and reading LDs, with similar LDs being found in 35 percent to 45 percent of first-degree relatives. Also, identical twins are more likely to have similar LDs than fraternal twins. Chromosomes 6 and 15 have been implicated frequently as possible genetic causes of LDs. Neuroimaging techniques, such as functional magnetic resonance imaging, have documented differences among dyslexic and nonreading-disabled individuals. Studies have found that in individuals with dyslexia, certain areas of the brain are different than in individuals without dyslexia. Nonetheless, there are no neuroanatomic or neuroelectric diagnostic tests that identify LDs in the brain. Although LDs are found more frequently in children subject to brain insult (such as premature birth and asphyxia), many children display LDs without any identifiable cause.

Outcomes

Learning disabilities do not disappear; rather, students compensate and learn bypass strategies, allowing for academic progress. The long-term outcome is variable, depending on the type of LD, degree of impairment, intelligence, environment, type of interventions provided, and presence of other disorders. For example, in the case of dyslexia, students often show improvement, but the underlying deficits in phonemic awareness skills prevent the individual from reading in an "automatic," appropriately speeded fashion.

Conclusions

To adequately understand an LD, the following areas must be considered: educational achievement, educational opportunity, cognitive functioning, potential emotional issues, peripheral sensory and neurological function (e.g., vision, hearing), family history, academic history, and age of onset of the LD. More specific tests need to be employed as necessary. Only in this way can a proper diagnosis and effective intervention plan be made.

See also: DEVELOPMENTAL DISABILITIES

Bibliography

American Academy of Child and Adolescent Psychiatry. "Practice Parameters for the Assessment and Treatment of Children and Adolescents with Language and Learning Disorders." *Journal of the Academy of Child and Adolescent Psychiatry* 37 (1998 supplement):46S–62S.

American Psychiatric Association. *The Diagnostic and Statistical Manual of Mental Disorders: DSM-IV.* Washington, DC: American Psychiatric Association, 1994.

Aylward, Glen. *Practitioner's Guide to Developmental and Psychological Testing.* New York: Plenum Medical, 1994.

Kavale, K. A., and S. R. Forness. *The Nature of Learning Disabilities: Critical Elements of Diagnosis and Classification.* Mahwah, NJ: Erlbaum, 1995.

Mather, Nancy, and William Healy. "Deposing Aptitude-Achievement Discrepancy as the Imperial Criterion for Learning Disabilities." *Learning Disabilities* 1 (1989):40–48.

Morris, Robin, Karla Stuebing, Jack Fletcher, Sally Shawitz, G. Reid Lyon, Donald Shankweiler, Leonard Katz, David Francis, and Bennett Shaywitz. "Subtypes of Reading Disability Variability around a Phonological Core." *Journal of Educational Psychology* 90 (1998):347–373.

Padget, S. Y. "Lessons from Research on Dyslexia: Implications for a Classification System for Learning Disabilities." *Learning Disability Quarterly* 21 (1998):167–178.

Pennington, Bruce. "Genetics of Learning Disabilities." *Journal of Child Neurology* 10 (1995 supplement):S69–S77.

Rourke, Byron. "Arithmetic Disabilities, Specific and Otherwise." *Journal of Learning Disabilities* 26 (1993):214–226.

Rourke, Byron. *Syndrome of Nonverbal Learning Disabilities.* New York: Guilford Press, 1995.

Shaywitz, Sally. "Dyslexia." *Scientific American* 275 (1996):98–104.

Shaywitz, Sally. "Dyslexia." *New England Journal of Medicine* 338 (1998):307–312.

Silver, Larry. "Introduction and Overview to the Clinical Concepts of Learning Disabilities." *Child and Adolescent Psychiatric Clinics of North America* 2 (1993):181–192.

Tomblin, J. B., and P. R. Buckwalter. "Studies of the Genetics of Specific Language Impairment." In R. Watkins and M. Rice eds., *Specific Language Impairments in Children.* Baltimore: Paul H. Brookes, 1994.

Glen P. Aylward

LOCKE, JOHN (1632–1704)

Born in Somerset, England, John Locke was a noted philosopher—the first of the British empiricists—political adviser, and physician. As a student at the Westminster School, Locke endured the typical mid-seventeenth-century educational regimen reserved for adolescent boys: strict adherence to rules, severe punishments, and rote memorization of both the principles of grammar and large selections of Latin and Greek verse. Undoubtedly, Locke's dissatisfaction with his education at Westminster was responsible, to a significant extent, for both his stalwart support of home schooling—the preferred method at the time for educating girls—and private tutors, as well as his forceful criticism of institutional education.

But much of Locke's view on education and the proper development of children—set forth in a series of letters to a cousin and later published as *Some Thoughts on Education*—also reflected his philosophical writings on the nature of knowledge and human understanding (though scholars differ on the precise relationship between these two bodies of work). In *An Essay Concerning Human Understanding*, Locke argued that the human mind at birth is a tabula rasa (blank slate), entirely devoid of any ideas or other mental content. All the content of the active human mind is derived from the data of sense experience, which is then transformed into increasingly complex ideas through reflection and reason. Crucial to Locke's philosophical view, and of great significance for his thoughts on education, was his emphasis on the role of experience in the acquisition of knowledge. Indeed, in the first paragraphs of *Some Thoughts on Education*, Locke contended that the depth and breadth of one's knowledge, both moral and practical, is overwhelmingly a product of education and experience, as opposed to natural intellect. Locke did recognize that children are born with differing aptitudes and inclinations, and he believed that, for the most part, these natural elements could not be significantly altered. It is for this reason, Locke argued, that curricula must be designed that fit the parameters of a child's natural genius. But without experience these aptitudes cannot be detected nor, of course, developed. And children are best able to develop their

John Locke (1632–1704) was a proponent of home schooling and private tutoring rather than the strict regimen that most adolescent boys were required to follow. (Bettmann/Corbis)

intellectual and social skills, according to Locke, through various kinds of play and the practicing of certain skills, rather than through rote memorization of assorted rules.

The interest in Locke's writings on education for his successors is clear: By the end of the nineteenth century *Some Thoughts on Education* had been through literally dozens of English editions, as well as several editions in French, German, and Italian.

Bibliography

Cleverly, John, and D. C. Phillips. *Visions of Childhood: Influential Models from Locke to Spock.* New York: Teachers College Press, 1986.

Simons, M. "Why Can't a Man Be More Like a Woman? (A Note on John Locke's Educational Thought)." *Educational Theory* 40 (1990):135–145.

Publications by Locke

The Works of John Locke: Some Thoughts on Education. London: Printed for Thomas Tegg, 1823.

Locke, John. *An Essay Concerning Human Understanding*, edited by Peter H. Nidditch. Oxford: Oxford University Press, 1975.

Richard M. Buck

M

MAINSTREAMING

Mainstreaming is the original term used for the requirement under the Individuals with Disabilities Education Act (IDEA) that children with disabilities be educated in the least restrictive environment (LRE). Under IDEA, states must assure that, to the maximum extent appropriate, children ages three to twenty-one who have disabilities have access to the general education curriculum and are educated with children without disabilities (for infants and toddlers, early intervention services must be provided in natural environments where age peers are typically found).

The term "mainstreaming" commonly refers to the integration of a child with a disability in regular education settings for part of the school day. As legal and social interpretations of IDEA have evolved, the term "mainstreaming" has been superceded by the term "inclusion," reflecting a new understanding of LRE that presumes full participation of children with disabilities in regular education settings while ensuring continuum of participation options based on a child's educational and social needs.

See also: DEVELOPMENTAL DISABILITIES; MENTAL RETARDATION

Bibliography

Accardo, Pasquale J., and Barbara Y. Whitman, eds. *Dictionary of Developmental Disabilities Terminology.* Baltimore: Paul H. Brookes, 1996.

Erwin, Elizabeth J., ed. "The Promise and Challenge of Supporting All Children in Natural Environments." *Putting Children First: Visions for a Brighter Future for Young Children and Their Families.* Baltimore: Paul H. Brookes, 1996.

Hocutt, Anne M. "Effectiveness of Special Education: Is Placement a Critical Factor?" *The Future of Children* vol. 6, no. 1 (1996):77–99.

Rogers, Joy. "The Inclusion Revolution." In Phi Delta Kappa Center for Evaluation, Development, and Research [web site]. *Research Bulletin* no. 11, May 1993. Available from http://www.pdkintl.org/edres/resbul11.htm: INTERNET.

Turnbull, H. Rutherford III, and Ann P. Turnbull. "Least Restrictive Appropriate Educational Placement." In *Free Appropriate Public Education: The Law and Children with Disabilities.* Denver: Love Publishing, 2000.

Donna M. Noyes-Grosser

MALNUTRITION

Malnutrition refers to any condition caused by excess or deficient food energy, protein, or nutrient intake, or by an imbalance of nutrients. Nutrient or energy deficiencies are classified as forms of undernutrition; nutrient or energy excesses are forms of overnutrition. Malnutrition can take two forms: primary, due to a lack, excess, or imbalance of a nutrient or nutrients in the diet; and secondary, which occurs as a result of a disease or illness that affects dietary intake, nutrient needs, or metabolism. Historically, the most common nutrient-related problems among U.S. children are obesity, iron-deficiency anemia, and dental cavities. Protein-energy malnutrition (PEM), a problem in developing countries, is not common in the United States but can occur secondary to trauma, disease, psychological problems, or medical treatment. PEM occurs in two forms: marasmus, in which the deficiency is primarily in energy-providing foods, and kwashiorkor, characterized by inadequate protein intake.

Inadequate maternal nutrition can affect fetal development. Although the body reserves of the mother are used to meet fetal growth needs, they cannot always insulate the fetus from dietary deficiencies. Inadequate nutrition can lead to a decrease in actual cell number and in cell size or growth. Cell number increases early in pregnancy; in the third trimester, size or growth of cells increases rapidly, along with number, and nutrient requirements are high. This active process continues after birth until one to two years of age. Restrictions that lead to decreased cell size can be reversed, but when the increase in cell number stops, it may be permanent.

See also: MARASMUS; MATURATION; MOTOR DEVELOPMENT; NUTRITION

Bibliography

Boyle, Marie A., and Diane H. Morris. *Community Nutrition in Action: An Entrepreneurial Approach.* St. Paul, MN: West Publishing, 1994.

Mahan, L. Kathleen, and Sylvia Escott-Stump. *Krause's Food, Nutrition, and Diet Therapy,* 9th edition. Orlando, FL: Saunders, 1996.

Worthington-Roberts, Bonnie, and Sue Rodwell Williams. *Nutrition throughout the Life Cycle.* New York: McGraw Hill, 2000.

Nicole B. Knee
Janice Dodds

MARASMUS

Marasmus is a form of emaciation and wasting in an infant due to protein-energy malnutrition. It is characterized by growth retardation in weight more than height so that the head appears quite large relative to the body. There is a progressive wasting of subcutaneous fat and muscle so that the skin appears loose. Severe prolonged marasmus may result in permanent retardation. Marasmus is common in Third World countries in situations with poor access to protein-rich food sources or where unsanitary water is associated with severe infant diarrhea and a corollary inability to absorb nutrients. The term "marasmus" is also used as roughly equivalent to "anaclitic depression," a term coined by René Spitz to refer to children who suffer from the early loss of a mother without a suitable substitute. Thus, marasmus has come to be associated with parental abuse or neglect that results in a failure to thrive. In some cases parents are uninformed regarding nutritional or emotional needs of children or are unable to provide sustenance because of poverty. In other cases such failure to thrive stems from emotional deprivation as a result of parental withdrawal, rejection, or hostility. It is hypothesized

that the emotional experiences of the child lead to shifts in the production of growth hormone.

See also: FAILURE TO THRIVE

Bibliography

Bennett, S. "Failure to Thrive." *Paediatrics and Child Health* 1 (1996):206–210.

Frongillo, Edward A. *Protein-Energy Malnutrition.* Vevey, Switzerland: Nestle Nutrition, 1999.

Giardino, Angelo P. *A Practical Guide to the Evaluation of Child Abuse and Neglect.* Thousand Oaks, CA: Sage, 1997.

Olson, Roberta A. *The Sourcebook of Pediatric Psychology.* Boston: Allyn and Bacon, 1994.

Larry P. Nucci

MASLOW, ABRAHAM H. (1908–1970)

Abraham Maslow is best known for his work on a theory of motivation and for his enormous impact on humanistic psychology, also known as the third force in psychology. Born April 1, 1908, in Brooklyn, New York, to Russian-Jewish immigrant parents, Maslow was the oldest of seven children. He attended City College of New York and Cornell University before transferring, in 1928, to the University of Wisconsin. During this time he married Bertha Goodman, with whom he would have two daughters. At the University of Wisconsin Maslow studied primate behavior, working with Harry Harlow, the experimental psychologist who became famous for his work with attachment behavior and baby rhesus monkeys. Maslow received his A.B. in 1930, his M.A. in 1931, and his Ph.D. in 1934. He worked as a Carnegie Fellow at Columbia University before accepting a position at Brooklyn College, where he taught and researched from 1937 to 1951. In 1951 he accepted a position at Brandeis University, where he remained until 1969. He served as president of the American Psychological Association from 1967 to 1968. After leaving Brandeis, Maslow worked as Resident Fellow at the W. Price Laughlin Charitable Foundation in California until his death of a massive heart attack on June 8, 1970.

Maslow is best known for his work in the area of motivation. Overall, he wanted to emphasize what was positive about humans, rather than focusing on the negative or deficient. Maslow used a holistic approach, which emphasizes the individual as a complete being rather than a collection of separate, and possibly disparate, components. He developed a theory of motivation that placed human needs into a hierarchy. This hierarchy of needs theory posits that every person must fulfill the most basic needs first, with other needs being addressed after lower needs are satisfied. Physiological needs such as oxygen and food are at the base of the hierarchy, followed by safe-

Abraham H. Maslow used a holistic approach in developing his theory of motivation. (UPI/Corbis Bettmann)

ty, belongingness, and esteem. Only when these needs have been satisfied can humans fully realize their potential. In realizing their potential and achieving everything they are capable of, an individual becomes a self-actualized person.

Among Maslow's better known works are *Motivation and Personality* and *Toward a Psychology of Being*. Maslow also published over a hundred articles and book chapters on a variety of topics.

See also: THEORIES OF DEVELOPMENT

Bibliography

Hoffman, E. *The Right to Be Human: A Biography of Abraham Maslow*. Los Angeles: Tarcher, 1988.

Publications by Maslow

"A Theory of Human Motivation." *Psychological Review* 50 (1943):370–396.

Toward a Psychology of Being, 2nd edition. New York: VanNostrand/Reinhold, 1968.

Motivation and Personality, 3rd edition, edited by Robert Frager, James Fadiman, and Ruth Cox. New York: Harper and Row, 1987.

Jennifer S. Feenstra

MATERNAL AGE

Extremes of maternal age are associated with adverse outcomes in pregnancy. Age at the time of delivery of less than sixteen years or greater than thirty-five years

meets the criteria for this definition. Young women have a higher incidence of premature delivery, high blood pressure, and small infants. In women over age thirty-five, chronic diseases such as diabetes and high blood pressure become more common. In addition, the aging of the developing eggs in the ovary is associated with an increased risk for spontaneous miscarriage and the birth of infants with chromosomal abnormalities such as Down syndrome and Edwards syndrome. As an example, at age thirty-five a woman's risk for the delivery of an infant with Down syndrome is 1 in 378; by age forty-five this risk has increased dramatically to 1 in 30. Tests that sample the amniotic fluid around the developing fetus (amniocentesis) or sample a small part of the placenta (chorionic villus biopsy) can be undertaken to determine if the chromosomal makeup of the fetus is normal.

See also: BIRTH; BIRTH DEFECTS; MILESTONES OF DEVELOPMENT; PREGNANCY

Bibliography

Bobrowski, Renee, and Sidney Bottoms. "Underappreciated Risks of the Elderly Multipara." *American Journal of Obstetrics and Gynecology* 172 (1995):1764–1767.

Hook, Ernest, Philip Cross, and Dina Schreinemachers. "Chromosomal Abnormality Rates at Amniocentesis and Live-Born Infants." *Journal of the American Medical Association* 249 (1983):2034–2038.

Satin, Andrew, Kenneth Leveno, Lynne Sherman, Nancy Reedy, Thomas Lowe, and Donald McIntire. "Maternal Youth and Pregnancy Outcomes: Middle School versus High School Age

Groups Compared to Women beyond the Teen Years." *American Journal of Obstetrics and Gynecology* 171 (1994):184–187.

Kenneth J. Moise Jr.

MATERNAL HEALTH

A comprehensive definition of maternal, or reproductive, health was one of many important contributions of the landmark United Nations International Conference on Population and Development (ICPD) held in September 1994 in Cairo, Egypt. The ICPD definition stated that "Reproductive health is a state of complete physical, mental, and social well-being and not merely the absence of disease or infirmity, in all matters relating to the reproductive system and to its functions and processes. Reproductive health therefore implies that people are able to have a satisfying and safe sex life and that they have the capability to reproduce and the freedom to decide if, when and how often to do so."

Measuring Maternal Health

The most common indicator of maternal health used internationally is maternal mortality, usually measured as the ratio of deaths to women while pregnant or within forty-two days of termination of pregnancy per 100,000 live births. Deaths are usually included only if the cause is related to or aggravated by the pregnancy or its management. Maternal mortality is a rare event in the United States. However, the 1998 ratio of 7.1 deaths per 100,000 live births was higher than the ratio in many other industrialized countries. No progress was observed in the United States in the 1990s, and disturbing differences persist in the incidence of maternal death among ethnic groups. African-American women have three times the risk of maternal mortality compared with white women, and the risk of death for Latinas or Hispanic women also appears to be significantly higher than the risk for white women.

In order to prevent maternal mortality and eliminate disparities, researchers must determine the fundamental causes of pregnancy-related deaths. Defining and measuring maternal morbidity is also critical because illnesses and complications of pregnancy are far more common than maternal deaths. While it is not easy to obtain an accurate count of all of the deaths that might be precipitated by pregnancy or childbirth, the legal requirement for registering deaths and filing death certificates assures a fairly high level of completeness. Measuring the morbidity that accompanies women's reproductive lives is much more difficult.

The U.S. Department of Health and Human Services, Office of Disease Prevention and Health Pro-

motion, developed an initiative called Healthy People, which establishes new health objectives for the nation every ten years. The overall goals of Healthy People 2010 are to increase longevity and quality of life and to eliminate health disparities in the population. One aim is to reduce maternal mortality by more than 50 percent, to an overall ratio of 3.3 deaths per 100,000 live births by the year 2010.

A similar objective for maternal morbidity cannot be set because severe complications throughout pregnancy are too difficult to measure reliably with existing data. Instead, Healthy People 2010 focused its attention on problems that occur during labor and delivery. Most women in the U.S. deliver their babies in hospitals with trained providers who record any complications to the mother and the newborn. In 1998, hospital discharge data indicated that women experienced complications of labor and delivery in nearly one-third (31.2) of every 100 deliveries. The objective for improving this rate is a target of twenty-four complications per 100 deliveries by the year 2010.

Two other maternal health outcomes were targeted for improvement in the Healthy People 2010 objectives, even though data that is gathered will not facilitate adequate monitoring of these events. The first is ectopic pregnancies, sometimes called tubal pregnancies, that result from the implantation and development of a fertilized egg in a woman's fallopian tubes or elsewhere outside the uterus. This condition, which can pose extreme danger to women and sometimes causes death if not detected and treated in a timely fashion, appears to be on the rise in the U.S. The second concern is postpartum complications, including depression as well as physical problems such as hemorrhage and infection.

Since reproductive health, according to the ICPD definition, encompasses positive aspects beyond the absence of disease or disability, many other indicators would be required to monitor maternal wellness. For example, women's psychological health, quality of life, level of satisfaction in intimate relationships, and overall physical condition would need to be measured. Indicators that track threats to women's reproductive health, such as domestic violence, toxic environmental exposures, and hazards in the workplace, should also be taken into account. Accessibility and quality of gynecology, family planning, abortion, preconception, prenatal delivery, and postpartum services are important issues to monitor. Since most women spend many more years raising children than they do bearing children, maternal well-being should encompass the experience of childrearing as well as women's development throughout the life cycle. Older women are often ignored in the realm of reproductive health, although menopause has become a topic of public discussion and reproductive cancers are receiving new attention.

Maternal Health and Child Health

Common sense as well as scientific evidence tells us that the health of women and the health of their children are closely related. Persistent infant health problems such as low birth weight and prematurity have been linked to maternal conditions that precede pregnancy, and may even be traced through previous generations in a woman's family. A woman in poor health who wants to become pregnant is more likely to experience infertility. Once she does become pregnant, she is less likely to have a healthy infant and less able to marshal the consistent energy and resources needed to promote childhood health. Women and their children share the same social and economic environments; poverty, inadequate housing, and unsafe neighborhoods create multiple stresses and potentially harmful exposures for women, children, and all family members.

In the late twentieth century there was an increase in public awareness and concern about infant health problems stemming from pregnant women's use of substances, including tobacco, alcohol, and illicit drugs, and from sexually transmitted diseases, including HIV and AIDS. Domestic violence is also understood as a public health problem affecting pregnant women and mothers. These behaviors and risks may be found throughout the entire population, but the consequences are often worse for disadvantaged women who have less access to health care and other support services.

Government programs that subsidize health care for children sometimes support women only while they are pregnant or recovering from childbirth. Gender discrimination or lack of support for women, as well as economic and racial inequities, is harmful to the health of families. Knowledge and understanding of the reciprocal needs of women, men, and children are needed to promote the physical and mental health of families and larger communities.

The developing fetus is most vulnerable to many influences soon after conception when women are often unaware of their pregnancies, especially in the case of an unintended pregnancy. Nearly half (49%) of pregnancies to women in the U.S. are not the result of conscious planning at the time of conception. Thus, healthy fetal development in the first trimester requires health screening and education among sexually active women before they become pregnant. *Preconceptional health care* is a model that provides guidelines for examination, counseling, and treat-

ment of women who may be thinking about getting pregnant. Universal recommendations for all women of childbearing age are likely to reach more potential mothers and may have long-term benefits for the women themselves, regardless of their decisions about childbearing. Examples of such recommendations include smoking cessation, HIV antibody testing, and consumption of vitamins containing folic acid for prevention of birth defects. Utilization of family planning services and routine preventive health care will help women plan the timing of wanted pregnancies and maintain their own health, thus helping them to improve the health of their children.

Prenatal care provides an important opportunity to address the unmet health needs of pregnant women. Although interventions during pregnancy are too late to promote optimal reproductive outcomes for many women, surveillance and care during pregnancy are important for the medical and psychological well-being of both mothers and children. Nutritional, educational, and psychosocial services for women and families are available in comprehensive prenatal care settings. An important role of prenatal care is to engage women in ongoing relationships with health-care providers, so they will have continuing contact with caring professionals after childbirth and during the interval before subsequent pregnancies.

The postpartum period is an important time for establishing positive family relationships, particularly because the social demands on new mothers are significant. In addition to routine preventive care, developmental screening, and treatment of any special needs in childhood, the best way to promote children's health is to ensure healthy mothers and well-functioning families. Physical health is basic to childrearing responsibilities, but psychological and other supports beyond the medical realm are also essential. Women shoulder the major burden of childcare in most families, a stressful job under the best of circumstances. Taking care of children with special health care needs is even more challenging, requiring guidance and respites for parents as well as supportive services to guarantee the best possible futures for the children.

Because motherhood has been perceived by society as central to women's identities, there is often a gap in access to and utilization of health services after women complete their childbearing years. Women live longer than men, but suffer from a higher rate of chronic diseases later in life. Some of these chronic conditions are influenced by women's reproductive histories, and the continuum of health-care needs is important throughout the life cycle. As more women have entered the workforce, they have accumulated social roles without obtaining relief from traditional responsibilities. As adults, "baby boomers" are becoming caretakers of aging parents while they are still providing support for their own children. Women in this "sandwich generation" deserve social recognition and support for maintaining their own health as they face these new physical and emotional challenges.

See also: POSTPARTUM DEPRESSION; PRENATAL CARE

Bibliography

Bennet, Trude. "Women's Health in Maternal and Child Health: Time for a New Tradition?" *Maternal and Child Health Journal* 1 (1997):253–265.

Bennet, Trude, Milton Kotelchuck, Christine E. Cox, Myra J. Tucker, and Denise A. Nadeau. "Pregnancy-Associated Hospitalizations in the United States in 1991 and 1992: A Comprehensive View of Maternal Morbidity." *American Journal of Obstetrics and Gynecology* 178 (1998):346–354.

Chavkin, Wendy, Vickie Breitbart, and Paul H. Wise. "Finding Common Ground: The Necessity of an Integrated Agenda for Women's and Children's Health." *The Journal of Law, Medicine and Ethics* 22 (1994):262–269.

Healthy People, 12/2000. In the U.S. Department of Health and Human Services, Office of Disease Prevention and Health Promotion [web site]. Available from http://www.health.gov/healthypeople/; INTERNET.

Rohweder, Catherine L., Tracy Schaffzin, and Allan Rosenfield. "Public Health Perspectives in the Care of Women and Children." In J. J. Sciarra ed., *Gynecology and Obstetrics*, revised edition. Philadelphia: J. B. Lippincott, 1995.

Zapata, B. Cecilia, and Trude Bennett. "Women's Health: A Life Cycle." In Jonathan B. Kotch ed., *Maternal and Child Health: Programs, Problems, and Policy in Public Health*. Gaithersburg, MD: Aspen Publishers, 1997.

Trude Bennett
Catherine Rohweder

MATURATION

Arnold Gesell, a psychologist, pediatrician, and educator in the 1940s, was very interested in child development. From his numerous observations of children, Gesell formulated a theory known as maturation. This theory stated that developmental changes in a child's body or behavior are a result of the aging process rather than from learning, injury, illness, or some other life experience. Gesell's idea of maturation was rooted in the biological, physiological, and evolutionary sciences. As a result, Gesell centered most of his theory on the power of biological forces, which he felt provided momentum for development to occur. Gesell and his contemporaries proposed that development follows an orderly sequence and that the biological and evolutionary history of the species decides the order of this sequence. Maturation supports the idea that each child's unique genetic and biological makeup determines the rate of development regardless of other potential environmental influences.

See also: GESELL, ARNOLD; MCGRAW, MYRTLE BYRAM; MOTOR DEVELOPMENT; STAGES OF DEVELOPMENT

Bibliography

Salkind, Neil J. "Arnold Gesell and the Maturational Approach." *Theories of Human Development.* New York: D. Van Nostrand, 1981.

Shaffer, David R. "The Concept of Development." *Developmental Psychology: Childhood and Adolescence*, 4th edition. Pacific Grove, CA: Brooks/Cole, 1989.

Joan Ziegler Delahunt

MCGRAW, MYRTLE BYRAM (1899–1988)

Born in Birmingham, Alabama, in 1899, Myrtle McGraw was a pioneer in the study of child growth and development in the 1930s and 1940s. She is best known for her experimental study of twins Johnny and Jimmy Woods. Her studies demonstrated that early stimulation accelerates motor development, enabling infants to learn challenging skills, such as swimming and roller skating, and to solve problems that require judgment and deliberation. She also disputed Yale psychologist Arnold Gesell's maturation theory, which held that genetic processes within the brain determine infant behavior. McGraw found that early development is not preset or straightforward but involves frequent changes in the pace and complexity of interactions between brain growth and behavior.

McGraw briefly attended Sneed Junior College, a seminary, before transferring to Ohio Wesleyan University where she attained her bachelor's degree in 1923. She continued her graduate education at Columbia University and Teachers College in 1924 and was awarded her master's degree and doctorate in psychology in 1925 and 1931, respectively. McGraw was a recipient of a Laura Spelman Rockefeller Fellowship from 1927 through 1929. During this time, she was a research assistant with the Institute for Child Development and an intern for the Institute for Child Guidance. She was appointed and served from 1930 to 1942 as associate director of the Normal Child Development Study at Babies Hospital, Columbia University. McGraw was appointed professor of psychology at Briarcliff College in 1953, headed an innovative laboratory for the study of infants and toddlers, and served as the head of the department of developmental psychology until 1972. In 1976 the Society for Research in Child Development bestowed upon McGraw its first award for distinguished contribution to child development.

McGraw had an extraordinarily close personal and intellectual relationship with philosopher John

Dewey, one of the founders of American pragmatism. She began exchanging letters with him as a teenager in 1916. McGraw considered Dewey to be her "intellectual godfather." He influenced her decision to attend graduate school and eventually advised and collaborated with her on studies of infant growth and development. Dewey urged McGraw to study how infants respond to uncertainty, because he believed that this would reveal how infants integrate their motor and cognitive abilities. Her studies supported Dewey's contention, outlined in his most important book, *Logic: The Theory of Inquiry* (1938), that inquiry is governed by judgments grounded in experience.

McGraw worked with scientists who challenged the behaviorist orthodoxy of the era, which reduced mind to reflex and equated learning with conditioning. Frederick Tilney, a neurologist and director of the Neurological Institute of New York and head of McGraw's studies, contended that the brain evolved to enable humans to acquire the intelligence needed to respond to the increased demand for coordinated behavior. McGraw demonstrated experimentally that for babies learning to walk or perform other forms of locomotion, maintaining balance poses the biggest challenge and accounts for the largest differences among babies in the strategies that they employ. Thus, learning to walk never presents the same problem for each individual. Toddlers must resolve the challenge of balance encountered in previous stages, the circumstances of which vary considerably among infants. George Coghill, a neuroembryologist and a project consultant, discovered that neural growth anticipates the acquisition of function. He believed that prelocomotor stepping, kicking, and other seemingly transient reflex behaviors are instrumental in the proper sequencing and integration of complex behaviors. McGraw's research supported this theory by showing that babies can learn how to stay afloat by adapting the movements involved in their being startled. Harvard University neuroanatomist Leroy Conel also made an important contribution to McGraw's studies by revealing the sequence in which the cerebral cortex, the part of the brain that coordinates sensory and motor information, becomes functional in early development. McGraw employed Conel's data to suggest how cortical control emerges gradually, affording infants increased awareness of and control over their actions.

McGraw's research remains controversial today because developmental psychologists disagree about how to interpret her work and often confuse it with Gesell's maturationism. Some scientists have incorrectly interpreted McGraw's assertion that infant behavior does not become fully integrated until after the onset of cortical control to mean that advanced brain

Myrtle McGraw watching Johnny Woods, twenty-two months, ascending a wooden slide. McGraw was known for her experimental work with the Woods twins, in which she proved that early stimulation accelerates motor development. (Mitzi Wertheim)

structures must be completely functional before behavior can occur. McGraw, however, explicitly acknowledged that "the problem of developmental or maturational relations between structure and function is more complex than the question of localization of function" (McGraw 1943, p. 4). McGraw never argued that the cortex caused or determined motor development. Nor did she ever find evidence of a one-to-one correspondence between a neural structure and a behavioral trait. Instead, she contended that a combination of cortical and subcortical structures support behavior during different periods of development. Moreover, Gilbert Gottlieb contended that McGraw can take credit for having first formulated a bidirectional theory, which holds that neural structures and processes not only support behavior but are changed as a result of novel experiences.

McGraw's research remains pertinent to contemporary developmental scientists who consider the nature-versus-nurture debate outmoded and who seek new methods to understand how the mind emerges from the integration of brain and behavior. McGraw focused on the processes of growth and learning and how infants respond differently to the competing and sometimes chaotic demands on motor and cognitive development. Her most important legacy was the belief that scientists and parents will fully grasp the lessons of development, if they just let babies be their teachers.

See also: DEVELOPMENTAL NORMS; INFANCY; STAGES OF DEVELOPMENT

Bibliography

Coghill, George. *Anatomy and the Problem of Behavior.* New York: Cambridge University Press, 1929.

Conel, Leroy. *The Post-Natal Development of the Human Cerebral Cortex,* Vol. 1: *Cortex of the Newborn.* Cambridge, MA: Harvard University Press, 1939.

Dalton, Thomas. "Was McGraw a Maturationist?" *American Psychologist* 51 (1996):551–552.

Dalton, Thomas, and Victor Bergenn, eds. *Beyond Heredity and Environment: Myrtle McGraw and the Maturation Controversy.* Boulder, CO: Westview Press, 1995.

Dalton, Thomas, and Victor Bergenn. "John Dewey, Myrtle McGraw, and *Logic:* An Unusual Collaboration in the 1930s." *Studies in History and Philosophy of Science* 27, no. 1 (1996):69–107.

Dalton, Thomas, and Victor Bergenn. "Myrtle McGraw: Pioneer in Neurobehavioral Development." In Gregory Kimble and Michael Wertheimer eds., *Portraits of the Pioneers in Psychology.* Washington, DC: American Psychological Association, 1998.

Gottlieb, Gilbert. "Myrtle McGraw's Unrecognized Conceptual Contributions to Developmental Psychology." *Developmental Review* 18 (1998):437–448.

Tilney, Frederick. *Master of Destiny.* New York: Hoeber, 1929.

Publications by McGraw

Growth: A Study of Johnny and Jimmy. New York: Appleton Century Crofts, 1935.

The Neuromuscular Maturation of the Human Infant. New York: Columbia University Press, 1943.

"Memories, Deliberate Recall and Speculations." *American Psychologist* 45 (1990):934–937.

Thomas C. Dalton
Victor W. Bergenn

MEDIATION

When a marriage is dissolving, the spouses must reach agreement on property division, spousal support, child custody, and parental visitation. With the advent of "no-fault" divorce laws, the process of reaching a settlement between the divorcing spouses has become increasingly private. The high costs associated with the more public and formal legal processes has led many divorcing spouses to seek a low-cost alternative: divorce mediation. Much has been written about the reasons for this trend toward the "privatization" of divorce, including the increase in no-fault divorce and the elimination of the "tender years" presumption, which used to influence judges to award child custody to the mother. When divorce

is no longer contingent on proving fault, and when the courts have no strong guidelines for making custody determinations, there are few compelling reasons to rely on legal intervention to dissolve a marriage.

Another influence on the growth of private approaches to determining divorce agreements has been the research on the effects of divorce on children's development. Divorce often results in the loss of contact with the noncustodial parent, less effective parenting, and reduced financial resources. These negative consequences have been linked to more behavior and peer problems in children. Studies have shown that cooperation between the ex-spouses on parenting issues, despite their continued personal conflict, can mitigate the negative effects of the divorce on children's development.

For these reasons, divorce mediation has emerged in recent years as a more suitable alternative to court-ordered approaches. Mediation holds the promise of being cheaper, takes less time to reach settlement, and can effectively prevent many custody disputes from going to court. By allowing the ex-spouses to reach agreement on child custody privately, the amount of conflict between the parents might diminish, the settlement might be fairer for both parties, and contact between the child and each parent can be maintained. These improvements in the period immediately following the divorce should then attenuate any short-term negative effects on the children and improve their adjustment. This article examines the evidence for the benefits of mediation and its effects on parent and child adjustment.

How Mediation Works

Mediation is defined as any strategy or approach to resolving conflict that arrives at a settlement agreeable to the parties. In divorce mediation, the spouses meet with an impartial third party to reach an agreement regarding child custody and other issues. Two forms of divorce mediation are generally recognized. Child custody mediation is specific to the issues of each parent's right to custody and visitation of their children. Comprehensive divorce mediation deals with other issues such as property distribution and spousal support. Some mediation programs involve an average of two or three sessions, whereas others may use as many as ten sessions.

Unlike adversarial methods of reaching divorce settlements, such as litigation or out-of-court negotiation between the spouses' lawyers, mediation occurs with one professional, assumes the parties will cooperate to reach an agreement rather than compete to get the most for themselves, and allows the spouses to make their own decisions. Although some forms of mediation may address underlying interpersonal or individual problems, mediation is unlike marriage therapy because it does not aim for reconciliation. The goal of mediation is for the couple to reach a fair settlement that allows the marriage to be dissolved.

As of 1994, five states (California, Maine, New Mexico, Oregon, and Wisconsin) required mediation as a mandatory first step in resolving child custody disputes, while seven states (Alaska, Colorado, Connecticut, Illinois, Iowa, Kansas, and Louisiana) provided for mediation as part of the state family courts on a discretionary basis, depending on the nature of the divorce disputes. As of 1999, some states still did not have statutes regarding mediation but allowed individual jurisdictions within those states to enact local rules, whereas in other states (Michigan and New Hampshire) mediation was voluntary, that is, the courts mentioned its availability to the parties involved.

In addition to court-based mediation, there is now a growing use of mediators in private practice. While court-based mediators often are social workers or other mental health professionals, private mediators tend to be attorneys, many of whom have also served as divorce attorneys. As divorce mediation becomes a "growth industry" for attorneys, questions have arisen about the appropriate role for lawyers and the potential ethical dilemma of dual representation. Researchers have raised questions about the appropriateness of mediation in cases of domestic violence or abuse. Mediation also may not be appropriate when other severe power imbalances exist between the two parties, such as in cases of alleged child abuse or neglect, mental health problems, or borderline intellectual functioning.

How Mediation Affects the Settlement Process

There are important limitations to studying the effects of mediation. First, the vast majority of divorce cases end in out-of-court settlements, with only 10 percent of cases going to trial. Other than mediation, settlements are reached out of court by negotiations between the parties' lawyers. In some mediation cases, each party's lawyers review the settlement before the agreement is presented to the court, a process that still involves lawyers and the courts. Second, the prevalence of privately held mediations is difficult to measure, because no reporting is required and the divorce judgment often does not indicate whether the settlement was arranged by a private mediator. Thus, it is sometimes hard to compare mediated and litigated settlements, especially among those that are

reached out of court. Finally, couples may "self-select" for mediation or litigation based on such factors as the degree of conflict and cooperation (more acrimonious disputes and less cooperative couples tend to bypass mediation) and socioeconomic factors such as employment, education, and income (parents with higher income, education, and employment status tend to select mediation, particularly private mediation).

Much of the research evaluating mediation has shown positive results, but there are some notable gaps. Mediation appears to improve the rate at which couples reach agreement. In a 2000 review of the literature, from 50 percent to 85 percent of mediated divorces reach agreement and most studies report agreement rates in the upper part of this range. Settlement rates are equally high for all forms of mediation and do not vary according to the amount of time the mediation required. Mediation also substantially reduces court caseloads by diverting some couples before they reach the court. Reports from Los Angeles County in the mid-1980s, shortly after California became the first state to mandate mediation, suggest that custody hearings may be reduced by as much as 75 percent. Evidence also supports the lower cost of mediation compared with litigation, and, because the settlement was reached cooperatively, mediation may reduce the number of couples who return to court, that is, the rate of relitigation. This is an important consideration in light of reports that as many as one-third of all litigated divorces involving child custody typically return to court within two years.

The evidence for the effects of mediation on relitigation rates is nevertheless mixed. One study that tracked couples for two years found that those who reached a divorce settlement through mediation were less than half as likely to return to court than those couples whose settlements were court-ordered. Also, mediated divorce settlements were reached in about half the time. In another two-year study, couples with mediated agreements were six times less likely to return to court than those whose disputes were settled in court. Although little research has followed couples beyond the two-year postsettlement period, one study tracked couples over a nine-year period but found no differences in relitigation between those who mediated and those who litigated the initial settlement. There was, however, a relatively high attrition rate of 48 percent, which is to be expected after nine years. There are other studies that have also reported no differences in relitigation rates.

Typically, after the initial settlement is reached in litigation, the custodial parent faces the possibility that the noncustodial parent will not comply with the court order, including both child support payments

Married couples wanting to separate may prefer mediation over the more detailed legal process of divorce for many reasons. Mediation varies widely, it is relatively brief, and focuses on the task of reaching settlement rather than improving adjustment. (Scott Roper/Corbis)

and custody arrangements. Because mediation is more cooperative, parents should show higher levels of compliance. Research supports this notion: In practically all studies, parents who used mediation reported fewer difficulties with compliance.

How Mediation Affects Parents and Children

The negative psychological effects of divorce on parents and children may be directly or indirectly a function of the adversarial approach, which often maintains and even fuels hostility between divorcing parents. Mediation should provide psychological benefits for both parents and children, such as decreasing bitterness and tension and increasing communication between the parents. The research findings are not completely clear, however. While some studies indicate that couples in mediation show greater cooperation and improved interpersonal relationships after the divorce settlement, some studies have found no consistent differences in psychological adjustment that could be attributed to the mediation itself. These inconsistent findings may be due to pre-

existing differences between the mediation and litigation groups. Other studies found that the couples who had mediation were more satisfied with the divorce settlement and reported doing much better up to one year following the settlement.

Mothers and fathers appear to differ in their satisfaction with mediated settlements. These differences, however, may be related to the type of custody presumption applicable in the states where the research was done and differences in custody outcomes between mediation and litigation. Generally, litigation is more likely to result in the award of sole custody to the mother. In states where the primary presumption of custody favors the mother in a sole custody arrangement, mothers tended to be more satisfied with their settlements than fathers. Mediation tends to produce more joint legal custody agreements, and in those states where the custody presumption favored sole mother custody, fathers who mediated were more satisfied than those who litigated. But in states where the custody presumption favored joint legal custody, both fathers and mothers who mediated were more satisfied than those who went to court.

Compared to litigation, mediated settlements also resulted in both parents maintaining greater involvement with their children. In one long-term study, nine years after the initial divorce settlement, couples who used mediation reported more contact with each other than those whose settlements were litigated. As well, both parents were more involved in their children's lives and reported more frequent communication with the other spouse about the child or children.

It is logical to presume that mediation will positively influence children's adjustment, by improving parental cooperation and communication and maintaining contact between the noncustodial parent and the children. Studies of the effects of divorce on children's adjustment strongly support the positive effects of increased parental cooperation and decreased conflict in the post-divorce period. For mediation, however, the research is surprisingly sparse. Studies have failed to show significant improvements for children as a result of the parents' mediation. This lack of empirical support parallels the mixed evidence on the benefits of mediation for the parents' adjustment.

The critical question is whether one should expect such enduring effects on children and parents. The benefits of mediation appear to occur primarily in the short term by improving compliance, reducing relitigation, and decreasing the time required for the couple to reach a settlement. While mediation has significant benefits over litigation, the research evidence is far from conclusive, particularly concerning the link with improved psychological adjustment of parents and their children. Mediation has an important place in helping families through the initial stress of divorce, but it should not be viewed as a solution for coping with the long-term issues that arise after the dissolution of a marriage.

See also: CHILD CUSTODY AND SUPPORT; DIVORCE

Bibliography

Beck, Connie J. A., and Bruce D. Sales. *Family Mediation: Facts, Myths and Future Prospects.* Washington, DC: American Psychological Association, 2001.

Dillon, Peter A., and Robert E. Emery. "Divorce Mediation and Resolution of Child Custody Disputes: Long-Term Effects." *American Journal of Orthopsychiatry* 66 (1996):131–140.

Emery, Robert E. *Renegotiating Family Relationships: Divorce, Child Custody, and Mediation.* New York: Guilford Press, 1994.

Emery, Robert E. *Sage Developmental Clinical Psychology and Psychiatry Series,* Vol. 14: *Marriage, Divorce, and Children's Adjustment.* Thousand Oaks, CA: Sage, 1999.

Emery, Robert E., and Melissa M. Wyer. "Divorce Mediation." *American Psychologist* 42 (1987):472–480.

Emery, Robert E., Sheila G. Matthews, and Melissa M. Wyer. "Child Custody Mediation and Litigation: Further Evidence on the Differing Views of Mothers and Fathers." *Journal of Consulting and Clinical Psychology* 59 (1991):410–418.

Hahn, Robert A., and David M. Kleist. "Divorce Mediation: Research and Implications for Family and Couples Counseling." *Family Journal: Counseling and Therapy for Couples and Families* 8 (2000):165–171.

Johnston, Janet R., and Linda E. G. Campbell. *Impasses of Divorce: The Dynamics and Resolution of Family Conflict.* New York: Free Press, 1988.

Kelly, Joan B. "The Determination of Child Custody." *Future of Children: Children and Divorce* 4 (Spring 1994):121–142.

Gary Resnick

MEIOSIS

Two types of nuclear division, mitosis and meiosis, occur in cell biology. Most human cells (called diploid cells) are formed through mitosis and contain forty-six chromosomes in twenty-three matched pairs. By contrast, meiosis produces haploid cells, each containing a single set of twenty-three unpaired chromosomes. Sex cells (sperm and ovum) are haploid.

Prior to meiosis, DNA is replicated within a diploid cell, resulting in four copies of each chromosome (now numbering ninety-two). Two successive divisions of the nuclear material occur during meiosis. As part of the process, homologous chromosomes—paired maternal and paternal chromosomes—exchange segments, thus recombining their genes. Four daughter haploid cells are formed, each with one-quarter of the genetic material (twenty-three chromosomes) of the original diploid cell. When haploid cells unite in sexual reproduction, each contributes half of the genetic

material that creates the offspring. Meiosis, therefore, contributes to the genetic diversity within species.

See also: MITOSIS

Bibliography

Alberts, Bruce, Dennis Bray, Alexander Johnson, Julian Lewis, Peter Walter, Keith Roberts, and Martin Raff. *Essential Cell Biology: An Introduction to the Molecular Biology of the Cell.* New York: Garland, 1998.

Maryann Wzorek Rossi

MEMORY

Memory is involved in almost every aspect of children's behavior, from everyday occurrences such as finding a misplaced toy, through the routine demands of learning formulas for a math test, to emotionally charged experiences such as explaining why a particular punishment was unfair. In this overview of memory development, the structure of the memory system will be examined, different types of memory processes will be defined, and age-related changes in memory capabilities from infancy through middle childhood will be described.

Overview of the Memory System

The multi-store model of memory developed by Richard Atkinson and Richard Shiffrin has guided research in memory and its development. The model is supported by extensive experimental evidence and is applied productively in work with individuals who have suffered brain injuries and students with typical learning characteristics as well as learning difficulties. In this information-processing model, illustrated in Figure 1, human memory is seen as operating in a manner analogous to that of a computer. The model depicts three separate memory stores that function as the hardware of the memory system: long-term memory, the sensory register, and working memory. Long-term memory, which is what people typically mean when they refer to memory, is a relatively permanent memory store with an apparently limitless capacity. It includes both semantic memory, a mental reference book that contains facts about the world, and episodic memory, a repository of stored traces of experienced events. It should be noted, however, that representations of learned material or personal experiences do not enter long-term memory directly. Information is moved through earlier stores to long-term memory.

Sights and sounds from the world enter the memory system through the sensory register. This store holds the icon of a visual display or the echo of a sound for a very brief period of time. Within only one second, information that an individual has not ex-

FIGURE 1

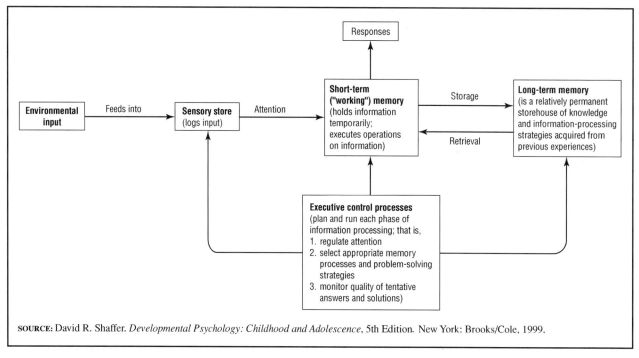

SOURCE: David R. Shaffer. *Developmental Psychology: Childhood and Adolescence*, 5th Edition. New York: Brooks/Cole, 1999.

tracted from the icon or echo is lost. Hence, much of what enters the senses never becomes part of long-term memory. Information that is identified by individuals is often maintained in working memory while the individual interprets it, transforms it, or uses it to solve problems. Applying the computer metaphor, the contents of working memory correspond to open files and running programs. Information moves from working memory into long-term storage when it is processed in a way that makes it meaningful to the individual.

The long-term memory store is often incorrectly described as containing complete and actual representations of past events. In contrast, long-term memory is understood by psychologists to be a reconstructive process. Memories can be altered when individuals encounter new material that interferes with stored information or make inferences that are added to a representation. A well-documented way in which inference occurs is through the operation of schemas, which are organized sets of facts (for example, beliefs about what happens during a visit to the doctor). In a classic study conducted in 1932, Frederick Bartlett read English research participants a story that described events that were inconsistent with their own life experiences and hence seemed bizarre. When they were later asked to recall the story, the participants distorted the actions that took place in a manner that made them consistent with their own culture.

In addition to the memory stores described above, mental strategies are an important component of the information processing system. Strategies correspond to the software of the computer. They are learned procedures that individuals use to direct attention, move information from working to long-term memory, or apply techniques for solving problems. A second grader who repeats a telephone number before dialing it is using verbal rehearsal, a simple memory strategy; a ninth grader who learns a new vocabulary word by using it to describe a principle he has previously learned is using elaboration, an especially effective strategy. Strategies make it possible for memory to be intentional, the term applied when information is deliberately learned or purposefully retrieved. In contrast, memory is described as incidental when information is acquired in the process of performing another activity.

It should be apparent from even this brief introduction that the components of information processing are constantly interacting as a system. The contents of the long-term store are important in encoding, the process of taking information from the world into the memory system. Information stored in long-term memory makes it possible to identify the stimuli in the sensory register so that it can be moved to another store. Knowledge from long-term memory enables the application of strategies or problem-solving procedures in working memory. The contents of permanent memory also determine to a large extent how meaningful new material is, and hence how it can be organized and accessed from the long-term store.

The information-processing model is particularly useful in understanding explicit memory, the type of memory of greatest interest to parents and teachers. Explicit memories are potentially conscious and can be described verbally or pictured in images. A child uses explicit memory when she describes a class field trip or edits a report by applying grammatical rules she has learned. In contrast, some information may affect task performance without entering the individual's conscious awareness. In this case, it is described as implicit memory. Implicit memory is assessed by indirect measurements, such as determining how much quicker individuals can add letters to complete a word when they have previously been presented with a target word, or by physiological indicators, such as changes in galvanic skin response.

Understanding children's memory requires identifying the age-related changes that occur in the components of the information processing system. The first significant advance, of course, is the emergence of memory in development. In the next section, the point in life at which the memory system can be considered to be "up and running" will be discussed. The following sections will examine the changes that occur during childhood in the memory stores and in the use of strategies. The importance of these transitions in children's everyday lives will be explored in each section.

The Developmental Onset of Memory

The memory stores described above are assumed to be universal and present throughout life. Indeed, there is evidence that the capacity to store information in long-term memory begins even before birth. In a well-controlled investigation conducted by Anthony DeCasper and Melanie Spence, the researchers asked pregnant women to read aloud a Dr. Seuss story during the last six weeks of their pregnancies, a point in prenatal development at which fetuses can hear. Shortly after birth, the newborns' recognition memory was tested by comparing their reactions to the familiar passages versus similar but new story excerpts, both of which were read by the babies' mothers. The assessment built on the knowledge that babies can learn to modify the time between bursts of sucking when a change in sucking is followed by the presentation of a stimulus that serves as a reinforcer. The newborns wore headphones and were given a pacifier that recorded their sucking bursts. They indeed modified the way they sucked when the change in sucking was followed by the familiar passage, but they did not do so with the unfamiliar passage. The fact that the old,

but not the new, passages served as reinforcers demonstrated that the babies could recognize the stimuli to which they were exposed before birth.

Although even very young infants can recognize sights, sounds, and smells they have previously encountered, the ability to recall an object or an experience develops later. Recall differs from recognition in that it requires coming up with a response as well as determining that it is correct. Some simple recall is present in the second half of the first year. As every babysitter knows, very young infants remain calm when their parents go out; by around seven months of age, however, separation protest is apparent. By about nine months of age, babies can imitate an action after a twenty-four-hour delay. Note that early recall is heavily dependent on cues and is limited to relatively brief time intervals. Recall continues to develop over the second year of life, corresponding to the development of the prefrontal cortex and other brain structures associated with explicit memory. Between age two and two and a half, toddlers can be expected to remember to stay away from common hazards, provide their first and last names when asked, repeat parts of nursery rhymes, and possess simple event schemas (also called scripts) for everyday events.

By age two and a half, as is well documented in the work of Robyn Fivush and her colleagues, children describe specific past experiences such as a trip to an amusement park. Such early memories, however, do not generally become a permanent part of autobiographical memory, the subset of episodic memory that represents individuals' own life histories. Most people do not recall anything that happened before they were three years of age. This phenomenon is described as infantile amnesia. Although the reasons for infantile amnesia are not completely understood, several factors appear to be important in explaining the developmental emergence of autobiographical memory. One of these is the maturation of the frontal lobes of the brain, which continues throughout early childhood. A second factor appears to be the emergence of the self-concept, which serves as a conceptual framework for the organization of memories. Another is the role of social interactions in maintaining early memories. Katherine Nelson has emphasized the importance of the child's participation in family discussions about past events for keeping early memories alive, a process described as reinstatement. Children are about three years old before they can actively participate in conversations about past events. Finally, some early memories may not be retrieved at later points in development because they are not effectively cued. Because the typical everyday environments of older individuals differ greatly from those of very young children, some potential memories may not be accessed.

Developmental Changes in Information Processing Capacity

Does the absolute capacity of the memory stores change with development? The answer to this question is unknown and, according to some experts, may be unknowable. It is clear, however, that memory span, a measure of working memory, improves reliably with age. Memory span is defined as the number of single words or digits individuals can report in order immediately after hearing them. It increases from about two items at age two to five items at age seven to seven items in adulthood. The amount of information that individuals can hold in memory at any one time determines at least in part what they can learn.

It appears that age-related improvements in the memory span are attributable to two factors: changes in the resources that are available in the information processing system and differences in the efficiency with which older children and adults apply these resources. One of the most important developmental changes in the information processing system is in the speed of processing. Robert Kail asked individuals from ages six to twenty-one to perform a variety of cognitive tasks ranging from mental addition to memory search. He found a remarkably similar pattern of age-related increases in reaction time in the performance of all of the tasks. It should be noted that speed of processing is important in executing many cognitive functions, from moving information from the sensory register to working memory to applying strategies. Hence, developmental differences in speed of processing can influence children's capabilities to perform a variety of academic and everyday tasks.

Processing capacity increases if more resources are available; it can also be enhanced if the resources necessary to perform the task can be decreased. Simply providing extra time for study or problem solving improves children's performance in some but not all tasks. Perhaps the most important determinant of task demands is the learner's relevant knowledge. Familiarity with the to-be-remembered material affects the memory process at every step of information processing. Imagine how difficult it would be, for example, for someone who speaks only English to remember a string of digits presented in another language.

Michelene Chi provided a classic demonstration of the importance of prior knowledge. In this investigation, children who were chess experts had better memories for chess positions than did nonexpert adults, even though the adults demonstrated the expected advantage in remembering digits. Here, prior knowledge of chess eliminated age differences in memory. Because children's knowledge bases increase as they get older simply through their experiences in the world, age differences in memory may be explained to a great extent by differences in task-relevant knowledge.

Changes in the knowledge base also affect the organization of information in long-term memory and hence partially determine whether or not material can be reported. As depicted in the semantic network model of memory, items are represented as nodes and the nodes for associated items are linked. Knowledge about a particular content domain (such as dinosaurs or soccer) creates semantic associations between previously unconnected items, resulting in the formation of connections between nodes. When one item is recalled, the activation spreads to associated items as well, increasing the likelihood that they will also be reported. Items that are represented as part of an extensive network of information within a content area are also less likely to be lost over time. Moreover, age differences in children's long-term event recall are minimized when younger and older children have high levels of prior knowledge about the to-be-remembered components of the experience.

Knowledge also enhances memory by making it easy to apply strategies for encoding and retrieving information. As discussed in the next section, the development of memory strategies is another important reason for age-related increases in children's ability to remember, especially in academic settings.

The Acquisition of Memory Strategies

A child's intentional memory shows dramatic improvement when he can effectively use memory strategies. These deliberate tactics for remembering develop over a lengthy period that spans the elementary and middle school years. Preschool children use very simple tactics for remembering in some special task settings; for example, a four-year-old can be expected to use a marker to denote an object's hiding place in preparation for subsequently finding it. Preschoolers do not, however, use mental strategies and indeed do not typically differentiate memory and perception. By age seven, most children spontaneously use rehearsal to enhance short-term memory performance. Retrieval strategies (such as going sequentially through the alphabet) begin to be spontaneously used around third grade. Children's self-directed use of organization, the ability to impose a semantic structure on the to-be-remembered items to guide memory performance, emerges later in the elementary school years. For example, a fifth grader could be expected to remember what to take on a school field trip by reviewing the activities involved and packing accordingly (e.g., "things to do on the bus," "what I need for the nature walk," "things I'll need at lunch") by herself. It is unlikely, however, that a third grader would use organization as a guide without the direction of an adult. Elaboration, a highly effective strategy that involves actively creating a representation integrating new information with existing information, may not be used spontaneously by children until early adolescence. An eighth grader may remember the definition of the word "fruition" by creating an image of a ripe pear on a bough, but it is unlikely that most sixth graders would do so.

Most students do not acquire optimally effective study skills, which can be considered forms of memory strategies, until adolescence. By the later elementary school years, children allocate more study time to test items that they have previously missed on practice tests; in contrast, younger elementary school children devote comparable amounts of attention to items that they have previously gotten correct and incorrect. By high school good students can be expected to take spontaneous and effective notes and to emphasize key information in studying.

Regardless of the strategy under consideration, its use emerges initially in highly supportive task settings. At early points in the acquisition of memory strategies, children use a strategy when adults instruct them to use the strategy but they do not generate the strategies spontaneously, a limitation described as a production deficiency. Additional preparation time, the use of familiar materials, and cues that may reduce memory demands are other factors that increase the likelihood that strategies will be used. When they are fully acquired, strategies are applied spontaneously in a wide array of task settings. Metamemory, or knowledge about the operation of the memory system, contributes to the development of strategies. Metamemory involves understanding the demands of the task and the relevant characteristics of the rememberer, as well as identifying and using effective task approaches and monitoring their effectiveness. In general, the development of metamemory increases with age, corresponding to changes in actual memory performance.

Fostering Children's Memory Development

Memory develops largely through social interaction, and consequently parents and teachers play a critical role in assisting children in developing good memories. During early childhood, everyday adult-child interactions provide the basis for memory development by fostering language development and helping children acquire scripts for common events. Conversations that include reminiscing about the recent past are significant in helping children understand what memory is and what should be remembered. Developing family traditions and participating in rituals encourage reminiscing.

When a child begins formal schooling, adults can contribute to the child's acquisition of metamemory and memory strategies by modeling their own approaches to tasks involving memory and discussing their memory failures. It is important that teachers and parents recognize that strategies develop over an extended period. Children's use of effective memory strategies in studying should be monitored, and adults should help children simplify tasks by providing external memory aids and other supports as needed. Informal instruction in the use of memory strategies should be incorporated into class presentations and assignments.

It is also important to keep in mind that memory is facilitated by advances in other domains of development. As examples, narrative skills increase children's abilities to provide reports of their personal experience; problem-solving techniques increase functional working memory capacity. The development of the knowledge base plays a vital role in memory performance. Hence, providing children with opportunities to learn about the world contributes significantly to their capacity to remember effectively.

See also: COGNITIVE DEVELOPMENT; LEARNING

Bibliography

Atkinson, Richard C., and Richard M. Shriffrin. "Human Memory: A Proposed System and Its Control Processes." In K. W. Spence and J. T. Spence eds., *The Psychology of Learning and Motivation: Advances in Research and Theory.* New York: Academic Press, 1968.

Chi, Michelene. "Knowledge Structures and Memory Development." In R. S. Siegler ed., *Children's Thinking: What Develops?* Hillsdale, NJ: Lawrence Erlbaum, 1978.

DeCasper, Anthony J., and Melanie J. Spence. "Prenatal Maternal Speech Influences Newborns' Perception of Speech Sounds. *Infant Behavior and Development* 9 (1986):133–150.

Fivush, Robyn, and Judith A. Hudson, eds. *Knowing and Remembering in Young Children.* Cambridge, Eng.: Cambridge University Press, 1990.

Howe, Mark. *The Fate of Early Memories: Developmental Science and the Retention of Childhood Experiences.* Washington, DC: American Psychological Association, 2000.

Kail, Robert. "Development of Processing Speed in Childhood and Adolescence." In H. W. Reese ed., *Advances in Child Development and Behavior.* San Diego: Academic Press, 1991.

Nelson, Katherine. "The Psychological and Social Origins of Autobiographical Memory." *Psychological Science* 1 (1993):1–8.

Molly Carter Imhoff
Lynne E. Baker-Ward

MENARCHE

Menarche refers to the first menstrual flow experienced by a girl during puberty. Menstruation means that the physiological and hormonal changes underlying reproductive processes have matured sufficiently to produce the endometrial lining of the uterus, which is sloughed off at the end of the menstrual cycle if implantation of a fertilized ovum has not occurred.

Menarche typically occurs after other pubertal changes are well established, and marks the completion of puberty. The mean age of menarche for girls in the United States is twelve, but it may occur normally from ages ten to sixteen. Early menstrual cycles are often irregular and may include no ovulation or multiple ovulations.

Menarche often is acknowledged by family or community rituals, recognizing the adolescent's entrance into womanhood and sexual potential. Challenges of adolescence for a girl include incorporating the new status and potential into her self-concept and coping with reactions of family and peers.

See also: ADOLESCENCE; MENSTRUAL CYCLE; PUBERTY

Bibliography

Grumbach, Melvin M., and Dennis M. Styne. "Puberty: Ontogeny, Neuroendocrinology, Physiology, and Disorders." In Jean D. Wilson and Daniel W. Foster eds., *Williams Textbook of Endocrinology*, 9th edition. Philadelphia: Saunders, 1998.

Herman-Giddens, Marcia E., Eric J. Slora, Richard C. Wasserman, Carlos J. Bourdony, Manju V. Bhapkar, Gary G. Koch, and Cynthia M. Hasemeier. "Secondary Sexual Characteristics and Menses in Young Girls Seen in Office Practice: A Study from the Pediatric Research in Office Settings Network." *Pediatrics* 99 (1997):505–512.

Lawrence G. Shelton

MENSTRUAL CYCLE

The menstrual cycle is a periodic flow of blood and cells from the lining of the uterus in human females and the females of most other primates, occurring about every twenty-eight days. The beginning of menstruation, or menarche (the first menstrual period), typically starts between the ages of ten and seventeen and is a sign of readiness for childbearing.

During each cycle, the lining, or endometrium, of the uterus experiences a rapid generation of cells and vein-filled channels in preparation for pregnancy. Halfway through the cycle, an ovum (egg) is released from an ovary. The ovum passes through the fallopian tube, and if fertilized by a sperm, the ovum is implanted in the uterus, and the thickened lining helps support the pregnancy. If the ovum is not fertilized, the tissue and blood are shed.

The many myths and taboos related to menstruation have caused some cultures to chastise it as "unclean" or a "curse." For a young girl, menarche is simply related to growth and body weight. Signs of puberty can begin after the age of eight, but early physical maturation may result in social pressure because of increased attention.

See also: ADOLESCENCE; CONTRACEPTION; MENARCHE; PUBERTY

Bibliography

Gorman, Christine. "Growing Pains: What Happens When Puberty Comes Too Soon in Your Child—and What You Can Do about It." *Time* (August 21, 2000):84.

Peters, Diane. "It's Wonderful Being a Girl." *Chatelaine* (June 2000):76.

Beth A. Kapes

MENTAL AGE

Mental age refers to an age-normed level of performance on an intelligence test, and it became a popular way of referring to "mental level" as measured by the Binet-Simon Scale of 1908. The Binet-Simon Scale identified the academic skills typical of specific age groups. In 1912 William Stern used chronological age as a denominator to be divided into mental age, resulting in an intelligence quotient. In 1916 Lewis Terman multiplied this intelligence quotient by 100 (to eliminate the decimal places) and called the result an IQ score. Terman's formula of mental age divided by chronological age multiplied by 100 became popularized as the formula for calculating a person's IQ. Adult intelligence does not change from year to year so the concept of mental age is less meaningful when discussing adults. Contemporary IQ tests use cumulative indexes to determine scores rather than the calculation of IQ scores based upon Terman's formula. A contemporary equivalent of mental age is the Standard Age Score of the Stanford-Binet IQ test, which was formulated in 1987.

See also: MILESTONES OF DEVELOPMENT

Bibliography

Anastasi, Anne. *Psychological Testing*. New York: Macmillan, 1988.

Fancher, Raymond. *Pioneers of Psychology*. New York: Norton, 1990.

Francine Smolucha

MENTAL DISORDERS

Children's mental health problems have emerged from a long history of misunderstanding and neglect to become the central concern of an active group of researchers and practitioners. The last few decades of the twentieth century witnessed an explosion of knowledge about the nature of disorders that affect children, their frequency of occurrence, their developmental course, and the effectiveness of treatments.

In both children and adults, mental disorders typically are defined in one of two ways: as a category or along a dimension. Categorical approaches are typified by the American Psychiatric Association's diagnostic criteria, as published in the *Diagnostic and Statistical Manual of Mental Disorders: DSM-IV*. The definitions of mental disorders in the *DSM-IV* are characterized predominantly by symptom criteria for diagnoses, as well as by taking into account impairment and, for some disorders, age of onset. For this approach, clinical interviews are the typical measurement.

In contrast to categorical approaches, dimensional approaches emphasize symptoms along a continuum from none or few symptoms to clinically significant levels of symptoms. The dimensional approach is typically measured by reliable and valid questionnaires administered to parents, teachers, or the children under study, with lists of behaviors that the respondent indicates as being characteristic of the child, sometimes or somewhat characteristic, or not characteristic of the child. Children are assigned a score along the continuum or are indicated as exceeding, or not, an empirically established cutoff for clinically significant levels of behavior problems or, at the next lower level, of borderline significance.

The mental disorders that children can develop are commonly divided into two groups: disruptive or externalizing behavior disorders (e.g., attention-deficit hyperactivity disorder, conduct problems) and emotional or internalizing behavior disorders (e.g., anxiety, depression). In addition, children also can develop other disorders that do not fit into this classification system, such as autism, schizophrenia, and eating disorders.

An important perspective within which to understand children's mental disorders is development. By its nature, children's behavior fluctuates over time. One of the biggest challenges for parents and practitioners is to distinguish between normal developmental changes and the emergence of a disorder (atypical changes). Development is also an important consideration in determining whether early signs of a disorder will emerge as a full-blown disorder, develop into a different disorder, or resolve into healthy functioning.

Disruptive or Externalizing Behavior Disorders

The disruptive or externalizing disorders consist of attention deficit hyperactivity disorder (ADHD), conduct disorder, and oppositional defiant disorder. Because the latter two are both considered disruptive behavior disorders, they are typically considered together.

Attention Deficit Hyperactivity Disorder

ADHD has as its primary symptoms inattention, impulsivity, and hyperactivity. Research has shown that inattention symptoms tend to cluster apart from symptoms of impulsivity and hyperactivity, while the latter two tend to cluster together. The *DSM-IV* maintains this distinction by including two sets of symptoms. In order to meet diagnostic criteria for ADHD, the child's parents or teachers must report the presence of at least six symptoms of inattention (e.g., is often easily distracted by extraneous stimuli) or six symptoms of hyperactivity-impulsivity (e.g., often fidgets with hands or feet or squirms in seat). In both cases, the symptoms must: (1) have been present and been causing impairment before age seven years; (2) have been present for six months or more; and (3) cause clinically significant impairment in terms of interpersonal or academic functioning in two or more settings and must differ from normal developmental expectations. Alternatively, behavior rating scales, on which respondents rate individual symptoms of ADHD, provide a dimensional, age-sensitive, quantitative assessment of ADHD-related problems, along with an indication of the level at which the scores are considered to be indicative of clinically significant problems.

Although reports vary depending on the criteria used, with *DSM-IV* based criteria the estimates of the incidence of ADHD are about 3 percent to 5 percent of the general population of children. As with the other externalizing disorders, it occurs much more frequently in boys than in girls, with a typical ratio of six to one in samples attained from treatment settings and three to one in community samples.

Although some children show signs of ADHD as early as infancy, for most children the first signs of behavior that differs from developmental expectations emerge between the ages of three and four years. Another common time for children to be first identified is at school entry.

No one knows exactly what causes ADHD. Biological factors are likely to include genetic transmission and pregnancy and birth complications, and may also include brain injury or lead exposure. Researchers have found strong evidence for the influence of genetics (although accounting for only 10 percent to 15 percent of the variance in ADHD symptoms) and neurobiological factors (with more support found for irregularities in brain structures than for neurochemical imbalances). The notion that sugar and other dietary factors cause ADHD has received little support. Family factors have not been found to play a clear role in causing ADHD, although family influences are known to be important in the developmental course and emergence of associated symptoms.

The frequent co-occurrence of other conditions and the extent to which ADHD symptoms cause problems in multiple settings (e.g. home, school) complicate treatment of ADHD. These characteristics contribute to the lack of consensus on the best treatment for ADHD as well as the understanding that no one approach works for all children and that many children with ADHD will benefit from a multifaceted treatment program. In addition, there is consensus that treatments must be ongoing and must be sensitive to children's developmental level and other strengths and needs of the child and the family. Stimulant medications, the most frequently used treatment, lead to dramatic improvements in symptoms in about 80 percent of children with ADHD. To treat the problems often associated with ADHD (e.g., conduct problems, depression), which have not been found to benefit from stimulant medications, parent management training (PMT) is an effective approach. Although there are many variations on PMT, standard features typically include providing parents with an understanding of the disorder and techniques for managing their child's behavior problems. Treatment approaches that combine stimulant medication with PMT have shown the greatest effectiveness. Although many other interventions are available, the evidence for their effectiveness is limited. At the beginning of the twenty-first century, a large study funded by the National Institute of Mental Health was underway and was evaluating the effectiveness of an intensive intervention combining medication, PMT, and classroom interventions. This study offered great promise for providing information on the best treatments for children with ADHD.

Conduct Problems (Disruptive Behavior)

The primary behaviors that fall into this category are aggression, noncompliance, defiance, and aversive interpersonal behavior. The *DSM-IV* categorizes children with the less severe form of disruptive behavior disorders as having oppositional defiant disorder (ODD). Symptoms of ODD include a pattern of negativistic, defiant, noncompliant, and argumentative behavior, lasting for at least six months and causing significant impairment in social or academic functioning. In contrast, aggression and violation of rules characterize conduct disorder (CD). The fifteen symptom-based criteria are clustered into four groups: (1) aggression to people and animals, (2) destruction of property, (3) deceitfulness or theft, and (4) serious violation of rules. From the dimensional perspective, ODD and CD are considered externalizing behavior problems, further distinguished as two subtypes: delinquent and aggressive.

Estimates of the frequency of occurrence among school-age children of ODD range from 5 percent to 25 percent and of CD from 5 percent to 20 percent. As with ADHD, both ODD and CD are more frequently diagnosed in boys than in girls. ODD is twice as common in males than females, although only before puberty; rates are about even in postpubertal males and females. The male to female ratio for CD is between two to one and three to one.

Children may be first diagnosed with ODD or CD at any point in childhood. ODD may be present as early as three years of age and is usually diagnosed by the early school years. Some researchers consider ODD to be a milder, earlier version of CD, although the matter is controversial. Only about 25 percent of children with ODD progress to the more severe CD. On the other hand, most children who meet the criteria for CD were previously diagnosed with ODD and had persisting ODD symptoms. Children with childhood-onset (i.e., before age ten years) of CD, who are more likely to be boys, have been found to be more likely to persist in antisocial behaviors over time. In a 1996 research report, Terri Moffitt and her colleagues delineated two alternative developmental pathways for children with conduct problems. The researchers described one group of these children, those with early onset and problems that persist, as following the life-course-persistent path, whereas those whose conduct problems first emerged later in adolescence and were typically limited to the teen years were described as following the adolescent-limited path.

The development of ODD or CD is likely to have origins in multiple factors associated with diverse pathways. Researchers have found evidence that several factors are related to the development of ODD, CD, or both: genetically based, early temperament difficulties (e.g., having lower frustration tolerance), neurobiological factors (e.g., low psychophysiological arousal), social-cognitive factors (e.g., cognitive distortions), family patterns of interaction (e.g., inadequate monitoring of the child's behavior), and family environmental stress and adversity (e.g., marital discord).

Evidence for the effectiveness of treatment of children with serious conduct problems is not promising. Although families are likely to be offered a range of treatment options, none of them has been shown to be strongly effective. As with ADHD, the treatments that are most likely to be effective include a combination of treatments targeting not only the child but also the family, school, and neighborhood. The most effective treatments also take into consideration the developmental status of the child and the developmental trajectory of conduct problems for the child, with the children most difficult to treat being those who are farther along in the trajectory. Three approaches to treatment that have at least some empirical support are parent management training (focused on teaching parents new skills for managing their child's behavior); cognitive problem-solving skills training (focused on changing children's perceptions and appraisals of interpersonal events); and multisystemic treatment (focused on the context within which the child functions, including family, school, neighborhood, and the legal system).

Emotional or Internalizing Disorders

Some children develop depression and anxiety, disorders that involve not only maladaptive thoughts and emotions but also maladaptive behaviors. It is important to distinguish these disorders from common depressed mood or childhood worries and fears. Knowledge of normal development of emotions and cognitions is helpful in making these distinctions.

Anxiety

Anxiety disorders in children are most likely to fall into the *DSM-IV* diagnostic categories of generalized anxiety disorder, simple phobia, separation anxiety disorder, obsessive-compulsive disorder, or posttraumatic stress disorder. Children diagnosed with generalized anxiety disorder have a consistent pattern, lasting six months or more, of uncontrollable and excessive anxiety or worry, with the concerns covering a broad range of events or activities. In addition to worry, symptoms include irritability, restlessness, fatigue, difficulty in concentrating, muscle tension, and sleep disturbances. Deborah Beidel found that this disorder commonly begins at around age ten, is persistent, frequently co-occurs with depression, and is often accompanied by a number of physical symptoms such as sweating, suffering from chills, feeling faint, and having a racing pulse.

In contrast to generalized anxiety disorder, children with the other anxiety disorders have a much more narrow focus of their concerns. Simple phobia is typically focused on a specific situation or object. With separation anxiety, children display excessive fear and worry about becoming separated from their primary attachment figures. This disorder is often expressed as school refusal or school phobia. Obsessive-compulsive disorder consists of specific obsessions

(abnormal thoughts, images, or impulses) or compulsions (repetitive acts). Posttraumatic stress disorder symptoms develop in reaction to having experienced or witnessed a particularly harrowing event. Symptoms include sleep disturbances, irritability, attention problems, exaggerated startle responses, and hypervigilance.

For phobias and separation anxiety disorder, it is particularly necessary to determine if a child's fears reflect typical concerns of the age group or are clinically significant. Onset of a fear at a time that is different from children's age-typical fears is often an important indication of clinical significance. Other important indications of clinical significance include fear reactions that are strong, persistent, and intense and that interfere with school, family, or peer relationships. Similarly, it is essential to distinguish symptoms of obsessive-compulsive disorder from typical childhood rituals and routines.

Although generalized anxiety disorder and specific phobias are among the most common disorders in children, the other anxiety disorders are rare. Diagnosis of anxiety disorders is particularly difficult because it is so dependent on self-reports from the children. Children may not recognize that their fears are excessive and typically do not complain about them, although they will go out of their way to avoid situations that evoke the anxiety.

The anxiety disorders are typically viewed as having their origins in learning experiences. Children may learn fears through imitation, instruction, or direct reinforcement. Similarly, compulsive behavior can develop from a chance occurrence when a child felt positive reinforcement for engaging in a particular behavior because it was associated with reduced anxiety.

Anxiety disorders that begin in childhood often persist into adulthood. Thus it is particularly important to treat them early. Behavioral or cognitive therapies have been most successful. Treatment typically involves a combination of graduated exposure to the feared situation and teaching the child adaptive and coping self-statements. The effectiveness and safety of using medications was the subject of several studies at the beginning of the twenty-first century; some early findings showed promising results from the use of antidepressants.

Depression (Mood Disorders)

Depression is another relatively common disorder that often first appears in childhood or adolescence. The *DSM-IV* includes the depression diagnoses of major depression and dysthymia. To be diagnosed with major depression, children must experience either depressed mood (or irritability) or

Depression is a relatively common mood disorder that often first appears during childhood or adolescence. (Custom Medical Stock)

loss of interest in their usual activities plus other symptoms such as sleep or appetite disturbance, loss of energy, or trouble concentrating. These symptoms must be present nearly every day for two weeks or more. For dysthymia, the symptoms are typically of a lower level of severity but persist for one year or more. For both disorders, the symptoms must cause impairment and must reflect a change from the child's usual level of functioning. Standardized questionnaires are also used to measure depression and determine whether a child's level of symptoms are in the nondepressed range or indicate mild, moderate, or severe levels of depression.

Studies of community samples have found that from 2 percent to 5 percent of children have mood disorders. Rates increase with age. Although rates are about equal for boys and girls in childhood, beginning at puberty girls are twice as likely as boys to receive a depression diagnosis. Depression is a recurrent disorder, with each additional episode increasing the likelihood of a recurrence.

Early stages in the emergence of depression are often missed because children are not likely to recognize or report their distress. Once a depression disorder emerges, it is typically persistent and progresses from relatively mild symptoms to more severe symptoms.

Genetics contribute to the likelihood of a childhood depression occurring, as do neurobiological factors and stress. Children with particular patterns of thinking, such as blaming themselves for negative outcomes while not giving themselves credit for positive outcomes, may be more vulnerable to depression than others.

Treatments that have been found to be successful often involve intervention into the psychosocial components of the disorder. For example, treatment may involve helping the children identify and modify maladaptive beliefs and perceptions, develop social skills and problem-solving abilities, and broaden their resources for coping with stress. A particularly effective focus in treatment of adolescents with depression has been on interpersonal relationships, addressing the stage-salient concerns of adolescents. Although they are often prescribed, evidence for the effectiveness of antidepressant medication in children and adolescents has been mixed, possibly because of the methodological challenges of studying medications during periods of still rapid development.

Other Disorders

The disorders included in this last category involve more extreme deviations from normal development than the externalizing and internalizing behavior disorders. Parents typically become extremely concerned when symptoms of these disorders emerge. Two of these disorders, autism and childhood schizophrenia, are considered pervasive developmental disorders in the *DSM-IV*, a term suggesting not only that the disorders emerge early but also that they affect all of the developing systems, including social, language, and cognitive-intellectual.

Autism

Autism is an extremely rare condition, occurring in fewer than 5 out of 10,000 individuals, possibly more common in males. Symptoms, which must emerge before the age of three years to meet *DSM-IV* diagnostic criteria, include impairment in social interaction (e.g., avoidance of eye contact) and communication (e.g., delayed or inadequate speech), as well as repetitive and stereotyped patterns of behavior, interests, or activities. Thus autism develops early and disrupts development in all key areas. The causes of autism are not known, but research findings center on genetic factors, including chromosome abnormalities, and brain injuries or anomalies in brain development. Research on treatment for autism has been controversial because parents understandably pursue a wide range of activities to help their children. Behavioral treatments of specific problematic behaviors have been shown to be successful and often involve teaching the parents the skills to manage their children's behavior. Evidence for the effectiveness of medications have been mixed but offer some promise.

Schizophrenia

Schizophrenia also is rarely diagnosed in children, probably occurring in fewer than 1 in 1,000 children, and the *DSM-IV* does not even include criteria for a specific category of childhood schizophrenia. In childhood, although not in adolescence, schizophrenia occurs more frequently in males than females. Symptoms include hallucinations and delusions, disorganized or incoherent speech, and disorganized behavior. Onset is typically in late childhood or adolescence following predominantly normal development. Once it emerges, the course of schizophrenia is characterized by episodes alternating with periods of improvement and relapse. The causes of schizophrenia are most likely genetic and other biological considerations. Treatment may involve the same antipsychotic medications that are used with adults. Research indicates that medications may be most effective when combined with a program of helping the family to manage the child's behavior and minimize stress levels.

Eating Disorders

The *DSM-IV* includes two eating disorders. Anorexia nervosa is characterized mainly by refusal to maintain even minimally normal body weight, symptoms of intense fear of gaining weight even though underweight, and disturbance in the perception or experience of one's body weight or shape. The second disorder, bulimia nervosa, is diagnosed when individuals engage repeatedly in binge eating alternating with inappropriate methods to prevent weight gain. Eating disorder symptoms and associated behaviors can also be measured with questionnaires. Eating disorders tend to be more prevalent in industrialized countries and are relatively rare, with prevalence estimates typically fewer than 2 percent, nearly all girls. Onset is typically around adolescence and may be associated with a stressful event. Causes are likely to include a combination of biological, family, and sociocultural factors as well as individual psychological characteristics of the child. Treatment, often resisted, requires coordination between medical attention and therapy, including behavioral intervention, training in self-monitoring, and the development of coping skills.

See also: ANTISOCIAL BEHAVIOR; ATTENTION DEFICIT HYPERACTIVITY DISORDER; AUTISM

Bibliography

American Psychiatric Association. *The Diagnostic and Statistical Manual of Mental Disorders: DSM-IV.* Washington, DC: American Psychiatric Association, 1994.

Arnold, L. Eugene, Howard B. Abikoff, Dennis P. Cantwell, C. Keith Connors, Glen Elliott, Laurence L. Greenhill, Lily Hechtman, Stephen P. Hinshaw, Betsy Hoza, Peter S. Jensen, Helena C. Kraemer, John S. March, Jeffrey H. Newcorn, William E. Pelham, John E. Richters, Ellen Schiller, Joanne B. Severe, James M. Swanson, Donald Vereen, and Karen C. Wells. "National Institute of Mental Health Collaborative Multimodal Treatment Study of Children with ADHD (the MTA): Design Challenges and Choices." *Archives of General Psychiatry* 54 (1997):865–870.

Barkley, Russell A. *Attention Deficit Hyperactivity Disorder: A Handbook for Diagnosis and Treatment.* New York: Guilford Press, 1990.

Barkley, Russell A. "Attention-Deficit/Hyperactivity Disorder." In E. J. Mash and R. A. Barkley eds., *Treatment of Childhood Disorders,* 2nd edition. New York: Guilford Press, 1998.

Beidel, Deborah C. "Assessing Anxious Emotions: A Review of Psychophysiological Assessment in Children." *Clinical Psychology Review* 9 (1989):717–736.

Biederman, Joseph, Stephen V. Faraone, Sharon Milberger, Jennifer G. Jetton, Lisa Chen, Eric Mick, Ross W. Greene, and Ronald L. Russell. "Is Childhood Oppositional Defiant Disorder a Precursor to Adolescent Conduct Disorder? Findings from a Four-Year Follow-Up Study of Children with ADHD." *Journal of the American Academy of Child and Adolescent Psychiatry* 35 (1996):1193–1204.

Hinshaw, Stephen P., Benjamin B. Lahey, and Elizabeth L. Hart. "Issues of Taxonomy and Comorbidity in the Development of Conduct Disorder." *Development and Psychopathology* 5 (1993):31–49.

Moffitt, Terri E., Avshalom Caspi, Nigel Dickson, Phil Silva, and Warren Stanton. "Childhood-Onset versus Adolescent-Onset Antisocial Conduct Problems in Males: Natural History from Ages Three to Eighteen Years." *Development and Psychopathology* 8 (1996):399–424.

Swanson, James M., Keith McBurnett, Diane L. Christian, and Tim Wigal. "Stimulant Medications and the Treatment of Children with ADHD." In Thomas H. Ollendick and Ronald L. Prinz eds., *Advances in Clinical Child Psychology.* New York: Plenum Press, 1995.

Waldman, Irwin D., Scott O. Lilienfeld, and Benjamin B. Lahey. "Toward Construct Validity in the Childhood Disruptive Behavior Disorders." In Thomas H. Ollendick and Ronald J. Prinz eds., *Advances in Clinical Child Psychology.* New York: Plenum Press, 1995.

Sherryl Hope Goodman

MENTAL RETARDATION

Mental retardation (MR) is a developmental disability, defined by looking at three aspects of a child. IQ score, adaptive functioning, and the age of onset determine where a child lies in the continuum of mental retardation.

A numerical component of MR is defined by an IQ intelligence test. An IQ test measures and predicts how well individuals learn in their environment. The average IQ score of a typical developing child falls between 80 and 119. An IQ score below 70 to 75 characterizes a child for further evaluations to determine if the child is mentally retarded. IQ levels below 75 are categorized into several levels. These levels represent the amount of support individuals with MR require. The four levels of support include: intermittent (IQ score 55–65), limited (IQ score 35–55), extensive (IQ score 25–35), and pervasive (IQ score 20–25).

Adaptive functioning, the way an individual functions in society, is another aspect required for a valid definition of MR. Included in adaptive functioning are intellectual, emotional, physical, and environmental considerations. Daily living skills such as dressing, personal hygiene, eating, and receptive and expressive communication, as well as safety awareness and other basic skills, are evaluated for adaptive functioning. A child must show poor development in at least two of the adaptive functioning categories to be considered mentally retarded.

The last aspect for a definition of MR is the age of onset of the preceding characteristics. Under the definition of MR from the American Association on Mental Retardation, the age of onset has to be in childhood before the age of eighteen. As discussed in the following section, MR can develop even before the baby is born.

Individuals who fall below the IQ standard, show poor adaptive functioning in two or more areas, and had the onset of these conditions occur in childhood are considered to be mentally retarded. This does not mean that the individual will not learn and develop but, instead, that intervention will be necessary to assist the individual with his or her development.

Causes of Mental Retardation

Individuals affected by MR comprise between 1 percent and 3 percent of the population. Mental retardation can be acquired from any of the following categories: prenatal, perinatal (at the time of birth), postnatal, and economic status.

Prenatal, or before birth causes, can be broken down into genetics, disturbances in the embryonic development, and acquired causes. MR is associated with more than 500 genetic diseases. Examples of genetically inherited MR are too many chromosomes, too few, and a combination of defective genes and abnormal genes inherited from the parents. Disturbances in the embryonic development include multiple birth defects as well as specific syndromes. Acquired causes include infections during the pregnancy; the mother drinking, smoking, or taking other drugs, including some prescribed medications; and other maternal health issues. If the mother's health is in jeopardy, it in turn jeopardizes the unborn child's health. Drinking, smoking, drug usage, malnutrition, and contraction of HIV all affect the fetus.

All of these health hazards can cause damage such as low birthweight, mental retardation, and other neurological damage.

Perinatal causes of MR include premature birth (birth before thirty-six weeks gestation), low birthweight, deprivation of oxygen to the fetus, and any undue stress put on the fetus at the time of birth.

Postnatal causes of MR include environment toxins and exposure to a childhood disease. There are vaccinations available to prevent the newborn from contracting damaging diseases. Whooping cough, measles, rubella, and mumps are all common childhood diseases for which the child can be immunized. Meningitis is another very serious disease that attacks the covering of the brain and spinal cord. This viral infection can cause permanent brain damage in infants. Any injury to the brain, including abuse or accident, can cause profound trauma to the developing brain. Toxins in the environment are also a cause of postnatal MR. One of the most important toxins is lead, the presence of which in paint has been a continuing issue. Symptoms of lead poisoning include lethargy, anemia, seizures, brain damage, and even death. Once lead poisoning is diagnosed, medications can assist with removing excess lead from the body. Even with medication, however, mental retardation may still be present.

The last category of causes of mental retardation is economic status. If a family lives in poor environmental conditions, the children in that family are at higher risk for disease, malnutrition, insufficient medical care, and understimulation, which can all lead to MR. Research has found that understimulation of the brain can cause irreversible damage to the brain and can lead to MR. Interacting with children is especially important in the first years of life to develop the neurons.

Prevention of Mental Retardation

The degree to which MR can be prevented has grown with the increased quality and quantity of medical technology, as well as the amount of education presented to expectant mothers. Technology allows medical staff access to the baby in the uterus. The amniotic fluid can be tested to determine some forms of defect in the fetus. Ultrasound allows the medical staff to see the baby in the uterus and determine if there is a physical defect. If a defect is found through one of these technologies, early intervention can be implemented either while the fetus is still in the uterus or directly after birth.

In addition to the prenatal techniques, newborn screenings have provided well over 2,000 newborns the opportunity for typical development. These screenings can prevent phenylketonuria (PKU), congenital hypothyroidism, Rh disease, and other abnormalities. PKU occurs in approximately 1 of every 14,000 births in the United States. PKU is a genetic disorder that causes difficulty for the body in breaking down the common food chemical, phyenylalanine. When phyenylalanine, an amino acid, builds up it can cause serious health and learning problems. Other preventive measures used to prevent mental retardation include reducing the presence of lead in the environment, using helmets and child safety seats, and educating people about the importance of using safety equipment. In addition, ensuring proper prenatal care for all pregnant women and seeking genetic counseling if there is history of birth defects will help prevent MR.

Public Policy Regarding Mental Retardation

Legislation passed in 1990 provided a clear path for the elimination of discrimination against people with disabilities. The Americans with Disabilities Act (ADA) protects persons with disabilities from discrimination in employment, government, public accommodations, commercial facilities, transportation, and telecommunications. The effectiveness of ADA lies with the advocates of this legislation. Demanding the compliance of every agency involved in the process is the advocate's responsibility. As each year passes, there will likely be fewer barriers for persons with disabilities.

Additional legislation includes IDEA (Individuals with Disabilities Education Act). IDEA states that every child, regardless of disability, will be provided a "free appropriate public education" in the "least restrictive environment to the maximum extent appropriate." Thus, children with disabilities are entitled to an education at public expense, with the added stipulation that the children be in the most contact possible with their nondisabled peers. This legislation was built on the existing public law 94-142 (PL 94-142), which ensures a child with a disability an individualized education plan (IEP). An IEP includes services the child requires, such as speech therapy and occupational therapy, as well as the child's goals and benchmarks to meet the goals.

PL 94-142 services begin from the child's third birthday. Before that, public law 99-457 (PL 99-457) serves children from birth through age two. Under these laws, states receive grants to provide services to children with disabilities. PL 99-457 requires an individualized family service plan (IFSP), which is similar to an IEP, except that instead of being child centered, it is family centered. Families with children who are

disabled often require extra support and training. Included in the IFSP are teaching strategies for the parents as well as educating the siblings in how to interact with and understand their sibling with a disability.

The Future of Accommodating Mental Retardation

Before these laws were passed, children with disabilities had a very difficult time gaining an education. Society underestimated their learning capabilities. The few chances children with disabilities were given to learn were unsuccessful because of the lack of an appropriate teaching method.

Today, there is the opportunity to start early intervention from birth. There is greater understanding about mental retardation and how it affects brain development, which in turn enables society to make the necessary accommodations for both children and adults with disabilities. Early intervention provides a stronger foundation for the child to learn and develop skills later in life.

Agencies throughout the United States and in other countries provide continuous services to families who qualify. The Association for Retarded Citizens, which was started in the 1950s, is one such organization. These services provide employment opportunities, socialization opportunities, and daily living assistance to adults with disabilities. The ultimate goal of these agencies is to teach the adult how to function as a part of society and with the most independence possible.

Conclusions

Since the 1960s, when President John F. Kennedy spoke of his public support of people with mental retardation, the field of knowledge has expanded. This is due at least in part to people with MR presenting their acquired skills in the areas of education, employment, and athletics. These people have shown that, when provided with the right opportunities, they will rise to the occasion and take advantage of their opportunities.

Society has advanced from institutionalization of persons with MR to independent living in some cases. The expansion of education from segregation to inclusion has benefited many students with MR, as well as their typically developing peers. As technology continues to move forward, more advances will take place within the realm of MR. The more skills learned by people with MR, the more opportunities they will be given. In accordance with the law, and a better understanding of MR, prospects for the future of people with MR look very bright.

See also: DEVELOPMENTAL DISABILITIES

Under legislative guidelines, children with disabilities are entitled to an education at public expense, with the added stipulation that the children be in the most contact possible with their nondisabled peers. (AP/ Wide World Photos)

Bibliography

"Introduction to Mental Retardation." In the Association for Retarded Citizens [web site]. Silver Springs, Maryland, 2001. Available from http://www.thearc.org/faqs/mrqa.html; INTERNET.

Matson, Johnny. L., and James A. Mulick, eds. *Handbook of Mental Retardation,* 2nd edition. Pergamon Press, 1991.

"Mental Retardation." In the University of Maryland Medicine [web site]. Baltimore, Maryland, 2001. Available from http://umm.drkoop.com/conditions/ency/article/001523.htm; INTERNET.

Plog, Stanley C., and Miles B. Santamour, eds. *The Year 2000 and Mental Retardation.* New York: Plenum Press, 1980.

"Public Law 94-142: The Individuals with Disabilities Education Act." In the Association for Retarded Citizens [web site]. Silver Springs, Maryland, 1992. Available from http://www. thearc.org/faqs/pl94142.html; INTERNET.

Richardson, Stephen A., and Helene Koller. *Twenty-Two Years: Causes and Consequences of Mental Retardation.* Cambridge, MA: Harvard University Press, 1996.

Rowitz, Louis, ed. *Mental Retardation in the Year 2000.* New York: Springer-Verlag, 1992.

Scheerenberger, R. C. *A History of Mental Retardation: A Quarter Century of Promise.* Paul H. Brookes, 1987.

Smith, R. S. *Children with Mental Retardation: A Parent's Guide.* Woodbine House, 1993.

Lisa A. Wertenberger

METACOGNITION

If cognition is defined as the way we think and process information, then metacognition can be defined as the way we think about our own thoughts. In other words, metacognition is thinking about thinking.

American psychologist John Flavell believes that metacognition consists of metacognitive knowledge and metacognitive experiences. Metacognitive knowledge can be knowledge about the way you or others think, knowledge that different tasks or problems require different types of cognitive demands, or knowledge about strategies that can enhance learning and performance. Metacognitive experiences, such as reflecting on thoughts or analyzing thoughts, examine how we use strategies to help us regulate and oversee our own learning.

In sum, metacognition consists of planning, evaluating, and monitoring problem-solving activities and the outcome of these activities. Research suggests that greater metacognitive abilities are associated with more successful problem solving. This finding has instructional applications, meaning that it may be possible to teach students to be more aware of their own learning processes and performance, how to regulate these processes, and to learn more effectively.

See also: THEORY OF MIND

Bibliography

Flavell, John. "Metacognition and Cognitive Monitoring: A New Area of Cognitive-Developmental Inquiry." *American Psychologist* 34 (1979):906–911.

Sally A. Srokowski

METHODS OF STUDYING CHILDREN

When a researcher decides to study children, the task usually begins by choosing a topic or behavior to study and then focusing on a basic method that will allow the information to be gathered in the most efficient and effective manner. Researchers of child development have a variety of research methods from which to choose. These methods differ in important ways. For example, in a case study, the research tends to not intrude very much into the lives of the subjects of the study, and experimental control is not a major concern of the researcher. Conversely, in an experimental or quasi-experimental study, the research is typically more intrusive, and the researchers desire a certain amount of experimental control. Understanding the strengths and weaknesses of each method plays an important role in deciding which one to use in a particular study.

The type of method the researcher chooses is driven by several factors: the hypothesis that is being tested or the research question that is being asked, the type of information that is being gathered, how the study is designed, the number of participants, and any ethical considerations that relate to the participants. No matter which method is used, it is imperative that the research be conducted according to scientifically accepted procedures.

One of the first tasks of the child development researcher is to decide on a basic method by which to collect information. Scientific inquiries generally fall into two broad categories: those conducted using qualitative methods and those conducted using quantitative methods. As the word "qualitative" implies, qualitative methods employ nonnumeric designs and attempt to study phenomena inductively, as a process, and in the place in which the phenomena occur. Conversely, the quantitative approach attempts to measure phenomena numerically and make conclusions deductively and with respect to outcomes or products. Both approaches are well represented in the study of children.

Qualitative Methods of Child Study

The major types of qualitative methods include observation, self-reports, and the case study. Researchers often choose to view behavior directly through some kind of systematic observation. There are a number of options depending upon the level of intrusion that is desired and the type of environment in which the observation is to occur. The least intrusive form of observation is called naturalistic. In conducting a naturalistic observation, the researcher observes behavior in a natural environment, such as in a home, day-care, or school setting. This can be an excellent way to observe what happens in the everyday setting. The drawback, however, is that the researcher has little control over the environment and, consequently, over any extraneous variables (factors other than the behavior being researched). Furthermore, the behavior may not be displayed very often, or at all, during the observation. To remedy this problem, the researcher may choose to set up the observation in a place where the conditions are the same for all participants. A laboratory setting or contrived classroom, for example, could be set up for this purpose. In such a setting, unfortunately, participants may not behave in the same way that they would in a normal setting. Regardless of how the observation is set up, data from observations, sometimes referred to as field notes, must be studied carefully for themes and major ideas.

The use of self-reports is another option for gathering information qualitatively. There are two forms of self-reports. The first is the interview method, in which the researcher poses questions to participants in either informal or formal settings and records the responses. The second form is the self-report instrument, in which participants respond to a questionnaire or some other type of structured instrument. Both forms have advantages and disadvantages. Structured instruments provide control over external and extraneous stimuli, permit comparisons of the responses, and aid in efficient data collection. Interviews may provide richer information and could tap aspects of the participants that go unmeasured in structured instruments, such as how the participants think and function in the natural setting. Unfortunately, the results of the open interview are difficult to use for comparison purposes among individuals or groups of individuals. The rich data gained through interviews could come at the cost of standardization, thereby ruling out comparisons across participant responses.

The third qualitative method of research is the clinical method, or case study. The case study allows the researcher to gain detailed information on one individual's development. The rich data provides an extensive picture of the developmental process of an individual. In turn this means that there is only one person in the study and that any conclusions that are drawn cannot be easily generalized to other individuals.

Quantitative Methods of Child Study

There are three types of quantitative methods of study: correlational, experimental, and quasi-experimental. To some degree each of these designs allows the researcher to identify relationships between different factors and to then specify the causes of these relationships. The initial responsibility of the researcher is to find the general design that tests the hypothesis with the maximum amount of clarity.

The correlational design is used to determine whether relationships exist between two or more variables. Ultimately the investigator wants to determine whether a change in one variable coincides with a change in a second variable. In a correlation design no variable manipulation occurs. For example, a child's behaviors are measured as they naturally occur, and a numerical index reflecting the relationship between the measures' outcomes is then computed. Usually, a correlation coefficient is used to calculate the strength and type (positive or negative) of relationship that exists. While the correlational design is extremely useful, it cannot be used to determine cause-effect relationships between variables. The primary reason for this is that variables other than the ones under study cannot be controlled, measured, or otherwise considered in the correlational design; such variables could influence the relationship between the variables under study. This kind of control is afforded only in designs in which variables can be manipulated and participants can be randomly assigned to groups.

An experimental design does allow cause-effect conclusions since variables can be manipulated and participants can be randomly assigned. With respect to manipulation of variables, the researcher must assign independent and dependent variables to the experiment. The independent variables are the various treatments that the participants receive (and that are manipulated by the researcher), while the dependent variable represents the responses of the participants. For example, an independent variable might represent the amount of direct reading instruction students receive, and the dependent variable might be reading achievement scores. In essence, the researcher wants the dependent variable to reflect the effect of being treated with the independent variable. Experimenter control of the independent variable (e.g., amount, duration, and type of treatment) partially affords the necessary confidence to reach cause-effect conclusions. In other words, differences in the dependent variable may then be attributed to the various treatments the participants received (in the example, differences in reading achievement scores may be attributed to the various amounts of direct reading instruction).

In order to say that the treatment has caused some effect (on the dependent variable), it is important that all the traits of the participants be about the same, especially those that could confound the study. One way to accomplish such group equality is to randomly assign participants to groups. In essence, when "chance" is the force behind who gets the various treatments, it is assumed that the groups contain participants who were more or less alike prior to receiving treatments.

The ability to gain the necessary control that allows for cause-effect conclusion is also an important shortcoming of the experimental design. Conducting research in a controlled setting may alter the natural behavior patterns of participants and therefore decrease the "ecological validity" of the results. The researcher must also stay within ethical bounds, meaning that treatments that have adverse physical or psychological effects on participants cannot be used. Finally, the requirement of random assignment may not be possible for ethical or practical reasons.

To counter the latter drawback to the experimental design, a researcher might turn to the quasi-experimental design. The quasi-experimental method permits the researcher to compare groups that have been manipulated but not randomly assigned. For example, in the above example of a study of the effect of direct reading instruction on reading achievement, suppose that homerooms have already been assigned in the school where the researcher intends to conduct the study. It may still be possible to treat different classes, but the researcher must take into account that the participants were not randomly assigned to the classes. In such a case, a quasi-experimental design could be used, but the researcher must temper any cause-effect conclusions because of the possibility that uncontrolled variables "caused" the results.

Finally, it may not be possible to manipulate variables or randomly assign participants to groups. In this case, a causal comparative design might be used. In the causal comparative method, already existing groups are studied (after the "independent variable" has already occurred) and group differences are studied on some dependent variable of interest. For example, a researcher might choose to study the intellectual development of children in orphanages compared to that of children raised in a home setting with their biological parents. The causal comparative design is often used to study treatments that would be unethical to impose on participants. Obviously, the causal-comparative design offers little of the control necessary to make cause-effect conclusions.

Longitudinal versus Cross-Sectional Studies

By the very nature of their field of study, child development researchers are concerned with change that occurs over time. This fact brings to light another research design choice that must be considered: longitudinal research versus cross-sectional research. Longitudinal studies involve studying the same group of participants over a particular time period. Cross-sectional studies involved studying groups of participants in different age groups at the same point in time. It would seem that longitudinal research would be the developmental researcher's first choice, but because of some of the disadvantages of that method, developmental researchers must sometimes use the cross-sectional method.

In a longitudinal study, a researcher performs repeated observations or testing at specified points during the participants' lives, thus allowing the observation of development. The time span involved may be anywhere from a few months to a lifetime. This design provides the best information about the continuity or discontinuity of behavior over time and allows for the individual tracking of patterns of behavior, as well as trends of development, within a similar group. The problems of this type of design can often override the benefits. It is expensive to study a large group of individuals over an extensive time span. Keeping up with these individuals can be costly and time consuming. Participants may move away from home and local communities, and therefore drop out of the study. Sometimes the participants become wise to the testing or observations and practice over repeated measures and contaminate the results. Cohort effects may also be a factor in the outcomes of longitudinal studies. Cohort effects are common characteristics or trends in development for one cohort or group that may not follow suit for another cohort. To try to alleviate some of these potential problems, researchers often study small groups of individuals; but this may make it difficult to generalize the findings to a larger group.

Cross-sectional studies are quick by nature in that a researcher does not have to follow the development of each individual. At the same time a researcher does not gain the rich data on individual development that can be garnered from longitudinal studies, since the evidence of change is inferred from differences between the age groups. The cross-sectional design is also affected by the cohort effect where age differences may show trends particular to a specific group

and not true developmental changes. Thus, while the cross-sectional design solves some the problems associated with a longitudinal design (e.g., subject dropout and cost), the cross-sectional design still suffers some disadvantages (e.g., age differences do not show age change and cohort effects).

Summary

Qualitative and quantitative research methods can be used in child development studies. The decision on which method to use is typically based on the research question of interest and how researchers have previously attempted to address the question. With respect to qualitative methods, the researcher's job is to study the topic in its natural context with as little intrusion as possible. In the quantitative method, the researcher's job, after conceptualizing the study, is to define the dependent and independent variables or decide whether this kind of control is possible. In instances where variables cannot be controlled, the researcher must use appropriate methods to control for differences or use correlations to determine how the variables may be related to each other. Using representative sampling is imperative to be able to generalize the study to other populations and settings. In either approach to child development research, the ability to uncover interesting data and to replicate it helps strengthen the field as a whole.

See also: THEORIES OF DEVELOPMENT

Bibliography

Graue, M. Elizabeth, and Daniel J. Walsh. *Studying Children in Context: Theories, Methods, and Ethics.* Thousand Oaks, CA: Sage, 1998.

Isaksen, Judith Graver. *Watching and Wondering: Observing and Recording Child Development.* Palo Alto, CA: Mayfield, 1986.

Lancy, David F. *Studying Children and Schools: Qualitative Research Traditions.* Prospect Heights, IL: Waveland Press, 2001.

Vasta, Ross. *Studying Children: An Introduction to Research Methods.* San Francisco: W. H. Freeman, 1979.

Terrill F. Saxon
Majka Woods Mitchell

MIDWIVES

A midwife is a person, usually a woman, who assists other women in giving birth. Typically, this assistance extends throughout pregnancy, labor, delivery, and the newborn period. Midwives focus on delivering healthy babies in as natural a manner as possible; they also provide health counseling to mothers and families. Although obstetricians and midwives have much knowledge and experience in common, they occupy different professions. While both are concerned with a healthy pregnancy and delivery, obstetrations are prepared to deal medically with complications. It is not uncommon for midwives and obstetricians to collaborate.

Since the 1970s, a small but growing proportion of North American women have chosen midwives to attend their births. Many of these midwives are registered nurses with formal midwifery training and certification by the American College of Nurse Midwives. There are also "lay" or "direct-entry" midwives, who have not been trained as nurses. Midwife deliveries may take place in hospitals, birth centers, or homes.

See also: BIRTH; NATURAL CHILDBIRTH; PREGNANCY; PRENATAL CARE

Bibliography

Lefèber, Yvonne, and Henk W. A. Voorhoeve. *Indigenous Customs in Childbirth and Child Care.* Assen, The Netherlands: Van Gorcum, 1998.

Rooks, Judith P. *Midwifery and Childbirth in America.* Philadelphia: Temple University Press, 1997.

Faye B. Steuer

MILESTONES OF DEVELOPMENT: OVERVIEW

Milestones of development are major turning points in childhood that help organize or direct other aspects of a child's development. Milestones occur in every area of development: physical and motor, social and emotional, and cognitive. Almost everyone experiences these environmental (e.g., nutrition and culture) factors. Not reaching a milestone or an extreme variation in timing may have an influence on the child's later development. One example of a physical milestone is the development of the ability to walk. Walking, rather than crawling, opens up the toddler's physical and perceptual world. A major social-emotional milestone is the development of an attachment to a major caregiver during the infant's first year. Secure attachment has been found to promote the child's later social and cognitive development.

See also: STAGES OF DEVELOPMENT

Bibliography

Abe, Jo Ann, and Carroll Izard. "The Devleopmental Functions of Emotions: An Analysis in Terms of Differential Emotions Theory." *Cognition and Emotion* 13 (1999):523–549.

Hay, Dale, and A. Angold. *Precursors and Causes in Development and Psychopathology.* New York: John Wiley and Sons, 1993.

Lee, Kang. *Childhood Cognitive Development: The Essential Readings.* Malden, MA: Blackwell, 2000.

Diane E. Wille

MILESTONES OF DEVELOPMENT

Human development is a complicated affair, progressing as the result of the continuous interaction of biologic and environmental factors. It is for this reason that no two people are exactly alike, not even identical twins. Despite such variability, there are aspects of development that are predictable, such that children throughout the world develop certain abilities and characteristics at about the same time. These universal accomplishments are termed "milestones"—guideposts that reflect normal, species-typical development.

The temporal regularity of these milestones implies that they are under biological control, little affected by the vagaries of the external world. This is only partially true, for all aspects of development are also influenced by environmental factors. Children inherit not only a species-typical genome (DNA), but also a species-typical environment, which begins prenatally and continues after birth as infants around the world are nurtured by adults in social settings. Subtle differences at both the genetic and environmental levels affect development of even these reliable milestones, so that experts are not able to specify the exact time children will display a particular characteristic but can state only approximately when they will appear. Variation around these average times is normal, with half of all children showing these characteristics sooner than average and half later than average.

In Tables 1–3 are partial lists of physical, cognitive, and social/emotional milestones, denoted separately for the periods of infancy, preschool, school age, and adolescence. Some of these milestones have great social significance. For instance, in some traditional societies, a girl's first menstrual period signals a move from childhood to adulthood; and, in American society, being out of diapers is a requirement for admission to some preschools.

Perhaps the first thing to note is that there are many more entries for infancy than for the other age groups. This is primarily because the accomplishments of the first two years of life are more under the influence of maturational factors than environmental ones. As children get older, their developmental pathways vary as a function of the societies they live in. For example, for children in literate societies, one could have included milestones related to reading. Reading, however, requires specific instruction that not all children receive; moreover, there are different writing systems, alphabets, and educational philosophies that result in different patterns of reading-related behavior even in literate cultures.

TABLE 1

Physical and Motor Development

Infancy (0-2 years)	Preschool (2-5 years)	School Age (6-10 years)	Adolescence (11-18 years)
Rolls over in both directions (2-5 months)	Enjoys rough & tumble play (2-2.5 years)	First permanent teeth erupt (6-7 years)	Growth spurt peak (girls: 11-14 years; boys: 13-16 years)
First teeth (5-7 months)	Has manual coordination to use simple tools (for example, spoons) (2-2.5 years)	Growth spurt begins for girls (9-10 years)	Secondary sexual characteristics for girls (11-15 years)
Sits unsupported; Crawls on hands and knees; Pulls self up to stand while holding on to objects (5-8 months)	Attains bowel and bladder control (2.5-4 years)		Secondary sexual characteristics for boys (12-17 years)
Walks without support (11-15 months)			First menstrual period (menarche) (12-13 years)
Begins running and climbing (18-24 months)			

SOURCE: *David F. Bjorklund and Jesse M. Bering.*

Physical Milestones

The list for physical development (Table 1) includes a number of familiar milestones for infants, most related to gaining control over their bodies so that they are able to move about on their own. The list of milestones for the preschool years will also be familiar. It is during this time that children become toilet trained and learn to use simple tools, such as forks and spoons. The first permanent teeth erupt around six years of age. Although children across the globe are typically weaned by age three or four, they are not able to eat an adult-style diet until they have most of their permanent teeth. This means that adults must specially prepare food for children years after they have stopped nursing. This is a pattern seen in no other animal and makes the period of "childhood" unique to the human species.

Physical growth is slow and gradual between the ages of about six and eleven, when the adolescent growth spurt begins (sometimes a bit earlier for girls). The rapid growth at this time, which occurs later for boys, coupled with the development of secondary sexual characteristics, marks the physical transition to adulthood. Girls' first menstrual period (menarche) usually occurs about two years after the onset of secondary sexual characteristics, and both boys and girls have a period of relative infertility, lasting several years, after they have become sexually mature. Although the pattern of puberty described here is universal, the average age at which girls reach puberty has been decreasing over the past two centuries, primarily because of better nutrition and health. There is also evidence that girls from high-stress, father-absent homes reach puberty earlier than girls from low-stress, father-present homes, reflecting the role that social factors can have on physical development.

Cognitive Milestones

Selected cognitive milestones are presented in Table 2. It is not until around seven or eight months that infants will search for an object hidden as they watch, believing, apparently, that the object continues to exist even though they no longer see it. First words are usually uttered late during the first year, and children's first two-word sentences are typically spoken between eighteen and twenty-four months of age. Language abilities develop rapidly during the third year of life, so that by age three and a half, most children are linguistic geniuses, being able to speak their native tongue proficiently (and far better than most adult second-language learners). Children have a difficult time taking the psychological perspective of others until about three and a half to four years of age. Until this time, they often believe that if they know something (for example, that a cookie has been moved from a box to a jar), other people should know it as well, even though others have different knowledge (not knowing the cookie was moved). Understanding that people's behavior is governed by beliefs and desires, which may be different from one's own, has been termed "theory of mind" and is the basis of all sophisticated human social interaction. Thinking

TABLE 2

Cognitive Development

Infancy (0-2 years)	Preschool (2-5 years)	School Age (6-10 years)	Adolescence (11-18 years)
Makes vowel sounds (coos) (2-3 months)	Language increases rapidly (2-3 years)	Understands substance doesn't change in quanity with change in appearance (conservation) (6-8 years)	Abstract thought (11-16 years)
Begins to babble (5-7 months)	Understands false beliefs (3-4 years)		
Recovers "hidden" objects (objects permanence) (6-9 months)	Shows knowledge of counting and simple arithmetic (2.5-4 years)		
Points out objects to others (10-12 months)			
Speaks first words (9-12 months)			
Recognizes self in mirror (15-24 months)			
Produces first two-word sentence (18-24 months)			
Plays make-believe (18-24 months)			

SOURCE: *David F. Bjorklund and Jesse M. Bering.*

TABLE 3

Social/Emotional Development

Infancy (0-2 years)	Preschool (2-5 years)	School Age (6-10 years)	Adolescence (11-18 years)
Social smile (2-3 months)	Shows signs of empathy (2-3 years)	Peer group membership/friends become important; dominance hierarchies are established (6-7 years)	Reduced interest in family, increased interest in peers (11-13 years)
May show wariness to unfamiliar people (5-8 months)	Plays cooperatively with other children (2.5-3.5 years)		Begins dating/heterosexual relationship (12-17 years)
Begins to show understanding of emotions in others (18-24 months)	Understands gender will not change over time or contexts (gender constancy) (4-5 years)		

SOURCE: *David F. Bjorklund and Jesse M. Bering.*

becomes more logical during the school years, and this is perhaps best reflected by conservation tasks, developed by the Swiss psychologist Jean Piaget. Beginning around six years of age, children realize, for example, that the amount of water one has is the same regardless of whether the container that holds it is short and fat or tall and skinny. Much before this time, the appearance of "more" in the tall container determines children's thinking in such situations. With adolescence comes abstract thought, again as first described by Piaget. Children are able to think

scientifically and are able to reflect upon what they already know.

Social/Emotional Milestones

Table 3 presents some social/emotional milestones. The social smile, observed early in infancy, reflects a general responsiveness to people, critical for an intensely social species such as *Homo sapiens*. Infants' attachment to their parents is sometimes reflected by a wariness of strangers and by distress when they are separated from their caregivers. By the pre-school years, children are able to identify emotions in others and can seemingly empathize with the feelings of others, as reflected, for instance, by a three-year-old bringing his tearful mother his teddy bear to comfort her. Although toddlers are interested in other children, friends typically do not become important until the early school years, at which time children enter the peer group and establish dominance hierarchies, often based on physical strength, especially among boys. Typically during this time, boys and girls segregate themselves into same-sex play groups. In adolescence, the peer group becomes increasingly important (although the family rarely loses its influence), and, coupled with the onset of puberty, heterosexual interests and behavior commence.

A milestone approach to development provides a quick glimpse at important acquisitions that children over the world experience. There is still much variability in when children attain these milestones, because of both biological (genetic) and environmental (societal) factors. And many culturally important phenomena that arise only with specific experiences (e.g., reading, religious practices) are not captured by knowledge of milestones. Nonetheless, milestones show what is universal in human development and give parents and educators an idea of how quickly children are progressing relative to a species-typical standard.

See also: STATES OF DEVELOPMENT; THEORY OF MIND

Bibliography

Belsky, Jay, Lawrence Steinberg, and Patricia Draper. "Childhood Experience, Interpersonal Development, and Reproductive Strategy: An Evolutionary Theory of Socialization." *Child Development* 62 (1991):647–670.

Bogin, Barry. *Patterns of Human Growth,* 2nd edition. Cambridge, Eng.: Cambridge University Press, 1999.

Wellman, Henry M. *The Child's Theory of Mind.* Cambridge, MA: MIT Press, 1990.

David F. Bjorklund
Jesse M. Bering

MISCARRIAGE

Miscarriage is a synonym for "spontaneous abortion" or "spontaneous pregnancy loss." A miscarriage occurs because of an abnormal fetus (usually within the first twelve weeks) or disruption of the uterus as a safe environment (more prevalent after thirteen weeks). Miscarriages are common, occurring in up to 19 percent of pregnancies.

Miscarriage usually leads to vaginal bleeding, abdominal cramping, and occasionally severe pelvic pain as the disrupted fetus and placenta pass through the cervix. The major concerns are the health of the mother; there are no medical interventions that will mitigate against fetal death.

Miscarriages are unanticipated and occur early during a time of frequent maternal ambivalence regarding the pregnancy. Grief is often prolonged, with self-reproach as to the cause of the miscarriage. Siblings usually experience turmoil due to various combinations of previous jealousy of the pregnancy, lack of parental emotional availability, and processing the reality of death.

See also: BIRTH; PREGNANCY; PRENATAL DEVELOPMENT

Bibliography

Reindollar, Richard H. "Contemporary Issues for Spontaneous Abortion: Does Recurrent Abortion Exist?" *Obstetrical and Gynecological Clinics of North America* 27 (2000):541–554.

Scroggins, Kathleen M., William D. Smucker, and Adarsh E. Krishen. "Spontaneous Pregnancy Loss: Evaluation, Management, and Follow-up Counseling." *Primary Care* 27 (2000):153–167.

Simpson, Joe L. "Fetal Wastage." In Steven G. Gabbe, Jennifer R. Niebyl, and Joe L. Simpson eds., *Obstetrics: Normal and Problem Pregnancies,* 3rd edition. New York: Churchill Livingstone, 1996.

Michael Storr

MITOSIS

Mitosis is the stage of the cell cycle at which chromosomal division occurs. This division precedes cytokinesis, or cell division, which leads to two daughter cells with identical nuclear DNA content. Between mitotic events, chromosomal DNA is replicated during the synthesis stage of the cell cycle. The process of mitosis is required whenever a somatic cell divides. In contrast to meiosis, which occurs in germ cells prior to the reproductive process, mitosis does not involve exchange of DNA between homologous chromosomes or a reduction in DNA content.

See also: MEIOSIS

Bibliography

Oak Ridge National Laboratory. "The Science behind the Human Genome Project." Available from http://www.ornl.gov/hgmis/ project/info.html; INTERNET.

David W. Threadgill
Robert E. Boykin

MONTESSORI METHOD

The Montessori Method is a system of education based on the beliefs of Maria Montessori. The most critical components of her method include the pre-

Maria Montessori (right) created a system of education based on skill development in specific areas, including practical living and language. (AP/Wide World Photos)

pared environment and the teacher. The Montessori classroom is usually divided into four areas: practical living, sensorial, math, and language. Each area contains beautifully crafted, authentic materials designed for independent use by the child in order to build skills in each of these areas, as well as to develop dispositions including self-direction, freedom, and order. Many Montessori materials are self-correcting, clearly indicating if they are being used successfully. The teacher's role is to carefully observe the children and introduce activities and modify the environment in order to support each child's exploration and growth. The Montessori Method has had a profound impact on the field of early childhood education both in terms of the materials and activities Maria Montessori developed and her approach to teacher observation and planning.

See also: PRESCHOOL

Bibliography

Lillard, Paula. *Montessori: A Modern Approach.* New York: Schocken Books, 1972.

Martha J. Buell

MORAL DEVELOPMENT

During the last half of the twentieth century, perceptions of increased school violence within the United States renewed public concern for children's moral development. The study of moral development includes the way individuals reason about morality, the emotions associated with morality, the actions or behavior demonstrating morality, and the socialization or teaching of morality. Morality is the level of agreement or disagreement with a system of moral rules or standards of right and wrong. Although some children as young as thirty-four months know the difference between morality and social custom, the distinction between the two concepts is often distorted. For example, many children considered flag burning to have moral consequences. Respect for a flag is a social convention or a culturally agreed upon and accepted custom, regulation, or protocol that changes with social opinion. Moral rules, however, rarely change. Considering this confusion, research concerning moral reasoning, emotionality, behavior, and socialization often overlaps with topics concerning other types of prosocial development.

Reasoning

Like Jean Piaget, the pioneer of cognitive theory, Lawrence Kohlberg, a prominent moral development researcher, believed that people's perceptions, attitudes, and actions are influenced by the way they think or reason. So, he studied the reasoning process employed to resolve ethical dilemmas, not the resulting judgments or rules that foster social justice. Through research, he discovered three progressive stages of moral reasoning: preconventional, conventional, and postconventional. Each stage has two phases. All six levels reflect a type of decision that could not be made at an earlier age. Even though an elementary-school-age child has an improved understanding of others' beliefs and thoughts, children between the ages of six and eleven tend to reason in preconventional or self-focused ways. At first, they are likely to make judgments that reflect the need to obey moral rules to avoid punishment, but in later elementary grades, reasoning is likely to reflect a need for reciprocity or in-kind treatment. A person's moral reasoning ability, however, develops over a lifetime and individuals, from the age of twelve on, tend to reason in conventional or community-focused ways.

First, they want to please others or receive social approval for following the community's rules. Later, they may think from a law-and-order perspective and value becoming a good citizen. The third stage, post-conventional or ideal-centered reasoning, occurs rarely.

These levels of reasoning may overrule the culture's standards and the individual's personal concerns. Initially, laws are important in ideal-centered analyses of moral dilemmas because they are agreed upon by the community, as a whole, and are created to help everyone. Infractions are accepted if the rules become harmful or if another party breaks the legal contract. Kohlberg suggested, however, that individuals would eventually reason using universal principles established through individual reflection—not legal standards or individual values—but there is little evidence to demonstrate that this stage of reasoning exists.

Evolutionary biologists criticize the validity of Kohlberg's last three stages because, unlike the first three stages, they do not foster the adaptation and cooperation necessary for species survival. Others assert that his moral reasoning levels do not reflect various religious beliefs, cultural values, economic circumstances, social situations, or individual interpretations of moral dilemmas. For example, replies to moral dilemmas frequently reflect either a care for others' perspective or a justice and rights perspective. Morality of care perspectives consider more responsibility toward, interest in, and nurturance of others. Morality of justice perspectives do not consider personal ideas of right and wrong, but reflect theoretical, visionary, and complex notions of morality. When assessing replies to moral dilemmas, some researchers have found that females more than males reflect a morality of care and that males more than females reflect a morality of justice. On the whole, however, Kohlberg's stages reflect a range of human possibility in moral reasoning and have provided a foundation for future theory and research.

Emotionality

A child's moral reasoning ability and behavior expands as emotions, other awareness, and self-awareness develop. People feeling guilt, the emotion of remorse over doing wrong, often feel empathy and are often motivated to confess and compensate. Feelings of guilt, as well as feelings of disgust, sadness, and empathic anger, also coincide with perceptions of injustice and immorality. Those with empathic and sympathetic temperaments or positive moods, in general, tend to exhibit more sharing, supporting, volunteering, helping, and less aggressive behavior, while intense negative emotions tend to lead to destructive or unproductive anger resolution. Feelings of shame that arise from situations in which the self has been challenged appear to be related to antisocial behavior. Shame and embarrassment tend to reflect others' evaluations and play a large role in conformity to social conventions.

The precursors to many emotions are self- and other awareness, which may occur as early as twelve or fifteen months of age. Guilt and other types of mental discomfort about moral and social transgressions begin to develop between fourteen and forty-six months. Additionally, empathic responding, reparative behavior, and awareness of right and wrong are first evident at twenty-four months. Children who demonstrate these feelings and behaviors also demonstrate fewer moral and social transgressions. Between ages seven and eleven the brain has adequately developed so that children can begin to understand moral issues and relate to their own feelings about moral behavior. During adolescence not only does complex moral reasoning increase, but so too does concern for others. Cognitive processing or thinking skills, however, tend to break down when people feel threatened or sad; therefore, it is understandable that adolescents may concentrate on their own needs and desires when the costs of helping others are great.

Behavior

Some people assert that society should be more concerned about moral behavior than moral reasoning. Children demonstrate prosocial and moral behavior when they share, help, cooperate, communicate sympathy, and otherwise demonstrate their ability to care about others and the community. Ideally, these behaviors are performed without the expectation of reward, as reflected in the later stages of moral reasoning. Moral behavior, however, often provides good feelings, kinship, and interconnection with others. The frequency and type of moral or prosocial behavior vary with the frequency and type of moral reasoning, the child's emotional development, the child's gender, and situational factors, including culture and religion. Human respect, concepts of success, and beliefs fostered by family and peers, as well as negative sanctions, are also related to the frequency of prosocial and antisocial behavior.

Children's ability to restrain unacceptable behavior begins to improve in toddlerhood. Children between the ages of seven and eleven, however, regard allegiance to peers as more important than cultural rules, so they often say that they would cheat, lie, or steal to help a friend in need. It is clear that children think about and make choices concerning morality and that peers have a great influence on moral behavior.

Socialization

Moral development is also fostered by the adult control and communication of cultural values, beliefs, and ethics. Less obvious types of support, such as role modeling, may also foster children's moral development. Active reflection, however, is more likely to lead to moral action than merely accepting social conventions and laws, so adult and peer discussion are necessary to foster moral development.

Political, academic, and social influences have encouraged schools to augment parent and peer influence. For example, Kohlberg was aware of increased school violence, and he believed that large schools fostered detachment and poor communication between staff and students. He also had observed high levels of moral development in Israeli kibbutzim, so he created Just Community high schools in which student-faculty groups developed their own rules of conduct through discussion, reason, and argument about fairness. Violations of the rules were subject to the group's criticism and discipline. Kohlberg asserted that moral development would occur when students shared in the responsibility of creating a moral environment. In fact, within these schools, the students' complex moral reasoning increased while antisocial behavior declined. The content of the moral issues addressed, however, was not the same from school to school and increased moral behavior did not extend beyond the school environment.

Providing children with opportunities to question their own moral reasoning and behavior will foster moral development, but discussing the intentions, perspectives, false beliefs, and judgments of characters within a moral dilemma may also foster moral development. When promoting moral and prosocial behavior, parents, teachers, and other important adults should employ activities suitable for the child's age. One study suggested that moral dilemmas should concern children doing familiar things in familiar settings so that moral issues are more easily understood. Many teachers recognize this need for age appropriate curricula; differences in age appropriateness, however, vary between cultures. Therefore, not only should maturational contexts be considered when creating moral development curricula, but so should experiential, cultural, and economic contexts.

The benefits of incorporating moral development in school curricula may extend beyond decreased antisocial and immoral behavior. Research suggests that it may also help children develop a theory of mind and enhance their social and academic success. Therefore, in an effort to prepare children for socially acceptable community involvement, schools should continue to develop and use appropriate curricula, and researchers should continue to explore the realms of moral development.

See also: KOHLBERG, LAWRENCE; STAGES OF DEVELOPMENT; THEORY OF MIND

Bibliography

Eisenberg, Nancy. "Emotion, Regulation, and Moral Development." *Annual Review of Psychology* 51 (2000):665–697.

Gabennesch, H. "The Perception of Social Conventionality by Children and Adults." *Child Development* 61 (1990):2047–2059.

Gilligan, C. *In a Different Voice: Psychological Theory and Women's Development.* Cambridge, MA: Harvard University Press, 1982.

Helwig, C. C., and A. Prencipe. "Children's Judgments of Flags and Flag Burning." *Child Development* 70, no. 1 (1999):132–143.

Kohlberg, Lawrence. *The Psychology of Moral Development: The Nature and Validity of Moral Stages.* San Francisco: Harper and Row, 1981.

Kohlberg, Lawrence, C. Levine, and A. Hewer. *Moral Stages: A Current Formulation and a Response to Critics.* Buffalo, NY: Karger, 1983.

Saarni, C. *The Development of Emotional Competence.* New York: Guilford Press, 1999.

Schweder, R. A., M. Mahapatra, and J. G. Miller. "Culture and Moral Development." In J. W. Stigler, R. A. Schweder, and G. Herdt eds., *Cultural Psychology: Essays on Comparative Human Development.* Cambridge, Eng.: Cambridge University Press, 1990.

Smetana, J. G., M. Killen, and E. Turiel. "Children's Reasoning about Interpersonal and Moral Conflicts." *Child Development* 62 (1991):629–644.

Tomlinson, J. "Values: The Curriculum of Moral Education." *Children and Society* 11, no. 4 (1997):242–251.

Turiel, E. *The Development of Social Knowledge: Morality and Convention.* Cambridge, Eng.: Cambridge University Press, 1983.

Walker, L. J., R. C. Pitts, K. H. Hennig, and M. K. Matsuba. "Reasoning about Morality and Real-Life Moral Problems." In Melanie Killen and Daniel Hart eds., *Morality in Everyday Life: Developmental Perspectives.* Cambridge, Eng.: Cambridge University Press, 1995.

Danae E. Roberts

MOTHERESE

Speech directed toward infants and young children displays special characteristics, such as heightened pitch, exaggerated intonation, and increased repetition of words and clauses, that differ from the speech adults use with one another. Such "motherese" or "infant-directed talk" is typical of fathers as well as mothers, nonparents as well as parents, and across diverse ages and socioeconomic groups. Motherese has been documented in a variety of cultures and across a typologically diverse set of languages, including English, Japanese, Hausa (a Nigerian language), and sign language. Infants prefer motherese to adult-directed speech, and they benefit from such interaction. For example, by enhancing attention, motherese promotes infants' processing of speech. Likewise, motherese helps infants to analyze the structure of speech by highlighting boundaries between important units, such as words and clauses. Research in the late 1990s suggested that motherese is actually part of a more general tendency to modify infant-directed interactions. For example, adults also modify at least some of their infant-directed bodily motions. Such "motionese" includes simplification and increased repetition of action. Thus motherese speech seems to be just one dimension of a whole constellation of infant-directed modifications.

See also: BABBLING AND EARLY WORDS; LANGUAGE DEVELOPMENT

Bibliography

Fernald, Anne, and Patricia Kuhl. "Acoustic Determinants of Infant Preference for Motherese Speech." *Infant Behavior and Development* 10 (1987):279–293.

Lieven, Elena. "Crosslinguistic and Crosscultural Aspects of Language Addressed to Children." In Clare Gallaway and Brian Richards eds., *Input and Interaction in Language Acquisition.* Cambridge, Eng.: Cambridge University Press, 1994.

Rebecca J. Brand
Dare A. Baldwin

MOTOR DEVELOPMENT

When babies are born, they are not able to move much on their own. Over time, a baby learns to move many parts of its body and control its muscles so it can hold its head up, sit up by itself, stand up, or pick up a toy. The process of motor development, however, does not happen overnight. Like many things, learning about the body and making it move takes time. Motor development is the process of learning how to use muscles in the body to move. The progression of acquiring motor skills goes from simple to complex.

Motor development happens in a predictable sequence of events for most children, but each child varies in age when each skill is mastered. For example, although most children begin to walk independently around twelve to fourteen months, some children are walking as early as nine months. Further, children differ in terms of the length of time it takes to develop certain motor skills, such as the baby who sits up, virtually skips crawling, and begins walking.

Transition from Reflex Movement to Voluntary Movement

At birth, babies have very little control over their bodies. They spend most of their time curled up in what is called a fetal position. This position is how the baby lay in the womb during the nine months of the mother's pregnancy. In addition to the fetal position, primitive reflexes dominate virtually all of a newborn baby's movements. Babies are born with these reflexive movements as a means for basic life preservation. The reflexes, which are controlled by lower levels of the brain, eventually give way to more sophisticated voluntary movements monitored by higher levels of the brain.

The first voluntary task of a newborn is learning to bring the arms and legs out straight in order to lie flat. This maneuver takes a lot of muscular energy, so the baby begins moving arms and legs around during the waking hours to develop coordination and strength. As babies move their bodies more in the first months of life, motor pathways begin to form in the brain. These pathways allow a baby to eventually perform motor movements without conscious thought.

Principles of Development

The process of motor development depends heavily on the maturation of the central nervous system and the muscular system. As these systems develop, an infant's ability to move progresses. The sequence of motor development follows an apparently orderly pattern. Arnold Gesell, a noted researcher in the field of child development, indicated through his studies that development does not proceed in a straight line. Instead, it swings back and forth between periods of rapid and slower maturation. Gesell and his colleagues also discovered from their infant observations made in the 1930s and 1940s that infant growth does indeed follow distinct developmental directions: cephalocaudal, proximal-distal, and general to specific.

Cephalocaudal Principle

First, most children develop from head to toe, or cephalocaudal. Initially, the head is disproportionately larger than the other parts of the infant's body. The cephalocaudal theory states that muscular control develops from the head downward: first the neck, then the upper body and the arms, then the lower trunk and the legs. Motor development from birth to six months of age includes initial head and neck control, then hand movements and eye-hand coordination, followed by preliminary upper body control. The subsequent six months of life include important stages in learning to control the trunk, arms, and legs for skills such as sitting, crawling, standing, and walking.

Proximal-Distal Principle

Second, children develop their motor skills from the center of their bodies outward, near to far or proximal-distal. This principle asserts that the head and trunk develop before the arms and legs, and the arms and legs before the fingers and toes. Babies learn to master control of upper arms and upper legs, then forearms and legs, then their hands and feet, and finally fingers and toes. An example of this is an infant's need to control the arm against gravity before being able to reach for a toy.

General to Specific Principle

Lastly, the general to specific development pattern is the progression from the entire use of the body to the use of specific body parts. This pattern can be best seen through the learned process of grasping. Initially, infants can grossly hold a bottle with both hands at about four months of age. After practice and time, twelve-month-old infants can hold smaller toys or food in each hand using a pincher grasp. This finger and thumb grasp is more precise than the grasping skill of an infant at four months. Just as the child develops a more precise grasp with time and experience, many other motor skills are achieved simultaneously throughout motor development. Each important skill mastered by an infant is considered a motor milestone.

Motor Milestones

Motor milestones are defined as the major developmental tasks of a period that depend on movement by the muscles. Examples of motor milestones include the first time a baby sits alone, takes a step, holds a toy, rolls, crawls, or walks. As discussed previously, the timing of the accomplishment of each motor milestone will vary with each child. "Motor milestones depend on genetic factors, how the mother and father progressed through their own development, maturation of the central nervous system, skeletal and bone growth, nutrition, environmental space, physical health, stimulation, freedom and mental health" (Freiberg 1987; Paplia and Wendkosolds 1987). Within the motor milestones exist two forms of motor development: gross motor development and fine motor development. These two areas of motor development allow an infant to progress from being helpless and completely dependent to being an independently mobile child.

Gross Motor Development

Gross motor development involves skills that require the coordination of the large muscle groups of the body, such as the arms, legs, and trunk. Examples of gross motor skills include sitting, walking, rolling, standing, and much more (see the list of gross motor milestones in Table 1). The infant's gross motor activity is developed from movements that began while in the womb and from the maturation of reflex behav-

ior. With experience, the infant slowly learns head control, then torso or trunk control, and then is rolling, sitting, and eventually walking. The first year of a baby's life is filled with major motor milestones that are mastered quickly when compared to the motor milestone achievements of the rest of the baby's development. In addition to the development of gross motor skills, a baby is simultaneously learning fine motor skills.

Fine Motor Development

Fine motor development is concerned with the coordination of the smaller muscles of the body, including the hands and face. Examples of fine motor skills include holding a pencil to write, buttoning a shirt, and turning pages of a book (see the list of fine motor milestones in Table 1). Fine motor skills use the small muscles of both the hands and the eyes for performance. For the first few months, babies spend a majority of time using their eyes rather than their hands to explore their environment. The grasping reflex, which is present at birth, is seen when a finger is pressed into the baby's palm; the baby's fingers will automatically curl around the person's finger. This grasping reflex slowly integrates and allows the development of more mature grasping patterns. At four months, babies will begin to more frequently reach out for toys with their arms and hands. The reach looks more like a swipe because the baby is learning how to control the arm and hand. Over time, babies learn how to make smoother and coordinated movements with their arms and hands.

Assessment of Gross Motor and Fine Motor Development

Many assessment tools exist to measure a child's performance in regard to gross and fine motor skills. Each assessment requires good observational skills from the evaluator, who is typically a developmental pediatrician, nurse, educator, occupational therapist, or physical therapist. Some assessments call for each item to be administered in a formal standardized manner, so that each child is tested the same way every time. These tests are also called normative-based because they compare individual performance to that of other children. Other measures encourage professionals to ask parents questions about their child and are based on informal observations of the child at play. These more informal tests are referred to as criterion-based assessments because they compare individual performance to a criterion or standard. Regardless of the type of assessment, each measure has the common purpose of evaluating the child's current ability to perform motor-related tasks. Professionals use the results of these assessments to

TABLE 1

Age	Gross motor skills	Fine Motor skills
One month	Turns head side to side on tummy; lifts head for a few seconds	Hands are closed; visually watching objects; grasp reflex present
Two months	Bends hips with bottom in the air; head bobs in sitting; legs give way in supported standing	Grasp reflex; holds hands together; holds rattle when placed in hands for a few seconds; hands more open
Three months	Pushing up on elbows while on tummy; head is steadier; sits with less support; rolls back to side and tummy to side	Begins swiping at objects, beginning to look from hand to object; hands clasped together at center of body
Four months	Head comes up with body when pulled to sit with fewer lags; able to sit up if helped	Shakes and plays with rattle in hands; puts fingers in mouth; holds on to dangling toy; begins reaching for toys
Five months	Lifts head by self; brings feet to mouth; brings hands to feet; rolls from back to tummy; pushes up on arms while on tummy; sits with little support; stands with help	Pulls down a suspended ring; picks up a small toy or spoon; begins to hold toys with two hands
Six months	Sits unsupported; stands with help; able to lift chest off floor while on tummy; rolling with leg starting first	Begins to reach with one hand; able to hold own bottle; able to pick up dropped object
Seven months	Crawls forward on belly; able to turn body while on tummy; placing hands out to the side for balance in sitting	Plays with paper; holds one cube and takes another; pulls out peg from pegboard; beginning to move toy from one hand to the other hand
Eight months	Beginning to turn with upper body in sitting; standing at the sofa; moves from tummy to sitting; beginning to crawl by self	Shakes toys; picks up small toy using the side of index finger and thumb; releases toys from hand; reach and grasp toy with one attempt
Nine months	Crawls by self; can sit for longer periods of time; may pull self to stand	Begins to show preference for dominant hand; begins to use finger and thumb to pick up small objects
Ten months	Stands alone for brief seconds; takes steps with hand held; goes from lying on back to pulling to stand	Begins to poke holes using index finger; hits toys with spoon; drinks from a cup; begins to roll ball
Eleven months	Reaches for furniture farther away; takes steps either direction while holding on to furniture	Pulls string to get toy; holds crayons to make marks; using finger and thumb to pick up very small objects
Twelve months	Walks unsupported a few steps; stands alone; moving quickly on hands and knees	Bangs objects together; drops object into cup; marks with pencil; attempts to stack blocks; turns many pages of a book at a time
Fifteen months	Begins to run; walks alone without falling; crawls up several steps; stoops to pick up toy; gets into standing without using hands	Scribbles with crayon after demonstration; unwraps toy; holds three cubes; inserts round shape into puzzle board
Eighteen months	Runs unsteadily; able to jump in place; falls frequently; able to get into chairs without help	Turning pages one or two at a time; builds three to four block towers; places toys into container; scribbles
Twenty-four months (two years)	Runs better; kicks ball; stoop to pick up toys without falling	Builds six block tower; turn pages one at a time; turns doorknob, imitates circular and vertical strokes
Three years	Able to ride tricycle; briefly balance on one foot; walk up stairs with alternating feet	Copies a circle design; recognizes reversals in puzzle pieces; cuts across paper with scissors; places objects in small openings; stacks nine block towers
Four years	Hops on one foot; throws ball overhead	Cuts out picture using scissors; copies circle and cross
Five years	Run on tiptoe; balances on foot	Print a few capital letters; establish hand dominance; begin to tie shoes
Six years	Catches ball with accuracy; hits ball with bat; jumps with rope turned by others or self; walks on balance beam	Cuts out more complex picture with scissors; writing more controlled; established handedness
Seven years	Running smoothly; participates in sports	Hands steadier; letters smaller
Eight years	Swims crawl stroke with difficulty; riding bike well	Individual finger movements more precise (learn musical instrument)
Nine years	More coordinated motor movements	Printing more uniforms; beginning cursive writing; increased strength in fingers
Ten years	Boys more speed and accuracy than girls; increase in muscle mass for greater strength	Hand size grows; increase in hand strength, grip, and function
Eleven years	Boys and girls differ greatly in motor abilities	Able to produce complex and intricate movements with hands
Twelve years	Large growth spurt beginning; more clumsy and uncoordinated, especially for boys	Continue to perform more advanced hand skills; able to manipulate small buttons for video games well
Thirteen years	Motivation to participate in vigorous activities which challenge body	Begin showing interest in using hands for crafts, vocational and academic skills
Sixteen years	More coordinated and better control over body; participate in team sports	Continue to use hands to learn skills such as typing or other vocational tasks

SOURCE: *Case-Smith and Denegan, "The Developmental Process," in Case-Smith, Allen, and Pratt, eds., Occupational Therapy for Children, (1996); "Developmental Milestones" (2000); "Early Learning Accomplishment Profile" (1988, 1995); Gormly and Brodzinsky, Life Span Human Development, (1996); "Including Your Child" (2000).*

decide whether intervention is needed and also to guide goal setting and outcome measurement.

Delays in Gross Motor and Fine Motor Development

When children are not able to perform the motor skills at the appropriate milestones, their motor development may need to be evaluated by a professional. When motor skills do not progress along a normal trend, a child may be at risk for missing out on potential learning and social experiences. Children who demonstrate potential motor delays are at risk for continuing these delays throughout later development. For example, a child who demonstrates weak hand strength and has difficulty coordinating finger movement may have trouble with handwriting in school.

Early Intervention

After 1986, legislation was passed at the state level to set up services that assist families who suspect their child may have some developmental delays. These services are called early intervention systems. The main purpose of early intervention is to offer evaluation and treatment to children from birth to age three and to their families. The professionals involved with early intervention are members of a team who test a child's skills to see where the child's current skills are in relation to the chronological age. Children who are not doing many motor activities typical of their age may be considered at risk or delayed. These children may not have the strength, coordination, or balance to do most things that others of their age can do. The professionals involved in early intervention include occupational therapists, physical therapists, speech language pathologists, special education teachers, nurses, doctors, social workers, and service coordinators. Each of these professionals help the child and family learn about ways to improve motor coordination so the child can function more independently.

Bibliography

Ames, Louise Bates, Clyde Gillespie, Jacqueline Haines, and Frances L. Ilg. *The Gesell Institute's Child from One to Six: Evaluating the Behavior of the Preschool Child.* New York: Harper and Row, 1979.

Case-Smith, Jane, ed. *Pediatric Occupational Therapy and Early Intervention,* 2nd edition. Woburn, MA: Butterworth-Heinemann, 1998.

Case-Smith, Jane, Anne S. Allen, and Pat Nuse Pratt, eds. *Occupational Therapy for Children,* 3rd edition. St. Louis, MO: Mosby, 1996.

Coleman, Jeanine G. *The Early Intervention Dictionary: A Multidisciplinary Guide to Terminology,* 2nd edition. Bethesda, MD: Woodbine House, 1999.

Davies, Douglas. *Child Development: A Practitioner's Guide.* New York: Guilford Press, 1999.

"Developmental Milestones." In the University of Maryland Medicine [web site]. Maryland, 2000. Available from http://umm.drkoop.com/conditions/ency/article/002006.htm; INTERNET.

"Early Learning Accomplishment Profile (Early LAP) Birth to Thirty-Six Months." Chapel Hill, NC: Chapel Hill Training-Outreach Project, 1988, 1995.

Freiberg, Karen L. *Human Development: A Life-Span Approach,* 3rd edition. Boston, MA: Jones and Bartlett, 1987.

Gormly, Anne V., and David M. Brodzinsky. *Life Span Human Development,* 6th edition. Fort Worth, TX: Harcourt Brace, 1996.

"Including Your Child." Appendix A: "Developmental Progress Chart." 1997. Available from http://www.ed/.gov/pubs/parents/Including/develop.html; INTERNET.

Karmiloff, Kyra, and Annette Karmiloff-Smith. *Everything Your Baby Would Ask, If Only He or She Could Talk.* New York: Golden Books, 1999.

Paplia, Diane E., and Sally Wendkosolds. *A Child's World: Infancy through Adolescence.* New York: McGraw-Hill, 1987.

Joan Ziegler Delahunt

N

NATURAL CHILDBIRTH

In natural childbirth, birth takes place with no medical intervention. Medical interventions during childbirth include: giving anesthesia for pain; giving other drugs such as Pitocin to speed up labor; performing an episiotomy, in which the perineum or the area between a woman's vagina and anus is cut, ostensibly to reduce tearing in that area; and attaching an electrode to the baby's scalp to monitor heart rate. In natural childbirth the idea is that the mother's body naturally knows what to do and unless there are problems, interventions are not necessary or desirable. Pain control consists of the use of different breathing patterns (such as the Lamaze method), imagery, massage, or related techniques. Mothers may be encouraged to walk around and try positions such as squatting. Both of these methods may help labor to go faster and better. In Western countries, midwives, nurses, or physicians may facilitate such births. These births can take place at home, at birthing centers, or in hospitals.

See also: BIRTH; CESAREAN DELIVERY

Bibliography

Garcia, Jo, Martina Corry, Dermot MacDonald, Diana Elbourne, and Adrian Grant. "Mothers' Views of Continuous Electronic Fetal Heart Monitoring and Intermittent Auscultation in a Randomized Controlled Trial." *Birth* 12 (1985):79–85.

Low, Lisa K., Julia S. Seng, Terri L. Murtland, and Deborah Oakley. "Clincian-Specific Episiotomoy Rates: Impact on Perinatal Outcomes." *Journal of Midwifery and Women's Health* 45 (2000):87–93.

Walker, Nancy C., and Beverley O'Brien. "The Relationship between Method of Pain Management during Labor and Birth Outcomes." *Clinical Nursing Research* 8 (1999):119–134.

Michael Lamport Commons
Patrice Marie Miller

NATURALISTIC OBSERVATION

Naturalistic observation is a technique used to collect behavioral data in real-life situations as opposed to laboratory or other controlled settings. This technique is most useful when little is known about the matter under consideration. Underlying the interpretation of data obtained through this procedure is the assumption that the investigator did not interfere with the natural order of the situation.

As an example of naturalistic observation, the study of parent-child interaction may involve videotaping the parent and child in their home either as they go about their daily routine or as they perform an activity given to them by the researcher. These videotaped interactions can then be taken back to the laboratory and analyzed using a variety of techniques in order to extract the desired information from them. This particular research technique has the advantage of making it easier for research participants to be involved in the study.

See also: METHODS OF STUDYING CHILDREN

Bibliography

Bakeman, R., and J. M. Gottman. *Observing Interaction: An Introduction to Sequential Analysis.* Cambridge, Eng.: Cambridge University Press, 1986.

Ray, W. J., and R. Ravizza. *Methods toward a Science of Behavior and Experience*, 2nd edition. Belmont, CA: Wadsworth, 1985.

E G Bishop

NEONATE

The term "neonate" is defined as any infant up to the age of twenty-eight days (i.e., through 27 days, 23 hours, and 59 minutes from the moment of birth). The neonatal period represents the end stage of newborn development that spans the entire time before birth (prenatal), starting with the fertilized embryo. Early embryonic development is described in stages that correspond to time periods during which human embryos develop specific morphological characteristics. Stage one begins at fertilization, spanning the first fifty-six days and ending as stage twenty-three. Next, at the fifty-seventh day, the "fetal period" begins; it ends with the completion of delivery outside of the mother. The neonate is unique in his/her vulnerability to the extrauterine environment resulting in higher risk for mortality and morbidity compared to later in infancy. Precise terminology is important for accurate interpretation and comparisons of databases related to newborn concerns.

See also: BIRTH; PRENATAL DEVELOPMENT

Bibliography

American Academy of Pediatrics and the American College of Obstetricians and Gynecologists. *Guidelines for Perinatal Care*, 4th edition. Washington, DC: American Academy of Pediatrics, 1997.

Moore, Keith, and T. V. N. Persaud. *The Developing Human, Clinically Oriented Embryology*. Philadelphia: W. B. Saunders, 1998.

Carol A. Miller

NUTRITION

Food and nutrition are at the heart of the normal growth and development of children. Without the nutrients that food provides, new tissue, skin, muscle, and bones cannot be added to the body and old parts cannot be repaired. At each of the four stages of childhood, different nutrition issues are priorities.

Infancy

Provision of adequate energy and nutrients is needed in the first year of life to support the most rapid growth and development period in a person's life. From birth to six months of age about 108 calories per kilogram per day are needed; by twelve months a baby needs about 100 calories per kilogram per day. Since babies can eat only a small volume of food to support rapid growth, they require nutrient-dense, highly caloric foods. Fat must contribute at least 30 percent of total calories to meet the demands of growth and development. Babies should double their birthweight by four to six months of age and triple it by one year. On average, their length will increase by 50 percent in the first year of life.

Mother's breast milk is the best source of nutrients for a newborn. A full-term infant's digestive system has been specially designed to digest breast milk. Whether by breast or by bottle, feeding on demand is best. Infants can self-regulate their food intake to match their nutritional needs, based upon internal hunger and satiety cues. Parents need to pay attention to their baby's cues and feed them accordingly. If a baby is bottle-fed and signals that he is full by pulling away or easily becoming distracted, consumption of the entire bottle is not necessary.

For the first four to six months, babies should be fed only breast milk or correctly prepared infant formula. Children under the age of twelve months should not have cow's milk. Between four and six months of age, children are usually developmentally ready to try moist, soft foods. To easily identify allergies, one food should be introduced at a time, with a three-day wait before the introduction of another new food. Parents should encourage the child to try new foods, one at a time. During the first year or so, children will learn to chew, swallow, and manipulate finger foods; drink from a cup; and eventually feed themselves. Of course, they will make lots of mess while learning these skills, so patience is important. Bottle-fed infants should be weaned from the bottle by twelve to fourteen months of age. There is no specific time to wean a breast-fed child; the longer a baby is on breast milk, the better it will be for her health and well-being.

Early Childhood

Children tend to be unpredictable, picky eaters during the early childhood phase of growth and development (one to four years of age). Parents should allow the child to explore new foods through touch, smell, and taste. It is normal to offer the child a new food five to ten times before he will try to eat it. A food that a child likes one day may not be one he likes the next day. Children may also eat a lot one day and very little the next. They usually eat just one or two foods per meal. This is normal behavior for a child and parents should not worry that the child is not eating enough. Children's growth rates and energy needs decrease during this period.

Parents should offer their children a variety of foods and act as role models by eating a variety of foods. Parents need to provide a structured, pleasant mealtime environment to help their child develop healthy eating behaviors. Parents are responsible for what, when, and where the child eats; children are responsible for whether they eat and how much they eat. Older preschool children may learn to like new foods more by participating in their preparation. Fat should not be restricted before age two; by age five, children should eat fewer high-fat foods and their total fat intake should not exceed 30 percent of total daily calories. Children under age two should be provided whole milk; after age two lower-fat milk options are appropriate. Parents should encourage the child to eat enough iron-rich foods, such as lean red meat or fortified cereals with juice that contains vitamin C, at the same meal. Daily regular activity is important to build a healthy habit and to balance a child's weight and food intake.

Middle Childhood

During middle childhood, regular food habits should be established. This includes eating three meals and two snacks every day. A variety of foods should be chosen with special attention to foods high in calcium (such as low-fat dairy products and dark green vegetables), and zinc and iron (such as low-fat animal products and fortified breakfast cereal). Overconsumption of foods high in fat (such as whole milk, table spreads, and cooking oil), saturated fat (full-fat dairy products, animal products, and solid cooking fats), and sodium (salt and cheese) need to be avoided. Participation in regular physical activity is important to reduce the risk of obesity and development of chronic disease such as coronary heart disease or hypertension.

During and just before a growth spurt, a child's appetite and food intake will increase. The percentage of body fat in older school-age children increases in preparation for the growth spurt during adolescence. Parents should be aware that a child's body image becomes very important at this time. The increased fat mass that naturally occurs during these periods, particularly among girls, can be alarming unless the family realizes that this is normal development. Some preadolescent children may become concerned that they are overweight and may begin to eat less, therefore compromising their normal growth and development. It can also lay the foundation for future psychological issues, such as eating disorders.

Adolescence

Adolescence is the second most rapid period of growth and development (the first being the first year of life), which leads to increased energy and nutrient

Adequate nutrition during adolescence ensures sexual maturation, linear growth, and peak bone mass. (UPI/Corbis Bettmann)

needs. Physical activity influences adolescents' growth and body composition as well as their propensity for obesity. Inadequate nutrition can delay sexual maturation, slow or stop linear growth and compromise peak bone mass as well as cognitive development, with the latter possibly affecting learning, concentration, and school performance. Studies continue to show that students achieve higher test scores if they consume a meal before the test. A boy's physical maturation tends to increase his satisfaction with his body because of increased size and muscular development. In contrast, a girl's physical maturation tends to decrease body satisfaction. Reassurance that fat accumulation in the hips, thigh, and buttocks is normal during adolescence will help to allay this anxiety.

Healthy eating habits, such as eating breakfast and not skipping meals, should continue to be promoted. Healthful food choices that are based on the Dietary Guidelines for Americans and the Food Guide Pyramid should be encouraged. Adolescents become more independent and make more of their own food choices. Parents should be encouraged to provide a variety of healthful foods at home and to make family mealtimes a priority.

In the average adolescent's diet, the intake of folate, iron, zinc, calcium, and vitamins A and B6 is inadequate. Consumption of green leafy and dark orange vegetables, whole grains, lean meat and fortified breakfast cereals, and low-fat dairy products will provide these nutrients and should be advocated. Although vitamin and mineral supplements can appear to be an easy solution, these do not provide other nutrients, such as fiber, which are found naturally in food. The best insurance for good health is to eat a variety of foods and enough to meet daily needs. Intake of fat, saturated fat, cholesterol, sodium, and sugar tends to be excessive. Obesity is an increasingly prevalent problem among adolescents and is contributed to by little physical activity and intake of high caloric, low-nutrient foods. Other nutritional concerns include inadequate intake of fruits, vegetables, and calcium-rich foods; excessive intake of soft drinks; unsafe weight loss practices; iron-deficiency anemia in girls; eating disorders; and hyperlipidemia, including high blood cholesterol.

Government Nutrition Assistance Programs

There are several government nutrition assistance programs that are available in health centers or clinics, schools, child-care centers, and licensed day-care homes. These programs assist families in meeting the nutritional needs of their children.

The Supplemental Nutrition Program for Low Income Women, Infants, and Children is a government program that provides nutrition education, vouchers for food, and referral for services for eligible women and children. Eligibility includes having a nutritional risk and an income that is less than the poverty level multiplied by 1.85.

The Child and Adult Care Food Program provides reimbursement to child-care providers—child-care centers and family day-care homes—for each child to have two meals and a snack. The provider must follow menu guidelines and report the menus in order to be reimbursed.

The National School Meal Program (NSMP), which includes lunch, breakfast, and special milk, is offered in almost every school in the country. The lunch provides one-third of a child's daily nutrient requirements; when breakfast is also provided, 40 percent of the requirements are met. If a school does not have a cafeteria, food may be brought in from a central kitchen or at least the special milk program will be available. With the increase of after-school programs, the NSMP is assisting in providing snacks for those programs. In the summer when school is not in session, day camps, recreation centers, and schools can sponsor the Summer Food Program, which provides lunches for children to eligible programs.

The Food Stamp Program was designed to provide coupons or electronic benefits to people with low incomes for the purchase of eligible food items. Income, household size, assets, housing costs, work requirements, and other factors determine eligibility and allotments. A study of data gathered in fiscal year 1998 found that 52.8 percent of all participants were children (age eighteen or younger).

See also: EXERCISE; MALNUTRITION; OBESITY; WOMEN, INFANTS, AND CHILDREN

Bibliography

Clark, Nancy. *Nancy Clark's Sports Nutrition Guidebook,* 2nd edition. Champaign, IL: Human Kinetics, 1996.

Dietz, William H., and Lorraine Stern, eds. *Guide to Your Child's Nutrition: Making Peace at the Table and Building Healthy Eating Habits for Life.* New York: Villard, 1989.

"Frequently Asked Questions [about Food Stamps]." In the U.S. Department of Agriculture, Food and Nutrition Service [web site]. Washington, DC, 2001. Available from http://www.fns.usda.gov/fsp/menu/faqs/faqs.htm; INTERNET.

Story, Mary, Katrina Holt, and Denise Sofka, eds. *Bright Futures in Practice: Nutrition.* Arlington, VA: National Center for Education in Maternal and Child Health, 2000.

U.S. Department of Agriculture, Center for Nutrition Policy and Promotion. *Tips for Using the Food Guide Pyramid for Young Children, Two to Six Years Old.* Washington, DC: U.S. Department of Agriculture, Center for Nutrition Policy and Promotion, 1999.

"Your Guide to Nutrition and Health Information on Federal Government Websites." Available at http://www.nutrition.gov; INTERNET.

Stacy L. Dubit
Janice Dodds
Nicole B. Knee

O

OBESITY

American culture values thinness. From supermodels to laptop computers, the American public equates thinness with beauty; yet, the prevalence of obesity in the United States is higher than at any time in history. Estimates of overweight and obesity among children and adolescents in the United States have doubled since the 1970s, to almost 25 percent in 2001. Once obesity develops in childhood or adolescence, there is a risk that it will persist into adult life. The risk appears to be greatest for children who are obese in the prepubertal years (between ages nine and thirteen), with more than 50 percent of such children remaining obese as adults, and for children with one or two obese parents.

William Dietz, of the Centers for Disease Control and Prevention (CDC), described three critical periods in the development of obesity, corresponding to periods of adipose tissue (the connective tissue where fat is stored) proliferation: gestation and early infancy, ages five to seven years, and adolescence. Body fat increases over the first twelve to eighteen months of life. Loss of "baby fat" over the subsequent eighteen months leads to a decrease in fatness, which lasts until the age of five to seven years, when the adiposity rebound occurs and fatness begins to increase again. Children who experience the adiposity rebound earlier, before five years and six months of age, are more prone to later obesity.

Definition

Obesity is a condition of excessive fatness. Fatness is often expressed as a percentage of body weight. Prepubertal boys and girls typically have about 15 percent of their body weight as fat, while the average adult male is 20 percent fat, and the average adult female is 30 percent fat. Body fatness is measured using a variety of techniques, such as body densitometry, electrical impedance, and skin-fold thickness. Total body weight, although it includes muscle, bone, and internal organs, in addition to body fat, can be used as an index of fatness, especially when expressed in relation to body height. A ratio of weight and height, called the body mass index (BMI), has been adopted for use in the assessment of children, adolescents, and adults. BMI is calculated by dividing the weight, in kilograms, by the square of the height, in meters (kg/m2). If pounds and inches are used, then the quotient (pounds divided by inches squared) multiplied by 704.5. For adult men and women, BMI greater than 25 signifies overweight, and BMI greater than 30 indicates obesity. During childhood, BMI varies by gender and normally increases with age. Obesity is determined with a graph or reference table that gives the eighty-fifth percentile for age (as a criteria for overweight) and the ninety-fifth percentile for age (as a criteria for obese) for boys and girls. In 2000 the CDC published revised percentile standards for BMI (see Table).

TABLE 1

Body Mass Index Values For Overweight And Obesity

Age	Males 85 Percentile	Males 95 Percentile	Females 85 Percentile	Females 95 Percentile
2	18.1	19.3	18.0	19.1
3	17.3	18.2	17.2	18.3
4	16.9	17.8	16.8	18.0
5	16.8	17.9	16.8	18.3
6	17.0	18.4	17.1	18.8
7	17.4	19.2	17.6	19.7
8	18.0	20.1	18.3	20.7
9	18.6	21.1	19.1	21.8
10	19.4	22.2	20.0	23.0
11	20.2	23.2	20.9	24.1
12	21.0	24.2	21.7	25.3
13	21.9	25.2	22.6	26.3
14	22.7	26.0	23.3	27.3
15	23.5	26.8	24.0	28.1
16	24.2	27.6	24.7	28.9
17	24.9	28.3	25.2	29.6
18	25.7	29.0	25.7	30.3
19	26.4	29.7	26.1	31.0

SOURCE: Adapted from the National Center for Health Statistics 2000: http://www.cdc.gov/nchs/about/major/nhanes/growthcharts/

Causes

Obesity is caused by a variety of factors, all of which result in an excess of caloric intake relative to the body's expenditure of energy (calories) at rest, during activity, and, in childhood and adolescence, for growth. Calorie intake in excess of these needs is converted to fat. Less than 2 percent of obesity in childhood is due to endocrinologic conditions, such as thyroid disease. An equally small percentage is due to genetic disorders (e.g., the Prader-Willi Syndrome). Though obesity "runs in families," the genetic contributions to fatness are not well understood. A shared environment also contributes to the hereditary pattern of obesity, with parental influences on diet and exercise during childhood and adolescence. Numerous studies have failed to precisely define the relative contributions of caloric intake and expenditure to the development of obesity. The difference in daily intake necessary to result in as much as a ten-pound difference in weight gain over the course of a year is actually as little as a hundred calories per day. Studies have shown that more time spent using television, VCRs, and video games is associated with a greater likelihood of obesity and that decreasing the amount of time spent watching television correlates with less weight gain.

Some interesting developmental factors may contribute to overconsumption of calories. These include difficult infant or child temperament, poor self-regulation of intake, and an "obese eating style," involving rapid eating and rapid consumption of calories. Studies of infant feeding have revealed a style of vigorous feeding, similar to the obese eating style, with rapid sucking, at higher pressure, resulting in greater caloric intake at a feed. Studies of children's ability to self-regulate dietary intake have found poorer self-regulation of eating in fatter girls and in children exposed to a highly controlling parenting style. Studies of child temperament have found that difficult children (low in rhythmicity, approach, and adaptability; high in intensity; and negative in mood) show more rapid weight gain, perhaps as a result of being overfed by parents who use feeding as a soothing technique, and may later use eating as a technique for comforting themselves.

Consequences

Obesity has significant medical consequences, especially for adults, but also for children and adolescents. Among adults, obesity is a major risk factor for heart disease, myocardial infarction (heart attack), strokes, cancer, and many other diseases. During adolescence and childhood, obesity can contribute to problems of the joints, especially the hips, knees, and spine, and more difficulty with chronic illnesses, such as asthma. Obesity affects the endocrine system, leading to changes in sex hormones, adrenal hormones, and the ability to respond appropriately to insulin. Type II diabetes has become more common during adolescence as the prevalence of obesity has increased. Sleep apnea, due to obstructed breathing during sleep, is more common among obese children and adolescents.

The psychological consequences of obesity are very important during childhood and adolescence. Though some studies have found similar prevalence of psychological problems in obese and normal weight children, obese children are often teased by other children, excluded from peer group activities, picked last (if at all) for sports teams, and shunned during social activities. Stigmatization of obesity is commonplace throughout the media, especially television, movies, and popular magazines. Unfortunately, poor self-esteem, depression, and the development of eating disorders occur often in individuals with histories of obesity. Obese adults are even discriminated against when they apply for jobs and during the application process for college.

Treatment

Obesity is not a disease that can be diagnosed on the basis of one or more blood tests or treated with one or a combination of medications. Until the true genetic contributions to the development of excessive fatness are better understood, treatment will remain a process of managing the balance between calorie intake and expenditure. This behavioral treatment process must support reduction in calorie intake, modification of food selection, reduction in sedentary time, and increase in caloric expenditure. Important components of change include the use of diet diaries, to help recognize needed diet change, and the careful replacement of unhealthy food choices with lower calorie items that supply adequate amounts of protein, carbohydrates, minerals, and vitamins. Similarly, increasing energy expenditure can be the result of reducing reliance on cars, public transportation, elevators, and other conveniences, while increasing the time spent walking, bicycling, or other ways of expending energy, such as using stairs.

Modification of diet and activity and change in the degree of obesity among children over the age of eight years can occur in weekly group treatment programs that also involve parents in separate group sessions. Three treatment program characteristics contribute most to positive results: comprehensive treatment (including a combination of behavioral modification procedures, a special diet, and an exercise program); explicit inclusion of behavior modification techniques; and focus on children with more severe obesity. The diet should emphasize calorie and fat reduction (tailored to the child's age and metabolic needs), include a simple categorization of foods understood easily by children, and be supervised by a health professional.

More aggressive approaches to weight loss being used in the treatment of adults are under investigation in the treatment of adolescents, including the use of medications, very low calorie diets, and surgery. Until recently, the use of medications in the treatment of obesity has been of relatively little benefit. In the late 1990s, success with medications such as phentermine and fenfluramine, found to decrease appetite or increase satiety, was tempered by the discovery of unexpected and potentially fatal side effects. Two newer medications, sibutramine, an appetite suppressant, and orlistat, a blocker of fat absorption in the intestine, show promising results in adult treatment and are undergoing clinical trials for use in adolescents.

In more extreme situations, caloric intake can be reduced dramatically with the use of very low calorie diets and obesity surgery, but should be considered for adolescents only after completion of puberty. These diets include anywhere from 300 to 800 calories per day, primarily as protein and carbohydrate, and should be instituted only with adequate medical supervision, since severe nutrient deficiencies and medical complications, such as fatal rhythm disturbances of the heart, can accompany them. Surgical treatments either reduce the capacity of the stomach, thereby inducing earlier satiety, or they decrease the length of the bowel, thereby reducing the bowel's capacity to absorb fat from the meal. Significant side effects in terms of abdominal discomfort, diarrhea, and potential nutrient deficiency are common.

With the difficulty in treating obesity at any stage of life, attention is turning toward understanding the possible role of prevention. Efforts are underway to develop behavioral and biochemical approaches to prevention, particularly in children identified as high risk, based on their early growth patterns and family history.

See also: EXERCISE; NUTRITION; PHYSICAL GROWTH

Bibliography

Epstein, Leonard H. "New Developments in Child Obesity." In Albert J. Stunkard and Thomas A. Wadden eds., *Obesity*. New York: Raven Press, 1993.

Hammer, Lawrence D. "The Development of Eating Behavior in Childhood." *Pediatric Clinics of North America* 39 (1992):379–394.

Hammer, Lawrence D., and Thomas N. Robinson. "Child and Adolescent Obesity." In Melvin D. Levine ed., *Developmental-Behavioral Pediatrics*. Philadelphia: Saunders, 1999.

Robinson, Thomas N., and William H. Dietz. "Weight Gain: Overeating to Obesity." In Abraham M. Rudolph ed., *Pediatrics*. Stamford, CT: Appleton and Lange, 1996.

World Health Organization. *Obesity: Preventing and Managing the Global Epidemic*. Geneva: World Health Organization, 1997.

Lawrence D. Hammer

OBJECT PERMANENCE

Object permanence refers to a set of commonsense beliefs about the nature, properties, and behavior of animate and inanimate objects. The first belief is that objects are permanent entities that exist continuously and independently of one's immediate actions on or perceptions of them. The second and third beliefs stipulate that objects are stable entities whose properties and behavior remain subject to physical laws regardless of one's immediate perception of them. According to Jean Piaget, a Swiss psychologist who formulated a major theory of cognitive development, the understanding that objects exist continuously emerges during stage four of the sensorimotor period (around eight months of age), when infants spontaneously search for and retrieve an object that they see being hidden. For Piaget, however, object permanence is not fully developed until the end of the sensorimotor period (around two years of age), when infants demonstrate through their manual search behavior that they can imagine the behavior and motion of hidden objects.

See also: COGNITIVE DEVELOPMENT; PIAGET, JEAN

Bibliography

Baillargeon, Renée. "The Object Concept Revisited: New Directions in the Investigation of Infants' Physical Knowledge." In C. E. Granrud ed., *Visual Perception and Cognition in Infancy.* Hillsdale, NJ: Lawrence Erlbaum, 1993.

Piaget, Jean. *The Construction of Reality in the Child,* translated by Margaret Cook. New York: Basic, 1954.

Andréa Aguiar

OBSERVATIONAL LEARNING

Observational learning is a powerful means of social learning. It principally occurs through the cognitive processing of information displayed by models. The information can be conveyed verbally, textually, and auditorially, and through actions either by live or symbolic models such as television, movies, and the Internet. Regardless of the medium used to present the modeled activities, the same psychological processes underlie observational learning. These include attention and memory processes directed to establish a conceptual representation of the modeled activity. This representation guides the enactment of observationally learned patterns of conduct. Whether the learned patterns will be performed or not depends on incentive structures and observers' actual and perceived competence to enact the modeled performances. Unlike learning by doing, observational learning does not require enactment of the modeling activities during learning. The complexity of the learning, however, is restricted by the cognitive competence and enactment skills of the learner.

See also: COGNITIVE DEVELOPMENT

Bibliography

Bandura, Albert. *Social Foundations of Thought and Action: A Social Cognitive Theory.* Englewood Cliffs, NJ: Prentice-Hall, 1986.

Schunk, Dale H. "Peer Modeling." In Keith Topping and Stewart Ehly eds., *Peer-Assisted Learning.* Mahwah, NJ: Lawrence Erlbaum, 1998.

Kay Bussey

ONLY CHILDREN

See: BIRTH ORDER AND SPACING

P

PARALLEL PLAY

Parallel play (or parallel activity) is a term that was introduced by Mildred Parten in 1932 to refer to a developmental stage of social activity in which children play with toys like those the children around them are using but are absorbed in their own activity and usually play beside rather than with one another. Children in this stage may comment on what they are doing or imitate what another child does, but they rarely cooperate in a task or engage in dramatic play or formal games with others. This stage occurs after solitary and onlooker play and before associated and cooperative play when children engage in more complex social interactions. Preschool children of all ages engage in parallel play, particularly when using sand, water, blocks, and art materials; this type of play appears to serve as a bridge to more complex cooperative activities.

See also: PLAY; SOCIAL DEVELOPMENT

Bibliography

Bakeman, R., and J. R. Brownlee. "The Strategic Use of Parallel Play: A Sequential Analysis." *Child Development* 51 (1980):873–878.

Parten, Mildred B. "Social Participation among Preschool Children." *Journal of Abnormal and Social Psychology* 27 (1932):243–269.

Rubin, K. H., William Bukowski, and J. G. Parker. "Peer Interactions, Relationships, and Groups." In William Damon and Nancy Eisenberg eds., *Handbook of Child Psychology,* Vol. 3: *Social, Emotional, and Personality Development.* New York: John Wiley, 1998.

Roberta R. Collard

PARENT-CHILD RELATIONSHIPS

In two significant articles on parenting, W. Andrew Collins and his colleagues, writing in *American Psychologist,* and Eleanor Maccoby, writing in *Annual Review of Psychology,* both noted that an enormous body of literature supports the important role of parents in shaping the development of children. Collins and his colleagues and Maccoby were responding in part to the contention of Judith Harris, author of *The Nurture Assumption,* that parental influence on child development may not be as great as the influence of genetic predispositions and the influence of peers. Maccoby persuasively argued that such a contention is out of date in view of genetic studies suggesting that experiences children have with parents and others can modify genetic influence and of the substantial body of literature showing the importance of parent-child relationships for a child's development. This large body of literature suggests that it is the quality of the parent-child relationship that is particularly important in understanding the course of the child's development; and that the parent-child relationship is coconstructed by the parent and the child, not something that comes from the parent alone. In this article, consideration is given to what aspects of parent-child relationships are associated with the development of competence and well-being in children and how the parent-child relationship changes over time and with development. Also considered are the factors that contribute to these qualities of parent-child relationships.

Infancy and the Preschool Years

In infancy and the preschool years amazing growth occurs in the child's capacity for self-control and self-regulation and in the internalization of standards for behavior. In his important book *Emotional Development,* Alan Sroufe noted that there is wide agreement among developmental psychologists about the role that a parent or caregiver plays in helping the child achieve self-control and self-regulation. The parent or caregiver helps the child develop her own self-regulation by soothing distress, enhancing alertness, and allowing the child the experience of self-regulation by sensitively responding to the child's signals of need for soothing or increased stimulation. Children who have experienced chaotic and inconsistent parenting do not have the experience of regulation to guide their own efforts, nor the confidence in the caregiver (and consequently in themselves) required for self-regulation. Additionally, children who have been pushed to independence at too early an age because the parent is emotionally unavailable or too strict tend to adopt rigid regulatory strategies, which they attempt to use on their own. They do not learn to turn to parents or others to help them with regulation. Sroufe noted that children whose interactions with their parents have been characterized by sensitive, responsive care from the parent—as opposed to overstimulating, intrusive care—have been found to be better able to handle frustration, be less hyperactive, have longer attention spans during the preschool years, and do better academically and emotionally in the early elementary years. In toddlerhood, willing compliance with parents is associated with parent interaction behaviors that are well coordinated with the child's. Children who have a secure, trusting relationship with their parents (having experienced responsive care) show greater self-reliance in the classroom, and less inclination to fall apart under stress, a greater curiosity and willingness to make a strong effort in the face of challenge, and greater flexibility and complexity in their play. Additionally, children with secure relationships with their parents have peer relationships characterized by greater commitment and emotional closeness, and by more positive emotions such children are also more empathic and supportive with other children when the partner is injured, distressed, or less able, but are assertive with aggressive partners.

Middle Childhood

Andrew Collins and his colleagues, in *Handbook of Parenting,* noted that in middle childhood (generally considered to be from ages five to ten), parents and children spend less time together and that cognitive changes on the part of children greatly expand their capacity for solving problems and gaining necessary information on their own. Other researchers have found that parental monitoring of their children's activities and whereabouts seems to be particularly important, as poor monitoring has been linked to antisocial behavior in middle childhood and adolescence. The effectiveness of monitoring depends on an attentive, responsive, warm relationship between the parent and child. Parents are more effective at monitoring when children are willing to be monitored and actively help parents know where they are and what they are doing. This occurs more often when the relationship between the parents and child is warm and close.

Attentive, responsive relationships between parents and their children in middle childhood are associated with the development of self-esteem, competence, and social responsibility in the child. Children generally perceive parents as sources of support, and children's perceptions that there are available adults with whom they can talk and discuss problems are correlated positively with prosocial behaviors and attitudes such as empathy and understanding of others. Parents' use of explanations that emphasize the impact of children's behavior on others is associated with helpful, emotionally supportive relationships toward others. These interchanges that benefit children occur within the context of involved, sensitive, and responsive relationships in which parents are willing to instruct and children are willing to receive the instruction. In contrast, parents' indifferent, unresponsive behavior toward children is associated with antisocial behavior in children. Antisocial tendencies in children place them at risk for peer rejection and school failure during middle childhood and for later involvement in antisocial behavior as adolescents and young adults.

Adolescence

Grayson Holmbeck and his colleagues, also writing in *Handbook of Parenting,* noted that the amount of warmth and responsiveness in the relationship between parent and child continues to be important in predicting positive outcomes during the adolescent years and even into the adult years. Warm and responsive relationships between adolescents and parents are associated with a variety of positive outcomes, including self-esteem, identity formation, socially accepted behavior, better parent-adolescent communication, less depression and anxiety, and fewer behavior problems. The challenge during adolescence is that warm, responsive, and involved relationships must be maintained at a time when the asymmetries in power that characterized earlier parent-child relationships are shifting to more equality.

Studies have concluded that the level of positive nurturing in the relationship between parents and their children is important to predicting positive outcomes throughout a child' developmental years. (Paul Barton/The Stock Market)

The shift to more equality is driven by the adolescent's more sophisticated social cognitive skills and broader contacts with the environment outside the family. The transition to adolescence involves biological, cognitive, social cognitive, emotional, self-definitional, peer relationship, and school context changes for the adolescent. Cognitive changes may result in more confrontations between parents and adolescents, as adolescents increasingly begin to question and debate parental rules and expectations. Andrew Collins and Brett Laursen have noted that although parent-child conflict typically increases during adolescence, the conflict can serve as an important signal to parents that parenting behaviors need to be modified in response to the changing developmental needs of their children. Thus, parent-adolescent conflict can serve an adaptive function, as conflict can be an impetus to change. Conflicts that occur in the context of generally warm, supportive family relationships may be more likely to help an adolescent's development progress.

Factors that Affect Parent-Child Relationships

Parent-child relationships do not occur in a vacuum, and the context in which the relationships develop are likely to affect the nature of the relationships. Such factors as birth order, financial and emotional

stress, social support, gender of the parent, infant temperament, and parent personality may influence qualities of the parent-child relationships and the impact of that relationship on the child's development. Marc Bornstein, in *Handbook of Parenting,* noted that mothers of first-borns engage with, respond to, stimulate, talk to, and express positive affection for their babies more than mothers of later-borns, even when there are no differences in first- and later-born behavior. Other researchers have found that financial and emotional stresses negatively affect the well being of parents and adversely affect their attentiveness and sensitivity to their children. Bornstein found that mothers who are supported emotionally by their husbands or other adults are less restrictive and punitive with their infants than are mothers without good social support. Mothers and fathers may provide different kinds of relationships and experiences for their children. Ross Parke suggested in his book *Fatherhood* that the relationships boys have with their fathers or available male figures may be particularly associated with the boys' competence with their peers. Infant temperament clearly influences adults. Having a baby who is easily soothed leads mothers to perceive themselves as more competent parents. Parental personality and functioning also has been found to be important in predicting parent-child relationships. Levels of parent psychopathology are related to qualities of the parent-child relationship and the child's adjustment. The interactions between depressed mothers and their infants are characterized by less positive and more negative emotions, less infant vocalization, and more passivity on the part of the infant.

Summary

A large body of literature and theory converges on the notion that it is the relationship between the parent and child that is critical for the positive development of children. Specifically, a common theme during childhood is that the way in which parents are able to sensitively regulate their parenting behavior based on the developmental needs of their children is a critical determinant of positive outcome. Additionally, the context in which the parent-child relationship occurs is important in affecting the qualities of that relationship.

See also: ANTISOCIAL BEHAVIOR; BIRTH ORDER AND SPACING; FATHERS; PARENTING

Bibliography

Bornstein, Marc, ed. "Parenting Infants." *Handbook of Parenting*, Vol. 1: *Children and Parenting*. Mahwah, NJ: Lawrence Erlbaum, 1995.

Collins, W. Andrew, and Brett Laursen. "Conflict and Relationships during Adolescence." In Carolyn Shantz and Willard Hartup eds., *Conflict in Child and Adolescent Development*. New York: Cambridge University Press, 1992.

Collins, W. Andrew, Eleanor E. Maccoby, Larry Steinberg, E. Mavis Hetherington, and Marc Bornstein. "Contemporary Research on Parenting: The Case for Nature and Nurture." *American Psychologist* 55 (2000):218–232.

Collins, W. Andrew, Michael Harris, and Amy Susman. "Parenting during Middle Childhood." In Marc Bornstein ed., *Handbook of Parenting*, Vol. 1: *Children and Parenting*. Mahwah, NJ: Lawrence Erlbaum, 1995.

Conger, Rand, and Glen Elder. *Families in Troubled Times: Adapting to Change in Rural America*. New York: Aldine De Gruyter, 1994.

Harris, Judith R. *The Nurture Assumption: Why Children Turn Out the Way They Do*. New York: Free Press, 1998.

Holmbeck, Grayson, Roberta Paikoff, and Jeanne Brooks-Gunn. "Parenting Adolescents." In Marc Bornstein ed., *Handbook of Parenting*, Vol. 1: *Children and Parenting*. Mahwah, NJ: Lawrence Erlbaum, 1995.

Maccoby, Eleanor. "Social-Emotional Development and Response to Stressors." In Norman Garmezy and Michael Rutter eds., *Stress, Coping, and Development in Children*. New York: McGraw-Hill, 1983.

Maccoby, Eleanor E. "Parenting and Its Effects on Children: On Reading and Misreading Behavior Genetics." *Annual Review of Psychology* 51 (2000):1–27.

McLoyd, Vonnie C. "Children in Poverty: Development, Public Policy, and Practice." In William Damon, Irving Sigel, and K. Ann Renninger eds., *Handbook of Child Psychology*. New York: Wiley, 1998.

Parke, Ross. *Fatherhood*. Cambridge, MA: Harvard University Press, 1996.

Patterson, Gerald. *Coercive Family Processes*. Eugene, OR: Castalia Press, 1982.

Sanson, Ann, and Mary Rothbart. "Child Temperament and Parenting." In Marc Bornstein ed., *Handbook of Parenting*, Vol. 4: *Applied and Practical Parenting*. Mahwah, NJ: Erlbaum, 1995.

Sroufe, L. Alan. *Emotional Development: The Organization of Emotional Life in the Early Years*. Cambridge, Eng.: Cambridge University Press, 1995.

Tolan, Patrick, and Rolf Loeber. "Antisocial Behavior." In Patrick Tolan and Bertram Cohler eds., *Handbook of Clinical Research and Practice with Adolescents*. New York: Wiley, 1993.

Martha J. Cox

PARENTAL LEAVE

Parental leave refers to the time taken off from work by employees to care for their children. The term is more inclusive than maternity or paternity leave in that it covers both mothers and fathers. By allowing either parent time off from work, employers offer families more options as to which parent will care for the child and which one will continue to be the wage earner.

Prior to August of 1993, employers in the United States were not required to implement parental leave policies. And many companies did not recognize that such flexibility and choice could be given to either parent of a child. Recognizing the need for a universal policy, the Clinton/Gore administration introduced the Family and Medical Leave Act in 1993. Through the provision of this act, most employees are guaranteed a protected job, with unpaid leave, in the event that birth and care of a newborn is needed, adoption or foster care has occurred, or an immediate family member needs care. While the act gives parents more choices and job security, it does not, mandate wage replacement during the leave period. As a result, many parents are reluctant to take the needed time off for fear of losing income.

In 1999 the Campaign for Family Leave Benefits was launched. The purpose of this campaign was to address the growing concern among Americans regarding unpaid parental leave in the United States. The campaign hopes to make family and medical leave more affordable for working parents in America through research, a clearinghouse, advocacy, public education, a family leave benefits network, and an advisory committee.

See also: SINGLE-PARENT FAMILIES; WORKING FAMILIES

Bibliography

"Campaign for Family Leave Benefits." In the National Partnership for Women and Families [web site]. 1998. Available from http://www.nationalparternship.org/workandfamily/fmleave/expansion/fli_launchmain.htm; INTERNET.

Decker, Kurt H. *Family and Medical Leave in a Nutshell.* St. Paul: West Publishing, 1999.

"Family and Medical Leave Act." In the Department of Labor [web site]. Available from http://www.dol.gov/dol/esa/fmla.htm; INTERNET.

Fried, Mindy. *Taking Time: Parental Leave Policy and Corporate Culture.* Philadelphia: Temple University Press, 1998.

Mandy D. Goodnight

PARENTING

Parenting is the process by which adults socialize the infants, children, and adolescents in their care. Methods such as monitoring, emotional closeness, discipline, control, and demands are used to shape society's younger members so that they behave appropriately for their future role in society. Parenting is at once both a careful dance between child and parent and a process that is heavily influenced by the larger social context. Urie Bronfenbrenner is well known for developing his ecological model, which describes the role of contexts such as family, peers, schools, and political climate in human development. Thus, social scientists no longer study parent-child interaction in a vacuum. Rather, the family is best understood as a social system with subsystems, including parent-child, marital, and sibling systems, that is enmeshed in the larger social context.

From time to time researchers have questioned how important parenting is to long-term outcomes for children. The answer over and over has been a resounding "very important." With such a broad constellation of influences on the developing child, how can one be so sure that differences in what average parents do really matters? The answer lies in the fact that parents affect their children directly and indirectly. Parents shape children by interacting with them directly. In addition, parents act in concert with institutions such as peers, schools, and media. Parents determine the neighborhood children are raised in, for example, which sets in motion a chain of events that heavily influences a child's future identity.

Quantitative Aspects of Parenting

A wealth of research findings indicate there is great variation within each type of family structure—such as two-parent, divorced, remarried, cohabiting, and single-parent—such that family structure alone is a very poor indicator of quality of home environment or child outcomes. Children can have their emotional, social, cognitive, and physical needs met in the context of diverse family structures when parents have the personal and economic resources and the desire to provide a healthy environment for chil-

dren in their charge. According to the U.S. Bureau of the Census, in 1999, 68 percent of children in America lived with two parents. This represented a drop from 77 percent in 1980. Among children living in two-parent households, 91 percent lived with both biological parents while 9 percent lived with a stepparent—more commonly a stepfather.

Who Is Socializing U.S. Children?

Despite progressive shifts in cultural attitudes regarding the appropriateness of mothers and fathers sharing caregiving activities and involvement with children, only small changes in actual parenting patterns are recorded by existing research completed after 1980. Fathers continue to spend less time than mothers with infants and children in the United States and other industrialized countries. When they are with their children, fathers are more likely than mothers to be involved in play rather than the children's routine maintenance such as feeding and grooming. Fathers also spend a greater amount of time on personal activities, such as watching television and reading, in comparison to mothers. Parenting infants, as opposed to children or teenagers, differs greatly with respect to the common activities and skill utilization parents have the opportunity to employ. Although qualitative changes in parenting are dramatic as children mature, the traditional division of labor between mothers and fathers persists through developmental changes.

Division of labor is not an issue for the growing number of parents who manage all the varied responsibilities for their children on their own. The substantial majority of single parents are mothers. In 1999 the Census Bureau reported that 23 percent of children lived with only their mothers while 4 percent lived with only their fathers. Other data indicated that growth of one-parent families was slowing. In particular, the number of single-father households was rising, while the number of single-mother households remained nearly constant between 1995 and 1998, after almost tripling from 1970 to 1995. Time and money continue to be the biggest challenges for mothers parenting alone. In America, the richest country in the world, 19 percent of children lived in poverty in 1998. This statistic reveals that many divorced or never-married mothers struggle to make ends meet. The median household income for single fathers is significantly higher than that of their female counterparts. Some of the financial difficulties faced by single parents may be assuaged by contributions made by cohabiting partners. Sixteen percent of children living with fathers and 9 percent of children living with mothers also lived with a parent's cohabiting partner.

Fluctuations in family structure have been accompanied by a changing American work force. From the 1960s on, much media, legislative, and academic attention has been devoted to mothers' increased presence in the workplace. Mothers have challenged societal gender norms as the proportion of employed mothers has steadily risen. Even as far back as 1980, 50 percent of American women were employed for pay and the typical woman worker was a mother. The percentage of mothers who held jobs and had children under age one continued to increase; according to the Census Bureau, 59 percent of mothers of infants worked in 1998—up from 38 percent in 1980. These numbers are compelling, and they have sparked a national debate regarding the effect of child care on the emotional, social, cognitive, and physical development of American children. Concern about overuse of child care may be quelled by data indicating that the majority of mothers of very young children are not employed full time. Children under age two are generally in home-based care when mothers do work. Children ages three to six are likely to be in a part-time or full-time center-based, preschool-type program. The extent to which center-based care is learning-focused varies widely; a minority of programs feature developmentally appropriate, effective learning environments. Good quality, learning-based preschool experience is related to positive long-term outcomes for children, especially children with lower-quality home environments. In addition, smaller amounts of state and federal monies are spent on social programs over time for individuals who attended a good-quality preschool.

In findings published in 1998–2000 from the most comprehensive study of early child care, the National Institutes of Child Health and Human Development (NICHD) Study of Early Childcare indicate that up to thirty hours per week of good-quality child care does not pose a threat to the cognitive, social, or emotional development of children ages zero to three who are from adequate home environments. The fact that American child-care facilities often do not rise to the level of "good" presents greater cause for concern. Further, in communities where a sufficient amount of good-quality child care is present, it is often unaffordable for many middle-class families.

Qualitative Aspects of Parenting

Many formulas for "correct" or effective parenting have been published since the 1930s, when behavioral scientists likened parenting babies to training animals with conditioning paradigms based on strict use of reward and punishment. Unlike other cultures, both industrialized and nonindustrialized, American society experiences wide swings in popular parenting wisdom espoused by parents, psychologists, and pediatricians. Present understanding of parent-child interaction has benefited from a context of reviewing existing research findings and examining long-term consequences of various approaches. There are two contemporary approaches to understanding the impact of parenting on children's development: typological and social interaction. Typological models focus on overall styles or types of parenting while the social interaction approach stresses the nature of specific exchanges between parent and child.

Parenting Style

The most widely appreciated typological approach to understanding parenting was developed by Diana Baumrind in 1973. Baumrind identified authoritative, authoritarian, and permissive parenting styles. Parenting style is a set of attitudes toward the child that a parent transmits to the child to create an emotional climate surrounding parent-child exchanges. Parenting style is different from parenting behaviors, which are characterized by specific actions and socialization goals. The combination of parental warmth and demandingness is central to conceptualization of parenting style. Authoritative parents display a warm, accepting attitude toward their children while maintaining firm expectations of and restrictions on children's behavior. Open communication between parent and child is facilitated within this emotional climate. Long-term outcomes for children and adolescents of authoritative parents are more favorable compared to outcomes for children of authoritarian or permissive parents. For instance, Baumrind found that adolescent sons of authoritative parents were more competent in comparison to children reared with other parenting styles.

The authoritarian parenting style is characterized by a harsh, rigid emotional climate combined with high demands and little communication. Baumrind found in her longitudinal study that boys with authoritarian parents were particularly vulnerable in terms of both cognitive and social competence. Permissive parents display warmth and acceptance toward their children but do not place demands or restrictions on children's behavior.

Behavioral scientists have continued to conduct research based on Baumrind's parenting styles. Findings have confirmed positive outcomes for offspring of authoritative parents, in particular, better academic achievement. Some findings indicate parenting styles may not be relevant cross-culturally since they are conceptually based in Western cultural values and parenting practices, which do not translate readily into other cultural socialization norms. Also, there has been a lack of research on the processes by which associations exist between parenting styles and social, cognitive, and emotional outcomes for children and adolescents.

Parent-Child Interaction

Behavioral scientists have also approached the question of how to best understand relations between the parental role and child outcomes through studying parent-child interaction. This method focuses on the dyadic relationship between one parent (historically the mother) and one child. From a family systems perspective, the dyadic relationship represents one piece of a larger puzzle. Nonetheless, emphasis on the dyadic relationship has been fruitful and has dominated decades of parenting literature. Parent-child interaction research has shown that the interaction between parent and child is linked to a variety of social outcomes including aggression, achievement, and moral development. Significant associations between parent-child interaction and child outcomes are impressive not because of their size, which is often small, but because of the unique influence they have on child development amid the array of other family, school, and community influences on any given child. Behavioral scientists have "turned over many stones" in their search for influential parental characteristics. Examples of parental qualities that have been repeatedly identified as salient predictors of positive development include parental responsiveness, lack of hostility and controlling parenting, and positive parental affect.

Studies conducted in the 1990s found unique effects for fathers' interaction apart from effects from mothers with respect to cognitive and social development. Thus, it is no longer accurate to view fathers' role in the household as instrumental (e.g., breadwinner) while mothers influence all emotional development. Despite the lesser amount of time fathers spend with children, fathers' interaction patterns contribute to children's emotional development apart from the influence of mothers. Further, parent-child interaction research has evolved from simply matching behaviors on the part of parents with behaviors displayed by their children. Contemporary work focuses on psychological processes that underlie associations between parenting and child adjustment, such as emotional understanding, emotional regulatory skills, mental representations, attributions and beliefs, and problem-solving skills.

Discipline

Whether one approaches parenting from a large-scale family climate perspective or a more fine-detail, parent-child interaction perspective, how to discipline children remains one of the most frequently asked questions from behavioral scientists and parents alike. Specifically, is physical punishment effec-

tive, and even if it is, is it damaging to children? A wealth of research indicates that physical punishment yields obedience out of fear, which quickly translates into transgressions when the fear is alleviated. That is, children do not continue to obey when the threat of punishment is lifted. Children are, however, likely to incorporate parents' rules into their normal repertoire of behavior when they have been consistently rewarded for their good behaviors. Reasoning, rather than punishment, has yielded effective socialization outcomes. Further, minor physical discipline such as spanking a child's buttocks in a controlled manner with an open hand is associated with higher levels of bullying aggression displayed by kindergartners as well as noncompliance among young children. Children learn what they live, and spanking clearly does not promote prosocial development based on current research knowledge.

Parental Monitoring and Involvement

Another practical and influential parenting behavior often studied and questioned is parental monitoring. Parental monitoring is a range of activities that includes the supervision of children's choice of social settings, activities, and friends. Monitoring of young children is direct in nature while for adolescents it is indirect in the form of management of social activities. A number of studies have shown that less monitoring and supervision of children's activities is associated with delinquent and antisocial behavior. After-school time and evening are particularly important segments of the day for parents to keep close tabs on preadolescents and adolescents by phone calling, asking questions, verifying answers, and, where possible, escorting and supervising kids. Children on their own after school, especially girls, are susceptible to peer pressure to engage in such activities as vandalism, cheating, and stealing.

Parental involvement is conceptually related to monitoring in that it involves the parents' management of the child's access to opportunities to develop socially, emotionally, physically, and cognitively, such as extracurricular activities and social circles. Parents act as a conduit for children to interface with institutional settings such as church, Brownies, Cub Scouts, library, and pool. Mothers more often than fathers maintain involvement with such organizations. Social class differences are related to children's use of community organizations and the level of maternal participation. Diminished participation by less advantaged families may be explained by lesser ability to pay and get time off from work to attend. Involved parents also act as social coaches in that they arrange opportunities for play and socialization through their own adult peer network.

Individual parents bring unique levels of personal resources to the parenting process, including the cumulative effects of upbringing, education, employment, and mental health. (AP/Wide World Photos)

Influences on Parenting Quality

Parenting is such a wildly complex and subtle process that it is necessary to use several levels of analysis in order to gain a well-rounded understanding of the entire process. For instance, from most fine-grained to most general, one can examine parent-child interaction, parenting style or family climate, the family as a system, and, finally, influences on parenting quality altogether external to the family.

Parental Employment

One factor external to the family, but important to the parenting process, is parental employment. Employment affects parents as individuals since the way they feel about work is often brought home after work, a process called spillover. Parents with very demanding jobs have been found in research studies to shy away from complex parenting tasks such as helping with homework. A disengaged parenting style is one in which a parent seeks to do the minimum required when interacting with offspring. This approach may be more likely when parents are emotionally and cognitively drained from work. Dis-

engaged parenting style has been shown to be related to poor outcomes for children. Jobs also affect parents' skills, attitudes, and perspectives through providing practice at the objective tasks that they perform on the job. From this point of view, jobs shape parents developmentally over time, reinforcing particular strengths and weaknesses.

Parental employment changes the allocation of responsibilities and power in the family. Children may be asked to be responsible for chores at an earlier age when both parents are employed. Although the data are not conclusive, fathers may take on more responsibility for running the household when mothers are employed. The adjustment each family member makes to the time management and effort jobs require of parents determines the effect employment has on children. In other words, with respect to children's development, employment versus nonemployment is less informative than details about the job and family functioning, such as quality of the home environment and parental involvement.

Socioeconomic Status

Socioeconomic status (SES) is a reliable predictor of parenting and child adjustment that is closely tied to parental employment. It is a complex variable based on income and education, along with other "social address" indicators, that determines many of the structural components of children's daily lives such as neighborhood, school district, extracurricular activities, health care, and nutrition. A number of studies have confirmed that there are SES differences in parenting practices and beliefs. Lower SES parents tend to be more authoritarian in their overall parenting style, with more controlling, restrictive, and disapproving parent-child interaction patterns. Parents' use of control strategies may be the result of dangerous living conditions.

Higher SES mothers tend to be more verbal when interacting with their children. Researchers are far from understanding why SES is such a reliable indicator of parenting factors. Current efforts are focused on developing more detailed information on how specific components related to SES—such as neighborhood, job quality, and family structure—affect parenting, and examining risk and resiliency models within this framework.

Individual Differences

Individual parents have unique levels of personal resources stemming from cumulative effects of upbringing, education, employment, and mental health, for instance. Therefore, parents bring themselves to the parenting equation—including their own developmental stage. The lifespan developmental model emerged in the 1970s and is built on the premise that human development is a lifelong process. Parents, therefore, are at a specific point in their own growth as they face their child's continually changing needs. For instance, mothers may be negotiating their own new identity as "homemaker" or "career woman" as they make decisions about bedtimes, child care, or nutrition. Similarly, marriages evolve over time. Marital happiness and stability is a good predictor of parenting quality whether or not parents fight in front of children. Marital discord can be draining emotionally and financially taxing, and may present many unique complications in between. These factors in the socioemotional lives of parents represent very real barometers of what parents have to give to child rearing.

In a similar vein, children bring to the careful dance of child rearing their own individual selves complete with desires, habits, and temperament. Temperament is the biological preparedness infants bring into the world that predisposes them to deal with social, cognitive, and perceptual challenges in particular ways. Children's responses to such chal-

lenges play a significant role in adaptation to their environment. During the 1990s there was increasing recognition that children's individual differences in a variety of behaviors shape the way parents respond to children. For instance, infants with difficult temperament are thought to elicit more arousal and distress from caregivers than their less difficult counterparts. Temperamental differences are thought to be modifiable depending on parental personality traits, among other environmental factors.

Parental Education

Finally, behavioral scientists have made efforts to determine whether parenting is modifiable through parental education. Many different programs for parent education exist, with varying success rates in the short and long term. The success of a program can be measured according to changed parenting or improvement in child adjustment. In general, more training has been shown to lead to better outcomes. Parent education programs commonly focus on positive forms of discipline, information about children's developmental stages, activities to enhance children's cognitive skills, and the importance of warmth combined with consistent rules. Longitudinal data from "welfare to work" studies indicate that parental education programs need to include a minimum of biweekly home visits and last over two years to be effective in terms of changed parental behavior. Such programs are prohibitively expensive. Thus, a high-quality parent education program can change the parenting of poorly educated, young, poor mothers, but these improvements are not necessarily related to better cognitive and social development for children. This may be because parenting is just one of the challenges disadvantaged families face. For instance, better parenting may not be able to completely eclipse environmental threats, such as poverty or domestic violence.

See also: FATHERS; GAY- AND LESBIAN-HEADED FAMILIES; PARENT-CHILD RELATIONSHIPS; SINGLE-PARENT FAMILIES

Bibliography

Baumrind, Diana. "The Development of Instrumental Competence through Socialization." In Anne D. Pick ed., *Minnesota Symposium on Child Psychology.* Minneapolis: University of Minnesota Press, 1973.

Eccles, Jacquelynne S., Allan Wigfield, and Ulrich Schiefele. "Motivation to Succeed." In William Damon and Nancy Eisenberg eds., *Handbook of Child Psychology: Social, Emotional, and Personality Development.* New York: Wiley, 1998.

NICHD Early Child Care Search Network. "The Effects of Infant Child Care on Infant-Mother Attachment Security: Results of the NICHD Study of Early Child Care." *Child Development* 68 (1997):860–879.

NICHD Early Child Care Search Network. "The Relationship of Child Care to Cognitive and Language Development."

Presented at the Society for Research in Child Development Meeting, April 3–6, 1997, Washington, DC.

NICHD Early Child Care Search Network. "Early Child Care and Self Control, Compliance, and Problem Behavior at Twenty-Four and Thirty-Six months." *Child Development* 69 (1998): 1145–1170.

U.S. Bureau of the Census. "Survey of Income and Program Participation." *March Current Population Survey.* Washington, DC: U.S. Government Printing Office, 1996.

U.S. Bureau of the Census. "Household and Family Characteristics." *March Current Population Survey.* Washington, DC: U.S. Government Printing Office, 1998.

U.S. Bureau of the Census. *March Current Population Survey.* Washington, DC: U.S. Government Printing Office, 1999.

Abigail Tuttle O'Keeffe

PEERS

See: ADOLESCENCE; FRIENDSHIP; SOCIAL DEVELOPMENT

PERSONALITY DEVELOPMENT

Personality psychology is considered the study of individual differences in behavior—how individuals behave differently from one another in various situations. Developmental personality psychologists are interested in understanding the ways individuals develop their unique patterns of responding to the environment based on genetic endowments and social histories. Also of interest is identifying the ways in which personality changes or is stable across development, as well as identifying early behavioral precursors that are predictive of later individual differences. From these multiple interests have come a number of perspectives on personality development relevant to the age period spanning infancy through adolescence (birth to twenty years of age).

Perspectives on Personality Development

Behavioral individuality in newborns is defined as temperament. A number of competing models of temperament have been proposed, but most generally view temperament as a construct that represents the early emerging, constitutionally based, behavioral individuality that is consistent over both time and situations. Conceptually, psychologists have differentiated infant temperament from childhood and adolescent personality by noting that temperament represents the more biologically based basic emotions, while personality represents the consistent behavioral repertoire developed by an individual out of her interactions with the social environment.

The course of personality development from temperamental beginnings has been described by some as a transition from temperament to personality or as an elaboration from basic dimensions of temperament to more complex dimensions of personality. By late childhood and adolescence, this behavioral transition or elaboration is apparent as behavior has become more purposefully directed and increasingly incorporates concepts like self-understanding.

A number of theories have been developed that outline different interactional processes of personality development, but most of the theories can be grouped into two categories: those that emphasize certain developmental environments in shaping an individual's personality and those that emphasize the individual's biology. A theoretical orientation that emphasizes either the environment or biology generally does not completely discount the position of the other, but rather stresses one factor over the other with respect to relative importance.

Attachment

Many personality theorists and researchers emphasize the importance to early personality development of the quality of attachment between infant and primary caregiver. Attachment is considered the enduring emotional tie that an infant forms with his caregiver, which helps to ensure a relationship style between caregiver and infant that fosters infant survival. Several models characterize the developmental progression of attachment formation. These models emphasize the universal, biologically based process of attachment as it unfolds across infancy and childhood.

Significant individual differences are not thought to occur in the actual process of attachment formation itself, but individual differences do occur in the quality or style of attachment. See Table 1 for a listing of the commonly agreed upon infant and childhood attachment patterns and their characteristic behaviors. These patterns of behavior have been identified through a laboratory procedure called the Strange Situation, which was developed by Mary Ainsworth and her colleagues. The Strange Situation is a standardized procedure that places the infant or young child in increasingly stressful separation-reunion situations with the caregiver.

Many contributing factors lead to differences in attachment style, but the developmental factor typically viewed as most important to attachment outcomes is caregiver responsiveness to infant needs. For example, a caregiver facilitates a secure attachment by consistently meeting the infant's needs. Infant needs may be satisfied by behaviors such as responding to crying, feeding when hungry, physical contact, and comforting during times of stress. If the infant's needs are met consistently, a secure attachment is

TABLE 1

Patterns of Attachment

Attachment Classification	Attachment Behavior
Secure attachment	☐ Prefers closeness to caregiver in novel situations ☐ Distressed by separation from caregiver ☐ Easily calmed upon return ☐ Prefers caregiver to strangers
Insecure–avoidant attachment	☐ Does not prefer closeness to caregiver in novel situations ☐ Does not become distressed by separation from caregiver ☐ Avoids contact upon return ☐ Shows little or no preference for caregiver over stranger
Insecure–resistant attachment	☐ Distressed in presence of caregiver in novel situations ☐ Upset by separation ☐ Is not calmed by return ☐ Resists contact with strangers
Insecure–disorganized–disoriented attachment	☐ Is confused and dazed in novel situations ☐ Bewildered during separations from caregiver ☐ Contradictory behaviors of seeking out (e.g., reaching out) and avoiding (e.g., look away) caregiver upon reunion

SOURCE: *Brady Reynolds.*

TABLE 2

Attachment Outcomes

Attachment Classification	Attachment Outcome Behavior
Secure attachment	☐ Rated by peers as less anxious ☐ High in social competence ☐ Describe parents favorably ☐ Invested in relationships ☐ Prefer mutually satisfactory solutions to interpersonal conflicts ☐ Usually adopt parents view of God as warm and trustworthy
Insecure–avoidant attachment	☐ Viewed by peers as hostile, lonely, and having little family support ☐ More likely to report parents with drinking problems ☐ Express disinterest in intimacy ☐ High breakup rates and less grieving following a breakup ☐ Prefer to work alone ☐ Most likely to be agnostic
Insecure–resistant attachment	☐ Rated by peers as most anxious of the three groups ☐ High levels of anxiety, depression, and loneliness ☐ Most likely to describe parents as unfair and intrusive ☐ Characterized as desperate for a romantic relationship

SOURCE: *Brady Reynolds.*

most likely formed through the infant learning to expect the caregiver's responsiveness and dependability.

If an infant's needs are not met consistently, then one of the insecure attachment patterns is more likely to develop. These insecure attachment patterns may lead to later peer and romantic relational problems in adolescence and early adulthood. Table 2 shows some adolescent and early-adulthood characteristics that researchers have found to be related to different earlier attachment patterns. Table 2 includes only the first three attachment styles listed in Table 1. Since the 1990s, researchers have identified the fourth attachment style, insecure-disorganized-disoriented, and have not studied the outcomes that might be associated with it.

Some research has revealed a relation between infant temperament and attachment style. Infants classified as temperamentally difficult—characterized by irritability, adverse reactions to changes in routine, and unpredictable endogenous rhythms, like wake/sleep cycles, are more likely to form one of the insecure attachment styles. This relation between temperament and attachment suggests that temperament can influence the process of attachment. For instance, a temperamentally difficult infant is in many ways more difficult and less satisfying to care for than a

more easygoing infant. The increased burden of caring for a difficult infant makes it less likely that the infant's needs will be met as consistently as those of the more temperamentally easygoing infant. These relationship differences between caregivers and temperamentally different infants stand to shape different attachment patterns.

Becoming increasingly popular in assessing the relative contributing factors in early personality development is the concept of goodness-of-fit between the developing infant or child and his or her environment. In the example above of the temperamentally difficult infant being more likely to form an insecure attachment, if the particular caregiver is not negatively affected by the difficult behaviors of the infant, then an insecure attachment is less likely to occur because of the good fit between the caregiver and infant. The goodness-of-fit between an infant or child and her environment is as important in determining developmental outcomes as different developmental factors (e.g., parental responsiveness, temperament) considered separately.

Friendship

Another important environmental influence for personality development is peer friendships. Research suggests that between 6 percent and 11 percent of school-age children have no friends, and there is clear evidence that these children are at increased risk for later social and emotional maladjustment. A lack of successful childhood friendships is also related to academic difficulties and dropping out of high school. The broad scope of childhood friendships as potentially a positive or negative developmental influence for personality is understandable in light of the amount of time children and adolescents spend with peers in both school and social settings.

Friendships take on greater importance as children grow older, with friendships accounting for an increasing amount of the child's time and experience. For young children, friendships serve to increase excitement during play and allow opportunities for the child to regulate his excitement. Maintaining friendships in middle childhood (generally considered to be between the ages of six and twelve) requires children to learn about behavioral norms and relate to others. And in adolescents, friendships are particularly important as the typical adolescent begins to rely on friendships for social support and as a resource for self-exploration. In adolescents, friendships provide an important opportunity for social referencing, which allows the adolescent to try on different social roles and ideals that are essential to the development of a sense of self.

Self-Concept

Related to adolescent friendships and personality development is an aspect of personality known as self-concept. Some personality theorists and researchers contend that the developing and changing view a person holds of herself is an important aspect of individual differences and is often neglected under the temperament or trait conceptions of personality. From this perspective, a person's self-concept (which incorporates such features as the individual's history, sense of competency, and goals for the future) is an important behavioral determinant that is more dynamic, malleable, and encompassing than temperament or personality traits.

A critical component in the development of one's self-concept is referencing, including temporal referencing, a self-comparison from an earlier time to a later time, and social referencing, a comparison of one's self to others. Temporal and social referencing yield the type of self-examination that serves to increase the stability of individual differences through an individual making behavioral and/or environmental changes to maintain a self-concept. The particular style of referencing most commonly adopted changes across the lifespan. Temporal referencing is most common in childhood and in old age when relatively rapid physical and cognitive changes are most apparent. Conversely, social referencing is most common in

adolescence and adulthood when individual change is less appreciable.

For adolescents, it is their emphasis on social referencing that makes having successful friendships especially important in the development of self-concept. Having successful friendships in adolescence leads to more interactive and positive comparisons between self and others. Without successful friendships, an adolescent is more isolated and is more likely to make negative comparisons. These negative comparisons during adolescence set a developmental trajectory toward low self-esteem and further social withdrawal in adulthood, making it difficult for such individuals to learn the social skills necessary to meet social support needs.

In regard to why some children and adolescents have more trouble making friends than others, evidence suggests that in some instances early individual differences in attachment and temperament predict later friendship problems or successes. For example, research has shown that children classified as insecure-avoidant are more likely than securely attached children to exhibit aggression, anger, and hostility in peer-group settings. Also, insecure-ambivalent children in such settings are more likely to exhibit social inhibition and a low threshold for frustration. These patterns of social behavior are predictive of peer rejection and lack of friendship. Similarly, research in infant and childhood temperament has revealed a predictive relation between friendship success and both overall emotionality and the ability of an infant or child to self-regulate emotional expression. Infants and children who are the most temperamentally emotional and the least capable of regulating their expression of emotion are on average less successful in developing and maintaining friendships.

In summary, research suggests that some early individual differences in attachment and temperament may lead to behavioral styles that ultimately undermine an individual's ability to successfully make and maintain friendships. The long-term effects of these individual differences could be harmful for the individual. With greater understanding and awareness of the elements and dynamics involved, however, interventions may be developed that help deflect the individual's development to more successful and healthy outcomes.

A Biological Perspective on Personality Development

From a more biological perspective, personality development is thought to be primarily governed by the biological maturation of the individual. Even environmental influences on development are viewed as largely under the influence of biologically based dispositions and characteristics. Personality developmentalists holding a strong biological orientation argue that environmental factors do not play a significant role in the development of individual differences, except in the case of extreme environmental deficiencies. An example of such a deficiency is the lack of early caregiver responsiveness described above, which is often found with the insecure attachment styles.

Biologically oriented personality theorists argue that specific environments cannot be required for species-typical developments such as individual differences. Rather, environments are viewed as providing, or not providing, opportunities for biological development to take place. All that is required for adaptive, functional development is a range of adequate environments.

As described above, early biologically based individual differences are often characterized as differences in temperament. Considerable evidence based on heritability research shows that individual differences in temperament have strong genetic foundations. These genetic foundations lead to individual differences in physiology, which in turn may influence environmental conditions in ways that channel environmental experiences to fit temperamental qualities. Put another way, biological determinants of personality development in some ways influence and shape the environmental conditions that influence development.

An infant's or child's biological characteristics bias his environmental experiences in a number of ways. First, as described earlier, there is goodness-of-fit—biologically based characteristics of an infant or child influence his fit with the environment, which indirectly shapes the quality of environmental experiences. Second, aspects of an individual's behavior stemming from his biology may consistently evoke certain types of behavior in others. For instance, a dispositionally timid or shy child may be ignored more in social contexts than an extroverted child who often initiates social exchange. Third, biologically based dispositions may lead to certain environmental preferences as an infant or child grows to increasingly select preferred environments. For example, an individual with a particularly high activity level may be drawn more to sports or other physical activities while someone less active may prefer comparatively sedentary activities. Finally, biologically based dispositions also may influence the way an individual experiences environmental conditions. For example, research has revealed very early individual differences in reactivity to novel or highly stimulating environments arising from differences in brain functioning. For highly reactive infants, novel or stimulating environments are aversive, and these infants are likely to withdraw from such environments because they are easily overstimulated. Given the same environment, however, less reactive infants are likely to be curious and want to explore.

All of these biologically based differences, which in some ways shape an individual's environmental experiences, lead to unique environmental influences on personality development that match the individual's biology. Thus, from a biological perspective, an individual's unique biology stands to influence the environment and therefore bias how the environment influences personality development.

A logical next question regarding biological influences on personality development concerns the structure of personality. With personality development having a biological component, there should be a degree of universality in overall personality structure. Research suggests that indeed there may be such a universal structure of personality.

The Developing Structure of Personality

In the field of personality psychology, there appears to be an emerging consensus that the structure of late-adolescent and adult personality can be comprehensively described by five broad factors, which are known as the "Big Five." These five factors are typically characterized as: Extroversion/Surgency, Agreeableness, Conscientiousness, Neuroticism/Emotional Stability, and Openness to Experience/Intellect. Using language-based instruments cross-culturally, the Big Five has been successfully identified in American English, German, Dutch, Portuguese, Hebrew, Chinese, Korean, and Japanese. Such findings support the idea that the Big Five is a universally applicable taxonomy of late-adolescent and adult personality.

In similar studies of infant and childhood individual difference dimensions, usually using parental or teacher ratings of temperament, five to seven dimensions are normally identified. Five of the dimensions are particularly robust and have been labeled Activity Level, Negative Emotionality, Task Persistence, Adaptability/Agreeableness, and Inhibition. The two other dimensions are less certain and have been labeled Rhythmicity and Threshold. Developmentally, the process of change from these earlier infant and childhood dimensions to the Big Five dimensions of late adolescence and adulthood appears to involve multiple early dimensions being subsumed under single Big Five dimensions. In other words, during the course of development, the organizational structure of individual difference dimensions changes, with

FIGURE 1

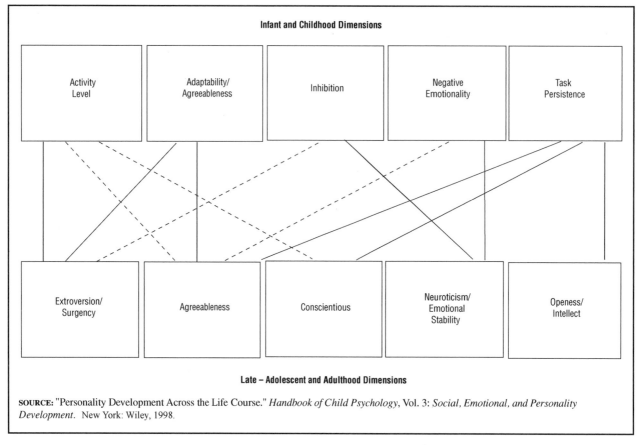

Infant and Childhood Dimensions

Activity Level

Adaptability/ Agreeableness

Inhibition

Negative Emotionality

Task Persistence

Extroversion/ Surgency

Agreeableness

Conscientious

Neuroticism/ Emotional Stability

Openess/ Intellect

Late – Adolescent and Adulthood Dimensions

SOURCE: "Personality Development Across the Life Course." *Handbook of Child Psychology*, Vol. 3: *Social, Emotional, and Personality Development*. New York: Wiley, 1998.

each of the Big Five dimensions being comprised of features from more than one of the earlier dimensions.

Figure 1 shows hypothesized relations between five of the individual difference dimensions of infancy and childhood and the different dimensions of the Big Five. The general relations outlined in Figure 1 are based on empirical evidence; more detailed research is required, however, before more specific conclusions can be drawn about the role of these early individual difference dimensions in the development of the Big Five. In Figure 1, the lines connecting specific dimensions of infancy and childhood to specific dimensions of the Big Five represent correlations between the earlier and later dimensions. The solid lines represent positive correlations, while the dashed lines represent negative correlations.

Apparent from Figure 1 should be the lack of one-to-one correspondence between early and later individual difference dimensions. Evidence suggests that this dimensional reorganization is more biologically determined than environmentally determined; meaning, as described earlier, that specific environmental conditions are not required for this reorganization to occur. Exactly how and when this

dimensional reorganization takes place, however, is not understood. Future research will examine more closely the age-related changes that take place in the organization of individual difference dimensions.

Conclusion

Individual differences in personality are universal in that they are found in all human populations. The roots of individual differences are no doubt bedded in evolutionary history, selected because of their improved adaptiveness to conditions in the environment. The specific personality qualities of an individual, which lead to individual differences between people, are not based so much in evolution, however, but are the product of many developmental factors.

The developmental study of individual differences in personality provides a rich source of data for the researcher and practitioner alike to use in understanding and predicting behavior. Without the study of individual differences, there could be no detailed analysis or explanation of why people often behave or develop very differently under seemingly equivalent environmental conditions. Understanding these differences and the development of these differences is fundamental not only to psychologists' understanding of behavior but also to parents, schoolteachers, social workers, policymakers, and anyone else working with other people. Because of its universality and its implications for understanding behavior, the study of individual differences is an essential part of any complete scientific study of behavior.

See also: MILESTONES OF DEVELOPMENT; STAGES OF DEVELOPMENT; TEMPERAMENT

Bibliography

Ainsworth, Mary, Mary Blehar, Everett Waters, and Sally Wall. *Patterns of Attachment.* Hillsdale, NJ: Lawrence Erlbaum, 1978.

Bates, John, and Theodore Wachs, eds. *Temperament: Individual Differences at the Interface of Biology and Behavior.* Washington, DC: American Psychological Association, 1994.

Bowlby, John. *Attachment and Loss,* Vol. 1: *Attachment.* New York: Basic, 1969.

Bowlby, John. *Attachment and Loss,* Vol. 3: *Loss, Sadness, and Depression.* New York: Basic, 1980.

Caspi, Avshalom. "Personality Development across the Life Course." In William Damon and Nancy Eisenberg eds., *Handbook of Child Psychology,* Vol. 3: *Social, Emotional, and Personality Development.* New York: Wiley, 1998.

Damon, William. *Social and Personality Development: Infancy through Adolescence.* New York: Norton, 1983.

Halverson, Charles, Jr., Geldolph Kohnstamm, and Roy Martin, eds. *The Developing Structure of Temperament and Personality from Infancy to Adulthood.* Hillsdale, NJ: Lawrence Erlbaum, 1994.

Harris, Judith. "Where Is the Child's Environment? A Group Socialization Theory of Development." *Psychological Review* 102 (1995):458–489.

Kohnstamm, Geldolph, Charles Halverson Jr., Ivan Mervielde, and Valerie Havill, eds. *Parental Descriptions of Child Personality: Developmental Antecedents to the Big Five?* Mahwah, NJ: Lawrence Erlbaum, 1998.

Mahler, Margaret, Fred Pine, and Anni Bergman. *The Psychological Birth of the Human Infant.* New York: Basic, 1975.

McAdams, Dan. "Can Personality Change? Levels of Stability and Growth in Personality across the Life Span." In Todd Heatherton and Joel Weinberger eds., *Can Personality Change?* Washington, DC: American Psychological Association, 1994.

Rothbart, Mary, and John Bates. "Temperament." In William Damon and Nancy Eisenberg eds., *Handbook of Child Psychology,* Vol. 3: *Social, Emotional, and Personality Development.* New York: Wiley, 1998.

Rubin, Kenneth, William Bukowski, and Jeffrey Parker. "Peer Interactions, Relationships, and Groups." In William Damon and Nancy Eisenberg eds., *Handbook of Child Psychology,* Vol. 3: *Social, Emotional, and Personality Development.* New York: Wiley, 1998.

Scarr, Sandra. "The Development of Individual Differences in Intelligence and Personality." In Hayne Reese and Michael Franzen eds., *Biological and Neuropsychological Mechanisms: Life-Span Developmental Psychology.* Mahwah, NJ: Lawrence Erlbaum, 1997.

Sperling, Michael, and William Berman, eds. *Attachment in Adults: Clinical and Developmental Perspectives.* New York: Guilford Press, 1994.

Wiggins, Jerry, ed. *The Five Factor Model of Personality: Theoretical Perspectives.* New York: Guilford Press, 1996.

Brady Reynolds

PETS

Pets are a ready source of companionship, comfort, and unconditional love for children, and they contribute to a child's emotional and physical well-being. As children care for pets, they learn about responsibility, friendship, sharing, and empathy toward both animals and humans. Studies have shown that pets also have a therapeutic value. Some hospitals have pet-assisted therapy programs through which companion animals, like dogs, visit young patients and comfort them through the soothing effects of petting and holding a soft, warm animal.

Selecting a pet takes careful consideration. Some families want a pet to share in all family activities. Some want to avoid animals with fur because of family allergies. Others prefer caged animals like gerbils, fish, or reptiles because they require less space and attention. Whatever the pet choice, it should reflect a family's needs, income, living space, and lifestyle.

See also: PERSONALITY DEVELOPMENT; SOCIAL DEVELOPMENT

Bibliography

Beck, Alan, and Aaron Katcher. *Between Pets and People: The Importance of Animal Companionship.* West Lafayette, IN: Purdue University Press, 1996.

"How Pets Help People." In the Humane Society of the United States [web site]. Available from http://www.hsus.org/programs/companion/pets_help_people.html; INTERNET.

"Selecting a Proper Pet: Practical Advice and Considerations." In the American Veterinary Medical Association [web site]. Available from http://www.avma.org/care4pets/avmabuy.htm; INTERNET.

Patricia Ohlenroth

PHENOTYPE

Phenotypes are the physical characteristics, such as eye color, displayed by an individual. Phenotype, often used in relation to specific variable characteristics or disease states manifested by an individual, contains no information about the underlying genetic determinants of the characteristics. The genotype contains the genetic information that is used to determine the range of potential phenotypes. Within this range, the environment and other nongenetic factors determine the final phenotype. For example, cystic fibrosis is a phenotype. Conversely, the description of a mutation in the gene that causes this disease is a genotype. The links between genes and particular normal and abnormal phenotypes are being identified using results of the Human Genome Project. Identification of these links is improving child health by providing genetic counselors with detailed information on the causes, phenotypic variability, and environmental factors that lead to birth defects and other diseases. Nongenetic factors influencing a phenotype that results from a particular genotype can be used by genetic counselors to suggest environmental or lifestyle changes that can lessen disease severity.

See also: GENETIC COUNSELING; GENOTYPE; HUMAN GENOME PROJECT

Bibliography

Oak Ridge National Laboratory. "The Science behind the Human Genome Project." Available from http://www.ornl.gov/hgmis/ project/info.html; INTERNET.

David W. Threadgill
Robert E. Boykin

PHENYLKETONURIA

Phenylketonuria (PKU) is due to a deficiency of phenylalanine hydroxylase, the enzyme that converts phenylalanine to tyrosine. High levels of phenylalanine accumulate in the body resulting in severe mental retardation, seizures, and a musty odor. PKU is an autosomal recessive genetic disorder. The incidence is 1 in 10,000 to 1 in 12,000 live births. PKU is detected on newborn screens, which are most sensitive when performed between forty-eight and seventy-two hours of life, and after the infant has been fed a diet containing protein. Phenylalanine levels are easily detected by a few drops of blood, and early treatment prevents complications making it a model disease for screening. Treatment includes a diet low in phenylalanine and frequent monitoring of blood levels. Dietary therapy should begin immediately in the newborn period. The duration of therapy is controversial. It is recommended that children maintain a very restrictive diet through the age of six, and they are encouraged to maintain some restriction throughout life.

See also: BIRTH DEFECTS; NUTRITION

Bibliography

Berry, Gerard. "Inborn Errors of Carbohydrate Ammonia, Amino Acid, and Organic Acid Metabolism." In H. William Taeusch and Roberta Ballard eds., *Avery's Diseases of the Newborn.* Philadelphia: W. B. Saunders, 1998.

Goodman, Stephen, and Carol Greene. "Metabolic Disorders of the Newborn." *Pediatrics in Review* 15 (1994):359–365.

Rezvani, Iraj. "Defects in Metabolism of Amino Acids." In Richard E. Behrman, Robert M. Kliegman, and Ann M. Arvin eds., *Nelson Textbook of Pediatrics.* Philadelphia: W. B. Saunders Company, 1996.

Meica M. Efird

PHYSICAL GROWTH

Physical growth usually refers to changes in size or mass; so it is correct to say that a child grows in stature (height) or body weight. Even though most people usually think of growth at the level of the whole child, the cells and internal structures that make up the child also grow, primarily by increasing in number or size. Consequently, auxologists (those who study child growth) may be interested in the growth of bones to help understand fractures and osteoporosis; the growth of the heart walls to help understand hypertension (high blood pressure) and heart disease; or the growth of adipose tissue (body fat) to help understand obesity.

The measurement of body dimensions such as those used in growth studies is called anthropometry. Past growth is usually measured as the size attained at a chronological age, for example the weight of a child at eight years old. Assessment of the rate of growth requires that a body dimension, such as weight, be measured twice over a period, and then the change is expressed in terms of the increment or velocity of growth, for example in pounds or kilograms per year.

Some physical changes in childhood are more complicated than just size or mass. These changes include alterations in body structures and functions and can be termed development. Physical developmental changes are as diverse as the closing of the fontanels (soft spots) in a baby's skull, the erupting of teeth, learning to walk, or the deepening of the voice of boys during adolescence.

Some developmental changes are considered maturational, or indicators of physical maturity. Maturation is the progression of developmental changes toward the characteristics of adults. Physical maturation occurs from the time of conception, but some of the most commonly recognized indicators of maturation become apparent during adolescence. Changes in body shape, breast development in girls, pubic hair development in both genders, and development of facial hair in boys are visible indicators of maturation toward adult appearance of the body, and they signal adult reproductive functioning. The cessation of the growth of long bones, associated with the final attainment of adult stature is also a maturational event.

Although growth and maturation are certainly related, distinguishing between them is important because some physiological and hormonal processes affect growth and maturation differentially, as do some diseases. It is easy to observe that children of the same size can differ in maturational status and that fully mature individuals (adults) can be of different sizes.

General Patterns

Growth differences between males and females begin before birth and continue until adulthood. Generally, boys are larger than girls throughout gestation, so that when they are born at full term (forty weeks), male newborns usually weigh about 150 grams (5.3 ounces) more than females, and are about one centimeter (0.4 inches) longer. Even though they are smaller than their male counterparts, female babies are usually more mature skeletally and neurologically at birth.

After birth, most body dimensions, such as stature, body circumferences, and weight, follow a similar pattern of growth: a period of very rapid growth in infancy, slower growth during middle childhood, a very rapid growth phase or spurt in adolescence, and a period of rapidly decelerating growth, ending with adult size. Obviously, some body dimensions, such as weight or fatness, can continue to change throughout adulthood. The different phases of postnatal growth can be appreciated more easily by looking at the rates of growth, or velocity, in addition to attained size.

On average, boys are taller and heavier than girls at every postnatal age, except from about nine to thirteen years. The reversal of size differences at these ages results from girls entering their adolescent growth spurt about two years earlier than boys. Boys usually end up about nine to thirteen centimeters (three to five inches) taller and seven to nine kilograms (fifteen to twenty pounds) heavier than girls at eighteen years of age. This is primarily because boys grow approximately two years longer than girls do before their spurt, and because the spurt of boys usually is more intense and lasts a little longer than that of girls.

Timing of Maturation

Different body structures and functions often mature at differing rates, and they achieve adult status at different average chronological ages. For example, the three tiny bones of the inner ear (the incus, malleus, and stapes) are mature before birth, while the last bone to achieve adult status (the clavicle or collarbone) does not do so until approximately twenty-five years of age.

Even within groups of healthy children, there is considerable variation in the timing of the same maturational processes and events. For example, the first menstrual period of girls, or menarche, signals achievement of one aspect of adult reproductive functioning and is a widely used maturational indicator. (The corresponding but less noticeable event in boys is the first production of sperm cells, or spermarche.) The average age at menarche for girls in the United States is approximately 12.8 years of age. About two-thirds of U.S. girls will attain menarche within one year of the average timing, and about 98 percent of all girls within two years. For healthy girls, this variation in the timing of menarche is due to inherited patterns from their parents. Age at menarche (and most other maturational timing) can be delayed by malnutrition and infectious disease, and less commonly by hormonal dysfunction.

The chronological age at which maturational events occur provides a measure of the relative timing of that event in the child's growth and development. In addition to menarche, other examples of maturational events whose timing may be of interest include onset of ossification of bony centers (visible in X rays), eruption of teeth, first walking, first appearance of pubic hair, the age when the adolescent spurt is at its peak velocity, and the final fusion of the growing centers of long bones.

Of course, these maturational events are really biological processes that occur progressively in the developing child and the "event" is really just an arbitrary point in the developmental process that has been defined by auxologists so that it can be measured more easily. Some maturational processes have been more or less arbitrarily defined in stages or grades so that the progress through the stages can be measured. The progressive development of the secondary sexual characteristics associated with sexual maturation is a common example where such stages have been applied. The development of breasts in girls, penis and scrotum in boys, and pubic hair in both genders have carefully described stages of development that pediatricians and endocrinologists use clinically and that are also used by researchers who are interested in normal and abnormal adolescent growth and maturation.

Nutrition, Health, and the Environment

Physical growth and maturation are often used as indicators of child health because they are sensitive to nutritional deficiencies, infection, and poverty. Growth is a very adaptable process that will slow in the face of extreme nutritional deficiency, for example, as a mechanism to conserve nutrients for body functions essential to the child's survival. Growth will resume or even catch up at faster rates than normal when the nutritional deficits are remedied. This sensitivity to health and environmental constraints makes growth an excellent indicator of the adequacy of nutrition and the health of individuals and of populations. As basic indicators of health, pediatricians compare the attained stature and weight of children and their rates of growth with the expected values for healthy children or with growth standards.

TABLE 1

Average Age at Menarche for Selected Countries

Country	Age (years)
Argentina	12.5
United States	12.8
Belgium	13.1
Norway	13.2
Nigeria (rural)	14.5
India (rural)	14.6
New Guinea	15.6
Nepal (high altitude)	16.2

SOURCE: Phyllis B. Eveleth, and James M. Tanner. *Worldwide Variation in Human Growth*, 2nd edition. Cambridge, England: Cambridge University Press, 1990.

In public-health studies comparing different populations or countries, the percentage of young children with very short stature (stunting) and the percentage of those whose weight is very low for how tall they are (wasting) are important indicators of nutritional and health conditions affecting children. In such studies, the average age at menarche, or of other maturational events, may be used to indicate the adequacy of general health and nutritional conditions.

Some examples of the average age at menarche from different countries are given in Table 1. Average ages of menarche greater than 13.5 years are usually considered to be associated with some general nutritional or health constraints in the country. In the case of Nepal, these issues are probably complicated by the people living at very high altitude, which may affect growth and maturation because of the reduced availability of oxygen to the body.

When nutritional energy (calories from food) is in excess of what the body uses and what is expended in physical activity, it is stored in adipose tissue. This fat tissue is accumulated within the body and subcutaneously (under the skin). The growth in weight of children and measurements of the thickness of the subcutaneous fat by calipers are used as indicators of overweight and obesity. Sometimes the weight of children is expressed as an index relative to stature (calculated by dividing the weight, in kilograms, by the square of stature, in meters) to yield the body mass index (BMI). BMI standards are also commonly used to define overweight and obesity and to relate these conditions to various health outcomes.

Physical growth includes many aspects of the biological development of children that can reflect genetics, nutrition, health, and the environment. The aspects of physical growth are central to the child's progress toward adulthood, and they inevitably interact with psychological, behavioral, and social aspects of the developing child.

See also: MENARCHE; MILESTONES OF DEVELOPMENT; MOTOR DEVELOPMENT; NUTRITION; OBESITY

Bibliography

Buckler, J. M. H. *A Reference Manual of Growth and Development*, 2nd edition. Oxford: Blackwell Science, 1997.

Eveleth, Phyllis B., and James M. Tanner. *Worldwide Variation in Human Growth*, 2nd edition. Cambridge, Eng.: Cambridge University Press, 1990.

Himes, John H., ed. *Anthropometric Assessment of Nutritional Status.* New York: Wiley, 1991.

Malina, Robert M., and Claude Bouchard. *Growth, Maturation, and Physical Activity.* Champaign, IL: Human Kinetics, 1991.

Tanner, James M. *Foetus into Man: Physical Growth from Conception to Maturity.* Cambridge, MA: Harvard University Press, 1990.

Tanner, James M., R. H. Whitehouse, and M. Takaishi. "Standards from Birth to Maturity for Height, Weight, Height Velocity, and Weight Velocity: British Children, 1965." *Archives of Disease in Childhood* 41 (1966):613–635.

John H. Himes
LaVell Gold

PIAGET, JEAN (1896–1980)

Jean Piaget's scientific career began at the age of eleven with the publication of a brief notice on an albino sparrow and lasted nearly seventy-five years, resulting in more than sixty books and five hundred articles. Although often referred to as a child psychologist, Piaget was trained as a zoologist and considered himself an epistemologist (a person who studies the nature and development of knowledge). Piaget's fascination with children's reasoning began with his work on early Intelligence Quotient (IQ) tests when he noticed that children's errors were systematic and followed a logic that was entirely different from that used by adults. Systematic observation of his own children and ingenious experiments and interviews with thousands of children and adolescents led Piaget to propose that knowledge develops in a series of stages. Each stage is marked by particular forms of thought that are constructed by the child through interaction with the world. This theory of stages coupled with Piaget's insistence that children play an active role in their own cognitive development had a profound impact on the field of education. Rather than viewing children as empty vessels to be filled with collections of facts, educators came to appreciate that children construct knowledge much like scientists do, by testing their ideas in action and by modifying their knowledge in response to environmental feedback. In a very real way, children produce their own development.

The roots of Piaget's theorizing can be seen in his autobiographical novel, *Recherche*, published in 1918 when he was just twenty-two years old. In it he describes a new science of organization that could be used to explain how it is that new and more powerful forms of knowledge can arise out of less powerful ones. Throughout his long career Piaget continued to explore this problem both in the thinking of children and in the history of science.

The breadth of Piaget's application of these ideas can be seen in the titles of some of his major works: *Judgement and Reasoning in the Child; The Origin of Intelligence in the Child; Construction of Reality in the Child; The Child's Conception of Number; Play, Dreams and Imitation in Childhood; Intelligence and Affectivity; Biology and Knowledge; Sociological Studies; Psychogenesis and the History of Science;* and *Towards a Logic of Meanings.* Recognition of Piaget's contributions include honorary doctorates from thirty-one universities and appointment to the Executive Council of United Nations Educational Scientific Cultural Organization (UNESCO).

See also: STAGES OF DEVELOPMENT

Bibliography

Bringuier, Jean Claude. *Conversations with Jean Piaget.* Chicago: University of Chicago Press, 1980.

Smith, Les. *Critical Readings on Piaget.* London: Routledge, 1996. In the Jean Piaget Society [web site]. Available from http://www.piaget.org; INTERNET.

Chris Lalonde

Jean Piaget's fascination with children's reasoning began with his work on early Intelligence Quotient (IQ) tests. (AP/Wide World Photos)

PLACENTA

The placenta is a disk-shaped organ that serves as the interface for maternal and fetal exchange of materials. It is formed early in pregnancy when the outer cell layer that envelops the developing embryo, the chorion, fuses with the uterine wall forming fingerlike projections called chorionic villi. Each villus, surrounded by a pool of maternal blood, contains a network of fetal capillaries through which nutrients and waste products are transferred (although there is no actual exchange of blood). Products harmful to fetal development, such as nicotine, cocaine, alcohol, some medications, and environmental pollutants, may also be transferred to the fetus. Upon completion of the pregnancy, the placenta is expelled from the uterus. For the purposes of diagnosis in cases of complications, physicians may examine the placenta. Complications involving the placenta itself include postpartum hemorrhage, placenta previa, preeclampsia, and intrauterine growth restriction.

See also: BIRTH; PREGNANCY; PRENATAL DEVELOPMENT

Bibliography

Begley, David J., Anthony Firth, and Robin Hoult. *Human Reproduction and Developmental Biology.* New York: Macmillan, 1980.

Faber, J. J., and Kent Thornburg. *Placental Physiology: Structure and Function of Fetomaternal Exchange.* New York: Raven Press, 1983.

Jansson, Thomas, and Theresa Powell. "Placental Nutrient Transfer and Fetal Growth." *Nutrition* 16 (7/8):500–502.

Vander, Arthur, Jane Sherman, and Dorothy Luciano. *Human Physiology: The Mechanisms of Body Function,* 5th edition. New York: McGraw-Hill, 1990.

Patricia Crane Ellerson

PLAY

All children play. From the infant squealing in delight during a game of peek-a-boo to the older child playing a game of basketball, children of all ages play and they play in all kinds of ways.

Play is recognized as an important part of a child's development. In fact, it is an important topic of study in many different disciplines. In the field of early childhood special education, play is valuable in assessing a child's level of development and in providing intervention. In psychology, therapists often watch children play to gain an understanding of children's problems and to help them deal with their emotions. The universal nature of play can also provide professionals working with children a basis for comparing typical and atypical development and behavior.

What Is Play?

In a preschool classroom, two four-year-old children pretend to go grocery shopping. One child methodically checks her grocery list and asks her friend what they need to buy. The other child places pretend groceries consisting of empty cans and boxes into his grocery sack. Once his sack is full, he asks his friend if she has any money in her purse to pay for the groceries. As she digs in her purse for the plastic coins and paper money, he approaches another child at the toy cash register to make his purchase.

As typical children grow and learn, they progress through stages of increasingly more complex levels of play. The above example illustrates a sophisticated level of play, where children pretend to be grocery shopping and take on the roles of shoppers, and employee. Jean Piaget, a well-known Swiss psychologist who extensively studied how children think, would have suggested that this example of play is reflective of the children's experiences and interactions with their environment. In his study of children and development, Piaget described play as a "child's work."

Holding views similar to Piaget's is Francis Wardle, an author and instructor at the University of Phoenix (Colorado), who defines play as "child-centered learning." Play then, is a natural, child-directed way for children to learn new concepts and to develop new skills that will provide the basis for success in future settings.

The Importance of Play

Through play, children learn the skills necessary to effectively participate in their world through play. Play provides children with natural opportunities to engage in concrete and meaningful activities that enhance physical, language, social, and cognitive development. During play, children increase their knowledge and understanding of self, others, and the physical world around them.

A child's motor development becomes increasingly more refined through the physical activity that play naturally provides. Through the manipulation of toys and materials, children develop small motor skills. Large motor skills are developed as a child runs, climbs, and throws a ball.

Play is also important for the development of children's language skills. Children experiment with language during play and use words to express their thoughts and ideas. As children become more sophisticated in their play skills, their language development becomes equally sophisticated. Children use language during play to solve problems and to communicate their desires.

During play, children are provided with opportunities for social interaction with peers. Children learn the importance of social rules and how to get along with others through play. It is during this social interaction that children learn to express and control their emotions and to resolve conflicts with others.

As children are encouraged to explore and manipulate objects and materials in their environment, cognitive skills are developed and challenged. Children gain confidence as they experience fun and success in play. This increased confidence encourages children to further explore their world and to seek out even more challenging activities. Ideas and concepts expressed by children during play increase and become more complex as their play skills increase and become more complex.

Elements of Children's Play

Depending upon the materials involved in play and the level of the child's development, individual experiences, and personality, children will demonstrate a variety of play skills. Children's play skills can be described as having social and cognitive elements. The social elements are identified as solitary, parallel, or social play. The cognitive elements of play are described as being sensorimotor, pretend, constructive, mastery, or games with rules. Table 1 provides a summary of the elements of play and the typical age at which they might be noted or observed.

The social elements of play describe the amount of social interaction that the child is engaged in, whereas the cognitive elements describe the complexity of the child's play skills. Social and cognitive play elements are interrelated and will often overlap. Children may demonstrate several social and cognitive elements during one play activity.

Social Elements of Play

Solitary play is simply that—play that a child engages in alone. The child is totally absorbed in the activity and is not reliant upon the actions or words of others. Examples of solitary play include an infant shaking a rattle in her crib and a preschooler quietly looking at a book by herself. Children of all ages engage in solitary play.

Parallel play differs from solitary play in that the child is observant of others. Children are engaged in parallel play when they play side-by-side, using the

TABLE 1

Elements of Play

Social Elements	Key Descriptors	Typical Age
Solitary Play	Child plays by self	All ages
Parallel Play	Child plays side-by-side, observing but not interacting with others	2-3 years
Social or Group Play	Child plays with others and starts to develop friendships	Emerges at 3-5 years

Cognitive Elements	Key Descriptors	Typical Age
Sensorimotor Play	Child engages in motor movements, reflexive and intentional	Birth through 2 years
Pretend Play	Child acts out adult roles, familiar actions and events	Emerges at 18 months, more symbolic at 3-4 years
Constructive Play	Child manipulates materials and objects resulting in an end product	Emerges at 3-4 years
Mastery Play	Child engages in motor play and pretend play simultaneously	Emerges at 4-5 years
Games with Rules Play	Child engages in organized activities such as board games and sports	Emerges at 5 years, pre-dominant in middle childhood

SOURCE: *Janet W. Bates.*

same toys and materials, but do not engage in social interaction. A child may notice what his peers are doing, but he will not directly attempt social contact. Parallel play is a common play pattern with children ages two to three.

Social or group play is commonly first observed during the preschool years or around three to five years of age. Group play experiences provide young children with opportunities to learn social rules such as sharing, taking turns, and cooperation. Most activities provided in a nursery school or preschool setting support social or group play in young children. It is during this stage that children begin to develop friendships.

Cognitive Elements of Play

In sensorimotor play, children engage in motor movements beginning with early reflexes and moving toward more intentional actions. These early actions are initially the result of trial and error; children learn through their actions that their behavior has an effect on the environment. As children develop, their actions become more sophisticated and as a result more deliberate. For example, sensorimotor play includes the reflexive behavior of an infant grasping a rattle placed in her hand, as well as the intentional behavior of an older infant picking up and shaking a rattle to make sound. The sensorimotor stage typically occurs from infancy through age two.

Pretend play usually begins around eighteen months of age. Children at the pretend play level are able to act out adult roles, actions, and events that are familiar to them. At about the age of three or four, pretend play skills become more symbolic. This means that children are able to substitute one object for another. The younger child "feeds" a baby doll with a toy bottle, whereas the older child is able to "feed" the baby with a wooden block, pretending that the block is the baby bottle. It is during this level of play that the child's own experiences directly influence and provide a foundation for their play.

It is at about the age of three to four that children develop an interest in constructive play. Children at the constructive level manipulate objects and materials in their world resulting in an end product, such as a chalk picture, a block tower, or a sand mountain. Here children draw designs on a piece of paper, build with blocks, play and dig in the sand, and so forth. As children become skilled in manipulating objects and materials in their environment, they also become more skilled in expressing thoughts, ideas, and concepts.

The child at the mastery play level is able to demonstrate skilled motor movements and engage in forms of imaginative or pretend play simultaneously. Children at this level move about their environment with ease, confident in their actions. A child at the mastery level would be able to run and jump over obstacles on a playground while pretending to be a cartoon superhero. Mastery play typically emerges around four to five years of age and continues to develop as the child encounters new play experiences and challenges.

By the age of five, children become interested in formal games that have rules and, at times, have two or more sides. Games with rules play is predominant during the middle childhood years, a time during which children's thinking becomes more logical. It is at this level of play that children begin to realize that activities such as Red Rover, Simon Says, and card games will not work unless everyone follows the same set of rules. This level of cognitive play is much more organized than the earlier levels described and may involve competition and defining criteria that establishes a "winner."

Play is important to all aspects of a child's development. Children learn ideas and concepts and enhance language, social, and motor skills through play. As Piaget so simply stated it: Play is a child's work.

See also: FRIENDSHIP; PARALLEL PLAY; SOCIAL DEVELOPMENT

Bibliography

Bredekamp, Sue, and Carol Copple. *Developmentally Appropriate Practice in Early Childhood Programs.* Washington, DC: National Association for the Education of Young Children, 1997.

Bronson, Martha R. *The Right Stuff for Children Birth to Eight: Selecting Play Materials to Support Development.* Washington, DC: National Association for the Education of Young Children, 1995.

Fernie, David. "The Nature of Children's Play." In the ERIC Clearinghouse on Elementary and Early Childhood Education [web site]. Champaign, Illinois, 1988. Available from http://npin.org/library/pre1998/n00373/n00373.html; INTERNET.

The Nemours Foundation. "The Power of Play: How Play Helps Your Child's Development." In the Kids Health for Parents [web site]. 1999. Available from http://www.kidshealth.org/parent/emotions/behavior/power_play.html; INTERNET.

Janet W. Bates

POSTPARTUM DEPRESSION

The postpartum period is a time of unrivaled demands and unique stresses, and is a developmentally challenging time for new parents even in the best of circumstances. During a normal postpartum experience, it is not unusual for new parents to experience heightened family and family-of-origin issues associated with the transition to parenthood. For example, adjustments usually need to be made in areas such as sleep schedules, employment, and role allocation. And, even for seasoned parents, there is the adventure of understanding the particular infant's unique temperament, needs, vulnerabilities, and strengths. The experience of depression in the mother during the postpartum period transforms an already challenging adventure into a potentially overwhelming one.

What Is Postpartum Depression?

There are three forms of postpartum depression, which vary greatly in terms of severity, duration, and impairment. The least severe (and most common) type is known as the "baby blues." This is a mild syndrome occurring in up to 80 percent of new mothers. It usually starts within the first few days following childbirth and may last from a few hours to several days. Although distressing, the symptoms (which generally include episodes of crying, mood swings, and worry) do not cause significant impairment for the mother. On the other hand, "postpartum psychosis" is a rare yet very severe psychiatric illness. In such cases, the symptoms, which include mood disturbances along with hallucinations or delusions, cause major impairment in the new mother's ability to function. This illness usually requires that the mother be hospitalized.

The third type of depression, known as "postpartum depression," occurs in approximately 15 to 20

percent of women following childbirth. It is a psychiatric syndrome, defined by the *Diagnostic and Statistical Manual of Mental Disorders: DSM-IV* as dysphoric mood (or loss of pleasure or interest in usual activities), coupled with symptoms such as sleep and appetite changes, cognitive disturbances, loss of energy, and/or recurrent thoughts of death, which co-occur for at least a two-week period. These symptoms cause significant distress and/or impairment in the new mother's functioning. It is important to note that these are the same symptoms used to diagnose a major depression at anytime during a person's life. The depressive syndrome is labeled a postpartum depression if the symptoms begin within the first three months following childbirth. On average, postpartum depression lasts for about four months, although it can vary considerably in length.

What Causes Postpartum Depression?

Depression during the postpartum period can best be considered an accident of timing; research has suggested that the rates, antecedents, course, and quality of depression during the postpartum period are similar to episodes experienced at other times in a woman's life. Although some research has suggested that negative life events during pregnancy and following delivery (such as financial difficulties, unemployment, and poor marital adjustment) may be associated with the onset of postpartum depression in new mothers, research in the late 1990s identified a previous instance of major depression as the most salient risk factor for postpartum depression.

What Are the Consequences of Postpartum Depression?

There has been an abundance of research on the influence of maternal depression in general on child outcome. This is for good reason—such research generally supports the notion that parental psychological distress (such as depression) is related to the development of negative parent-child interaction and family relationship patterns, which are associated with poor child outcomes. Depressed mothers as a group provide more negative self-reports regarding various aspects of family life, including dissatisfaction in relationships with their spouses and children, as well as stress and uncertainty regarding their own role as parents. Maternal depression has also been associated with disruptions in family unit functioning.

Not only are mothers affected by postpartum depression, the children of depressed mothers also exhibit a variety of impairments in social, psychological, and emotional functioning. More specifically, maternal depression during the postpartum period has

The least severe and most common type of postpartum depression is known as the "baby blues," a mild syndrome occurring in up to 80 percent of new mothers that usually starts within the first few days following childbirth and may last from a few hours to several days. (Karen Huntt Mason/Corbis)

been associated with problems for infants such as increased levels of distress/irritability, protest, withdrawal, and avoidance of social interaction. Maternal postpartum depression has been related to insecure parent-infant attachment in some studies but not others. Researchers need to provide a better understanding of how the timing, chronicity, and intensity of the mother's depression are related to the infant's development. In general, even though maternal depression in the postpartum period has been found to be problematic for mothers and infants, it is important to keep in mind that depressed mothers "don't always look as bad as they feel" (according to researchers Karen Frankel and Robert Harmon) and that they likely have the ability in most cases to provide "good enough" parenting to their young children.

Are Interventions Effective in Treating Postpartum Depression?

There have been two main approaches for treating postpartum depression, neither of which has had much empirical testing. The first strategy is to focus directly on the individual woman, with the main goal of reducing her depressive symptoms. As discussed above, postpartum depression is by definition a major depression that occurs during the postpartum period. There is ample evidence to suggest that major depression can effectively be treated with psychopharmacological intervention (i.e., antidepressant medication). Mothers (and physicians) are generally

reluctant, however, to use medication during the postpartum period given potential complications associated with breast-feeding. Alternatively, individual psychotherapy has been used to help improve the moods of depressed women. For example, Michael O'Hara and his colleagues reported in 2000 that interpersonal psychotherapy (IPT) was an effective treatment for reducing depressive symptoms, and improving social adjustment, in women with postpartum depression. Initially, IPT involves identifying depression as a medical disorder that occurs within an interpersonal context. The next stage of treatment focuses on current interpersonal challenges identified by the patient (i.e., difficulties with a partner or extended family, role transitions, and/or losses related to the birth). The final stage of treatment consists of reinforcing the patient's competence related to symptom reduction, as well as future-oriented problem solving related to the potential recurrence of depressive symptoms.

The second general strategy for treatment is to focus on maladaptive relationship patterns or parenting practices that are often associated with maternal postpartum depression, in order to improve and enhance parent-infant interactions. There are a number of techniques that have been examined, including relationship-based intervention conducted in the family's home, interaction guidance, and touch or massage therapy for infants. Although these approaches vary in technique, all are generally designed to enhance maternal sensitivity, responsivity to infant cues, and positive parent-infant interaction. Primary outcomes are examined in terms of improvement in factors such as infant regulatory capacities, social-emotional development, and parent-infant attachment. In addition, reduction in maternal depressive symptoms is usually reported, although this is not the direct focus of the intervention. Overall, improvements are noted, although minimal information is available to determine the duration or the specific effects.

Summary

There are several important points to consider in regard to postpartum depression. First, postpartum depression has been linked to adverse infant and family outcomes. Postpartum depression has been associated with problematic infant development, poor parent-child interactions, and unhealthy family functioning. Recent research has suggested that it is the quality of family functioning that is the key to promoting positive child outcomes.

Second, the best intervention for postpartum depression is early identification. Women at risk for postpartum depression can be identified early (even during pregnancy) by determining whether the woman has a history of depression. Past history of depression is one of the most consistent findings for the prediction of postpartum depression.

Third, once the risk for maternal depression has been identified, steps can begin immediately to prevent adverse outcomes for mother and child. Early identification of depression is most critical—that is, before the baby is born. Even prior to the onset of full-blown disorder, services can be put in place to facilitate parenting competence, enhance parent-child relationship quality, and/or reduce intensity of depressive symptoms by connecting mothers with appropriate community services.

Finally, interventions are effective in ameliorating symptoms of postpartum depression. Much research has focused on the treatment of mothers' depressive symptoms. Treatment strategies for postpartum depression also need to include family development plans that account for each family's unique strengths and needs, an emphasis on strengthening family relationships by highlighting the role of fathers and other important caregivers, and the promotion of positive parenting and parental competence. Without question, giving support to families who are experiencing significant risks such as maternal depression is ultimately in the best interest of children.

See also: BIRTH; PARENTING; PREGNANCY

Bibliography

American Psychiatric Association. *Diagnostic and Statistical Manual of Mental Disorders: DSM-IV.* Washington, DC: American Psychiatric Association, 1994.

Campbell, Susan B., and Jeffrey F. Cohn. "Prevalence and Correlates of Postpartum Depression in First-Time Mothers." *Journal of Abnormal Psychology* 100 (1991):594–599.

Campbell, Susan B., and Jeffrey F. Cohn. "The Timing and Chronicity of Postpartum Depression: Implications for Infant Development." In Lynne Murray and Peter J. Cooper eds., *Postpartum Depression and Child Development.* New York: Guilford Press, 1997.

Campbell, Susan B., Jeffrey F. Cohn, C. Flanagan, S. Popper, and Meyers. "Course and Correlates of Postpartum Depression during the Transition to Parenthood." *Development and Psychopathology* 4 (1992):29–47.

Cooper, Peter J., and Lynne Murray, eds. "The Impact of Psychological Treatments of Postpartum Depression on Maternal Mood and Infant Development." In *Postpartum Depression and Child Development.* New York: Guilford Press, 1997.

Cowan, Carolyn P., and Phillip A. Cowan. *When Partners Become Parents.* New York: Basic, 1992.

Cummings, E. Mark, and P. T. Davies. "Maternal Depression and Child Development." *Journal of Child Psychology and Psychiatry* 35 (1994):73–112.

DeMulder, Elizabeth K., and Marian Radke-Yarrow. "Attachment with Affectively Ill and Well Mothers: Concurrent Correlates." *Development and Psychopathology* 3 (1991):227–242.

Dickstein, Susan, and Ronald Seifer. "Longitudinal Course of Depression in Women from Pregnancy to Postpartum." Paper presented at the biennial meeting of the Marce Society, Iowa City, IA, 1998.

Dickstein, Susan, Ronald Seifer, Lisa C. Hayden, Masha Schiller, Arnold J. Sameroff, Gabor Keitner, Ivan Miller, Steven Rasmussen, Marilyn Matzko, and Karin Dodge-Magee. "Levels of Family Assessment II: Impact of Maternal Psychopathology on Family Functioning." *Journal of Family Psychology* 12 (1998):23–40.

Downey, Geraldine, and J. C. Coyne. "Children of Depressed Parents: An Integrative Review." *Psychological Bulletin* 108 (1990):50–76.

Field, Tiffany, N. Grizzle, F. Scafidi, and S. Abrams. "Massage Therapy for Infants of Depressed Mothers." *Infant Behavior and Development* 19 (1996):107–112.

Field, Tiffany M., Nathan A. Fox, J. Pickens, and T. Nawrocki. "Relative Right Frontal EEG Activation in Three- to Six-Month-Old Infants of 'Depressed' Mothers." *Developmental Psychology* 31 (1995):358–363.

Frankel, Karen A., and Robert J. Harmon. "Depressed Mothers: They Don't Always Look as Bad as They Feel." *Journal of the American Academy of Child and Adolescent Psychiatry* 35 (1996):289–298.

Heinicke, Christoph M., N. R. Fineman, G. Ruth, S. L. Recchia, D. Guthrie, and C. Rodning. "Relationship-Based Intervention with At-Risk Mothers: Outcome in the First Year of Life." *Infant Mental Health Journal* 20 (1999):349–374.

McDonough, Susan. "Interaction Guidance: Understanding and Treating Early Caregiver-Infant Relationship Disturbances." In Charles Zeanah ed., *Handbook of Infant Mental Health.* New York: Guilford Press, 1993.

McGrath, Ellen, Gwendolyn P. Keita, Bonnie R. Strickland, and Nancy F. Russo. *Women and Depression: Risk Factors and Treatment Issues.* Washington, DC: American Psychological Association, 1990.

Milgrom, J., P. R. Martin, and L. M. Negri. *Treating Postnatal Depression.* Chichester, Eng.: Wiley, 1999.

Murray, Lynne, and Peter J. Cooper, eds. "The Role of Infant and Maternal Factors in Postpartum Depression, Mother-Infant Interactions, and Infant Outcomes." In *Postpartum Depression and Child Development.* New York: Guilford Press, 1997.

O'Hara, Michael W. "Interpersonal Psychotherapy for Postpartum Depression." Paper presented at the biennial meeting of the Marce Society, Iowa City, IA, 1998.

O'Hara, Michael W., J. A. Schlechte, D. A. Lewis, and E. J. Wright. "Prospective Study of Postpartum Blues." *Archives of General Psychiatry* 48 (1991):801–806.

O'Hara, Michael W., S. Stuart, L. L. Gorman, and A. Wenzel. "Efficacy of Interpersonal Psychotherapy for Postpartum Depression." *Archives of General Psychiatry* 57 (2000):1039–1045.

O'Hara, Michael W., Ellen M. Zekoski, Laurie H. Philipps, and Ellen J. Wright. "Controlled Prospective Study of Postpartum Mood Disorders: Comparison of Childbearing and Nonchildbearing Women." *Journal of Abnormal Psychology* 99 (1990):3–15.

Parke, Ross D., and Barbara R. Tinsley. "Family Interaction in Infancy." In Joy D. Osofsky ed., *Handbook of Infant Development,* 2nd edition. New York: Wiley, 1987.

Weissman, Myrna M., G. D. Gammon, K. John, K. R. Merikangas, V. Warner, B. A. Prusoff, and D. Sholomskas. "Children of Depressed Parents." *Archives of General Psychiatry* 44 (1987):847–852.

Weissman, Myrna M., and J. C. Markowitz. "Interpersonal Psychotherapy: Current Status." *Archives of General Psychiatry* 51 (1994):599–606.

Susan Dickstein

POVERTY

One of every five children in the United States lives in a family with income below the official poverty level, despite general agreement that this poverty threshold ($14,630 in 2001 for a family of three) is out of date and too low when considering current housing costs and other family expenditures (e.g., child care, health care). Arloc Sherman of the Children's Defense Fund reports that one in three children in this country will experience at least one year of poverty before they reach age sixteen. Minority children are disproportionately represented, especially among those who experience persistent poverty. As summarized by Suniya Luthar of Columbia University, one in four African-American children experiences ten to fifteen years of poverty; this is a rare phenomenon for Anglo children.

When addressing the incidence of childhood poverty, it is also important to consider what Daniel Hernandez of the National Academy of Sciences and Institute of Medicine defines as relative poverty. This is the minimum income required to purchase those items that society considers essential to decent and respectable living, the minimum level required to avoid the stigma of living in inhumane conditions. Hernandez defined relative poverty as 50 percent of the median income for a given year, adjusted for family size. Given this definition, about one in three children in the United States lives in relative poverty.

Causes of Poverty

What are the causes of childhood poverty or low family income? The most obvious answer is that the parents make low wages for their work. Full-time work at or near the minimum wage is insufficient to move even a small family above the poverty level. What characteristics are associated with low income for families? Parents in poor families tend to be younger and less educated than parents in nonpoor families; they are also more likely to be single or divorced. The rise in childhood poverty since the 1970s is associated with an increase in single-parent families. It would be a mistake, however, to view single parenthood as a major cause of child poverty independent of economic factors. Custodial parents experience significant declines in family income following divorce or separation. Also, single parents often have difficulty balancing the demands of parenting (e.g., picking up a sick child from child care) and the demands of job advancement or promotion. Finally, family stress and conflict caused by poverty can be responsible for divorce or separation; Sherman reports that poor parents separate twice as frequently as do nonpoor parents.

Consequences of Poverty

Children who grow up in families with low incomes are significantly more likely to experience a wide range of problems and poor developmental outcomes than children from wealthier families. Greg Duncan from Northwestern University and Jeanne Brooks-Gunn from Columbia University have summarized extensive research findings that substantiate significant associations between poverty and children's health, cognitive development, behavior problems, emotional well being, and problems with school achievement. For example, children from poor families are 1.7 times more likely to be born with low birthweight, 2 times more likely to repeat a grade in school, 2 times more likely to drop out of school, and 3.1 times more likely to have an out-of-wedlock birth than children from nonpoor families. The specific aspects of poverty that are most destructive, as well as the specific outcomes of poverty, vary across different ages and developmental levels. For example, inadequate nutrition is associated with low birthweight, an important measure of well-being for infants that is predictive of later behavior problems and poor school achievement. As another example, the effects of in-

One of every five children in the United States lives in a family with income below the official poverty level. Children who grow up in families with low incomes are significantly more likely to experience a wide range of problems and poor developmental outcomes. (Library of Congress)

come on children's intelligence are most apparent for children who experience poverty in early childhood (two to five years of age).

When examining the consequences of poverty, it is important to recognize several patterns. First, the effects of poverty are usually nonlinear, meaning that the consequences of income differences below or near poverty levels are substantially greater than comparable differences at higher income levels. Differences in outcomes between children from families living at 50 percent of the poverty level versus 100 percent of the poverty level are large and significant. In contrast, income differences among middle or upper class families make little or no difference for children. Second, persistent poverty can be particularly destructive for children, compared to short-term poverty. For example, Brooks-Gunn and Duncan reported that children who experienced poverty during four to five of their first five years experienced a full nine-point decline in intelligence test scores compared to children who experienced no poverty; fewer years of poverty resulted in a four-point decline in test scores. Third, it is important to recognize that different risk factors (e.g., poverty, father absence, maternal depression, low parental education) are cumulative in their effects. Poor children experience more risks than do nonpoor children. Luthar argued that the effects of poverty are qualitatively different and worse for contemporary

children (compared to earlier generations) because of the accumulation of multiple risks in poor families. Finally, it is important to recognize that the effects of poverty can be interactive as well as cumulative. That is, research indicates that poor children are more vulnerable to further negative influences than are children from families with higher incomes. For example, Pamela Klebanov, of Columbia University, and her colleagues found that family risk factors had greater negative effects on infant intelligence for poor children than for nonpoor children.

Poverty influences aspects of children's lives that child development experts have long recognized as essential to normal development. For example, economic stress interferes with positive, high-quality parent-child interactions. As another example, children living in poor families are often socially isolated and/or painfully aware of the shame and stigma associated with poverty. In a research study, the author found that children who most frequently went hungry were also most likely to report that adults criticized or disapproved of them. Child development experts recognize the importance of positive self-esteem to healthy development. Of course, living in a poor family also increases the chances of living in a poor neighborhood with more exposure to violence and less social support for families than in other neighborhoods. Klebanov and her colleagues found that neighborhood poverty had significant effects on children's developmental test scores as early as age three (beyond the effects of family risks and family income). Stressful parent-child relationships, social isolation and shame, and poor neighborhoods are examples of potential mediators or pathways through which poverty produces negative outcomes for children. Researchers have identified a number of other mediators of the effects of poverty on children, including low-quality child care, inadequate health care, the inability to provide a rich and stimulating learning environment in the home, chronic exposure to violence, and poor parental mental health.

Some of the most impressive research findings on childhood poverty come from statistical analyses of large data sets in which pure effects of family income have been isolated from the effects of other factors often associated with poverty (e.g., single parenthood, low parental education). Duncan and Brooks-Gunn and their colleagues demonstrated that family income significantly predicted children's academic achievement and ability, even after removing any predictive power associated with family risk factors that often go along with poverty. Such findings are particularly important in invalidating arguments that poor outcomes for poor children result from other factors besides income level (e.g., character flaws in families, negative effects of welfare, low education levels, single parenting). On the other hand, such an approach to statistical analyses may also represent an unfair or overly rigorous test of whether poverty matters for children. As also noted by Luthar, one will necessarily underestimate the consequences of poverty if one eliminates or ignores any influences of poverty that are also associated with common causes of that poverty (e.g., low parental education, single parenthood). In the real world, poverty naturally coexists with other important family risk factors.

Programs for Children Living in Poverty

This review suggests a number of policies and programs that should be helpful to children living in poverty. For example, research identifying pathways for the influences of poverty reinforces the need for programs designed to provide stimulating learning environments (e.g., Head Start), to strengthen poor neighborhoods, to improve the quality of child care available to low-income families, and to provide mental health services for parents. Robert St. Pierre and Jean Layzer, researchers with Abt Associates, have summarized the successes and failures of various programs designed to improve the "life chances of children in poverty." They conclude that intensive early childhood programs, with follow-up as children enter school, can have significant positive effects. In con-

trast, research has failed to demonstrate that parenting education yields positive outcomes for children. St. Pierre and Layzer suggested that most comprehensive two-generation programs (focusing on both parents and children) have failed because of their erroneous focus on coordinating existing services instead of adding intensive programs needed by vulnerable children. These researchers concluded that "without the societal will to make direct and dramatic changes in the economic circumstances of low-income families, policymakers will have to continue to rely on programs such as the ones reviewed in this article as a second-best solution to helping low-income families." (St. Pierre and Layzer 1998, p. 19). Overall, the research on children and poverty indicates that the most successful programs for producing positive child outcomes will be those that reduce family poverty.

See also: HEAD START; HEALTH INSURANCE

Bibliography

Brooks-Gunn, Jeanne, Greg Duncan, and Nancy Maritato. "Poor Families, Poor Outcomes: The Well-Being of Children and Youth." In Greg Duncan and Jeanne Brooks-Gunn eds., *Consequences of Growing Up Poor.* New York: Russell Sage Foundation, 1997.

Duncan, Greg, and Jeanne Brooks-Gunn. "Family Poverty, Welfare Reform, and Child Development." *Child Development* 71 (2000):188–196.

Hernandez, Daniel. "Poverty Trends." In Greg Duncan and Jeanne Brooks-Gunn eds., *Consequences of Growing Up Poor.* New York: Russell Sage Foundation, 1997.

Klebanov, Pamela, Jeanne Brooks-Gunn, Cecilia McCarton, and Marie McCormick. "The Contribution of Neighborhood and Family Income to Developmental Test Scores over the First Three Years of Life." *Child Development* 69 (1998):1420–1436.

Luthar, Suniya. *Poverty and Children's Adjustment.* Thousand Oaks, CA: Sage, 1999.

Sherman, Arloc. *Poverty Matters: The Cost of Child Poverty in America.* Washington, DC: Children's Defense Fund, 1997.

St. Pierre, Robert G., and Jean I. Layzer. "Improving the Life Chances of Children in Poverty: Assumptions and What We Have Learned." *Social Policy Report: Society for Research in Child Development* 12, no. 4 (1998):1–27.

Linda J. Anooshian

PREGNANCY

Pregnancy is one of the most important watershed events in a woman's life. Some regard the nine-month gestation as one of the happiest times in their lives, others as the most arduous test of patience that they have ever experienced. It is certain, however, that from both a physical and personal perspective, a woman is undeniably changed by this event. What follows is basic information regarding the developmental changes that the woman and fetus undergo during the course of a gestation.

Maternal Development

A woman's physical state begins to change from as early as the implantation of the fertilized egg and continues to change throughout gestation. The ability of a woman to alter herself to support and nurture the development of another being within her own body is one of nature's most impressive feats. From a physiologic standpoint, the maternal body remodels almost all of its organ systems, from heart to hormones, to prepare for the upcoming nine-month gestation. These changes result in the various signs and symptoms characteristic of pregnancy.

In general, a typical gestation, or pregnancy, lasts nine months or three trimesters of three months. Trimesters are used to mark significant milestones in a pregnancy. For example, most spontaneous miscarriages occur prior to the end of the first trimester. The end of the second trimester usually is a good time to recheck maternal lab values, such as the blood count, and to screen for diabetes in pregnancy. From an obstetrician's standpoint, a gestation is measured in weeks. Because different women have different tendencies toward ovulation (some ovulate earlier in their menstrual cycles, some later), it is difficult to establish a gestational age from the time of fertilization. Instead doctors and midwives calculate the gestational age from a more reliable indicator: the first day of the woman's last normal menstrual period. This starting time is usually about two weeks prior to ovulation. The due date can be quickly calculated using a simple formula: adding seven days to the date of the start of the last normal menstrual period, then subtracting three months. The resulting month and day represent the expected delivery date of a full-term gestation.

One of the most obvious signals of pregnancy is the interruption of a woman's menstrual cycle. This sign is most reliable in women who have regular, consistent menses (menstrual flows). A period that is ten days late or more in a woman with regular menses can be considered a strong indicator of pregnancy. This suspicion is strengthened if a woman goes on to skip her next period altogether. This qualification changes for women who have a history of skipping periods or have erratic cycles that are affected by environmental or physical stressors. For these women, a pregnancy test is the best way to ascertain pregnancy.

What is the most reliable way to determine whether a woman is pregnant? There are dozens of home pregnancy tests available. These are good initial measures to use. Although some companies state that their tests are greater than 97 percent accurate, some individuals fail to use these tests properly, which can result in a lower than expected accuracy rate. Studies done in the early 1980s and 1990s showed that the accuracy rates of home pregnancy tests ranged from 70 percent to 83 percent for women who were actually pregnant. The best way to obtain a diagnosis is to undergo a blood test ordered by a doctor and performed by trained technicians. These tests use chemical analysis to measure the presence of a hormone called human chorionic gonadotropin (HCG). HCG is produced by placental cells and is expressed in maternal blood and urine almost immediately from the day the embryo implants in the uterus. These biochemical tests determine the level of hormone in a woman's blood sample. Increasing levels of HCG, along with the other symptoms and signs of pregnancy, provide the most reliable, consistent, and reproducible results for determining pregnancy.

Other symptoms of pregnancy that are commonly seen include nausea, fatigue, changes in urinary habits, and ultimately the perception of fetal movement. Episodes of nausea and occasional vomiting, also known as "morning sickness," occur around six weeks from the start of a woman's last menstrual period. Typically, the woman experiences a few episodes of nausea and vomiting, most commonly for a few hours during the morning. These episodes usually pass by the end of the first trimester. Occasionally, women will have more serious episodes of vomiting marked by increased frequency and intolerance of any food or liquid intake. This condition, known as hyperemesis gravidarum, can persist throughout pregnancy. Treatment entails the use of antinausea medications, and if cases are severe enough, hospitalization for intravenous rehydration.

Changes in urinary habits are noted during the first trimester. At that time, the growing uterus begins to exert more force on the bladder, producing the sensation of fullness and increasing the number of trips to the bathroom. As pregnancy continues, the uterus expands out of the pelvis, relieving some pressure on the bladder and decreasing urinary frequency. As the time of labor approaches, however, the fetus "drops" into the pelvis and reexerts pressure on the bladder, resulting in a return of frequent urination.

The first sensation of fetal movement, also known as the "quickening," is reported by most women to occur between sixteen and twenty weeks. These movements are described as "fluttering" or "tickles" in the abdomen. First-time mothers usually report that the quickening occurs later than women who have previously gone through pregnancy. Although this event is not fully diagnostic of pregnancy by itself, it is a milestone that is noted by many obstetricians and is a good way to roughly judge the gestational age of the pregnancy.

In addition to these self-reported symptoms of pregnancy, an obstetrician can use ultrasonography to definitively identify an early gestation. Using transvaginal ultrasound techniques, an obstetrician can identify a gestational sac as early as two weeks, although four to five weeks is the norm. A yolk sac can be seen as early as three weeks but should be clearly seen by six weeks. At seven weeks, the earliest picture of the developing fetus, known as the fetal pole, can be detected. By eight weeks, the fetal heart can be seen contracting. From this gestational age to about twelve weeks, the size of the fetus, measured from the top of the head to the hips (the crown-rump length), can be compared with the gestational age based on a woman's last menstrual period. These two measures are used to determine the gestational age of the pregnancy and to predict the pregnancy's due date.

As the pregnancy progresses, the uterus continues to enlarge. By twelve weeks of gestation, the uterus becomes perceptible through the abdominal wall. This is usually noticed as a small lump that protrudes from the lower abdomen, slightly above the pelvic bone (pubic symphysis) at the level of the start of pubic hair growth. Starting at twenty weeks, a measurement is regularly taken from the pubis to the top, or fundus, of the uterus during an obstetrical visit. The bladder must be empty to produce an accurate measurement. The resulting measurement in centimeters should roughly equal the number of weeks of pregnancy, with an error of plus or minus two centimeters. This measurement, called the fundal height, may indicate that the fetus is not growing properly (i.e., is too small or too big). If an abnormal result is obtained, an ultrasound can usually be done to check fetal growth and the level of amniotic fluid in the womb. This general principle is applicable to single fetal gestations only, because twins and other multiple pregnancies necessarily produce a larger fundal height.

In addition to these changes in physical stature, the pregnant woman goes through a series of amazing physiologic changes that affect all aspects of the maternal body. From a metabolic perspective, pregnancy necessitates an increased maternal need for nutrients, water, and energy (calories). The fetus is dependent on the expectant mother for all nutritional needs and oxygenation, and it extracts what it needs at the woman's expense. Thus, the woman herself needs to gain weight and increase her caloric consumption to meet her own needs and those of the fetus. The National Research Council's dietary guidelines recommend that pregnant women increase their caloric intake by approximately 300 kilocalories per day. Specifically, a nonpregnant woman requires approximately 2,200 kilocalories per day. A pregnant woman should thus consume 2,500 kilocalories per day.

The demand for iron also increases during pregnancy. The body uses iron to carry oxygen in the blood, which is ultimately transported to the fetus. Thus, it is recommended that women increase their iron intake, especially during the second and third trimesters, when the fetus does the bulk of its growing to reach its physical size. Usually, adequate amounts of iron can be obtained through ingestion of iron rich foods, such as liver, and dark leafy vegetables, such as spinach. Some sources have found, however, that the amount of iron provided by both normal dietary intake and maternal storage is insufficient to meet pregnancy demands. In fact, the National Academy of Sciences and the American College of Obstetrics and Gynecology recommend that pregnant women receive a supplement of 30 milligrams of iron per day. Most obstetricians recommend that a woman stay on her prenatal vitamin, which should supply enough iron to cover the recommended amount. It is also common practice to check the level of blood (via the hematocrit and hemoglobin tests) both at the start and in the third trimester of pregnancy. If the expectant mother is found to be anemic, she is started on additional iron supplements (ferrous sulfate tablets).

In addition to the increased demand for nutrients, increasing the intake of water is vital to the maintenance of pregnancy. Higher levels of total body water are required to provide the increased fluid volume needed to meet the demands of increased blood flow and circulation to the developing baby. Thus, the pregnant woman's kidney system begins to retain water. Maintaining adequate amounts of fluid intake is also important, as it is easier for pregnant women to become dehydrated, which can lead to preterm contractions.

The summation of all these dietary and metabolic changes can be seen in the recommendations for weight gain in pregnancy. In a normal nonobese woman, a twenty-five to thirty-five pound weight gain is recommended. This value fluctuates depending on the prepregnancy weight of a woman; specifically, an underweight woman may gain up to forty pounds, while it is recommended that overweight women limit their weight gain to fifteen to twenty pounds. Usually, three to six pounds are gained in the first trimester, with a subsequent gain of one-half to one pound per week thereafter until term. Weight should be measured at every obstetrical visit. If a woman does not show a ten-pound weight gain by the mid-second trimester, her nutritional status should be reviewed. A woman with below average weight gain is at higher risk of producing a low-birthweight and intrauterine growth-restricted infant. Likewise, obese women

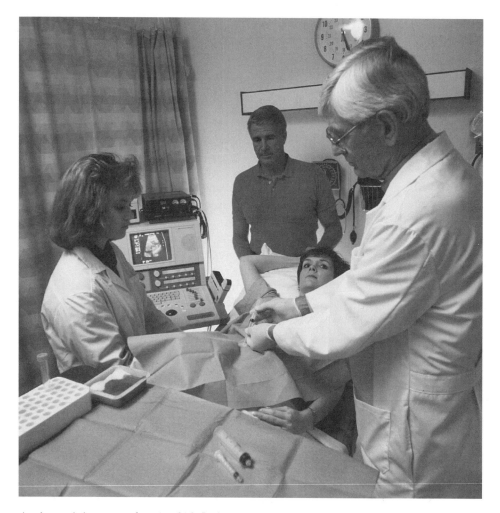

Amniocentesis is a prenatal test in which fluid is extracted from the amniotic sac via the uterus of a pregnant woman. The results of the test can indicate whether or not the infant will have a chromosomal problem, such as a genetic disease. (Pete Saloutos/The Stock Market)

should be careful about their weight gain as they have an increased risk of producing a large for age (macrosomic) baby, with its associated higher risk of difficult delivery and cesarean delivery.

As each week of the pregnancy passes, the woman will be able to gauge the progression of her pregnancy only through the increasing size of her belly and the amount of activity felt in her uterus. She may not be fully aware of the extent of change occurring with the fetus. Hidden within the woman is a process that is no less fascinating than the changes the woman is undergoing.

Fetal Development

The first trimester is the most critical period for fetal development. It is at this point that the fertilized egg begins to develop from a mass of disparate cells into an organized whole that is truly the sum of its individual specialized parts. The start of the third week

after fertilization marks the beginning of the embryonic period. At this point, the fertilized egg begins to differentiate its cells into the beginnings of the placenta and the body of the future fetus. By the end of the fourth week after ovulation, the embryo is roughly four to five millimeters (0.16 to 0.2 inches) long, and heart activity can be seen on ultrasound. By the end of the sixth week, the embryo is roughly two centimeters (three-quarters of an inch) long and has a definitive head separate from the body. A vast amount of organ development occurs before many women realize that they are indeed pregnant, highlighting the importance of attention to the health of women as they anticipate pregnancy.

The fetal period is usually considered to start by the eighth week after fertilization. By this time, the period most crucial to organ and structural development has passed. Development from this period consists of the growth and maturation of structures that were formed during the embryonic period. According to *Williams Obstetrics,* a primary textbook in the obstetrical field, the milestones in fetal development can be marked every four weeks of the fetus's menstrual/gestational age.

At twelve weeks from the last menstrual period, the fetus is clearly visible by transvaginal ultrasound and may be visualized by abdominal technique depending on the quality of the equipment and the size of the expectant mother. Fingers and toes are differentiated from each other, and fingernails are present. The external genitalia are starting to develop, but it is difficult to determine gender at this point.

By sixteen weeks, the fetus can be seen by abdominal ultrasound. The fetus now weighs approximately 110 grams (four ounces) and has well-developed lower limbs. Intestines, stomach, and bladder should be visible. The sex of the baby can be reliably determined at this point, with fetal cooperation, of course. At this time, most pregnant women undergo screening tests of their blood to check for possible problems with Down syndrome or spina bifida. An ultrasound to assess anatomy and to look for any signs of structural defects is usually done at this age.

The end of the twentieth week represents the midpoint of pregnancy. The average fetus weighs approximately 320 grams (eleven ounces) and is approximately sixteen centimeters (six and one-quarter inches) long. At this point, some scalp hair may be seen in ultrasound images, and the body is covered with a fine, downy hair called lanugo.

The twenty-fourth week represents a major milestone as hospitals with high-tech (level 3) neonatal intensive care nurseries and neonatal specialists consider fetuses at this age to be viable. Unfortunately, fetuses born at this age are extremely premature. The skin is wrinkled, with small amounts of subcutaneous (below the skin) fat present; thus, they have tremendous problems maintaining body temperature. They weigh only 630 grams (twenty-two ounces) and have poorly developed lungs, which necessitates the use of ventilators to assist breathing.

At twenty-eight weeks, the fetus is now roughly twenty-five centimeters (nine and three-quarter inches) long and can weigh approximately 1,100 grams (two pounds, six ounces). By this point, the fetus that is delivered will have eyes partially open, limbs that can move energetically, and may be able to cry. Most fetuses born at this point will survive under the care of a high-tech, level 3 neonatal intensive care unit.

By thirty-two weeks, the average fetus weighs roughly 1,800 grams (three pounds, fifteen ounces), and measures approximately 28 centimeters. The skin is wrinkled and red, but the body begins to fill out with more deposition of subcutaneous fat. This represents another major milestone as the chances of the other problems of prematurity, such as hemorrhages in the brain or the eye and problems with the intestines, drop considerably. The biggest problems facing babies born at this age involve lung development and function.

The thirty-sixth week represents another important milestone. At this point, the baby measures approximately thirty-two centimeters (twelve and one-half inches) and weighs approximately 2,500 grams (five pounds, eight ounces). The body is filled out with subcutaneous fat. Although babies born at this age are still technically "preterm" (infants are considered term at thirty-seven to forty weeks), most women who go into labor at this age would not be stopped with medications. Babies born at this age have an excellent chance of survival.

Finally, at forty weeks, the goal of gestation is reached. At this age, the average baby measures thirty-six centimeters (fourteen inches) and weighs approximately 3,400 grams (seven pounds, seven ounces). The skin is smooth and pink, the body is plump, and the lungs generally function well. It should be noted that these stages of development represent general characteristics only. There is always a large degree of variability in fetal development, much of which is influenced by variable factors such as genetic makeup (e.g., chromosomal defects), characteristics of the parents (e.g., size, weight, race) and characteristics of the pregnancy (e.g., toxemia, maternal smoking, bleeding during the pregnancy). At times, the gestation may go past forty weeks. This occurrence is not uncommon. In fact, very few deliveries occur at exactly forty weeks. In cases where pregnancies go "post-term," the women should be followed normally. Most obstetricians will institute measures to induce delivery if the woman does not go into labor on her own past forty-two weeks. At this point, there is concern that the fetus will grow too big and an increased chance of cesarean delivery. Furthermore, the placenta has a finite "lifespan," and gestations that continue too long past the due date have a higher risk for placental failure, which could harm the safety of the fetus.

Although the gestation itself represents a relatively short period in a woman's life, the physical and personal changes that pregnancy brings about in a woman last throughout her lifetime. Clearly, pregnancy is a task that should not be met without preparation and assistance.

See also: BIRTH; CONTRACEPTION; PRENATAL CARE; PRENATAL DEVELOPMENT; REPRODUCTIVE TECHNOLOGIES

Bibliography

Cunningham, F. Gary, Paul C. MacDonald, Norman F. Gant, Kenneth J. Leveno, Larry C. Gilstrap, Gary D. Hankins, and Steven L. Clark, eds. *Williams Obstetrics.* Stamford, CT: Simon and Schuster, 1997.

Doshi, M. L. "Accuracy of Consumer Performed In-Home Tests for Early Pregnancy Detection." *American Journal of Public Health* 76 (1986):512–514.

Gabbe, Steven G., Jennifer R. Niebyl, and Joseph L. Simpson, eds. *Obstetrics: Normal and Problem Pregnancies.* New York: Churchill and Livingstone, 1997.

Jeng, L. L., R. M. Moore, R. G. Kaczmarek, P. J. Placek, and R. A. Bright. "How Frequently Are Home Pregnancy Tests Used? Results from the 1988 National Maternal and Infant Health Survey." *Birth* 18 (1991):11–13.

National Research Council. *Recommended Dietary Allowances,* 10th edition. Washington, DC: National Academy Press, 1989.

Valanis, B. G., and C. S. Perlman. "Home Pregnancy Testing Kits: Prevalence of Use, False-Negative Rates, and Compliance with Instructions." *American Journal of Public Health* 72 (1982):1034–1036.

Garrett Lam

PREMATURE INFANTS

Premature infants are those who are born too soon, that is, born before the normal length of time in pregnancy that is typically needed for a fetus to develop, mature, and thrive postnatally. The average length of pregnancy is thirty-nine to forty weeks, which is the approximate duration of pregnancy needed for the fetus to reach full development and maturity. Infants delivered between the thirty-seventh and forty-first week of pregnancy are typically referred to as "term" or "mature" births. "Preterm" or "premature" birth is defined as delivery before the thirty-seventh week of pregnancy and "postterm" or "postmature" births are those occurring at forty-two weeks and beyond. Preterm deliveries are further delineated as either "very preterm" (before the thirty-third week) or "moderately preterm" (between the thirty-third and thirty-sixth weeks).

The use of the expression "prematurity" has changed over time. It once was used to refer to any early or small birth, thereby encompassing births that occurred before term and births of infants of low birthweight (less than 2,500 grams [5 pounds, 8 ounces]). It became apparent, however, that not all low birthweight infants were born preterm and that not all preterm births were low birthweight. Many low birthweight infants are term births that are small in size due to growth-related complications. These two different types of low birthweight infants—those preterm and those small for their duration of gestation—were recognized to reflect distinct medical problems, and as a result, more specific labels were needed to refer to each type of birth according to its birth-weight, duration of gestation, and birthweight for gestation. It is now the convention to clearly distinguish between births that are preterm, low birthweight, and/or "small for gestational age." For single live births born to U.S. resident mothers between 1995 and 1997, 9.6 percent were preterm and 6.1 percent were low birthweight. Of these low birthweight deliveries, 61.9 percent were preterm. Simultaneously, only 39 percent of preterm births were low birthweight.

The duration of the pregnancy prior to delivery in completed weeks is referred to as the gestational age of the newborn and thereby establishes if the delivery is preterm. The duration of pregnancy is traditionally measured as the interval from the date of the mother's last menstrual period to the date of birth. This approach for defining gestational age at delivery is derived from obstetrical practice and overestimates by approximately two weeks the interval from conception to birth. Alternate approaches to estimating the gestational age have been developed and include physical and neurological assessments of the newborn and prenatal ultrasound measures of fetal size (body length, femur length, and skull diameter and circumference).

Knowledge of gestational age is essential for the appropriate medical management of both the pregnancy and the newborn infant as gestational age serves as a proxy measure for the extent of fetal development and the fetus's readiness for birth. As an indicator of newborn maturity, gestational age is closely associated with the newborn's chances for survival during the first year and the likelihood of developing neonatal complications. Moreover, knowledge of a preterm infant's gestational age is necessary for assessing developmental progress in infancy.

Gestational age is also used by public health professionals to calculate a variety of statistical indicators that are useful for monitoring the health status of populations and assessing the need for and impact of targeted public health interventions. Preterm and very preterm percentages in populations may reflect the prevalence of a variety of health-related concerns, including infections, psychosocial and physical stresses, poor nutrition, and substance abuse.

Between 1981 and 1996 in the United States, annual preterm rates rose from 9.4 percent to 11 percent of live births, a 17 percent increase (see Figure 1). Although infant mortality rates declined during the same period, the ongoing increase in preterm rates is a matter of considerable concern. Indeed, increasing rates of preterm birth are recognized as a pregnancy related crisis in the United States. Approximately three-quarters of neonatal deaths and nearly one-half of the long-term neurological damage seen

FIGURE 1

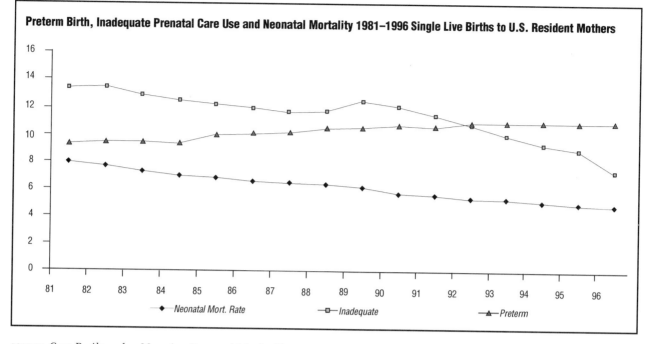

Preterm Birth, Inadequate Prenatal Care Use and Neonatal Mortality 1981–1996 Single Live Births to U.S. Resident Mothers

SOURCE: *Greg R. Alexander, Mary Ann Pass, and Martha Slay.*

in children have been attributed to preterm birth. Preterm infants have an increased risk of developmental delay, cerebral palsy, mental retardation, sensory impairment, learning and school-related problems, and other disabilities. Moreover, the health-care costs associated with an extremely small baby or early birth are more than ten times greater than those of normal weight infants. The persistent disparity in infant mortality rates among ethnic groups in the United States has also been related to ethnic differences in preterm birthrates. Further, high preterm birthrates in the United States have been identified as a major contributor to this nation's relatively poor ranking for infant mortality among developed countries.

Considerable effort was expended in the United States during the last few decades of the twentieth century to reduce the rates of preterm delivery and low birthweight. In 1985 the Institute of Medicine promoted increasing access to prenatal care and improving the content of care as a means to improve the rates of these adverse perinatal outcomes. Since then, considerable effort has been expended to improve prenatal care and reduce preterm births. Between 1981 and 1995, the percent of women starting prenatal care in the first trimester increased 6.1 percent, from 76.9 percent to 81.6 percent. Over the same period, the percent of women with adequate utilization of prenatal care increased 37.9 percent, from 29.3 percent to 40.4 percent, while the percent of women who inadequately used prenatal care decreased 33.3

percent, from 13.5 percent to 9 percent. Notwithstanding improvements in access to and use of prenatal care, preterm and low birthweight rates in the United States continued to increase (see Figure 1). By 1995, a *Future of Children* report on low birthweight concluded that prenatal care in its present form "does little to prevent low birth weight or preterm birth" (Shiono and Behrman 1995). Other reviews in the late 1990s also concluded that there is little done during the standard prenatal care visit to reduce the risk of very low birthweight or to prevent preterm delivery.

Several explanations can be proposed for the ongoing increase in preterm birthrates in the United States. The possible factors driving these trends include:

• changes in vital record reporting (i.e., very preterm infants once reported as fetal deaths are now being registered as live births);

• a rising incidence of multiple births, the infants from which are more likely to be preterm;

• an increase in the percentages of unmarried and older aged mothers, who are at greater risk of having a preterm delivery; and

• changes in obstetric practice that have lead to earlier delivery of pregnancies deemed at risk of a poor outcome.

Improvements in the early and adequate use of prenatal care services, coupled with developments in obstetric and neonatal practice and technology (e.g., surfactant, steroids, ultrasound), may lead to earlier diagnosis of problems and resultantly to an earlier cesarean delivery, which, while further decreasing the risk of maternal, fetal, and even infant mortality, may potentially increase the rate of moderate preterm delivery. In all, the rise in preterm birthrates in the United States during the 1990s may stem largely from attempts to improve reporting, fertility, and survival rather than from a major rise in high-risk behavioral and medical factors.

The limited success of the efforts to reduce rates of preterm birth in part stems from preterm birth being a single outcome (i.e., being born too early) that results from multiple causes, most of which are still poorly understood. Only between 25 and 40 percent of preterm births can be explained with currently known risk factors, including single marital status; low socioeconomic status; previous preterm birth; maternal illness (e.g., hypertension); cocaine and tobacco use; multiple second trimester spontaneous abortions; gestational bleeding; urogenital infections; multiple gestations; placental, cervical, and uterine abnormalities; and black race of mother (which may reflect a complex array of socioeconomic, cultural, biological, and behavioral risk characteristics). The major clinical classifications of preterm birth are spontaneous preterm labor, preterm rupture of membranes before the onset of labor, and indicated preterm delivery for pregnancy complications. Nevertheless, as each of these clinical presentations have multiple causes, more recent efforts have focused on establishing the many unique antecedents and biological causes for preterm birth. Accordingly, the discovery and development of a single prevention or intervention strategy to markedly reduce the present level of preterm births is highly unlikely and probably unrealistic. In spite of the many risk factors for preterm birth that have been identified, only a few of these risk factors, such as cigarette smoking, can be considered modifiable during the current pregnancy. In the early twenty-first century, research efforts to further understand the determinants of preterm birth are focusing on the role of infections, stress, socioeconomic deprivation, pregnancy anxiety, hormones, nutrition, and fetal growth restriction.

See also: BIRTHWEIGHT; HIGH RISK INFANTS; INFANT MORTALITY; PREGNANCY

Bibliography

Alexander, Greg. "Preterm Birth: Etiologies, Mechanisms, and Prevention." *Prenatal and Neonatal Medicine* 3, no. 1 (1998):3–9.

Alexander, Greg, and Marilee Allen. "Conceptualization, Measurement, and Use of Gestational Age: I. Clinical and Public Health Practice." *Journal of Perinatology* 16, no. 2 (1996):53–59.

Allen, Marilee, Greg Alexander, Mark Tompkins, and Thomas Hulsey. "Racial Differences in Temporal Changes in Newborn Viability and Survival by Gestational Age." *Pediatric and Perinatal Epidemiology* 14, no. 2 (2000):152–158.

American Academy of Pediatrics and the American College of Obstetricians and Gynecologists. *Guidelines for Perinatal Care*, 3rd edition. Washington, DC: American Academy of Pediatrics and the American College of Obstetricians and Gynecologists, 1992.

Berkowitz, Gertrud, and Emile Papiernik. "Epidemiology of Preterm Birth." *Epidemiological Review* 15 (1993):414–443.

Goldenberg, Robert, and Dwight Rouse. "Prevention of Premature Birth." *New England Journal of Medicine* 339 (1998):313–320.

Guyer Bernard, Marian MacDorman, Joyce Martin, Donna Hoyert, Stephanie Ventura, and Donna Strobino. "Annual Summary of Vital Statistics, 1998." *Pediatrics* 104 (1999):1229–1247.

Institute of Medicine Committee to Study the Prevention of Low Birth Weight. *Preventing Low Birth Weight.* Washington, DC: National Academy Press, 1985.

Klebanoff, Mark. "Conceptualizing Categories of Preterm Birth." *Prenatal and Neonatal Medicine* 3, no. 1 (1998):13–15.

Kogan, Michael, Joyce Martin, Greg Alexander, Milton Kotelchuck, Stephanie Ventura, and Fredric Frigoletto. "The Changing Pattern of Prenatal Care Utilization in the United States, 1981–1995: Using Different Prenatal Care Indices." *Journal of the American Medical Association* 279 (1998):1623–1628.

Kramer, Michael. "Determinants of Low Birth Weight: Methodological Assessment and Meta-Analysis." *Bulletin of the World Health Organization* 65 (1987):663–737.

Lewit, Eugene, Linda Schurrmann Baker, Hope Corman, and Patricia Shiono. "The Direct Cost of Low Birth Weight." *Future of Children* 5, no. 1 (1995):35–56.

McCormick, Marie. "The Contribution of Low Birth Weight to Infant Mortality and Childhood Morbidity." *New England Journal of Medicine* 312 (1985):82–89.

Paneth, Nigel. "The Problem of Low Birth Weight." *Future of Children* 5, no. 1 (1995):19–34.

Shiono, Patricia, and Richard Behrman. "Low Birth Weight: Analysis and Recommendations." *Future of Children* 5, no. 1 (1995):4–18.

Greg R. Alexander
Mary Ann Pass
Martha Slay

PRENATAL CARE

Prenatal care refers to medical care and other health-related services offered during pregnancy to ensure the well-being of the mother and her future offspring. Medical visits for prenatal care follow the pattern recommended by the American College of Obstetricians and Gynecologists (ACOG): an initial visit in the first trimester, one visit every four weeks through twenty-eight weeks of gestational age, then a visit every two weeks until thirty-six weeks, and then a visit every week through forty weeks (or until delivery). This pattern results in thirteen prenatal care visits for a normal length pregnancy. The emphasis on more visits at the end of pregnancy reflects the historical roots of prenatal care in the detection of preeclampsia/eclampsia, a systemic hypertensive-related disorder that traditionally was the leading cause of maternal mortality.

The initial prenatal care visit involves taking a thorough obstetric history; establishing the gestational age of the fetus and the expected due date; assessing the initial level of risk to ensure appropriate level of treatment; initiating serial surveillance of fetal and maternal biologic markers to ensure that the pregnancy is following a normal developmental trajectory (e.g., physical exams, laboratory tests); and providing general prenatal education and psychosocial support. Subsequent visits involve continued serial surveillance, psychosocial support, and childbirth and postpartum education. Women with high-risk conditions, such as diabetes, elevated blood pressure, sexually transmitted diseases, and twins, may be followed more closely or referred to high-risk prenatal care specialists.

While the timing of prenatal care visits is well established, the content of the visits continues to evolve. New tests and procedures—such as alpha-fetoprotein, amniocentesis, genetic testing, sexually transmitted disease detection, and ultrasound—have emerged and have increased the physician's capacity to monitor the health of the mother and the growing fetus.

Although prenatal care as a formal medical service began in the early 1900s as part of the newly emerging obstetric profession's efforts to reduce maternal mortality, more recently the primary focus of prenatal care has increasingly shifted toward improving the health of the newborn. This shift has been accompanied by an expansion of prenatal health care to address a broader, more comprehensive range of health and social services that affect infant health. In 1965, as part of the War on Poverty, the federal Maternal and Infant Care project provided funds, for the first time, for social workers, health educators, and nutritionists to augment traditional medical services at the then newly inaugurated community health centers. This broadening of prenatal care reflected recognition of the larger social health context of a pregnancy, the limits of medical care alone to improve birth outcomes, and the increased focus on infant outcome.

Increasing Access to Prenatal Care

The 1980s saw a proliferation of public and private efforts to increase access to comprehensive prenatal care, as health experts concluded that such care was the public health solution for reducing the high infant mortality rates in the United States and for decreasing racial disparities in poor birth outcomes. The seminal 1985 Institute of Medicine report on Preventing Low Birthweight (LBW), in particular, strongly encouraged public efforts to increase the availability and comprehensiveness of prenatal care to reduce LBW. The report noted that prenatal care was widely perceived to be effective at reducing LBW and was cost effective ($3.38 saved for every dollar spent); it envisioned a more comprehensive version of prenatal care with strong psychosocial content.

Numerous federal, state, and philanthropic efforts were undertaken in this period. The U.S. National Commission to Prevent Infant Mortality was established; the Healthy Mothers, Healthy Babies Coalition was formed; the March of Dimes initiated the program Toward Improving the Outcome of Pregnancy; numerous state infant mortality commissions were started; and several new federal infant mortality reduction programs were undertaken (e.g., Healthy Futures/Healthy Generations, Healthy Start Initiative). A major federal report on the Content of Prenatal Care, published in 1989, also increased the focus on psychosocial and comprehensive prenatal care.

The most significant achievement of this period was the expansion of Medicaid in the late 1980s, which increased eligibility for prenatal care services by delinking Medicaid eligibility from welfare eligibility (specifically, the Aid to Families with Dependent Children program), and fostered more comprehensive prenatal care by allowing Medicaid to pay for numerous nonmedical prenatal services. Medicaid now could enroll and pay for the costs of prenatal care and delivery of all poorer women (those with an income of less than 185 percent of the poverty level), regardless of their marital status. Medicaid could also pay for any case-management, home visitation, nutrition, social work, and health education services that are needed. By the early twenty-first century, Medicaid was covering the costs of more than 40 percent of births in the United States.

In 1980, the U.S. government set as one of its 1990 National Health objectives that 90 percent of all pregnancies begin prenatal care in the first trimester. By the end of the twentieth century, the United States had still not reached this goal, and it therefore became a Healthy People 2010 objective. According to federal statistics from 1998, 82.8 percent of all mothers began prenatal care in the first trimester. This figure rose steadily in 1990s from 75.8 percent, after a decade-long period of no change. The increase in early usage was most likely due to the numerous federal efforts initiated in the late 1980s. The figures also revealed substantial disparities by race: 87.9 percent of white mothers started prenatal care in the first tri-

There has been a recent refocusing of prenatal care to address issues of maternal health, such as diabetes, obesity, and hypertension. For many women, regular exercise and careful dietary controls throughout pregnancy have led to better overall maternal health. (Owen Franken/Corbis)

mester, compared to 73.3 percent of black, 74.3 percent of Hispanic, and 83.1 percent of Asian mothers.

More comprehensive utilization measures, such as the Kotelchuck Adequacy of Prenatal Care Utilization (APNCU) Index, also use number of visits and length of gestation, in addition to the timing of initial care, to assess the ACOG prenatal care standards. These indexes suggest an even more somber picture of prenatal care usage in the United States. For example, the APNCU Index reveals that only 74.3 percent of pregnant women have adequate prenatal care, 13.8 percent intermediate care, and 16.9 percent inadequate care, with correspondingly worse figures for African Americans, Hispanic Americans, and Asian Americans. Interestingly, more than 31 percent of U.S. women have more than the ACOG recommended number of visits, a percentage that increased substantially from the 24 percent level of 1990.

Barriers to the Use of Prenatal Care

A variety of barriers to the use of prenatal care have been identified. In 1988 the Institute of Medicine cited four groups of barriers: financial; inadequate systems capacity; organization, practices, and atmosphere of prenatal services; and cultural/personal. Financial barriers have largely, but not completely, been addressed by the recent expansions of Medicaid eligibility and by reforms in health insurance, which have mandated pregnancy coverage. Immigration status and enrollment barriers, however,

still influence access to Medicaid coverage. Transportation remains a major structural barrier to care in both urban and rural areas. Teens generally start prenatal care late. Organizational and personal factors, such as disrespect by providers, lack of planned pregnancy, not valuing prenatal care, and fear of detection of drug usage, remain substantial barriers to early and continuous prenatal care.

The content of care should be equal for all women, regardless of the source of their care, but this may not be the case. In general, prenatal care is more comprehensive in public clinics (including that among equally low-income women, public clinics make more referrals to the federal Women, Infants, and Children (WIC) nutrition program than private doctor's offices do). There is some evidence that providers offer different prenatal care content depending on the race and social class of their clients. And white women participate in childbirth education classes much more often than do African-American women.

The Relation between Prenatal Care and Birth Outcomes

Although it is widely believed that prenatal care is associated with better birth outcomes, the actual association is more complex. Early case-control/correlational research in the 1960s and 1970s generally showed a small positive association between increased medical prenatal care and decreased low birthweight and infant mortality. More recent, rigorous studies, however, have not generally demonstrated significant associations with improved birth outcomes.

Several factors complicate this widely assumed positive association. First, the association between prenatal care visits and birth outcomes is not linear but U-shaped. Both less (inadequate) care and more (possibly medically needy) care are associated with increased poor birth outcomes. Second, women who participate in prenatal care enhancement programs may be a more self-selected group of health-conscious women, a factor that may be more important to improving birth outcomes than their use of more enhanced prenatal care. Third, research has not consistently demonstrated a strong impact of psychosocial factors on LBW, prematurity, and infant mortality. Much attention has shifted to the role of infectious diseases, such as bacterial vaginosis, in occurrences of prematurity, an example of a biologic factor in contrast to social factors. Fourth, almost all the late twentieth century improvements in infant mortality rates resulted from improvements in keeping LBW babies alive through improved neonatal care, not the prevention of low birthweight infants (the presumed pathway of prenatal care). And finally, there has been an increase in LBW and prematurity rates in the United States, despite simultaneous broad improvements in prenatal care overall. The policy and programmatic enthusiasm of the 1980s and 1990s for access to comprehensive prenatal care to address poor birth outcomes and racial disparities had greatly diminished by the early twenty-first century.

Trends in Prenatal Care

Several new trends in prenatal care efforts have emerged. First, reflecting the popular aphorism that "you can't solve a lifetime of ills in nine months of a pregnancy," there has been an increasing focus on pre-conceptual care. Pre-conceptual care tries to detect and treat key maternal health issues prior to the beginning of the pregnancy. Examples include reduction of smoking, initiation of diabetes treatment, dietary improvement, and family planning. Pre-conceptual care links prenatal/reproductive care to the broader women's health movement. Second, there has been an increasing focus on providing specific "proven" prenatal care content rather than simply increasing the number of generic prenatal care visits. In this way, prenatal care has increasingly focused on such areas as smoking reduction, substance use reduction, diabetes treatment, WIC/nutrition supplementation, folic acid consumption, genetic testing, and HIV treatment. Third, there has been a further expansion of prenatal care psychosocial content to address newer and possibly more potent health risk factors, such as spousal violence and environmental risks. Finally, there has been a refocusing of prenatal care to once again address issues of maternal health and to not simply focus on birth outcomes (i.e., examining the impact of pregnancy on women's health, not simply the impact of women's health on pregnancy outcomes). Such an orientation focuses on prenatal to postnatal continuities in maternal depression, obesity, hypertension, and diabetes, as well as postpartum linkage to health services and satisfaction with care.

Beyond attempting to reduce the number of infants born small and premature, U.S. public health and clinical efforts to improve prenatal care usage and content have not generally been directly linked to child development programs. The federal funding sources that address these two developmental periods have been generally quite distinct. The temporal focus of some of the relevant professions has not generally overlapped, which further adds to their discontinuity. For example, obstetricians and public health maternity workers may have little interaction with pediatricians.

There are, however, increasing areas of overlap between prenatal care and child development efforts. There is increased recognition that many of the same high-risk families are being seen in both public prenatal care and child development programs. Maternal well-being (both physical and psychosocial) is critical in both the prenatal and postnatal periods. Comprehensive prenatal care now includes many of the same interventions as child development: home visitation, parent education, etc. In turn, the child development community is increasingly recognizing the importance of prenatal factors (including prenatal care) on subsequent infant and child functioning. There is a growing number of federal programs that try to improve both the reproductive and child developmental domains, including Medicaid, WIC, Early Intervention, and Title V. The newly revised Healthy Start program (the largest federal initiative dedicated to reproductive health) also has a focus on maternal and infant health from pregnancy through the first two years of an infant's life.

Prenatal care remains primary care for women in pregnancy. Its impact on both maternal health and newborn health reflects the evolving knowledge about its content and society's ability to ensure universal access.

See also: BIRTHWEIGHT; HEALTHY START; INFANT MORTALITY; PREGNANCY

Bibliography

Alexander, Greg, and Carol Korenbrot. "The Role of Prenatal Care in Preventing Low Birth Weight." *The Future of Children* 5 (1995):103–120.

Alexander, Greg, and Milton Kotelcuck. "Quantifying the Adequacy of Prenatal Care: A Comparison of Indices." *Public Health Reports* 111 (1996):408–418.

Fiscella, Kevin. "Does Prenatal Care Improve Birth Outcomes? A Critical Review." *Obstetrics and Gynecology* 85 (1995):468–479.

Kogan, Michael, Greg Alexander, Milton Kotelchuck, and David Nagey. "Relation of the Content of Prenatal Care to the Risk of Low Birth Weight." *Journal of the American Medical Association* 271 (1994):1340–1345.

Kogan, Michael, Joyce Martin, Greg Alexander, Milton Kotelchuck, Stephanie Ventura, and Fredric Figoletto. "The Changing Pattern of Prenatal Care Utilization in the United States, 1981–1995, Using Different Prenatal Care Indices." *Journal of the American Medical Association* 279 (1998):1623–1628.

Merkatz, Irwin, Joyce Thompson, Patricia Mullen, and Robert Goldenberg. *New Perspectives on Prenatal Care.* New York: Elsevier Science Publishing, 1990.

Milton Kotelchuck

PRENATAL DEVELOPMENT

The end result of a successful pregnancy is that miracle called a child, which begins as a simple zygote and becomes a fertilized ovum during the first of three stages, or trimesters, of prenatal development. During the nine months, or approximately 266 days, of prenatal development, the zygote divides into billions of cells, which eventually become differentiated from one another while new systems and parts become integrated.

Ovum or Germinal Stage

Almost right after conception, cell division begins. While the zygote is splitting and new cells are created, it moves through the mother's fallopian tube toward the uterus, the place it will call home and where it will receive nourishment for the rest of its prenatal days. As with any other "egged" living thing, the yolk of the ovum provides all necessary nourishment.

By the time the cell cluster arrives at the uterus on the first stop of this journey, the process known as differentiation is just beginning. Here cells separate into groups according to their future roles. At this point the blastocyst (fertilized ovum) is a hollow ball of cells. Part of these cells will begin to form four membranes that help protect the growing organism. These membranes will eventually become the yolk sac, the allantois (which later becomes part of the circulatory system), the amnion (which soon forms the amniotic sac, the fetus's bubble-like home), and the chorion, which later becomes the placenta.

The blastocyst literally "floats" for some time in the uterus, and by the sixth day after conception it finds its home by implanting itself in the uterine wall. This is a critical point in gestation, because if the blastocyst does not implant itself properly and at the right time and in the right place, the cell mass will die before it can reach the embryo stage. If all goes well, the blastocyst will be firmly embedded about two weeks after conception.

Embryo Stage

During the forty-six-day embryo stage, the embryo grows to a length of more than one inch (2.5 centimeters). By the end of the embryo stage many body systems will be in operation, and the embryo will begin to appear human-like.

The embryo takes nourishment and oxygen and releases waste products through the umbilical cord, which links it with the placenta. The umbilical cord contains three blood vessels through which the embryo's blood circulates to and from the placenta.

The placenta is a disk-shaped mass of tissue six to eight inches (15.2 to 20.3 centimeters) long and one inch (2.5 centimeters) thick and weighs about one pound (.45 kilogram). Implanted in the inner wall of the uterus, it serves as a two-way filter between the bloodstream of the mother and the embryo. The placenta makes it possible for the mother to carry on life functions such as digestion, excretion, circulation, and respiration for the embryo. Into the placenta, by way of two arteries in the umbilical cord, the embryo deposits such waste material as carbon dioxide. The mass of blood vessels on the mother's side of the placenta then absorbs the wastes into her bloodstream. The embryo receives, through the vein in the umbilical cord, fresh nutrients (oxygen, amino acids, sugar, fats, and minerals) from the mother's bloodstream, and hormones, antibodies, and other necessary substances by the same route.

The placenta acts as a highly permeable membrane and as a natural screen to keep out many—but unfortunately, not all—harmful substances. Thus, the unborn child receives only materials with molecules that are small enough to pass through the screen. At the same time that the embryo is taking shape, the amniotic sac is developing into a protective chamber. By the end of the eighth week this sac completely surrounds the embryo. The watery fluid inside keeps the embryo from being jostled by any sudden movements of the mother or by accidents that may happen to her, such as a fall. The amniotic sac also keeps the embryo at a constant temperature.

During the embryonic period, three layers of cells are differentiated. The outer layer, or ectoderm, de-

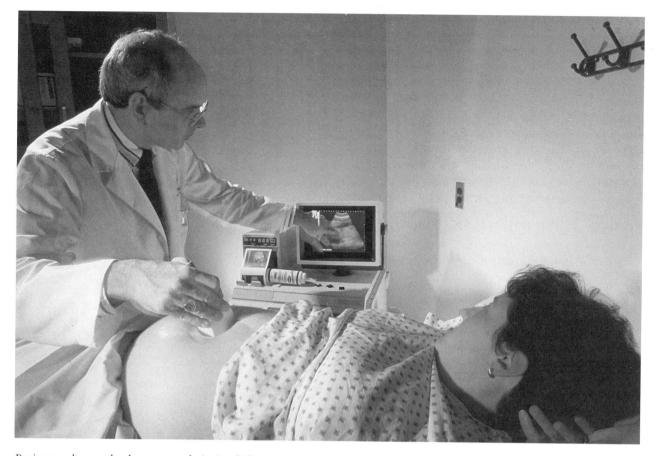

During an ultrasound a doctor uses a device in which sound waves detect bones and tissue in a woman's uterus. Ultrasounds can be used to confirm pregnancy, determine the gender of the baby, detect physical abnormalities or multiple fetuses, and evaluate fetal growth and health. (Richard Nowitz, FPG International)

velops into sensory cells, skin, and the nervous system. The middle layer, or mesoderm, becomes the excretory system, muscles, and blood. The inner layer, the endoderm forms the digestive system, lungs, and thyroid gland.

By the end of the third week of development the embryo's heart is beating and its nervous system is forming rapidly. After the fourth week the legs are curled and the eyes have appeared as dark circles. During the fifth and sixth weeks arms and legs can be seen. After eight weeks all of the major body organs are present. The liver is making blood cells, and the kidneys are removing waste products. The mouth, nose, eyes, and head are clear and distinct. The head is roughly half the total body size at this time. Fingers and toes are blunt, and ribs show under the fetus' skin.

The eight-week time span of embryonic development is a particularly vulnerable period in human growth. Chemicals, drugs, hormones, or viruses present in the mother's system can very easily affect the embryo, as is described in more detail below in the section on "Prenatal Environmental Influences."

Fetal Stage

The fetal stage begins in the ninth week of pregnancy and continues until the birth of the baby, usually about thirty weeks later.

The thrill of the first-time mother feeling the movements of the fetus in the fourth or fifth month of pregnancy is unforgettable. By this time, the fetus can open and close its mouth, swallow, and make certain head movements. It may even suck its thumb. The fastest growth period for the fetus is the fourth month, when it almost doubles in length, reaching six inches (15.2 centimeters) from crown to rump. Limbs become sensitive to touch, and a heartbeat can be heard with a stethoscope, a thrilling and sometimes mystifying experience for parents-to-be.

The fetus is becoming more of an individual during this stage. Some fetuses move around a great deal while others are relatively quiet. The fetus' sense of hearing has also begun to function during this period, as evidenced by startled reactions to loud sounds.

After five months the skin of the fetus is fully developed. Hair, nails, and sweat glands are apparent, and the fetus even sleeps and wakes and keeps almost regular hours. In month six the eyelids can open, and the fetus can open and close its eyes. It may now weigh as much as twenty-four ounces (680 grams). During month seven the eyes can distinguish light from dark, and the brain has more control over body systems than before. The most important aspect of this particular time in development is that an infant born prematurely now has a fair chance for survival. In the last two months the fetus gains about eight ounces (227 grams) per week and gets ready for birth.

Prenatal Environmental Influences

With increasingly sophisticated technology, the fetus has been studied and is considered to be an active agent in its own development. Many scientists believe that anything that affects the environment of the fetus can have an effect upon development beginning at conception and not at birth.

Environment does indeed begin to influence the individual as soon as he or she is conceived. As the zygote undergoes mitosis (cell division), the new cells themselves become part of the mother's environment, and through their particular physical and chemical influence they guide and control the development of further new cells. Different genes are activated or suppressed in each cell, so that while one group of cells is developing into brain tissue, another is giving rise to the heart, another to the lungs, and another to the skeletal system. Meanwhile, the lump of cells is surrounded by the larger environment of the mother's uterus, and this environment is surrounded by the mother and the world in which she lives.

The great majority of women have uncomplicated pregnancies and give birth to healthy babies, and for many years it was believed that the baby in the uterus was completely insulated from outside influences. Scientists now know that this is not entirely true. Environmental influences ranging from radioactivity and stress in the outside world to drugs, chemicals, hormones, and viruses in the mother's bloodstream can affect prenatal development.

Such threats affect the health of the fetus in several ways. This is because the body organs and parts develop at different speeds and go through definite phases. First they go through a phase of rapid multiplication in the number of cells. Then there is an increase in both the number of cells and in cell size. In the third and final phase of development, cell size continues to increase rapidly, but cell division slows down.

When a body part or organ system is growing most rapidly both in cell number and size, this is known as a critical period. If an environmental factor, such as a chemical or virus, interferes with growth during the critical period, development of that organ system will be permanently affected.

The effect of environmental influences varies, therefore, in accordance with the stage of prenatal development in which the environmental factor is encountered, as well as the intensity of the threat, as shown in Table 1.

During the first three months of pregnancy, tissues and important body systems develop in the embryo. Adverse influences during this period will affect the basic structure and form of the body and may have particularly serious effects on the nervous system. Physical development can be arrested and irreparable malformation may occur. For example, many women who took the once-available drug Thalidomide during the first three months of pregnancy gave birth to children with serious defects. When taken toward the end of pregnancy, however, the drug did not seem to have any negative effects.

Teratogens
The scientific study of congenital abnormalities caused by prenatal environmental influences is known as teratology (from the Greek word *teras*, meaning "marvel" or "monster"), and the environmental agents that produce abnormalities in the developing fetus are called teratogens.

Drugs
Chemicals (over-the-counter and prescribed pharmaceuticals as well as illegal substances) can cause a wide range of congenital abnormalities that account for about 10 percent of birth defects. The severity of the abnormality depends on the amount of the chemical the mother is exposed to, the developmental stage of the fetus, and the period of time over which the mother's exposure to the chemical takes place.

In terms of narcotics, women who are addicted to heroin, morphine, or methadone give birth to addicted babies. Soon after birth, the babies show symptoms of withdrawal, including tremors, convulsions, difficulty breathing, and intestinal disturbances.

Smoking and Nicotine
Cigarette smoking has already been shown to have dire consequences for the smoker, and it can be hazardous for the fetus and the newborn child. The results of studies of thousands of pregnancies in the United States and elsewhere, encompassing various ethnic, racial, and cultural groupings, indicate that the fetus and newborn are significantly affected by cigarette smoking during pregnancy.

Maternal smoking increases the risk of spontaneous abortions, bleeding during pregnancy, prema-

TABLE 1

Potential Impact of Teratogens during Prenatal Development

	Embryo Stage						WEEK OF DEVELOPMENT Fetal Stage			Full Term
	3	4	5	6	7	8	9–12	13–16	17–36	38
Central Nervous System	M	M	M	M	m	m	m	m	m	m
Eyes			M	M	m	m	M	m	m	m
Heart	M	M	M	M	m	m	M	m	m	
Arms/Legs		M	M	M	M	m	M	m	m	
Palate				M	M	M	M	m	m	m
Teeth					M	M	M	m	m	m
Genitalia					M	M	M	m	m	m

m=minor damage to fetus / M=major damage to fetus

SOURCE: *Neil J. Salkind.*

ture rupture of the amniotic sac, and fetal deaths and deaths of newborns. Women who smoke during pregnancy give birth to babies who are about one-half pound (225 grams) lighter (on the average) and smaller in all dimensions (for example, length and head circumference) than babies of nonsmokers, are born prematurely, and have other health problems.

Alcohol

The effects of alcohol are almost undisputed. Fetal alcohol syndrome (FAS), identified in 1973, is perhaps one of the best known and best documented outcomes of drinking, affecting approximately one out of every 750 births. And it is not just the heavy drinker who may place her fetus in danger. It has been found that women having one or more drinks daily were three times more likely to miscarry than women who had less than one drink daily.

FAS is a pattern of malformations in which the most serious effect is mental retardation. Other possible complications include permanent growth retardation, malformations of the face, brain damage, hyperactivity and learning disabilities, and heart defects.

Even if a child does not suffer from FAS, the effects of alcohol consumption can be significant. Although these children do not manifest the characteristics discussed above, they are at high risk for such problems of children of alcoholics as hyperactivity and learning disabilities. Results of research also indicate that moderate drinking can affect the later development of a child's intelligence as measured by IQ scores at age four.

The Mother

Since the mother's body is the chief element in the fetus' environment, the mother's physical condition can significantly affect the baby's development.

Among the maternal factors known to influence the fetus are disease, age, diet, reactions associated with a certain blood component, and prolonged stress.

Even a mother's knowledge of what is taking place in her body can be important. Some research has shown that mothers who consumed potentially teratogenic drugs during pregnancy had very little information about these drugs and even less information about their effect during pregnancy.

Diseases

Since the placenta cannot filter out extremely small disease carriers, such as viruses, children can be born with malaria, measles, chicken pox, mumps, syphilis, or other venereal diseases that have been transmitted from the mother.

Rubella is the most widespread of the viruses that have a teratogenic effect. If a pregnant woman contracts rubella in the first three months of pregnancy, she is likely to give birth to a child with a congenital abnormality such as heart disease, cataracts, deafness, or mental retardation. Interestingly, there is not a direct relationship between the severity of the disease in the mother and its effect on the fetus. For example, women who have had mild attacks of rubella have given birth to babies with severe abnormalities.

Although rubella might be the most widespread disease, acquired immunodeficiency syndrome (AIDS) is by far the most frightening and the one that has received the most publicity. The vast majority of children with AIDS contracted the disease sometime between early pregnancy and birth. The disease is usually transmitted from the mother through the uterus during pregnancy or is acquired by the offspring at birth.

As of the early twenty-first century, there was not a cure for AIDS, and the majority of efforts at controlling the disease focused on education in an effort to get potential female AIDS victims to take the proper precautions and avoid sexual relationships with high-risk males, usually those involved with drugs. Significant progress was being made, especially concerning children.

Toxemia is a frightening condition that is potentially fatal for the mother and the fetus. It is characterized by high blood pressure, swelling, and weight gain due to a buildup of fluid in the body tissues, and the presence of protein in the mother's urine. In severe cases the woman may go into convulsions or coma, placing a tremendous strain on her, which is carried over to the fetus. Women with toxemia frequently give birth to premature babies or to babies smaller than average for their gestational age. Like many other types of blood-pressure disorders, however, toxemia can be treated through medication and diet.

Anoxia is a condition in which the brain of the baby does not receive enough oxygen to allow it to develop properly. Anoxia can cause certain forms of epilepsy, mental deficiency, cerebral palsy, and behavior disorders. If the amount of brain damage is not too severe, however, it may be possible to compensate for the disorder to some extent. Epilepsy can often be controlled with drugs, for instance, and many children with cerebral palsy can learn to control their affected muscles.

Age

Teenage mothers and those over thirty-five years of age have a higher risk of miscarriage, premature birth, and some birth defects than mothers in the prime childbearing years. Some of the reasons are fairly obvious. Very young mothers have not yet completed their own development, and the reproductive system may not be quite ready to function smoothly or effectively. In older women the reproductive system may be past its most efficient functioning.

In both cases, pregnancy puts an extra strain on a body that is not fully able to bear it. Furthermore, there is some reason to think that a woman's ova may deteriorate with age, leading to a greater risk of birth defects. Women have all their ova in partly developed form when they are born. So a woman who becomes pregnant at age thirty-seven, for example, is "using" an ovum that has been more or less exposed to thirty-seven years' worth of harmful chemicals, radiation, virus infections, and whatever else has happened to her body. This may explain why, for instance, Down syndrome is most common in children born to mothers over forty years of age.

It is quite possible that men's sperm may also be susceptible to chemicals and radiation effects over time. Furthermore, there may be genetic disorders that cause changes in sperm structure.

Diet and Physical Condition

Just as other aspects of physical health are important, so is the mother's diet. While physicians and researchers have long realized that pregnancy puts additional demands on the mother's body, they used to assume that the fetus' nutritional needs would be met first, even at the mother's expense.

The current opinion, however, is that the prenatal development of the fetus and its growth and development after birth are directly related to maternal diet. Women who follow nutritionally sound diets during pregnancy give birth to babies of normal or above-normal size. Their babies are less likely to contract bronchitis, pneumonia, or colds during early infancy and have better developed teeth and bones. The mothers have fewer complications during pregnancy and, on the average, spend less time in labor. The less time in labor, the easier the birth and the less stress the mother and child experience.

But if the mother's diet is low in certain vitamins and minerals when she is pregnant, the child may suffer from specific weaknesses. Insufficient iron may lead to anemia in the infant, and a low intake of calcium may cause poor bone formation. If there is an insufficient amount of protein in the mother's diet, the baby may be smaller than average and may suffer from mental retardation, with almost 20 percent fewer brain cells. Mothers who are also physically small (under 100 pounds [45 kilograms] in total body weight) are risky for pregnancy as well because of the stress that pregnancy can place on them.

The Rh Factor

The Rh-positive factor is an inherited genetically dominant trait in the blood that can result in a dangerous situation for the fetus. When blood containing the Rh factor (that is, Rh-positive blood) is introduced into blood without the Rh factor (Rh-negative blood), antibodies to combat the Rh factor are produced. If an Rh-negative woman mates with an Rh-positive man, the resulting child may have Rh-positive blood. Any small rupture in the capillaries of the placenta will release the Rh factor into the mother's bloodstream, causing her body to produce the antibodies needed to fight it. The antibodies in the mother's blood will then cross the placenta into the fetal bloodstream and attack its Rh-positive red blood cells, depriving the fetus of oxygen. The result may be a miscarriage, possible brain defects, or even death to the fetus or newborn child. Only in circumstances involving an Rh-negative mother and an Rh-positive child does this danger exist.

This condition in the child is called fetal erythroblastosis. Firstborn children are not threatened, because the mother's blood has not had time to produce a large amount of antibodies, but the risk increases with each pregnancy. In the past, erythroblastosis was always fatal, but now medical techniques can minimize the harmful effects of Rh incompatibility. After the birth of an Rh-positive child, the Rh-negative mother can be given an injection of the drug Rhogam to reduce the buildup of antibodies in her blood. If this is not done, future Rh-positive children will be endangered by the high antibody level. A doctor who suspects an Rh incompatibility between mother and fetus can measure her antibody level and induce labor if the antibody count becomes too high. Immediate and complete blood transfusions to the newborn infant can then eliminate the mother's antibodies from its blood. If the fetus is not yet mature enough to survive after birth, a blood transfusion may be possible in utero.

Stress

If a mother is extremely anxious (about her pregnancy, her abilities as a mother, or any other problems in her life), the unborn child may be affected. Although the baby's nervous system is separate from the mother's, strong emotions in the mother such as rage, fear, and anxiety cause a great increase of hormones and other chemicals in her bloodstream. These substances pass through the placenta wall, and it is believed that they can reproduce the mother's physiological state in the fetus.

Exercise

The benefits of exercise are unquestioned. People who regularly exercise live longer for a variety of reasons. Their circulatory and respiratory systems get exercise and function more efficiently. Exercise tends to increase energy, make sex more enjoyable, decrease depression, increase self-confidence, and suppress appetite, which helps maintain an ideal weight-to-height ratio. There is also a social component to exercise (getting out of the house, being with other adults) that provides an incentive to continue. When the human body is in better condition, it can better fight off diseases, and when struck with illness, it reacts in a more positive fashion.

One longitudinal study examined the relationship between exercise and pregnancy, focusing on the levels of fatigue that women experience during childbirth and the association between fatigue and several maternal factors. The best predictors for fatigue among these women were examined. The set of possible predictors included whether the women took formal childbirth education classes, their average amount of sleep, whether they exercised during the last trimester of pregnancy, whether they worked during the last trimester of pregnancy, their anxiety level, and whether they had been medicated prior to

the interview. When admitted to the hospital, the best predictors of fatigue were anxiety, amount of sleep, and medication. Two hours after admission, the best predictors were previous fatigue, medication, and work. Four hours after admission, the variables were medication, previous fatigue, exercise, and childbirth education. Six hours after admission, the predictors with the greatest influence were previous fatigue, medication, exercise, and work. Within twenty-four hours after delivery, the greatest predictor of fatigue was previous fatigue.

Although exercise in a couple of instances seemed to be associated with fatigue, for the most part it did not seem to be one of the best predictors for fatigue. Along with the other benefits mentioned earlier, it would seem that exercise helps lessen a woman's fatigue during childbirth.

Conclusion

Never before has the importance of prenatal care for the developing child been so apparent. With increases in research and knowledge of what factors can affect the zygote, embryo, and fetus, the likelihood that such factors can have a negative impact on the well-being of the child and the mother is greatly decreased.

See also: BIRTH; PREGNANCY; PREMATURE INFANTS

Bibliography

Boyd, Susan. *Mothers and Illicit Drugs: Transcending the Myths.* Toronto: University of Toronto Press, 1999.

"Pregnancy and Prenatal Care." In the Make Way for Baby [web site]. Pompano Beach, Florida, 2000. Available from http://www.2bparent.com/pregnancy.htm; INTERNET.

"Prenatal Development and Birth." In the George Mason University [web site]. Fairfax, Virginia, 2001. Available from http://classweb.gmu.edu/awinsler/ordp/prenatal.html; INTERNET.

Priest, Judy, and Kathy Attawell. *Drugs in Conception, Pregnancy, and Childbirth.* London: Thorsons Publications, 1998.

Neil J. Salkind

PRESCHOOL

Most children begin their formal schooling at the age of five or six. Many children, however, have experience with organized educational programs before that time. Indeed, these "preschool" programs are quite popular in today's society. This article briefly reviews the history of preschool programs in the United States, differences in the philosophies guiding such programs, their impact on children's development, cultural differences in preschool programs, and finally the movement toward inclusion of children with special needs in preschool.

History and Demographics

Preschool programs began in earnest in the United States during the first quarter of the twentieth century. The philosophical foundations for these programs can be traced to the belief, popularized during the seventeenth century, that early childhood is a unique period of life during which the foundation for all subsequent learning is established. The early programs often began informally and involved the efforts of women who took turns caring for each other's children. The first public preschool program began at the Franklin School in Chicago in 1925 with the support of the Chicago Women's Club.

The popularity of preschool as an option for young children increased dramatically after the 1970s. In 1970, for example, only 20 percent of three- and four-year-olds participated in organized education programs. In 1998, approximately half of all children in this age range attended a full-time preschool program. The increasing popularity of preschool has been fueled in part by an increase in the number of women entering the work force as well as by a belief among many parents and educators that children need early preparation for elementary school.

Program Differences

There are many different types of preschool programs, from those that strive to accelerate the academic progress of children who are otherwise developing at a normal pace to those that attend more to the social and emotional needs of the children. Such program differences often reflect deeper philosophical differences in beliefs about young children and the goal of preschool. Such differences can be seen by considering two programs currently popular in the United States: the Montessori approach, which has a long history in this country, and the Reggio Emilia approach, which is relatively new to this country.

The Montessori approach was developed in the early twentieth century by Maria Montessori, an Italian physician and educator. In this approach, children are allowed choices and opportunities to pursue their own interests by moving freely from one activity center to another; the activities available to children, however, are designed to foster cognitive growth rather than social or emotional growth. In fact, Montessori teachers encourage preschoolers to work independently and to persist at challenging cognitive tasks, while minimizing interactions with peers. Teacher interactions, too, tend to be minimal, with teachers serving mainly to model ways in which children can use curricular materials.

The Reggio Emilia approach was started in 1945 in Reggio Emilia, a small community in northern Italy. It emerged from the efforts of parents who sought high-quality care for their children and educator Loris Malaguzzi, who provided the philosophical foundation. Proponents view the preschooler as highly competent and as inherently curious and social. They further see development as resulting from the child's active involvement with the physical and social worlds and from repeated experiences that provide the opportunity for reflection and for constructing increasingly more flexible representations of those experiences. In practice, this philosophy entails the use of group projects that evolve according to the children's interests, an emphasis on children communicating their ideas to others, and children learning to express ideas through multiple media. Perhaps the hallmark of this approach is the extensive support and collaboration of the community, including parents and the government.

Impact of the Preschool Experience

There are both advantages and disadvantages for children who attend preschool compared to children who do not. Advantages include more collaborative interactions with peers, increased social competence, and greater expressiveness. Disadvantages include less compliance with adult demands and heightened aggressiveness toward peers. It is important to recognize, however, that the extent and nature of the impact of preschool may depend on a number of factors, including the length of time in the program, the child's family environment, and the particular characteristics a child brings to the program. Most important, however, is the quality of the preschool program. High-quality programs, for example, have been found to foster language development, whereas increased aggression may be more likely for children in low-quality care.

Developmentally Appropriate Practices

What makes a program "high quality"? High quality is defined by a number of factors, including a low child-teacher ratio, adequate physical space, a staff whose members are highly experienced, and a wealth of play and curricular materials. Most importantly, however, high-quality programs are defined by developmentally appropriate practices.

Developmentally appropriate programs have five characteristics. First, these programs attempt to facilitate not only cognitive development but also social and emotional development, focusing on areas such as learning to take turns, learning to respect others, and feeling good about one's accomplishments. Sec-

The Head Start program served as a preschool model to provide equal educational opportunities for "at risk" children. (Shelley Gazin/Corbis-Bettmann)

ond, these programs allow children to develop at their own pace and to pursue their own interests. Third, these programs allow children to control their own learning by relying on discovery and exploration rather than on drill and practice or other teacher-controlled activities. Fourth, developmentally appropriate programs provide activities matched to an individual child's current level of functioning, with the aim being for the child to participate in activities that require skills just slightly in advance of those already in the child's repertoire. Finally, developmentally appropriate programs have a realistic academic orientation—one that introduces some basic academic skills but without attempting to push children too far academically.

Developmentally appropriate practices have been shown to lead to positive child outcomes. In a study by Luigi Girolametto, Elaine Weitzman, Riet van Lieshout, and Dawna Duff, for example, the researchers found that preschoolers talked more and in more sophisticated ways when their teachers used developmentally appropriate language (e.g., open-ended questions, utterances that followed rather than redirected the children's attention) rather than developmentally inappropriate language (e.g., commands and test questions, which reflected the teacher's "agenda" rather than the children's interests). There is also evidence that preschool programs designed to "speed up" children's academic progress, which are by definition developmentally inappropriate, lead to a number of undesirable outcomes, including less creativity, a less positive attitude about school, and no lasting positive impact on academic performance.

Cultural Variations

Cross-national comparisons conducted in the late 1990s raised concerns about declining achievement for students in the United States, especially as compared to students in Japan and other Asian countries. In making such comparisons, it is important to recognize that any nation is a diverse collection of cultures, philosophies, and educational practices. Ignoring such diversity can lead to stereotyped conceptions of another country's or culture's educational practices. It is possible in some instances, however, to identify a modal, or most popular, educational philosophy or practice for a particular country. This makes it possible to compare countries in terms of these modal philosophies or practices, provided that one is careful to avoid overgeneralizations.

Many people in the United States mistakenly believe that Asian students typically participate in highly academically oriented preschool programs. In fact, American preschools are more likely than are programs in Japan or other Asian countries to have the goal of providing children an academic head start. The majority of Japan's preschool programs, for example, are organized around the goal of teaching children to work as members of a group. This entails fostering persistence, concentration, and a willingness to forestall individual rewards. In Japan, instruction in reading and writing during the preschool years has traditionally been seen as the province of the family and occurs largely at home. In contrast to the group orientation of many preschools in Japan, preschools in the United States stress independence and self-confidence. Interestingly, there is evidence of an increasing trend toward providing an academic head start to preschoolers in Japan, although this often leads to clashes between educators and families who have more "traditional" values.

Inclusion of Preschoolers with Special Needs

In the 1980s and 1990s, there was an ever-increasing emphasis on educating children with special needs (e.g., learning disabilities) alongside typically developing peers in the "regular" classroom rather than in separate, "special" classes that enroll only children with disabilities. Although mandated by federal laws and regulations, this move toward inclusion has been controversial. Nevertheless, there has been considerable research documenting the potential benefits of inclusion at all levels of education, including the preschool level. These benefits are not typically seen on standardized measures of achievement but rather on social and cognitive behaviors within the classroom. Moreover, these benefits are seen for typically developing children as well as for children with special needs. Inclusion, however, may not alleviate all the problems of children with special needs. For example, children with cognitive disabilities in inclusive classrooms participate in fewer social interactions with peers and have fewer friends than do typically developing preschoolers in the same classes. It is important to recognize that there is considerable variability among inclusive preschool programs in both their educational quality and the extent to which there is an active attempt to fully include children with special needs in the "life" of the classroom. Not surprisingly, educational quality and the

nature of the inclusive practices affect the outcomes for preschoolers with special needs.

See also: HEAD START; MONTESSORI METHOD

Bibliography

Abbeduto, Leonard. *Taking Sides: Clashing Views on Controversial Issues in Educational Psychology.* Guilford, CT: Dushkin/McGraw-Hill, 2000.

Beatty, B. *Preschool Education in America.* New Haven, CT: Yale University Press, 1995.

Berger, Kathleen. *The Developing Person through Childhood and Adolescence.* New York: Worth, 2000.

Clarke-Stewart, K. Alison, and Greta Fein. "Early Childhood Programs." In Paul H. Mussen ed., *Handbook of Child Psychology*, Vol. 2: *Infancy and Developmental Psychopathology.* New York: Wiley, 1983.

Girolametto, Luigi, Elaine Weitzman, Riet van Lieshout, and Dawna Duff. "Directiveness in Teachers' Language Input to Toddlers and Preschoolers in Day Care." *Journal of Speech, Language, and Hearing Research* 43 (2000):1101–1114.

Guralnick, Michael. "Family and Child Influences on the Peer-Related Social Competence of Young Children with Developmental Delays." *Mental Retardation and Developmental Disabilities Research Reviews* 5 (1999):21–29.

Hendrick, Joanne, ed. *First Steps toward Teaching the Reggio Way.* Upper Saddle River, NJ: Prentice-Hall, 1997.

Holloway, Susan. "Divergent Cultural Models of Child Rearing and Pedagogy in Japanese Preschools." In E. Turiel ed., *Development and Cultural Change: Reciprocal Processes.* San Francisco: Jossey-Bass, 1999.

Howes, Carollee. "Children's Experiences in Center-Based Child Care as a Function of Teacher Background and Adult-Child Ratio." *Merrill Palmer Quarterly* 43 (1997):404–425.

Odom, Samuel. "Preschool Inclusion: What We Know and Where We Go from Here." *Topics in Early Childhood Special Education* 20 (2000):20–27.

Santrock, John. *Child Development,* 8th edition. Boston: McGraw-Hill, 1998.

U.S. Department of Education, National Center for Education Statistics. *Preprimary Enrollment.* Washington, DC: U.S. Department of Education, National Center for Education Statistics, 1998.

Yen, Sue-Chen, and Jean Ispa. "Children's Temperament and Behavior in Montessori and Constructivist Early Childhood Programs." *Early Education and Development* 11 (2000):171–186.

Zigler, Edward, and Matia Finn Stevenson. *Children in a Changing World: Development and Social Issues,* 2nd edition. Pacific Grove, CA: Brooks/Cole, 1993.

Leonard Abbeduto
Patti Beth

PROSOCIAL BEHAVIOR

The term prosocial behavior describes acts that demonstrate a sense of empathy, caring, and ethics, including sharing, cooperating, helping others, generosity, praising, complying, telling the truth, defending others, supporting others with warmth and affection, nurturing and guiding, and even the altruistic act of risking one's life to warn or aid another. Because many of these behaviors are found in a variety of other animal species, and some appear early in human infancy, their source is believed to be at least partly genetic. Additional sources of influence are suggested by the hundreds of studies that reveal age-related increases in the production of human prosocial acts that parallel increases in moral reasoning, the ability to see the perspective of others, and experiencing and showing emotional concern. Adults and peers can also increase the degree of a child's prosocial behavior by modeling and labeling it, discussing, and rewarding it when it appears in the child's actions. Differences in temperament, personal experiences, cultural expectations, and the nature of the situation also influence children' prosocial behavior.

See also: ALTRUISM; SOCIAL DEVELOPMENT

Bibliography

Berk, Laura. *Child Development,* 5th edition. Boston: Allyn and Bacon, 2000.

Eisenberg, Nancy, and Richard Fabes. "Prosocial Development." In *Handbook of Child Psychology,* Vol. 3: *Social, Emotional, and Personality Development,* 5th edition, edited by William Damon. New York: John Wiley and Sons, 1998.

Honig, Alice, and D. S. Wittmer. "Helping Children Become More Prosocial: Ideas for Classrooms, Families, Schools, and Communities." *Young Children* 51 (1996):62–70.

Vasta, Ross, Marshall Haith, and Scott Miller. *Child Psychology: The Modern Science,* 3rd edition. New York: John Wiley and Sons, 1999.

Edward J. Forbes III

PUBERTY

Puberty is the time of life in which physical and hormonal changes take place in the body making it capable of reproduction. It occurs primarily during early adolescence. Changes can begin as early as age nine or as late as age seventeen. Nutrition, health, and genetic factors determine when a child starts puberty. Girls usually start puberty earlier than boys. First changes are internal; external changes are noticeable in the development of breasts and appearance of pubic hair. The sequence of changes for girls are as follows:

- Ovaries increase production of estrogen
- Internal sex organs begin to grow larger
- Breast bud stage
- Pubic hair begins to appear
- Weight spurt begins
- Peak height spurt
- Peak muscle and organ growth (also, hips become wider)
- Menarche (first menstruation)
- First ovulation
- Final pubic hair pattern
- Full breast growth

Boys' changes are also initially internal. The first external signs are growth of the scrotum and appearance of pubic hair. The sequence of changes for boys are as follows:

- Testes increase production of testosterone and progesterone
- Testes and scrotum grow larger
- Pubic hair begins to appear
- Penis growth begins
- First ejaculation
- Weight spurt begins
- Peak height spurt
- Peak muscle and organ growth (also, shoulders become broader)
- Voice lowers
- Facial hair appears
- Final pubic hair pattern

See also: ADOLESCENCE; MATURATION; MENARCHE

Bibliography

Bell, Ruth. *Changing Bodies, Changing Lives,* 3rd edition. New York: Random House, 1998.

Harris, Robie H. *It's Perfectly Normal.* Cambridge, MA: Candlewick Press, 1994.

Jane L. Abraham

R

RACIAL DIFFERENCES

Discussing racial differences in the field of psychology is problematic. The term "race" can be defined as a distinct biological group of people who share inherited physical and cultural traits that are different from the shared traits in other races. By definition, therefore, race implies racial differences. No scientific basis exists for notions of racial differences as biological, genetically inherited differences. Race is a social construction. Race and racial differences do not really exist. Rather, they have a social reality—they exist within the context of culture and the environment. Ideas of race and meanings of racial differences are determined by people in their interactions and through the negotiation of the meaning of race in everyday situations, circumstances, and contexts.

The problem with the study of racial differences is that the ambiguity surrounding definitions and meanings of race and racial differences precludes us from understanding variability in behavior and/or processes of development. When race was used as a study variable in most behavioral research of the past, it was assumed to be the explanation for any differences found in behavior or the construct being studied. Therefore, researchers misled readers to assume that the differences were due to genetic differences. In reality, instead of helping clarify human variability, race merely identifies another aspect of that variability.

Historical View of Race

Historically, scientists defined race as being a biological entity. In the late 1700s and early 1800s, scientists' claims of hierarchies among the races were used to justify slavery and segregation in addition to social, political, and economic dominance over and oppression of blacks by whites. Race was defined by skin color, hair texture, and other physical features. Moreover, researchers believed that a person's race was related to intellectual, spiritual, and moral qualities that they inherited and that the races were unequal in this regard. While scientists were not able to, and still have not been able to, scientifically validate this idea of race, this notion has continued to be perpetuated over time.

In the early 1900s, social scientists—specifically psychologists, anthropologists, and sociologists—began to realize that differences in behavior, morality, religiosity and spirituality, culture, and intelligence were the result of environmental factors, including history and education, not genetic inheritance. As a result, the concept of race in psychology generally has come to mean inheritable, physical characteristics. If race refers to inherited physical characteristics, then one would expect that there would be genetic markers for racial characteristics that scientists can identify, just as there are genes for eye color or biological sex, for example. In other words, if being black, white, or Asian causes a person to have the bone structure, facial features, hair texture, or skin complexion that they do, there ought to be some gene or chromosomal marker that scientists can identify that is responsible for race. No such markers exist for all members of any one race. No genes or hereditary factors are shared by every Asian, or every black, or every white person. Moreover, specific traits such as the ones listed previously vary more within each racial group than they do between racial groups.

America has always been multiethnic and multiracial. As more immigrants settle in the United States, and people marry interethnically and interracially, ethnic and racial heterogeneity continues to increase. Racial and ethnic minority children and adolescents are the largest growing segment of the U.S. population. Changes in the "face" of America demand that individuals try to understand developmental processes operating in children from varying racial and ethnic backgrounds, as well as other factors that influence the differences in children's development. Looking at similarities and differences in development helps researchers identify universal principles and processes that occur across all cultures, races, and ethnicities.

Standardized Tests and Race

A variety of race comparative studies have been conducted in the field of psychology and, more specifically, in child development. Race comparative studies on self-esteem, identity formation, out-of-school activity participation, risk taking, parenting style, and parental monitoring number in the thousands. Perhaps the most controversial area of study of racial and ethnic differences has been in intellectual performance. Many African-American and Native-American children score, on average, twelve to fifteen points lower than their European-American peers on standardized IQ tests. Hispanic-American children's scores fall between African-American and European-American children's, whereas Asian-American children's scores tend to be at the same level as scores of European-American children. It is important to note that neither IQ, future academic performance, nor life success can be predicted from an individual's race or ethnicity.

Researchers have suggested several possible explanations to account for racial and ethnic differences in intellectual performance. The first explanation is that standardized IQ tests and testing procedures are culturally biased toward European-American middle class knowledge and experiences. According to Janet E. Helms, IQ tests are designed to measure cognitive skills and information that middle class European-American children are more likely to have acquired. Researchers have attempted to make IQ tests more culturally fair, so members of minority groups and

lower socioeconomic status are not placed at an instant disadvantage when taking them. A completely culture-free test, however, is good in theory, but not so feasible yet in practice.

Another explanation that has been suggested for racial and ethnic differences in intellectual performance is that minority children are not motivated to do their best on standardized tests. John U. Ogbu suggested that negative stereotypes about minority children's abilities may influence their ideas about their future educational success and career prospects. Children may feel that because of societal prejudice and discrimination they may not be able to get ahead in life, so the effort that they make and how well they score on a test is irrelevant. Furthermore, Ogbu suggested that African-American children may associate academic achievement and doing well on tests with "acting white" rather than with the values of their own group. Thus, they may avoid doing well because of the fear of being rejected by their own racial or ethnic group for behaving in ways valued by or associated with the majority culture. Claude M. Steele suggested that minority children and adolescents may experience stereotype threat—the fear that they will be judged to have traits associated with negative appraisals and/or stereotypes of their race or ethnic group (e.g., African Americans are not smart in reading; Hispanics just cannot do math; African Americans are simply intellectually inferior)—which produces test anxiety and keeps them from doing as well as they could on tests. According to Steele, minority test takers experience anxiety, believing that if they do poorly on their test they will confirm the stereotypes about inferior intellectual performance of their minority group. As a result, a self-fulfilling prophecy begins, and the child performs at a level beneath his or her inherent abilities.

In 1994, in their book *The Bell Curve*, Richard J. Herrnstein and Charles Murray suggested that differences in IQ are the result of genetic differences between the races and cannot be explained simply on the basis of test bias or socioeconomic status differences. They also suggested that these IQ differences were responsible for higher rates of poverty, unemployment, and welfare dependence in minority groups as compared to majority groups. Arthur R. Jensen agreed with the genetic hypothesis and proposed that humans inherit two types of intellectual abilities: Level I abilities, related to memorization and short-term memory, and Level II abilities, which deal with problem solving and abstract reasoning. Jensen believed that all children perform Level I tasks equally well, but that European-American children perform Level II tasks better than children from other racial groups. Herrnstein and Murray were met

Changes in the "face" of America demand that individuals try to understand developmental processes operating in children from varying racial and ethnic backgrounds. (Tony Arruza/Corbis)

with extreme protest from many researchers who felt their claims were exaggerated, if not completely false. Critics suggested that Herrnstein and Murray's research was not scientifically rigorous. All findings relied upon a single data set, ignoring a century of research in the social sciences; the standardized tests used in their research measured academic instruction rather than inherent ability; the comparison groups were poorly designed; and they repeatedly overinterpreted weak relationships in the data. Moreover, *The Bell Curve* failed to explain within-racial-group differences in IQ. Similarly, neither the genetic hypothesis nor Herrnstein and Murray's theory of intellectual performance could account for multiracial children's IQ scores or the scores of adopted children.

The last and most compelling proposed explanation for racial differences in intellectual performance is that differences are the result of environmental circumstances. The subject of racial differences cannot easily be separated from the subject of socioeconomic class. Racial and ethnic group membership, in fact, is highly related to socioeconomic stratification. There

is a direct correlation between parental income and education with standardized test scores. The scores of minority test takers tend to be lower, because minority children and adolescents on average come from families with lower incomes than do European-American children and adolescents. Furthermore, poor children and children from minority groups, who are more likely to be of lower socioeconomic status, are more likely to grow up in circumstances that do not favor intellectual development. Lack of access to resources and economic hardship can affect intellectual growth. Poor nutrition, poor health care, and living in chronic poverty or violent neighborhoods are just some of the factors that can combine to produce less than optimal learning environments.

Cultural Differences vs. Racial Differences

The direction of research on racial differences is beginning to move away from the race-comparative framework, which has cultivated the deficit perspective—the idea that minority children are inherently deficient or pathologic in some way—toward adopting race-homogenous frameworks, looking at within-ethnic-group variability, and the particular influence of the cultural context. A focus on intragroup and cultural differences rather than racial differences has more potential explanatory power for behavior and developmental processes. This movement has the potential to decrease the perpetuation of traditional notions of racial categories and subsequent stereotyping and racism, might legitimize race as a scientifically valid variable in behavioral research, and may lead to a meaningful recognition of social, economic, and cultural factors that contribute to differences in children's behavior and development.

See also: AFRICAN-AMERICAN CHILDREN; ASIAN-AMERICAN CHILDREN; HISPANIC CHILDREN; SOCIAL CLASS

Bibliography

Fraser, Steven, ed. *The Bell Curve Wars: Race, Intelligence, and the Future of America.* New York: Basic, 1995.

Helms, Janet E. "Why Is There No Study of Cultural Equivalence in Standardized Cognitive Ability Testing?" *American Psychologist* 47 (1992):1083–1101.

Herrnstein, Richard J., and Charles Murray. *The Bell Curve: Intelligence and Class Structure in American Life.* New York: Free Press, 1994.

Jensen, Arthur R. *Genetics and Education.* New York: Harper and Row, 1972.

McLoyd, Vonnie C., and Laurence Steinberg, eds. *Studying Minority Adolescents: Conceptual, Methodological, and Theoretical Issues.* Mahwah, NJ: Lawrence Erlbaum, 1998.

Montagu, Ashley. *Race and IQ.* New York: Oxford University Press, 1999.

Ogbu, John U. "Black Education: A Cultural-Ecological Perspective." In Harriette Pipes McAdoo ed., *Black Families.* Beverly Hills, CA: Sage, 1988.

Steele, Claude M. "A Threat in the Air: How Stereotypes Shape Intellectual Identity and Performance." *American Psychologist* 52 (1997):613–629.

Teper, Shirley. *Ethnicity, Race, and Human Development: A Report on the State of Our Knowledge.* New York: Institute on Pluralism and Group Identity of the American Jewish Committee, 1977.

LeShawndra N. Price

READING

Reading can be an activity of extremes; either a person read or he cannot. What has to happen to be able to read? Why is it easy for some children and difficult for others? Reading is not an unlearned skill, such as talking, that starts developing at birth. The ability to read and write does not develop by itself; a child needs instruction to be able to read. When and where should that reading instruction begin?

The Emergent Reader: The Infant and Toddler Years

In the first few months after birth, children begin to play with sounds. Their cooing turns to babble as they attempt to imitate the sounds that they hear. They love to play games such as pat-a-cake and peek-a-boo, and manipulate objects. Adults need to talk to babies using simple language and acknowledge their language attempts to support their oral language development. It is during this time of play that infants begin their pathway to reading.

First readings with infants should include cardboard books, which are sturdy and allow the infant to handle the book without concern about pages being ripped. Most readings with a toddler center around vocabulary building, such as by asking him to point to different items in a picture. Toddlers can identify more items through this type of labeled reading than by actually talking. A toddler might not be able to voice the word if you point to an elephant, but if you ask him to show you an elephant, he will be able to point to a picture of one. As toddlers increase their vocabulary, they begin to imitate language around them by speaking in simple sentences; "I want cookie," "I go bye-bye," and "I have book" are a few examples. This oral language is the foundation for the development of literacy.

Precursors to Reading: The Preschool Years

To encourage vocabulary development, it is important for children to be engaged in meaningful conversations with others. Children need to exchange ideas about their feelings and thoughts. Children are often imitators of what they see and hear, and they need to experience reading and writing behaviors that will encourage their interest in and enjoyment of reading and writing.

Among the first words that children recognize or read are those found on fast-food signs, the names of their favorite foods and favorite toys, the names they use for their parents, and their own name. To encourage reading, children need to be exposed to print every day; during this daily reading, print concepts are introduced that are necessary for the preschooler to learn to read. These concepts are understood when a child can:

- show where the front of a book is;
- realize that there are words on a page;
- point to the words as they are read;
- understand that one reads from left to right;
- show where the story starts on a page; and
- show the beginning and ending of a word.

After reading a story to a child give her the opportunity to talk about the story. She can tell you her favorite part of the story; you might also encourage her to retell the story in her own words. Children enjoy rereading the books that have been read to them. They will pull out the same book to be read again and again. They may even "read" their books by looking at the pictures and telling the story. This pretend reading, known as book talk, provides another brick in the foundation of their reading pathway.

If a child were retelling the story "The Three Little Pigs," he would probably include the language: "I will huff and puff and blow your house down." The words "huff" and "puff" are not typically in a child's basic vocabulary. These are examples of book talk words; using such words shows that the child has retold the story using the language from the book. Normally these book words are important to the story structure or story meaning.

Book talks, story retellings, singing songs, and noticing rhymes in words are ways that children like to play with words. A child is ready to begin formal reading instruction when she is recognizing symbols, demonstrating vocabulary knowledge by using book talk, and identifying word patterns with rhymes.

Beginning to Read: Kindergarten and Primary Grades

Formal reading instruction begins when a child is introduced to the letters in the alphabet. This typically occurs in kindergarten or the primary grades of elementary school. Children must learn that the written word is made up of letters that are symbols for the sounds they hear. Children must match those known sounds with letters. To help children match the sounds that they hear to letters, they need opportunities to use different literacy tools such as writing lists, making signs in block building, writing notes, and using icons and words when exploring computer games.

Children's writing experiences should allow the flexibility to use nonconventional forms of writing at first, what is called inventive spelling. These spelling attempts show where they are developmentally in their reading. Children go from hearing the beginning sound, then the ending sound, before they begin to look at letters in the middle of a word. If they attempt to spell the word "jump" with a "j," they are looking at the beginning letter of a word when they read. If they spell "jump" with "jp," that would indicate that they are looking at both the beginning and ending letters of words when they read. When children look at both the beginning and ending sounds, they are then ready to look at the letters in the middle of the word. At this point children would spell "jump" either "jup" or "jop." To help children look at the entire word, they should be encouraged to stretch out the sounds they hear: "j-u-m-p."

In this beginning stage of reading, children "read" from matching what they hear to letters in the word. Having the children stretch out the word "jump" to hear the individual sounds will help them realize that there are four different sounds. When they can hear and identify those four different sounds they will be able to read and write "jump" with conventional spelling. Once children understand this letter sound match, they should be encouraged to write on their own as the next step in their literacy development.

In addition to being read to, children need to be encouraged to read independently. In the early stages of learning, children depend on illustrations to help them read a story. Before having a child read, have him look at and discuss what he sees in the pictures. This process, known as a picture walk, helps the child gather words he needs to read the story and is also an opportunity to teach any unfamiliar vocabulary found in the book. For example, while doing a picture walk the child tells you he sees a crocodile but the word on the page is "alligator." A parent would tell the child, "yes that does look like a crocodile, but it is really an alligator." When the child is reading the book and he comes to the word "alligator," he will be able to read the word successfully because of the discussion during the picture walk.

As children master high frequency words, they begin to look at words in chunks or parts (st-amp, fl-oat, gl-ad). They will start to recognize common blends (st, pl, br) and digraphs (ew, ar, ou). To become independent readers, children need to know several strategies to help them decode an unknown word. These strategies include: using the picture, sounding out the word, looking for sound chunks in a word, rereading the sentence, skipping the word, and thinking about the story.

During this early reading stage, it is very important that children continue to be read to. They need to be read meaningful stories and informational stories daily to continue to build vocabulary meanings of unknown words.

Reading to Learn: Second Grade through High School

Once a child can decode words using a variety of strategies, the focus of reading changes from word recognition to comprehension and reading fluency. Reading becomes an opportunity to learn as children read a variety of texts. Their reading success depends

As part of reading development, children must learn that the written word is made up of letters that are symbols for the sounds they hear. (Access)

on the skills learned in the early stages of reading. Children begin to make connections from one topic to another and are able to consider several viewpoints while reading.

Summary

Reading and writing are complex skills, and each child has a unique learning pattern and her own timing in acquiring the skills necessary to become a reader and writer. The age a child learns to read depends on the individual's background of literature and print. If given exposure to appropriate literacy experiences and good teaching during early childhood, most children will learn to read at age six or seven. A few children will learn to read at four, some at five, and others will need intensive individual support to learn to read at eight or nine. Literacy experiences that help a child learn to read are daily exposure to print, vocabulary development, book retellings, and an understanding of print concepts.

See also: LANGUAGE DEVELOPMENT

Bibliography

Griffith, Priscilla, and Mary Olson. "Phonemic Awareness Helps Beginning Readers Break the Code." *International Reading Association* 45 (1992):516–523.

"Learning to Read and Write: Developmentally Appropriate Practices for Your Children. A Joint Position Statement of the International Reading Association (IRA) and the National Association for the Education of Young Children (NAEYC)." *Reading Teacher* 52 (1998):192–216.

Reading Is Fundamental, Inc. (RIF). Available from http://www.rif.org/home.html; INTERNET.

Victoria L. Davids

REFLEXES

A reflex is an involuntary or unlearned response to some type of stimulus. For example, when the cheek of a newborn child is stroked, she will turn toward the direction of the stimulation. This is the rooting reflex. There are many of these reflexes that are present at birth, most of which tend to disappear within the first year of life. While the purpose of such reflexes as rooting and sucking is fairly clear (getting a good jump on learning how to feed), the function of others is not fully understood. For example, the tonic neck reflex is where an infant forms fists with both hands and usually turns her head to the right. This may have something to do with a preference for one side of the body over the other. Pediatricians are interested in the presence or absence of reflexes primarily because they reflect the level of maturity of the central nervous system.

See also: BRAZELTON NEONATAL ASSESSMENT SCALE; INFANCY

Bibliography

Miller, Linda G., and Kay M. Albrecht. *Innovations: The Comprehensive Infant Curriculum.* Beltsville, MD: Gryphon House, 2000.

Tirosh, E. "Neonatal Neurobehavioural Assessment as Related to Growth in Infancy." *Journal of Reproductive and Infant Psychology* 18, no. 1 (2000):61–66.

"Your Baby's Amazing Reflexes" [web site]. Available from http://www.i5ive.com/article.cfm/developmental_psychology/46602; INTERNET.

Neil J. Salkind

REINFORCEMENT

Reinforcement generally refers to the increase or strengthening of a particular response following the delivery or removal of a stimulus or event. Given that this is perhaps the most fundamental process in operant learning theory, it is critical to understand the difference between positive and negative reinforcement. Simply stated, positive reinforcement involves the presentation or delivery of something "positive," and negative reinforcement involves the removal, reduction, or termination of something "negative." It is important to note that both processes have the same effect; that is, they both strengthen or reinforce particular behaviors. This is a critical point, given that negative reinforcement is often mistakenly equated with punishment.

More specifically, positive reinforcement is a process in which a stimulus is presented following a particular behavior, thereby strengthening that behavior. The stimulus is referred to as a "reinforcer" and is roughly synonymous with the word "reward." The following is a simple example of positive reinforcement: Clarice's teacher provided lavish praise (a positive reinforcer) after Clarice used the word "please." Clarice's use of this word was positively reinforced; thus, she will be more likely to say "please" in the future.

Negative reinforcement is a process that involves the removal or reduction of a negative or unwanted stimulus after a behavior occurs, thereby strengthening that behavior. Negative reinforcement involves responding to "escape" from an annoying or aversive stimulus (i.e., a negative reinforcer or "punisher").

The following example demonstrates how Adam's gift-giving behavior was negatively reinforced: Adam's angry girlfriend, Holly, was not speaking to him. To escape this aversive and unpleasant situation, Adam gave Holly a bouquet of roses. The act of giving roses led to the removal of an unwanted and aversive situation (i.e., Holly began speaking to him again); thus, Adam's behavior was negatively reinforced. As a result, Adam will be more likely to give roses to his angry girlfriend in the future.

See also: LEARNING; SKINNER, B. F.

Bibliography

Chiesa, M. *Radical Behaviorism: The Philosophy and the Science.* Boston, MA: Authors Cooperative, 1994.

Iwata, Brian. "Negative Reinforcement in Applied Behavior Analysis: An Emerging Technology." *Journal of Applied Behavior Analysis* 20 (1987):361–378.

Martin, Gary, and Joseph Pear. *Behavior Modification: What It Is and How to Do It,* 6th edition. Upper Saddle River, NJ: Prentice Hall, 1996.

Skinner, B. F. *Science and Human Behavior.* New York: Macmillan, 1953.

Skinner, B. F. *Contingencies of Reinforcement: A Theoretical Analysis.* New York: Appleton-Century-Crofts, 1969.

Laurie A. Greco

RELIGION

From the earliest stages of birth through adolescence, religion can play a role in providing a framework for a child's life and world view. A strong religious background can help children and adults individually and together answer life's most significant questions, respond to difficult challenges, and make important decisions. Religion conveys a sense of the sacred or holy, often reflected in views of a god. Each religion consists of rituals, symbols, stories, values, and role models, which guide and shape a child's ways of being and acting in the world. Parents draw upon these different elements in passing on a religious tradition to their children, often sharing the responsibility for educating their children with a religious school and a religious institution such as a church, synagogue, or mosque.

Bibliography

Fowler, James W. *Stages of Faith: The Psychology of Human Development and the Quest for Meaning.* San Francisco: Harper and Row, 1981.

Goodman, Roberta Louis. "Faith Development: A Jewish View." In Audrey Friedman Marcus and Raymond Zwerin eds., *The New Jewish Teachers Handbook.* Denver: ARE Publishers, 1994.

Roberta Louis Goodman

REPRODUCTIVE TECHNOLOGIES

Reproductive technologies encompass a group of clinical laboratory procedures involving the extracorporeal (occurring outside the body) manipulation of gametes (eggs and sperm) and developing embryos to assist in the achievement of fertilization, implantation, and pregnancy. Common procedures to assist fertilization include: artificial insemination, in which sperm are physically introduced into the vagina or uterus to facilitate fertilization in vivo (within the body); in vitro fertilization, in which eggs are combined with sperm outside of the body; intracytoplasmic sperm insertion, in which individual sperm are physically introduced into individual eggs; and in vitro maturation, in which immature eggs are allowed to mature appropriately in vitro prior to fertilization. Procedures to assist implantation include: embryo transfer, in which developing embryos are placed physically into the uterus; and assisted hatching, in which the protective shell surrounding the developing embryo is compromised to allow the embryo to escape and implant. Embryo cryopreservation involves procedures that permit the storage of embryos at extremely cold temperatures to maintain viability for subsequent intrauterine transfers.

See also: ARTIFICIAL INSEMINATION; SURROGATE MOTHERING

Bibliography

Keel, Brooks A., Jeffrey V. May, and Christopher J. De Jonge, eds. *Handbook of the Assisted Reproduction Laboratory.* Boca Raton, FL: CRC Press, 2000.

Kempers, Robert D., Jean Cohen, Arthur F. Haney, and J. Benjamin Younger, eds. *Fertility and Reproductive Medicine.* Proceedings of the XVI World Congress on Fertility and Sterility, October 1998. Amsterdam: Elsevier Science, 1998.

New York State Task Force on Life and the Law, Health Education Services. *Assisted Reproductive Technologies: Analysis and Recommendations for Public Policy.* Albany, 1998.

Jeffrey V. May

RESILIENCY

Resilience is a descriptive name given to unexpectedly positive outcomes in the face of negative predictors for child development. The unexpectedness of the outcomes appears to have influenced at least three of the major researchers in the field. While tracking children of drug-addicted women in London, Michael Rutter is reported to have doubted his study when he found that at least one-fourth of the children seemed healthy and capable. When Norman Garmezy studied the children of severely depressed women and found that some of the children seemed healthy, he also doubted his own diagnosis of the mothers. Other re-

search of pathologies led him in the direction of studying the attributes of competence in children. Yet another researcher drawn into the "why not" question was Emmy Werner, known for her longitudinal study of native Hawaiians born in 1955. The study originally focused on the vulnerability of children exposed to several serious risk factors. When one-third of the children successfully coped with the risk factors, however, she changed the focus to look at the roots of resiliency.

How Resiliency Works

Resiliency is the result of a complex interaction between risk factors and protective factors. A closer look at the risk factors reveals three main categories. One category includes life events that tend to trigger disorders; such events include catastrophes, natural disasters, and other traumatic circumstances. Another category is chronic adversity in the home or neighborhood, which predisposes the child to vulnerability; included in this category are poverty, violence, substance abuse, poor prenatal care, and parental psychopathology. Third, the absence of protective factors is itself a risk factor. There is an interactive effect among the risk factors that tend to escalate their impact. Single stress factors do not have a critical impact but combinations do, and additional difficulties compound the impact of all existing risk factors.

There are several ways to look at resiliency and the impact of stress on adaptation. At times the risk factor is seen as having a strengthening or steeling effect, inoculating the individual as the challenge is confronted. In other models risks are not the only elements at work. There are also a wide variety of factors that protect children from the hazards and stresses they face. These protective factors function by increasing resistance to risk, making the stress more tolerable. They may also be seen to alleviate the effects of stress, thus fostering adaptation and competence. These factors can be organized into three groups: personal disposition, family environment, and outside support systems.

Growing Up Resilient

For the newborn, good health is a protective factor. Another is being an easy baby, that is, an active and good-natured baby with an easy temperament. These babies elicit a positive response from the primary caretaker. The age of the opposite sex parent is an influence but it differs: younger mothers for resilient males but older fathers for resilient females. Spacing is protective if there are two years or more between children, as is having four or fewer children in a family. Other protective factors important in infancy are the mother's workload and the number and type of alternative caretakers available to the mother. The amount of attention given by the mother or primary caretaker is yet another. In considering these factors it is easy to see the interaction among them.

As the child grows, the care-giving style of the parents comes to the forefront as a protective factor. This is a realm where self-esteem can be fostered and the child can acquire areas of skill and mastery. Socialization within the family works as a strengthening shield when trust, autonomy, initiative, and affective ties are encouraged. Families fostering resilience often include relatives with similar values and beliefs who are available to pitch in when the parent or parents are not present. Also common is either a brother, or sister, or close friend who takes care of the other children.

Interestingly, an intact family is not a consistent factor. A father's absence is not the determining factor in resilience—more important is the overall coping and functioning of the family, with low discord. An organized home environment that includes structure and monitoring does contribute to fostering resilience.

Other caring relationships develop in school. Along with extended family members, teachers are extremely important as confidants, mentors, or positive role models. During middle childhood and adolescence, encouraging school environments are a powerful factor. A school buffers stress when it provides a place to excel at something—to be recognized and feel good about one's self has a definite buffering effect. Schools that foster resilience have high expectations for children and provide them with opportunities for participation and contribution. In such empowering schools, students' self-esteem, self-efficacy, and positive values are reinforced. Additional supportive environments include churches, clubs, and organizations that furnish positive role models. Through these, caring adults lessen the effects of the risk factors. The community at large can also contribute, when it makes good public health care available and provides high levels of public safety.

Profile of a Resilient Child

Resilience happens when the factors protecting the child outweigh the hazards and handicaps. A child with roots of resiliency is an optimistic, well-balanced person. This child has effective problem-solving and communication skills. Resilient children are generally efficient at getting other people to help out and have at least an average IQ. They also most likely have an area of ability that is recognized and appreciated by those around them. A hopeful outlook

is observed, with faith in the future and a sense of meaning in life. A good sense of humor is common, as is efficient impulse control and social skills.

Resilient children do not run a straight line to success. In adolescence, resilient youths may report higher levels of anxiety and depression. Resilient youths rely more heavily on practical coping skills than well-adjusted adolescents who have not been exposed to multiple risks. Resilient youths also struggle more with self-esteem and may experiment with antisocial or illegal activities, although this is not a predictor of similar later activities in adulthood.

There is a temptation to think of resilient children as super-kids who are invincible and stand up well under stress. After all, they can be identified as high risk due to their being poor or coming from families with a history of violence, crime, or substance abuse. They may come from a large family, with parents who have a minimal education or even mental health problems. Maybe they were even born with some congenital disease. Yet somehow, protective factors are also in place and they are beating the odds. Showing signs of being well-liked, well-adjusted, functioning children, it is no wonder they seem "survivors." One researcher described resilient people as a "checkerboard of scars and strengths."

Resilience-Based Programs

A resilience-based approach is already being used in many youth development, school improvement, and health-risk behavior prevention programs. Some programs have risk-focused strategies, such as the health program that seeks to reduce the exposure to threat. Others focus on improving the number or quality of resources available. Yet others seek to mobilize basic human adaptation strategies such as supporting cultural traditions, fostering secure relationships, or teaching effective coping strategies. Programs exist that include all three types of strategies.

In the early twenty-first century, research was evolving from the identification of the traits of resilience to resilience as a dynamic developmental process. The latter research was seeking to understand the precise nature of the interaction of resilience and risk factors in order to improve health, social, and academic outcomes. In providing a framework for the programs mentioned, it is considered the responsibility of adults to provide the external protective factors or assets while fostering the internal resilience traits of young people. The basic external assets include caring relationships, high expectations, and meaningful participation in home, school, and community. The internal assets encompass social competence, autonomy and sense of self, and sense of meaning and purpose.

The study of resilience holds the key to helping strengthen children's chances of succeeding in spite of many obstacles. The good news is that the past is not a prison, survivors exist who escaped and beat the odds. Their strengths can be identified along with strategies and processes to enhance the developmental process. Resilience can be cultivated.

See also: PERSONALITY DEVELOPMENT; STRESS

Bibliography

Glanz, Meyer, and Jeanette Johnson, eds. *Resilience and Development: Positive Life Adaptations.* New York: Klewer Academic/ Plenum, 1999.

ResilienceNet. "Information for Helping Children and Families Overcome Adversities." A collaboration of Assist International and ERIC Clearinghouse on Elementary and Early Childhood Education [web site], 2000. Available from http:// resilnet.uiuc.edu; INTERNET.

Werner, Emily, and Ruth Smith. *Overcoming the Odds: High-Risk Children from Birth to Adulthood.* Ithaca, NY: Cornell University Press, 1992.

Sandra K. Sloop

RESPIRATORY DISTRESS SYNDROME

Respiratory distress syndrome (RDS) is a disorder of lung function frequently affecting premature infants. Infants born at less than thirty-two weeks gestation are at the highest risk. RDS is caused by the inability of immature lungs to produce sufficient amounts of the chemical surfactant. Without surfactant, the small air sacks of the lungs collapse, resulting in poor exchange of oxygen and respiratory distress. RDS may be severe enough to cause respiratory failure and the need for support with a ventilator. Generally, RDS lasts three to five days; infants with mild cases recover quickly. Sicker infants may require long-term respiratory support and can develop chronic lung disease. RDS may be prevented and treated with the administration of surfactant into the lungs of at-risk or affected newborns. Preventing premature birth and treating pregnant women with steroid therapy prior to a premature birth decreases the chances of immature lungs and RDS. However, RDS remains a leading cause of death for premature infants.

Bibliography

Linden, Dana, Emma Paroli, and Mia Doron. *Preemies: The Essential Guide for Parents of Premature Babies.* New York: Pocket Books, 2000.

Spafford, P. S. "Use of Natural Surfactants to Prevent and Treat Respiratory Distress Syndrome." *Seminars in Perinatology* 17, no. 4 (1993):285–294.

Taeusch, H William, and Roberta Ballard. *Avery's Diseases of the Newborn.* Philadelphia: W. B. Saunders, 1998.

Diane D. Marshall

RETENTION

Retention, sometimes called flunking, is the practice of having a child repeat a grade in school to help the child acquire the academic and social skills needed for success in later grades. Most research, however, has found that simply repeating the same grade is not very effective. Although children who are retained often perform better during their second year in the same grade, their gains usually shrink or disappear in subsequent years. Moreover, children who are retained are more likely to develop a bad attitude toward school and are more likely to drop out of school than nonretained children with similar levels of poor achievement.

Since the mid-1990s, public policies against social promotion (i.e., advancing children to the next grade despite poor achievement, to keep them with children of the same age) have spurred the development of programs to help struggling children avoid retention. The same programs, such as extra tutoring, summer school, and increased use of classroom aides, could also help retained children gain more from their experience.

See also: MILESTONES OF DEVELOPMENT

Bibliography

Karweit, Nancy L. "Grade Retention: Prevalence, Timing, and Effects." In the Johns Hopkins University CRESPAR [web site]. Baltimore, Maryland, 1998. Available from http:// www.csos.jhu.edu/crespar/reports/report33chapt1.htm; INTERNET.

Riley, Richard W., Marshall S. Smith, and Terry K. Peterson. "Taking Responsibility for Ending Social Promotion: A Guide for Educators and State and Local Leaders." In the U.S. Department of Education [web site]. Washington, DC, 1999. Available from http://www.ed.gov/pubs/socialpromotion/title.html; INTERNET.

Shepard, Lorrie A., and Mary L. Smith. *Flunking Grades: Research and Policies on Retention.* London: Falmer Press, 1989.

Pamela P. Hufnagel

RH DISEASE

Rhesus disease (or Rh disease) is caused when Rh-positive red blood cells from a fetus enter the maternal circulation of an Rh-negative woman. This usually happens at the time of delivery, but it can occur at other times during pregnancy, such as spontaneous miscarriage or abortion. These cells are recognized as foreign to the mother's immune system, and antibodies are formed to destroy them. In the next pregnancy, these antibodies can cross the placenta and cause anemia (low blood count) in the developing fetus. Rhesus-immune globulin is administered routinely at seven months in pregnancy and after delivery in Rh-negative women. Although 99 percent effective in preventing Rh disease, reports from the 1990s indicate that 1 to 6 infants per 1,000 live births have evidence of the effects of Rh disease. Pregnant women with an antibody concentration of greater than 1:16 are monitored with serial ultrasounds and amniocenteses to measure possible destruction of fetal blood. In some cases, the fetus can be given red blood cells while still in the womb; this is done through an intrauterine transfusion.

See also: INFANT MORTALITY; PREMATURE INFANTS; PRENATAL DEVELOPMENT

Bibliography

Chavez, Gilberto, Joseph Mulinare, and Larry Edmonds. "Epidemiology of Rh Hemolytic Disease of the Newborn in the United States." *Journal of the American Medical Association* 265 (1991):3270–3274.

"Prevention of RhD Alloimmunization." *American College of Obsetricians and Gynecologists Practice Bulletin* 4 (1999).

Ventura, Stephanie, Joyce Martin, Sally Curtin, and T. J. Mathews. "Births: Final Data for 1997." *National Vital Statistics Reports* 47 (1999):1–96.

Kenneth J. Moise Jr.

Acording to Jean-Jacques Rousseau, childhood is a distinct and precious period of life, functioning according to its own laws and developmental stages. (AP/Wide World Photos)

ROUSSEAU, JEAN-JACQUES (1712–1778)

Jean-Jacques Rousseau, a Genevan by birth, was a major contributor to modern political and educational theory and practice; he also set in motion what is known as the romantic movement in art, music, and literature. Shortly after Rousseau's birth on June 28, 1712, his mother died, leaving the child-rearing duties to the father, who shared his enthusiasm for books with his son but who otherwise provided little support. At the age of ten Rousseau was apprenticed to an engraver, but before the terms of the contract were fulfilled, he fled. At sixteen, abandoned by his father, he found himself in the home of the twenty-nine-year-old Madame de Warens, ostensibly to receive religious instruction. They became intimate friends and lovers. In 1745 Rousseau met Thérèse Levasseur, an uneducated washerwoman, who became his mistress and eventually his wife, but not before giving birth to five children, each of which was placed in a foundling home.

Rousseau was variously employed as tutor, secretary, and music copyist, but he valued his independence too much to be harnessed to a conventional career. In 1750 Rousseau found his true calling as a writer with his prize-winning essay, "A Discourse on the Arts and Sciences." His opera, *The Village Soothsayer* (1752), added to his reputation. There followed a series of original works for which Rousseau is best known today: *A Discourse on the Origins of Inequality* (1755); *Julie, or the New Eloise* (1761); *Émile, or On Education* and *The Social Contract* (1762); and *Confessions* (1771). His last work, *Reveries of a Solitary Walker,* was completed shortly before his death on July 2, 1778.

Three key ideas are central to Rousseau's view of children and their development. First, to an age known as the Age of Reason, which put its faith in science and technology, Rousseau preached instead the primacy of feeling and sensation and the centrality of matters of the heart. Second, against the prevailing doctrine of original sin, Rousseau proclaimed the basic goodness of human nature and the innocence of childhood. Third, Rousseau took issue with the notion that children were but imperfect adults. In Rousseau's view, depicted in *Émile,* childhood is a distinct and precious period of life, functioning according to its own laws and developmental stages. The persuasiveness of Rousseau's ideas has significantly influenced contemporary approaches to children and their development.

Bibliography

Cranston, Maurice. *Jean-Jacques: The Early Life and Work of Jean-Jacques Rousseau, 1712–1754.* Chicago: University of Chicago Press, 1991.

Cranston, Maurice. *The Noble Savage: Jean-Jacques Rousseau, 1754–1762.* Chicago: University of Chicago Press, 1991.

Cranston, Maurice. *The Solitary Self: Jean-Jacques Rousseau in Exile and Adversity.* Chicago: University of Chicago Press, 1997.

Dent, N. J. H. *Rousseau: An Introduction to his Psychological, Social, and Political Theory.* New York: Basil Blackwell, 1989.

Wokler, Robert. *Rousseau.* Oxford, Eng.: Oxford University Press, 1995.

Publications by Rousseau

Rousseau, Jean-Jacques. *Émile, or On Education,* translated by Allan Bloom. New York: Basic, 1979.

Jim Hillesheim

RUBELLA

Rubella is the clinical manifestation of infection caused by the rubella virus, which was first isolated in 1962. The timing of infection before or after birth determines the two principal clinical syndromes. Infection in the postnatal period produces a relatively mild disease that is primarily notable for an erythematous rash (a rash caused by capillary congestion) and swollen lymph nodes. Infection during pregnancy can result in specific fetal anomalies defining the congenital rubella syndrome.

In postnatal infection (also known as German measles), the rash of rubella first appears on the face and spreads to the rest of the body. The rash consists of combined flat and raised (maculopapular) erythematous lesions that typically resolve after several days. A low-grade fever may be present. Swollen lymph nodes, particularly of the head and neck, have been commonly reported. Cough, sore throat, and headache may precede or accompany the appearance of rash. Complications of rubella infection in the postnatal period include joint complaints (arthritis and arthralgia), central nervous system infection (encephalitis), and a decrease in platelet number (thrombocytopenia). Joint complaints are more common in females than males and more frequent in older age groups (i.e., adolescents and adults).

Congenital rubella syndrome refers to specific birth defects caused by infection of the fetus with the rubella virus. Since the 1940s, it has been known that rubella infection in a pregnant woman could have adverse effects on the fetus. The risk to the fetus of developing congenital rubella syndrome is greatest when infection occurs early in the pregnancy. In congenital rubella syndrome, defects typically affect the eyes, ears, brain, and heart.

Between 1962 and 1965, an epidemic of rubella occurred in the United States. In 1964 alone, an estimated twenty to thirty thousand cases of congenital rubella syndrome occurred. A vaccine against rubella was licensed in the United States in 1969. Universal immunization against rubella has resulted in dramatic declines in both postnatal rubella and congenital rubella syndrome of over 97 percent. Between 1997 and 1999, only 792 cases of laboratory-confirmed rubella and 24 cases of congenital rubella syndrome were reported in the United States. The National Notifiable Diseases Surveillance System along with the National Congenital Rubella Syndrome Registry monitor the number of cases of congenital rubella syndrome.

At the start of the twenty-first century, cases of postnatal rubella and the congenital rubella syndrome occurred primarily because of lapses in vaccination. Prevention of congenital rubella syndrome requires that immunization rates remain high in order to prevent the spread of rubella in the community. Vaccination is aimed at children and at women of reproductive age who were not vaccinated as children. Children receive a first dose of rubella-containing vaccine (combined with mumps and measles vaccines as the MMR) at one year of age and a second dose between four and six years of age. In the United States, infants with congenital rubella syndrome are often born to mothers who emigrated from countries that do not routinely immunize against rubella. Because of this, women of reproductive age should be screened for immunity against the rubella virus (i.e., tested for the presence of antibodies against rubella, which indicates protection) during premarital and prenatal health-care visits.

See also: BIRTH DEFECTS; IMMUNIZATION; PRENATAL DEVELOPMENT

Bibliography

Centers for Disease Control and Prevention. "Measles, Rubella, and Congenital Rubella Syndrome—United States and Mexico, 1997–1999." *Morbidity and Mortality Weekly Report* 49 (2000):1048–1050, 1059.

Cherry, James D. "Rubella Virus." In Ralph D. Feigin and James D. Cherry eds., *Textbook of Pediatric Infectious Diseases.* Philadelphia: Saunders, 1998.

Parkman, P. D. "Making Vaccination Policy: The Experience with Rubella." *Clinical Infectious Diseases,* supplement 2 (1999):140–146.

Alan Uba

RURAL CHILDREN

The delivery of rural mental health services focuses on understanding and responding to emotional and behavioral needs of children in the 2,303 "rural" communities that, according to the United States Census Bureau, have fewer than 2,500 residents. The proportion of the rural population involved with farming has decreased markedly over the past fifty years, leading the young and better educated to migrate to urban settings. Also, more disabled persons tend to migrate to centers where more specialized services are available. As a result, the rural population is older, less educated, socially conservative, and living longer than its urban counterpart. Diagnostically, this trend appears linked to heightened levels of affective and alcohol-related disorders. Understaffed and geographically stretched providers of health services must overcome resistance to acknowledging emotional disorders, seeking treatment, and complying with interventions for children. Rural providers tend to be general practitioners who themselves experience isolation, as increasing demands for services and a constant need to overcome stigma are the norm. As a result, rural children may receive diagnoses and treatment only after emotional problems have become more advanced.

See also: POVERTY

Bibliography

U.S. Department of Health and Human Services. *Mental Health: A Report of the Surgeon General.* Rockville, MD: U.S. Department of Health and Human Services, Center for Mental Health Services, National Institutes of Health, National Mental Health Institute, 1999.

Raymond P. Lorion
Michael Blank

S

SCHIZOPHRENIA

See: MENTAL DISORDERS

SCHOLASTIC APTITUDE TEST

The Scholastic Aptitude Test (SAT) is a standardized college admission test, consisting of a verbal portion and a mathematics portion, that was developed by the Educational Testing Service of Princeton, New Jersey. Verbal reasoning is examined by the test taker's ability to correctly analyze and complete analogies, sentence completion problems, and reading comprehension passages. Mathematical reasoning is tested through the completion of multiple-choice items covering areas such as algebra and geometry, as well as questions that require the student to produce original answers. With possible scores ranging from 200 to 800 on each section, individual scores are based on a comparison of the student's performance and the performance of students taking the test in the past, such that the average score is approximately 500 for each section. Students traditionally take the SAT in eleventh or twelfth grade as a part of their college admission portfolio. While colleges and universities have traditionally used SAT scores to predict student success, some critics argue that the test is biased against certain racial, ethnic, and economic groups, and have advocated its exclusion from the admissions process.

See also: STANDARDIZED TESTING

Bibliography

Educational Testing Service. "Frequently Asked Questions and Answers." In the College Board [web site]. Princeton, New Jersey, 2001. Available from http://www.collegeboard.com/sat/html/students/faq.html; INTERNET.

University of California. "UC and the SAT." In the University of California [web site]. Berkeley, California, 2001. Available from http://www.ucop.edu/ucophome/commserv/sat/welcome.html; INTERNET.

Scott Weckerly

SCHOOL VOUCHERS

Under most education systems, government funding is allocated to state-run schools that enjoy the exclusive right to offer public education services. School vouchers are an alternative funding mechanism in which parents receive a voucher that can be redeemed at any state-run or independent school of their choice. According to economists ranging from the eighteenth century's Adam Smith to contemporary Nobel laureate Milton Friedman, parental choice, competition between schools, and other market forces improve educational quality and lower costs for all families.

The states of Maine and Vermont have had small-scale voucher programs operating since the 1800s, but attention in the early twenty-first century was focused on more recent systems such as the one serving Milwaukee, Wisconsin. Critics argue that vouchers violate the separation of church and state (because parents can use them at private schools run by religious organizations), and that they fail to serve the most needy and difficult to educate. Others caution that existing programs are too limited to offer the benefits of a true education marketplace. Defenders point to court rulings and mounting experimental evidence to rebut these charges.

See also: CLASS SIZE; HOME SCHOOLING

Bibliography

Coulson, Andrew J. *Market Education: The Unknown History.* New York: Transaction Books, 1999.

Henig, Jeffrey R. *Rethinking School Choice: Limits of the Market Metaphor.* Princeton, NJ: Princeton University Press, 1994.

Levin, Henry M. *Privatizing Education: Can the School Marketplace Deliver Freedom of Choice, Efficiency, Equity, and Social Cohesion?* Boulder, CO: Westview Press, 2001.

Lieberman, Myron. *Privatization and Educational Choice.* New York: St. Martin's Press, 1989.

Merrifield, John. *The School Choice Wars.* Lanham, MD: Scarecrow Education, 2001.

Andrew Coulson

SELF-CONCEPT

The self-concept is the accumulation of knowledge about the self, such as beliefs regarding personality traits, physical characteristics, abilities, values, goals, and roles. Beginning in infancy, children acquire and organize information about themselves as a way to enable them to understand the relation between the self and their social world. This developmental process is a direct consequence of children's emerging cognitive skills and their social relationships with both family and peers. During early childhood, children's self-concepts are less differentiated and are centered on concrete characteristics, such as physical attributes, possessions, and skills. During middle childhood, the self-concept becomes more integrated and differentiated as the child engages in social comparison and more clearly perceives the self as consisting of internal, psychological characteristics. Throughout later childhood and adolescence, the self-concept becomes more abstract, complex, and hierarchically organized into cognitive mental representations or self-schemas, which direct the processing of self-relevant information.

See also: PERSONALITY DEVELOPMENT

Bibliography

Damon, William, and Daniel Hart. *Self-Understanding in Childhood and Adolescence.* New York: Cambridge University Press, 1988.

Harter, Susan. "The Development of Self-Representations." In *Handbook of Child Psychology,* Vol. 3: *Social, Emotional, and Personality Development,* 5th edition, edited by William Damon and Nancy Eisenberg. New York: John Wiley and Sons, 1998.

Lewis, Michael. "Social Knowledge and Social Development." *Merrill-Palmer Quarterly* 36 (1990):93–116.

Jeannette M. Alvarez

SELF-FULFILLING PROPHECY

The term self-fulfilling prophecy most often refers to a phenomenon where students perform to a level consistent with their teachers' preconceived expectations for them. In a classic study conducted in 1968, researchers told elementary school teachers that some of their students had been identified as having marked potential for intellectual growth. In fact, however, the designated students had been selected randomly. Eight months later, the students who had been identified as intellectual "bloomers" showed greater gains on an Intelligence Quotient (IQ) test than other students in the school. This result became known as the Pygmalion effect, in reference to George Bernard Shaw's play by the same name, and underlies recommendations that teachers should hold high expectations for all students.

Teacher expectations can influence students' motivation and achievement in two ways. First, inaccurate judgments of a student's effort and ability may bias evaluation of that student's performance. Second, teachers tend to challenge, interact with, and praise students of whom they have higher expectations. Expectations that are too low can lead to decreases in motivation, engagement, and learning.

Bibliography

Rosenthal, Robert, and Lenore Jacobson. *Pygmalion in the Classroom: Teacher Expectation and Student Intellectual Development.* New York: Holt, Rinehart and Winston, 1968.

Stipek, Deborah. *Motivation to Learn: From Theory to Practice,* 3rd edition. Boston: Allyn and Bacon, 1998.

Lynley H. Anderman
Tierra M. Freeman

SELFISHNESS

Unlike the more commonly studied topic of egocentrism, which focuses on cognitive-developmental barriers to effective social functioning caused by young children's inability to appreciate others' perspectives, the concept of selfishness emphasizes motivational barriers to effective social behavior caused by an individual's unwillingness to balance self-enhancing and other-enhancing goals in situations calling for cooperation, sharing, or consideration for others. Indeed, the term selfishness is generally considered inappropriate for self-centered behavior that can be attributed to ability deficits. That is why this label is rarely used to describe the social behavior of infants and young toddlers who have not yet developed certain rudimentary social-cognitive and social-emotional capabilities. In contrast, as children approach adolescence, the failure to balance powerful self-interests (e.g., autonomy, material gain, emotional gratification, social superiority) with the interests of others can increasingly be attributed to weak integrative motives (e.g., lack of concern for others' welfare or norms of social responsibility).

See also: EGOCENTRISM; SELF-CONCEPT

Bibliography

Damon, William. *Greater Expectations: Overcoming the Culture of Indulgence in Our Homes and Schools.* New York: Free Press, 1996.

Eisenberg, Nancy, and Paul Mussen. *The Roots of Prosocial Behavior in Children.* New York: Cambridge University Press, 1989.

Ford, Martin. "Motivational Opportunities and Obstacles Associated with Social Responsibility and Caring Behavior in School Contexts." In J. Juvonen and K. Wentzel eds., *Social Motivation: Understanding Children's School Adjustment.* New York: Cambridge University Press, 1996.

Martin E. Ford

SENSORY DEVELOPMENT

Everything humans do involves using one or more senses. It is through the senses that infants discover the world. Without one's senses, the brain would be an eternal prisoner within the confinement of one's skull. Humans experience these sensations through interactions with the environment; interpreting the meaning of these sensations for actions is called sensory processing. When a child uses her senses to discover a new object, she creates a neuronal pathway in the brain. The more often she stimulates her senses from her environment, the more likely she is to create new neuronal pathways and strengthen old neuronal pathways in the brain.

Sensory development begins during gestation and continues throughout childhood. There are seven sensory processes: taste, smell, touch, hearing, seeing, body position sense (called proprioception), and movement sensations (called vestibular input). Below is a brief discussion of each sense, its purpose, and the stages of its development; how infants stimulate their senses; and why sensory stimulation is important for infants.

Touch

Several touch receptors make up the somatosensory system. The infant experiences the sense of touch by any direct contact to the skin. The sensory receptors for touch send messages to the brain, through neurons, concerning temperature, pain, and the texture and pressure of objects applied to the skin.

The somatosensory system begins to develop during gestation. The nervous system, which is the message carrier to the brain for the senses, begins to develop at the third week of gestation. At the ninth week of gestation the sensory nerves have developed and are touching the skin. By the twenty-second week of gestation, the fetus is sensitive to touch and temperature. At birth, the sense of touch can be observed through the infant's reflexes when it comes in contact with different stimuli. One example is the rooting response. This is when an infant will reflexively turn its head in the direction of a touch to its cheek.

It is important for adults to understand what types of touch stimulation a specific infant needs. For example, infants who fall asleep only when rocked and like to be cuddled may prefer firm pressure against the body. One way to apply this pressure is by swaddling infants. This firm pressure relaxes excited neurons that are sending messages back and forth from the surface of the skin to the brain. Some infants are content to lie or sit and play in one spot; this does not mean that they are not as curious as other infants, but that they can absorb only so much stimulation at one time. By contrast, other infants who are constantly exploring by reaching out to touch various objects and textures are more likely seeking stimulation.

Taste and Smell

Taste and smell are chemical senses; they process information by processing chemical changes in the air and in objects on the tongue. These are primitive sensory systems that are intimately involved with early developmental activities such as feeding, eating, and recognizing family members compared to strangers. In this way, these are protective senses; they enable the organism to survive, both through recognizing familiarity for safety purposes and by enabling the infant to identify food for nourishment.

The taste buds become apparent during the eighth week of gestation, and by the fourteenth week the taste sensation is formed. At birth, infants express positive and aversive facial responses to tastes. The sense of smell is apparent at birth as an infant begins to recognize and prefers its mother's scent. As infants begin to develop, it is important to observe their reaction to the different sensations of sweet, sour, bitter, and salty, as well as to textures, to know what they like or dislike.

Taste is a chemical sense that allows humans to process information through different sensations—such as sweet or salty—as well as textures. (Robert J. Huffman/Field Mark Publications)

Movement Sensations

The movement sensations, or vestibular system, is a sensory area that is not often discussed in literature but is important to development. The vestibular system involves one's balance and works in conjunction with other senses. The vestibular system is designed to answer questions that relate to the human body, such as "Which way is up?" and "Where am I going?" This is accomplished by measuring the position of the head through the combined efforts of the five sensory organs in the inner ear, a process that enables one to maintain one's balance.

During gestation, the vestibular system is immature but operating by the ninth week and continues to mature throughout gestation and after birth. The vestibular system is important for an infant to be able to hold its head steady when being held upright, sitting up, standing, and walking. It is easy to recognize when the vestibular system is sending different messages to the brain than what is actually taking place. Examples include infants falling over when sitting and falling down when walking. In these instances, the vestibular system is sending a different message to the infant's brain in relation to what is happening with its body.

Auditory System

The auditory system begins to develop next. Around the fifth week of gestation the ear begins to form, and by the twenty-fourth week of gestation all hearing structures are in place. By the end of gestation, the auditory system is reasonably mature and continues to develop throughout the first year after birth. Infants demonstrate this sense by turning their head or eyes toward a sound. Newborns are more likely to respond to higher frequencies than lower frequencies. Also, repetition and longer duration increase the likelihood of infants hearing and responding to a sound. Adults can encourage infant stimulation through musical toys that use repetitive sounds and higher pitched tones.

Visual System

The visual system begins to develop around the ninth and tenth week of gestation and continues developing until three years after birth. At birth, infants are able to detect motion, can focus on an object about eight inches away, are sensitive to brightness, and have red and green color vision. By the end of the second month, infants are able to track smooth pattern movements and begin to discriminate between colors. During the third month, infants are better able to focus on objects farther away and are beginning to develop depth perception, both of which continue to develop until age two or three. Many toy companies gear toys that have geometric shapes and are black and white for newborns, and toys that are brightly colored and have patterns for infants about three months and older. These toys encourage development as the infant's neuronal pathways are being established.

Body Position Sense

The seventh sense, body position sense, or proprioception, works in conjunction with other senses. Proprioception is the movement and position of the limbs and body in relation to space. Proprioceptors are located in muscles and joints and are triggered by bodily movements. Proprioceptors, combined with vision, the sense of touch, and input from the vestibular system, help infants reach such milestones as rolling over, crawling, and walking.

Sensory Systems in Concert

The sensory systems work in concert with each other to enable an infant to engage with the environment and gain control over the body and its capabilities. Consider a sensory explanation of what one might observe when watching a six-month-old infant playing ball using all seven senses. As he touches and hits the ball, the infant receives cues as to whether the ball is hard or soft, smooth or rough. He discovers the texture and taste using his tongue to lick the ball when it is near or in his mouth, as well as any odors by smelling the ball. The infant receives visual stimulation by the color of the ball and by watching it roll or bounce. The auditory system is triggered when a noise, such as a thud, ring, or squeak is made as the infant hits the surface of the ball, throws it, or shakes it. The vestibular system is activated as the infant is sitting up, maintaining his balance. Finally, the infant uses proprioception as he is moving his arms and legs in space while throwing, pushing, or hitting the ball and watching it with his eyes and maintaining his balance.

Adults can encourage sensory development in their infants by providing a safe and stimulating environment for discovery. Sensory exploration is important to infant development, specifically for establishing new neuronal pathways in the brain and strengthening already developed neuronal pathways.

See also: METHODS OF STUDYING CHILDREN; MILESTONES OF DEVELOPMENT

Bibliography

Coren, Stanley, Lawrence Ward, and James Enns. *Sensation and Perception*, 4th edition. Fort Worth: Harcourt Brace College, 1994.

Dunn, Winnie. "Sensory Dimensions of Performance." In C. Christiansen and C. Baum eds., *Occupational Therapy: Overcoming Human Performance Deficits*. Thorofare, NJ: Slack, 1991.

Kandel, Eric, James Schwartz, and Thomas Jessell. *Principles of Neural Science*, 4th edition. New York: McGraw-Hill, 2000.

Erin Nash Casler

SEPARATION ANXIETY

Separation anxiety is characterized by an intense emotional reaction on the part of a young child to the departure of a person with whom the child has established an emotional attachment. Signs of separation anxiety, such as crying when the caregiver prepares to leave, typically emerge around six to eight months when infants have formed a representation of their caretakers as reliable providers of comfort and security. Distress reactions peak around fourteen to twenty months at which time toddlers may follow or cling to

caregivers to prevent their departure. Although most children show signs of separation anxiety, the intensity of an individual child's distress varies depending on: (1) the availability of another caregiver with whom the child has a close bond; (2) the familiarity of the situation; (3) previous experience with the caretaker leaving; and (4) the child's sense of control over the situation. Gradually, separation anxiety becomes less intense and less frequent, diminishing by age two.

See also: ATTACHMENT; PARENT-CHILD RELATIONSHIPS; STRANGER ANXIETY

Bibliography

Bowlby, John. *Attachment and Loss*, Vol. 3: *Loss*. New York: Basic, 1980.

Becky Kochenderfer-Ladd

SEX AND GENDER DIFFERENCES

See: GENDER-ROLE DEVELOPMENT

SEX EDUCATION

Sex education usually refers to programs offered in schools, typically from grades five through twelve, that cover sexuality and reproduction. Sexuality refers to the quality or state of being sexual and includes all thoughts and behaviors that have to do with an individual as a sexual being. For example, bodily changes at puberty, decisions to engage in kissing, petting, or having sexual intercourse, and using or not using contraceptives can be included under the broad term "sexuality." Sex education programs are also called family life education, sexuality education, and reproductive health education. Sometimes sex education is offered in the form of human immunodeficiency virus (HIV) education. In 1999 more than 93 percent of all public high schools in the United States offered courses on sexuality or HIV. Sex education is not a required subject in all school districts, and programs can vary from an entire course on human sexuality to integration of information in biology, health education, physical education, and consumer and family science (home economics) classes. Many programs allow parents to choose whether or not they want their son or daughter to participate.

Originally, sex education was started in schools to teach students about physical and sexual maturation. Over the years the goals became decreasing the incidence of teen pregnancy, delaying the onset of sexual activity among teens, and decreasing the rates of sexually transmitted diseases (STDs) and HIV cases. Studies conducted from the 1980s to the early twenty-first century indicated that few sex education

The nature of sex education can vary widely from one school district to another. Programs can range from abstinence-based models to more controversial approaches, such as this 1991 high school condom "give away." (Rotolo/Gamma Liaison Network)

programs achieved these goals. Increase in reproductive knowledge did not necessarily lead to responsible decision making about sexual choices. Improving access to contraceptives did not decrease teen pregnancy or increase use of contraceptives. But there have been many things learned from both successful and unsuccessful programs as is discussed below.

Basically, sex education programs are divided into two approaches: abstinence-only and abstinence-based. Abstinence-only education focuses on abstinence (not having sexual intercourse) as the only choice for adolescents until marriage. Other birth-control measures are not taught. Abstinence-based education covers all birth-control methods with a greater emphasis on abstinence as the method of choice. Abstinence-only programs increased in number, comprising only 2 percent of all sex education programs in 1988 but 23 percent in 1999. There was increased federal and state funding for abstinence-until-marriage education as part of the 1996 federal welfare reform legislation.

Ninety-three percent of Americans support teaching sexuality education to high school students and 84 percent support sexuality education to middle/junior high school students. In spite of this support, sex education in schools is a controversial issue on federal, state, and local levels. The controversy surrounding abstinence-only versus abstinence-based programs centers around the belief that teaching students how to use birth-control methods will only encourage them to be sexually active. Politics plays a

part in which policies are adopted in school districts. The federal government increased funding for abstinence-only programs in the later 1990s. This, along with increased funding for HIV and AIDS prevention programs and for teen pregnancy prevention programs, has contributed to state and local trends toward encouraging abstinence-only programs. Additionally the conservatism of the administration of George W. Bush, along with the strength of religious conservatives in some areas of the country, has contributed to the growing number of abstinence-only programs in schools.

Research has thus far failed to support the claim that knowledge of birth-control methods actually increases sexual activity. There was a decrease in teenage sexual activity and adolescent pregnancy rates from 1991 to 1997. Sexual activity rose again, however, from 1997 to 1999. Abstinence accounts for about one-quarter of the decline in pregnancy, while three-quarters is due to better use of contraceptives, especially long-term methods. In a 1999 survey, the Centers for Disease Control and Prevention found that 65 percent of students have sexual intercourse before the end of high school. Adolescents are having sex at a younger age and are engaging in high-risk behaviors such as having multiple sex partners.

Topics included in sex education vary from program to program. Typically puberty is discussed, especially in the early adolescent years. Many programs also cover physiology, STDs, HIV/AIDS, pregnancy, and parenthood. Less frequently covered topics include pregnancy prevention information (except for abstinence), sources of family planning services, the most likely time for pregnancy to occur, abortion, and sexual orientation. These latter subjects are the basis for community-based controversy about sex education. As mentioned earlier, some people believe giving certain information teenagers will encourage their sexual activity, cause an increase in the abortion rate, or bring about more homosexuality.

In fact, in the late 1990s effective sex education programs were shown to delay adolescents' sexual activity and increase contraceptive use among adolescents who have sexual intercourse. From years of study of sex education programs, researchers have found that some programs are more successful than others in reducing sexual activity or increasing safe sexual practices. Sex education programs that are effective:

1. focus on reducing one or more sexual behaviors that lead to unintended pregnancy or HIV/STD infection;
2. use social learning theories that have been used by other health promotion programs that are successful;
3. give clear messages;
4. provide basic, accurate information about the risks of unprotected intercourse and ways to avoid unprotected intercourse;
5. include activities that address social pressures on sexual behaviors;
6. provide modeling and practice of communication, negotiation, and refusal skills;
7. use a variety of teaching methods to involve students and get them to personalize the information;
8. incorporate information appropriate to the age, sexual experience, and culture of the students;
9. last long enough to complete important activities adequately;
10. select teachers or peers who believe in the program and provide training for them.

Programs with these components can be effective with high-risk youth, that is, students who are most likely to use drugs and alcohol, be sexually active, and/or drop out of school.

It has also been found that the goals of reducing the rates of pregnancy and childbearing can also be reached by youth programs that address issues of poverty, unemployment, and school performance. Examples of these include the Youth Incentive Entitlement Employment Program, the Teen Outreach Program,

and the American Youth and Conservation Corps. The reasons for the positive impact of these programs are not fully known, but the programs do address factors that put adolescents at high risk for being sexually active such as poverty, lack of future orientation, problems at schools, social disorganization, and lack of feeling connected.

The future of sex education programs in the twenty-first century will depend on the national political climate and local community reactions. Although 86 percent of registered voters in a national survey agreed that sex education should be taught in the public schools, the political environment will certainly influence the future direction of sex education.

See also: ADOLESCENCE; SEXUAL ACTIVITY

Bibliography

Darroch, Jacqueline E., David J. Landry, and Susheela Singh. "Changing Emphases in Sexuality Education in U.S. Public Secondary Schools, 1988–1999." In the Alan Guttmacher Institute [web site]. New York, 2000. Available from http://www.agi-usa.org/pubs/journals/3220400.html; INTERNET.

Kirby, Douglas. "Reflections on Two Decades of Research on Teen Sexual Behavior and Pregnancy." *Journal of School Health* 69, no. 3 (1999):89–94.

"Trend toward Abstinence-Only Sex Ed Means Many U.S. Teenagers Are Not Getting Vital Messages about Contraception." In the Alan Guttmacher Institute [web site]. New York, 2000. Available from http://www.agi-usa.org/pubs/archives/newsrelease3205.html; INTERNET.

Wilson, S. N. "'Sexuality Education': Our Current Status, and an Agenda for 2010." In the Alan Guttmacher Institute [web site]. New York, 2000. Available from http://www.agi-usa.org/pubs/journals/3225200.html; INTERNET.

Jane L. Abraham

SEXUAL ACTIVITY

Sexuality is an aspect of human development across the lifespan. The rapid biological and psychosocial changes that occur during adolescence enhance the importance of sexuality during this critical period. During puberty, hormones increase adolescents' attraction to potential sexual partners and enables their bodies to reproduce. Psychosocial development enhances teens' abilities to negotiate sexual relationships and to realize that their physically mature bodies encourage adultlike interactions, including romantic relationships and a greater degree of autonomy from parents. This article reviews a number of adolescent sexual issues, including sexual activity, contraception, sexually transmitted infections (STIs), and reproduction. In addition, the issues of substance use, violence, and sexual orientation as related to adolescent sexual behavior are discussed.

Adolescent Sexual Behavior

Overall, fewer high school students are choosing to have sexual intercourse than in the past. The Alan Guttmacher Institute (AGI) reported in 1999 that one in five adolescents (ages fifteen to nineteen) had not had intercourse. Yet, in 1999, 49.9 percent of teens in grades nine through twelve reported ever having had sexual intercourse, a decline from 54.1 percent in 1991. According to the 1999 Youth Risk Behavior Survey (YRBS), produced by the Centers for Disease Control and Prevention (CDC), black students (71.2%) are about 50 percent more likely to be sexually experienced than Hispanic (54.1%) and white students (45.1%). Older students (grades eleven and twelve; 58.7%) were more likely to have had sex than those in ninth and tenth grades (42.7%). Among male and female students, 36.3 percent reported having had sex within the previous three months with higher percentages among black students (53%) and twelfth graders (50.6%).

More than 8 percent of adolescent students (grades nine through twelve) reported having had sexual intercourse before age thirteen. According to the 1999 YRBS, male students (12.2%) were almost three times as likely as female students (4.4%) to have had intercourse before age thirteen. Black students were the most likely to have had sex by that age (20.5%). Males in grades nine and ten also reported initiating sex earlier than their eleventh and twelfth grade peers.

Nationwide figures from the CDC show that 16.2 percent of students (grades nine through twelve) in 1999 reported having had four or more sexual partners, a decline from 18.7 percent in 1991. More male students (19.3%) reported multiple partners than female students (13.1%). Black students (34.4%) more frequently reported sex with multiple partners than Hispanic (16.6%) and white students (12.4%).

Underscoring the importance of contraception is the reality that teens experience a disproportionate share of STIs and unintended pregnancies. In the 1999 CDC survey, 58 percent of students in grades nine through twelve reported that they or their partner used a condom during last sexual intercourse. By gender, 65.5 percent of males and 50.7 percent of females reported condom use. Black students (70%) were more likely to report condom use than Hispanics (55.2%) and whites (55%). From 1991 to 1999, the percentage of teens (grades nine through twelve) that used a condom at last intercourse increased from 46.2 percent to 58 percent. Concerning oral contraception, only 16.2 percent of students reported use of the birth control pill before last sexual intercourse. Overall, white female students in grades eleven and twelve reported the highest use of oral contraception. Yet the 1995 National Survey of Adolescent Males revealed that even adolescents who have successfully used contraception do not use it consistently.

Consequences of Adolescent Sexual Behavior

One sexual encounter can lead to pregnancy or an individual's sexually transmitted infection. AGI finds that every time a teenage woman has sex she has a 1 percent risk of contracting human immunodeficiency virus (HIV), a 30 percent risk of contracting genital herpes, and a 50 percent risk of contracting gonorrhea. The U.S. Department of Health and Human Services (DHHS) reports that although adolescents (ages fifteen to nineteen) represent less than 16 percent of the population of reproductive age (ages fourteen to forty-four), youth account for almost 27 percent of new STI infections (4 million of 15 million new STIs). Based on the 1999 YRBS, female adolescents (ages fifteen to nineteen) had the highest rate of chlamydia (about 2,484 per 100,000) and gonorrhea infection (534 cases per 100,000) among all U.S. women (404.5 cases per 100,000 and 130 cases per 100,000, respectively).

Sherry Murphy reported that in the United States in 1998, HIV infection was the ninth leading cause of death among persons fifteen to twenty-four years of age. Using YRBS data, the CDC found that although the national number of acquired immunodeficiency syndrome (AIDS) cases diagnosed annually had declined, changes in infection rates among individuals aged thirteen to twenty-four had not followed the same downward trend. By 1999 more than 800 youth (ages thirteen to nineteen) had been diagnosed with AIDS. Adolescent females (64%) and black youth (56%) represented a greater proportion of those diagnosed. Sexually active teenagers face an increased risk for STIs because they often are unable or reluctant to obtain education, birth control, and services for infection screening and treatment.

Among the world's developed countries, the United States has one of the highest teen pregnancy rates—double the rate of France and nine times that of the Netherlands and Japan. In 1994 teenagers aged fifteen to eighteen experienced the highest percentage of unintended pregnancies (71.1%), more than twice that of people aged thirty to thirty-four (33%). According to 1999 YRBS data, 6.3 percent of all sexually active students reported a pregnancy or impregnation of a partner. Female students in grades eleven and twelve (8.1% and 13.8%, respectively) were significantly more likely to have been pregnant than females in lower grades (4.8%). By race, black stu-

TABLE 1

Adolescent Sexual Behaviors, 1999

GENDER	Ever had sexual intercourse			Currently sexually active[1]			First sex intercourse before age 13			≥4 sex partners during lifetime			Condom use at last sex[6]			Birth control pill use at last sex[6]			Pregnancy or got partner preg.			Alcohol or drug use at last sex[6]		
	F[2]	M[3]	T[4]	F	M	T	F	M	T	F	M	T	F	M	T	F	M	T	F	M	T	F	M	T
Race/Ethnicity																								
White[5]	44.8	45.4	45.1	34.7	31.3	33.0	3.5	7.5	5.5	12.7	12.1	12.4	47.6	63.0	55.0	25.9	15.7	21.0	5.8	3.0	4.3	21.5	33.7	27.4
Black[5]	66.9	75.7	71.2	50.3	55.8	53.0	11.4	29.9	20.5	21.3	48.1	34.4	64.5	75.3	70.0	11.9	3.4	7.7	14.1	12.7	13.4	9.3	26.6	18.1
Hispanic	45.5	62.9	54.1	34.0	38.5	36.3	4.4	14.2	9.2	10.5	23.0	16.6	43.0	66.1	55.2	10.5	5.4	7.8	6.2	6.6	6.4	14.4	30.0	22.5
Grade																								
9	32.5	44.5	38.6	24.0	29.1	26.6	5.5	17.7	11.7	7.9	15.6	11.8	63.1	69.5	66.6	12.8	11.3	12.0	4.8	4.2	4.5	20.0	30.0	25.6
10	42.6	51.1	46.8	32.0	33.9	33.0	5.1	13.9	9.4	10.1	21.4	15.6	55.3	70.0	62.6	12.8	5.9	9.3	4.9	5.5	5.2	17.7	28.7	23.1
11	53.8	51.4	52.5	39.5	35.4	37.5	4.5	7.8	6.2	15.1	19.4	17.3	50.0	69.3	59.2	18.4	11.6	15.3	8.1	3.7	5.9	20.0	38.2	28.6
12	65.8	63.9	64.9	53.0	48.1	50.6	2.1	7.6	4.8	20.6	20.6	20.6	41.1	55.9	47.9	31.4	17.3	24.9	13.8	6.7	10.3	17.0	27.9	22.0
TOTAL	47.7	52.2	49.9	36.3	36.2	36.3	4.4	12.2	8.3	13.1	19.3	16.2	50.7	65.5	58.0	20.4	11.8	16.2	7.6	5.0	6.3	18.5	31.2	24.8

[1] Respondent reported sexual intercourse during the three months prior to survey administration

[2] Female

[3] Male

[4] Total

[5] Non-Hispanic

[6] Among students who reported current sexual activity

SOURCE: Centers for Disease Control and Prevention, Youth Risk Behavior Survey, 1999

dents (13.4%) were significantly more likely than white students (4.3%) to have been pregnant or to have gotten someone pregnant. AGI found that between 1990 and 1996, the national teen pregnancy rate (among those age fifteen to age nineteen) declined 17 percent, from 117 pregnancies per 1,000 women to 97 per 1,000. By race, however, the figures were not as promising. During the same period, the national pregnancy rate for black teens (ages fifteen to nineteen) decreased from 224 pregnancies per 1,000 to 179 per 1,000, while the Hispanic rate basically stayed the same (163 per 1,000 in 1990; 165 per 1,000 in 1996).

In 1998, 12.3 percent of all U.S. births occurred to teens. This teen birthrate has been decreasing over time. Between 1991 and 1996, the teen birthrate decreased 12 percent, from 62.1 births per 1,000 women to 54.4 births per 1,000, as reported by AGI. Between 1986 and 1996, the proportion of teen pregnancies that ended in abortion fell 31 percent; the number of abortions attributed to adolescent women (ages fifteen to nineteen) declined from 42.3 per 1,000 women in 1986 to 29.2 per 1,000 in 1996. Abortion rates appear to be declining because fewer teens are becoming pregnant and fewer pregnant teens are terminating their pregnancy by abortion.

Other Adolescent Sexuality Issues

Adolescent substance use increases the likelihood of risky adolescent sexual behavior, including multi-

ple sexual partners and early initiation of sexual intercourse. Among students who reported current sexual activity in the YRBS, 24.8 percent had used alcohol or drugs at last sexual intercourse. Male students (31.2%) were more likely to have used such substances than females (18.5%). In examining the data by race, both white male (33.7%) and female students (21.5%) were more likely than Hispanic (male: 30%; female: 14.4%) and black students (male: 26.6%; female: 9.3%) to have combined alcohol or drugs with their last sexual experience.

Substance use has also been associated with sexual violence among adolescents. In 1998, of the almost half million cases of victim-reported rape, 43 percent of the victims reported the offender was under the influence of alcohol and/or drugs. Alcohol has been deemed the chief date-rape drug on U.S. college campuses.

The 1999 YRBS data revealed that 8.8 percent of American students (grades nine through twelve) had been forced to have sexual intercourse against their will. Female students (12.5%) were more than twice as likely to report that they had been victims of sexual aggression than male students (5.2%). By race, black (11.6%) and Hispanic students (10.5%) were more likely to report forced sexual intercourse than white students (6.7%).

A final adolescent sexuality issue that is often ignored is sexual orientation. In 1998 Robert Bidwell wrote that the prevalence of sexual minority youth (e.g., gay, lesbian, bisexual, transgender) was undetermined. Yet it is important to consider sexual orientation in relation to other sexual risk behaviors and adolescent health in general. Sexually active gay adolescents are at particular risk for HIV infection. In 1999, according to the CDC, 46 percent of reported HIV infections among adolescent males (ages thirteen to nineteen) were attributed to male-to-male sexual contact. In addition to medical risks, the DHHS found that lesbian, gay, and bisexual youth face discrimination, hatred, isolation, and an increased risk for suicide.

It is evident that adolescents can and do take a great number of sexual risks. Unprotected intercourse has the ability to create life (pregnancy) or to end life (HIV infection). Fortunately, researchers have found a number of relevant avenues of prevention. These include addressing factors related to neighborhoods (e.g., socioeconomic status, joblessness), peers (e.g., sexually active friends), families (e.g., family instability, single-parent households, sibling sexual activity), and individuals (e.g., academic motivation, depression). Adolescents certainly have much to gain through more comprehensive prevention efforts.

See also: ADOLESCENCE; SEX EDUCATION

Bibliography

Alan Guttmacher Institute. *Sex and America's Teenagers.* New York: Alan Guttmacher Institute, 1994.

Alan Guttmacher Institute. *Facts in Brief: Teen Sex and Pregnancy.* New York: Alan Guttmacher Institute, 1999.

Alan Guttmacher Institute. *Teenage Pregnancy: Overall Trends and State-by-State Information.* New York: Alan Guttmacher Institute, 1999.

Bidwell, Robert. "Sexual Orientation and Gender Identity." In Stanford Friedman, Martin Fisher, S. K. Schonberg, and E. M. Alderman eds., *Comprehensive Adolescent Health Care.* St. Louis, MO: Mosby Publishing Service, 1998.

Centers for Disease Control and Prevention. "Fact Sheet: Youth Risk Behavior Trends from CDC's 1991, 1993, 1995, 1997, and 1999 Youth Risk Behavior Surveys." In the Centers for Disease Control and Prevention [web site]. Atlanta, Georgia, 2000. Available from http://www.cdc.gov/nccdphp/dash/yrbs/trend.htm; INTERNET.

Centers for Disease Control and Prevention, Division of STD Prevention. *Sexually Transmitted Disease Surveillance, 1999.* Atlanta, GA: U.S. Department of Health and Human Services, 2000. Available from http://www.cdc.gov/nchstp/dstd/Stats_Trends/1999SurvRpt.htm; INTERNET.

Centers for Disease Control and Prevention, Division of HIV/AIDS Prevention. *Need for Sustained HIV Prevention among Men Who Have Sex with Men.* Atlanta, GA: U.S. Department of Health and Human Services, 2000. Available from http://www.cdc.gov/hiv/pubs/facts/msm.htm; INTERNET.

Centers for Disease Control and Prevention, Division of HIV/AIDS Prevention. *Young People at Risk: HIV/AIDS among America's Youth.* Atlanta, GA: U.S. Department of Health and Human

Services, 2000. Available from http://www.cdc.gov/hiv/pubs/facts/youth.htm; INTERNET.

Henshaw, Stanley. "Unintended Pregnancy in the United States." *Family Planning Perspectives* 30 (1998):24–29.

Murphy, Sherry. "Deaths: Final Data for 1998." *National Vital Statistics Report* 48, no. 11. Hyattsville, MD: U.S. Department of Health and Human Services, Centers for Disease Control and Prevention, National Center for Health Statistics, 2000. Available from http://www.cdc.gov/nchs/data/nvs48_11.pdf; INTERNET.

U.S. Department of Health and Human Services. *Report of the Secretary's Task Force on Youth Suicide.* Washington, DC: U.S. Department of Health and Human Services, 1989.

U.S. Department of Health and Human Services. *Healthy People 2010: Objective 25: Sexually Transmitted Diseases.* Washington, DC: U.S. Department of Health and Human Services, 2000.

Ventura, Stephanie, Joyce Martin, Sally Curtin, T. J. Matthews, and Melissa Park. "Births: Final Data for 1998." *National Vital Statistics Report* 48, no. 3. Hyattsville, MD: U.S. Department of Health and Human Services, Centers for Disease Control and Prevention, National Center for Health Statistics, 1998. Available from http://www.cdc.gov/nchs/data/nvs48_3.pdf; INTERNET.

Laurie L. Meschke
Elyse Chadwick

SHYNESS

When an infant or toddler is confronted with strangers, either adults or children, an initial reaction of reticence and withdrawal is generally accepted and understood. Being cautious with strangers, animal or human, served for millions of years as a built-in safety device and was advantageous for survival. But from age three or four onward, most parents in modern societies like to see their children overcome their natural inhibitory tendencies soon after being introduced to other people. Cultures differ in their acceptance of shyness. In the United States, having an outgoing personality is highly valued, and thus parents worry when their child is socially inhibited by temperament, fearful when confronted by strangers, says as little as possible when in the company of unfamiliar people, and prefers playing alone. In other cultures, such as in Sweden, shy, reserved behavior is preferred to bold, attention-getting behavior, and consequently shyness is seen as less of a problem. In both cultures however, when people who were shy as children become adults, they tend to marry a few years later than adults who were not shy in childhood.

See also: PERSONALITY DEVELOPMENT; SOCIAL DEVELOPMENT

Bibliography

Kerr, Margaret, William Lambert, and Daryl Bem. "Life Course Sequelae of Childhood Shyness in Sweden: Comparison with the United States." *Developmental Psychology* 32 (1995):1100–1105.

Rubin, K. H., and Jens B. Asendorpf, eds. *Social Withdrawal, Inhibition and Shyness*. Hillsdale, NJ: Lawrence Erlbaum, 1992.

Dolph Kohnstamm

SIBLINGS AND SIBLING RELATIONSHIPS

Although psychologists first began to study siblings and their relationships during the nineteenth century, it was not until the late twentieth century when they began to focus on the family related features of sibling relationships. Early research was devoted to examining the effects of siblings' age spacing and birth order. Scientists found, however, that these had little to do with children's emotional and social development. During the 1980s and 1990s, psychologists became more interested in the family as a unit. This encouraged them to study the ways in which brothers and sisters influence each other's development and their families' well-being, as well as the family's influence on sibling relationships.

Parents, as well as scientists, know that sibling relationships can either enhance or disrupt family harmony and child development. For a long time, parents have named conflict between siblings as one of the most common and persistent problems that they encounter in rearing their children. At the beginning of the twenty-first century, this issue is particularly important for several reasons. First, more parents are working full-time. Because of this, many siblings care for their younger brothers and sisters before and after school. If siblings in this situation fight frequently, the younger children are not likely to receive the kind of care that they need. Second, sibling relationships tend to remain the same throughout life. Brothers and sisters who get along well as children are likely to continue to have a positive relationship when they are adolescents and adults. On the other hand, sibling rivalry that started in childhood can continue well into adulthood and result in a distant relationship between the siblings. Given the extent to which siblings can support each other emotionally, it is important to understand the foundations of sibling relationship quality.

Individual Siblings' Temperaments

Personal characteristics of the children involved in a sibling relationship are important in determining the kind of relationship that they will have. One of the most thoroughly studied characteristics is temperament, which is defined as the style of behavior that a person uses when relating to other people or to the surrounding environment. It develops early in life, is at least partly determined by a person's genetic make-up, and remains essentially the same across the life-span. Although siblings share a considerable part of their genetic makeup, children in the same family can have quite different temperaments. Some children are calm and easygoing, whereas others are impatient and easily upset. Not surprisingly, easygoing children experience less conflict in their sibling relationships than impatient children do. When one sibling is easygoing and another is impatient, the kind of relationship that they have depends on which sibling has the easygoing temperament. Sibling relationships run more smoothly when the easygoing sibling is older than the impatient one, because older children usually take charge of the situation when they are with their younger siblings.

Skills That Siblings Learn from One Another

This taking charge helps both siblings develop important life skills. Children's development is enhanced when they interact with people who occupy a variety of roles. Observations of siblings' everyday behavior with one another have revealed that older siblings act as teachers, managers, and helpers when playing with their younger brothers and sisters, and the younger siblings assume the corresponding learner, managee, and helpee roles. In such situations, siblings learn not only about their own roles but also about the corresponding ones.

Cooperation and a general sense of goodwill between siblings certainly can enhance children's development. As in any close relationship, though, conflict is bound to arise. This conflict need not be damaging to the relationship. It can provide an opportunity for siblings to vent their emotions, express their feelings, and practice open communication. Both conflict and friendliness between siblings help children learn to consider other people's feelings, needs, and beliefs. Both kinds of behavior may be necessary to give children a variety of experiences in learning to deal with others. A balance of friendliness and conflict in sibling relationships can provide a unique opportunity for children to develop social and behavioral skills that will enable them to manage anger and disagreements and provide help and comfort to others. Learning these skills in their relationships with their siblings helps children form positive relationships with their friends and adjust well to the social demands that they encounter in school.

Parents' Guidance and Sibling Conflict

The ways in which parents handle their children's disagreements and quarrels is an important means through which they help siblings form positive

A balance between friendliness and conflict in sibling relationships can provide a unique opportunity for children to develop important social and behavioral skills. (Corbis)

relationships with one another. With young children, parents must usually intervene in siblings' arguments to prevent older siblings from taking advantage of younger ones. This intervention is most effective when parents talk with the children about the problem, discuss the children's feelings and needs, explain their own feelings about the issues, and enforce rules for the children's treatment of one another. For siblings in middle childhood and adolescence, parents' consistent enforcement of rules that emphasize equality and fairness helps siblings develop respect for one another as they work out their own disagreements. Conflict in sibling relationships also decreases when parents treat their children impartially and keep the discussion friendly when talking with their children about sibling relationship problems.

Sibling Relationships in the Family System

Siblings and the other members of the family are part of a system in which one person's behavior affects everyone else. Likewise, relationships between some family members can influence relationships between other members. For example, the relationship be-

tween a mother and father can affect the children's relationships with one another. Psychologists who study children's responses to conflict between their parents have found that the parents' anger at one another causes negative emotional reactions in the children, who often direct these reactions toward others. The result is often sibling relationships in which children exchange little positive behavior and much negative behavior. This, however, is not always the case. Some older siblings respond to their parents' fights by becoming more caring and kind toward their younger brothers and sisters, to protect them from the distress arising from the adults' conflict. Parents' individual problems can also affect sibling relationships by influencing individual children's emotional states. The unpleasant feelings that arise from dealing with a depressed or hostile parent may make it more difficult for children to behave pleasantly toward their brothers and sisters.

Psychologists have found that conflict between parents and parents' personal problems influence sibling relationships through parent-child relationships. If parents' problems lead them to behave in a hostile manner toward their children, sibling relationships will be disrupted. If parents do not become hostile, however, marital problems and parental depression are far less likely to affect sibling relationship quality. The same is true for parents' relationships with impatient children. Parents who are able to form positive relationships with such children, even though the children's temperaments make it difficult to deal with them, may be able to smooth out the problems these children experience in their sibling relationships. Children with difficult temperaments who experience positive relationships with their parents will learn how to treat others positively, including their siblings.

When parents' relationships with their children are not equally positive, though, sibling relationships can be affected negatively. Ever since Sigmund Freud formulated his theories about sibling rivalry, psychologists have found that discrepancies in parents' treatment of their children create negative feelings between siblings. This is particularly likely to happen when parents direct unequal amounts of intrusiveness, responsiveness, positive emotions, and negative emotions toward their children, and when they discipline one child more than another for the same behavior. Sensitive parenting, however, often requires that children in the same family be treated differently. Children of different ages have different needs related to their stages of development, and children with different temperaments need their parents to respond to them in ways that best suit the children's personalities. Treating siblings differently is most likely to affect their relationships negatively when the children interpret their parents' behavior as a sign that their parents are less concerned about them, or that they are less worthy of love, than their brothers and sisters. Children are less likely to draw such conclusions when parents give each child the attention and nurturing that he or she needs.

Conclusion

Sibling relationships are, in and of themselves, important as children relate to one another and influence the social world in which they grow and develop. The social and psychological skills that children gain through sibling interactions are also useful throughout their lives in a wide variety of other social relationships. Children's personalities can have positive or negative influences on the relationships that they develop with their siblings. Parents can also influence the nature of sibling relationships, both through direct guidance and through the types of relationships that they form with each other and with each of their children.

See also: BIRTH ORDER AND SPACING; SOCIAL
 DEVELOPMENT

Bibliography

Brody, Gene H., ed. *Sibling Relationships: Their Causes and Consequences.* Norwood, NJ: Ablex, 1996.

Brody, Gene H. "Sibling Relationship Quality: Its Causes and Consequences." *Annual Review of Psychology* 49 (1998):1–24.

Brody, Gene H., Zolinda Stoneman, and J. Kelly McCoy. "Contributions of Family Relationships and Child Temperaments to Longitudinal Variations in Sibling Relationship Quality and Sibling Relationship Styles." *Journal of Family Psychology* 8 (1994):274–286.

Brody, Gene H., Zolinda Stoneman, and J. Kelly McCoy. "Forecasting Sibling Relationships in Early Adolescence from Child Temperaments and Family Processes in Middle Childhood." *Child Development* 65 (1994):771–784.

Bronfenbrenner, Urie. *The Ecology of Human Development.* Cambridge, MA: Harvard University Press, 1979.

Cummings, E. Mark, and Donna Smith. "The Impact of Anger between Adults on Siblings' Emotions and Behavior." *Journal of Child Psychology and Psychiatry* 25 (1989):63–74.

Dunn, Judy, and Carol Kendrick. *Siblings: Love, Envy, and Understanding.* Cambridge, MA: Harvard University Press, 1979.

Hetherington, E. Mavis. "Parents, Children, and Siblings Six Years After Divorce." In Robert A. Hinde and Joan Stevenson-Hinde eds., *Relationships within Families: Mutual Influences.* New York: Oxford University Press, 1988.

Howe, Nina, and Hildy S. Ross. "Socialization, Perspective-Taking, and the Sibling Relationship." *Developmental Psychology* 26 (1990):160–165.

MacKinnon, Carol E. "An Observational Investigation of Sibling Interactions in Married and Divorced Families." *Developmental Psychology* 25 (1989):36–44.

Stocker, Clare, Judy Dunn, and Robert Plomin. "Sibling Relationships: Links with Child Temperament, Maternal Behavior, and Family Structure." *Child Development* 60 (1989):715–727.

Gene H. Brody
Eileen Neubaum-Carlan

SICKLE CELL ANEMIA

Sickle cell anemia is a genetic disease caused by a single recessive mutation in hemoglobin. Individuals who inherit this recessive gene from both parents exhibit symptoms, while those who inherit only one copy of the gene typically do not exhibit symptoms and are resistant to malaria. About 1 in 12 African Americans worldwide carry the trait, and about 1 in 400 have the disease. Sickling of red blood cells causes them to clump together and impedes the passage of red blood cells in the circulatory system. Painful vaso-occlusive crises are influenced by the frequency of other globin mutations, as well as psychological stress. Thus, many individuals have complications from the disease, whereas others are relatively healthy. The physical signs include slow growth, lethargy, jaundice, anemia, poor feeding, enlargement of liver and spleen, and delay in sexual maturation. Psychosocial symptoms include embarrassment, poor self-esteem, depression, and fear.

There is no cure, but there have been significant advances in life expectancy and treatment.

See also: GENOTYPE

Bibliography

Conyard, Shirley, Muthuswamy Krishnamurthy, and Harvey Dosik. "Psychological Aspects of Sickle-Cell Anemia in Adolescents." *Health and Social Work* vol. 5 (1980):20–26.

DeRoin, Dee Ann. "Sickle Cell Anemia." Written for Clinical Reference Systems, 1998, on NBCi [web site]. Available from http://br.nbci.com/lmoid/resource/0,566,-2770,00.html; INTERNET.

National Library of Medicine. "Sickle Cell Disease in Newborns and Infants: A Guide for Parents." In the Wellness Web [web site], 2001. Available from http://wellweb.com/index/qsickle.htm; INTERNET.

Kathryn S. Lemery

has an extensive lexicon but it also operates as a rule-governed, grammatical system. Most linguists now recognize ASL and other sign languages used in deaf communities as full and genuine languages.

See also: AMERICAN SIGN LANGUAGE; HEARING LOSS AND DEAFNESS

Bibliography

Bonvillian, John D. "Sign Language Development." In Martyn Barrett ed., *The Development of Language*. East Sussex, Eng.: Psychology Press, 1999.

Klima, Edward S., and Ursula Bellugi. *The Signs of Language*. Cambridge, MA: Harvard University Press, 1979.

Wilbur, Ronnie B. *American Sign Language: Linguistic and Applied Dimensions,* 2nd edition. Boston: College-Hill Press, 1987.

John D. Bonvillian

SIGN LANGUAGE

Sign languages are the principal means of communication among members of deaf communities, with most countries having their own distinct sign language. In the United States, American Sign Language (ASL) is the language typically used by persons who have grown up deaf. Sign languages have gained considerable attention outside of deaf communities through the use of signs to foster communication in minimally verbal hearing persons (e.g., children with autism) and with nonhuman primates.

For centuries, sign languages were viewed as primarily pantomimic—not true languages at all. This belief helped support the oral approach to deaf education, a strategy that eschewed signing and focused on speech. Oralists advised parents of deaf children to shun all forms of manual communication and to promote spoken language acquisition through speech training, hearing amplification, speech reading, and writing. Sadly, many young people failed to attain sufficient speech mastery through this approach. As a result, many schools for deaf students today embrace a total communication approach. In this approach, all avenues of communication, including signing, are used to foster deaf students' language skills.

The pioneering research of William Stokoe (1919–2000) did much to alter the view that sign languages were not true languages. Stokoe identified three aspects of sign formation that distinguish one ASL sign from another: the place where the sign is made, the configuration and orientation of the hands, and the hand and arm movement forming the sign. These sign formational aspects function in a manner similar to that of phonemes in spoken languages. Subsequent studies demonstrated that ASL not only

SINGLE-PARENT FAMILIES

Although the term "single-parent family" is a familiar one, upon careful examination, the precise definition of a single-parent family becomes less clear. Families are frequently (although not exclusively) identified on the basis of shared residential space and the presence of emotional bonds and support relationships among members. "Single parent" implies that a solo mother or father is responsible for the care of one or more children under the age of eighteen within such a family. For the purposes of this article, single-parent families will be defined according to these guidelines.

Such a definition, however, oversimplifies the diversity of circumstances that may define the lives of single-parent families. For example, single parents are usually fathers or mothers, but they are sometimes single grandparents raising grandchildren. Single parents may represent any of a variety of sexual orientations. They may be biological, adoptive, or foster parents. They may have arrived at their current life circumstances through divorce, separation, or death of a spouse, or may never have married at all. They may have become single parents during adolescence (often because of an unplanned pregnancy) or in early or middle adulthood (because of an unplanned pregnancy, through a deliberate decision to become a single parent, or because of a divorce, separation, or death of a spouse). In many cases, families classified as single parent by researchers or census takers actually involve a committed residential coparenting relationship, but one that is not legally recognized. Finally, many families progress through a variety of family structures over time (e.g., outside-of-marriage adolescent single parenthood, followed by marriage and subsequent postdivorce single parenthood). This diversity and fluidity among single-parent families is typically underrecognized in research and by the media.

The Prevalence of Single-Parent Families in America

It has been predicted that half of all American children born in the 1990s will spend some part of their childhood in single-parent homes. Figures available from the U.S. Bureau of the Census (which yielded all of the statistics presented here) indicate that the percent of American homes that were single parent in composition increased dramatically from 1970 (when 18.5% of homes were single parent) to 1999 (27.7%).

Such increases are accounted for by rising divorce rates (5.7% of first-time marriages ended in divorce in 1970, while 18.5% of such marriages ended in divorce in 1998) and an increase in the number of women who give birth to or adopt children outside of marital relationships. Women giving birth outside of marital relationships include adolescent mothers and increasing numbers of older, more affluent (and predominantly white) women, who have elected to become single parents through either out-of-marriage births or adoption. Such women are called single mothers by choice.

There are ethnic differences in the prevalence of single-parent families. In 1999 the rate of single-parent families among black families was 56 percent; among Hispanic families, 32 percent; and among white families, 20 percent. Higher rates of black single-parent families result from higher rates of out-of-marriage adolescent childbearing within this group and higher divorce rates among black women.

The Well-Being of Children Raised in Single-Parent Homes

When compared to their peers from traditional two-parent homes, children raised in single-parent homes are at risk for a number of less desirable outcomes. Such outcomes include both lower academic performance and a higher incidence of behavioral problems. It would be a mistake to conclude, however, that such negative outcomes were the direct consequence of the number of parents in the home or, as has been suggested on occasion, the absence of a father figure in a child's life. Instead, children are adversely affected by circumstances that co-occur with single-parent family configurations (such as economic disadvantage, residential instability, and interparental conflict) or are the consequence of such configurations (such as disrupted parenting). Such circumstances are not uniformly present in the lives of all single-parent families. Consequently, children from different types of single-parent families are at differential risk for adverse outcomes associated with their living arrangements.

A greater percentage of single-parent families (57.4% in 1999) than two-parent families (6.3%) live below the poverty line. The percentage of single-parent families below the poverty line is highest for adolescent single mothers and lowest for widowed mothers. In addition, a higher percentage of single mothers than single fathers lives below the poverty line. Economic disadvantage is linked with lower academic achievement and increased behavioral problems among children. Fewer economic resources are also linked with residential instability, which further contributes to children's academic and behavioral difficulties. Differences in well-being for children from single-parent families versus two-parent families typically disappear when differences in economic circumstances are taken into account.

Families that attain their single-parent status through marital dissolution are disproportionately more likely to experience both residential instability and higher rates of interparental conflict (both prior and subsequent to marital disruption). Children who are exposed to interparental conflict are more likely to experience difficulties with regard to psychological and behavioral adjustment and academic achievement. Again, once levels of interparental conflict are taken into account, differences in well-being for children from single-parent families versus two-parent families are reduced.

Finally, children from all family types are at risk when they experience parenting that is inadequate in terms of warmth, control, or monitoring. Less than optimal parenting is more likely to be observed in families that are experiencing economic stress and among adolescent mothers (although a large part of this association may be explained by the greater likelihood that adolescent single mothers will experience economic disadvantage). Psychologist Mavis Hetherington has found that the parenting skills of mothers tend to diminish in the years immediately following divorce, and children who are exposed to such disruptions in parenting experience concurrent psychological, behavioral, and academic difficulties. As mothers adjust to their new single-parent status, however, their parenting improves, as does their children's well-being.

Single Fathers Compared to Single Mothers

The overwhelming majority of single-parent families are headed by mothers (84% of all single-parent families in 1998), rather than fathers (16%). Still, the

Children in single-parent homes do well when they experience parenting that is adequate in terms of warmth, control, and monitoring. (Hurewitz Creative/Corbis)

number of single fathers has increased since the 1970s (9% of all single-parent homes were father-headed in 1970). The circumstances surrounding the single-parent status of men versus women differ. The greatest percentage of single fathers gained custody of children as the result of parental divorce. Single fathers are more likely to gain custody of children when mothers have either chosen not to retain custody or are perceived to be incompetent. Single fathers are more likely to have custody of older rather than younger children and of boys rather than girls. By and large, the challenges for single fathers and single mothers are similar and include the difficulties of combining parenting responsibilities and employment, and economic disadvantage. On average, single fathers have higher standards of living than do single mothers, which decreases potential stresses within the family. Yet single mothers have been reported to have warmer and more structured relationships with their children than do single fathers. Several studies have indicated that once economic factors are taken into account, children from single-mother families fare better than children from single-father families. Such differences may be accounted for by these parenting differences or by the afore-mentioned differences in the circumstances surrounding the father custody arrangement.

Conclusion

In summary, single-parent families increased in number and as a percentage of all families from the 1970s to the 1990s. Single-parent families represent a diverse group of parents raising children on their own through a diverse set of circumstances. To understand the ways in which being raised in a single-parent family affects the lives of children, it is necessary to consider the individual circumstances of families in regard to economic disadvantage, residential instability, parenting competencies, and interparental conflict.

See also: FATHERS; PARENTING; WORKING FAMILIES

Bibliography

Amato, Paul R. "Diversity within Single-Parent Families." In David H. Demo, Katherine R. Allen, and Mark A. Fine eds., *Handbook of Family Diversity*. New York: Oxford University Press, 2000.

Biblarz, Timothy J., and Adrian E. Raftery. "Family Structure, Educational Attainment, and Socioeconomic Success: Rethinking the 'Pathology of Matriarchy.'" *American Journal of Sociology* 105 (1999):321–365.

Heath, Terri, ed. "Single Mothers, Single Fathers." Special issue of *Journal of Family Issues* 20, no. 4 (1999).

Hetherington, Mavis, Martha Cox, and Roger Cox. "Effects of Divorce on Parents and Children." In Michael E. Lamb ed., *Nontraditional Families: Parenting and Child Development*. Hillsdale, NJ: Lawrence Erlbaum, 1982.

Weinraub, Marsha, and Marcy B. Gringlas. "Single Parenthood." In Marc H. Bornstein ed., *Handbook of Parenting*, Vol. 3: *Status and Social Conditions of Parenting*. Hillsdale, NJ: Lawrence Erlbaum, 1995.

Anne C. Fletcher

SKINNER, B. F. (1904–1990)

Burrhus Frederic (B. F.) Skinner was born in Susquehanna, Pennsylvania. His main contribution to the study of human and nonhuman behavior was to establish a psychology in which behavior is understood in scientific, naturalistic terms. For example, he explained behavior in terms of an ongoing stream of public and private events, not in terms of popular, cultural concepts such as ego, mind, or free will. Skinner's contributions were foundational to the field of behavior analysis.

Skinner received a B.S. in English from Hamilton College (New York) in 1926, failed in a brief literary career, and turned to psychology, receiving his Ph.D. from Harvard University in 1931. In groundbreaking research, he experimentally analyzed the "voluntary" behavior of individual organisms (rats), using equipment he himself designed and built (e.g., the operant chamber or "Skinner box"). Skinner's main interests were how behavior was learned and, once learned, how it was maintained. Skinner formalized, first, the principle of reinforcement, which states that behavior is learned because of its consequences (e.g., reinforcers), and, second, the concept of the contingencies of reinforcement. As for the latter, he discovered an important class of contingencies—schedules of reinforcement (e.g., the number of responses per reinforcer)—that maintained predictable patterns of behavior over time (e.g., high and low rates). The most representative presentation of Skinner's early research is *The Behavior of Organisms* (1938).

Although Skinner never conducted research with humans, he systematically interpreted human behavior in terms of the basic behavioral principles (e.g., *Science and Human Behavior*, 1953). His best known scholarly interpretation was *Verbal Behavior* (1957), which set off a debate about the role of mind and behavior in the analysis of language; the repercussions of the debate still linger. His more popular interpretations included *Walden Two* (1948) and *Beyond Freedom and Dignity* (1971), which addressed the human

The work of psychologist B.F. Skinner helped form the foundation for behavioral analysis studies. (Psychology Archives, University of Akron)

condition and how to improve it. Skinner rarely applied his psychology directly. This was undertaken by others, especially in the fields of developmental disabilities, education, and clinical psychology, who became known as applied behavior analysts and behavior therapists.

Skinner did, however, address topics in developmental psychology, mainly child rearing and education, and invented important apparatuses (e.g., teaching machines, the "air crib"—a controlled physical space for infants). In the 1950s and 1960s his principles, concepts, and theory were extended to child development by other behavior analysts, notably Donald Baer, Sidney Bijou, and Jacob Gewirtz.

See also: BEHAVIOR ANALYSIS

Bibliography

Bjork, Daniel W. *B. F. Skinner: A Life*. New York: Basic Books, 1993.

Nye, Robert D. *The Legacy of B. F. Skinner: Concepts and Perspectives, Controversies and Misunderstandings*. Pacific Grove, CA: Brooks/Cole, 1992.

Publications by Skinner

The Behavior of Organisms: An Experimental Analysis. New York: Appleton-Century-Crofts, 1938.

Walden Two. New York: Macmillan, 1948.

Science and Human Behavior. New York: The Free Press, 1953.

Verbal Behavior. New York: Appleton-Century-Crofts, 1957.

Beyond Freedom and Dignity. New York: Knopf, 1971.

Brian D. Midgley

Edward K. Morris

SLEEPING

Sleep is known to play an important role in the health and well-being of children. But sleeping, although restful, involves more than resting. Despite the peaceful appearance of the sleeping child, sleep is an active process with cycles of physiological arousal alternating between intense activity and profound tranquility.

Stages, States, and Cycles

Two sleep states have been identified: rapid eye movement (REM) sleep, and non-REM (NREM) sleep. REM sleep is a state of heightened arousal characterized by uneven breathing, heart rate, and blood pressure; intense electrical brain activity; loss of muscle tone; and darting eye movements. NREM sleep is marked by reduced brain activity; regular patterns of heart rate, breathing, and blood pressure; and general body quiescence.

For older children and adults, NREM sleep can be further differentiated into four progressively deeper levels, with stages three and four (also called delta or slow-wave sleep) representing the deepest levels. This slow-wave activity emerges at about three to six months, peaks during early childhood, and then decreases during adolescence.

Because infant sleep patterns do not approximate adult patterns until well into the first year, infant sleep states are described differently. Infants slip easily back and forth among several states of arousal that include three awake states (crying, waking activity, and quiet alertness), a transitional state (drowsiness), and two sleeping states (active and quiet sleep). Quiet sleep resembles NREM sleep in adults, but might include occasional startle movements or sucking. Active sleep, although similar to adult REM sleep, is characterized by much movement of the limbs, as well as twitching, smiling, and rapid eye movements beneath closed or partially closed lids. Brain wave patterns are highly similar to awake patterns.

Sleeping patterns are cyclical and are controlled by two biological "clocks." The first, which originates in the suprachiasmatic nucleus of the hypothalamus, controls daily cycles. Cycles develop before birth and can be detected in utero at about twenty weeks; as the clock matures, however, there is a gradual change from multiple cycles to a single daily pattern. The second clock, originating in the pons section of the brain stem, regulates the alternation between REM and NREM sleep. Here, too, maturational changes can be seen. Newborns typically fall first into REM sleep, whereas older children may not experience REM for three hours and the adult pattern (about ninety minutes after falling asleep) is not established until adolescence.

Functions of Sleep

Despite the fact that sleep is a dominant activity during the early years, surprisingly little is known about why humans sleep. Aside from general agreement that sleep has restorative functions, evidence linking sleep to various waking behaviors is largely circumstantial. Sleep appears to play a role in behavioral regulation and in emotional and cognitive functioning. (Irritability, overactivity, and decreased attention span have been associated with sleep disruptions in children.) Sleep may also facilitate the consolidation of memories and, in older children and adults, REM sleep is associated with dreaming.

Whether or not infants dream is not known; REM sleep, however, may be important to infants in other ways. Newborns spend approximately 50 percent of sleep time in REM, an impressive amount when compared to six-month-olds whose REM approximates that of adults (25–30% of sleeping time). Many researchers believe that the heightened activity occurring during REM sleep stimulates brain growth.

Measuring Sleep

Researchers use a variety of techniques to study sleep. These include parental reports, sleep diaries, direct observations, and videotaping, as well as more complicated techniques that involve recordings of heart rate, brain waves, eye and muscle activity, oxygen saturation, and airflow. Actigraphy (recording of movements via a small device worn on the arm or leg) is also used to record sleep patterns.

Developmental Trends in Sleep

Patterns of sleep and wakefulness undergo striking changes from infancy through adolescence, but within any given age group, there is great variability. Newborns do not sleep for long stretches. Instead, they experience about seven sleep periods daily, totaling about sixteen hours. Somewhere around three months, many infants begin to sleep for at least five continuous hours during the night. Like children and adults, infants awaken briefly a few times during the night but 70 percent of one-year-olds are able to soothe themselves back to sleep. Self-comforting techniques such as thumb sucking, face stroking, and body rocking are frequent. By one year, sleep time averages twelve hours distributed into a long sleep period at night and two daytime naps.

Across early childhood, daytime naps gradually disappear, resulting in decreased daily sleep. By age four, children sleep about eleven hours per day and many have given up napping. Not only do preschoolers sleep less than infants, they also fall asleep differently. Young children are often reluctant to go to sleep, and bedtime rituals may take on a predictable pattern with children who have been tucked in perhaps requesting a drink of water or another goodnight kiss. Children over the age of three are also more likely than younger children to depend on a favorite blanket or teddy bear to help them fall asleep.

By six to ten years of age, children are generally "good sleepers," sleeping soundly for about ten hours at night and staying alert during the day. But as they approach puberty, sleep patterns undergo further change. Studies in the United States, Europe, and elsewhere reveal an increasing tendency among adolescents to sleep less, to go to bed later, to develop different patterns of sleep on weekends and weeknights, and to report increased daytime sleepiness. But contrary to popular belief, adolescents do not necessarily need less sleep. Although optimal sleep time for adolescents is about nine hours per night, most adolescents average less than eight hours. This is unfortunate because inadequate sleep is associated with poor school performance, mood and behavioral problems, and increased risk for automobile accidents.

A study of school-age children in Israel showed that sleep habits identified in adolescents may be drifting down to younger ages. In addition, girls in the study slept more and moved less in sleep than boys, a finding that has also been observed in newborns. Overall, however, researchers have found relatively few gender differences in sleeping patterns.

Sleep Requirements

It is not clear how much sleep is optimal for children because most studies have been based on small samples. Until developmental norms are established for large representative samples of children and adolescents, parents may need to monitor their child's behavior. A child who has difficulty waking in the morning, or is consistently sleepy, irritable, and inattentive during the day, may not be getting enough sleep.

Sleep Disorders

Two general categories of sleep disorders are recognized. Dyssomnias are problems with the initiation or maintenance of sleep, or with sleep that is inefficient. These include common sleep timing problems such as frequent night wakings and difficulty falling asleep at night or difficulty waking in the morning. Dyssomnias also include relatively rare problems such as obstructive sleep apnea (associated with enlarged tonsils and adenoids) and narcolepsy (sudden daytime sleep attacks).

Parasomnias occur during sleep but are not associated with insomnia or excessive sleepiness. Common parasomnias in children include head banging or rocking (exhibited by about 58% of children) and nightmares (most commonly of being attacked, falling, or dying). Nightmares are not the same as the rarer sleep terrors, a disorder in which a child, although asleep, appears to be awake and terrified. In sleep terrors, the child is screaming and incoherent with a glassy-eyed stare, profuse sweating, and rapid heart rate and respirations. The child is difficult to rouse and calm, and in the morning retains no memory of the episode. Both nightmares and sleep terrors occur during the transition from NREM sleep to REM sleep. They generally resolve with age. Other parasomnias are teeth grinding (bruxism), sleepwalking, and sleep talking. Bed-wetting (enuresis) is also considered a parasomnia if it continues after the age of five in the absence of physical or psychiatric pathology.

Dreaming

Children's dreams have often been described as bizarre and fantastical in nature. Early theories of children's emotional development (e.g., psychoanalytic theory, which maintained that dreams are wish fulfillments) contributed to this view. But how dreams are studied may also play a role. Dreams reported after they occur may have been recalled because they were bizarre. David Foulkes showed in laboratory studies that if children were awakened during REM sleep and asked to describe their dreams, a different picture emerged. Although some dreams contained bizarre elements, children generally dreamed about familiar people, settings, and actions. In addition, dreams changed with age. It was not until about age eight or nine that dream reports began to include narratives that featured activity by dream characters with the self as a participant. Foulkes concluded that dreaming in children is linked to general intellectual development with dream construction dependent on abstract, representational thought.

In general, empirical research on children's dreams has been sparse. While knowledge of many aspects of sleeping in childhood has grown since the 1950s, relatively little is known about the intriguing topic of children's dreams.

See also: APNEA; MILESTONES OF DEVELOPMENT

Bibliography

Anders, Thomas F., and Lisa A. Eiben. "Pediatric Sleep Disorders: A Review of the Past Ten Years." *Journal of the American Academy of Child and Adolescent Psychiatry* 36, no. 1 (1997):9–20.

Carskadon, Mary A. "Patterns of Sleep and Sleepiness in Adolescents." *Pediatrician* 17 (1990):5–12.

Carskadon, Mary A., ed. *Encyclopedia of Sleep and Dreaming.* New York: Macmillan, 1993.

Foulkes, David. *Children's Dreams: Longitudinal Studies.* New York: Wiley, 1982.

Kahn, André, Bernard Dan, José Groswasser, Patricia Franco, and Martine Sottiaux. "Normal Sleep Architecture in Infants and Children." *Journal of Clinical Neurophysiology* 13, no. 3 (1996):184–197.

Mindell, Jodi A., Judith A. Owens, and Mary A. Carskadon. "Developmental Features of Sleep." *Child and Adolescent Psychiatric Clinics of North America* 8 (1999):695–725.

Sadeh, Avi, Amiram Raviv, and Reut Gruber. "Sleep Patterns and Sleep Disruptions in School-Age Children." *Developmental Psychology* 36 (2000):291–301.

Wolfson, Amy R., and Mary A. Carskadon. "Sleep Schedules and Daytime Functioning in Adolescents." *Child Development* 69 (1998):875–887.

Mabel L. Sgan
Beverly J. Roder

SMILING

While people often think of smiling as only an indication that a child might find something funny, it is actually one of the most important forms of social communication. Smiling appears within the first few weeks of life as a response to a human voice and becomes a full-fledged social smile at about three months of age. As a social behavior it encourages parents to interact with developing infants and thereby helps ensure the infant will be cared for as well as socialized into the culture, which the parents represent. In other words, it promotes bonding. Child development specialists have studied smiling and have found it to be a complex behavior that is integral to a child's healthy development. For example, the more infants smile, the more time their mothers spend with them. Children who do not smile early and often are not just unhappy. Rather, there is some other issue at hand that needs professional attention.

See also: PERSONALITY DEVELOPMENT; SOCIAL DEVELOPMENT

Bibliography

Bailey, Kimberly. "What's in a Smile?" [web site]. Available from http://bipolar.about.com/health/bipolar/library/weekly/aa000802a.htm?rnk=r8&terms=smiling; INTERNET.

Farris, Marinelam R. "Smiling of Male and Female Infants to Mother vs. Stranger at Two and Three Months of Age." *Psychological Reports* 87 (2000):723–728.

Neil J. Salkind

SOCIAL CLASS

Social class is a concept that has been discussed and argued about throughout the ages. Many different theories exist concerning a workable definition. The basis often used for describing social class comes from nineteenth-century German theorist Karl Marx. He believed in a three-class system consisting of capitalists, workers, and petty bourgeoisie. Since then, sociologists have provided new conceptualizations of social class. These conceptualizations include social class as more than just an economic measure. Many define social class as more of a social status, meaning people in a specific class share similar experiences, background, and position in society. Other factors that influence social class rankings are occupational prestige and general opinion of others in the community. The concept of social status from German sociologist Max Weber (1864–1920) is used by a number of American sociologists when explaining social class. Weber saw property, skills, and education all contributing to the concept of social class. His view is similar to and sometimes used interchangeably with socioeconomic status.

Classes are apparent in every large, complex society, such as the United States. In this type of society, roles are divided so that the group may function efficiently. Social classes continue to exist within society because people have learned how to live within them and have passed this knowledge on to the next generation. People, or families, often associate with those who are similar. They may have similar careers, incomes, and goals in life. By sticking together, people reinforce the presence of social classes. These classes extend across generations because social class is somewhat inherited. A middle-class family cannot give birth to an upper-class baby. The child is born into the social class of the parents. As the child grows, he will most likely form friendships with others similar to him, once again reinforcing the social class system.

Categories

Social classes may be described differently for each region of the country, but most observers would agree upon three general classes: upper, middle, and lower. Because of the broad nature of these categories, the three main classes are often split into six, more descriptive categories: upper-upper, lower-upper, upper-middle, lower-middle, upper-lower, and lower-lower. The additional classes help to discriminate who falls into which class, but there is still some ambiguity. The way in which each class is defined depends on the perspective one takes. Someone in upper-upper class may label upper-middle class people differently than someone in the lower-middle class would label them. Although definitions may differ, a generality in American class structure is the criteria required to gain the acceptance of a particular class. The process begins with money, which influences behavior and material goods, which in turn influences participation with the group, which finally leads to acceptance by the social class. This last aspect of acceptance is needed for an individual or family to "belong" to a certain social class.

Measurement

When measuring social class, which is often used simultaneously with socioeconomic status, the characteristics of the male father figure are most often used to represent the status of the children. This approach seems logical when assessing children from two-parent, intact families. The father figure approach may not always be an accurate portrayal of most families in society. With a high rate of divorced, stepparent, and single-parent, often female, families, looking at the father's income not only may be inaccurate but may sometimes be impossible. Therefore, when measuring the socioeconomic status of children it may be best to examine the characteristics of the person who heads the family whether that person is a male or a female. Since social class is about more than just money, researchers may want to consider other features besides the basic financial feature. Nonmaterial resources and social environment are factors that influence social class as well.

Income is the most recognized form of measuring social class or socioeconomic status, but it may not always be the best indicator. Children often do not know how much their parents make and adults are sometimes hesitant to answer. Some people take the "income question" very personally because of the stigma that often accompanies level of income. Nonmaterial resources also factor in determining class. This category contains information about education, including the highest degree attained and the highest grade in school completed. It is important to know the educational background of the parents when children are being studied because it helps provide insight into the kind of educational support the children receive at home, such as encouragement and help on homework. Social environment is the third suggested contributor for measuring social class or socioeconomic status. This refers to the environment around children, especially that of family structure.

Poverty is also associated with social class. The U.S. Bureau of the Census publishes yearly reports on the amount of income that constitutes the poverty threshold. In 2000 the poverty threshold for a family of four was $17,761. Along with poverty information, it is also helpful to know the occupation of the parents. Information regarding occupational prestige scores is available from the Census Bureau and the U.S. Department of Labor.

Effects

The effects of social class can be felt anywhere. Almost every aspect of society is influenced in some manner by social class. The magazines one reads, the television shows one watches, and the clothes a person buys affect social class. School, work, religious, and home lives are also linked to the influence of social classes. Schools and the workplace are greatly influenced by social class. The look of employment is changing because workers can no longer expect to work their way up through a company. Many companies look outside of the company for people with the right educational background instead of hiring from within. This greatly limits the potential for advancement of workers who lack formal education. For people to move up in the social hierarchy, they must obtain higher education. Instead of spending years at a lower level position, people are spending more time in school and moving directly into management. Thus the change in the workplace influences the educational system.

Social class also plays a part in families, especially in the development of children. Youth are often taught to fit in with their social class, thus developing a personality that correlates with social status. Educational systems can help or hinder the prospect of social mobility. Although many teachers work hard to ensure against favoritism, this is not always possible, partly because of the stigma attached to social class. Teachers may give special opportunities to certain groups. They may also wrongly anticipate the knowledge or potential of specific classes of children. For example, children from high-class families are sometimes viewed as being more intelligent than those from lower social classes. Sometimes more attention will be invested in the children who have more knowledge attributed to them. The idea that upper-class children are smarter has been passed down throughout the ages, but there is no conclusive evidence to back it up. In fact, lower-class children do not have lower IQ scores than upper-class children as previously suspected. This means there must be a glitch in the system somewhere because a greater number more of high social class children are going on to college and getting jobs with advancement potential while lower-class children are in positions without hope of advancement. The lack of money in lower social classes may contribute to the problem, but the presence of social class in the educational system may be contributory as well. Thus it is vital to study how the effects of social class are entering into classrooms and helping to determine the future of children.

Social class is often used when researching children. Despite its frequent use, it is difficult to use social class as a reliable variable. The lack of a consistent definition is one of the reasons. Each researcher uses a different definition of social class, thus making it difficult to study it as a variable across research. Not only does the definition of social class cause a problem, so does measuring it. Once again there is not a specific assessment process used universally. The reporting of social class contributes to the lack of reliability as well. Since social class is often self-reported, it is difficult to assure the accuracy of the information collected. Even if the data is accurate, social classes are not the same in each region or city. What constitutes upper class in one location may be middle class in another. The lack of consistency involved in researching social class accounts for the difficulty in using it as a reliable variable.

Conclusion

Although it may be difficult to get a universal definition for social class and the inconsistency surrounding it is abundant, there are reasons to continue researching this concept. Social class has a large impact on how children are raised, how they are schooled, and even whom they are friends with. For these reasons, it is important that social class be taken into account when studying child development, as long as the limitations are understood.

See also: POVERTY; RACIAL DIFFERENCES; SOCIAL DEVELOPMENT

Bibliography

Argyle, Michael. *The Psychology of Social Class.* London: Routledge, 1994.

Brantlinger, Ellen A. *The Politics of Social Class in Secondary School: Views of Affluent and Impoverished Youth.* New York: Teachers College Press, 1993.

Levine, Rhonda F. *Social Class and Stratification: Classical Statements and Theoretical Debates.* Lanham, MD: Rowman and Littlefield, 1998.

Warner, W. Lloyd, Marchia Meeker, and Kenneth Eells. *Social Class in America: A Manual of Procedure for the Measurement of Social Status.* Chicago: Science Research Associates, 1949.

Linda K. McCampbell

SOCIAL COGNITION

The study of social cognition focuses on how people think about and make sense of themselves, others, and the world of social affairs. This cognitive approach highlights the active role that people play in organizing, interpreting, and "constructing" the social world within which they live and interact. Conceptual structures or schemas—internalized knowledge or information—are assumed to play a central role. These structures, derived from previous experiences, are the basis for mental representations (re-presenting objects and events not physically present), and they serve as a frame of reference for interpreting, storing, processing, and using information and experiences. The development of well-differentiated and integrated cognitive structures enables people to select, process, and use social information in a relatively efficient, automatic fashion. Nevertheless, as a comprehensive research review by Richard E. Nisbett and Lee Ross demonstrated, automatic processing increases the likelihood that novel social information may be distorted and biased in a manner consistent with a person's existing conceptual structures. For instance, social stereotyping involves automatically categorizing an individual in terms of a conceptual structure that represents a particular group of people.

Developmental Changes in Social-Cognitive Reasoning

A primary process in social-cognitive development involves distinguishing oneself from others. Infants express a sense of self-recognition and a rudimentary understanding that they exist independent from their mothers (e.g., showing distress when separated) within the first year of life. Subsequently, children come to understand that people are active agents with "minds" who think, plan, have intentions, pretend, may hold erroneous beliefs, are influenced by inner desires and motives, and the like.

Considerable research on social-cognitive development has been inspired and informed by the theory of cognitive development formulated by the Swiss psychologist Jean Piaget (1896–1980). Drawing on Piagetian theory and research, John H. Flavell in 1985 identified a number of developmental trends in social cognition. One deals with a change in reasoning from surface to depth. Young children deal with social situations in a superficial, concrete fashion. They focus almost exclusively on salient, external features of others, and are easily deceived by impressions and appearances. Adolescents are better able to go beyond surface appearances and make inferences about peoples' psychological motives and states. A second theme involves the development of metacognition. "Meta" means to transcend; metacognition involves thinking about thoughts and cognitive processes. Not only does this promote introspective self-awareness and self-examination, it also enhances the ability to effectively plan, monitor, and regulate personal behavior.

Developmental improvement in abstract and hypothetical thinking enables children to begin to think in terms of general personality traits and characteristics as well as environmental factors when explaining actions. Hypothetical reasoners are able to go beyond concrete reality and consider how social situations and institutions ideally should be. A decline in egocentrism is a fourth theme identified by Flavell. Egocentrism is a failure to accommodate or adjust a cognitive structure to fit new information; the experience or information is distorted to fit an existing structure. Assume a preschool child is facing you and you raise your left hand. If asked which hand you raised, the child would say, "your right." Preschool children are able to mentally internalize and represent the relevant information—assimilate it to a cognitive schema—but they remain bound quite closely to their own perceptual perspective. Correctly answering the question, however, requires a child to "mentally rotate" the representation 180 degrees. More to the point, the relational nature of many social concepts requires children to mentally take different standpoints. The number of sisters in a family depends on whose point of view is taken: If Tommy has two sisters, Nicole and Kelly, how many sisters does Kelly have? Egocentric children have difficulty shifting their thinking from the perspective of Tommy (two) and that of Kelly (one).

David Elkind noted in a 1980 article that egocentrism may take different forms during development. Adolescents, for instance, may be tied to their own conceptual perspective. They can think about the thoughts of others as well as their own (metacognition). They may mistakenly assume, however, that others are thinking about the same ideas and concepts as they themselves are. Technically speaking, they are egocentric in that they assimilate the thoughts of others to their own cognitive structures. Imagine two teenagers preoccupied with their own feelings and anxieties. Even though they may be talking past each other in a social exchange, each may infer that the other has the same understanding as her own. Elkind explains that adolescents' egocentric thoughts about the thinking of others constitute an imaginary audience that adolescents strategically play to and become self-conscious about: Being self-constructed, it "knows" every blemish and shortcoming the adolescent frets about.

These themes provide a general summary of the major aspects of social-cognitive development. It should be mentioned that late-twentieth-century neo-Piagetian researchers, such as Robbie Case, suggested that the process may be more continuous and complex, with information-processing factors—such as cognitive resources, memory functions, and automatization of strategies—playing an influential role.

Reasoning within Different Social Domains

Social reasoning is influenced by the particular social activity, institution, interpersonal problem, or group being thought about. Research, however, has demonstrated developmental consistencies in social-cognition across various social topics and domains. Representative examples of three lines of research follow: perceptions of others, moral reasoning, and thinking about political issues.

Perceptions of Others

How people conceptualize and understand others is a primary consideration in social reasoning. William Livesley and Dennis Bromley asked children of different ages to describe familiar people. The youngest children offered behavioristic, egocentric accounts, highlighting physical features (e.g., tall, wears glasses) and stereotypical qualities (e.g., nice, mean). Older children were more likely to go beyond external, surface features and use more inner psychological qualities (i.e., traits, abilities, interests). By adolescence, attempts to explain rather than simply describe other people were offered. Adolescents went beyond categorical assertions and attempted to justify and qualify their claims about others. People were seen not only as possessing unique blends of traits but also as being contradictory (e.g., happy people can have dark moods).

Moral Reasoning

According to Lawrence Kohlberg, reasoning about moral situations and dilemmas also proceeds along the developmental progression described above. Children of different ages were given a series of moral dilemmas designed to determine how they construed, understood, and attempted to resolve moral conflicts. (For instance, after exhausting all legal possibilities, should the husband of a dying wife steal an excessively expensive drug that would cure her?) The youngest children focused on external factors such as the presence or absence of punishment and made judgments on an egocentric, self-centered basis: How will he benefit or suffer in the here and now? ("He should steal it, it's his wife; he needs her.") Older children began to internalize and represent moral rules, values, and standards. These children, however, conformed to the conventions in a rigid, inflexible, absolutist manner: It is a question of duty or obedience to the rules of the social order. ("He has to obey the law!") Kohlberg found that some adolescents, by no means all, displayed a post-conventional approach to moral reasoning and attempted to go beyond the concrete rules and laws and deal with more abstract principles and rights. These adolescents acknowledged the relativist nature of any given law yet emphasized the need for contractual agreements to protect the rights of individuals.

Political Reasoning

A similar progression in reasoning about political institutions has been identified. Joseph Adelson and Robert O'Neil asked participants to imagine that a large group of disgruntled people decided to move to a deserted island to establish a new government. They were then questioned about the pros and cons of various social rules, authority structures, and political processes. Young children thought about political processes in concrete, egocentric, absolutist terms. They focused on specific, present-oriented activities and self-serving issues. For example, they were willing to grant authorities unrestricted, unilateral power to ensure nothing went wrong. Adolescents were more likely to shift away from a concrete, authoritarian stance; some expressed concern about the rights of individuals as well as the collective welfare. They were more idealistic and they reasoned in a relativistic manner, attempting to envision possibilities and scenarios that might occur in the future. For instance, they considered the need to limit governmental powers because of the possibility that some leaders might become capricious or corrupt.

Conclusion

From these examples one might get the impression that social-cognitive reasoning in adolescence and beyond should be complex, logical, and rational. Research reviewed by Susan Fiske and Shelly Taylor demonstrates, however, that because of limited cognitive resources and motivational biases people may frequently become "cognitive misers" who expend as little deliberate mental effort as possible in social situations. As a result, social cognition in adulthood may be marked by numerous distortions and biases, especially when reasoning is automatic rather than intentional and conscious. For instance, adults often reason in a self-serving fashion (they take more credit than they deserve for successes, and vice versa when it comes to setbacks), overgeneralize and stereotype in social situations, and engage in biased searches for information that will confirm existing expectations.

See also: SOCIAL DEVELOPMENT

Bibliography

Adelson, Joseph J., and Robert P. O'Neil. "Growth of Political Ideas in Adolescence: The Sense of Community." *Journal of Personality and Social Psychology* 4 (1966):295–306.

Case, Robbie. *Intellectual Development: Birth to Adulthood.* New York: Academic Press, 1985.

Elkind, David. "Strategic Interactions in Early Adolescence." In Joseph J. Adelson ed., *Handbook of Adolescent Psychology*. New York: Wiley, 1980.

Fiske, Susan T., and Shelly E. Taylor. *Social Cognition,* 2nd edition. New York: McGraw Hill, 1991.

Flavell, John H. *Cognitive Development,* 2nd edition. Englewood Cliffs, NJ: Prentice-Hall, 1985.

Flavell, John H., and Patricia H. Miller. "Social Cognition." In William Damon ed., *Handbook of Child Psychology,* 5th edition, Vol. 2: *Cognition, Perception, and Language,* edited by Deanna Kuhn and Robert S. Siegler. New York: Wiley, 1998.

Kohlberg, Lawrence. "Moral Stages and Moralization: The Cognitive-Developmental Approach." In Thomas Lickona ed., *Moral Development and Behavior: Theory, Research, and Social Issues.* New York: Holt, Rinehart, and Winston, 1976.

Livesley, William J., and Dennis B. Bromley. *Person Perception in Childhood and Adolescence.* London: Wiley, 1973.

Nisbett, Richard E., and Lee Ross. *Human Inference: Strategies and Shortcomings of Social Judgment.* Englewood Cliffs, NJ: Prentice-Hall, 1980.

Michael D. Berzonsky

SOCIAL DEVELOPMENT

By nature, people are social creatures—it is evolutionarily adaptive that, during all periods of life, interaction with others occurs. From infancy to adulthood, however, the way in which the interaction takes place, as well as with whom, changes. During infancy, interactions occur primarily with parents and family members. During childhood the frequency of interactions with same-age peers increases, though parental support is still important. Adolescence marks the increased centrality of interactions with peers and the emergence of romantic relationships. Both of these events forecast the progression into adulthood, during which individuals become autonomous from parents and often begin families of their own.

The developing person is affected by multiple socializing forces, including biological, parental, peer, and cultural factors. The results of these forces include one's views of the self and others, one's personality, and one's behaviors (e.g., aggression) when interacting with others. Moreover, these socializing forces and the complex array of outcomes show both normative trends and interindividual variability across development.

Biological and familial factors are important socializing agents in infancy, while peer relationships become more important in childhood and adolescence. This is not meant to imply, however, that other socializing agents play no role during certain periods of development. Similarly, the focus in this article on particular topics during only one period of development should not be taken to mean that these topics are not salient aspects of social development during other periods.

Infancy and Preschool: An Emphasis on Biology and Parenting

Even before a child is born, much has occurred in terms of social development. Genetic and prenatal biological factors play a large, persistent role in determining later social behavior. After birth, parents and other family members are the key socializing agents of the preschooler's development.

By studying monozygotic (i.e., identical) and dizygotic (i.e., fraternal) twins, as well as adopted siblings, behavioral geneticists have concluded that genetic factors account for 40 to 70 percent of the variability in certain characteristics. Sandra Scarr described how genes contribute directly to children's characteristics and indirectly influence social development through three processes: passive effects, in which children's genes are related to the parenting of their biological parents; evocative effects, by which children elicit certain types of behaviors from others; and active effects, through which children seek out environments that best fit their genetic makeups.

Although it is clear that genetic makeup plays a crucial role in social development, it is less certain exactly what biological mechanisms account for this influence. Certainly, many innate factors affecting social behavior are common to nearly all infants. For instance, infants will cry when distressed, and they actively attend to and seek attention from caregivers. Infants have differences, however, in their genetic makeups, and researchers have searched for ways in which these differences are expressed. Perhaps the most widely studied aspect is temperament, which consists of several components related to emotional reactivity and regulation. Infants described as having "difficult temperament" are those who are fussy, become upset easily, and are not easily soothed. Other infants are considered inhibited—they are timid and fearful, become easily upset by intense stimuli, and are also not easily soothed. Infants with "easy temperaments" are outgoing and respond positively to social stimuli (i.e., do not show excessive fear), and are easily soothed when they do become upset. Temperament is rather stable across time and exerts powerful eliciting effects on parents' and other family members' behaviors toward the child across development.

Parenting practices also play a crucial role in infants' social development. Certain parenting practices, such as feeding and protecting, are necessary for the infant's survival and are performed by nearly all parents. Parents vary considerably, however, in the degree to which they are permissive, are warm or rejecting, and are consistent in the form of discipline they apply. Many of these factors are incorporated into Diana Baumrind's three typologies of parenting: authoritative parenting, in which parents are warm and responsive to the child, yet place limits on the child's behavior; authoritarian parenting, in which parents place strict limits on the child's behavior, with violation of these limits harshly punished, and in which there is little parental warmth; and permissive parenting, in which parents are warm and nurturing without placing limits on the child's behavior. There is ample evidence that authoritative parenting is associated with positive social development, whereas authoritarian and permissive parenting are associated with negative development (e.g., conflictual relationships).

These parenting styles are influential throughout development, but may be especially important in the formation of attachment security in infancy. According to John Bowlby, nearly all infants form an attachment bond to their caregivers, and this bond is evolutionarily adaptive in promoting a balance between exploring the world and seeking safety with the caregiver. Mary Ainsworth demonstrated that there are important differences in infants' attachment styles, depending on the history of caregiver availability and responsiveness. Secure attachment is related to a history of warm and consistent parenting, avoidant attachment to parental negativity and rejection, and resistant attachment to inconsistent parenting. These attachment styles influence social behavior not only with parents, but also with siblings and peers. Securely attached children are the most socially competent with others, while avoidant toddlers are hostile and aggressive, and resistant toddlers are socially inhibited in their interactions with others.

These early influences likely exert influence on later social behavior through the formation of social cognitions, or mental representations of the social world. Albert Bandura described three classes of social cognitions that guide social behavior: self-efficacy is the perception of one's ability to enact a behavior (e.g., "how well am I able to maintain a conversation with a peer?"); outcome expectations are the expected consequences if one enacts a behavior (e.g., "if I converse with this boy will he want to be my friend?"); and outcome values are the values placed on the expected outcomes (e.g., "do I want him as my friend?"). The behaviors of parents and other family members shape these early social cognitions, which are further shaped by interactions with peers in childhood.

Childhood and Early Adolescence: An Emphasis on Peers

Children spend much of their time with similar-age peers. Meaningful interactions between peers begin in infancy—infants direct and respond to each other's smiles and vocalizations. As preschoolers age, their interactions with peers become increasingly complex, progressing from solitary play to onlooking (child watches others but does not join), parallel play (child plays beside but not with others), associative play (child plays with others), and cooperative play (child plays with others using coordinated roles). As children age they engage in more of the latter forms of play, though the former types of play are not entirely abandoned. Moreover, the topics of play change during childhood, from constructive play (e.g., block building) to dramatic play to games with formal rules.

This increased complexity of play is paralleled by increased complexity of social behavior. This, as well as the increased time spent with peers, has led psychologists to focus much of their attention on the peer relations of children and adolescents. Topics of study include children's acceptance or rejection by the larger peer group, friendships, and aggressive and prosocial behaviors toward others. Researchers have also examined gender differences in each of these aspects of development.

The terms "popularity" and "rejection" are used to describe the degree to which children are liked or disliked by their peers. Certain types of behavior are consistently related to group acceptance throughout childhood. Popular children, who are liked by many of their peers and disliked by few, tend to be sociable, often do well in school, and are generally not aggressive. Rejected children, on the other hand, who are disliked by many of their peers and liked by few, are often aggressive or withdrawn, have poor social skills, and do not do well in school. Despite these generalizations about popular and rejected children, however, these groups are heterogeneous (i.e., children in these groups vary in their characteristics and/or behaviors). Some children are rejected because their aggressive, disruptive behavior is annoying to peers, while other children are rejected because they are timid and socially anxious. Children may be popular by behaving prosocially, being academically competent, and being leaders, while other popular children are aggressive or delinquent, but are seen as "cool" by their peers. Importantly, behaviors that are valued or devalued by peers are dependent upon group norms, which are influenced by surrounding societal and cultural values.

Whereas friendships of younger children center around concrete reciprocities (e.g., sharing toys) and those of older children emphasize self-disclosure and loyalty, friendships at all ages are based on mutual liking, reciprocity of positive behavior, and seeking the other's presence. Both having friends and the quali-

ties of friendships are predictors of later development. For instance, having friends during childhood predicts having romantic relationships in adolescence and feelings of self-worth in adulthood, having supportive friendships predicts academic achievement during school transitions, and having protective friends can reduce peer victimization. It must be remembered that friendships are defined by two members, and the characteristics that make a child a desirable friend to one peer may not make that child desirable to another. Children tend to have friends who are similar to them in demographic characteristics (e.g., age, race, gender), academic abilities (e.g., intelligence, school achievement), and social behavior (e.g., aggression, attachment styles). Not only do children tend to form friendships with those who are similar, but friends also tend to influence each other such that they become more similar over time.

The frequency of aggressive behavior remains fairly constant during childhood, but physical forms of aggression (such as hitting and pushing) displayed in younger children tend to be replaced with verbal aggression (such as teasing and threatening) among older children. Highly aggressive children are often rejected by their peers, and aggressive behavior is often associated with academic failure. Despite often being rejected by the larger peer group, however, aggressive children typically have as many friends as nonaggressive peers, most commonly with other aggressive children. These deviant friends reinforce the child's aggression, and, when combined with academic failure and the loss of socialization from mainstream peers, may lead to later delinquency and antisocial behavior. The experience of being the victim of peer aggression can lead to negative outcomes—both personal (e.g., depression, anxiety, low self-esteem) and interpersonal (e.g., rejection, few friends)—which in turn further perpetuate peer abuse. These consequences are not limited to the period during which the child is victimized; chronic victimization can lead to low self-esteem and depression that persists into adulthood.

The frequency of prosocial behavior, behavior meant to assist others, increases during childhood, then remains relatively constant during adolescence. Nancy Eisenberg and Richard Fabes suggested that acts of prosocial behavior are based upon the development of prosocial moral reasoning, which involves increasing concern for others and ability to understand their suffering. Across childhood, prosocial behavior is related to popularity, the presence of friendships, and high quality friendships.

It is important to keep in mind that differences exist between boys and girls. Boys tend to play differently and in larger groups than girls. Boys' friend-

Boys tend to play differently and socialize in larger groups than girls, with friendships delineated by common activities, such as sports. (Shelley Gazin/Corbis)

ships are marked by common activities whereas girls' are marked by intimacy. Boys are more aggressive than girls, and girls tend to use aggression that is more social (e.g., excluding someone from a group) than physical in nature. There is less evidence, however, that the causes and consequences of these social behaviors differ for boys and girls. For example, although aggression is more common in boys, the same cognitions that motivate aggressive behavior appear to operate for both genders, and behaving aggressively often leads to peer rejection for both boys and girls. Rather than focusing on the differences in boys' and girls' behavior in general, Eleanor Maccoby suggested that it may be more important to focus on how boys

and girls interact among themselves and with each other. During childhood, interactions occur almost exclusively with same-sex peers when children are given a choice (e.g., on playgrounds). When required to interact, the power-assertive behavior typical in boys' groups results in boys dominating the interactions (e.g., playing with the more desirable toys). Girls in these interactions, who are accustomed to the supportive style typical in girls' groups, find this style aversive and the boys unresponsive to change. When possible, the girls will discontinue interaction or seek proximity to an adult whose presence can reduce the boys' dominating style.

Adolescence and Adulthood: Completing the Cycle

Whereas opposite-sex interactions are infrequent in childhood, they increase during adolescence. Much of this increase is due to the emergence of romantic attraction, which is a product of both biology (i.e., pubertal maturation) and societal standards. Adolescent dating can be both a positive and negative socializing influence—it can be a source of intimacy, expanded social competency, and heightened self-esteem and peer status, but it can also be a source of jealousy, abuse, and damage to self-esteem. Adolescent romantic relationships are based upon many of the same principles as children's friendships (such as mutual liking, positive behavior, and proximity seeking), but physical attractiveness also becomes important in the selection of romantic partners. Although the rule that opposites attract may sometimes apply, adolescent romantic relationships (like childhood friendships) are typically characterized by similarity in race, academic achievement, activities, attitudes, and physical attractiveness.

In adolescence there is also an increasing desire for autonomy—of separating from parents and becoming an independent adult. This desire may lead to heightened family conflict (e.g., arguments about time spent with peers) and defiant behaviors (e.g., affiliation with antisocial peers and engagement in delinquent activities). These manifestations of autonomy striving have resulted in the frequent use of the term "adolescent storm" in referring to this age. The intensity of this storm, however, is heavily influenced by parenting styles (e.g., authoritative parenting is associated with less problematic autonomy development), family characteristics (e.g., single-parent and divorced families may impede autonomy or intensify conflict), peer relations (e.g., dating and involvement with peers are frequent sources of conflict), cultural values (e.g., the importance placed on autonomy and deference to parents affect the occurrence and expression of conflict), and generational differences (e.g., differences between parents and children in beliefs about appropriate behavior may be a frequent source of conflict). Healthy individuation involves a gradual shifting of balance between autonomy and connectedness with parents—of gaining independence while maintaining quality relationships with parents.

The importance of romantic relationships and individuation during adolescence is congruent with events common in adulthood—marriage and beginning one's own family. The characteristics of these relationships are based upon previous social learning. Adults often interact within their romantic relationships in a manner similar to how their parents interacted with each other, because as children they observed these interactions. Direct experiences with parents and peers also affect these relationships. For example, securely attached children are more likely to be securely attached with their spouses in adulthood, and childhood friendships based on intimacy and trust are likely to foster these types of relationships with later romantic partners. These past experiences also influence parenting behavior. Thus, the familial environment in which a child is raised is to some extent replicated in the environment these adults provide for their children, though relations with peers and romantic partners modify this continuity.

Limitations, Controversies, and Future Directions

Despite all that is known about social development in the home and the peer context, there is still much to be learned about the bidirectional influences across these two contexts. The works of Ross Parke and Gary Ladd have illuminated some of the linkages from the home to the peer group. For instance, it is known that secure attachment is associated with peer acceptance and quality friendships, while insecure (avoidant or resistant) attachment is related to rejection, having fewer friends, and involvement in aggression (either as the aggressor or victim). Social development in the home appears to contribute to social outcomes with peers through the development of social competence (or incompetence). The impact of the peer context on social behavior in the home, however, is less well known. Previous studies have too often been concurrent (i.e., examining factors in the home and peer group at the same time), preventing the elucidation of temporal primacy (i.e., did home factors precede behavior and status in the peer group, or vice versa?). Researchers have recognized this limitation, and future longitudinal research will likely provide answers to this ambiguity.

Judith Harris challenged the notion that parent-child interactions affect social development outside of the home context. Based upon the premise that socialization in dyads (e.g., parent-child, child-friend) does not generalize beyond that dyad, Harris proposed that the primary source of socialization is the peer group. According to Harris, parents' influence is limited to the selection of the child's peer group (e.g., attending a particular school, affiliating more or less with one's racial or ethnic group). As might be expected, this proposition has elicited a great deal of controversy, and has been criticized by some developmental researchers; perhaps it has also prompted researchers to more carefully consider threats to their assumptions of socializing influences.

The beginning of the twenty-first century is an exciting time for social development researchers—much has been learned and it is likely that the rate of learning will rapidly accelerate in the future. As knowledge of human genetics increases, the focus on *how much* behavior is affected by genes is likely to shift to *how* behavior is affected by genes. Additionally, although much has been learned about biological, familial, and peer socializing influences during infancy, childhood, and adolescence, long-term studies considering multiple contexts are needed to examine the interactive effects of these influences on social development.

See also: FRIENDSHIP; PARENTING; PLAY; STAGES OF DEVELOPMENT

Bibliography

Ainsworth, Mary D. S. "Infant-Mother Attachment." *American Psychologist* 34 (1979):932–937.

Asher, Steven R., and John D. Coie, eds. *Peer Rejection in Childhood.* New York: Cambridge University Press, 1990.

Bandura, Albert. *Social Foundations of Thought and Action.* Englewood Cliffs, NJ: Prentice Hall, 1986.

Baumrind, Diana. "Current Patterns of Parental Authority." *Developmental Psychology Monographs* 4 (1971):1–103.

Bowlby, John. *Attachment and Loss,* Vol. 1: *Attachment.* New York: Basic, 1969.

Bukowski, William M., Andrew F. Newcomb, and Willard W. Hartup, eds. *The Company They Keep: Friendship in Childhood and Adolescence.* New York: Cambridge University Press, 1996.

Dishion, Thomas J., Joan McCord, and François Poulin. "When Interventions Harm: Peer Groups and Problem Behavior." *American Psychologist* 54 (1999):755–764.

Eisenberg, Nancy, and Richard A. Fabes. "Prosocial Development." In William Damon ed., *Handbook of Child Psychology,* 5th edition, Vol. 3: *Social, Emotional, and Personality Development,* edited by Nancy Eisenberg. New York: Wiley, 1998.

Harris, Judith R. "Where Is the Child's Environment? A Group Socialization Theory of Development." *Psychological Review* 102 (1995):458–489.

Hodges, Ernest V. E., and David G. Perry. "Personal and Interpersonal Consequences of Victimization by Peers." *Journal of Personality and Social Psychology* 76 (1999):677–685.

Maccoby, Eleanor E. "Gender and Relationships: A Developmental Account." *American Psychologist* 45 (1990):513–520.

Parke, Ross D., and Gary W. Ladd, eds. *Family-Peer Relationships: Models of Linkage.* Hillsdale, NJ: Lawrence Erlbaum, 1992.

Plomin, Robert, and John Crabbe. "DNA." *Psychological Bulletin* 126 (2000):806–828.

Rubin, Kenneth H., William M. Bukowski, and Jeffrey G. Parker. "Peer Interactions, Relationships, and Groups." In William Damon ed., *Handbook of Child Psychology,* 5th edition, Vol. 3: *Social, Emotional, and Personality Development,* edited by Nancy Eisenberg. New York: Wiley, 1998.

Scarr, Sandra. "Developmental Theories for the 1990s: Development and Individual Differences." *Child Development* 63 (1992):1–19.

Vandell, Deborah L. "Parents, Peer Groups, and Other Socializing Influences." *Developmental Psychology* 36 (2000):699–710.

Noel A. Card
Jenny Isaacs
Ernest V. E. Hodges

SPATIAL ABILITIES

Spatial ability refers to skill in perceiving the visual world, transforming and modifying initial perceptions, and mentally recreating spatial aspects of one's visual experience without the relevant stimuli. Several categories of spatial abilities may be distinguished. Spatial orientation is the ability to keep track of objects or locations in space even after a rotation or movement to a new location; spatial perception involves determining spatial relationships with respect to gravity or one's own body in spite of distracting information; and spatial manipulation involves the ability to mentally rotate two- or three-dimensional figures rapidly and accurately.

Spatial abilities develop, in part, when children manipulate and explore objects and environments. In general, there tends to be a strong relationship between how well one performs on verbal tasks and nonverbal tasks. However, some people are more skillful in one area than another, and some researchers argue for recognizing and valuing people's strengths with different abilities.

See also: PLAY

Bibliography

Gardner, Howard. *Frames of Mind: The Theory of Multiple Intelligences.* New York: Basic Books, 1985.

Linn, Marcia, C., and Anne C. A. Petersen. "Emergences and Characteristics of Sex Differences in Spatial Ability: A Meta-Analysis." *Child Development* 56 (1985):1479–1498.

Michael E. McCarty

SPOCK, BENJAMIN (1903–1998)

Born in New Haven, Connecticut, and trained as a medical doctor, Benjamin "Ben" Spock was best known for his books on child care and parenting. More copies of the many editions of his book, *Baby and Child Care,* were sold than any other book in the world, with the exception of the Bible.

Benjamin McLane Spock was the first of six children born to Mildred and Benjamin Ives Spock. Many of Spock's beliefs about child care originated with his own upbringing and his helping to care for his siblings. At his mother's charge, he attended progressive, private schools throughout his childhood. In

Benjamin Spock's name became synonymous with child rearing and development after the publication of his 1946 book The Common Sense Book of Baby and Child Care. *(Library of Congress)*

1921 Spock began his first year at Yale University, followed by a summer job as a counselor for disabled children. At the home for crippled children, Spock watched an orthopedic operation, at which point he decided to become a pediatrician. He was graduated from college and remained at Yale for the first two years of medical school.

While at Yale, Spock met Jane Cheney. He and Cheney corresponded for many years and married in 1927. They moved to New York City and Spock transferred from Yale to Colombia University to complete his medical training. He graduated at the top of his class in 1929. His good grades and dedication helped Spock secure an internship at a Presbyterian hospital. In order to help with finances, Jane Spock found a job as a research assistant, exploring the relationship between psychology and illness. This was a novel concept at the time, and Jane Spock's experiences with Freudian psychoanalysis affected her husband's views on psychology and medicine.

In 1931 Spock began another internship in pediatrics, but he felt strongly that he needed training in psychology as well. After an extensive search for a program that addressed both psychology and medicine, and finding that no such program existed, Spock settled on a residency at Cornell University's Payne Whitney Psychiatric Clinic. In the late 1930s,

he opened a pediatric practice where he applied Freudian theory to his assessment of children's needs.

In 1946 Spock published the first edition of his famous book, *The Common Sense Book of Baby and Child Care*. Although he never mentioned Freudian theories, he clearly applied them in his books. In the later editions of the book, Spock changed some of his advice in response to advancing research and theory in child development. Throughout his career, he continued to serve as a pediatrician and political activist and to write books about child care, specific points of child development, family values, disabled children, parenting practices, and politics.

See also: THEORIES OF DEVELOPMENT

Bibliography

Maier, Thomas. *Dr. Spock: An American Life*. New York: Harcourt Brace, 1998.

Publications by Spock

Spock, Benjamin, and Marion O. Lerrigo. *Caring for Your Disabled Child*. New York: Macmillan, 1965.

Spock, Benjamin, and Steven Parker. *Dr. Spock's Baby and Child Care*. New York: Pocket Books, 1998.

Diane B. Leach

STAGES OF DEVELOPMENT

Imagine a playground full of children on a warm summer day. A toddler tentatively makes her way across the sand to retrieve a shovel then, with a smile of triumph, retreats to her mother's side. Nearby a pair of two-year-olds dig in the sand side by side, practically touching yet seemingly unaware of one another. A band of boisterous five-year-olds rush past them, chasing an imagined pirate on a tumultuous sea. A quick survey of these intersecting scenes shows that these groups of children are clearly going about the business of learning and play in very different ways, at increasing levels of sophistication. Over the years, developmental psychologists have confronted the question of how best to characterize these changes in both cognitive and social functioning. Is it a simple matter of children adding to their repertoire of skills and knowledge as they get older (quantitative change), or do higher levels of functioning actually represent a reorganization of the previous level of functioning, much in the way that a caterpillar goes through discrete stages of life on the way to becoming a butterfly (qualitative change)? "Stage models" of development are based on a combination of these two types of conceptualizations. Psychologists have developed such models for understanding and explaining both cognitive and psychosocial development.

Stages of Cognitive Development

Jean Piaget was among the first psychologists to wrestle with the question of how a child develops from simple-thinking newborn to cognitively sophisticated adolescent and adult. Over a lifetime of grappling with this question, he developed a theory of cognitive development in which he identified four major stages or "periods" of development. Underlying this theory are the ideas that each stage of development is a self-contained unit, that each builds upon the preceding stage, that each proceeds from a loosely defined unit into a tightly integrated model, and that children proceed through these stages in a universal, fixed order.

Piaget's stage model centers around the concept of schemas, that is, basic units of knowledge that serve as the building blocks of and framework for intellectual development. Infants in the first couple of years of life, according to Piaget, are capable only of forming simple schemas based on their actual physical encounters with the world: They must experience the world through their senses or motor actions (e.g., touch it, grab it, suck on it, bang it, throw it) in order to know anything about it. Piaget thus termed this the sensorimotor period of development. In the sensorimotor period, schemas are simple. For example, the very young infant develops a sucking schema; that is, the infant organizes information according to what can be sucked (fingers, pacifier, teething ring) and how sucking actions can vary (hard or soft, fast or slow). As the child grows and experiences new things in the world, schemas become more complex.

Perhaps the crowning achievement of the sensorimotor period is the development of the idea that things exist independent of the child, even when the object is out of sight. This amazing new ability is called object permanence. According to Piaget, this knowledge (reflected in the toddler's continued search for an object even after it has been hidden) reflects an ability on the part of the child to form a mental representation of the object and thus allows the child to be able to think about the object without having to experience it via the senses or motor activity.

The ability to form mental representations opens up a whole new world of learning and imagination for children in the preoperational period (roughly from age two to seven years). They engage in pretend play ("there's a monster coming; hide!"); they can role play ("I am the mommy, you are the baby"); they can imagine something even when nothing is there at all (for example, "eating" a seven-course meal off an empty toy dish); they can use one object to stand for another (for example, using a shoe box as a bus). Somewhere around age six or seven, according to Pia-

get, children enter the concrete operational period of development. Now they become capable of performing simple "mental operations" such as adding, sorting, or ordering objects. They are no longer bound by their own perceptions of things; rather, they recognize that others have their own perspectives and that objects have their own constant properties. Nevertheless, children's ability to perform these operations is limited to real, concrete objects and to the here and now. Once they can apply such operations to abstract concepts and possibilities (usually around age eleven or older), they are said to have reached Piaget's final stage, the formal operational period.

Piaget's theory of cognitive development is a perfect example of a stage theory of development. New information is being added as children grow and experience the world, but there are also qualitative shifts in the way that information is organized to help the child understand the world. Piaget's theory is still the springboard for much of the research on cognitive development that has taken place in the years since his death. Some of this later work, however, has shown that modifications must be made to the original theory.

First, it now seems that the characteristics of the stages that Piaget described are less consistent and less global than he had portrayed. As their ways of thinking mature, children will sometimes show more sophisticated ways of thinking in just one area, or with one type of task, or with one set of objects. For example, contrary to Piaget's belief, not all preoperational children are invariably egocentric (i.e., incapable of taking the perspective of others). Children's performances on some of the classic Piagetian tasks seem to be dependent in part on how familiar the children are with the objects, how well they understand the instructions, what experience they have with similar tasks, etc. Furthermore, it appears that some of Piaget's beliefs about young children's limited abilities may have arisen as a function of a limitation of his research methods. As researchers have uncovered increasingly clever and technologically advanced ways to tap the mental activity of young infants, they have found that even very young infants understand, remember, and can learn far more than Piaget ever realized. In summary, then, psychologists now think of cognitive development as proceeding in terms of gradual changes to higher levels of thinking rather than sudden advances from one style of thinking to another, more sophisticated style.

Stages of Psychosocial Development

Like those who have studied cognitive development, researchers in the field of psychosocial development have also developed stage theories to

TABLE 1

Erikson's Stages of Psychosocial Development

Approximate Age	Stage	Description
First year	Trust vs. Mistrust	Infants learn to trust that their needs will be met, or they learn to mistrust the world
2-3 years	Autonomy vs. Shame and Doubt	Children learn to do things and make choices for themselves, or they become doubtful of their own worth and abilities
4-5 years	Initiative vs. Guilt	Children learn to define personal goals and seek to fulfill them, or they develop a sense of guilt over having such personal desires
6 years to puberty	Industry vs. Inferiority	Children develop a feeling of competence to learn things and to work on projects, or they develop a feeling of worthlessness
Adolescence	Identity vs. Role Confusion	Adolescents "find themselves"; they define themselves by choosing certain roles that suit them, or they become confused about what role is best for them
Early adulthood	Intimacy vs. Isolation	Young adults become able to enter into close, personal relationships (both intimate friendships and romantic relationships) with others, or they retreat into a world of solitude
Middle age	Generativity vs. Stagnation	Adults become interested in efforts that aid the next generation (having children, working to help make the world a better place), or they become self-centered and inactive
Old age	Integrity vs. Despair	Older adults reflect on their lives, satisfied with what they have done, or they feel regret over what they have done or failed to do

SOURCE: *Virgina D. Allhusen.*

understand and explain children's development in this domain. By far the most notable and global stage theory of social development comes from the work of Erik Erikson. A psychoanalyst by training, his stage model had roots in Freudian theory but took as its points of departure a lifespan approach to understanding development and a recognition of the impact of culture and society on development.

Erikson characterized social development as proceeding through eight distinct stages that cover the entire lifespan; these stages are summarized briefly in Table 1. Within each stage, a central crisis presents itself. Typically this crisis relates to some important issue confronting the individual at that point of development. Erikson identified a positive and a negative possible outcome for each stage. If development is to proceed favorably, each stage must be resolved in such a way that the positive outweighs the negative. Otherwise, the individual carries the burden of that negatively resolved stage throughout life, constantly facing it but perhaps eventually resolving it in a more favorable direction.

Erikson also recognized that culture and society play an important, ever-expanding role in directing the course of development and determining the out-

come of each crisis. At first, the infant's "society" consists primarily of the mother. As the child grows and goes out into the world, however, that circle of influence is expanded to include other adults, peers, and social institutions such as school, churches, and political structures.

In Erikson's theory, the individual is constantly in search of an identity. People seek to define themselves at each stage of development; that definition varies with the stage, but in the best-case scenario there is always a positive "reinvention" of the self such that the person decides that he or she is inherently good, worthy, capable, and lovable. Development in one stage is influenced by the positive or negative outcomes of all the previous stages, much in the same way that Piaget's successive stages of cognitive development were thought to build upon previous stages. Thus, for example, in the scenario where all crises are resolved positively, babies in their first year of life (through experiences with the mother or other primary caretaker) learn to trust that their needs will be met. This gives them the courage and confidence to go out and explore the world once they are able to crawl or walk away from the mother, and to do things for themselves. With support and success in these efforts, by age four or so they develop a desire to go after personal goals, confident that they will succeed in whatever they try. Adolescence marks a special crisis period in Erikson's theory, as this is a time when children face adulthood and seek to define what kind of adult they will be (in Erikson's terms, they face an "identity crisis"). Armed once more with the confidence that they are good, competent, and worthy people, young adults are able to open up their deepest, most vulnerable sides to loved ones, building intimate relationships. They turn their efforts to the good of society, and, in old age, take stock of their lives with satisfaction at their accomplishments and contributions. Thus Erikson's theory, like Piaget's, is a perfect example of a stage model of development. Each stage has its own unique features and issues, yet looking across the stages one can easily trace the impact of previous stages on subsequent development and outcomes.

Summary

Returning for a moment to the scene on the playground, Piaget's and Erikson's stage theories help show that children at these various ages are not simply just adding to their experience and knowledge base as they grow older in the way that a person glides up an escalator at a smooth and steady pace. Instead, their development is more like walking up a grand staircase with multiple plateaus. Within a level they are always making advances, and those advances taken together help prepare them for the next level. Once they reach that next higher level, they are facing a new set of issues, perhaps functioning in a qualitatively different way, but building nevertheless upon their rich experience of previous levels.

See also: ERIKSON, ERIK; MILESTONES OF DEVELOPMENT; OBJECT PERMANENCE; PIAGET, JEAN; PLAY

Bibliography

Erikson, Erik H. *Identity: Youth and Crisis*. New York: Norton, 1968.

Ginsburg, Herbert, and Sylvia Opper. *Piaget's Theory of Intellectual Development*, 3rd edition. Englewood Cliffs, NJ: Prentice-Hall, 1988.

Gross, Francis L. *Introducing Erik Erikson: An Invitation to His Thinking*. Lanham, MD: University Press of America, 1986.

Miller, Patricia H. *Theories of Developmental Psychology*, 3rd edition. New York: Freeman, 1993.

Piaget, Jean, and Bärbel Inhelder. *The Psychology of the Child*. New York: Basic, 1969.

Siegler, Robert S. "Children's Thinking: How Does Change Occur?" In Franz E. Weinert and Wolfgang Schneider eds., *Memory Performance and Competencies: Issues in Growth and Development*. Hillsdale, NJ: Lawrence Erlbaum, 1995.

Virginia D. Allhusen

STANDARDIZED TESTING

Standardized testing is a commonly misunderstood term. In actuality, a standardized test requires adherence to identical administration and scoring of items/tasks across people, time, and places. This uniformity is reflected in clearly defined procedures in examiner's manuals, test books, and scoring guides.

Many types of standardized tests exist, including achievement, psychological, and licensure assessments. These tests may include a combination of open-ended and multiple-choice questions designed to measure a particular trait, such as mathematics, intelligence, or a job skill. An excellent example of a standardized achievement test is *TerraNova: Multiple Assessments Edition.*

Standardization studies for these tests typically involve large nationally representative samples. These studies finalize administration and scoring procedures, establish test timing, and quantify student performance under the standardized procedures. Study participants are selected to accurately and fairly represent minority and socioeconomic groups across geographical regions and/or other demographic variable(s). This standardization procedure permits comparison of future students to the standardized group's performance.

See also: SCHOLASTIC APTITUDE TEST

Bibliography

Abbott, Susan. *Standardized Testing*. Westminster, CA: Teacher Created Materials, 1997.

National Education Association of the United States. *Standardized Testing Issues: Teachers' Perspectives*. Washington, DC: National Education Association, 1977.

Linda J. McGarvey-Levin

STATE CHILDREN'S HEALTH INSURANCE PROGRAM

The Balanced Budget Act of 1997 (Public Law 105-33) established the State Children's Health Insurance Program (SCHIP) as Title XXI of the Social Security Act. This legislation, which involved the largest expansion of children's health insurance coverage in over thirty years, enables states to provide health insurance coverage to low-income children under age nineteen who are uninsured and ineligible for Medicaid.

Not since the enactment of Medicaid has there been a greater investment in children's health care in the United States. Title XXI provided over $40 billion in federal grants to states over a ten-year period. States were required to contribute a defined share of funds in order to obtain federal matching funds.

This legislation provided states flexibility in how they design their program. States can choose one of three approaches: (1) expand the current Medicaid program, (2) create or expand a separate state children's health insurance program, or (3) use a combination of both approaches. The majority of states created a non-Medicaid SCHIP program for at least some of their SCHIP-eligible children. Fifteen states created a non-Medicaid SCHIP program only, and nineteen states created a state program in combination with a Medicaid expansion. The remaining nineteen states used SCHIP funds to expand Medicaid only.

See also: HEALTH INSURANCE; POVERTY

Bibliography

American Academy of Pediatrics. *State Approaches to Title XXI.* Elk Grove Village, IL: American Academy of Pediatrics, 2000.

Beth K. Yudkowsky

STEPFAMILIES

Each year approximately one million American children and adolescents will experience their parents' divorce. Most of their parents (70–75%) will remarry or begin living with a new partner within three to five years. These new families are labeled stepfamilies or blended families. The 1996 United States census indicated that 32 percent of African-American, 16 percent of Hispanic, and 15 percent of Caucasian children live in stepfamilies. Approximately one-fourth of all American children will live in a stepfamily before they reach adulthood. Most children and adolescents who live in stepfamilies live with their biological mother—17 percent of children are in the father's custody after the divorce. More than half of second marriages end in divorce within the first five years. Consequently, children in stepfamilies may experience a second divorce. Research indicates that the more divorces children experience, the more they are negatively affected.

Children's and Adolescents' Adjustment in Stepfamilies

Children and adolescents in stepfamilies tend to develop more problems than children and adolescents in intact families. Children in stepfamilies are more likely than children in intact families to have academic problems, to have externalizing or internalizing disorders, to be less socially competent, and to have problems with parents, siblings, and peers. About a third of adolescents become disengaged from their stepfamilies and consequently may be more like-

ly to become sexually active at an early age, to be involved in delinquent activities, to be involved with drugs or alcohol, and to drop out of high school. When children or adolescents raised in stepfamilies reach adulthood, they are more likely to divorce than children raised in intact families. But it is important to note that although children in stepfamilies are more likely to have problems than children in intact families, the majority of children in stepfamilies are normally adjusted.

One would expect that children and adolescents in stepfamilies would be better adjusted than children and adolescents in single-parent divorced families. Stepfamilies have more resources than single-parent divorced families, including two parents to share child rearing and more financial resources. Surprisingly, a large body of research indicates that children and adolescents in stepfamilies have the same level of adjustment problems as children and adolescents in divorced single-parent families. One reason for this similarity between the adjustment of children in stepfamilies and single-parent divorced families may be that stepfamilies experience significant stresses within their family interactions. It may take five to seven years for a new stepfamily to stabilize and begin to function smoothly. From a family systems perspective, stepfamilies begin with a weak family system. Instead of a healthy family system (a strong, well-established marital bond, strong child bonds to both parents, and little outside interference), stepfamilies typically begin with a new and relatively weak marital coalition, a strong parent-child relationship, a weak or conflicted stepparent-child relationship, and with the outside involvement of the noncustodial parent. In addition, children in stepfamilies may have to adjust to less attention from their biological parent, to parenting from a new stepparent, and to new sibling relationships.

What Affects Children's and Adolescents' Adjustment to Stepfamilies?

Several factors may affect how well a child adjusts to a stepfamily. First, the child's gender is a factor. Girls have more difficulty than boys adjusting to stepfamily life. In stepfamilies that include the child's biological mother and a stepfather, girls are more likely than boys to be resistant to the stepfather. In single-parent divorced families, mother-daughter relationships often are exceptionally close; consequently, when mothers remarry, girls may view new stepfathers as threats to their previously close relationships with their mothers. In contrast, boys' overall adjustment is likely to improve after their mothers' remarriage. Mother-son relationships in single-parent divorced families typically are conflicted and coercive; consequently, boys may appreciate new stepfathers as alternative supportive parents and masculine role models. In stepfamilies that include the child's biological father and a stepmother, the stepmother may be seen as an intruder in the previously close father-child relationship. Girls may have trouble adjusting to the new stepmother, particularly because most girls maintain a close relationship with their noncustodial mother, but girls generally adjust to the new stepmother and benefit from the new relationship.

The second area that may affect a child's adjustment to a stepfamily is the age of the child. Young children adapt most easily, whereas early adolescents have the most difficulty adjusting to new stepfamilies. The adjustment is particularly difficult for early adolescents because, in addition to the new stepfamily, they are adjusting to puberty and new sexual feelings, becoming more independent from the family, experiencing egocentrism and self-consciousness, and being exposed to new peer pressures to experiment with sexuality and drugs or alcohol. These multiple stressors make it more likely that the adolescent may react negatively to the new stepparent, making it difficult to build a relationship. In addition, stepparents may be hesitant to monitor adolescents for fear of threatening the stepparent-adolescent relationship; consequently, these adolescents may be more likely to get into trouble.

Individual differences in temperament, intelligence, and behavioral patterns also may affect how well children adjust to stepfamilies. Children with easygoing temperaments, high intelligence, and good behavior are more likely to evoke positive responses from their parents and stepparents, making it more likely that these children will receive the support needed to adjust. In contrast, the stresses of living in a stepfamily are likely to magnify children's and adolescents' preexisting problems. Consequently, children with difficult temperaments or with preexisting behavior problems are likely to evoke negative reactions from their parents and new stepparents, thereby reducing the amount of support these children receive.

Parenting factors also may affect children's adjustment to stepfamilies. Children are more likely to have problems adjusting to stepfamilies if both adults bring children into the new stepfamily because parents tend to have closer relationships with their biological children. Stepchildren perceive the closer relationships between stepparents and their biological children as differential or nonequal treatment and resent their stepsiblings.

In addition, because of the stresses of adjusting to a new marriage, mothers (during the first year of the

America's most famous stepfamily—the Brady Bunch. This television sitcom was centered on two single parents, each with three children, who married to become one big family. Episode themes dealt with issues related to having new brothers, sisters, and stepparents. (Kobal Collection)

remarriage) are likely to provide less control and monitoring and to be more negative toward their children. Mothers' parenting tends to improve after the first year and eventually becomes similar to mothers in intact families. Adolescents in stepfamilies are still more likely than adolescents in intact families to experience mother-adolescent disagreements and low levels of supervision.

Stepfathers typically initially assume a polite, nondisciplinarian role in stepfamilies partly because stepchildren (especially stepdaughters) tend to reject stepfathers' attempts at discipline. Eventually, stepfathers and stepdaughters may become involved in conflict focused on the stepfathers' authority. Consequently, stepfathers often become less supportive, less positive, and less involved in discipline than fathers in intact families. Stepfathers' disengagement from parenting is associated with poor child and adolescent adjustment. The most positive outcomes occur with younger children (especially boys) when the stepfather initially forms a warm relationship with the child and supports the mother's discipline, and later begins to provide authoritative discipline (warmth with moderate control). Early adolescents adjust best when stepfathers begin immediately to establish a warm, supportive relationship with moderate amounts of control.

In contrast, stepmothers often immediately become more involved in discipline. If the biological father supports the stepmother's discipline attempts, children generally receive more effective parenting from both parents. Stepmothers perceive parenting as more challenging than mothers in intact families, although research suggests that stepmothers are actually less negative and coercive in their interactions with their stepchildren than mothers in intact families. Stepmothers who provide authoritative parenting, providing warmth and moderate control, have stepchildren who are better adjusted than the stepchildren of stepmothers who provide authoritarian or neglectful parenting.

Suggestions for Parents in Stepfamilies

Children's and adolescents' adjustment in stepfamilies can be encouraged several ways. First, parents can help children and adolescents adjust to stepfamilies by taking into account issues related to gender and age. The most successful stepfamilies have parents who are flexible and able to adjust to the varying demands that children's gender, age, and individual differences place on parents. Parents should have realistic expectations of new family relationships and should not expect close bonds immediately. Parents also should be aware that fathers and mothers in stepfamilies face different challenges and try to provide support for their partner's parenting. A strong marriage is the foundation of a successful new stepfamily. Finally, parents should work together to create warm, supportive relationships with their children and stepchildren. One technique for doing so is to create new family traditions to add to the traditions of the original families. In conclusion, although children's and adolescents' development in stepfamilies can be adversely affected by many factors, with parental support, most children and adolescents in stepfamilies do not develop significant problems.

See also: DIVORCE; MEDIATION; PARENTING

Bibliography

Booth, Alan, and Judith Dunn. *Stepfamilies: Who Benefits? Who Does Not?* Hillsdale, NJ: Lawrence Erlbaum, 1994.

Ganong, Lawrence, and Marilyn Coleman. *Remarried Family Relationships.* Thousand Oaks, CA: Sage, 1996.

Hetherington, E. Mavis. *Coping with Divorce, Single Parenting, and Remarriage: A Risk and Resilience Perspective.* Mahwah, NJ: Lawrence Erlbaum, 1999.

Anne Dopkins Stright

STRANGER ANXIETY

Stranger anxiety is discomfort at the approach of an unfamiliar person. Babies differ greatly in how they show it: some cry vigorously, cling and hide their faces, or merely become subdued and wary. Because of differences among researchers with regard to behaviors used as evidence of stranger anxiety, there is disagreement about when it first occurs. Clearly, however, by the time they are one year old, most babies react with some degree of stranger anxiety. These reactions show that they can discriminate between familiar and unfamiliar people, an accomplishment of cognitive development. As the child continues to grow, new ways of showing discomfort appear. Preschoolers, for instance, may whisper or refuse to talk when strangers make a near approach. Babies and preschoolers who have had considerable experience encountering strangers or who are approached by a stranger while an attachment figure is closeby may show little or no stranger anxiety.

See also: ATTACHMENT; SEPARATION ANXIETY

Bibliography

Morgan, George, and Henry N. Ricciuti. "Infants' Responses to Strangers during the First Year." In Brian M. Foss ed., *Determinants of Infant Behavior.* New York: Wiley, 1969.

Sroufe, L. Alan. "Wariness of Strangers and the Study of Infant Development." *Child Development* 48 (1977):731–746.

Anne McIntyre

STREET CHILDREN

Street children are defined as often unsupervised children who work, play, and/or live in street environments. As of 1998, there were about 1.5 million children in the United States categorized as out-of-school, homeless, runaway, throwaway, and system youths (i.e., youths in foster care, institutions, shelters, and group homes). More than 100 million street children are found in poor countries of Africa, Asia, and Latin America. Street children are broadly subgrouped into children on the street (working) and of the street (living and working). Factors that contribute to homelessness and street children include poverty; physical, emotional, and sexual abuse; abandonment and family indifference; desire for a better life; and the lure of the street. Street children exhibit many physical health problems (such as respiratory and skin disorders, malnutrition, and anemia), emotional health problems (such as depression, anxiety, psychosis, and suicidal tendencies), and health-compromising behaviors (such as substance abuse, prostitution, violence, and delinquency). Intervention efforts have included reuniting families, providing shelter, and improving access to counseling, health care, education, and vocational training.

See also: DELINQUENCY; MALNUTRITION; POVERTY

Bibliography

Raffaelli, M., and R. W. Larson. *Homeless and Working Youth around the World: Exploring Developmental Issues.* San Francisco: Jossey-Bass, 1999.

Evelyn K. Kumoji
Debra Mekos

STRESS

Children are confronted with many challenges throughout their childhood. What types of challenges do children encounter at various ages? How do stressful experiences influence their psychological and physical health? How do children's personal qualities and their environments affect how they react to these challenges? These are all questions that psychologists have been trying to answer to learn more about the causes and consequences of stress in children's lives and to develop programs that help children cope with stress.

Conceptualizations and Types of Stress

The study of stress has a long and rich history, which is characterized by diverse perspectives on how to examine stress and its impact on people's lives. In one early definition from 1974, Hans Seyle conceptualized stress in terms of external events that elicited certain distress responses, called the general adaptation syndrome. This approach proved valuable in elucidating the effects of the environment on physiological functioning, but it created the difficulty of disentangling the stressor itself from individuals' responses to stress. Two other perspectives have received more attention in the investigation of stress in children. The first "stimulus-based" approach, pioneered in 1967 by Thomas H. Holmes and Richard H. Rahe, viewed stress in terms of exposure to disruptive or demanding environmental circumstances. This definition emphasized that stress can be defined based on objective characteristics of one's environment. The second "transactional" approach, advocated in 1984 by Richard S. Lazarus and Susan Folkman, incorporated not only environmental events and conditions but also individuals' subjective appraisals of

As children move through adolescence, they begin to experience stress more intensely. Studies have shown that adolescent boys are particularly vulnerable to noninterpersonal stress, such as school-related difficulties. (Robert J. Huffman/Field Mark Publications)

these circumstances. According to this perspective, individual perceptions of events may determine their stressfulness.

Regardless of whether the definition focuses on objective events or on the transaction between external events and internal appraisals, several types of stress may emerge in the lives of children. Daily hassles and minor life events involve everyday occurrences—such as interpersonal conflicts, pressures at school, or minor physical illnesses—that may accumulate over time to pose a threat to well-being. Chronic strains involve ongoing stressful conditions, such as family adversity (e.g., marital conflict, mental illness in a parent), relationship problems (e.g., social isolation), or economic hardship. Acute, severe stressors involve traumatic events such as the death of a close family member, victimization, or exposure to a natural disaster. Finally, normative stressors involve events or situations that occur as a part of typical development, such as starting school or moving away from home for the first time.

Stress across Development

Research has suggested that children experience increasing stress as they move through adolescence. Some research has focused on the entrance into adolescence itself as one type of normative experience that accounts for higher levels of stress during this stage. This transition is characterized by both biological challenges associated with puberty, as well as social challenges such as moving into middle school and developing cross-sex relationships. Moreover, there is an accumulation of other types of stressful events during adolescence that exceed those experienced prior to this period. Interestingly, some studies have suggested that the nature of stress during adolescence may differ in girls and boys. For example, Karen D. Rudolph and Constance Hammen found that adolescent girls experience particularly high levels of interpersonal stress, such as conflicts with parents and friends, whereas adolescent boys experience particularly high levels of noninterpersonal stress, such as school-related difficulties.

Interactions between Stress and Development

A large body of evidence links a variety of stressors to poor psychological and physical health in children. For instance, cumulative and chronic stresses have been found to be associated with heightened emotional distress (e.g., anxiety, depression, low self-esteem), behavior problems (e.g., aggression, delinquency), and physical illness. Traumatic stressors, such as physical or sexual victimization, may lead to severe disturbances such as posttraumatic stress symptoms. Even stress ensuing from normative events may interfere with children's adjustment. For example, work by Jacquelynne Eccles and Carol Midgley demonstrated that school transitions may undermine achievement and emotional well-being in some adolescents, particularly girls. Importantly, many of these studies have demonstrated that exposure to stress predicts increases in adjustment problems over time, suggesting that stress exerts a potentially long-term influence on children's developmental course rather than merely a temporary disruption.

Protective and Risk Factors

Although research consistently has documented problematic consequences of stress, all children do not respond to stress in the same way. Hence, it is critical to understand when stress is likely to impair psychological and physical well-being and when stress may contribute to less adverse, or even positive, outcomes. This issue has been addressed through efforts to identify characteristics of children and their environments that either heighten (risk factors) or attenuate (protective factors) the adverse effects of stress.

A range of personal and environmental characteristics play a role in determining how children react to stress. In terms of psychological characteristics of youth, children's views of themselves and their competencies may influence their responses. For instance, children who attribute negative events in their lives to internal, stable, and global characteristics (e.g., "I failed a test because I am stupid"), and who feel a lack of control over important outcomes in their lives show increased vulnerability to depression in response to stress. In contrast, high levels of academic and social competence, high self-esteem, and adaptive coping styles may help children to deal effectively with stress, thereby protecting them against negative consequences. External resources, such as the presence of a supportive family environment or strong friendships, also may buffer children from the harmful effects of stress, but this possibility needs to be explored further before definitive conclusions can be drawn.

Children's responses to stress also may differ according to their gender and their age. Some research has shown that girls and boys display different types of vulnerability. In particular, girls may be more likely to respond to stress with emotional distress, such as feelings of anxiety and depression, whereas boys may be more likely to respond to stress with behavior problems, such as aggression. So far, little consistent evidence has emerged regarding the impact of particular types of stress across development, but it is possible that certain stressors may be more or less salient at different life stages. For instance, school-related stress may become particularly important during middle childhood, whereas friendship-related stress may become particularly important during early adolescence.

An area that has received little attention concerns the positive consequences of stress. It has been said "whatever does not kill us makes us stronger." This statement reflects the rather counterintuitive idea that, under some circumstances, the experience of stress actually may promote healthy development. For instance, encountering stressful situations may enhance children's strategies for coping with future stress or may strengthen social bonds as children seek support or advice from friends and family. Moreover, successful coping experiences may foster a sense of self-efficacy and increase children's self-esteem. An interesting direction for future research will be to distinguish when stress acts as a threat that undermines healthy development and when stress acts as a challenge that stimulates mastery or growth.

Remaining Questions and Implications

Despite well-established linkages between stress and adjustment across development, the field of life-stress research in children is still in its infancy. Additional research is needed to address several unanswered questions concerning the role of stress in development and to help guide the design of appropriate interventions. For example, the premise underlying the majority of life-stress research is that exposure to certain environmental demands overwhelms children's coping abilities, thereby precipitating psychological and health-related problems. Nevertheless, this focus on how stress affects children's development is somewhat limited. Instead, Rudolph and Hammen argued in a 1999 article that a more complete understanding of the developmental context of stress requires consideration of not only how children react to external events and circumstances but also how they construct and contribute to their environments. This stress-generation approach highlights the importance of studying characteristics of children that lead them to create stressful conditions, which then interfere further with their development.

Also, researchers have only begun to examine the processes through which stress undermines children's development. Thus, researchers need to learn more about how and why different types of stress create emotional, behavioral, and physical problems in children, as well as why some children are more likely to generate stress in their lives.

A more in-depth understanding about the complex linkages between stress and developmental outcomes is essential for the creation of effective intervention programs. Identifying personal qualities of children or environmental contexts that either exacerbate or dampen the negative effects of stress will provide essential information about how health professionals, teachers, and parents can promote effective coping strategies. Moreover, discovering which types of stress create a risk for particular problems and exploring how these effects occur will facilitate the development of targeted intervention programs that are tailored to the needs of the individual. Finally, identifying which children may be at highest risk for exposure to, or generation of, stress will lay the groundwork for early intervention programs designed to prevent the onset of the complicated cycle linking stressful life experiences and unhealthy development.

See also: RESILIENCY; VIOLENCE

Bibliography

Eccles, Jacquelynne S., and Carol Midgley. "Stage-Environment Fit: Developmentally Appropriate Classrooms for Young Adolescents." In Russell E. Ames and Carole Ames eds., *Research on Motivation in Education.* New York: Academic Press, 1989.

Hammen, Constance. "Life Events and Depression: The Plot Thickens." *American Journal of Community Psychology* 2 (1992):179–193.

Holmes, Thomas H., and Richard H. Rahe. "The Social Readjustment Rating Scale." *Journal of Psychosomatic Research* 11 (1967):213–218.

Lazarus, Richard S., and Susan Folkman. *Stress, Appraisal, and Coping.* New York: Springer, 1984.

Rudolph, Karen D., and Constance Hammen. "Age and Gender as Determinants of Stress Exposure, Generation, and Reactions in Youngsters: A Transactional Perspective." *Child Development* 70 (1999):660–677.

Seyle, Hans. *Stress in Health and Disease.* Woburn, MA: Butterworth, 1976.

Karen D. Rudolph

SUBSTANCE ABUSE

Adolescent substance abuse and its resulting harms are major concerns of parents, policymakers, teachers, and public health officials. Nevertheless, experimentation with substances, particularly alcohol and tobacco, is progressively more common behavior from pre- to late adolescence. When adolescents try substances a few times, with peers, this experimentation is generally not associated with any long-term impairment of functioning. Experimentation is considered problematic when substance use occurs at a very young age, with increasing frequency, while the child is alone, or in the context of behavioral or emotional difficulties. If use becomes more frequent, negative consequences can develop, including impairment at school or work, legal problems, accidents, and interpersonal difficulties. Substance use becomes abuse when an adolescent suffers negative and harmful consequences because of the use of substances—and yet continues using. Substance abuse has been strongly linked to risky sexual behavior, delinquent behavior, and low school achievement. Heavy and prolonged substance use can result in drug dependence, with a syndrome of significant distress if the drug use is stopped or reduced.

Adolescents tend to follow a particular pattern of involvement with drugs. Typically, the first substance an adolescent uses is one that is legal for adults (tobacco or alcohol). The next stage is often experimentation with marijuana. Tobacco, alcohol, and marijuana have been labeled "gateway drugs" because they precede the use of other harder drugs. High frequency of use and early age of initiation are both associated with movement to higher stages of substance use.

Early initiation of substance use is linked to substance abuse and dependence. A 1997 study by Bridget Grant and Deborah Dawson found that more than 40 percent of individuals who began drinking before age fourteen developed a dependence on alcohol. In comparison, only 10 percent of those who began drinking at age twenty or older developed alcohol dependence. Similarly, individuals who began using drugs at an early age tend to experience greater drug problems. A 1993 study conducted by Denise Kandel and Kazuo Yamaguchi found that adolescents who use harder drugs, such as cocaine or crack, began using one of the gateway drugs (cigarettes, alcohol, or marijuana) two years earlier than adolescents who did not advance to harder drugs. Most smokers begin smoking as teenagers. More than 90 percent of individuals who become regular smokers begin before the age of nineteen.

Trends in Substance Use

The Monitoring the Future study, conducted by Lloyd Johnston, Patrick O'Malley, and Jerald Bachman, tracked the prevalence of adolescent substance use among American eighth, tenth, and twelfth grade students each year from the mid-1970s into the twenty-first century. The study focused on three categories of substances: illicit drugs, alcohol, and cigarettes. It also examined gender and racial/ethnic differences in substance use.

Illicit Drugs

Illicit drug use peaked in the 1970s, decreased steadily until the early 1990s, and then increased during the 1990s, with a slight decline and leveling off at the close of the decade. Marijuana is the most common illicit drug used. In 2000, more than half (54%) of American high school seniors reported using some type of illicit drug in their lifetimes. Reported prevalence rates among tenth and eighth grade students that year were lower (46% and 27%, respectively). In 2000, one-quarter of twelfth grade students reported using an illicit drug during the previous month, followed by 23 percent of tenth graders and 12 percent of eighth grade students.

Alcohol

Alcohol use increased throughout the 1970s, peaking at the end of the decade; it then steadily decreased in the 1980s and remained fairly stable during the 1990s. In the 2000 survey, 80 percent of twelfth grade students reported having tried alcohol at least once, and 62 percent reported having been drunk at least once. Seventy-one percent of tenth grade students had tried alcohol (49 percent had been drunk at least once), and 52 percent of eighth grade students had tried alcohol (25 percent had been drunk at least once). One-half of high school seniors, 41 percent of tenth graders, and 22 percent of eighth graders reported drinking alcohol in the previous thirty days.

Cigarettes

Cigarette use peaked in the mid-1970s, declined substantially for a few years, remained relatively stable in the mid-1980s and early 1990s, increased during the mid-1990s, and experienced a slight decrease in the last few years of the twentieth century for eighth and tenth graders. According to results from 2000, over half of twelfth graders (63%) and tenth graders (55%) reported smoking a cigarette in their lifetimes, while 41 percent of eighth graders had smoked. The reported prevalence rates for smoking during the previous thirty days were 31 percent of twelfth grade students, 24 percent of tenth graders, and 15 percent of eighth graders.

Gender and Racial/Ethnic Differences

Male students have higher lifetime and thirty-day prevalence rates than their female counterparts for marijuana use for all grades reported. Senior males report more illicit drug use of other types in the previous thirty days than females, but there is little gender difference in tenth or eighth grade. Males also tend to use alcohol more than females, which becomes more apparent by twelfth grade. Across all grades, males and females seem to have almost equal rates of daily cigarette smoking. African-American students report lower lifetime, annual, thirty-day, and daily illicit drug use prevalence rates than white and Hispanic students. African-American students also have the lowest prevalence rates of alcohol use, being drunk, and binge drinking.

Approaches to Preventing Substance Abuse

In order to prevent substance abuse among young people, both supply and demand reduction strategies are critical. Supply reduction strategies include any method used to reduce the availability of drugs, such as border patrols, confiscation of drug shipments, and penalties for drug use and drug dealing. In recent years, "community" police officers have been increasingly used in neighborhood and secondary school settings to prevent the local sale and distribution of drugs. Within the realm of legal substances, such as alcohol and tobacco, effective supply reduction strategies include increasing taxes, increasing the legal age of use, increasing law enforcement, reducing product advertising, reducing the number of sales outlets, and imposing penalties for sales of these products to minors.

Demand reduction strategies are designed to reduce the demand for drugs. Prevention and treatment are part of demand reduction. Prevention attempts to reduce demand by decreasing risk factors and increasing protective factors associated with substance abuse, while treatment is designed to decrease demand by stopping substance abuse in addicted or abusing individuals.

Prevention programs are organized along a targeted audience continuum—that is, the degree to which any person is identified as an individual at risk for substance abuse. Universal prevention strategies address the entire population (e.g., national, local community, school neighborhood) with messages and programs aimed at preventing or delaying the use of alcohol, tobacco, and other drugs. Selective prevention strategies target subsets of the total population that are deemed to be at risk for substance abuse by virtue of their membership in a particular population segment—for example, children of adult alcoholics, dropouts, or students who are failing academically. Indicated prevention strategies are designed to prevent the onset of substance abuse in individuals who do not meet medical criteria for addiction but who are showing early danger signs, such as truancy, falling grades, and cigarette smoking.

Research shows that there are many risk factors for drug abuse, each having a different impact depending on the phase of development. Risk factors can be associated with individual characteristics as well as social contexts. Individual risk factors include: genetic susceptibility to addiction, high sensation seeking, impulsive decision making, conduct problems, shyness coupled with aggression in boys, rebelliousness, alienation, academic failure, and low commitment to school.

Family risk factors include: substance abusing or emotionally disturbed parents; perceived parent permissiveness toward drug/alcohol use; lack of or inconsistent parental discipline; negative communication patterns and conflict; stress and dysfunction caused by death, divorce, incarceration of parents or low income; parental rejection; lack of adult supervision; poor family management and communication; and physical and/or sexual abuse. School risk factors include: ineffective classroom management, failure in school performance, truancy, affiliations with deviant peers, peers around deviant behaviors, and perceptions of approval of drug using behaviors in the school, peer, and community environments.

Certain protective factors have also been identified. These factors are not always the opposite of risk factors, and their impact varies along the developmental process. The most salient protective factors include: strong bonds with the family; experience of parental monitoring with clear rules of conduct within the family unit and involvement of parents in the lives of their children; success in school performance; and strong bonds with prosocial institutions such as the family, school, and religious organizations. Other factors—such as the availability of drugs, alcohol, and tobacco, and beliefs that substance use by young people is generally tolerated—also influence a number of youth who start to use drugs.

A young boy rolls a marijuana cigarette. Adolescents are most likely to experiment with alcohol and tobacco before trying marijuana—all are considered to be "gateway drugs." (Joan Slatkin/Archive Photos, Inc.)

During the 1990s, the federal government made a concerted effort to test and disseminate prevention programs that met rigorous scientific standards for effectiveness. For example, school districts had to select effective programs and evaluate their progress toward specific goals for reduction of substance use by students, in order to receive funding through the Safe and Drug Free Schools program. Agencies such as the National Institute on Drug Abuse and the Center for Substance Abuse Prevention funded national and local studies to test whether youth who participate in prevention programs actually experience a reduction in risk factors, an increase in protective factors, and/or reductions in substance use. Federal agencies, scientific societies, and private foundations developed criteria for assessing the evidence about the effectiveness of various approaches and programs, and many provided recommendations to the public about particular programs and approaches through web sites and print media. Changing behavior is exceedingly complex, but informed efforts by parents, schools, and communities can help protect young people from the harms of substance abuse.

See also: ADOLESCENCE; CONFORMITY; PARENT-CHILD RELATIONSHIPS

Bibliography

Grant, Bridget F., and Deborah A. Dawson. "Age at Onset of Alcohol Use and Its Association with *DSM-IV* Alcohol Abuse and Dependence: Results from the National Longitudinal Alcohol Epidemiologic Survey." *Journal of Substance Abuse* 9 (1997):103–110.

Johnston, Lloyd D., Patrick M. O'Malley, and Jerald G. Bachman. *Monitoring the Future National Survey Results on Drug Use, 1975–1999,* Vol. 1: *Secondary Students.* Bethesda, MD: National Institute on Drug Abuse, 1999.

Johnston, Lloyd D., Patrick M. O'Malley, and Jerald G. Bachman. "Monitoring the Future National Results on Adolescent Drug Use: Overview of Key Findings, 2000." Available from http://www.monitoringthefuture.org; INTERNET.

Kandel, Denise B., and Kazuo Yamaguchi. "From Beer to Crack: Developmental Patterns of Drug Involvement." *American Journal of Public Health* 83 (1993):851–855.

Kandel, Denise B., Kazuo Yamaguchi, and Kevin Chen. "Stages of Progression in Drug Involvement from Adolescence to Adulthood: Further Evidence for the Gateway Theory." *Journal of Studies on Alcohol* 53 (1992):447–457.

Denise Hallfors
Laura E. Frame

SUDDEN INFANT DEATH SYNDROME

Sudden infant death syndrome (SIDS) refers to the sudden unexpected death of an infant under the age of one year who prior to the event was considered to be completely healthy. The diagnosis also requires that a review of the clinical and environmental history, death scene investigation, and autopsy fail to reveal an alternative explanation of the death. In other words, the diagnosis of SIDS remains a diagnosis of exclusion.

Incidence

SIDS remains the primary cause of death for infants between one month and six months of age. Prior to 1991 the incidence rates of SIDS in the United States ranged between 1.2 and 2 per 1,000 live births. Of the developed countries of the world, some, including Sweden, Hong Kong, and Japan, reported rates as low as 0.3 to 0.5 per 1,000 live births. Others, such as Australia (especially Tasmania), New Zealand, and Northern Ireland reported rates as high as 3–7 per 1,000 live births. In 1995, three years after the Academy of Pediatrics issued guidelines recommending placing infants in the nonprone position (i.e., not lying on the stomach) for sleeping, Michael Malloy and his colleagues published a study noting a 33 per-

cent drop in the incidence of SIDS within the United States. Other countries reported similar experiences after adopting infant sleep position changes. This lowered incidence was maintained for succeeding years, but it remains to be seen if additional decreases will occur with increasing compliance with the recommended sleep positioning guidelines.

Epidemiological Factors

While the cause of SIDS remains elusive, multiple studies have documented consistent epidemiological factors associated with higher SIDS risks in some groups of infants. Risk factor categories include maternal and prenatal, neonatal (newborn), postneonatal, geographic, and race/ethnicity groupings.

Maternal and prenatal risk factors constitute a lengthy list of biological and environmental conditions. These include shorter interpregnancy interval, increased placental weight, low socioeconomic status, nutritional deficiency, anemia, urinary tract infection, intrauterine hypoxia (oxygen deficiency), fetal growth retardation, smoking, drug exposure, poor prenatal care, young age, lower education, and increased number of pregnancies. Several studies have identified maternal smoking as a significant risk factor. The National Institute of Child Health and Human Development (NICHD) conducted a large study in the United States of 757 SIDS cases with two matched control groups. Seventy percent of the SIDS mothers in this study smoked. When compared with the control groups, the risk for infants of mothers who smoked is doubled and progressively increases as the number of cigarettes smoked per day increases. These infants also die at younger ages. Constriction of blood vessels leading to chronically diminished oxygen delivery to fetal tissues is thought to be the mechanism by which smoking increases the risk of SIDS.

Neonatal risk factors include poor growth, asphyxia (inadequate oxygen delivery to body tissues), prematurity, and low birthweight. As the gestational age decreases, the relative risk of SIDS increases. This is also true of birthweight. The incidence of SIDS in preterm infants whose birthweight is greater than 1,500 grams (3 pounds, 5 ounces) is about 8 per 1,000 live births, compared to preterm infants with birthweights less than 1,500 grams, where the risk rises to 10 per 1,000 live births. Postnatally, male sex, age (two to four months), bottle feeding, overheating, smoking exposure, soft bedding materials, no pacifier use, and prone sleeping position have been identified as significant factors that independently increase the risk of SIDS.

Geographic and race/ethnicity factors play an additional role in increasing the relative risks. SIDS rates increase during cold weather months, in economically poor countries, and in infants of black race or Native-American ethnicity. Worldwide, groups such as Gypsy, Maori, Hawaiian, and Filipino also have increased SIDS rates.

Pathologic Findings

Extensive work has been done in an attempt to determine distinguishing pathological abnormalities that if present at autopsy would definitively identify SIDS as the cause of death. While there are findings that are commonly present at autopsy, no gross anatomical or microscopic abnormalities have been found that are distinct to SIDS. Nevertheless, a thorough postmortem (autopsy) examination demonstrating the absence of a causative abnormality is crucial to the diagnosis of SIDS. Especially important is not missing evidence of child abuse such as signs of (1) suffocation, (2) blunt trauma to the head, ribs, or extremities, and (3) retinal hemorrhages seen in shaken baby syndrome.

Commonly described findings in the central nervous system include: (1) increase in brain weight, presumably due to disordered development of the brain, (2) delayed myelination (maturation) of nerve cells, (3) gliosis (scarring) of brain-stem cells, (4) areas of leukomalacia (degeneration of brain tissue that occurred weeks to months earlier), and (5) abnormal dendritic spine density in selected areas of the brain stem. Evidence of chronic oxygen deprivation—such as persistence of brown fat around the adrenal glands, red blood cell production in the liver, and gliosis of the brain stem—add support to the theory that abnormal respiratory regulation may be the mechanism underlying SIDS.

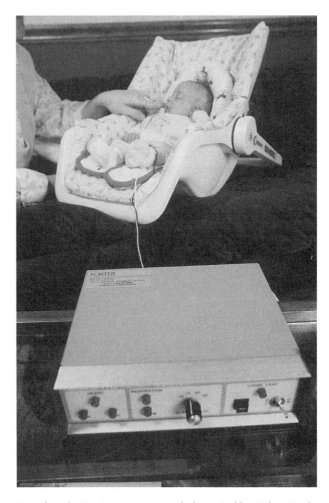

An infant sleeping in a car seat attached to a Sudden Infant Death Syndrome (SIDS) monitor. There are documented incidences of SIDS occurring even when the infants were being properly monitored, the machinery was fully functioning, and the resuscitative efforts were started promptly and correctly. This suggests that while abnormal breathing patterns are found in infants who subsequently die of SIDS, this is probably not the primary mechanism. (David H. Wells/Corbis)

Mechanism (Pathophysiology)

Current thinking regarding the mechanism of SIDS is focused on disordered regulation of the cardiorespiratory systems. The primary area of physiological regulation in humans is within the brain stem, which is located anatomically at the base of the brain. Abnormal findings on autopsy (as described in the above section), combined with clinical observations of abnormal regulatory control, support the view that delayed maturation or disruption of brain stem function results in the infant's lack of ability to respond when breathing and circulation patterns are insufficient to maintain life.

Several areas of respiratory regulation have been studied. Abnormalities of breathing patterns—such as recurrent brief apneic episodes, prolonged apneic event, and periodic breathing—have been observed in infants who later died of SIDS. The ability to electronically monitor and record breathing patterns in infants sparked enthusiasm for screening and monitoring of infants felt to be at high risk for SIDS.

However, experience has proven this intervention is not reliable in detecting which infants with abnormal breathing patterns will actually subsequently die of SIDS. In addition, multiple false alarms from the monitoring equipment resulted in high noncompliance rates in the home setting.

Diminished respiratory responsiveness to excessive buildup of carbon dioxide (hypercarbia) or to excessively low levels of oxygen (hypoxia) has also been found in infants at risk for SIDS. Nevertheless, the ability to discriminate between these infants and those not at risk who may have similar diminished responsiveness is lacking as of 2001.

A third respiratory regulation control mechanism is the arousal response. When experiencing hypocarbia or hypoxia, a normal sleeping infant will arouse and increase respiratory efforts in response to this life-threatening situation. Infants lacking sufficient arousal responsiveness will continue sleeping, becoming progressively more hypoxic, resulting in cardiorespiratory failure and sudden death.

Other mechanisms that are thought to be associated with the occurrence of SIDS include abnormal cardiac rhythms and increased body and/or environmental temperatures. It is likely that the pathophysiology of SIDS involves complex interactions between abnormal regulatory control systems and epidemiological risk factors such as poor intrauterine growth, exposure to smoking, prone sleep positioning, and prematurity.

Management

When a previously healthy infant is found unexpectedly dead, it is intensely emotionally traumatic. Caregivers blame themselves and each other. Families can be torn apart as a result of such an experience. For these reasons, proper management by experienced professionals is essential. A thorough investigation to determine the true cause of death is required. Other causes of sudden unexpected deaths of infants that have been mistakenly labeled as SIDS include congenital abnormalities of the heart and brain, metabolic disorders, occult infection (an infection that had escaped discovery), and accidental and nonaccidental trauma. Nonaccidental trauma or child abuse mistaken for SIDS has been highlighted by several high-profile cases in both the United States and Europe. The recommended approach when an infant is found unexpectedly dead consists of a thorough investigation at the scene to detail the environmental circumstances. This should be followed by a careful review of the infant's medical, social, and family histories, followed by a complete postmortem examination by an experienced forensic pathologist. In some cases, laboratory studies on family members may be indicated. Counseling of parents is essential so that they have accurate information as to the cause of their infant's death and the implications for future children, as well as for emotional support. Community resources should be provided for ongoing support.

Prevention

Although a definitive cause of SIDS remains unknown and there are no methods to predict which infants will die from SIDS, parents should be educated about strategies that will lessen the likelihood of a SIDS event. Parents should be advised to place infants on their backs for sleeping, provide a firm mattress, avoid loose clothing and blankets in the crib, avoid overheating their infant, breast-feed, and take their infant for regular medical care.

See also: INFANCY; INFANT MORTALITY

Bibliography

American Academy of Pediatrics. "Changing Concepts of Sudden Infant Death Syndrome: Implications for Infant Sleeping Environment and Sleep Position." *Pediatrics* 105 (2000):650–656.

American Academy of Pediatrics. "Distinguishing Sudden Infant Death Syndrome from Child Abuse Fatalities." *Pediatrics* 107 (2001):437–441.

Back to Sleep Campaign. "Reduce the Risk of Sudden Infant Death Syndrome (SIDS)" (brochure). Washington, DC: Back to Sleep Campaign, 1994.

Butlerys, Marc G., Sander Greenland, and Jess Kraus. "Chronic Fetal Hypoxia and Sudden Infant Death Syndrome: Interaction between Maternal Smoking and Low Hematocrit during Pregnancy." *Pediatrics* 86 (1990):535–540.

Hunt, Carl E., guest ed. "Apnea and SIDS" (special issue). *Clinics in Perinatology* 19, no. 4 (1992).

Hunt, Carl E. "Sudden Infant Death Syndrome." In Waldo E. Nelson ed., *Nelson Textbook of Pediatrics.* Philadelphia: Saunders, 1996.

Jeffery, Heather, Angelique Megevand, and Megan Page. "Why the Prone Position Is a Risk Factor for Sudden Infant Death Syndrome." *Pediatrics* 104 (1999):263–269.

Klonoff-Cohen, Hillary S., Sharon L. Edelstein, Ellen Lefkowitz, Indu P. Srinivasan, and David Kaegi. "The Effect of Passive Smoking and Tobacco Exposure through Breast Milk on Sudden Infant Death Syndrome." *Journal of the American Medical Association* 273 (1995):795–798.

Malloy, Michael H., and Daniel H. Freeman. "Birth Weight and Gestational Age-Specific Sudden Infant Death Syndrome Mortality: United States, 1991 versus 1995." *Pediatrics* 105 (2000):1227–1231.

Carol A. Miller

SUICIDE

Suicide is defined as the deliberate killing of oneself. Tragically, suicide is a problem that affects people of all ages, but most dramatically, adolescents and young adults. In fact, suicide is the most rapidly growing cause of death among youth between the ages of fifteen and twenty-four. In the mid-1990s, the National Center for Health Statistics ranked suicide as the third-leading cause of adolescent death, as it claimed the lives of approximately 5,000 American teenagers and young adults. In addition, the number of recorded deaths by suicide is apparently an underestimate of reality since a large number of completed suicides go unreported or are labeled as accidents.

Suicide attempts are defined as intentional, self-inflicted, and life-threatening acts that do not result in death. During adolescence, the documented prevalence rates of suicide attempts are higher than at any other time in the human lifespan. According to the Centers for Disease Control and Prevention (CDC), about one-half million adolescents and young adults attempt suicide each year with as many as 6 percent of high school males and 11 percent of high school females reporting at least one suicide attempt.

Suicidal ideation is broadly defined as a range of thoughts an individual may have related to the act of committing suicide. Suicidal ideation can range from thoughts that others might be better off if the person were dead to very specific, detailed planning for completing suicide. Signs of suicidal ideation may be expressed behaviorally, in written form, or through speech. Several surveys conducted in the mid-1990s suggest that 10 percent to 15 percent of adolescents have meaningful suicidal thoughts within a one-week or one-month time span. The CDC reported that in 1991 about 27 percent of high school students reported having thought seriously about attempting suicide and 16 percent reported having made a detailed suicide plan.

These facts and statistics become more meaningful when one considers what these findings suggest for a typical high school with an enrollment of 2,000 students. It is quite likely that in such a setting, approximately 500 students will have thoughts of suicide during the school year, 50 students will actually make a suicide attempt during the year, and 1 student will complete suicide once every four years.

Adolescent suicide is a reality that, although difficult and frightening for most of society to think about and discuss, can often be prevented. The key is for people to be informed about the potential reasons individuals might engage in suicidal behavior, the types of individuals who are at risk of engaging in suicidal behavior, the common myths about suicide, the warning signs of suicide, and the actions to take if one suspects a suicide might be attempted. An introductory examination of this vital information follows.

Reasons for Suicidal Behavior

Why do people kill themselves? This is an extremely difficult question to answer. Although there are many ideas or theories about why people commit suicide, there is no single comprehensive theory that describes and explains all life-threatening behaviors. The major theories of suicide can be categorized into sociological theories, psychological theories, and biological theories. In general, sociological theories are based on the idea that suicide results from the level and amount of control society has over an individual and the effects of social conditions and social changes

on the person. Psychological theories of suicide typically focus on conflicts within the individual; the role of one's thought processes, emotions, and personality characteristics; the person's developmental stage; and the ways in which the person's family functions. Finally, biological theories are based on the examination of biological aspects of suicide such as the influence of genetics, hormone levels, and neurotransmitter levels in the brain.

Suicidal acts take on very different meanings based upon the lenses one uses to examine each individual case of suicide. It is tempting to make sense of suicidal behavior by applying one of the many theories that have been developed by researchers to explain suicidal behavior. It appears, however, that the most complete understanding requires one to look beyond theories and ideas to the concrete evidence. Rather than asking why someone would commit suicide, the question can be rephrased as follows: What problem or problems was the person trying to solve?

Based upon the ways in which adolescents attempt to kill themselves, those who work with suicidal teens have found that most do not really want to die. When adolescents attempt suicide, most do it in their own homes, which is the place they are most likely to be found, and between the hours of 4 P.M. and midnight, which is the time of the day when someone in the family is most likely to be around. Thus, the chance of rescue is high, and those who hope for rescue do not really want to die. It appears then, that suicidal teens are simply attempting to solve one or more problems occurring in their life, but they, unfortunately, choose a permanent solution to their temporary problems. These teens are looking for a way to escape the emotional and physical pain that results from the problems they perceive or experience in their lives, and suicide appears to be a sure way to make the pain stop.

Those Who Are at Risk

People at risk of suicide come from a wide variety of backgrounds. There is not a special set of characteristics or personality traits that are common to all suicides. Unfortunately, suicide knows no boundaries. This is obvious since all kinds of youth end their own lives regardless of age, gender, ethnicity, economic background, and mental or physical state. Nevertheless, there are some general risk factors that apply to a large number of suicidal teens that may make suicide more likely for a given individual.

In general, adolescents are at higher risk for engaging in suicidal behaviors following a significant loss such as the death of a friend or family member, parental divorce or separation, or a breakup with a boyfriend or girlfriend. Teens who are depressed, involved with alcohol or other drugs, or are victims of physical, emotional, or sexual abuse have a higher potential for suicide. There is also heightened risk for those who have attempted suicide in the past or who come from a home where someone has committed suicide.

Research shows that adolescent females attempt suicide more often than adolescent males, but that males complete suicide at a higher rate. The most likely reason for this is that males tend to choose methods that are more lethal (e.g., gunshot, hanging, automobile crash), whereas females often use methods that are considered less lethal (e.g., drug overdose, slashing of wrists, carbon monoxide poisoning).

The rates of attempted suicide among gay and lesbian populations are two to six times greater than suicide rates for the general population. These statistics suggest that gay youth are at a greater risk for suicide than their straight counterparts. Finally, suicide risk is higher for teens who are gifted, have learning disabilities, or are pregnant or responsible for a pregnancy.

Warning Signs of Suicide

Most people who are suicidal put out warning signs to the public as a cry for help. They either directly or indirectly tell or show others about their suicide plan. Direct verbal threats such as "I am going to kill myself," "I am going to swallow a bottle of aspirin," or "By the weekend I will be dead" leave nothing to the imagination. These statements should be taken seriously, no matter how overdramatic they may sound, because very few people make such serious statements for the sake of just being funny. Indirect verbal threats are much more subtle and, therefore, more difficult to pick up on. Indirect threats tend to slide right into regular conversations and may easily be overlooked if one is not aware of these subtle cues. Statements such as "I hate my life," "Sometimes I wish I were dead," or "I just can't go on any longer" are all potential clues that someone may be thinking about suicide and that should lead anyone hearing the statement to act to prevent it.

In addition to direct and indirect verbal threats, suicidal people often exhibit a number of behaviors that serve as warning signs. Such signs include sudden changes in behavior related to eating and sleeping patterns, performance at school, physical appearance and hygiene, participation in activities and hobbies, and interactions with friends and family. When people suddenly stop acting like themselves for days or weeks, it is usually a signal that something has gone wrong in their lives and that this behavior should be examined further.

Teens who are making plans to die often try to tie up loose ends before they attempt to take their own life. They do this in a number of ways, including giving away the things that matter most to them, getting their rooms organized and their lockers or work spaces cleaned out, returning borrowed materials, and paying loans. These behaviors are not suspicious in and of themselves, but in combination with other suicide warning signs, these acts may serve as signals that the adolescent does not plan to be alive much longer.

Finally, teens who suddenly become aggressive, rebellious, or disobedient or who engage in risky or self-destructive behavior are also exhibiting signs that could be related to suicidal intent. These behaviors should not be ignored.

Actions to Take to Prevent Suicide

Adolescents who are suicidal need someone who will talk with them openly and honestly, who will listen attentively, and who will find them the help that they need. In order to help prevent a suicide from occurring, one must be informed of the questions to ask when suicide is suspected, the dos and don'ts of interacting with a person contemplating suicide, and who to contact for further assistance.

When signs of suicide have been observed, it is important to reach out to the person to find out what is going on. A good way to do this is by asking questions and listening attentively without making judgments. The goal is to get the person who may be considering suicide to talk about his or her problems out in the open. Specifically, there are four important questions that need to be asked directly: (1) Are you thinking about killing yourself? (2) How do you plan to do it? (3) When do you plan to do it? and (4) Where do you plan to do it? Contrary to popular belief, such candor will not give a person dangerous ideas or encourage a suicidal act. In fact, these questions not only allow the helper to assess the danger so she knows who to contact for further assistance, but also give the helpee permission to talk about suicide and the thoughts and problems that may be occurring. Such action can be a relief to individuals who are suicidal because it shows that someone is taking them seriously.

Some important information to remember when helping a person through a suicidal crisis is to remain calm even if what is said is shocking, to remain positive and never give up hope, and to know one's own limits and when it is time to seek outside help. One should never make promises to keep a person's suicide plans a secret. Instead, the helper should suggest that the suicidal person turn to help from trusted adults (e.g., parents, teachers, coaches), crisis hotlines, or trained professionals (e.g., counselors, therapists, doctors). Most importantly, one should never leave an individual in crisis alone, and one must act quickly if the person appears to be in danger.

See also: MENTAL DISORDERS; PERSONALITY DEVELOPMENT

Bibliography

Berman, Alan, and David Jobes. *Adolescent Suicide: Assessment and Intervention.* Washington, DC: American Psychological Association, 1991.

Kirk, William. *Adolescent Suicide.* Champaign, IL: Research Press, 1993.

Maris, Ronald, Morton Silverman, and Silvia Canetto. *Review of Suicidology, 1997.* New York: Guilford Press, 1997.

Nelson, Richard, and Judith Galas. *The Power to Prevent Suicide.* Minneapolis: Free Spirit Publishing, 1994.

Page, Randy. "Youth Suicidal Behavior: Completions, Attempts, and Ideations." *High School Journal* 80, no. 1 (1996):60–65.

Popenhagen, Mark, and Roxanne Qualley. "Adolescent Suicide: Detection, Intervention, and Prevention." *Professional School Counseling* 1, no. 4 (1998):30–36.

Robbins, Paul R. *Adolescent Suicide.* Jefferson, NC: McFarland, 1998.

Jeana L. Magyar-Moe

SURROGATE MOTHERHOOD

Surrogate motherhood is a practice in which one woman (the surrogate mother) intentionally becomes pregnant and gives birth to an infant who will be adopted by another woman (the adoptive mother), as arranged by a legal contract prior to conception. The surrogate mother may be impregnated by artificial insemination with the adoptive mother's husband's semen or may have implanted in her uterus an embryo conceived in vitro (outside the body). The contract frees the surrogate mother of parental rights and responsibilities; it may guarantee financial support and payment of medical costs but does not involve a direct payment for the child. Relevant ethical issues include reproductive freedom and rights, informed consent of the surrogate mother, and the best interests of the child. Roman Catholicism and Islam object to the procedure. In practice, some problems have occurred when surrogate mothers have been reluctant to give up children, and some adoptive parents have refused to accept children.

See also: PARENTING; REPRODUCTIVE TECHNOLOGIES

Bibliography

American Academy of Pediatrics. Committee on Bioethics and Committee on Early Childhood, Adoption, and Dependent Care. "Policy Statement." *American Academy of Pediatrics News* 9, no. 7 (1992).

Jean Mercer

SWADDLING OF INFANTS

Swaddling is the practice of binding or wrapping an infant in bands of cloth. An ancient custom, it is practiced in places as diverse as rural China, the American Southwest, Eastern Europe, and the Peruvian highlands. The reasons given for swaddling are also varied and include keeping the infant warm and protected in cold climates and at high altitudes, developing obedience, facilitating holding, and ensuring the baby's physical safety. Empirical studies have demonstrated that swaddling does serve to maintain higher, more stable temperatures inside the infant's microenvironment. Swaddling has also been studied, with limited success, as a possible technique for managing pain, enhancing neuromuscular development, and lengthening the sleep time of high-risk infants. Although swaddling retards motor performance while the baby remains wrapped, infants quickly catch up once swaddling is discontinued. A few studies have also suggested that swaddling may increase the risk of sudden infant death syndrome or of respiratory infections.

See also: INFANCY; SLEEPING

Bibliography

Li, Yan, Jintao Liu, Fengying Liu, Guamg ping Guo, Tokie Anme, and Hiroshi Ushijima. "Maternal Childrearing Behaviors and Correlates in Rural Minority Areas of Yunnan, China." *Developmental and Behavioral Pediatrics* 21 (2000):114–122.

Tronick, Edward, R. B. Thomas, and M. Daltabuit. "The Quechua Manta Pouch: A Caretaking Practice for Buffering the Peruvian Infant against the Multiple Stressors of High Altitude." *Child Development* 65 (1994):1005–1013.

Robin L. Harwood
Xin Feng

SYMBOLIC THOUGHT

Symbolic thought is the representation of reality through the use of abstract concepts such as words, gestures, and numbers. Evidence of symbolic thought is generally present in most children by the age of eighteen months, when signs and symbols ("signifiers") are used reliably to refer to concrete objects, events, and behaviors ("significates"). The hallmark of symbolic thought is language, which uses words or symbols to express concepts (mother, family), abstract references to transcend concrete reality (comfort, future), and allows intangibles to be manipulated (mathematical symbols). According to Jean Piaget, imitation plays an important role in the development of symbolic thought because the child is able to imagine behaviors observed in the past and to recreate them as imitated behaviors. Thus, a repertoire of signifiers is built that becomes connected to significates through assimilation of events and actions to those signifiers. The development of language arises from symbolic functions, which in turn facilitates development of symbolic thought.

See also: PIAGET, JEAN

Bibliography

Piaget, Jean. *Psychology of Intelligence.* New Jersey: Littlefield, Adams, and Company, 1966.

Dennis L. Molfese
Victoria J. Molfese
Julia Robinson

T

TABULA RASA

English philosopher John Locke (1632–1704) proposed that the mind of the newborn infant is a tabula rasa, or blank slate, on which experience writes. Although research on infant cognition has shown that this view is too extreme, some psychologists (known as empiricists) continue to believe that development is primarily a process of learning from the environment. Other psychologists (known as nativists) believe that knowledge emerges through a developmental process directed primarily by the genes.

Most contemporary psychologists, however, are interactionists. Rejecting the nativist/empiricist (or nature-nurture) dichotomy, interactionists argue that development is an ongoing interaction of genetic and environmental forces. Psychologists known as constructivists, moreover, acknowledging the interactive roles of genes and environment, add that the mind itself is an active agent in the construction of knowledge. Thus psychologists continue to debate how much knowledge we should attribute to the infant at birth and how development proceeds from there.

See also: INFANCY

Bibliography

Moshman, David. *Adolescent Psychological Development: Rationality, Morality, and Identity.* Mahwah, NJ: Lawrence Erlbaum, 1999.

Spelke, Elizabeth, and Elissa Newport. "Nativism, Empiricism, and the Development of Knowledge." In William Damon ed., *Handbook of Child Psychology,* 5th edition, Vol. 1: *Theoretical Models of Human Development,* edited by Richard Lerner. New York: Wiley, 1998.

David Moshman

TAY-SACHS DISEASE

Tay-Sachs disease is a rare, inherited degenerative disorder of the nervous system associated with deficiency of the enzyme β-hexosaminidase A (HEXA). When the condition is present, a particular lipid, called a ganglioside, accumulates in the cells of the central nervous system. Functional and anatomical abnormalities result, and are clinically manifested by motor disturbances, seizures, speech problems, psychiatric illness, and dementia. Age of onset and clinical severity depend upon the magnitude of the enzyme deficiency. The classic or infantile form is rapidly progressive, leading to death within the first few years of life. Adult onset cases are milder and the disease may not be life threatening. Certain ethnic groups, such as those of Ashkenazi Jewish, French Canadian, or Turkish origin, are more commonly affected. Research is directed toward understanding the biological activity of gangliosides and the effects of their excessive accumulation. As there is no cure, intervention involves identifying those who carry the genetic defect in order to provide reproductive counseling to them.

See also: GENOTYPE

Bibliography

Gravel, Roy A., Joe T. R. Clarke, Michael M. Kaback, Don Mahuran, Conrad Sandhoff, and Kinuko Suzuki. "The GM$_2$ Gangliosidoses." In Charles R. Scriver, Arthur L. Beaudet, William S. Sly, and David Vale eds., *The Metabolic and Molecular Basis of Inherited Disease,* 7th edition. New York: McGraw-Hill, 1995.

MacQueen, Glenda M., Patricia I. Rosebush, and Michael F. Mazurek. "Neuropsychiatric Aspects of the Adult Variant of Tay-Sachs Disease." *The Journal of Neuropsychiatry and Clinical Neurosciences* 10 (1998):10–19.

Patricia I. Rosebush

TEENAGE PREGNANCY

Teenage pregnancy has long been a topic of concern and controversy in the United States. On one hand it has been characterized as an "epidemic," and President Clinton referred to teen pregnancy as "our most serious social problem" in his 1995 State of the Union Address. Conversely, some research evidence suggests that young maternal age may not be the cause of all adverse consequences commonly associated with teen pregnancy. This article discusses the incidence of teenage pregnancy and trends in birth rates, research on the consequences of teen childbearing for mothers and their children, and the implications of these findings for current policy and intervention strategies.

Incidence of Teenage Pregnancy

Teenage pregnancy rates include those pregnancies that result in live births as well as those ending in induced abortions or other fetal losses. The National Center for Health Statistics estimates that in 1996 the pregnancy rate was 98.7 per 1,000 women aged fifteen through nineteen years, for a total of approximately 893,000 pregnancies. In that year, just over half (55%) of these pregnancies resulted in a live birth, with 30 percent ending in induced abortion, and 15 percent in fetal loss.

Pregnancy and birth rates among teenagers have varied considerably over time. Figure 1 depicts rates of birth among women aged fifteen through nineteen years from 1940 to 1999. Teen birth rates were at their highest from the late 1940s through the early 1960s, mirroring the elevated rates seen among all women of childbearing age during this time period, commonly referred to as the "baby boom." More recently, birth rates showed a relatively modest increase in the late 1980s and early 1990s, and declined steadily thereafter. Data for 1999 indicated that the teenage birth rate in that year fell to a record low of 49.6 births per 1,000.

Teen births tend to be concentrated in later adolescence, with two-thirds of the total births in 1999 occurring to women eighteen or nineteen years of age. Birth rates also vary among teens by race and ethnicity. Non-Hispanic white teenagers have historically had much lower birth rates than other groups. African-American teenagers ranked highest of any group until 1994, after which marked declines led their rates to track somewhat below those of Hispanic teens.

Teenage Pregnancy and Later Outcomes

Becoming a mother as a teenager is associated with higher risk for a number of poor outcomes. Teen mothers are less likely to finish high school, less successful in the job market, less likely to marry, and more likely to rely on public assistance than women who have children after their teen years. In addition, children of teen mothers generally do not fare as well as other children. They tend to score less optimally on assessments of cognitive development and academic achievement, and also tend to exhibit more problem behaviors than other children.

Although teen pregnancy is associated with this myriad of unfavorable outcomes, it has become widely acknowledged that such outcomes should not simply be interpreted as being caused by early childbearing itself. This is because teen births do not occur randomly among women in the population, but rather are experienced by women who themselves are much more likely to have come from disadvantaged backgrounds. Teenage mothers are up to twice as likely as other women, for example, to have grown up in single-parent families. Many teen mothers have spent much of their own childhood in poverty, often living in impoverished neighborhoods characterized by poor schools, inferior public services, and limited career options. Since people who come from disadvantaged backgrounds are generally at higher risk for poorer outcomes, it is very difficult to sort out whether the long-term difficulties experienced by teen mothers and their children are due to early childbearing, or are the result of the mothers' preexisting economic and social disadvantages.

During the 1990s, researchers used innovative methods to try to better understand the actual consequences of teen childbearing. Arline Geronimus and her colleagues studied pairs of sisters in their late twenties and thirties in which one of the pair had a birth while a teenager and the other did not. Since both sisters were raised in the same conditions, this strategy provided a way to control for many aspects of background disadvantage when examining ways that outcomes differed for the teen and nonteen mothers. Using data from several nationally repre-

FIGURE 1

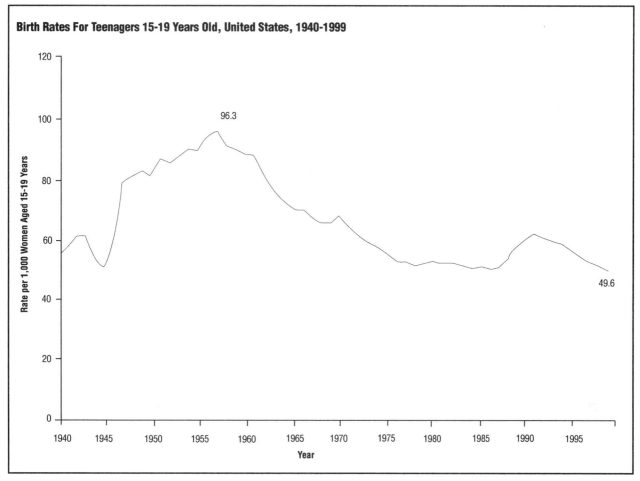

Birth Rates For Teenagers 15-19 Years Old, United States, 1940-1999

SOURCE: *Figure adapted from National Center for Health Statistics. Vital Statistics of the United States, 1968, Vol 1: Natality. Washington, DC: Public Health Service, 1970; National Center for Health Statistics. Vital Statistics of the United States, 1992, Vol 1: Natality. Washington, DC: Public Health Service, 1995; Ventura, Stephanie J., Joyce A. Martin, Sally C. Curtin, T. J. Mathews, and M. M. Park. "Births: Final Data for 1998." National Vital Statistics Reports 48 (3). Hyattsville, MD: National Center for Health Statistics, 2000; Sally C. Curtin, and Joyce A. Martin. "Births: Preliminary Data for 1999." National Vital Statistics Reports 48 (14). Hyattsville, MD: National Center for Health Statistics, 2000.*

sentative surveys, they found that the long-term "costs" of teen childbearing were lower than previously thought. Results based on one of the surveys indicated that future incomes and employment status were not significantly different among teen and older mothers. Similar analyses done by Geronimus and others (and replicated by Saul Hoffman and associates using data from another survey) did show somewhat lower incomes and poorer economic status among teen mothers when compared to their sisters who were not teen mothers. Although findings varied in different surveys, all of these studies consistently demonstrated that previous research, which did not account for background disadvantage, tended to overstate the negative consequences of teen childbearing.

More recently, Joseph Hotz and colleagues compared mothers who gave birth as teenagers, with women who became pregnant at the same age but suffered miscarriages and subsequently delayed childbearing for at least three or four years. Their results indicated that, on average, those who gave birth actually had significantly higher incomes later on than women who had delayed childbearing. In this study there was no difference among the groups of mothers in the likelihood of obtaining a high-school level education, although teen mothers were more likely to obtain a GED than a high school diploma. Teen mothers also tended to have more births by age thirty than the other mothers, and had spent a greater proportion of this time interval unmarried.

Studies have also examined the consequences of teen motherhood for children. For example, Kristin

Moore and associates compared outcomes among children of teen and nonteen mothers, using a set of standard statistical controls in their analyses for maternal background factors and other characteristics. They found that children of teen mothers experienced a significantly lower quality home environment, and children born to teens aged seventeen or younger were at a significant disadvantage with respect to cognitive development and academic achievement. Using their sister-pair strategy as a more comprehensive way to control mothers' background disadvantage, Geronimus and colleagues found that children of teen mothers actually did better than children of nonteen mothers on several cognitive and achievement tests; and on other tests, no significant differences among the children were observed.

In sum, research findings highlight the important and previously underemphasized role that disadvantaged conditions prior to pregnancy play in the poor outcomes seen among teen mothers and their children. There is general consensus that earlier studies exaggerated the consequences of teen childbearing because they failed to effectively take these background factors into account. The true nature and the extent of the outcomes caused by teen childbearing remain controversial, largely due to the fact that the data currently available with which to study them have significant limitations. More definitive answers will require the development of larger and more detailed surveys that follow childbearing women and their children over longer periods of time, as well as improved research methods for quantifying causal effects with increased certainty.

Public Policy and Teenage Pregnancy

Just as there is a lack of consensus about the consequences of teenage pregnancy, the optimal focus for public policy and intervention is also in dispute. Some experts reason that because the disadvantaged circumstances in which many women grow up are a predominant factor impacting teen birth rates, policies and programs would be most effectively directed at ameliorating that disadvantage and developing positive life options for young women. Others, however, maintain that in the absence of conclusive research findings to the contrary, targeted interventions such as the National Campaign to Prevent Teen Pregnancy initiated in 1996 have potential benefits and should continue to be pursued.

It is clear that teenage pregnancy fell steadily over the 1990s in the United States, with reductions seen for each of the three pregnancy outcomes (live births, induced abortions, and fetal losses). The National Center for Health Statistics noted several concurrent trends related to teen pregnancy rates over this period. First, rates of sexual activity among teenagers appear to have stabilized and perhaps declined, as measured by teens' responses in several national surveys. In addition, increases have been reported in condom use and in the availability and adoption of other effective birth control methods including injectable and implantable contraceptives. These behavioral trends may well have been influenced by educational and contraceptive-related intervention programs; however, it is also important to note that they occurred during a period of remarkable, sustained economic expansion. This expansion increased the opportunities available to teenagers, making higher educational and occupational goals more desirable and attainable and in the process providing a powerful impetus for behavior change.

See also: BIRTH; FATHERS; POVERTY; PREGNANCY; SEX EDUCATION; SEXUAL ACTIVITY

Bibliography

Curtin, Sally C., and Joyce A. Martin. "Births: Preliminary Data for 1999." *National Vital Statistics Reports* 48 (14). Hyattsville, MD: National Center for Health Statistics, 2000.

East, Patricia, and Leanne Jacobson. "Adolescent Childbearing, Poverty, and Siblings: Taking New Direction from the New Literature." *Family Relations* 49 (2000):287–292.

Geronimus, Arline, and Sanders Korenman. "The Socioeconomic Consequences of Teen Childbearing Reconsidered." *Quarterly Journal of Economics* 107 (1992):1187–1214.

Geronimus, Arline, and Sanders Korenman. "Maternal Youth or Family Background? On the Health Disadvantages of Infants with Teen Mothers." *American Journal of Epidemiology* 137 (1993):213–225.

Geronimus, Arline, Sanders Korenman, and Marianne Hillemeier. "Does Young Maternal Age Adversely Affect Child Development? Evidence from Cousin Comparisons in the United States." *Population and Development Review* 20 (1994):585–609.

Hoffman, Saul. "Teenage Childbearing Is Not So Bad After All . . . Or Is It? A Review of the New Literature." *Family Planning Perspectives* 30 (1998):236–249.

Hotz, V. Joseph, Susan McElroy, and Seth Sanders. "The Impacts of Teenage Childbearing on the Mothers and the Consequences of Those Impacts for Government." In Rebecca A. Maynard ed., *Kids Having Kids.* Washington DC: Urban Institute Press, 1997.

Moore, Kristin, Donna Morrison, and Angela Greene. "Effects on the Children Born to Adolescent Mothers." In Rebecca Maynard ed., *Kids Having Kids.* Washington DC: Urban Institute Press, 1997.

National Center for Health Statistics. *Vital Statistics of the United States, 1968,* Vol. 1: *Natality.* Washington: Public Health Service, 1970.

National Center for Health Statistics. *Vital Statistics of the United States, 1992,* Vol. 1: *Natality.* Washington: Public Health Service, 1995.

"Recent Accomplishments of the National Campaign to Prevent Teen Pregnancy." Available from http://www.teenpregnancy.org/accom.htm; INTERNET

Ventura, Stephanie J., and Mary Anne Freedman. "Teenage Child-bearing in the United States, 1960–1997." *American Journal of Preventive Medicine* 19(1S) (2000):18–25.

Ventura, Stephanie J., Joyce A. Martin, Sally C. Curtin, T. J. Mathews, and M. M. Park. "Births: Final Data for 1998." *National Vital Statistics Reports* 48 (3). Hyattsville, MD: National Center for Health Statistics, 2000.

Ventura, Stephanie J., William Mosher, Sally C. Curtin, Joyce Abma, and Stanley Henshaw. "Trends in Pregnancies and Pregnancy Rates by Outcome: Estimates for the United States, 1976–96." *Vital and Health Statistics* 21 (56). Hyattsville, MD: National Center for Health Statistics, 2000.

Marianne M. Hillemeier

TELEVISION

Since the middle of the twentieth century, television has grown from a novelty to a fixture in 99 percent of American households. Over time, the character of the medium also changed dramatically. Once offering only three principal broadcast networks, viewers' choices now may extend to more than a hundred channels. By 1999, 78 percent of homes with children and adolescents received at least basic cable, enabling children to grow up with a wide variety of general audience and child-oriented programming.

Television's introduction was accompanied by excitement and optimism, followed almost immediately by criticisms and concerns about its impact on children's development. Critics linked television to every ill effect from hyperactive toddlers to violent youth, prompting consideration of regulations for children's television. Regulations have varied over the years and have come to focus on requirements for educational programming, limitations on commercial time in children's programming, and implementation of a content rating system. Changes in regulations have been fueled not only by political shifts but also by ongoing research on children's use of television and television's influences on children's development.

How Do Children Use Television?

To understand television's potential impact on development, one must consider how much children watch television, how they direct their attention, and what they comprehend.

How Much Do They Watch?

Children are consumers of a variety of media, including computers, video games, print media, videotapes, music, and television. Although television is the most commonly used medium, viewing time varies with age. From two to seven years of age, children's viewing time is about two hours per day. Increasing through childhood, it peaks at about three and a half hours per day during middle school before dropping off to about two and a half hours per day during adolescence. The family environments of those who view more television tend to share certain characteristics: parents who watch a lot of television, television left on as background noise, and a television in the child's room.

How Do They Watch?

Children often have been characterized as "zombie" viewers who stare mindlessly at television for hours. Instead, naturalistic and laboratory studies of how children watch television indicate that children typically divide television viewing among a variety of activities. At all ages, children primarily monitor television content with short looks and only occasionally engage in extended looks at the television. Just as total viewing time changes across age, the percentage of time children spend actually looking at the television increases through middle school then drops slightly during adolescence.

Another common misconception is that the changing sights and sounds of television passively "capture" young children's attention. Certain formal, noncontent features of television production do sometimes cause children to orient automatically (e.g., a sudden loud noise, a rapid movement). Nevertheless, many features that attract or hold children's attention are informative, signaling content that children are likely to find relevant or entertaining. For example, the presence of children's voices, peculiar voices, sound effects, animation, and puppets cue children to the child-relevance of the content. Children's ongoing comprehension also influences their attention. If children are making sense of a program and judging it to be "for them," they are more likely to keep attending to it than if it seems confusing or adult-oriented.

What Do They Understand?

Many have claimed that until late in elementary school, children make little sense of most programs because they are poor at selecting important events, connecting events, and inferring causes of events. Nonetheless, if plots depend on concrete action sequences, if dialogue and action support one another, and if story events relate to children's experiences, even preschool children can understand relatively complex stories.

To comprehend a televised story, one must understand information that is conveyed by production techniques. For example, a viewer needs to infer that a cut between a shot of a house's exterior and a shot of characters at a kitchen table conveys the exact location of the characters. Young children are capable of making such inferences, if they comprehend simple

Displacement theory suggests that time spent with television leads to a decrease in more valuable activities, such as reading and imaginative play. While evidence supporting this proposal is mixed, children who view television most heavily seem to spend less time engaged in activities that encourage cognitive development. (Robert J. Huffman/Field Mark Publications)

relations in time and space. Another component of effective comprehension is appreciating that not all story events are equally important to the plot. Some of the most important events are those that can be connected as causes or consequences of other events. Contrary to claims that young children are unselective and insensitive to such connections, events with many connections are remembered best as early as the preschool years.

There are, of course, limits on young children's comprehension of television programs and considerable development in comprehension skills during middle childhood and adolescence. Not until later in elementary school do children become consistent at understanding complex production techniques (e.g., flashbacks) and characters' emotions, intentions, and motivations. Older children and teens also become more skilled at connecting groups of events to an overall theme. With age, children add to their store of world knowledge and so become capable of appreciating a wider variety of situations.

How Are Children Affected by Television?

Television may influence children's development in a variety of ways. Two broad areas for consideration are effects on children's cognitive development and academic achievement and effects on children's social development and relationships with others.

Does Television Affect Thinking and Achievement?

Parents and teachers have long voiced concerns regarding television's potential effects on children's thinking and school achievement. A basis for these concerns is displacement theory, which proposes that time spent with television takes time away from more valuable activities, such as reading and imaginative play. Evidence supporting this proposal is mixed. Children who view television most heavily do seem to spend less time engaged in activities that encourage cognitive development and in turn show the lowest achievement. For light to moderate television viewers, program content, family interaction, and opportunities for other activities moderate television's effects on children's achievement and creativity.

Does Television Affect Behavior with Others?

Concern regarding television's effects on children's social development has been most apparent in the longstanding debate over the link between televised violence and children's aggression, but extends to other areas such as development of stereotypes, understanding and expressing emotions, and problems such as substance abuse and eating disorders. Several overlapping theories offer reasons why television may exert effects.

Arousal theory emphasizes physiological responses that can be produced by television programs. Programs causing emotions also produce bodily responses, such as increased heart rate from excitement during a violent or suspenseful show. The excitement of shows that produce physical arousal will attract many children. This theory, however, also predicts that with increased exposure, children need stronger stimulation to reach the same level of arousal and emotional reactions, and so they can become desensitized to violence and other themes that provoke emotions. Perhaps the most compelling evidence for this perspective is that children show reduced responses to real-life aggression after viewing televised violence.

Social cognitive theory, developed by psychologist Albert Bandura, stresses that children learn many social behaviors by observing those modeled by others. Children are more likely to try a behavior if they can identify with the person modeling the behavior and the model is successful at achieving a goal or obtaining a reward. Heavy exposure to television characters who succeed by behaving in aggressive, violent, or stereotypical ways may encourage children to use similar strategies in their own lives. Numerous studies provide evidence that heavy exposure to televised violence is linked to increased aggressive behavior in children and adolescents.

Script theories address ways in which television influences the development of children's knowledge and beliefs about the world. Based on experiences with real and media events, children build representations of what to expect in certain situations or of certain people. In turn, children's expectations may guide their behaviors. Children who observe frequent aggressive solutions to conflict situations are more likely to expect others to behave aggressively. One specific version of script theory, cultivation theory, proposes that heavy viewing leads people to see the world as it is portrayed on television. For example, television programs overrepresent the occurrence of violence and exaggerate the presence and the power

of white males. Consistent with cultivation theory, heavy viewers are relatively likely to see the world as mean and threatening and to develop ethnic and gender stereotypes.

Some evidence supports each of these theories. Results from any single study, however, cannot establish a clear causal link from television to a particular behavior. The strongest argument is possible when multiple sources of evidence converge, as is the case for the conclusion that viewing televised violence contributes to aggressive behavior. Even here, heavy viewing of violent television is only one contributor to the development of aggressive behavior, and is most likely to affect children who are prone to aggressive behavior for other reasons (e.g., children from families or cultures in which aggression is an acceptable response to conflict).

What Can One Do about Television and Children?

Parent activism has spurred the development of broadcasting regulations, which in turn may exert some influence on children's viewing. Direct parental involvement, however, may have the greatest potential to affect the nature of television's impact on children's development. When children are young, it is relatively simple for parents to provide guidance concerning the amount and kind of viewing children do. Such guidance can help establish viewing habits that will continue to exert an influence as children get older and exercise more independent choice. If preschoolers learn to be selective about program choices and understand that there are many ways to spend their time, they may be less apt to fall into uncritical heavy viewing later in childhood. As children get older, parents can assist them in viewing critically and can avoid creating an environment that assigns television undue importance (e.g., a television in the child's room). Together, federal regulations and parental vigilance may help television contribute positively to children's development.

See also: SOCIAL DEVELOPMENT; VIOLENCE

Bibliography

Anderson, Daniel R., and Patricia A. Collins. *The Impact on Children's Education: Television's Influence on Cognitive Development.* Washington, DC: Office of Educational Research and Improvement, 1988.

Bryant, Jennings, and J. Alison Bryant, eds. *Television and the American Family,* 2nd edition. Mahwah, NJ: Lawrence Erlbaum, 2001.

Calvert, Sandra. *Children's Journeys through the Information Age.* Boston: McGraw-Hill College, 1999.

Huston, Aletha C., and John C. Wright. "Mass Media and Children's Development." In William Damon, Irving Sigel, and K. Ann Renninger eds., *Handbook of Child Psychology,* 5th edition,

Vol. 4: *Child Psychology in Practice,* edited by Jane B. Smith. New York: Wiley, 1997.

Kaiser Family Foundation. *Kids and Media at the New Millennium.* Menlo Park, CA: Kaiser Family Foundation, 1999.

Murray, John P. "Studying Television Violence: A Research Agenda for the Twenty-First Century." In Joy K. Asamen and Gordon L. Berry eds., *Research Paradigms, Television, and Social Behavior.* Thousand Oaks, CA: Sage, 1998.

Neuman, Susan B. *Literacy in the Television Age.* Norwood, NJ: Ablex, 1991.

Elizabeth Lorch
Clarese Lemberger

TEMPER TANTRUMS

Temper tantrums are disruptive behaviors in the form of angry outbursts that may be physical (hitting, biting, pushing), verbal (crying, screaming, whining), or persistent grouchiness and petulance. Tantrums are common in young children; up to 80 percent of two- and three-year-olds experience tantrums, and 20 percent have daily tantrums.

Tantrums consistent with normal toddler development reflect a striving for emotional independence and limited expressive language skills during frustrating events. Other contributing factors include the child's temperament. Intense, persistent children, shy, fearful children, and those with frequent episodes of stranger anxiety are more likely to experience tantrums. A delay in language development, hearing impairment, and disorders of the central nervous system may limit coping strategies and lead to tantrums.

A child's environment modifies the frequency and intensity of temper tantrums. Behavioral expectations and responses to disruptive behaviors by parents, teachers, and other caretakers have a strong influence on tantrums. Intolerance for minor temper outbursts, negative verbal or physical responses, inconsistent responses, and a limited understanding of normal development in young children affect the nature of tantrums. Parent education and principles of behavior modification applied to discipline form the foundation for an effective parental response.

See also: DISCIPLINE; PARENTING

Bibliography

Stein, Martin T. "Difficult Behaviors: Temper Tantrums to Conduct Disorders." In Abraham M. Rudolf ed., *Rudolf's Pediatrics,* 20th edition. Stamford, CT: Appleton and Lange, 1996.

Martin T. Stein

TEMPERAMENT

The word "temperament" is used frequently in everyday speech. People will refer to another person, or even an object, as "temperamental." To social scientists, temperament is not a set of behaviors per se; it is not an ability, such as thinking, or a set of actions, such as playing. Instead, temperament is a behavioral style. It is not what a person does, but how that person does it. It is not that the boy cries, but that he cries frequently. It is not that the girl walks, but that she walks quickly.

In 1987 a prominent cognitive psychologist, Robert McCall, created a definition of temperament that included elements common to the four main theories of temperament at the time. According to McCall, temperament is defined as biologically based individual differences in reactions to the world; these reactions are relatively stable across development. Temperament is not personality but is one of the bases of later personality differences. Personality characteristics include traits and behaviors that are acquired after infancy and some that are not influenced by biological factors. Habits, goals, and self-perceptions are aspects of people's personalities, but they are not temperament traits. Given the complexity of the definition, it may be helpful to discuss the three elements common to all temperament characteristics: (1) the individual differences are present at birth, (2) the differences are inherent in the person, and (3) the differences are stable across development.

Three Common Elements of Temperament Characteristics

The first factor common to all temperament characteristics is that these individual differences are present at birth. Sigmund Freud was the first psychologist to discuss personality development. The purpose of his theory, however, was to explain the common human experience. Freud argued that all children were born with biological drives (e.g., hunger, thirst) that need to be satisfied in order to ensure personal survival. Three mental structures (the id, the ego, and the superego) emerge during childhood and struggle with each other to create the individual's personality. According to Freud, personality differences are not present at birth. Instead, these differences emerge during childhood as each child resolves internal conflict in different ways and in different family contexts. By adolescence, children have developed unique coping styles that are stable into adulthood. Temperament researchers, on the other hand, argue that differences in reactions to the world are present at birth. In addition, few believe that children are constantly struggling to resolve internal conflict during childhood. Children are born with unique behavioral styles that influence their development from the womb until death.

The second element common to all temperament characteristics is that these differences are inherent in the person. Temperament is a biologically based reaction to the world. This does not mean that all temperamental differences are genetically inherited. This is the foundation of Arnold Buss and Robert Plomin's EAS theory of temperament, with EAS standing for the traits found to be heritable during infancy (emotionality, activity, and sociability). Other researchers, however, also include prenatal influences on children's behavior. The idea that traits are biologically based does not mean that these characteristics are resistant to environmental influences. All temperament theorists argue that social experiences can and will change a child's temperament. Inherent simply means that these behavioral styles are not due to parenting. Infants' unique reactions to the world have biological roots. For instance, many children born to mothers addicted to drugs have very difficult temperaments; these children cry often, are hard to console, and do not like to be held. Their behavior is thought to be due to the influence of the drugs on the developing fetus in the womb. Other children may inherit from their parents a tendency to be emotional or shy.

As early as 1699, the philosopher John Locke maintained that children are born with different behavioral tendencies. He also believed that the environment was the strongest force in development. To Locke, social experiences, not temperamental differences, shaped behavior across development. This was the predominant view of children's development until the 1960s and 1970s. During this time, Alexander Thomas and Stella Chess published their classic books about the role of temperament in parent-child relationships and children's social and emotional development. Thomas and Chess argued that children's behavioral problems do not always stem from bad parenting. Instead, some children come into this world with temperament styles that make disciplining them a challenge. Even competent, caring parents may have difficult children and these parents need help learning how to manage their sons and daughters.

Other child psychologists at this time also asserted that children are born equipped with behavioral biases and abilities that affect later development. The cognitive psychologist Jean Piaget described infants as active participants in their own experiences who are motivated to learn how to adapt in their environments. By the end of the 1980s, the child was no longer seen as a piece of clay to be molded into an obedient citizen, but as a force to be guided into a competent adult. It was in this intellectual context that the notion took hold that children are born with unique temperament characteristics.

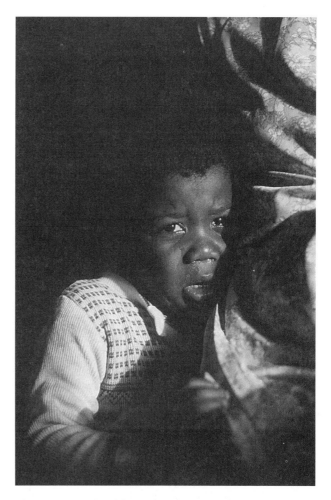

There is some evidence that early temperament traits predict behavior in adolescence and adulthood. It is easier to predict the future behavior of people with extreme temperament styles than of those who fall in the middle. (Nathan Benn/Corbis)

The third component of all definitions of temperament is that behavioral styles are relatively stable across development. Temperament characteristics can and will change in response to parenting and other social forces. The idea is that the early roots of adult personality can be seen from the beginning. Several studies have included groups of individuals who were followed from birth to adulthood. The findings from these studies regarding stability are mixed. Children's temperament traits do appear to be quite stable through infancy and into childhood. Jerome Kagan and his colleagues studied two extreme groups of children from infancy to adolescence. Members of the first group, behaviorally inhibited children, were very shy and fearful in unfamiliar situations. Members of the second group, behaviorally uninhibited children, were very gregarious and assertive in novel settings. The researchers found that the inhibited children were at greater risk for later social and emotional problems compared to the uninhibited children.

Others have found that children who withdraw from situations or who throw tantrums have more marital and work-related problems in adulthood compared to other children. Temperament measures are good tools to help uncover early adjustment problems. Predicting adult personality from infant temperament, however, is not as easily achieved for those in the middle range compared to those at the extreme ends. Some children change in response to their experiences with their parents, teachers, and peers. In addition, children begin to exert conscious control over their behavioral tendencies during childhood. Part of healthy development is learning how to adapt to the demands of different contexts. Some active children learn restraint and some emotional children learn peacefulness.

Measuring Temperament

While researchers tend to agree on the basic definition of temperament, they differ on the types of temperament styles they investigate. According to McCall, most temperament studies focus on four dimensions: activity, reactivity, emotionality, and sociability. Activity is the intensity and rate of a child's movement and speech. How much does the child move around during play or at her desk at school? Reactivity is the intensity of a child's approach or withdrawal from a situation and how long the child is interested in and stays in the situation. How much does a child withdraw from novel toys or new situations? Emotionality is the degree to which a child expresses negative or positive emotions and how often she expresses them. Does a child get upset easily or become angry quickly? Sociability is the tendency to initiate social contact and the preference to be with others. Is the child friendly?

Not all temperament characteristics fit neatly into these four dimensions. Shyness, for example, has been investigated as an aspect of reactivity (i.e., the tendency to withdraw from new social situations) and as the opposite end of sociability (i.e., the tendency to not want to be around people). While many researchers have focused on one or more of these dimensions, others have categorized children based on combinations of traits and styles.

Thomas and Chess divided children into three categories based on nine temperament dimensions: activity level, approach-withdrawal in new situations, adaptability, threshold of responsiveness, intensity of reactions, quality of mood, distractibility, persistence, and rhythmicity of biological functions (e.g., sleeping, feeding, needing to be changed). They were interested in the "goodness-of-fit" between the children's characteristics and their social environments. Forty percent of the children in their study were classified as "easy" babies. These children adapted easily to new situations, were sociable and playful, and had regular biological functions. These children were not too reactive or emotional, and so they were easy to parent. Another 15 percent of the babies fell into the "slow-to-warm-up" category. These children withdrew from new situations somewhat, took a little longer to adapt to environments, and were less active. They needed more attention and time compared to easy babies, but they adapted to their surroundings without too much trouble. About 10 percent of the infants were classified in the "difficult" temperament category. Children with difficult temperaments were very emotional, had irregular biological functions, and had intense negative reactions to new situations. These children were the most difficult to parent and required a great deal of effort, time, and patience. The remaining children fell into more than one category or could not be classified.

Dimensions of temperament are measured in a variety of ways. Parents are interviewed about their children's behavior at home, and teachers are interviewed about the children's behavior at school. Depending on the dimension being assessed, these adults may be asked about children's reactions to new toys or people (i.e., reactivity) or about their energy levels (i.e., activity). Parent and teacher reports of children's behavior may be limited to that context and influenced by their own perceptions of the world (i.e., they may be biased). So, scientists also use behavioral and observational methods to assess children's temperament. Activity level in infancy, for example, can be measured using a device that measures the number of times a baby's arms and legs move. Most of the time, trained researchers observe the children at home, at school, or in a novel environment (e.g., a playroom in a researcher's laboratory). Coders look for visible signs of the child's underlying temperament style. For example, a child who approaches an unfamiliar student on a school playground and talks to the new child would be coded as high in sociability.

Some dimensions of temperament have to be assessed in specific contexts. Reactivity and shyness, for instance, must be observed in novel situations because the behavior of interest may not appear in familiar contexts or may appear for only some children. For example, children who are withdrawn in unfamiliar situations are considered temperamentally shy. Children who are withdrawn in both familiar and unfamiliar situations, on the other hand, are considered anxious and possibly at risk for developing an anxiety disorder. Sometimes children's behavior is ambiguous, so researchers will measure changes in children's physiology as well. Shy children, for instance, tend to experience a higher heart rate when they are in new situations compared to when they are at home. Children are also asked to report their perceptions of their temperament style after around the age of eight. This is when most children are able to report their own behaviors and preferences in a reliable manner. Few studies, however, include self-report measures because most temperament studies focus on children in infancy and early childhood.

Biological Factors

Since theorists have argued that temperament has biological roots, many studies have focused on genetic and neurological correlates of different behavioral styles. Most (if not all) temperament dimensions appear to be moderately heritable, with shyness showing the highest heritability. That is, the more closely people are genetically related, the more alike they are in temperament. Much of the evidence supporting this conclusion comes from twin studies, which compare the behavioral similarity of monozygotic (identical) twin pairs to dizygotic (fraternal) twin pairs. Monozygotic twins inherit identical genotypes because they develop from the same fertilized egg. In contrast, dizygotic twins inherit, on average, 50 percent of their segregating genes. If genetic differences across people are associated with temperament differences across people, then identical twin similarity should be twice as high as fraternal twin similarity. Plomin and others found that this is true for temperament characteristics such as emotionality, activity level, sociability, and shyness.

Interestingly, some studies show that identical twins are more than twice as similar as both fraternal twins and other pairs of relatives (e.g., parents and their children and biologically related siblings). How could this be? David Lykken and his colleagues hypothesized that temperament (and personality) differences are associated with genetic effects that do not run in families. These genetic effects are the result of complex interactions across loci at the level of the genome and across behaviors at the level of the developing person. Only identical twins inherit all the genes associated with these higher-order interactions, and so they will be much more similar to each other compared to other pairs of genetically related relatives. Some social scientists maintain that high identical twin similarity on temperament measures is due to monozygotic twin assimilation effects (i.e., parents treat identical twins more alike compared to fraternal twins) or to measurement problems (i.e., measures are not sensitive enough to detect moderate to low fraternal twin or sibling similarity). Still, few research-

ers would argue that temperament is completely determined by the environment.

During the 1990s, the search for biological correlates of temperament differences expanded to include investigations of brain activation patterns. Scientists found brain activation differences between children who approach new situations (i.e., behaviorally uninhibited children) compared to children who withdraw from novel contexts (i.e., behaviorally inhibited children). Even though temperament styles appear to be linked to genetic, physiological, and neurological processes, temperament researchers still consider environmental factors to be very important.

Environmental Factors

Thomas and Chess argued that children's temperament characteristics interact with parenting to produce children's positive or negative adjustment. Their concept of the goodness-of-fit between the parent and the child is similar to the notion of attachment developed by John Bowlby. Attachment is the dynamic relationship between the child and the caregiver. Human infants are born vulnerable and need the security of a consistent, attentive, warm caregiver in order to feel safe enough to explore the world. Caregivers give children verbal and nonverbal clues about the nature of the environment and provide them with a secure base to return to when they feel anxious or threatened.

Mary Ainsworth advanced the attachment literature by creating a laboratory measure of attachment called the Strange Situation. During this procedure, the child and caregiver are separated and reunited several times in a laboratory playroom. During the separation episodes, the child is left alone with a strange adult or in a strange room for short periods. The level of distress the child exhibits after the caregiver returns is the index of the strength of the attachment relationship. Securely attached infants will become upset during separation, but can be easily consoled by the caregiver when reunited. Insecurely attached infants will show one of two different reactions to the situation. In one group, the insecurely attached infants showed little distress when left alone and freely interacted with a stranger. In a second group, the infants were very distressed when left alone and could not be comforted by their caregivers upon their return. Many temperament researchers have pointed out that the Strange Situation is not equally strange (or scary) for all children. Very emotional or shy children may react strongly to the novel context, while very sociable children may show no distress at all. Some researchers even contend that Ainsworth's measure of attachment is really assessing temperament styles. Attachment researchers counter that the procedure measures the relationship between the caregiver and the child, which is partly a reflection of how well the caregiver copes with the child's unique behavioral style.

Many social scientists believe that temperament and parenting are both related to children's development, but in different ways. For instance, in a study of more than a hundred infants, Grazyna Kochanska found that differences in the mother-child relationship predicted whether children were securely or insecurely attached, while the children's temperament style predicted which type of reaction they displayed in the Strange Situation.

In another study, Kochanska found support for Thomas and Chess's goodness-of-fit concept. Two different parent-child relationships when the children were toddlers predicted the development of conscience in children when they were five years old. Fearful children did better with mothers who used gentle discipline, while fearless toddlers did better with mothers who were very responsive. To Thomas and Chess, healthy development occurs when parents are able to work with a child's temperament and influence their child's reactions to the world. Socialization happens and parenting is important, but each parent-child relationship will be unique because each child is unique.

It is important to note that Thomas and Chess's studies in the 1960s and 1970s were based on the ideal characteristics for an infant reared in Western society. Culture also plays a role in the fit between the child and his environment. For instance, Mary Rothbart and others have found that parents in the United States and the People's Republic of China described their children using the same dimensions. Chinese infants, however, were lower in activity level compared to American children, a finding that has been replicated in other studies. In addition, the implications of certain temperament styles for children's development differ across cultures. Shyness or behavioral inhibition is associated with adjustment problems in the United States and Canada; the same temperament style, however, is associated with healthy development in China. What is considered a difficult temperament style depends on the culture, context, and characteristics of the family.

See also: ATTACHMENT; PARENTING; PERSONALITY DEVELOPMENT

Bibliography

Asendorpf, Jens B. "Abnormal Shyness in Children." *Journal of Child Psychology and Psychiatry and Allied Disciplines* 43 (1993):1069–1081.

Buss, Arnold H., and Robert Plomin. *Temperament: Early Developing Personality Traits.* Hillsdale, NJ: Lawrence Erlbaum, 1984.

Cole, Michael, and Sheila R. Cole. *The Development of Children,* 4th edition. New York: Worth Publishers, 2000.

Goldsmith, Hill H., Arnold H. Buss, Robert Plomin, Mary K. Rothbart, Alexander Thomas, Stella Chess, Robert A. Hinde, and Robert B. McCall. "Roundtable: What Is Temperament? Four Approaches." *Child Development* 58 (1987):505–529.

Kagan, Jerome. *Galen's Prophecy: Temperament in Human Nature.* New York: Basic, 1994.

Kochanska, Grazyna. "Multiple Pathways to Conscience for Children with Different Temperaments: From Toddlerhood to Age Five." *Developmental Psychology* 33 (1997):228–240.

Kochanska, Grazyna. "Mother-Child Relationship, Child Fearfulness, and Emerging Attachment: A Short-Term Longitudinal Study." *Developmental Psychology* 43 (1998):480–490.

Lykken, David T., Matt McGue, Auke Tellegen, and T. J. Bouchard. "Emergenesis: Genetic Traits that May Not Run in Families." *American Psychologist* 47 (1992):1565–1577.

Rothbart, Mary K., Stephan A. Ahadi, and David E. Evans. "Temperament and Personality: Origins and Outcomes." *Journal of Personality and Social Psychology* 78, no. 1 (2000):122–135.

Thomas, Alexander, and Stella Chess. *Temperament and Development.* New York: Bruner/Mazel, 1977.

Shirley McGuire

TERATOGENS

A teratogen is an environmental agent that can adversely affect the unborn child, thus producing a birth defect. Teratogens include infectious agents, such as rubella, syphilis, and herpes, and chemicals. Chemical exposures can occur through lifestyle choices (e.g., alcohol, smoking, drugs) or exposure to environmental hazards (e.g., X rays, certain environmental chemicals). The teratogenicity, or nature and extent of harm to the fetus, is influenced by fetal genetic vulnerability, type and amount of teratogen, and timing of the exposure during pregnancy. For example, certain teratogens may have adverse effects only during critical periods of fetal development or after a certain amount of exposure. There are possible exceptions to these principles in which teratogenic exposures may not result in negative effects. There are also agents and conditions with possible, but unproven, effects on fetuses. Therefore, it is important to check with a knowledgeable source for possible consequences of exposure.

See also: DEVELOPMENTAL DISABILITIES; PRENATAL DEVELOPMENT

Bibliography

Brendt, Robert, and David Beckman. "Teratology." In Robert Eden, Frank Boehm, Mary Haire, and Harry Jonas eds., *Assessment and Care of the Fetus: Physiological, Clinical, and Medicolegal Principles.* Norwalk, CT: Appleton and Lange, 1990.

Kolberg, Kathleen J. Sipes. "Environmental Influences on Prenatal Development and Health." In Thomas Whitman, Thomas Merluzzi, and Robert White eds., *Life-Span Perspectives on Health and Illness.* Mahwah, NJ: Lawrence Erlbaum, 1999.

McCormick, Marie C., and Joanna E. Siegel, eds. *Prenatal Care: Effectiveness and Implementation.* Cambridge, Eng.: Cambridge University Press, 1999.

O'Rahilly, Ronan, and Fabiola Muller. *Human Embryology and Teratology.* New York: Wiley-Liss, 1992.

Schettler, Ted, Gina Solomon, Maria Valenti, and Annette Huddle. *Generations at Risk: Reproductive Health and the Environment.* Cambridge, MA: MIT Press, 1999.

Deena R. Palenchar

THEORIES OF DEVELOPMENT

Why are humans the way they are? Why is it that the abilities of children seem so different than those of adults? What can one do to help children become fully developed adults? These are the kinds of questions that theorists of human development try to answer.

As it is easy to imagine from questions that are so broad, the answers theorists offer are equally broad, typically telling more about people in general than about what any one person is likely to do on a particular day. Furthermore, given such questions, the answers theorists arrive at are not always the same. In some cases this is because different theorists study different aspects of human development; in other cases it is because different theorists do their work using different sets of assumptions.

These differing assumptions reflect theoretical debates about four things. First, they reflect a debate about what in fact one should look at in order to measure the course of human development—should it be someone's actual behavior or the presumed internal psychological processes that might be reflected in behavior? Second, theorists debate how best to portray humans—are humans autonomous, self-directed individuals or ones acting largely in response to external events? Third, theorists differ as to the generalizability of their findings—is there one theory that explains the development of all people in all places at all times or are there many theories, each specific to a historical time and place? Finally, theorists differ as to the actual methods that should be used to divine the answers to all of these questions.

One useful way to understand these different approaches to the study of human development is to think of them as reflecting relatively distinct worldviews. A worldview is not a theory but something larger. It represents a set of assumptions that a theory may draw upon to serve as the foundation of that theory's investigations. Three worldviews are evident in the work of developmental theorists. They are referred to as the Mechanistic Worldview, the Organismic Worldview, and the Contextualist Worldview. Theories that share the same worldview, even if they are not studying the exact same thing, are nevertheless said to belong to the same family of theories.

The Mechanistic Worldview

Theories built on a Mechanistic Worldview reflect a belief that behavior and behavior change are predictable, lawful phenomena that can, theoretically at least, be fully understood through the use of systematic, objective empirical research methods (empirical meaning that the methods rely on observation or experimentation). Secondly, mechanists believe that behavior is caused by either factors external to the individual (efficient causes) or those defining the individual's biological makeup (material causes). Efficient causes include such things as parenting style, educational opportunities, and peer group composition. Material causes include inherited genetic characteristics and more general biological qualities such as temperament or information processing capability.

Two prominent examples of work within a Mechanistic Worldview are the operant conditioning model, most closely associated with B. F. Skinner (1904–1990), and the behavior genetic model, associated with the work of Robert Plomin and Sandra Scarr, among others. These two models are very contradictory. Skinner's work reflects the nurture side of the nature-nurture debate, while Plomin and Scarr's work reflects the nature side of the debate.

Operant Conditioning Model

Skinner's operant conditioning model examines the relationship between a behavior and its consequence. As a model of human development, the operant model is seen as a means of understanding how life experiences influence an individual's actions. It demonstrates how changes in the consequences of one's behavior can in turn modify that behavior. In essence, responses are more likely to increase if followed by a positive (i.e., desirable) consequence and less likely if followed by a negative (i.e., undesirable) consequence. Skinner also found that the timing or schedule of the contingent reinforcement is an equally significant variable. Continuous reinforcement is generally seen as more effective in establishing a response; variable or intermittent reinforcement is seen as more effective at maintaining a response at a high level once it has been established.

Skinner restricted his actual work to laboratory animals—pigeons and mice in particular—but he made it clear in his writings that he saw these general principles as governing the behavior of all species, human or otherwise. Further, others working in this tradition have demonstrated that these principles of operant conditioning are very useful in helping to untangle complicated family dynamics as well as the more subtle forms of observational learning.

Behavior Genetic Model

Behavior genetic models offer a different approach to answering the perennial nature-nurture debate. Through elaborate statistical procedures, behavior geneticists attempt to determine how much of the difference in a group of individuals can be said to be due to genetic factors and how much to environmental factors. Behavior genetic research with humans cannot, of course, involve selective breeding (the preferred technique when working with animals), so behavior genetic researchers look for situations that they believe allow for "experiments in nature." The two most common research designs for humans involve comparing individuals of different degrees of genetic relatedness and comparing adopted children to both their biological and adopted parents. Behavior genetic researchers report that both types of studies show a significant genetic contribution to many human characteristics, including intelligence and personality. That is, identical twins appear more similar than fraternal twins or siblings, who are in turn more similar than cousins, who are in turn more similar than unrelated individuals. Further, adopted children share many characteristics with their biological parents, even if they are adopted at birth.

The Organismic Worldview

Those favoring an Organismic Worldview recognize both efficient and material causes as important but place even more emphasis on what they see as formal and final causes. Formal causes reflect the organizational quality of all living systems, while final causes reflect organicists' belief that human development is a directional process. To use an analogy, when hydrogen and oxygen are combined to form water, a substance is created with properties radically different than either of its two constituents. At room temperature, hydrogen and oxygen each exists as a gas but water exists as a liquid. Water is very good for putting out fires, while oxygen and hydrogen actually have the opposite effect. As such, the emerging properties of water are radically different from the properties of the individual elements of which it is comprised. In the same way, organicists argue that humans are each more than the sum of their parts and that humans are actively involved in their own construction.

Two of the major theoretical traditions within the Organismic Worldview are the psychoanalytic models associated with the work of Sigmund Freud (1856–1939) and Erik Erikson (1902–1994), and the cognitive developmental model associated with the work of Jean Piaget (1896–1980).

Freud's Psychoanalytic Model

Freud's work, although highly controversial both then and now, is important because it helps highlight the importance of the early bonds between a parent and a child and helps show how experiences early in life may influence subsequent life experiences.

It is ironic that Freud's theory, one of the most controversial theories of child development, is based not on a careful examination of children but rather on clinical interviews he conducted with adult patients in the course of his psychiatric practice in Vienna at the turn of the twentieth century. Freud, the clinician, believed that his adult patients' problems stemmed from their early childhood experiences, and as a result his approach to therapy was to help them regress to those early experiences so that the traumatic nature of the experiences could be uncovered and therefore resolved.

Freud saw activity during the first year of life, what he called the oral stage, centered on the mouth and the process of learning to take in, both in the biological and psychological sense, those things that initially are external to the infant. Because this taking in or incorporating is pleasurable to the child, Freud saw those associated with the process, most notable the mother and the father, as also acquiring positive value in the eyes of the infant. To Freud, a psychic force, the id, regulated these early efforts on the part of the infant. The id exists in the infant's subconscious and has the sole purpose of reducing tension and increasing gratification.

By age two or three, during the anal stage, the focus of activity shifts from the oral region to the anal region, with issues of retention and elimination, again, at both the biological and psychological levels, becoming paramount. Because the child is now being asked to learn to balance power and control, a second psychic force, the ego, emerges as a regulatory mechanism. Unlike the id, the ego resides partly in consciousness and partly in unconsciousness and as such serves to help the child become socialized; that is, it helps the child recognize that she must respond to considerations other than her own immediate gratification.

The preschool years witness the phallic stage and a further shift in focus to the genitalia and issues of sex role identification. Freud sees this process as one of conflict for the child because the child initially sees the same-sex parent as a competitor for the affections of the opposite-sex parent rather than as a mentor and role model. Successful resolution of the conflict comes about through the emergence of a third psychic force, the superego. The superego resides entirely in the child's consciousness and is, in essence, the child's conscience. It is the superego that helps the child recognize the legitimacy of society's social expectations for the child.

Middle childhood brings a respite to the child, a time Freud called the latency stage. According to Freud, from age five to thirteen children's efforts are directed at establishing same-sex friendships, strengthening ties with parents, and meeting the social and intellectual demands imposed by school and society.

The adolescent years witness the emergence of the genital stage. Again the focus is on the genitalia but it has shifted from parent-child issues to issues of establishing intimacy with a same-age peer. How successful the adolescent and young adult is in establishing adult sexual relationships is, to Freud, largely a function of how successfully earlier stages were resolved.

Erikson's Psychoanalytic Model

Erikson's revision of Freud's theory reflected his belief in the interpersonal nature of human development. Erikson offered a sequence of eight developmental stages—or as he called them, psychosocial tasks—that must be successfully accomplished for a person to become fully developed. Erikson's first psychosocial task involves developing a basic sense of trust and is seen as the major developmental milestone for the infant. Developing a basic sense of trust comes about through the interactions with the infant's primary caregivers. The more predictable and appropriate the interactions, the more easily a sense of trust is established.

Erikson's remaining seven psychosocial tasks then follow in sequence, each associated with a particular period of the lifespan. Toddlers are expected to use their sense of trust to venture forth and establish a basic sense of autonomy. The preschooler, in turn is asked to develop a sense of initiative. By middle childhood, this sense of initiative is now expected to more fully develop into a sense of industry. One characteristic of Erikson's work that is well illustrated in these first four stages is their nested nature. For successful completion, each requires resolution at all previous levels. No resolution halts development; partial resolution restricts further development.

By adolescence, individuals are asked to form a sense of identity, which is seen as forming the foundation for the establishment of a sense of intimacy, the defining event of the early years of adulthood. Intimacy typically leads to some form of permanent bond, which in turn often leads to parenthood and the opportunity to develop a sense of generativity, or concern for the next generation. Finally, toward the end of life, one is asked to form a sense of ego integrity, to accept the life you have led as the life you have led.

Piaget's Cognitive Development Model

Unlike Erikson who focused on interpersonal relationships, Piaget focused on children's cognitive development, in particular on the cognitive structures or mechanisms that are available to individuals of different ages to help them make meaning out of their everyday experiences. Piaget saw this effort to make meaning as reflecting a desire to maintain an equilibrium or balance between the individual and his context. New experiences create a degree of disequilibrium, which the individual tries to adapt to either by drawing on previous experiences to make sense of the new one (a process Piaget referred to as assimilation) or by making the necessary cognitive changes to adapt to the new situation (a process of accommodation). This continual process of assimilation and accommodation leads to the changes in the individual's cognitive organization that were of interest to Piaget.

Piaget saw this developmental process as occurring in a sequence of four periods or stages. The first, the sensory-motor period, typically occurs during the first two years or so of life. It is marked by Piaget's observation that infants are initially unable to act or behave on the basis of their mental representations (literally, re-presentations) of their experiences but rather act on the basis of their sensory and motor impressions of these experiences. To Piaget's infant, what something means is based on whatever sensory or motor interactions the infant is able to have with the object, person, or experience.

Gradually over the second and third years of life, young children begin to acquire the ability to act, in a very elementary fashion, on their mental representations of objects, people, and events. This preoperational period, which typically lasts until ages five to seven, is characterized by the child's growing use of language, the increasing ability to engage in pretend play and imitation, and a growing ability to understand simple functional relationships. These young children, however, still have difficulty in appreciating the fact that others do not see things from the same perspective as they do (what Piaget referred to as egocentric thought), and they are still relatively easily fooled by how things appear to be rather than how they must be.

As children enter middle childhood around age five to age seven, they move into the period of concrete operational thought. They are now no longer easily fooled by their perceptions because they have the cognitive skills necessary to have their logic "correct" their perception. Concrete operational children demonstrate the cognitive skills necessary to arrange, organize, and classify information; use the types of logical operations necessary for the understanding of mathematical and scientific operations; and modify their comments to reflect the perspective of the listener.

Beginning in adolescence and continuing throughout the adult years, formal operational adults are potentially able to apply logic to all situations—hypothetical or real. Piaget saw this ability to have "thought take flight" as a partial explanation for the expansiveness of adolescent behavior and even for the difficulty adolescents and young adults have in initially settling into productive adults lives.

The Contextualist Worldview

Although there are many differences between a mechanistic and an organismic worldview, they nevertheless share one important characteristic—they each view the process of development as universal. This emphasis on universality is one of the ways in which these two worldviews can be contrasted to the third, Contextualism. Contextualists do not believe that there are universal laws of development; rather, they argue that the forces that contribute to development are specific to historical time and social place.

Contextualists make their nonuniversal argument for two reasons: one empirical and one conceptual. From an empirical perspective, they argue that there is more than enough variability in the data comparing individuals and groups from different settings to raise serious questions about the assumption that human development reflects the same universal set of variables. From a conceptual perspective, contextualists argue that since it is impossible to ever have an objective (i.e., context-free) perspective on human development, then it is impossible to make judgments that are not culturally based.

Lev Vygotsky's (1896–1934) cultural-historical theory of human development is a good example of a theory rooted in a Contextualist Worldview since it places great emphasis on the role of culture in both defining and then transmitting the sign and symbol systems used in that culture. Sign and symbol systems are the ways cultures note and code information. They are reflected in the nature of the language, in ways for quantifying information, in the expression of the arts, and more generally in the ways people establish, maintain, and transmit social institutions and relationships across generations.

Vygotsky saw language as the defining characteristic of humans as a species, the one element that distinguishes humans from other species. Language allows for a shared communication, which in turn allows for collective effort or labor. This effort, in turn, sets the foundation for the progressive evolution of culture across generations. To Vygotsky, culture is a uniquely human phenomenon, allowing history to replace biology as the defining element in the lives of humans.

Of the various elements of Vygotsky's theory, the one that continues to receive the most attention, is his concept of the zone of proximal development (ZPD). Vygotsky saw the ZPD as the mechanism through which a culture's sign and symbol systems were passed from generation to generation; not surprisingly, many educators see it as the key element in the educational process of children. The ZPD represents an interval between what a child (or adult) is able to do alone and what that person can do with the support of a more skilled person. For activity in the ZPD to be educationally meaningful, the teacher must have a clear sense of both what the child should learn and the child's current interests and abilities. In essence, intersubjectivity needs to be established between teacher and child so that the learner understands the goals of the teacher, and the teacher understands the child's present level. A failure to establish intersubjectivity indicates that the teacher will be ineffective in helping the child acquire new information because the strategies the teacher uses to help support the child's learning will be ineffective or inappropriate.

In addition to highlighting the educational process, the ZPD also highlights another important element of Vygotsky's theory, namely, the notion that the intermental always precedes the intramental. By this Vygotsky meant that all knowledge is first acquired as social knowledge and only later is it internalized and comprehended by the child. It is because all knowledge is first transmitted as social knowledge that the cultural-historical context of a particular culture is so important in understanding and defining an individual's development.

People sometimes tend to think of theories as abstract and not useful, as something only academics argue or care about. Actually nothing could be further from the truth. Theory is the foundation upon which all everyday ideas about human behavior and development are based. In the words of psychologist Kurt Lewin (1890–1947), "there is nothing so useful as a good theory."

See also: DEVELOPMENTAL NORMS; ERIKSON, ERIK; FREUD, SIGMUND; MILESTONES OF DEVELOPMENT; PIAGET, JEAN; SKINNER, B.F.; VYGOTSKY, LEV

Bibliography

Bandura, Albert. "Human Agency in Social Cognitive Theory." *American Psychologist* 44 (1989):1175–1184.

Bandura, Albert, and S. A. Ross. "Transmission of Aggression through Imitation of Aggressive Models." *Journal of Abnormal and Social Psychology* 63 (1961):575–582.

Burman, Erica. *Deconstructing Developmental Psychology.* London: Routledge, 1994.

Burman, Erica. "Continuities and Discontinuities in Interpretive and Textual Approaches in Developmental Psychology." *Human Development* 39 (1996):330–345.

Chandler, Michael. "Stumping for Progress in a Post-Modern World." In E. Amsel and K. A. Renninger eds., *Change and Development: Issues of Method, Theory, and Application.* Mahwah, NJ: Lawrence Erlbaum, 1997.

Cole, Michael. "Cross-Cultural Research in the Sociohistorical Tradition." *Human Development* 31 (1988):137–157.

Erikson, Erik. *Childhood and Society.* New York: Norton, 1950.

Erikson, Erik. *Identity: Youth and Crisis.* London: Faber, 1968.

Erikson, Erik. *Identity and the Life Cycle.* New York: Norton, 1980.

Erikson, Erik. *The Life Cycle Completed.* New York: Norton, 1997.

Freud, Sigmund. *The Interpretation of Dreams.* New York: Modern Library, 1900.

Freud, Sigmund. *The Ego and the Id.* London: Hogarth Press, 1927.

Gergen, Kenneth. "Stability, Change, and Chance in Understanding Human Development." In N. Datan and H. W. Reese eds., *Life-Span Development Psychology.* New York: Academic Press, 1977.

Gilligan, Carol. *In a Different Voice.* Cambridge, MA: Harvard University Press, 1982.

Goldhaber, Dale. *Theories of Human Development: An Integrative Approach.* Mountain View, CA: Mayfield, 2000.

Overton, Willis. "The Structure of Developmental Theory." In H. W. Reese ed., *Advances in Child Development and Behavior.* San Diego: Academic Press, 1991.

Patterson, Gerald. "Maternal Rejection: Determinant or Product for Deviant Child Behavior?" In W. W. Hartup and Z. Rubin eds., *Relationships and Development.* Hillsdale, NJ: Lawrence Erlbaum, 1986.

Pepper, Stephen. *World Hypotheses: A Study in Evidence.* Los Angeles: University of California Press, 1961.

Plomin, Robert. *Development, Genetics and Psychology.* Hillsdale, NJ: Lawrence Erlbaum, 1986.

Plomin, Robert. *Genetics and Experience: The Interplay between Nature and Nurture.* Thousand Oaks, CA: Sage, 1994.

Reese, Hayne, and W. F. Overton. "Models of Development and Theories of Development." In L. R. Goulet and P. B. Baltes eds., *Life-Span Developmental Psychology.* New York: Academic Press, 1970.

Rogoff, Barbara. *Apprenticeship in Thinking: Cognitive Development in Social Context.* New York: Oxford University Press, 1990.

Scarr, Sandra, and K. McCartney. "How People Make Their Own Environments: A Theory of Genotype-Environment Effects." *Child Development* 54 (1983):424–435.

Scarr, Sandra, and A. Ricciuti. "What Effects Do Parents Have on Their Children?" In L. Okagaki and R. J. Sternberg eds., *Directors of Development: Influences on the Development of Children's Thinking.* Hillsdale, NJ: Lawrence Erlbaum, 1991.

Skinner, Burris F. *The Behavior of Organisms: An Experimental Analysis.* New York: Appleton-Century-Crofts, 1938.

Skinner, Burris F. *Walden Two.* New York: Macmillan, 1948.

Skinner, Burris F. *Science and Human Behavior.* New York: Free Press, 1953.

Vygotsky, Lev. *Thought and Language.* Cambridge, MA: MIT Press, 1962.

Vygotsky, Lev. *Mind in Society.* Cambridge, MA: Harvard University Press, 1978.

Dale E. Goldhaber

THEORY OF MIND

Theory of mind (ToM) is the understanding of the mental states of others, including their intentions, desires, beliefs, and emotions. Around the age of eighteen months, a child is able to understand the intentions of other people. This progresses until the ages of three to four-and-a-half when children begin to understand others' states of knowledge and belief. Janet Astington, a long-time ToM researcher, has found that children's performance on standard false belief tasks was associated with their production of joint proposals and explicit role assignments during pretend play. Success at joint play may have some dependence on representing differing and conflicting beliefs and goals with the other participant in the play session. For social development, it is necessary for children to be able to communicate this information amongst themselves. With no knowledge about the mind or their playmate's beliefs, these pretend play interactions are quite difficult to execute successfully.

See also: COGNITIVE DEVELOPMENT; EMOTIONAL DEVELOPMENT

Bibliography

Astington, Janet W. "Intention in the Child's Theory of Mind." In Douglas Frye and Chris Moore eds., *Children's Theories of Mind: Mental States and Social Understanding.* Hillsdale, NJ: Lawrence Erlbaum, 1991.

Astington, Janet W. *Child's Discovery of the Mind.* Cambridge, MA: Harvard University Press, 1993.

Astington, Janet W., Paul L. Harris, and David R. Olson, eds. *Developing Theories of Mind.* Cambridge, Eng.: Cambridge University Press, 1990.

Frye, Douglas, and Chris Moore, eds. *Children's Theories of Mind: Mental States and Social Understanding.* Hillsdale, NJ: Lawrence Erlbaum, 1991.

Harris, Paul L., Carl N. Johnson, Deborah Hutton, and Giles Andrews. "Young Children's Theory of Mind and Emotion." *Cognition and Emotion,* 3, no. 4 (1989):379–400.

Heyes, Cecilia M. "Theory of Mind in Nonhuman Primates." *Behavioral and Brain Sciences* 21, no. 1 (1998):101–134.

Perner, Josef, Ted Rufman, and Susan R. Leekam. "Theory of Mind Is Contagious: You Catch It from Your Sibs." *Child Development* 65 (1994):1228–1238.

Sara Salkind

THREE MOUNTAIN TASK

The Three Mountain Task was developed by Jean Piaget and Bärbel Inhelder in the 1940s to study children's ability to coordinate spatial perspectives. In the task, a child faced a display of three model mountains while a researcher placed a doll at different viewpoints of the display. The researcher asked the child to reconstruct the display from the doll's perspective, select from a set of pictures showing the doll's view, and identify a viewpoint for the doll specified by a picture of the display. Some children around age four did not distinguish between their own view and that of the doll, a tendency interpreted by Piaget as evidence of egocentrism. Egocentrism was considered an indication of the preoperational period, a stage that preceded logical thinking. Research since the 1970s has shown young children's perspective-taking ability to be affected by a variety of situational variables.

See also: CONSERVATION; PIAGET, JEAN

Bibliography

Piaget, Jean, and Bärbel Inhelder. *The Child's Conception of Space.* New York: Norton, 1967.

Gary L. Allen

TITLE V (MATERNAL AND CHILD HEALTH SERVICES BLOCK GRANT)

In the United States the provisions of Title V of the Social Security Act (SSA) have their origins in the First Maternity and Infant Act (or Sheppard-Towner Act) of 1921, a grant-in-aid program that provided federal funds to states for the establishment of maternal and infant welfare and hygiene agencies. Passed in 1935, Title V extended new funding to states to provide maternal and child health services, specifically for early detection, treatment and rehabilitation for "conditions which lead to crippling," child welfare services, and vocational rehabilitation. Among the more important changes that have occurred to Title V since it was passed are the establishment of special projects in 1963, the consolidation of categorical MCH services into the Maternal and Child Health Block Grant in 1981, and the move toward greater accountability in 1989. By the end of the twentieth century, Title V, a $870-million program, remained the statutory basis of maternal and child health services in state and local health departments across the United States.

See also: POVERTY

Bibliography

Lesser, Arthur. "The Origin and Development of Maternal and Child Health Programs in the United States." *American Journal of Public Health* 75 (1985):590–598.

Margolis, Lewis, George Cole, and Jonathan Kotch. "Historical Foundations of Maternal and Child Health." In Jonathan Kotch ed., *Maternal and Child Health: Programs, Problems, and Policy in Public Health.* Gaithersburg, MD: Aspen Publishers, 1997.

Schmidt, William, and Helen Wallace. "The Development of Health Services for Mothers and Children in the United States." In Helen Wallace, Richard Nelson, and Patrick Sweeney eds., *Maternal and Child Health Practices,* 4th edition. Oakland, CA: Third Party Publishing, 1994.

VanLandighem, Karen, and Catherine Hess. "Maternal and Child Health at a Critical Crossroads." In Helen Wallace, Gordon Green, Kenneth Jaros, Lisa Paine, and Mary Story eds., *Health and Welfare for Families in the Twenty-First Century.* Sudbury, MA: Jones and Bartlett, 1999.

Jonathan Kotch

TOUCH

Touch typically refers to the provision of tactile/kinesthetic stimulation to the newborn and young infant with the intended goal of facilitating early growth and development. Also known as "massage therapy," sensory experiences include stroking, holding, and passive movements. When applied to preterm infants who suffer from a lack of responsive, developmentally appropriate stimulation, positive effects include less need for ventilatory support, better orienting to the social environment, healthier changes between sleep and wake states, and shorter hospitalization. Beneficial effects depend on the duration, amount, and timing of stimulation—including the infant's stress level. Evidence suggests that massage therapy is an effective intervention with infants of depressed mothers and children suffering from painful procedures and neuromuscular and immune disorders. Research supports suggestions that stimulation increases nervous system components, which lower physiological arousal and production of stress hormones. These changes may then lead to better infant interactions with the social and nonsocial environments, and efficient metabolization of nutrients and enhanced immune function, all of which are essential for optimal growth and development.

See also: INFANCY; PREMATURE INFANTS

Bibliography

Field, Tiffany M. "Massage Therapy Effects." *American Psychologist* 53 (1998):1270–1281.

Lester, Barry M., and Edward Z. Tronick, eds. "Stimulation and the Preterm Infant" (special issue). *Clinics in Perinatology* 17, no. 1 (1990).

Philip Sanford Zeskind

TOYS

Toys, or objects whose main intended use is for play, have the potential to enhance development (creative building blocks) or to alter or hinder development (violent video games). Toys are the primary tools of childhood that allow children to extend their play beyond what can be done through imagination, voice, or action alone. The careful selection of toys by adults, as well as mediation of their use, is an important way to facilitate the optimal development of children. As children grow, the use of toys typically changes from simple and physical (banging a block) to representational (pretending a block is a cup) to more complex and mental (playing board games). There tend to be gender differences in toy preferences: many girls prefer relation-based toys, whereas many boys prefer action-based toys. The influences of cultural expectations on these preferences cannot be separated from possible biological influences. There are also great individual differences in toy preferences regardless of gender.

See also: PLAY

Bibliography

Bergen, Doris, ed. *Readings from Play as a Medium for Learning and Development*. Olney, MD: Association for Childhood Education International, 1998.

Fleming, Dan. *Powerplay: Toys as Popular Culture*. Manchester, Eng.: Manchester University Press, 1997.

Goldstein, Jeffrey H., ed. *Toys, Play and Child Development*. Cambridge, Eng.: Cambridge University Press, 1994.

Hughes, Fergus P. *Children, Play, and Development*. Needham Heights, MA: Allyn and Bacon, 1998.

Steffen Saifer

TRUANCY

Truancy is defined as unexcused absences from school without parents' knowledge. Causes of truancy may include social (e.g., peer pressure), family (e.g., low parental involvement, discord, abusive or neglectful environment), and individual factors (e.g., low IQ, drug or alcohol use, psychological disorder). As such, frequent truancy may signal other difficulties in a child's life. Chronic truancy has been associated with delinquency (e.g., daytime burglary, vandalism, running away, lying), poor academic performance, and dropout rates. It may be predictive of criminal behavior in adulthood among children who also engage in other forms of delinquent behavior and have a history of conduct problems from an early age. Truancy should be distinguished from school refusal, which is defined as staying home from school with parents' knowledge due to emotional distress about attending. Whereas truancy is commonly associated with antisocial behavior, school refusal has been linked to anxiety disorders.

See also: DELINQUENCY

Bibliography

"Manual to Combat Truancy." Prepared by the U.S. Department of Education (July 1996). Available from http://www.ed.gov/pubs/Truancy/; INTERNET.

Pamela L. Schippell

TURNER SYNDROME

Turner syndrome (genotype 45, XO) is a chromosomal anomaly arising from the failure of chromosomes to separate properly during meiosis (cell division in sex cells in which the chromosomal number is halved). In 60 percent of the cases an egg lacking an X chromosome (or a sperm lacking an X or Y chromosome) unites with a normal sex cell to produce a zygote, or fertilized egg, bearing a single X chromosome. In the remaining cases, an X chromosome is lost from some cells during early embryonic development, resulting in mosaics that have both normal cells and X-deficient cells (genotype XO/XX). Mosaics include individuals with two or more distinct cell populations due to a genetic change or error soon after conception.

Turner syndrome occurs in 1 out of 2,500 live female births, although miscarriage is the result for 99 percent of the fetuses. Clinical features, which vary widely, include short stature, webbed neck, low-set ears, drooping eyelids, skeletal deformities, hearing problems, reduced secondary sexual development, and sterility. Behavioral features include poor directional sense and poor mathematical ability. Verbal intelligence has been considered normal, although studies conducted during the last decade of the twentieth century suggest an increased risk for speech and language problems. Families may be advised to seek hormonal treatment and educational assistance for these children.

See also: BIRTH DEFECTS; GENOTYPE

Bibliography

Plomin, Robert, John DeFries, Gerald McClearn, and Peter McGuffin. *Behavioral Genetics*, 4th edition. New York: Worth, 2001.

Simpson, Joe, Marion Verp, and Leo Plouffe, Jr. "Female Genital System." In Roger Stevenson, Judith Hall, and Richard Goodman eds., *Human Malformations and Related Anomalies*, vol. 2. New York: Oxford University Press, 1993.

Van Borsel, John, Inge Dhooge, Kristof Verhoye, Kristel Derde, and Leopold Curfs. "Communication Problems in Turner Syndrome: A Sample Survey." *Journal of Communication Disorders* 32 (1999):435–446.

Nancy L. Segal

TWIN STUDIES

Throughout history, across all cultures, people have been fascinated with twins. In addition to interest in the close emotional ties and biological similarities that twins may share, reports of special twin languages and twin extrasensory perception (ESP) help people to explore ideas of what it means to be human. Twin language is a form of creole that some twins develop and most outgrow at an early age. Mostly anecdotal evidence of twin ESP typically focuses on one twin feeling phantom pain when her co-twin is injured. Beyond this intrinsic interest, twins are very useful for science. Identical twins share the same genetic code and thus are natural clones. How similar or different are they to each other? How important are genes and environment for development? Because identical twins share all of their genes, it is the environment—rather than genetics—that accounts for any differences between them. In a study design that includes both identical and fraternal twins, a researcher can estimate the relative influence of genes and environments on behavioral differences among people.

Identical, or monozygotic, twinning occurs when one egg is fertilized by one sperm then splits after conception into two genetically identical halves. These twins share all of their genes and are the same sex. Fraternal, or dizygotic, twinning occurs when two eggs are released by the mother and fertilized by two separate sperm. Fraternal twins share on average half of their genes, just like typical siblings. They can be the same sex or opposite sex. About two-thirds of all twins are fraternal.

People differ from one another because of the complex interaction between their genetic endowment and their environment. Effects of genes and environments cannot be separated for individuals, but they can be separated at the population level through twin studies. Twins are the same age as each other, and in the twins-reared-together design, they are raised in the same home. Heritability is implied if identical twins (who share all of their genes) are more similar to each other than fraternal twins (who share half of their genes) for the trait under study. Other less common types of twin studies include the twins-reared-apart design, which focuses on twins who were adopted into separate homes when they were infants. These twins do not share their environments so genetic influences are thought to account for their similarities. A more experimental approach is the co-twin control design; one twin receives treatment while the other twin is studied as the control. For example, one twin may attend an after-school program to enhance gymnastic ability and the other will not. Learning effects are examined by comparing the twins' gymnastic abilities before and after the program.

Twin studies yield heritability estimates. Heritability is the proportion of the differences among individuals on a particular trait that are due to genetic differences. For example, the heritability of childhood attention deficit hyperactivity disorder (ADHD) is around 80 percent. Thus, most of the differences among individuals on symptoms of ADHD are due to genetic differences. On the other hand, the heritability of childhood delinquency is approximately 20 percent to 40 percent, suggesting that both genes and environment account for individual differences in delinquency. There are several important limitations to the heritability statistic that are often misunderstood. Heritability describes the variance, or the differences among people, in a particular population at that time. It does not apply to the development of single individuals nor to differences between populations.

Heritability also can change at different points in the lifespan as genes turn on and off and environmental conditions change. Behavior that is heritable is modifiable by environmental conditions to a great degree. It is important to emphasize that genetic influences are not deterministic but rather increase the probability of the behavior in some environments. Early brain development, for example, follows a genetic program with many opportunities for environmental modification. Appropriate prenatal nutrition is needed for proper dentition, and visual experience is needed for proper sight.

Arnold Gesell was one of the first to use the twin method to study early development. He noticed that identical twins were very similar both physically and behaviorally and used the identical co-twin control method to examine the effects of training on physical development. He studied a pair of twins, neither of whom could climb stairs when they were forty-six weeks of age. One twin was given daily practice and encouragement to climb stairs, while the co-twin had no stairs in his environment. After six weeks of practice, the trained twin could climb the stairs and the co-twin could not. One week later, however, the co-twin could also climb the stairs. Replicating this result in several similar studies, Gesell demonstrated that physical training can cause physical skills to appear sooner but that identical co-twins who were trained later performed the same after a relatively shorter period of training. Gesell later became interested in individual differences and the individual's role in creating his or her own environment. At the beginning of the twenty-first century, this dynamic view of person-environment relationships was being studied with newer sophisticated statistical techniques.

Contemporary twin studies have underscored the ways in which the environment influences human behavior. Studies show that the majority of environmental influences on behavior act to make siblings different from each other. This does not mean, however, that global family variables, such as parenting style, are unimportant for the development of children's behavior. Common factors, such as parenting style, can affect individuals differently and thus may contribute to individual differences. The impact of

Three generations of identical female Russian twins. There is some evidence that identical twins are more likely to be dressed alike; there is no evidence, however, that this increased similarity is linked to the types of behaviors that psychologists typically study, such as mental abilities or psychopathology. (Gerald Davis/Phototake NYC)

environmental factors on behavior and development is specific to each child, depending on individual characteristics, such as personality. Thus, parenting is influenced by child characteristics as well as parental characteristics.

Using simultaneous equations model fitting, the classic twin design has been expanded to the multivariate case to examine whether or not the same genetic and environmental factors influence two or more behaviors. This approach is useful for studying etiology, in which a researcher investigates why two behaviors—such as depression and anxiety—are likely to occur together. Using the same example, results from twin studies in childhood (conducted by Anita Thapar and Peter McGuffin) and adulthood (conducted by Ken S. Kendler and colleagues) suggest that a shared genetic factor primarily accounts for the co-occurrence of depression and anxiety. In addition, specific measures of genes (e.g., variations of the dopamine receptor gene) and environments (e.g., socioeconomic status) can be incorporated into the model to determine their individual effect. And assumptions of the twin method can be systematically tested.

There are two main assumptions of the twin design. The first is that twins are representative of the general population. Are twins and single-born children comparable? Because obstetrical complications and congenital anomalies are more common in twins, behaviors that are confounded with these complications are more common in twins. These differences might be important for some characteristics. In fact, twins are overrepresented in cerebral palsy and cognitive delays. On the other hand, twins are comparable on temperament and personality measures, and the proportion of twins in psychiatric clinics is no greater than the proportion for the population as a whole.

The second main assumption of the twins-reared-together design is equality of environments. Are identical and fraternal twins equally influenced by environments that are important for the behavior under study? If this assumption is violated, then the increased similarity of identical twins over fraternal twins may be partially due to environmental, rather than genetic, factors. For example, there are greater discrepancies in birthweight between identical twins than fraternal twins. Also, high maternal age influences fraternal twinning rates. Maternal age can affect parenting style and congenital anomalies. Some fraternal twin parents conceive twins because they used fertility treatments. Thus, it is important that investigators control for these differences when studying related factors. When environmental similarities are found between identical twins, it seems to be the result of (rather than the cause of) behavioral similarity. This finding suggests that environments are not independent of genetic characteristics.

All research designs have assumptions. It is important that investigators are aware of these assumptions and how they limit the conclusions that can be drawn from the study results. One way to test assumptions is to compare the findings of multiple studies using different methodologies. The results of twin studies can be verified by comparing them to findings from family and adoption studies, for example.

Twin designs are embedded in the context of the larger behavior genetic research paradigm. Behavior geneticists study the genetic influences on individual differences in behavior. The behavior genetic paradigm begins with specifying the behavior of interest. Whether or not biological relatives are more likely to also express the behavior is explored next. If so, heritability can be estimated from adoption and twin studies. Relationships with the brain can then be identified. If brain function is related to the behavior and they share genetic influences, this suggests a specific pathway from gene function to behavior. Also, the molecular genetic evidence can be explored. What particular genetic variations are associated with the behavior? Animal models can then be designed to elucidate various components of the system. Investigators are working at all of these levels of the paradigm, and results at one level inform research at another level. Twin studies and other behavior genetic designs are powerful approaches for studying development.

See also: GESSELL, ARNOLD; MATURATION; STAGES OF DEVELOPMENT

Bibliography

Gesell, Arnold, and Helen Thompson. "Twins T and C from Infancy to Adolescence: A Biogenetic Study of Individual Differences by the Method of Co-twin Control." *Genetic Psychology Monographs* 24, no. 1 (1941):3–122.

Goldsmith, H. Hill, Irving Gottesman, and Kathryn S. Lemery. "Epigenetic Approaches to Developmental Psychopathology." *Development and Psychopathology* 9 (1997):365–387.

Goldsmith, H. Hill, Kathryn S. Lemery, Kristin A. Buss, and Joseph Campos. "Genetic Analyses of Focal Aspects of Infant Temperament." *Developmental Psychology* 35 (1999):972–985.

Kendler, Ken S., Michael C. Neale, Ronald C. Kessler, Andrew C. Heath, and Lindon J. Eaves. "Major Depression and Generalized Anxiety Disorder: Same Genes, (Partly) Different Environments?" *Archives of General Psychiatry* 49 (1992):716–722.

Lemery, Kathryn S., and H. Hill Goldsmith. "Genetically Informative Designs for the Study of Behavioural Development." *International Journal of Behavioral Development* 23 (1999):293–317.

Plomin, Robert, John C. DeFries, Gerald E. McClearn, and Michael Rutter. *Behavioral Genetics,* 3rd edition. New York: Freeman, 1997.

Rowe, David C. *The Limits of Family Influence: Genes, Experience, and Behavior.* New York: Guilford Press, 1994.

Rutter, Michael, and Jane Redshaw. "Growing Up as a Twin: Twin-Singleton Differences in Psychological Development." *Journal of Child Psychology and Psychiatry and Allied Disciplines* 32 (1991):885–895.

Rutter, Michael, Judy Silberg, and Emily Simonoff. "Whither Behavioral Genetics? A Developmental Psychopathological Perspective." In Robert Plomin and Gerald E. McClearn eds., *Nature, Nurture, and Psychology.* Washington, DC: American Psychological Association, 1993.

Segal, Nancy L. *Entwined Lives: Twins and What They Tell Us about Human Behavior.* New York: Penguin Putnam, 1999.

Thapar, Anita, and Peter McGuffin. "Anxiety and Depressive Symptoms in Childhood: A Genetic Study of Comorbidity." *Journal of Child Psychology and Psychiatry* 38 (1997):651–656.

Kathryn S. Lemery

U

ULTRASOUND

Ultrasound is a method of assessing the fetus using low-frequency sound waves to reflect off fetal tissue. The ultrasound transducer produces ultrasound waves, which bounce off tissue at different speeds depending on its density. Most commercial ultrasound equipment emits energy that is much lower than the determined maximum safety standard. There are no known reports of fetal damage from conventional diagnostic ultrasound.

There is no uniform agreement as to when ultrasound should be performed during pregnancy. Nevertheless, ultrasound has become the predominant method for determining fetal age, assessing fetal anatomy, and monitoring fetal growth. The American Institute of Ultrasound in Medicine recommends that ultrasound be used in the first trimester to determine fetal age, number, and viability (via visualization of fetal heart activity). In the second and third trimesters, the fetus can be scanned for anatomic abnormalities, fetal growth, amniotic fluid volume, and placental location.

See also: AMNIOCENTESIS; BIRTH; BIRTH DEFECTS; PREGNANCY

Bibliography

Creasy, Robert K., and Robert Resnik. *Maternal-Fetal Medicine.* Philadelphia: Saunders, 1999.

Gabbe, Steven, Jennifer R. Neibyl, and Joseph L. Simpson. *Obstetrics: Normal and Problem Pregnancies.* New York: Churchill Livingstone, 1997.

Garrett Lam

UMBILICAL CORD

The lifeline of the fetus during its stage of intrauterine development, the umbilical cord averages 50 to 60 centimeters (20 to 23 inches) in length in a full term pregnancy and connects the fetus to the placenta. Contained within the cord are one umbilical vein, which transfers from the placenta the oxygen and nutrients necessary for fetal growth and development, and two umbilical arteries, which return the carbon dioxide and metabolic waste products produced by the fetus back to the placenta for elimination by the mother. These blood vessels are wrapped within a protective spongy material called Wharton's jelly.

Umbilical cords are often coiled, an arrangement that is thought to protect the blood vessels from the external compressive forces of uterine contractions. Some infants are born with the umbilical cord wrapped around the neck or a body part. Rarely, fetal movements can actually tie a knot in the cord. For the most part, fetuses can tolerate these stresses well and do not end up with major problems.

See also: BIRTH; PREGNANCY

Bibliography

Creasy, Robert K., and Robert Resnik. *Maternal-Fetal Medicine.* Philadelphia: Saunders, 1999.

Gabbe, Steven, Jennifer R. Neibyl, and Joseph L. Simpson. *Obstetrics: Normal and Problem Pregnancies.* New York: Churchill Livingstone, 1997.

Garrett Lam

V

VIDEO GAMES

Some early video games, as well as many recent ones, were and are self-consciously educational and prosocial. Most would agree that video games of the 1970s, such as *Pong,* carried little more developmental risk than a game of table-tennis. The primary criticism at the time was that they fostered sedentary behavior in children. Many surveys of video games of the 1990s, however, tend to reveal both violent and sexist content. More serious criticisms include the promotion of short-term and long-term aggressive behavior through exposure to on-screen violence and the formation of negative gender stereotypes through exposure to passive, sexualized, and/or victimized female characters. Other research suggests that children's prosocial behavior may be reduced by playing video games. Technology improvements have allowed photorealistic effects, which lend credence to the view that negative effects found for television viewing may be true for playing video games as well. Nevertheless, findings for long-term developmental effects are not consistent. The conservative assessment is that more study is needed.

See also: INTERNET; TELEVISION; VIOLENCE

Bibliography

Cesarone, Bernard. "Video Games and Children." In ERIC Digest [web site]. Urbana, Illinois, 1994. Available from http://www.ed.gov/databases/ ERIC_Digests/ed365477.html; INTERNET

Dietz, T. L. "An Examination of Violence and Gender Role Portrayals in Video Games: Implications for Gender Socialization and Aggressive Behavior." *Sex Roles* 38 (1998):425–442.

Van Schie, E. G. M., and O. Wiegman. "Children and Video Games: Leisure Activities, Aggression, Social Integration, and School Performance." *Journal of Applied Social Psychology* 27 (1997):1174–1194.

Derrald W. Vaughn

Heather Kelly

VIOLENCE

Violence in the United States is widely viewed, by policymakers and researchers, as an epidemic and a major public-health problem. Particularly in the wake of high-profile school shootings that occurred in the late twentieth century, the American public has shown increasing concern about violent adolescents and the harmful effects that exposure to violence has on children and adolescents. While high rates of lethal violence warrant attention, many more youth are exposed to chronic, nonlethal violence and aggression in their homes, schools, and communities. Violence rates generally follow economic trends and affect all youth, although poor, urban, and minority youth are most at risk. This article provides an overview of the incidence of violence, including suicide and homicide, among children and adolescents and its effects on them, and briefly reviews the effectiveness of intervention and prevention approaches to mitigating violence and its effects.

The Incidence of Violence Affecting Youth

After their peak in 1993, national crime rates, including juvenile crime rates, declined. Between 1993 and 1997 victimization from serious violent crime dropped 25 percent for adults, from 4.2 to 3 million, and 33 percent for youth, from 1,230,000 to 830,000. While this decline is encouraging, overall rates of violent crime remain alarmingly high. For instance, victimization rates for youth under age fifteen in the United States dramatically exceed those in other industrialized countries, particularly when firearm use is considered. Juveniles are twice as likely as adults to be victims of serious violent crimes and three times as likely to be victims of simple assault.

Juvenile Homicide

Juvenile homicide is the most severe and disturbing type of youth violence. The distinction between homicide and nonlethal violence may be somewhat arbitrary, however, because similar actions can produce either lethal or nonlethal outcomes.

Juvenile Victims

At the beginning of the twenty-first century in the United States, homicide was the second leading cause of death for youths age ten to nineteen. Homicide is the first leading cause of death for black male youths. Of all murder victims in 1997 (18,200 victims or 7 per 100,000 people living in the U.S.), 11 percent (2,100 victims or 3 per 100,00 juveniles living in the U.S.) were under age eighteen. Most juvenile victims (71%) were male black youths. Although black youth comprised only about 15 percent of the juvenile population, they were five times as likely as white youth to be homicide victims in 1997. This is a decrease from 1993 when the ratio was seven to one, but the ratio remained high compared with the early 1980s. Juvenile homicide rates for Latino youth appear comparable to those for blacks; for Native Americans the rates of violent victimization are the highest.

Despite some published reports, students are safer at school than elsewhere. Compared with nonurban youth, urban youth are at greater risk for violent victimization, including homicide, in any setting. All children are at highest risk for victimization in the hours immediately after school.

Firearm use among youths is a serious issue. Homicides of youths age fifteen to seventeen are more likely to involve firearms than for any other age group. In this age group, 86 percent of all homicides involved firearms. Rates of firearm-related juvenile homicide increased dramatically between 1987 and 1993, from about 800 victims (41% of juvenile homicides) to about 1,700 victims (61% of juvenile homicides), and showed some decline along with other crime statistics to about 1,200 victims (56% of juvenile homicides) in 1997. However, the rates of juvenile homicide with a firearm have continued to exceed those where no firearm was used.

Juvenile Perpetrators

Patterns of violent crime committed by youths generally mirror those for the general population. Juveniles committed approximately 12 percent of all murders in 1997. It is estimated that in 1997, of 18,200 murders committed, about 2,300 murders were committed by juveniles. Unlike murders committed by adults, 44 percent of all murders by juveniles involved more than one perpetrator (often including a young adult). Ninety-three percent of juvenile murderers were male, 56 percent were black, and 88 percent were between the ages of fifteen and seventeen. Juvenile murderers are more concentrated in urban areas and are usually the same race as their victims.

Violence and Gangs

Gangs are active in urban, suburban, and rural areas. Most gang members are male (92%) and nearly half (40%) are under age eighteen. While the number of gangs and gang members decreased in the late 1990s, youth gangs remain responsible for a disproportionate share of all violent and nonviolent crime. Rates of violence are significantly higher for gang members than for non-gang members, and the rates are higher during gang membership than before or after.

Violence and Drug Use

Surveys of high school seniors show that the risk for perpetration of and victimization by violent and nonviolent crime is higher among students who use illicit drugs. Using multiple "hard" drugs was associated with the highest rates of violence.

Juvenile Suicide

Although not interpersonal violence, suicide is a form of violent death affecting youth. While suicide risk, contrary to homicide risk, is higher for adults than for juveniles, adolescent suicide gets much more attention. Seven percent of all suicides in 1996 involved youth age nineteen and under. For every two young people murdered in the United States, one commits suicide. Youth suicide victims are overwhelmingly male (8 of 10), white (8 of 10), and teenage. Suicide rates for black male youth are parallel to but lower than those for white males. Females are more likely to "attempt" suicide. Between 8 percent and 9 percent of all youths have attempted suicide.

Clinical and epidemiological comparisons between youth suicide and homicide show that their rates tend to be similar, although homicide rates are higher. The fact that the rates are parallel over time suggests that they respond to similar social pressures, such as economic changes.

Child Abuse/Domestic Violence

Younger children are more likely to be victims of violence by family members. Between 1980 and 1997, most murdered children under age six were killed by a family member, whereas most adolescents were killed by an acquaintance or stranger. Differing definitions of child abuse and domestic violence among states and across settings (e.g., legal, medical) make it difficult to determine prevalence precisely. In 1993, nearly 3 million children were maltreated or endangered in the United States; of these, 43 percent were abused. From 1987 to 1996, the number of reported cases of abuse doubled. It is estimated that more than 10 million U.S. children are exposed to marital violence each year.

An Ecological Framework for Understanding Violence

To understand the effects of violence on child development, an ecological framework is useful. Violence is seen as embedded in layers of the child's ecological world. For instance, intrafamilial violence (child maltreatment and domestic violence) occurs in the child's immediate environment. Community (and school) violence occurs where the child and family interact with the social systems of the outside world. Media and societal violence occur in the larger social context. An ecological framework also aids in understanding what protects against and what raises the risk for poor outcome of children exposed to violence by considering the role of child, parents, and peers, and family and community resources.

The Effects of Violence on Children

Some children are exposed to a single severe violent event, such as being caught in sniper fire while leaving school. The negative impact of such exposure is well documented, with these children demonstrating traumatic effects such as reexperiencing and avoiding the trauma, and overreactivity.

Many children, though, are affected by chronic, pervasive forms of violence (e.g., witnessing drug deals, hearing gunfire, fighting) that occurs in multiple areas of their lives (e.g., home, neighborhood,

Violence can be introduced into children's lives through many channels, including media elements like video games that feature realistic weaponry and high "body counts." (Anthony Snyder/Corbis)

school). They may experience such violence directly as victims, as witnesses or by knowing someone who has been victimized. Some researchers have proposed the concept of multiple risk, suggesting that as children are exposed to an increasing number of risk factors (including violence in multiple spheres), their likelihood for suffering poor outcomes increases disproportionately. In these children, although they may suffer symptoms of trauma seen in children exposed to single violent events, it is more likely that broader declines in functioning are evident, including increased depression and anxiety, increased aggressive and antisocial behavior, decreased social competence, increased delinquency, moral disengagement, as well as decreased academic performance.

It has been widely observed that not all children exposed to violence—even severe, pervasive, and chronic violence—show poor outcomes. At the beginning of the twenty-first century, research was beginning to identify the factors that influence the path from violence exposure to outcome and was considering the role of a wide range of contextual influences.

Violence Prevention and Intervention Programs

Violence prevention and intervention efforts for youth have been developed to target different groups and needs. Primary prevention programs are generally population-based, involving youth, peers, teachers, schools, and families, and are designed to promote prosocial behavior. Many of these programs target elementary school-age children. Secondary prevention and treatment programs target youth who are at high risk for exposure to violence or becoming violent. Tertiary intervention targets youth who are already perpetrators or victims. The most promising components of intervention programs appear to target social-cognitive skills such as perspective taking, generating alternative solutions, building peer negotiation skills, avoiding violence, and improving self-esteem. Such programs are generally considered most effective at the primary and secondary prevention levels.

Violence among youth and affecting youth is not an isolated phenomenon. Patterns of violent crime among youth follow larger societal patterns. Although the courts in the late twentieth century and into the new century tended toward punishment of juvenile offenders, research shows that programs favoring rehabilitation are better. For children exposed to multiple risk factors and levels of violence, single types of intervention, such as a school curriculum, are insufficient. Societal approaches to reducing violence must include a broad array of both governmental and private initiatives. Because the use of firearms accounts for a sustained high level of juvenile homicide rates, governmental regulations targeted toward decreasing access to weapons is necessary. And because more and more children are without parent supervision in the after-school hours when children are most likely to be victims of violence, increasing funding for after-school programs is another key factor in reducing violence and its effects on children.

See also: CHILD ABUSE; DOMESTIC VIOLENCE; JUVENILE DELINQUENCY; SUICIDE; VIDEO GAMES

Bibliography

Eron, Leonard, Jacquelyn H. Gentry, and Peggy Schlegel, eds. *Reason to Hope: A Psychosocial Perspective on Violence and Youth.* Washington, DC: American Psychological Association, 1994.

Garbarino, James, Nancy Dubrow, Kathleen Kostelny, and Carole Pardo, eds. *Children in Danger: Coping with the Consequences of Community Violence.* San Francisco: Jossey-Bass, 1992.

Goldstein, Arnold P., and Jane Close Conoley, eds. *School Violence Intervention: A Practical Handbook.* New York: Guilford Press, 1997.

Holden, George W., Robert Geffer, and Ernest N. Jouriles, eds. *Children Exposed to Marital Violence: Theory, Research, and Ap-*
plied Issues. Washington, DC: American Psychological Association, 1998.

Holinger, Paul C., Daniel Offer, James T. Barter, and Carl C. Bell. *Suicide and Homicide among Adolescents.* New York: Guilford Press, 1994.

Osofsky, Joy D., ed. *Children in a Violent Society.* New York: Guilford Press, 1997.

Snyder, Howard N., and Melissa Sickmund. *Juvenile Offenders and Victims: A National Report.* Washington, DC: Office of Juvenile Justice and Delinquency Prevention, 1999.

Trickett, Penelope K., and Cynthia J. Schellenbach, eds. *Violence against Children in the Family and in the Community.* Washington, DC: American Psychological Association, 1998.

U.S. Department of Justice, Bureau of Justice Statistics. *Sourcebook of Criminal Justice Statistics, 1998,* edited by Kathleen Maguire and Ann L. Pastore. Washington, DC: U.S. Government Printing Office, 1999.

Tanya F. Stockhammer

VYGOTSKY, LEV (1896–1934)

Lev Semenovich Vygotsky was a developmental psychologist known for his sociocultural perspective. Born into a middle-class Jewish family in Orsha, Russia, Vygotsky's faith and social standing shaped many of his choices and views. Academically successful, Vygotsky entered Moscow University in 1913, where he studied law, being one of the few professions that allowed Jews to live outside restricted areas. He simultaneously attended Shaniavsky University to study social sciences. After an impressive presentation of his doctoral dissertation on William Shakespeare's play *Hamlet*, entitled *Psychology of Art*, Vygotsky was invited to join the research staff at the Psychological Institute in Moscow, where he met Alexander Luria, who was to become his colleague and collaborator.

Vygotsky posited two types of psychological functioning: "natural," consisting of biological growth, both physical and cognitive development; and "cultural," consisting of learning to use psychological and cultural tools, including signs, symbols, and language. Both natural and cultural functioning act in a mutually facilitative integrated process. Whereas Jean Piaget (1896–1980), Vygotsky's Swiss contemporary, proposed that instruction should follow development, Vygotsky saw development and learning as acting together to create higher psychological functioning. He suggested that learning and development are facilitated in a hypothetical region called the zone of proximal development (ZPD). This region represents the distance between the child's independent cognitive ability and the child's potential with the help of an adult or more competent peer. Thus, the child's natural ability is expanded upon through learning and does not fully mature without instruction. For example, in *Thought and Language*, Vygotsky examined language, a socially acquired tool, and identified stages that begin with speech for the purpose of requests. This speech eventually becomes internalized into thought.

As war, poverty, famine, and social change took their toll on the children of Russia, Vygotsky turned his attention to children with disabilities. Considered ahead of his time, Vygotsky suggested that children with and without disabilities be educated together. He recognized that necessary social and cultural developments would be more likely to occur in an integrated environment and that isolation caused by an inability to participate in collective activities might have an even more deleterious effect than the original problems.

Vygotsky died of tuberculosis at age thirty-seven before he was able to offer a comprehensive theory of child development. His early death, Soviet dictator Josef Stalin's ban on Vygotsky's works for political reasons, the Cold War, and the popularity of Piaget's ideas caused Vygotsky's theories to reach the West slowly. Nevertheless his ideas on socialization, language, and children with disabilities have influenced modern child developmentalists throughout the world.

See also: THEORIES OF DEVELOPMENT

Bibliography

Berk, Laura E., and Adam Winsler. *Scaffolding Children's Learning: Vygotsky and Early Childhood Education.* Washington, DC: National Association for the Education of Young Children, 1995.

Kozulin, Alex. *Vygotsky's Psychology.* Cambridge, MA: Harvard University Press, 1990.

Publications by Vygotsky

Mind in Society, edited by Michael Cole, Vera John-Steiner, Sylvia Scribner, and Ellen Souberman. Cambridge, MA: Harvard University Press, 1978.

The Vygotsky Reader, edited by René Van Der Veer and Jaan Valsiner. Cambridge, Eng.: Blackwell, 1994.

Carrie Lazarus
Laraine Masters Glidden

Psychologist Lev Vygotsky viewed development and learning as partners in the creation of higher psychological functioning. (Archives of the History of American Psychology)

W

WAR

While the effects of war on adults, and the countries in which they live, have long been studied and fairly well understood, the effects of war on children were largely ignored until the late twentieth century. Increased scrutiny by the press, "instant news," and twenty-four-hour cable coverage brought the ravages of war and children's circumstances into people's homes. For example, studies have shown that more than two-thirds of the children in the Balkan conflicts of the 1990s were afraid they were going to die, and an estimated 500,000 were traumatized by what they were forced to witness. Most countries recognize that children need special protection (but are often unable to provide it), with the minimum protective measures being that children must be shown special care appropriate for their circumstances, they should not be separated from their parents, they should not be recruited to fight in war if they are under fifteen years of age, and they should be evacuated from areas of danger to protected areas.

See also: EMOTIONAL DEVELOPMENT; VIOLENCE

Bibliography

Qouta, Samir, Eyad El Sarraj, and Raija Leena Punamaeki. "Mental Flexibility as Resiliency Factor among Children Exposed to Political Violence." *International Journal of Psychology* 36, no. 1 (2001):17.

Smith, Patrick, Sean Perrin, William Yule, and Sophia Rabe Hesketh. "ADRA Dialogues with Security Council on Effects of War on Children." In the Adventist Development and Relief Agency of Australia [web site]. Available from http://www.adra.org.au/news/2000/28b_7_00.htm 2001; INTERNET.

Neil J. Salkind

WECHSLER INTELLIGENCE SCALE FOR CHILDREN

Originally developed by David Wechsler in 1949, the third edition of the Wechsler Intelligence Scale for Children (WISC) was published in 1991. This standardized test is designed to measure children's (six to sixteen years of age) intellectual functioning in two broad areas. Verbal subtests require language skills similar to those used in schools, such as vocabulary and knowledge of general information. Performance subtests measure abstract reasoning in visual-motor abilities, such as constructing a puzzle.

Scores on the test consistently and accurately predict academic achievement. The WISC is one of the most commonly used tests for assessing a child's strengths and weaknesses in a variety of intellectual abilities. WISC scores can be used in conjunction with other information to diagnose learning difficulties. Although useful in diagnosis, the WISC does not provide information on intervention strategies.

See also: INTELLIGENCE

Bibliography

Groth-Marnat, Gary. *Handbook of Psychological Assessment,* 3rd edition. New York: Wiley, 1999.

Kaufman, Alan S. *Intelligence Testing with the WISC-III.* New York: Wiley, 1994.

Kaufman, Alan S., and Elizabeth O. Lichtenberger. *Essentials of WISC-III and WPPSI-R Assessment.* New York: Wiley, 2000.

Sattler, Jerome M. *Assessment of Children,* 4th edition. San Diego, CA: J. M. Sattler, 1992.

Jo Ellen Vespo

WELFARE PROGRAMS

The history of welfare programs in the United States is a controversial one. Although many other nations in the world have welfare systems, some of which provide certain kinds of assistance for all citizens, the United States has always been divided in terms of what welfare means and who should receive welfare benefits. The welfare system in America underwent significant changes in the late 1990s in order to reduce the number of people receiving certain types of welfare benefits. This occurred as a result of political and economic changes that caused American society to reexamine the meaning of its welfare programs against a rising tide of concern about and disdain for public assistance. In order to understand the welfare system of the early twenty-first century, however, it is important to first understand and reflect upon the inception and history of welfare in the United States.

Early History of Welfare in the United States

Prior to the Great Depression of the late 1920s and 1930s, there was no systematic federal service for providing help or relief to struggling citizens. State programs were fragmented, and charity was sporadically offered by various church organizations and community efforts. As the impact of the Great Depression spread across the United States, it was clear that some type of system was necessary in order to curtail the devastating effects of poverty and joblessness. President Franklin Roosevelt proposed a massive overhaul of the government by devising the New Deal in the 1930s, which was essentially a package of various social and welfare benefits aimed at relieving the effects of the Great Depression. The reality of this new welfare state would provide debate and controversy in political, social, and economic realms from that point forward.

Social Security

Although many Americans believe that welfare benefits to mothers and children were among the most costly and widely used welfare programs, in truth the biggest expenditures were funneled toward the Social Security program, developed in 1935. The Social Security Act (SSA) was targeted at several groups, including the elderly, the totally disabled, and families with children of deceased workers. Social Security was considered to be a universal program, in the sense that it was to provide coverage for all working Americans, as it continues to do. With this program, benefits were paid to individuals retiring from work at a preset age. The amount of benefits received was directly tied to the amount of money a person earned during her work history. Furthermore, if an adult or a child were deemed to have a significant disability that prevented the individual from working, then benefits would be paid to that individual through the Social Security Disability Income program, in the case of an adult, or the Supplemental Security Income program, in the case of a child. Finally, if a working parent were to die, then a specified amount of benefits would be paid to the surviving family. The Social Security program continues to provide benefits in this fashion, although it has been a source of some controversy, particularly because all individuals are entitled to these benefits, regardless of how much money they have or earn.

Employment Programs

The New Deal initiative with the second highest amount of funding was related to employment benefits, namely unemployment insurance and workers' compensation. Through the unemployment insurance program, workers who lose their jobs (not because of misbehavior or quitting) are allowed to collect a set amount of compensation, which is typically limited in duration to twenty-six weeks or less. Like Social Security, benefits are available to workers at all levels, with benefits being higher for upper-income jobs. Once individuals collect unemployment insurance, they must work for an additional period before being eligible to receive benefits again.

Workers' compensation is a welfare benefit that provides medical and cash assistance to individuals who are injured on the job. It is limited to job injuries only and provides aid to those who are not permanently disabled. Both unemployment insurance and workers' compensation continue to be provided in much the same fashion in the early twenty-first century, and both programs are considered universal, because they provide coverage to all working Americans.

Aid to Families with Dependent Children

Perhaps the most controversial welfare programs were and continue to be those related to mothers, children, and the poor. This third tier of welfare pro-

In 1933, as part of the New Deal, President Roosevelt created Aid to Families with Dependent Children (AFDC). Essentially, individuals had to qualify for benefits by demonstrating need and by maintaining minimal assets of their own. (Stephen Ferry, Gamma Liaison Network)

grams, which received the least amount of initial funding compared to the other two, primarily targeted single mothers with children. In 1933 as part of the New Deal, Roosevelt created Aid to Families with Dependent Children (AFDC), which was a means-tested program. In its inception, this program was designed to be a short-term, transitional solution to the problems faced by single poor women with children, many of whom were minorities as well. Small cash benefits were offered to recipients, although the recipients were monitored by caseworkers who maintained a high degree of latitude in determining who would receive benefits and how much they would get. Although recipients were not expected to work, some Americans soon worried that these individuals were taking advantage of the system and that the benefits awarded to them were undeserved. The AFDC program quickly became the most stigmatizing welfare program to evolve from the New Deal.

Welfare Programs of the 1960s

As the use of these New Deal welfare programs exploded over several decades, the administrations of John F. Kennedy and Lyndon B. Johnson of the 1960s saw a resurgence of public interest in issues regarding minorities, the poor, and children. During this time, new welfare programs were created to help address the continued spread of poverty, homelessness, hunger, and medical problems—difficulties that plagued many of America's citizens. The Food Stamp Act of the 1960s attempted to address the nation's problem of hunger by providing another means-tested program for the poor, the disabled, and single-parent households, in the form of food stamps. Also established was the Medicaid program, which was means-tested and offered medical care to poor children, people with disabilities, and the elderly. Unlike Medicare, the health insurance program for the elderly, Medicaid involved financial contributions from the states. These programs continued to exist into the twenty-first century, although many restrictions and time limitations had been added.

Welfare Reform

Although history shows that efforts were made, in particular decades and through particular political administrations, to address the effects of poverty, homelessness, and hunger on American citizens, there has always been controversy about the effectiveness of the means-tested programs, such as AFDC, food stamps, and Medicaid. Furthermore, the growth of AFDC, which had reached a peak of 14.2 million recipients by 1994, concerned many Americans. Consequently, in 1996 a sweeping welfare reform package entitled the Personal Responsibility and Work Opportunity Act (PRWOA) was passed by Congress and signed into law by President Bill Clinton. It effectively eliminated the nearly sixty-year-old entitlement welfare program initiated by Roosevelt. PRWOA remanded the responsibility for certain welfare programs back to the states. Block grants, in the amount of $16.5 billion, representing funds that would have been part of AFDC, were distributed to states in hopes that more effective and creative programs would be developed, based upon the particular needs of each state.

Within the PRWOA legislation, the new welfare program is called Temporary Assistance for Needy Families (TANF), and it differs significantly from the old AFDC program in many ways. One significant difference is that recipients are no longer guaranteed or entitled to receive assistance. Furthermore, TANF stipulated that eligible recipients of cash assistance must be working within two years of receiving benefits. Likewise, in an effort to address concerns about long-term welfare dependency, TANF placed a five-year, lifetime limit on receiving assistance except for a certain 20 percent of recipients who are considered to fall within a "hardship" category. Many states have opted to reduce the five-year cap to an even fewer number of years, which is allowed under the PRWOA legislation. The TANF policy is clear that only pregnant women and families with children are eligible for the assistance, although states have been given a certain amount of latitude in determining how they spend their federal block grant monies.

Since the enactment of TANF, the number of people on welfare has been reduced dramatically. By 1999, only 7.2 million recipients remained on welfare, compared to the 14.2 million of 1994. This 7.2 million figure included 2.6 million families and 5.1 million children. Policy analysts contended that several factors contributed to the decline in welfare numbers, including an improved American economy and tougher work requirements of the welfare programs. From the late 1990s into the initial years of the twenty-first century, recipients moved more quickly off of welfare than in the past, and fewer people began receiving benefits for the first time.

Analysis of Welfare Reform

At the start of the twenty-first century, advocates of welfare reform were pleased with the declining welfare caseloads and viewed the reform as a success. Opponents of welfare reform argued that poverty had not really been reduced, only the number of people receiving welfare benefits. The research regarding welfare reform was mixed, and any number of articles were available to point to either the success or failure of welfare reform. A *New York Times* article from January 23, 2000, indicated that the welfare-to-work policies had actually helped improve academic achievement of low-income students. The article went on to suggest that certain welfare programs empha-

sizing increased work and increased income improved the lives of children significantly. The author, however, did not mention that research existed suggesting that many children and families continued to live below the poverty line, despite increased income from work.

An article from the February 21, 2001, issue of the *Boston Globe* reported on a discrepancy in public opinion and policy analysis regarding the implications of welfare reform. Although some evidence confirmed that many recipients were leaving the welfare rolls and then finding and keeping jobs, other evidence showed that hunger and poverty continued to be significant issues that were not being addressed by the reform policy. The article reported that whereas 14 percent of families had reported hunger while receiving welfare benefits, 22 percent of families reported hunger after leaving welfare.

Conclusion

The issues surrounding welfare and welfare reform are controversial, political, and difficult to resolve. Almost seventy years after the formation of the welfare state, debate continued about who deserves and who does not deserve benefits. With TANF scheduled to be reauthorized and reevaluated in 2002, the successes and failures of U.S. welfare programs were certain to make for interesting policy discussions well into the twenty-first century.

See also: POVERTY; STATE CHILDREN'S HEALTH INSURANCE PROGRAM; WOMEN, INFANTS, AND CHILDREN

Bibliography

Ellwood, David T. *Poor Support: Poverty in the American Family*. New York: Basic, 1988.

Morales, Armando, and Bradford W. Sheafor. *Social Work: A Profession of Many Faces*. Boston: Allyn and Bacon, 1989.

Noble, Charles A. *Welfare as We Knew It: A Political History of the American Welfare State*. New York: Oxford University Press, 1997.

Pear, R. "Gains Reported for Children of Welfare-to-Work Families." *New York Times* (January 23, 2000):A11.

Ranalli, R. "Welfare Reform's Success an Issue." *Boston Globe* (February 21, 2001):10.

Schneider, Anne L., and Helen M. Ingram. *Policy Design for Democracy*. Lawrence: University Press of Kansas, 1997.

U.S. Department of Health and Human Services [web site]. 2001. Available from http://www.acf.dhhs.gov; INTERNET.

Walkowitz, Daniel J. *Working with Class*. Chapel Hill: University of North Carolina Press, 1999.

Kim Harrison

WOMEN, INFANTS, AND CHILDREN

Women, Infants, and Children (WIC) is a food assistance and nutrition program that provides supplemental food, nutrition education, and access to health care for pregnant women, women up to six months postpartum, women breast-feeding infants up to one year old, infants, and children under age five. Participants qualify based on nutritional risk and income at or below 185 percent of the federal poverty level. (The Food Stamp Program income cut-off is 130 percent of the federal poverty level.) Participants receive monthly coupons for food rich in protein, iron, calcium, vitamin A, and vitamin C (such as milk, cheese, eggs, fruit juice, cereal, peanut butter, legumes, infant formula, and infant cereal). The United States Department of Agriculture (USDA) funds the program; services are provided at the local level through health services, social services, and community agencies. The program's purpose is to provide nutrient-dense foods and nutrition education at critical periods of growth and development to prevent health problems and improve the health status of low-income women and children in the United States.

See also: NUTRITION; POVERTY

Bibliography

Boyle, Marie A., and Diane H. Morris. *Community Nutrition in Action: An Entrepreneurial Approach.* St. Paul, MN: West Publishing, 1994.

Story, Mary, Katrina Holt, and Denise Sofka. *Bright Futures in Practice: Nutrition.* Arlington, VA: National Center for Education in Maternal and Child Health, 2000.

Nicole B. Knee
Janice Dodds

WORKING IN ADOLESCENCE

One hallmark of a successful transition to adulthood is the development of career aspirations and an identity as someone who works. It is during adolescence that these issues become particularly salient.

Developmental Roots of Industry, Identity, and Employment

According to Erik Erikson's work in the early 1960s, the primary developmental task of adolescence is to achieve a sense of identity, to determine who one is and what one's place in society will be. This task lays the groundwork for educational and career choices and the eventual attainment of adult self-sufficiency. The roots of the attitudes and skills necessary for the successful resolution of this developmental task of adolescence begin in infancy and early childhood.

Attachment theorists have proposed that infants are genetically endowed to experience satisfaction in exploring and manipulating the environment, a developmental antecedent of employment. In the early 1960s, Erikson, R. Havinghurst, and Donald Super noted the importance of the early childhood years for the development of attitudes and skills associated with working. During the third stage of Erikson's theory of psychosocial development, around age five, children experience pleasure in using tools and interacting with their environment; and during latency, his fourth stage, children internalize a work principle. Havinghurst proposed that between five and ten years of age children establish "identification with a worker" and during early adolescence (ten to fifteen years of age) children acquire habits of industry.

Through schoolwork, chores, and the requirements of hobbies, children learn how to apply themselves, set goals, work in teams, and accomplish tasks. Super concurred that vocational concerns develop gradually over the course of early childhood and then become more salient in adolescence. For Super the primary task of adolescence was the crystallization of a vocational preference, which involves the formulation of ideas about work and self, and could then evolve into an occupational self-concept. He took the position that a vocational self-concept is a reflection of a person's overall self-concept but more specialized in that it shapes educational and employment activities. Research has shown that by seventh grade children have developed work-relevant cognitions, attitudes, and feelings that are quite similar to those of adolescents and adults.

Advantages and Disadvantages of Adolescent Employment

Despite the importance of early childhood and family factors in the development of an adolescent's sense of industry and vocational development, little research has been conducted to determine the specific influences on this key developmental outcome. Researchers have proposed that early positive experiences with employment significantly contribute to the adolescent's emerging sense of industry and identity. Based on belief in the positive benefits of youth employment, federal policy and government legislation have expanded opportunities for youths to develop work experiences (e.g., the Job Training Partnership Act and its forerunner, the Comprehensive Employment and Training Act of 1973). The goal of encouraging young people to assume part-time employment during their high school years has been widely endorsed for many years. In 1999 Julian Barling and E. Kevin Kelloway determined that the average high school student works the equivalent of a part-time job; by the time of graduation from high school, 80 percent will have held at least one part-time job.

The perceived potential benefits of youth employment include earning money, gaining relevant work experience, achieving autonomy, easing the transition from school to work, and developing work attitudes. Youth employment also provides employers with a ready supply of unskilled and inexpensive labor. Further, parents approve, believing that such experiences foster independence, responsibility, and improved attitudes toward school.

Further endorsements of youth employment come from Katherine Newman, who studied the employment experiences of Harlem youths and published her results in 1996. She found that although many young adults were in low-wage, seemingly dead-end "McJobs," these employment experiences also had many (sometimes hidden) benefits. Despite the fact that these jobs were tiring, boring, stressful, poorly compensated, stigmatized, and offered limited opportunities for advancement, the youths perservered because of a strong work ethic and a desire to develop and sustain an identity as someone who works. Further, these jobs allowed the teens to contribute to the survival of their poverty level households, leading to increased self-esteem and pride. Some youths were motivated by these low-end jobs to save part of their earnings for future educational and job training opportunities, essentially turning a dead-end job into a stepping stone for a career. Newman also found that participation in an employment setting shifted the youths' reference group away from out-of-school peers, into the workplace, and onto employed adult role models.

Contrary to the prevailing wisdom regarding the value of youth employment, some researchers have concluded that it can be harmful to academic and social development. For example, Jerald Bachman and John Schulenberg found in their nationally representative sample of high school seniors, that work intensity (the number of hours worked per week) was associated with behavioral problems as well as diminished time for sleep, eating breakfast, exercising, and dating. These findings, however, do not negate the potential for part-time work to be beneficial when experienced under the right circumstances. Defining the optimal type of job and intensity of work experience for producing positive effects in high school seniors is a task for future researchers. In particular, attention needs to be paid to the quality of the work experience in addition to its quantity. Further, Bachman and Schulenberg compared outcomes for employed versus not-employed youth in school. They did not examine the impact of employment specifi-

cally for out-of-school youths for whom employment (as opposed to postsecondary education) is the most viable pathway to adult self-sufficiency.

Youth Employment for Out-of-School and Disadvantaged Youth

In light of the importance of youth employment for disadvantaged youths, it is unfortunate that they face what researchers have called a "web of mutually reinforcing circumstances and behaviors" that makes a successful attachment to the labor market extremely difficult. Such circumstances include the deterioration of the labor market in urban communities, overwhelming personal and family issues that would distract even the most dedicated student and worker, and a mismatch between employer demands and the skills of entry-level workers. Indeed, lack of skills and lack of preparation for the workforce have been cited as among the most important reasons for the failure of youths to obtain long-term employment.

Lack of preparation for the transition from school to work is problematic for many minority youths. In general, high school students are ill-prepared for the world of work, a problem that is exacerbated by high school guidance counselors' exclusive focus on postsecondary education. An Educational Testing Service survey published in 1981 found that almost half of all students never talked to a guidance counselor about possible future occupations. These non-college-bound youths received little or no support or guidance in making a successful transition to the work force, often leading to a period of "floundering" as these young adults entered the labor market. As Gary Orfield and Faith Paul noted, "students not bound for college need the most help, receive the least assistance, are equipped with the most limited information, and experience the greatest risks in the job market" (Mendel 1995). Minority youths comprise one of several groups for whom this chaotic entry into the labor market is particularly harmful. According to Richard Kazis, the employment picture for black and Hispanic young Americans who do not make it to college is so bleak that it constitutes a serious school-to-work crisis.

Access to and identification with adults who have developed labor force attachments are also critical to an adolescent's successful entry into employment. Yet Edwin Farrell found in 1990 that at-risk minority youths have limited involvement with gainfully employed adult role models. Their understanding of the process of getting and maintaining employment was often limited, unrealistic, and inaccurate. Taken together, these data paint a picture of disadvantaged youths who are more likely to fail in school and less likely to build a foundation upon which to create an adult life in which they can support themselves and their families.

Demographic Trends and the Future

Demographic trends at the start of the twenty-first century are likely to increase the difficulty that disadvantaged youths will face in finding their place in the labor market. The total number of sixteen- to twenty-four-year-olds in the nation's population is projected to rise steadily through the year 2010, to 38.7 million, almost 7 million more than in 1995. Along with the expansion in the supply of young workers will be the increase in competition for low wage jobs and the increasingly technological nature of even minimum wage jobs. Thus, there will be a continued high incidence of employment and earning problems among many of the nation's out-of-school youths.

Several steps need to be taken to facilitate the successful transition to employment for disadvantaged and out-of-school youths. First, all youths must be encouraged to stay in school, and schools must provide the literacy and interpersonal skills necessary for successful integration into college, vocational training, and employment. Second, career counseling must be expanded to recognize that many high school seniors will not attend postsecondary education but are ready to pursue meaningful employment experiences. Third, intervention programs that have been proven successful at enhancing the employment experiences of disadvantaged and out-of-school youths need to be made available to all eligible individuals. Fourth, youths in minimum wage jobs need to be encouraged to apply a portion of their earnings to further their education and training. And finally, postsecondary educational opportunities need to be made available to all youths regardless of financial income. With these policies, programs, and practices in place, every youth will have a better chance to achieve the key developmental task of adolescence.

See also: ADOLESCENCE; WORKING FAMILIES

Bibliography

Bachman, Jerald G., and John Schulenberg. "How Part-Time Work Intensity Relates to Drug Use, Problem Behaviors, Time Use, and Satisfaction among High School Seniors: Are These Consequences or Merely Correlates?" *Developmental Psychology* 29 (1993):220–235.

Barling, Julian, and E. Kevin Kelloway, eds. "Introduction." *Young Workers*. Washington, DC: American Psychological Association, 1993.

Erikson, Erik. *Childhood and Society*. New York: Norton, 1963.

Farrell, Edwin. *Hanging In and Dropping Out: Voices of At-Risk High School Students*. New York: Teachers College Press, 1990.

Havinghurst, R. "Youth in Exploration and Man Emergent." In Henry Borow ed., *Man in a World of Work*. Boston: Houghton-Mifflin, 1964.

Kazis, Richard. *Improving the Transition from School to Work in the United States*. Washington, DC: American Youth Policy Forum, 1993.

Mendel, Richard. *The American School-to-Career Movement: A Background Paper for Policymakers and Foundation Officers*. Washington, DC: American Youth Policy Forum, 1995.

Newman, Katherine. "Working Poor: Low Wage Employment in the Lives of Harlem Youth." In Julia A. Graber, Jeanne Brooks-Gunn, and Anne C. Peterson eds., *Transitions through Adolescence: Interpersonal Domains and Context*. Mahwah, NJ: Lawrence Erlbaum, 1996.

Orfield, Gary, and Faith Paul. *High Hopes, Long Odds*. Indianapolis: Indiana Youth Institute, 1994.

Super, Donald E. "Vocational Development in Adolescence and Early Childhood: Tasks and Behaviors." In Donald E. Super, R. Starishevsky, N. Matlin, and J. P. Jordan eds., *Career Development: Self Concept Theory*. New York: College Entrance Examination Board, 1963.

Amy J. L. Baker

WORKING FAMILIES

The employment of mothers has been increasing to the point that it is now the modal pattern in the United States. In 1960, fewer than 30 percent of all mothers of children under age eighteen were in the labor force; forty years later, fewer than 30 percent were *not* in the labor force. Further, 64 percent of all married mothers with preschool children were in the labor force at the beginning of the twenty-first century, as were 73 percent of divorced mothers and 67 percent of the mothers who had never married. In fact, in two-parent families with infants one year old and under, 62 percent of the mothers were employed, a figure more than double the rate in 1975. Thus, most families in the early twenty-first century are "working families." There is considerable public interest in how this shift affects families and children, and it is a research area to which developmental psychologists have given considerable attention.

To understand the impact of maternal employment, it is important to realize that this change has been accompanied by other interrelated changes. Modern technology has diminished the amount of necessary housework and food preparation, women are more educated, marriages are less stable, life expectancy has been increased and youthfulness has been extended, expectations for personal fulfillment have expanded, and traditional gender-role attitudes are less widely held. There have also been changes in child-rearing practices, and the adult roles for which children are being socialized are not the same as previously. The increased employment of mothers is both an effect of these changes and also an influence on them. In addition, the accompanying social changes operate to modify the effects of maternal employment on the family and children.

For example, attitudes about women's roles have changed markedly over the years. The decrease in gender-role traditionalism is one of the factors that has led to the increased employment of mothers. The increased entry of mothers into the labor force itself, however, has also affected attitudes about gender roles. As more mothers seek employment, maternal employment has become more acceptable. In addition, it has affected the division of labor in the home. In dual-earner families, more than three-fourths of the mothers work full-time, thus decreasing the amount of time available for housework and child care. Studies of the family division of labor have long shown that when mothers work, fathers help more with housework and child care. In 1997 James T. Bond, Ellen Galinsky, and Jennifer E. Swanberg conducted a national-sample study to replicate a study from twenty years earlier. The new study found that fathers had become more active in household tasks and child care over the years. Although employed married mothers still do more housework and child care than their husbands, the difference has decreased. Attitudes have also changed. Not only is there more acceptance of mothers working, but there is also more acceptance of fathers helping with housework and child care. These changes, in turn, have modified the effects of employment on children and the stress on mothers. Research by Lois Hoffman and Lise Youngblade has shown that more active participation of fathers in child care and the resultant higher morale of the mothers have positive effects on children's academic performance and social adjustment.

School-Age Children

Most of the research over the years has compared school-age children of employed and nonemployed mothers in terms of academic and social competence. The results have failed to confirm the once widely held belief that mothers' employment would have negative effects on children. Indeed, effects seem mainly positive. The results, however, have not been the same across gender and social class. The most consistent pattern of positive outcomes has been for daughters of employed mothers.

In an extensive 1999 study, Hoffman and Youngblade examined how the mother's employment status affected child outcomes and then focused on why these effects occur. Daughters with employed mothers were found to have better academic and social skills, more independence, and a greater sense of effi-

cacy, a view that their own actions are important determinants of what happens to them. Having an employed mother itself was related to the daughter's view that women are competent, and this was enhanced when there was a less traditional division of labor between parents. The view that women are competent increased the girls' sense of efficacy, and efficacy predicted social and academic competence. In addition, the data indicated that employed mothers across social class, mothers' marital status, and ethnicity, were less likely to use authoritarian and coercive discipline. This discipline style was particularly harmful for girls and was associated with a low sense of efficacy and shy, withdrawn behavior. Thus the employment status of mothers was linked to family effects that helped explain child outcomes.

Although the finding of higher scores on various cognitive and social adjustment measures for daughters of employed mothers has been consistent over the years, the results for sons have been mixed. Some of the earlier studies found higher academic scores for sons of employed mothers, others found no difference, and a few found lower scores for sons, but only in the middle class. In the study by Hoffman and Youngblade, children with working mothers scored higher on all cognitive measures across gender, socioeconomic status, ethnicity, and mothers' marital status. The researchers suggested that the differences between the earlier studies and their own 1999 study reflected the change in fathers' roles over the decades.

Nevertheless, while the sons of employed mothers in the middle class obtained higher cognitive scores, they did not show better social adjustment. In fact, ratings by teachers and peers indicated that, in the middle class, sons of employed mothers who worked full-time engaged in more acting-out and aggressive behavior at school. This pattern was in contrast to sons of employed mothers in the blue-collar class and in poverty who showed less acting-out behavior, less aggression, and better social adjustment generally. An explanation for this class difference given by the researchers was that, although full-time homemakers across class used more authoritarian discipline than employed mothers, the discipline in the middle class was rarely harsh or severe. In the lower socioeconomic groups, and particularly among poor single mothers, this was not the case and harsh discipline was more common for full-time homemakers, though, paradoxically, so was permissiveness.

In addition, in the blue-collar and poverty classes, employed mothers were more likely than full-time homemakers to use a style of control developmental psychologists call "authoritative." Authoritative parenting is a style where parents support their control

A working mother helps her child get ready for school. When children are of school age, working families still have to deal with issues of control and supervision when work hours and school hours do not overlap. (Reflections Photolibrary/Corbis)

with reasons and explanations and allow some input from the child. It is a more common pattern in the middle class generally, but there it was not related to the mother's employment status. Thus, differences between employed and nonemployed mothers in the quality of parenting were more pronounced in the blue-collar and poverty groups, and these differences were linked to child outcomes.

An important reason maternal employment made such a difference in mothers' parenting styles in the lower-class families has to do with the mothers' sense of well-being. Although previous research has often shown that employed mothers have a higher sense of well-being than full-time homemakers, this result is most consistently found for mothers in the blue-collar and poverty groups. This was also true in the Hoffman and Youngblade study. In these lower-income families, the employed mothers scored lower on a measure of depressive mood and higher on a measure of positive morale. Further, for this group, the mothers' sense of well-being was shown to be the link between employment and more positive parenting styles. Employment status was not related to either measure in the middle class.

It may seem strange that employment has a more positive effect on mothers whose work may not be as interesting as the work available to more educated mothers. What these mothers value, however, is not the job itself, but the increased social support and stimulation provided by coworkers, the marked advantages that their wages bring to their families, and the greater sense of control that they feel over their lives. This is particularly true for poor single mothers who are often lonely and depressed, and for whom wages can make a major economic difference.

Infants and Toddlers

The research on infants and toddlers with working mothers has taken a different approach. At these early ages, it is very difficult to measure child outcomes that have long-term predictability, so studies have focused more on mother-child interaction or resorted to long-term designs. Studies of infants have examined the quantity and quality of mother-child interactions, and particular attention has been given to the security of the mother-infant attachment. The studies looking at quantity and quality suggest that although employed mothers spend less time with the infant during the workweek, they are more highly interactive when with them. The studies of attachment have produced mixed results, complicated by measurement difficulties. Most studies found mothers' employment status unrelated to the quality of the mother-infant attachment, but a few found that attachment was less secure when the mother was employed full-time. The most extensive investigation of these issues is an ongoing study conducted by a team of researchers under the auspices of the National Institute of Child Health and Human Development (NICHD). In this study, as reported in 1997, neither the child's age at the onset of employment nor the amount of nonmaternal care was found to be related to the security of attachment. What was important was the quality of the mother-child interaction and particularly the mother's sensitivity to the child's needs.

Nonmaternal Care

When mothers are employed, there are often times when both school-age and preschool children need nonmaternal care. A considerable amount of research has been conducted on the effects of nonmaternal care on preschoolers. Previous research on the effects of daycare indicated that although the daycare experience was often associated with higher cognitive competence, it was also associated with less compliance and more assertiveness with peers. The NICHD study, as reported in 1998, found that the major variables predicting children's negativity were the mother's sensitivity and her psychological adjustment. Both higher quality of nonmaternal care and greater experience in groups with other children predicted socially competent behavior. It was also the case, however, that more time in child care and less stable care predicted problematic and noncompliant behavior. On the whole, the results indicated that the home environment is the major influence on child outcomes, but that the quality and stability of the nonmaternal care does have an effect.

When children are of school age, working families still have to deal with issues of control and supervision when work hours and school hours do not overlap. An increasing number of schools and community organizations have responded by setting up after-school and before-school programs as well as supervised lunchrooms. Neighbors, relatives, and older siblings often fill in. Some children, however, return from school to an empty house. The effects of such unsupervised care vary widely depending on whether the child stays in the home and is governed by set rules and telephone contact, where the child spends this time if not in the home, and the safety of the neighborhood. For children of all ages, however, the prevalence of working families has brought with it a need for community programs and affordable, stable, high-quality nonparental care—a need that has not yet been met. This is an important social issue that needs to be addressed given that most families today are working families.

See also: LATCHKEY CHILDREN; PARENT-CHILD RELATIONSHIPS; SINGLE-PARENT FAMILIES

Bibliography

Bond, James T., Ellen Galinsky, and Jennifer E. Swanberg. *1997 National Study of the Changing Workforce.* New York: Families and Work Institute, 1998.

Clarke-Stewart, Alison. "Infant Day Care: Maligned or Malignant?" *American Psychologist* 44 (1989):266–273.

Hoffman, Lois W., and Lise M. Youngblade. *Mothers at Work: Effects on Children's Well-Being.* New York: Cambridge University Press, 1999.

National Institute of Child Health and Human Development, Early Child Care Research Network. "The Effects of Infant Child Care on Mother-Infant Attachment Security: Results of the NICHD Study of Early Child Care." *Child Development* 68 (1997):860–879.

National Institute of Child Health and Human Development, Early Child Care Research Network. "Early Child Care and Self-Control, Compliance, and Problem Behavior at Twenty-Four and Thirty-Six Months." *Child Development* 69 (1998):1145–1170.

Warr, Peter, and Glenys Parry. "Paid Employment and Women's Psychological Well-Being." *Psychological Bulletin* 91 (1982):498–516.

Lois Wladis Hoffman

APPENDIX A

31.   Racial and Ethnic Composition
32.   Reading Achievement
33.   Serious Violent Juvenile Crime Rate
34.   Youth Neither Enrolled in School Nor Working
35.   Youth Victims of Serious Violent Crime

TABLE 1

Access to Health Care: Percentage of Children under Age 18 Covered by Health Insurance[a] by Type of Health Insurance, Age, Race, and Hispanic Origin, 1987–1998

Characteristic	1987	1988	1989	1990	1991	1992	1993	1994	1995	1996	1997	1998
All health insurance												
Total	87	87	87	87	87	87	86	86	86	85	85	85
Age												
Ages 0–5	88	87	87	89	89	89	88	86	87	86	86	84
Ages 6–11	87	87	87	87	88	88	87	87	87	85	86	85
Ages 12–17	86	86	86	85	85	85	83	85	86	84	83	84
Race and Hispanic origin												
White, non-Hispanic	90	90	90	90	90	90	89	89	90	89	89	89
Black	83	84	84	85	85	86	84	83	85	81	81	80
Hispanic[b]	72	71	70	72	73	75	74	72	73	71	71	70
Private health insurance												
Total	74	74	74	71	70	69	67	66	66	66	67	68
Age												
Ages 0–5	72	71	71	68	66	65	63	60	60	62	63	64
Ages 6–11	74	74	75	73	71	71	70	67	67	67	68	68
Ages 12–17	75	76	76	73	72	71	69	70	71	70	70	65
Race and Hispanic origin												
White, non-Hispanic	83	83	83	81	80	80	78	77	78	78	78	79
Black	49	50	52	49	45	46	46	43	44	45	48	47
Hispanic[b]	48	48	48	45	43	42	42	38	38	40	42	43
Government health insurance[c]												
Total	19	19	19	22	24	25	27	26	26	25	23	23
Age												
Ages 0–5	22	23	24	28	30	33	35	33	33	31	29	27
Ages 6–11	19	18	18	20	22	23	25	25	26	25	23	23
Ages 12–17	16	16	15	18	19	19	20	20	21	19	19	19
Race and Hispanic origin												
White, non-Hispanic	12	13	13	15	16	17	19	18	18	18	17	16
Black	42	42	41	45	48	49	50	48	49	45	40	42
Hispanic[b]	28	27	27	32	37	38	41	38	39	35	34	31

[a] Children are considered to be covered by health insurance if they had public or private coverage at any time during the year. Some children are covered by both types of insurance; hence, the sum of public and private is greater than the total.

[b] Persons of Hispanic origin may be of any race.

[c] Government health insurance for children consists mostly of Medicaid, but also includes Medicare, SCHIP (the State Children's Health Insurance Program), and CHAMPUS (Civilian Health and Medical Program of the Uniformed Services). CHAMPUS is being replaced by Tricare.

SOURCE: U.S. Census Bureau, unpublished tables based on analyses from the March Current Population Survey.

TABLE 2

Activity Limitation: Percentage of Children under Age 18 with Any Limitation in Activity Resulting from Chronic Conditions[a] by Age, Gender, Poverty Status, Race, and Hispanic Origin, Selected Years 1984–1997

Characteristic	1984	1990	1991	1992	1993	1994	1995	1996	1997[b]
Children ages 0–17									
Total	5.0	4.9	5.8	6.1	6.6	6.7	6.0	6.1	6.5
Gender									
Male	5.9	5.6	6.8	7.1	7.8	7.9	7.4	7.4	8.3
Female	4.0	4.2	4.7	5.0	5.3	5.6	4.6	4.7	4.7
Poverty status									
Below poverty	7.1	6.7	8.8	9.2	9.5	9.7	9.2	9.7	8.8
At or above poverty	4.4	4.6	5.1	5.3	5.9	6.0	5.4	5.3	6.4
Race and Hispanic origin									
White, non-Hispanic	4.9	5.0	5.8	6.0	6.7	6.6	6.0	5.7	7.0
Black, non-Hispanic	5.6	5.5	6.7	7.5	7.7	8.9	7.3	8.4	7.3
Hispanic[c]	4.7	4.1	5.5	5.3	5.6	5.7	5.8	6.3	4.8
Children ages 0–4									
Total	2.5	2.2	2.4	2.8	2.8	3.1	2.7	2.6	3.4
Gender									
Male	2.7	2.6	2.7	3.3	3.1	3.4	3.3	3.3	4.2
Female	2.3	1.7	2.1	2.2	2.5	2.7	2.0	1.7	2.7
Poverty status									
Below poverty	4.0	3.0	4.3	4.5	4.3	5.2	3.9	4.9	4.5
At or above poverty	2.0	2.0	2.0	2.3	2.4	2.5	2.4	1.7	3.2
Race and Hispanic origin									
White, non-Hispanic	2.3	2.1	2.4	2.5	2.4	2.7	2.7	1.8	3.6
Black, non-Hispanic	3.3	2.9	3.2	4.2	4.7	5.0	3.5	4.8	4.5
Hispanic[c]	2.5	2.0	1.8	2.5	2.7	3.1	2.5	3.4	2.4
Children ages 5–17									
Total	6.1	6.1	7.2	7.5	8.1	8.2	7.4	7.5	7.7
Gender									
Male	7.3	6.9	8.5	8.7	9.8	9.7	9.0	9.0	9.9
Female	4.8	5.2	5.9	6.2	6.4	6.7	5.6	5.9	5.5
Poverty status									
Below poverty	8.7	8.5	11.0	11.7	12.2	11.9	11.8	12.1	10.7
At or above poverty	5.5	5.6	6.4	6.6	7.2	7.4	6.5	6.6	7.5
Race and Hispanic origin									
White, non-Hispanic	6.0	6.2	7.1	7.4	8.4	8.1	7.2	7.1	8.2
Black, non-Hispanic	6.7	6.7	8.2	9.0	9.0	10.6	8.9	9.8	8.3
Hispanic[c]	5.8	5.1	7.2	6.7	7.1	7.0	7.5	7.7	5.9

[a] Chronic conditions usually have a duration of more than 3 months, e.g., asthma, hearing impairment, diabetes. Persons are not classified as limited in activity unless one or more chronic conditions are reported as the cause of the limitation.

[b] In 1997, the National Health Interview Survey was redesigned. Data for 1997 are not strictly comparable with earlier data.

[c] Persons of Hispanic origin may be of any race.

SOURCE: Centers for Disease Control and Prevention, National Center for Health Statistics, National Health Interview Survey.

TABLE 3

Adolescent Birth Rate by Age, Race, and Hispanic Origin, Selected Years 1980–1998

(Live births per 1,000 females in specified age group)

Characteristic	1980	1985	1990	1991	1992	1993	1994	1995	1996	1997	1998
All races											
Ages 10-14	1.1	1.2	1.4	1.4	1.4	1.4	1.4	1.3	1.2	1.1	1.0
Ages 15-17	32.5	31.0	37.5	38.7	37.8	37.8	37.6	36.0	33.8	32.1	30.4
Ages 18-19	82.1	79.6	88.6	94.4	94.5	92.1	91.5	89.1	86.0	83.6	82.0
Ages 15-19	53.0	51.0	59.9	62.1	60.7	59.6	58.9	56.8	54.4	52.3	51.1
White, total											
Ages 10-14	0.6	0.6	0.7	0.8	0.8	0.8	0.8	0.8	0.8	0.7	0.6
Ages 15-17	25.5	24.4	29.5	30.7	30.1	30.3	30.7	30.0	28.4	27.1	25.9
Ages 18-19	73.2	70.4	78.0	83.5	83.8	82.1	82.1	81.2	78.4	75.9	74.6
Ages 15-19	45.4	43.3	50.8	52.8	51.8	51.1	51.1	50.1	48.1	46.3	45.4
White, non-Hispanic											
Ages 10-14	0.4	—	0.5	0.5	0.5	0.5	0.5	0.4	0.4	0.4	0.3
Ages 15-17	22.4	—	23.2	23.6	22.7	22.7	22.8	22.0	20.6	19.4	18.4
Ages 18-19	67.7	—	66.6	70.5	69.8	67.7	67.4	66.1	63.7	61.9	60.6
Ages 15-19	41.2	—	42.5	43.4	41.7	40.7	40.4	39.3	37.6	36.0	35.2
Black, total											
Ages 10-14	4.3	4.5	4.9	4.8	4.7	4.6	4.6	4.2	3.6	3.3	2.9
Ages 15-17	72.5	69.3	82.3	84.1	81.3	79.8	76.3	69.7	64.7	60.8	56.8
Ages 18-19	135.1	132.4	152.9	158.6	157.9	151.9	148.3	137.1	132.5	130.1	126.9
Ages 15-19	97.8	95.4	112.8	115.5	112.4	108.6	104.5	96.1	91.4	88.2	85.4
Black, non-Hispanic											
Ages 10-14	4.6	—	5.0	4.9	4.8	4.7	4.7	4.3	3.8	3.4	3.0
Ages 15-17	77.2	—	84.9	86.7	83.9	82.5	78.6	72.1	66.6	62.6	58.8
Ages 18-19	146.5	—	157.5	163.1	162.9	156.7	152.9	141.9	136.6	134.0	139.0
Ages 15-19	105.1	—	116.2	118.9	116.0	112.2	107.7	99.3	94.2	90.8	88.2
Hispanic [a]											
Ages 10-14	1.7	—	2.4	2.4	2.6	2.7	2.7	2.7	2.6	2.3	2.1
Ages 15-17	52.1	—	65.9	70.6	71.4	71.7	74.0	72.9	69.0	66.3	62.3
Ages 18-19	126.9	—	147.7	158.5	159.7	159.1	158.0	157.9	151.1	144.3	140.1
Ages 15-19	82.2	—	100.3	106.7	107.1	106.8	107.7	106.7	101.8	97.4	93.6
American Indian/Alaska Native											
Ages 10-14	1.9	1.7	1.6	1.6	1.6	1.4	1.9	1.8	1.7	1.7	1.6
Ages 15-17	51.5	47.7	48.5	52.7	53.8	53.7	51.3	47.8	46.4	45.3	44.4
Ages 18-19	129.5	124.1	129.3	134.3	132.6	130.7	130.3	130.7	122.3	117.6	118.4
Ages 15-19	82.2	79.2	81.1	85.0	84.4	83.1	80.8	78.0	73.9	71.8	72.1
Asian/Pacific Islander											
Ages 10-14	0.3	0.4	0.7	0.8	0.7	0.6	0.7	0.7	0.6	0.5	0.4
Ages 15-17	12.0	12.5	16.0	16.1	15.2	16.0	16.1	15.4	14.9	14.3	13.8
Ages 18-19	46.2	40.8	40.2	43.1	43.1	43.3	44.1	43.4	40.4	39.3	38.3
Ages 15-19	26.2	23.8	26.4	27.4	26.6	27.0	27.1	26.1	24.6	23.7	23.1

— = not available

[a] Persons of Hispanic origin may be of any race. T rend data for Hispanics are affected by expansion of the reporting area in which an item on Hispanic origin is included on the birth certificate as well as by immigration. These two factors affect numbers of events, composition of the His panic population, and maternal and infant health characteristics. The number of States in the reporting area increased from 22 in 1980 to 23 and the District of Columbia (DC) in 1983-87, 30 and DC in 1988, 47 and DC in 1989, 48 and DC in 1990, 49 and DC in 1991-92, and 50 and DC in 1993. Rates in 1981-88 were not calculated for Hispanics and white, non-Hispanics because estimates for these populations were not available. Recent declines in teenage birth rates parallel but outpace the reductions in birth rates for unmarried teenagers (POP6A). Birth rates for married teenagers have fallen sharply in the 1990s, but relatively few teenagers are married.

SOURCE: Centers for Diease Control and Prevention, National Center for Health Statistics, National Vital Statistics System. Ventura, S.J., Martin, J.A., Curtin, S.C., Mathews, T.J., and Park. M.N. (2000). *Births: Final data for 1998. National Vital Statistics Reports, 48* (3). Hyattsville, MD: National Center for Health Statistics. Mathews, T.J., Ventura, S.J., Curtin, S.C., and Martin, J.A. (1998) Births of Hispanic origin, 1989–95. *Monthly Vital Statistics Report, 46* (6 , Supplement). Hyattsville, MD: National Center for Health Statistics, Taffel, S.M. (1984). Birth and fertility rates for States: United States, 1990. *Vital and Health Statistics, 42* (Series 21). Hyattsville, MD: National Center for Health Statistics.

TABLE 4

Alcohol Use: Percentage of Students Who Reported Having Five or More Drinks in a Row in the Past Weeks by Grade, Gender, Race, and Hispanic Origin, Selected Years 1980–1999

Characteristic	1980	1985	1990	1991	1992	1993	1994	1995	1996	1997	1998	1999
8th–graders												
Total	–	–	–	12.9	13.4	13.5	14.5	14.5	15.6	14.5	13.7	15.2
Gender												
Male	–	–	–	14.3	13.9	14.8	16.0	15.1	16.5	15.3	14.4	16.4
Female	–	–	–	11.4	12.8	12.3	13.0	13.9	14.5	13.5	12.7	13.9
Race and Hispanic origin[a]												
White	–	–	–	–	12.7	12.6	12.9	13.9	15.1	15.1	14.1	14.3
Black	–	–	–	–	9.6	10.7	11.8	10.8	10.4	10.4	9.0	9.9
Hispanic[b]	–	–	–	–	20.4	21.4	22.3	22.0	21.0	20.7	20.4	20.9
10th–graders												
Total	–	–	–	22.9	21.1	23.0	23.6	24.0	24.8	25.1	24.3	25.6
Gender												
Male	–	–	–	26.4	23.7	26.5	28.5	26.3	27.2	28.6	26.7	29.7
Female	–	–	–	19.5	18.6	19.3	18.7	21.5	22.3	21.7	22.2	21.8
Race and Hispanic origin[a]												
White[s]	–	–	–	–	23.2	23.0	24.5	25.4	26.2	26.9	27.0	27.2
Black	–	–	–	–	15.0	14.8	14.0	13.3	12.2	12.7	12.8	12.7
Hispanic[b]	–	–	–	–	22.9	23.8	24.2	26.8	29.6	27.5	26.3	27.5
12th–graders												
Total	41.2	36.7	32.2	29.8	27.9	27.5	28.2	29.8	30.2	31.3	31.5	30.8
Gender												
Male	52.1	45.3	39.1	37.8	35.6	34.6	37.0	36.9	37.0	37.9	39.2	38.1
Female	30.5	28.2	24.4	21.2	20.3	20.7	20.2	23.0	23.5	24.4	24.0	23.6
Race and Hispanic origin[a]												
White	44.3	41.5	36.6	34.6	32.1	31.3	31.5	32.3	33.4	35.1	36.4	35.7
Black	17.7	15.7	14.4	11.7	11.3	12.6	14.4	14.9	15.3	13.4	12.3	12.3
Hispanic[b]	33.1	31.7	25.6	27.9	31.0	27.2	24.3	26.6	27.1	27.6	28.1	29.3

– = not available

[a]Examples for race and Hispanic origin represent the mean of the specified year and the previous year. Data have been combined to increase subgroup sample sizes, thus providing more stable estimates.

[b]Persons of Hispanic origin may be of any race.

SOURCE: Johnson, L.D., O'Malley, P.M., and Bachman, J.G., (1999). *National survey results on drug use from the Monitoring the Future Study, 1975–1998* (NIH Publication No. 99–4660). Bethesda, MD: National Institutes of Health, National Institute on Drug Abuse, and Institute for Social Research. University of Michigan, Press release of December 17, 1999, and unpublished data from Monitoring the Future, University of Michigan.

TABLE 5

Birth Rates for Unmarried Women by Age of Mother, Selected Years 1980–1998

(Live births to unmarried women per 1,000 in specific age group)

Age of mother	1980	1985	1990	1991	1992	1993	1994	1995	1996	1997	1998
Total ages 15-44	29.4	32.8	43.8	45.2	45.2	45.3	46.9	45.1	44.8	44.0	44.3
Age group											
Ages 15-17	20.6	22.4	29.6	30.9	30.4	30.6	32.0	30.5	29.0	28.2	27.0
Ages 18-19	39.0	45.9	60.7	65.7	67.3	66.9	70.1	67.6	65.9	65.2	64.5
Ages 20-24	40.9	46.5	65.1	68.0	68.5	69.2	72.2	70.3	70.7	71.0	72.3
Ages 25-29	34.0	39.9	56.0	56.5	56.5	57.1	59.0	56.1	56.8	56.2	58.4
Ages 30-34	21.1	25.2	37.6	38.1	37.9	38.5	40.1	39.6	41.1	39.0	39.1
Ages 35-39	9.7	11.6	17.3	18.0	18.8	19.0	19.8	19.5	20.1	19.0	19.0
Ages 40-44	2.6	2.5	3.6	3.8	4.1	4.4	4.7	4.7	4.8	4.6	4.6

Note: Nonmarital birth rates for 1989-93 are somewhat understated because births to unmarried women were substantially underreported in Michigan and Texas; data since 1994 have been reported on a complete basis. Thus, the overall increase in nonmarital birth rates between 1980 and 1994 is acurately recorded here, However, the rates for 1989-93, if computed on the basis of complete data, would have been higher than the rates shown here, and the peak years for the rates would have occurred in the early 1990s rather than in 1994. Ventura, S.J., Martin, J.A., Curtin, S.C., and Mathews, T.J. (1996). Advance report of final natality statistics, 1994. *Monthly Vital Statistics Report*, 44 (11, Supplement). Hyattsville, MD: National Center for Health Statistics.

SOURCE: Centers for Disease Control and Prevention, National Center for Health Statistics, National Vital Statistics System. Ventura, S.J., Martin. J.A., Curtin, S.C., Mathews. T.J., and Park, M.M. (2000). Births: Final data for 1998. *National Vital Statistics Reports*, 48 (3), Hyattsville, MD: National Center for Health Statistics.

TABLE 6

Child Poverty: Percentage of Related Children under Age 18 Living below Selected Poverty Levels by Age, Family Structure, Race, and Hispanic Origin, Selected Years 1980–1998

Characteristic	1980	1985	1990	1991	1992	1993	1994	1995	1995	1997	1998
Under 100 percent of poverty											
Children all families											
Related children	18	20	20	21	22	22	21	20	20	19	18
White, non-Hispanic	—	—	12	12	12	13	12	11	10	11	10
Black	42	43	44	46	46	46	43	42	40	37	36
Hispanic[a]	33	40	38	40	39	40	41	39	40	36	34
Related children under age 6	20	23	23	24	26	26	25	24	23	22	21
Related children ages 6–17	17	19	18	20	19	20	20	18	18	18	17
Children in married-couple families											
Related children	—	—	10	11	11	12	11	10	10	10	9
White, non-Hispanic	—	—	7	7	7	8	7	6	5	5	5
Black	—	—	18	15	18	18	15	13	14	13	12
Hispanic[a]	—	—	27	29	29	30	30	28	29	26	23
Related children under age 6	—	—	12	12	13	13	12	11	12	11	10
Related children ages 6–17	—	—	10	10	10	11	10	9	9	9	9
Children in female-householder families, no husband present											
Related children	51	54	53	56	55	54	53	50	49	49	46
White, non-Hispanic	–	–	40	41	40	39	38	34	35	37	33
Black	65	67	65	68	67	66	63	62	58	55	55
Hispanic[a]	65	72	68	69	66	66	68	66	67	63	60
Related children under age 6	65	66	66	66	66	64	64	62	59	59	55
Related children ages 6–17	46	48	47	50	49	49	47	45	45	45	42
All children[b]	18	21	21	22	22	23	22	21	21	20	19
Under 50 percent of poverty											
Children in all families											
Related children	7	8	8	9	10	10	9	8	8	8	8
White, non-Hispanic	—	—	4	5	5	5	4	3	4	4	4
Black	17	22	22	25	27	26	23	20	20	20	17
Hispanic[a]	—	—	14	14	15	14	17	16	14	16	13
Under 150 percent of poverty											
Children in all families											
Related children	29	32	31	32	33	33	32	32	31	30	29
White, non-Hispanic	—	—	21	21	21	22	21	19	19	19	18
Black	57	59	57	60	60	61	58	56	56	51	52
Hispanic[a]	—	—	55	58	58	60	58	59	57	56	52

— = not available

[a]Persons of Hispanic origin may be of any race.

[b]Related and non-related children.

Note: Estimates refer to children who are related to the householder and who are under age 18. The poverty level is based on money income and does not include noncash benefits, such as food stamps. Poverty thresholds reflect family size and composition and are adjusted each year using the annual average Consumer Price Index (CPI) level. The poverty threshold for a family of four was $16,660 in 1998. The levels shown here are derived from the ratio of the family's income to the familys poverty threshold. Related children include biological children, adopted children and stepchildren of the householder and all other children in the household related to the householder (or reference person) by blood, adoption, or marriage. For more detail, see U.S. Census Bureau, Series P-60, No. 207.

SOURCE: U.S. Census Bureau, March Current Population Survey, *Current Population Reports*, Consumer income, Series P-60, various years.

TABLE 7

Childhood Immunizations: Percentage of Children Ages 19 to 35 Months Vaccinated for Selected Diseases by Poverty Status, Race, and Hispanic Origin, 1994–1998

Characteristic	Total					Below poverty					At or above poverty				
	1994	1995	1996	1997	1998	1994	1995	1996	1997	1998	1994	1995	1996	1997	1998
Total															
Combined series (4:3:1:3)[a]	69	74	77	76	79	61	67	69	71	74	72	77	80	79	82
Combined series (4:3:1)[b]	75	76	78	78	81	66	67	71	73	76	77	79	81	80	83
DTP (4 doses or more)[c]	76	79	81	81	84	69	71	73	76	80	79	81	84	84	86
Polio (3 doses or more)	83	88	91	91	91	78	84	88	90	90	85	89	92	92	92
Measles-containing[b]	89	90	91	91	92	87	85	87	86	90	90	91	92	92	93
Hib (3 doses or more)[e]	86	92	92	93	93	81	88	88	90	91	88	93	93	94	95
Hepatitis B (3 doses of more)[f]	37	68	82	81	87	25	64	78	80	85	41	69	83	85	88
Varicella[g]	—	—	12	26	43	—	—	5	17	41	—	—	15	29	44
White, non-Hispanic															
Combined series (4:3:1:3)[a]	72	77	79	79	82	—	68	68	70	77	—	79	81	76	83
Combined series (4:3:1)[b]	78	79	80	80	83	—	—	70	73	79	—	—	82	82	84
DTP (4 doses or more)	80	81	83	84	87	—	—	72	76	82	—	—	85	85	88
Polio (3 doses or more)	85	89	92	92	92	—	—	88	90	91	—	—	93	92	93
Measles-containing[d]	90	91	92	92	93	—	—	86	85	91	—	—	93	93	94
Hib (3 doses or more)[e]	87	93	93	94	95	—	—	87	90	92	—	—	94	95	96
Hepatitis B (3 doses or more)[f]	40	68	82	85	88	—	—	75	80	87	—	—	83	85	88
Varicella[g]	—	—	15	28	42	—	—	6	17	37	—	—	16	29	43
Black, non-Hispanic															
Combined series (4:3:1:3)[a]	67	70	74	73	73	—	66	70	72	72	—	75	78	80	74
Combined series (4:3:1)[b]	70	72	76	74	74	—	—	73	72	74	—	—	80	78	76
DTP (4 doses or more)[c]	72	74	79	78	77	—	—	75	76	77	—	—	82	80	79
Polio (3 doses or more)	79	84	90	90	88	—	—	88	90	88	—	—	92	91	87
Measles-containing[d]	86	86	89	90	89	—	—	88	88	89	—	—	91	92	90
Hib (3 doses or more)[e]	85	89	90	92	90	—	—	87	92	90	—	—	92	94	90
Hepatitis B (3 doses or more)[f]	29	65	82	83	84	—	—	79	82	86	—	—	86	84	83
Varicella[g]	—	—	9	21	42	—	—	3	16	40	—	—	13	27	44
Hispanic[h]															
Combined series (4:3:1:3)[a]	62	69	71	72	75	—	65	68	71	73	—	72	74	77	79
Combined series (4:3:1)[b]	68	72	73	74	77	—	—	70	72	76	—	—	75	77	80
DTP (4 doses of more)[c]	70	75	77	77	81	—	—	73	75	79	—	—	79	80	83
Polio (3 doses or more)	81	87	89	90	89	—	—	88	89	90	—	—	90	90	90
Measles-containing[d]	88	88	88	88	91	—	—	88	86	91	—	—	89	89	93
Hib (3 doses of more)[e]	84	90	89	90	92	—	—	88	89	92	—	—	90	92	94
Hepatitis B (3 doses or more)[f]	33	69	80	81	86	—	—	79	79	83	—	—	82	84	88
Varicella[g]	—	—	8	22	47	—	—	6	18	44	—	—	11	25	48

— = not available

[a] The 4:3:1:3 combined series consists of 4 doses of diphtheria and tetanus toxoids and pertussis vaccine(DTP), 3 doses of polio vaccine, 1 dose of a measles-containing vaccine (MCV), and 3 doses of *Haemophilus influenzae* type b (Hib) vaccine.

[b] The 4:3:1 combined series consists of 4 doses of diphtheria and tetanus toxoids and pertussis vaccine (DTP), 3 doses of polio vaccine, and 1 dose of a measles-containing vaccine (MCV).

[c] Diphtheria and tetanus toxoids and pertussis vaccine.

[d] Respondents were asked about measles-containing vaccine, including MMR (measles-mumps-rebella) vaccines.

[e] *Haemophilus influenzae* type b (Hib) vaccine.

[f] The percentage of children 19 to 35 months of age who received 3 doses of hepatitis B vaccine was low in 1994, because universal infant vaccination with a 3-dose series was not recommended until November 1991.

[g] Recommended in July 1996. Administered on or after the first birthday.

[h] Persons of Hispanic origin may be of any race.

SOURCE: Centers for Disease Control and Prevention, National Center for Health Statistics and National Immunization Program, National Immunization Survey.

TABLE 8

Cigarette Smoking: Percentage of Students Who Reported Smoking Cigarettes Daily in the Previous 30 Days by Grade, Gender, Race, and Hispanic Origin, 1980–1999

Characteristic	1980	1985	1990	1991	1992	1993	1994	1995	1996	1997	1998	1999
8th-graders												
Total	—	—	—	7.2	7.0	8.3	8.8	9.3	10.4	9.0	8.8	8.1
Gender												
Male	—	—	—	8.1	6.9	8.8	9.5	9.2	10.5	9.0	8.1	7.4
Female	—	—	—	6.2	7.2	7.8	8.0	9.2	10.1	8.7	9.0	8.4
Race and Hispanic origin[a]												
White	—	—	—	—	7.7	8.8	9.7	10.5	11.7	11.4	10.4	9.7
Black	—	—	—	—	1.4	1.8	2.6	2.8	3.2	3.7	3.8	3.8
Hispanic[b]	—	—	—	—	7.3	7.2	9.0	9.2	8.0	8.1	8.4	8.5
10th-graders												
Total	—	—	—	12.6	12.3	14.2	14.6	16.3	18.3	18.0	15.8	15.9
Gender												
Male	—	—	—	12.4	12.1	13.8	15.2	16.3	18.1	17.2	14.7	15.6
Female	—	—	—	12.5	12.4	14.3	13.7	16.1	18.6	18.5	16.8	15.9
Race and Hispanic origin[a]												
White	—	—	—	—	14.5	15.3	16.5	17.6	20.0	21.4	20.3	19.1
Black	—	—	—	—	2.8	3.1	3.8	4.7	5.1	5.6	5.8	5.3
Hispanic[b]	—	—	—	—	8.4	8.9	8.1	9.9	11.6	10.8	9.4	9.1
12th-graders												
Total	21.3	19.5	19.1	18.5	17.2	19.0	19.4	21.6	22.2	24.6	22.4	23.1
Gender												
Male	18.5	17.8	18.6	18.8	17.2	19.4	20.4	21.7	22.2	24.8	22.7	23.6
Female	23.5	20.6	19.3	17.9	16.7	18.2	18.1	20.8	21.8	23.6	21.5	22.2
Race and Hispanic origin[a]												
White	23.9	20.4	21.8	21.5	20.5	21.4	22.9	23.9	25.4	27.8	28.3	26.9
Black	17.4	9.9	5.8	5.1	4.2	4.1	4.9	6.1	7.0	7.2	7.4	7.7
Hispanic[b]	12.8	11.8	10.9	11.5	12.5	11.8	10.6	11.6	12.9	14.0	13.6	14.0

— = not available

a Estimates for race and Hispanic origin represent the mean of the specified year and the previous year. Data have been combined to increase subgroup sample sizes, thus providing more stable estimates.

b Persons of Hispanic origin may be of any race.

SOURCE: Johnston, L.D., O'Malley, P.M., and Bachman, J.G. (1999). *National survey results on drug use from the Monitoring the Future Study, 1975–1998* (NIH Publication No. 99-4660). Bethesda, MD: National Institutes of Health, National Institute on Drug Abuse, and Institute for Social Research, University of Michigan. Table 2-2. Data are from the study, Monitoring the Future, University of Michigan. Press release of December 17, 1999, and unpublished data from Monitoring the Future, University of Michigan.

TABLE 9

Difficulty Speaking English: Children Ages 5 to 17 Who Speak a Language Other than English at Home, and Who are Reported to Have Difficulty Speaking English[a] by Race, Hispanic Origin, and Region, Selected Years 1979–1995

Characteristic	1979	1989	1992	1995[b]
Children who speak another language at home				
Number (in millions)	3.8	5.3	6.4	6.7
Percentage of children ages 5–17	8.5	12.6	14.2	14.1
Race and Hispanic origin				
White, non-Hispanic	3.2	3.5	3.7	3.6
Black, non-Hispanic	1.3	2.4	4.2	3.0
Hispanic[c]	75.1	71.2	76.6	73.9
Other, non-Hispanic[d]	44.1	53.4	58.3	45.5
Region[e]				
Northeast	10.5	13.5	16.2	15.1
Midwest	3.7	4.9	5.6	5.9
South	6.8	10.7	11.1	11.7
West	17.0	24.2	27.2	26.4
Children who speak another language at home and have difficulty speaking English				
Number (in millions)	1.3	1.9	2.2	2.4
Percentage of children ages 5–17	2.8	4.4	4.9	5.1
Race and Hispanic origin				
White, non-Hispanic	0.5	0.8	0.6	0.7
Black, non-Hispanic	0.3	0.5	1.3	0.9
Hispanic[c]	28.7	27.4	29.9	31.0
Other, non-Hispanic[d]	19.8	20.4	21.0	14.1
Region[e]				
Northeast	2.9	4.8	5.3	5.0
Midwest	1.1	1.3	1.6	2.3
South	2.2	3.8	3.5	3.4
West	6.5	8.8	10.4	11.4

[a] Respondents were asked if the children in the household spoke a language other than English at home and how well they could speak English. Categories used for reporting were "Very well," "Well," "Not well," and "Not at all." All those reported to speak English less than "Very well" were considered to have difficulty speaking English based on an evaluation of the English-speaking ability of a sample of the children in the 1980s.

[b] Numbers in 1995 may reflect changes in the Current Population Survey because of newly instituted computer-assisted interviewing techniques and/or because of the change in the population controls to the 1990 Census-based estimates with adjustments.

[c] Persons of Hispanic origin may be of any race.

[d] Most in this category are Asians/Pacific Islanders, but American Indian/Alaska Native children also are included.

[e] Regions: Northeast includes Connecticut, Maine, Massachusetts, New Hampshire, New Jersey, New York, Pennsylvania, Rhode Island, and Vermont. Midwest includes Illinois, Indiana, Iowa, Kansas, Michigan, Minnesota, Missouri, Nebraska, North Dakota, Ohio, South Dakota, and Wisconsin. South includes Alabama, Arkansas, Delaware, District of Columbia, Florida, Georgia, Kentucky, Louisiana, Maryland, Mississippi, North Carolina, Oklahoma, South Carolina, Tennessee, Texas, Virginia, and West Virginia. West includes Alaska, Arizona, California, Colorado, Hawaii, Idaho, Montana, Nevada, New Mexico, Oregon, Utah, Washington, and Wyoming.

Note: All nonresponses to the language questions are excluded from the tabulations.

SOURCE: U.S. Census Bureau, October (1992 and 1995) and November (1979 and 1989) Current Population Surveys. Tabulated by the National Center for Education Statistics.

TABLE 10

Early Childhood Care and Education: Percentage of Children Ages 3 to 5[a] Who Are Enrolled in Center-Based Early Childhood Care and Education Programs[b] by Child and Family Characteristics, Selected Years 1991–1999

Characteristic	1991	1993	1995	1996	1999
Total	53	53	55	55	59
Gender					
Male	52	53	55	55	61
Female	53	53	55	55	58
Race and Hispanic origin					
White, non-Hispanic	54	54	57	57	59
Black, non-Hispanic	58	57	60	65	73
Hispanic[c]	39	43	37	39	44
Other	53	51	57	45	66
Poverty status[d]					
Below poverty	44	49	45	44	52
At or above poverty	56	53	59	59	62
Family type					
Two parents	50	52	55	54	59
One or no parent	54	54	56	58	61
Mother's highest level of education[e]					
Less than high school graduate	32	33	35	37	40
High school graduate/GED	46	43	48	49	51
Vocational/Technical or some college	60	60	57	58	63
College graduate	72	73	75	73	74
Mother's employment status[e,f]					
Worked 35 hours or more per week	59	61	60	63	64
Worked less than 35 hours per week	58	57	62	64	63
Looking for work	43	48	52	47	55
Not in labor force	45	44	47	43	53

[a] Estimates are based on children who have yet to enter kindergarten.
[b] Center-based programs include day care centers, Head Start programs, preschool, nursery school, prekindergarten, and other early childhood programs.
[c] Persons of Hispanic origin may be of any race.
[d] Poverty estimates for 1991 and 1993 are not comparable to later years because respondents were not asked exact household income.
[e] Children without mothers in the home are not included in estimates dealing with mother's education or mother's employment status.
[f] Unemployed mothers are not shown separately but are included in the total.

SOURCE: U.S. Department of Education, National Center for Education Statistics, National Household Education Survey.

TABLE 11

Family Reading: Percentage of Children Ages 3 to 5[a] Who were Read to Every Day in the Last Week by a Family Member by Child and Family Characteristics, Selected Years 1993–1999

Characteristic	1993	1995	1996	1999
Total	53	58	57	53
Gender				
Male	51	57	56	51
Female	54	59	57	54
Race and Hispanic origin				
White, non-Hispanic	59	65	64	61
Black, non-Hispanic	39	43	44	41
Hispanic[b]	37	38	39	33
Poverty status[c]				
Below poverty	44	48	46	38
At or above poverty	56	62	61	58
Family type				
Two parents	55	61	61	57
One or no parent	46	49	46	42
Mother's highest level of education[d]				
Less than high school graduate	37	40	37	38
High school graduate/GED	48	48	49	44
Vocational/technical or some college	57	64	62	53
College graduate	71	76	77	70
Mother's employment status[d,e]				
Worked 35 hours or more per week	52	55	54	48
Worked less than 35 hours per week	56	63	59	55
Not in labor force	55	60	59	60

[a] Estimates are based on children who have yet to enter kindergarten.

[b] Persons of Hispanic origin may be of any race.

[c] Poverty estimates for 1993 are not comparable to later years because respondents were not asked exact household income.

[d] Children without mothers in the home are not included in estimates dealing with mother's education or mother's employment status.

[e] Unemployed mothers are not shown separately but are included in the total.

SOURCE: U.S. Department of Education, National Center for Education Statistics, National Household Education Survey.

TABLE 12

Family Structure and Children's Living Arrangements: Percentage of Children under Age 18 by Presence of Parents in Household, Race, and Hispanic Origin, Selected Years 1980–1999

Race, Hispanic origin, and family type	1980	1985	1990	1991	1992	1993	1994	1995	1996	1997	1998	1999
Total												
Two parents[a]	77	74	73	72	71	71	69	69	68	68	68	68
Mother only[b]	18	21	22	22	23	23	23	23	24	24	23	23
Father only[b]	22		333			3	3	4	4	4	4	4
No parent	4	3	3	3	3	3	4	4	4	4	4	4
White, non-Hispanic												
Two parents[a]	—	—	81	80	79	79	79	78	77	77	76	77
Mother only[b]	—	—	15	15	16	16	16	16	16	17	16	16
Father only[b]	—	—	333			3	3	3	4	4	5	4
No parent	—	—	2	2	1	1	3	3	3	3	3	3
Black												
Two parents[a]	42	39	38	36	36	36	33	33	33	35	36	35
Mother only[b]	44	51	51	54	54	54	53	52	53	52	51	52
Father only[b]	23		443			3	4	4	4	5	4	4
No parent	12	7	8	7	7	7	10	11	9	8	9	10
Hispanic[c]												
Two parents[a]	75	68	67	66	65	65	63	63	62	64	64	63
Mother only[b]	20	27	27	27	28	28	28	28	29	27	27	27
Father only[b]	22		334			4	4	4	4	4	4	5
No parent	3	3	3	4	3	4	5	4	5	5	5	5

— = not available

[a] Excludes families where parents are not living as a married couple.

[b] Includes some families where both parents are present in the household, but living as unmarried partners.

[c] Persons of Hispanic origin may be of any race.

Note: Family structure refers to the presence of biological, adoptive, and stepparents in the child's household. Thus, a child with a biological mother and stepfather living in the household is said to have two parents.

SOURCE: U.S. Census Bureau, Martal status and living arrangements, *Current Population Reports,* annual reports. (Beginning in 1995, detailed tables are available on the Census Bureau web site.)

TABLE 13

Food Security: Percentage of Children under Age 18 in Households Experiencing Food Insecurity by Level of Hunger and Poverty Status, Selected Years 1995–1999

Characteristic	1995	1998	1999
All children			
Food insecure without hunger	13.3	15.0	13.1
Food insecure with moderate or severe hunger	6.1	4.7	3.8
Food insecure with moderate hunger	5.1	4.0	3.3
Food insecure with severe hunger	1.0	0.7	0.5
Below poverty			
Food insecure without hunger	28.7	34.5	32.2
Food insecure with moderate or severe hunger	15.6	14.2	11.8
Food insecure with moderate hunger	12.9	11.8	10.2
Food insecure with severe hunger	2.8	2.4	1.6
At or above poverty			
Food insecure without hunger	8.2	10.3	8.7
Food insecure with moderate or severe hunger	3.0	2.3	1.9
Food insecure with moderate hunger	2.7	1.9	1.6
Food insecure with severe hunger	0.4	0.4	0.3

Note: The Food Security Scale, the percentage of children under age 18 in households experiencing food insecurity with moderate to severe hunger , is based on the food security scale derived from data collected in the Food Security Supplement to the Current Population Survey. The food security scale provides a near-continuous measure of the level of food insecurity and hunger experienced within each household. A categorical measure based on the scale classifies households according to four designated levels of severity of household food insecurity: food secure, food insecure without hunger, food insecure with moderate hunger, and food insecure with severe hunger. Food-secure households do not report a pattern of difficulty obtaining enough or acceptable quality food. Food-insecure households without hunger report having difficulty obtaining enough food, reduced quality of diets, anxiety about their food supply, and increasingly resorting to emergency food sources and other coping behaviors, but do not report indicators of hunger. Food-insecure households with moderate hunger report food insecurity and a pattern of indicators of hunger for one or more adults and, in some cases, for children. Food-insecure households with severe hunger report multiple indicators of both adults' and children' s hunger. For a detailed explanation of the U.S. Department of Agriculture/Department of Health and Human Services Food Security Measurement scale, see Food and Nutrition Service (1997), Household food security in the United States in 1995 and 2000. Guide to measuring household food security, Alexandria, VA: Food and Nutrition Service.

Data for 1996 and 1997 are not strictly comparable with data for 1995, 1997 and 1999 due to methodology differences. In previous reports, data for 1995 were made consistent with 1996 and 1997 data. In this report, the 1996 and 1997 data have been omitted, but the 1995 data are retained because, although screened on a different basis than the revised method adopted in 1998 and 1999, this had little effect on prevalence estimates. The 1996 and 1997 data, however, cannot readily be adjusted to be comparable.

SOURCE: U.S. Census Bureau, Food Security Supplement to the Current Population Survey.

TABLE 14

General Health Status: Percentage of Children under Age 18 in Very Good or Excellent Health by Age and Poverty Status, Selected Years 1984–1997

Age and poverty status	1984	1990	1991	1992	1993	1994	1995	1996	1997[a]
Children ages 0–17									
Total	78	81	80	80	79	79	81	80	81
Poverty status									
Below poverty	62	66	65	65	64	64	65	64	68
At or above poverty	82	84	83	83	83	83	85	84	86
Children ages 0–4									
Total	79	81	81	80	80	81	81	81	84
Poverty status									
Below poverty	66	69	68	67	68	68	66	68	74
At or above poverty	82	84	84	84	84	84	86	85	88
Children ages 5–17									
Total	77	80	80	80	79	79	81	79	81
Poverty status									
Below poverty	60	64	64	64	63	62	64	62	65
At or above poverty	81	84	83	83	82	82	85	83	85
Children ages 5–17									
Total	77	80	80	80	79	79	81	79	81
Poverty status									
Below poverty	60	64	64	64	63	62	64	62	65
At or above poverty	81	84	83	83	82	82	85	83	85

[a] In 1997, the National Health Interview Survey was redesigned. Data for 1997 are not strictly comparable with earlier data.

SOURCE: Centers for Disease Control and Prevention, National Center for Health Statistics, National Health Interview Survey.

TABLE 15

Healthy Eating Index: Overall and Component Mean Scores for Children, 3-Year Average 1994–1996

Component	Ages 2–3 All	Ages 4–6 All	Ages 7–10 All	Ages 11–14 Females	Ages 11–14 Males	Ages 15–18 Females	Ages 15–18 Males
Overall HEI score	73.8	67.8	66.6	63.5	62.2	60.9	60.7
1. Grains	8.3 (54)	7.2 (27)	7.6 (31)	6.7 (16)	7.2 (29)	6.3 (17)	7.5 (34)
2. Vegetables	5.9 (31)	4.9 (16)	5.1 (20)	5.5 (24)	5.4 (23)	5.8 (26)	6.3 (35)
3. Fruits	7 (53)	5.3 (29)	4.3 (18)	3.9 (14)	3.5 (9)	3.1 (12)	2.8 (11)
4. Milk	7.2 (44)	7.4 (44)	7.6 (49)	5.2 (15)	6.2 (27)	4.2 (12)	6.1 (28)
5. Meat	6.3 (28)	5.3 (14)	5.5 (17)	5.7 (15)	6.5 (28)	5.8 (21)	6.9 (36)
6. Total fat	7.4 (40)	7.3 (38)	7.2 (35)	7.2 (37)	6.8 (33)	7.1 (38)	6.8 (34)
7. Saturated fat	5.4 (27)	5.6 (28)	5.7 (28)	5.8 (31)	5.7 (32)	6.6 (42)	6 (35)
8. Cholesterol	9 (83)	8.9 (83)	8.7 (80)	8.5 (78)	7.6 (69)	8.4 (77)	6.7 (58)
9. Sodium	8.8 (64)	8.1 (53)	6.8 (54)	7.1 (39)	5.2 (21)	6.9 (37)	3.7 (51)
10. Variety	8.4 (64)	7.9 (53)	8.1 (54)	7.8 (51)	8.1 (58)	6.7 (37)	7.8 (51)

Note: Percentage of children meeting the dietary recommendations for each component appears in parentheses.

The Healthy Eating Index examines the diet of American children ages 2 to 18. The Index consists of 10 components, each representing different aspects of a healthful diet.

Components 1 to 5 measure the degree to which a person's diet conforms to the U.S. Department of Agriculture's Food Guide Pyramid serving recommendations for the five major food groups: grains (bread, cereal, rice, and pasta), vegetables, fruits, milk (Milk, yogurt, and cheese), and meat/meat alternatives (meat, poultry, fish, dry beans, eggs, and nuts). Component 7 measures saturated fat consumption as a percentage of total food energy intake. Components 8 and 9 measure total cholesterol intake and total sodium intake, respectively. And component 10 measures the degree of variety in a person's diet.

Each component of the Index has a maximum score of 10 and a minimum score of 0. Intermediate scores are computed proportionatel y. High component scores indicate intakes close to recommended ranges or amounts. The maximum combined score for the 10 components is 100. An HEI score above 80 implies a good diet, an HEI score between 51 and 80 implies a diet that needs improvement, and an HEI score less than 51 implies a poor diet.

SOURCE: U.S. Department of Agriculture, Center for Nutrition Policy and Promotion, Continuing Survey of Food Intakes by Individuals.

TABLE 16

Illicit Drug Use: Percentage of Students Who Have Used Illicit Drugs in the Previous 30 Days by Grade, Gender, Race, and Hispanic Origin, Selected Years 1980–1999

Characteristic	1980[a]	1985	1990	1991	1992	1993	1994	1995	1996	1997	1998	1999
8th-graders												
Total	—	—	—	5.7	6.8	8.4	10.9	12.4	14.6	12.9	12.1	12.2
Gender												
Male	—	—	—	5.8	6.4	8.7	11.9	12.7	14.6	13.3	11.9	12.6
Female	—	—	—	5.4	7.1	8.1	9.6	11.9	14.1	12.3	11.9	11.7
Race and Hispanic origin [b]												
White	—	—	—	—	5.9	7.1	8.7	18.9	13.2	13.7	12.4	11.3
Black	—	—	—	—	3.8	5.1	7.4	9.1	10.5	10.8	10.2	11.1
Hispanic[c]	—	—	—	—	10.2	12.3	15.7	16.7	16.5	15.9	15.9	17.0
10th-graders												
Total	—	—	—	11.6	11.0	14.0	18.5	20.2	23.2	23.0	21.5	22.1
Gender												
Male	—	—	—	12.1	11.3	15.2	20.5	21.1	24.3	24.8	22.5	23.7
Female	—	—	—	10.8	10.5	12.5	16.1	19.0	21.9	21.0	20.5	20.4
Race and Hispanic origin [b]												
White	—	—	—	—	12.1	13.1	16.4	19.7	22.4	23.8	23.1	22.6
Black	—	—	—	—	5.2	6.1	11.4	15.5	17.0	17.7	16.4	15.8
Hispanic[c]	—	—	—	—	12.7	15.0	18.0	20.6	22.5	24.2	24.2	23.8
12th-graders												
Total	37.2	29.7	17.2	16.4	14.4	18.3	21.9	23.8	24.6	26.2	25.6	25.9
Gender												
Male	39.6	32.1	18.9	18.4	15.9	20.4	25.5	26.8	27.5	28.7	29.1	28.6
Female	34.3	26.7	15.2	14.1	12.7	15.9	18.3	20.4	21.2	23.2	21.6	22.7
Race and Hispanic origin [b]												
White	38.8	30.2	20.5	18.6	16.8	17.8	21.4	23.8	24.8	26.4	27.5	27.0
Black	28.8	22.9	9.0	7.2	7.3	9.1	14.3	18.3	19.7	20.0	19.4	20.2
Hispanic[c]	33.1	27.2	13.9	14.7	14.6	15.6	18.3	21.4	22.6	23.9	24.1	24.4

— = not available

[a] Beginning in 1982, the question about stimulant use (i.e., amphetamines) was revised to get respondents to exclude the inappropriate reporting of nonprescription stimulants. The prevalence rate dropped slightly as a result of this methodological change.

[b] Estimates for race and Hispanic origin represent the mean of the specified year and the previous year. Data have been combined to increase subgroup sample sizes, thus providing more stable estimates.

[c] Persons of Hispanic origin may be of any race.

Note: Illicit drugs include marijuana, cocaine (including crack), heroin, hallucinogens (including LSD and PCP), amphetamines, and nonmedical use of psychotherapeutics.

SOURCE: Johnston, L.D., O'Malley, M.M., and Bachman, J.G. (1999). *National survey results on drug use from the Monitoring the Future Study, 1975–1998* (NIH Publication No. 99-4660), Bethesda, MD: National Institutes of Health, National Institute on Drug Abuse, and Institute for Social Research, University of Michigan. Table 2-2. Data are from the study, Monitoring the Future, University of Michigan. Press release of December 17, 1999, and unpublished data from Monitoring the Future, University of Michigan.

TABLE 17

Income Distribution: Percentage of Related Children under Age 18 by Family Income Relative to the Poverty Line, Selected Years 1980–1998

Poverty level	1980	1985	1990	1991	1992	1993	1994	1995	1996	1997	1998
Extreme povety	6.6	8.1	8.3	9.3	9.9	9.6	9.4	7.9	8.4	8.5	7.6
Below poverty, but above extreme poverty	11.3	12.0	11.6	11.8	11.7	12.4	11.9	12.2	11.4	10.8	10.7
Low income	24.0	22.8	21.8	22.2	22.0	22.2	22.0	22.5	22.7	21.4	21.2
Medium income	41.4	37.7	37.0	35.7	34.9	33.4	33.7	34.5	34.0	34.4	33.5
High income	16.8	19.4	21.3	21.0	21.5	22.3	23.1	22.8	23.5	25.0	27.0
Very high income	4.3	6.1	7.4	7.0	7.3	8.4	9.1	8.9	9.2	10.1	11.2

Note: Estimates refer to children who are related to the householder and who are under age 18. The income classes are derived from the ratio of the family's income to the family's poverty threshold. Extreme poverty is less than 50 percent of the property threshold (i.e., between $8,330 and $15,659 for a family of four in 1998). Low income is between 100 and 199 percent of the poverty threshold (i.e., between $16,660 and $33,319 for a family of four in 1998). Medium income is between 200 and 399 percent of the poverty threshold (i.e., between $33,320 and $66,639 for a family of four in 1998). High income is 400 percent of the poverty threshold or more. Very high income is 600 per cent of the poverty threshold and over. [These income categories are similar to those used in the *Economic report to the President* (1998). A similar approach is used by Hernandez, D. (1993), *America's children,* except that Hernandez uses the relationship to median income to define his categories. For either method, the medium and high income categories are at similar levels of median family income.]

SOURCE: U.S. Census Bureau, March Current Population Survey.

TABLE 18

Mathematics Achievement: Average Scale Scores of Students Ages 9, 13, and 17 by Age and Child and Family Characteristics, Selected Years 1982–1996

Characteristic	1982	1986	1990	1992	1994	1996
Age 9						
Total	219	222	230	230	231	231
Gender						
Male	217	222	229	231	232	233
Female	221	222	230	228	230	229
Race and Hispanic origin						
White	224	227	235	235	237	237
Black	195	202	208	208	212	212
Hispanic[a]	204	205	214	212	210	215
Age 13						
Total	269	269	270	273	274	274
Gender						
Male	269	270	271	274	276	276
Female	268	268	270	272	273	272
Race and Hispanic origin						
White	274	274	276	279	281	281
Black	240	249	249	250	252	252
Hispanic[a]	252	254	255	259	256	256
Parents' education						
Less than high school	251	252	253	256	255	254
Graduated high school	263	263	263	263	266	267
Some education after high school	275	274	277	278	277	278
Graduated college	282	280	280	283	285	283
Age 17						
Total	299	302	305	307	306	307
Gender						
Male	302	305	306	309	309	310
Female	296	299	303	305	304	305
Race and Hispanic origin						
White	304	308	310	312	312	313
Black	272	279	289	286	286	286
Hispanic[a]	277	283	284	292	291	292
Parents' education						
Less than high school	279	279	285	286	284	281
Graduated high school	293	293	294	298	295	297
Some education after high school	304	305	308	308	305	307
Graduated college	312	314	316	316	318	317

[a] Persons of Hispanic origin may be of any race.
Note: Data on parents' level of education are not reliable for 9-year-olds.
The mathematics proficiency scale ranges from 0 to 500:
  Level 150: Simple arithmetic facts
  Level 200: Beginning skills and understandings
  Level 250: Numerical operations and begining problem solving
  Level 300: Moderately complex procedures and reasoning
  Level 350: Multi-step problem solving and algebra

SOURCE: U.S. Department of Education, National Center for Education Statistics, National Assessment of Educational Progress (NAEP), *1996 Trends in academic progress*.

TABLE 19

Mortality Rate for Children Ages 1 to 4 by Age, Gender, Race, Hispanic Origin, and Cause of Death, Selected Years 1980–1989

(Deaths per 100,000 children in each group)

Characteristic	1980	1985	1990	1991	1992	1993	1994	1995	1996	1997	1998*
Ages 1–4											
Total[a]	63.9	51.8	46.8	47.4	43.6	44.8	42.9	40.6	38.3	35.8	34.4
Gender											
Male	72.6	58.5	52.4	52.0	48.0	49.5	47.3	44.8	42.2	39.7	37.5
Female	54.7	44.8	41.0	42.7	39.0	39.9	38.2	36.2	34.3	31.8	31.2
Race and Hispanic origin[b]											
White	57.9	46.6	41.1	41.7	38.1	38.3	36.5	35.1	32.9	31.6	29.9
White, non-Hispanic[c]	—	45.3	37.6	38.7	36.3	36.4	35.1	33.9	32.1	31.1	29.3
Black	97.6	80.7	76.8	79.7	73.2	79.1	77.2	70.3	67.6	59.2	61.4
Hispanic[c,d]	—	46.1	43.5	43.6	41.7	42.0	39.1	36.7	33.6	31.3	30.0
Asian/Pacific Islander	43.2	40.1	38.6	30.4	26.9	30.5	25.3	25.4	25.1	25.1	18.7
Leading causes of death											
Unintentional injuries	25.9	20.2	17.3	17.5	15.9	16.4	15.9	14.5	13.8	13.1	—
Cancer	4.5	3.8	3.5	3.5	3.1	3.3	3.3	3.1	2.7	2.9	—
Birth defects	8.0	5.9	6.1	5.7	5.5	5.1	4.5	4.4	4.1	3.8	—
Homicide	2.5	2.5	2.6	2.8	2.8	2.9	3.0	2.9	2.7	2.4	—
Heart disease	2.6	2.2	1.9	2.2	1.8	1.9	1.8	1.6	1.4	1.4	—
Pneumonia/influenza	2.1	1.6	1.2	1.4	1.2	1.2	1.1	1.0	1.1	1.2	—
Injury-related deaths by cause											
All injuries (intentional and unintentional)	28.9	23.0	19.9	20.5	18.7	19.4	19.0	17.4	16.7	15.5	—
Motor vehicle traffic related	7.4	5.9	5.3	5.0	4.7	4.8	5.0	4.5	4.5	4.3	—
Drowning	5.7	4.4	3.9	3.9	3.5	3.7	3.1	3.5	3.2	3.1	—
Fire and burns	6.1	4.8	4.0	4.3	4.0	4.1	4.2	3.1	3.0	2.5	—
Firearms	0.7	0.7	0.6	0.6	0.7	0.7	0.6	0.6	0.5	0.5	—
Suffocation	1.9	1.4	1.3	1.4	1.3	1.4	1.2	1.3	1.3	1.1	—
Pedestrian (non-traffic)[e]	1.5	1.1	0.9	0.9	0.8	0.8	0.9	0.7	0.8	0.7	—
Fall	0.9	0.6	0.6	0.6	0.4	0.4	0.4	0.3	0.3	0.3	—

— = not available

*Preliminary data.

[a]Total includes American Indians/Alaska Natives.

[b]Death rates for American Indians/Alaska Natives are not shown separately, because the numbers of deaths were too small for the calculation of reliable rates.

[c]Trend data for Hispnics and white, non-Hispanics are effected by expansion of the reporting area in which an item on Hispanic origin is included on the death certificate as well as by immigration. These two factors affect numbers of events, composition of the Hispanic population, and health characteristics. Tabulations are restricted to a subset of the States with the item on the death certificate and that meet a minimal quality standard. The quality of reporting has improved substantially over time, so that the minimal quality standard was relaxed in 1992 to those areas reporting Hispanic origin on at least 80 percent of records. The number of States in the reporting area increased from 15 in 1984 to 17 and the District of Columbia (DC) in 1985; 18 and DC in 1986-87; 26 and DC in 1988; 44 and DC in 1989; 45, New York State (excluding New York City), and DC in 1990; 47, New York State (excluding New York City), and DC in 1991; 48 and DC in 1992; and 49 and DC in 1993-96. The population data in 1990 and 1991 do not exclude New York City. Data for 1998 are preliminary due to incomplete reporting for California.

[d]Persons of Hispanic origin may be of any race.

[e]Includes death occurring on private property. Pedestrian deaths on public roads are inlcuded in motor vehicle traffic related.

SOURCE: Centers for Disease Control and Prevention. National Center for Health Satistics, National Vital Statistics System.

TABLE 20

Mortality Rate among Adolescents Ages 15 to 19 by Gender, Race, Hispanic Origin and Cause of Death, 1980–1997

(Deaths per 100,000 adolescents ages 15–19)

Characteristic	1980	1985	1990	1991	1992	1993	1994	1995	1996	1997
Total, all races										
All causes	97.9	80.5	87.8	89.0	84.3	86.9	86.8	83.5	78.6	74.8
Injuries	78.1	62.8	71.0	71.6	67.2	69.7	69.5	66.1	62.4	58.5
Motor vehicle traffic	42.3	33.1	32.8	30.9	27.8	28.3	29.0	28.3	28.2	27.0
All firearm	14.7	13.3	23.3	26.4	26.2	27.8	28.2	24.5	21.2	18.8
Firearm homicide	7.0	5.7	13.8	16.4	16.7	17.8	17.7	15.4	13.2	11.6
Firearm suicide	5.4	6.0	7.4	7.4	7.3	7.4	7.8	7.0	6.1	6.0
Males										
White, non-Hispanic										
All causes	—	105.1	108.7	104.1	97.1	98.0	99.0	96.0	92.1	90.1
Injuries	—	86.2	89.9	85.6	78.6	80.2	80.6	77.2	75.1	72.3
Motor vehicle traffic	—	47.6	48.2	44.3	39.0	41.1	41.1	38.5	39.3	37.1
All firearm	—	17.0	21.0	22.1	21.0	21.1	22.3	19.9	16.9	16.3
Firearm homicide	—	3.7	4.0	4.4	4.9	5.0	5.1	4.5	3.6	4.3
Firearm suicide	—	10.5	13.6	14.2	13.1	13.1	13.6	12.6	11.0	10.5
Black, non-Hispanic										
All causes	—	121.1	201.9	235.0	225.6	238.8	239.5	209.3	191.7	169.9
Injuries	—	92.6	174.7	205.5	196.1	209.7	208.3	177.2	163.1	143.6
Motor vehicle traffic	—	16.0	28.8	30.0	26.9	27.3	29.4	29.6	28.4	29.6
All firearm	—	49.2	120.7	145.0	145.7	157.8	156.1	124.9	113.0	93.8
Firearm homicide	—	39.1	105.7	126.5	122.9	134.2	131.3	106.0	95.2	80.6
Firearm suicide	—	4.9	8.6	9.1	12.8	11.7	13.9	10.7	9.5	8.7
Hispanic [a]										
All causes	—	121.3	132.2	143.2	141.9	146.3	145.4	131.6	119.9	107.1
Injuries	—	103.7	116.6	127.0	123.8	127.8	128.8	115.3	102.8	90.6
Motor vehicle traffic	—	42.8	41.0	36.3	32.9	35.0	35.2	33.1	31.2	27.7
All firearm	—	31.2	52.0	66.2	69.6	68.6	71.5	68.5	51.9	45.1
Firearm homicide	—	20.9	40.0	51.9	55.9	54.1	55.2	49.6	40.9	33.2
Firearm suicide	—	6.7	8.6	8.8	9.7	10.9	10.7	9.6	7.2	8.5
Females										
White, non-Hispanic										
All causes	—	46.4	45.5	46.9	43.2	44.2	43.4	44.3	43.1	43.8
Injuries	—	33.7	33.2	34.3	31.4	31.4	31.3	32.3	31.4	31.8
Motor vehicle traffic	—	22.5	23.2	24.0	21.6	21.0	22.3	22.9	22.2	22.5
All firearm	—	3.8	4.0	4.0	3.8	4.2	4.1	3.7	3.5	3.3
Firearm homicide	—	1.1	1.4	1.5	1.8	1.5	1.7	1.7	1.4	1.3
Firearm suicide	—	2.2	2.3	2.2	1.8	2.3	2.1	1.8	1.9	1.9
Black, non-Hispanic										
All causes	—	43.4	54.9	53.5	52.2	54.8	57.7	57.8	54.8	50.5
Injuries	—	20.4	30.7	30.6	29.2	32.0	31.5	33.3	31.7	27.7
Motor vehicle traffic	—	6.1	9.3	8.9	9.4	8.5	10.7	10.9	12.8	10.7
All firearm	—	6.4	12.1	13.0	12.6	16.0	13.7	14.5	12.0	9.6
Firearm homicide	—	4.8	10.3	11.5	10.7	14.4	11.4	12.6	10.2	7.8
Firearm suicide	—	*	****				2.0	1.7	*	1.6
Hispanic [a]										
All causes	—	33.6	35.7	38.9	37.1	38.7	36.7	37.7	35.3	33.7
In juries	—	20.7	23.0	24.6	23.1	25.3	23.3	24.5	22.1	21.5
Motor vehicle traffic	—	10.7	10.5	11.4	11.9	11.6	12.0	13.0	11.3	12.6
All firearm	—	4.5	6.9	7.6	6.7	8.1	7.5	6.1	4.2	4.7
Firearm homicide	—	*	4.9	5.7	5.5	5.7	5.8	4.8	2.4	3.2
Firearm suicide	—	*	*****					*	*	*

— = Data not available

* Number too small to calculate a reliable rate.

[a] Persons of Hispanic origin may be of any race.

SOURCE: Centers for Disease Control and Prevention, National Center for Health Statistics, National Vital Statistics System.

TABLE 21

Number of Children under Age 18 in the United States by Age, Selected Years 1950–1999 and Projected 2000–2020

Number (in millions)

Age group	1950	1960	1970	1980	1990	1991	1992	1993	1994	1995	1996	1997	1998	1999	Projected 2000	Projected 2010	Projected 2020
All children	47.3	65.5	69.8	63.7	64.2	65.1	66.1	67.0	67.9	68.5	69.1	69.6	69.9	70.2	70.4	72.1	77.2
Age group																	
Ages 0–5	19.1	24.3	20.9	19.6	22.5	22.9	23.2	23.4	23.6	23.6	23.3	23.1	22.9	22.8	22.7	24.0	26.3
Ages 6–11	15.3	21.8	24.6	20.8	21.6	21.9	22.0	22.2	22.4	22.6	23.0	23.4	23.7	24.0	24.1	23.4	25.6
Ages 12–17	12.9	18.4	24.3	23.3	20.1	20.4	20.9	21.4	22.0	22.4	22.7	23.0	23.2	23.4	23.5	24.6	25.2

SOURCE: U.S Census Bureau, *Current Population Reports,* Estimates of the population of the United States by single years of age, color, and sex; 1900 to 1959 (Series P-25, No. 311); Estimates of the population of the United States, by age, sex, and race: April 1, 1960, to July 1, 1973 (Series P-25, No. 519): Preliminary estimates of the population of the United States by age, sex, and race: 1970 to 1981 (Series P-25, No. 917); *Methodology and assumptions for the population projections of the United States: 1999 to 2100* (Population Division Working Paper No. 28); and unpublished vintage 1998 estimates tables for 1980-98 that are available on the Census Bureau website.

TABLE 22

Percentage of Beginning Kindergartners with Selected Knowledge and Skills by Mother's Education, Fall 1998

Characteristic	Total	Mother's education — Less than high school	High school diploma or equivalent	Some college, including vocational/technical	Bachelor's degree or higher
Reading proficiency [a]					
Letter recognition	66	38	57	69	86
Beginning sounds	29	9	20	30	50
Ending sounds	17	4	11	17	32
Print familiarity [a,b,c]					
0 skills	18	32	23	17	8
1 skills	21	28	23	20	14
2 skills	24	24	24	24	23
3 skills	37	17	30	39	56
Engagement in prosocial behavior [b,d]					
Accept peer ideas					
Never/sometimes	26	31	27	25	24
Often/very often	74	69	73	75	76
Form friendships					
Never/sometimes	23	30	25	22	19
Often/very often	77	70	75	78	81
Comfort others					
Never/sometimes	49	58	50	47	43
Often/very often	51	42	50	53	57
Approaches to learning [b,d]					
Persists at tasks					
Never/sometimes	29	39	30	27	21
Often/very often	71	61	70	73	79
Eager to learn					
Never/sometimes	25	38	28	22	17
Often/very often	75	62	72	78	83
Pays attention					
Never/sometimes	34	45	36	32	25
Often/very often	66	55	64	68	75

[a] Estimates are based on first-time kindergartners who were assessed in English (approximately 19 percent of Asian children and approximately 30 percent of Hispanic children were not assessed).

[b] Percentages may not sum to 100 due to rounding.

[c] Print familiarity skills in this report consist of knowing that print reads left to right, where to go when a line of print ends, and where the story ends.

[d] Estimates based on first-time kindergartners. Frequency of behaviors is based on teachers' reports.

Note: The ECLS-K reading assessment domain includes the following five proficiency levels: level 1, recognition of upper and lower case letters of the alphabet; levels 2 and 3, phonological sensitivity at the subword level (e.g., knowledge of letter and sound relationships at the beginning and at the end of words): level 4, ability to read common words; and level 5, comprehension of written text. This table presents information on only the first three levels. For more details, see West J., Denton, K., and Germino-Hausken, E., (2000). *America's kindergartners: Findings from the early childhood longitudinal study, Kindergarten Class of 1998-99, Fall 1998* (NCES 2000-070). Washington, DC: National Center for Education Statistics.

SOURCE: U.S. Department of Education, National Center for Education Statistics, Early Childhood Longitudinal Study, Kindergarten Class of 1998-89.

TABLE 23

Percentage of Children Ages 2 to 18 by Age and Diet Quality as Measured by the Healthy Eating Index, 1994–1996

Age	1994			1995			1996		
	Good diet[a]	Needs improvement[a]	Poor diet[a]	Good diet[a]	Needs improvement[a]	Poor diet[a]	Good diet[a]	Needs improvement[a]	Poor diet[a]
Ages 2–5	26	63	11	27	68	5	24	68	8
Ages 6–12	13	75	12	11	82	7	12	75	13
Ages 13–18	8	69	23	5[b]	76	19	6	74	20

[a] A Healthy Eating Index (HEI) score above 80 implies a good diet, an HEI score between 51 and 80 implies a diet that needs improvement, and an HEI score less than 51 implies a poor diet.
[b] Sample size relatively small to make reliable comparisons.

SOURCE: U.S. Department of Agriculture, Center for Nutrition Policy and Promotion, Continuing Survey of Food Intakes by Individuals.

TABLE 24

Percentage of Children Ages 2 to 18 by Age, Poverty Status, and Diet Quality as Measured by the Healthy Eating Index, 3-Year Average 1994–1996

Characteristic	Good diet[a]	Needs improvement[a]	Poor diet[a]
Age 2–5			
At or below poverty	19	70	11
Above poverty	28	65	7
Ages 6–12			
At or below poverty	10	78	12
Above poverty	12	78	10
Ages 13–18			
At or below poverty	3[b]	72	25
Above poverty	7	74	19

[a] A Healthy Eating Index (HEI) score above 80 implies a good diet, an HEI score between 51 and 80 implies a diet that needs improvement, and an HEI score less than 51 implies a poor diet.

[b] Sample size relatively small to make reliable comparisons.

SOURCE: U.S. Department of Agriculture, Center for Nutrition Policy and Promotion, Continuing Survey of Food Intakes by Individuals.

TABLE 25

Percentage of Children by Type of Care Arrangement for Children from Birth through 3rd Grade by Children and Family Characteristics, 1995 and 1999

Characteristic	Parental care only		Type of nonparental care arrangement							
			Total in nonparental care[b]		Care in a home[a]				Center-based program[c]	
					By a relative		By a nonrelative			
	1995	1999	1995	1999	1995	1999	1995	1999	1995	1999
Total	49	46	51	54	20	23	15	14	23	27
Age/grade in school										
Ages 0–2	51	49	50	51	23	25	19	17	12	16
Ages 3–6, not yet in kindergarten	26	23	74	77	19	23	17	16	55	59
Kindergarten	56	52	44	49	18	19	14	13	16	22
1st–3rd grade	62	57	38	43	18	21	10	9	13	18
Race and Hispanic origin										
White, non-Hispanic	49	48	51	52	17	19	17	16	24	28
Black, non-Hispanic	40	34	60	66	31	35	10	11	27	35
Hispanic[d]	58	53	42	47	23	24	10	11	13	19
Other	49	42	51	58	22	29	11	12	25	29
Poverty status										
Below poverty	56	50	44	50	23	27	9	10	18	23
At or above poverty	46	45	54	55	19	21	17	15	25	29
Mothers's highest level of education[e]										
Less than high school graduate	67	59	33	41	18	22	6	9	13	17
High school gradrate/GED	51	48	49	52	22	27	13	11	19	23
Vocational/technical or some college	44	43	56	57	22	23	17	16	25	29
College graduate	40	43	60	57	14	15	22	17	34	34
Mother's employment status[e]										
35 hours or more per week	22	22	78	78	32	34	25	21	33	37
Less that 35 hours per week	42	45	58	55	25	25	19	17	24	26
Looking for work	64	60	36	40	15	21	4	6	20	21
Not in the labor force	76	75	24	25	7	7	4	4	15	18

[a]Relative and nonrelative care can take place in either the child's own home or another home.

[b]Some children participate in more than one type of nonparental care arrangement. Thus, details do not sum to the total percentage of children in nonparental care.

[c]Center-based programs include day care centers, prekindergartens, Nursery schools, Head Start programs, and other early childhood education programs.

[d]Persons of Hispanic origin may be of any race.

[e]Children without a mother in the home are excluded from estimates of mother's highest level of education and mother's employment status.

SOURCE: U.S. Department of Education, National Center for Education Statistics, National Household Education Survey.

TABLE 26

Percentage of Children under Age 18 Living in Areas That Do Not Meet at Least One of the Primary National Ambient Air Quality Standards, 1990–1998

	1990	1991	1992	1993	1994	1995	1996	1997	1998
Total	31	35	22	24	25	32	20	21	24
Pollutant									
Ozone	26	28	18	21	20	29	17	19	21
Carbon monoxide	9	8	6	5	6	5	5	4	4
Particulates	8	9	10	3	5	10	3	3	3
Lead	2	6	2	2	2	2	2	1	2
Nitrogen dioxide	4	0	0	0	0	0	0	0	0
Sulfur dioxide	1	2	0	1	0	0	0	0	0

Note: Percentages were based on the number of children living in counties not meeting a national ambient air quality standard, divided by the total population. Population of children were based on the 1990 Census.

For more information on the emissions standards that are used in claculating these percentages, please see the following report: Office of Air Quality Planning and standards. (1998). National air quality and emissions trends report, 1997. Research Triangle Park, NC: U.S. Environmental Protection Agency.

The standards can also be found at http://www.epa.gov/oar/aqtrnd97/chapter2.pdf.

SOURCE: U.S. Environmental Protection Agency, Office of Air and Radiation, Aerometric Information Retrieval System.

TABLE 27

Percentage of Children Under Age 18 Living in Various Family Arrangements by Race and Hispanic Origin, 1996

Characteristic	Total	White, non-Hispanic	Black, non-Hispanic	Other, non-Hispanic	Hispanic
Total children ages 0 to 17					
Number (in thousands)	71,494	46,657	11,033	3,377	10,428
Living with two parents	**70.9**	**79.0**	**36.9**	**78.8**	**68.2**
Two bio./adopt. married	62.4	70.1	29.9	72.7	58.7
Two bio./adopt. cohab.	1.8	1.4	1.8	1.5	4.2
Bio./adopt. parent and step. married	6.4	7.3	4.9	4.6	4.8
Bio./adopt. parent and step. cohab.[a]	0.3	0.2	0.3	0.1	0.4
Living with a single parent	**25.4**	**18.5**	**54.9**	**18.0**	**27.5**
Single mother	20.6	13.4	50.2	14.6	23.3
Single mother with partner	2.1	2.1	2.3	1.6	2.4
Single father	2.1	2.4	1.7	1.3	1.3
Single father with partner	0.4	0.4	0.3	0.2	0.4
Stepparent	0.2	0.2	0.3	0.3	0.1
Stepparent with partner	0.0	0.0	0.0	—	—
Living with no parents	**3.7**	**2.5**	**8.2**	**3.2**	**4.3**
Grandparent	1.8	1.1	5.1	1.7	1.4
Other relatives only-no grandparent	0.8	0.4	1.6	0.9	1.3
Nonrelative only-not foster parent(s)	0.4	0.4	0.4	0.1	0.3
Other relatives and nonrelatives	0.3	0.2	0.3	0.4	0.3
Foster parent(s)	0.4	0.3	0.7	0.1	0.7
Own household or partner of householder	0.1	0.1	0.1	—	0.2
Children ages 0 to 4					
Number (in thousands)	19,960	12,759	3,073	871	3,257
Living with two parents	74.3	84.3	35.5	81.8	70.0
Two bio./adopt. married	68.4	79.0	30.3	76.6	60.5
Two bio./adopt. cohab.	4.1	3.4	3.5	4.4	7.3
Bio./adopt. parent and step. married	1.8	1.7	1.7	0.8	2.1
Bio./adopt. parent and step. cohab.[a]	0.1	0.1	—	—	0.1
Living with a single parent	23.0	14.1	58.1	17.7	26.4
Single mother	20.0	11.2	55.7	14.8	22.0
Single mother with partner	1.6	1.5	1.1	1.1	2.7
Single father	0.9	1.0	0.8	1.1	0.7
Single father with partner	0.3	0.2	0.3	—	0.8
Stepparent	0.2	0.1	0.2	0.7	0.2
Stepparent with partner	0.0	0.0	—	—	—
Living with no parents	2.6	1.6	6.4	0.6	3.6
Grandparent	1.5	0.9	4.5	0.6	1.3
Other relatives only-no grandparent	0.4	0.3	0.8	—	0.5
Nonrelative only-not foster parent(s)	0.2	0.2	0.2	—	0.2
Other relatives and nonrelatives	0.1	0.1	0.1	—	0.4
Foster parent(s)	0.4	0.1	0.8	—	1.1
Own household or partner of householder	—	—	—	—	—

SOURCE: U.S. Census Bureau.

TABLE 28

Percentage of Households with Children under Age 18 That Report Housing Problems by Type of Problem, Selected Years 1978–1997

Household type	1978	1983	1989	1993	1995	1997
All households with children						
Number of households (in millions)	32.3	33.6	35.7	35.5	37.3	37.0
Percent with						
Any problems	30	33	33	34	36	36
Inadequate housing[a]	9	8	9	7	7	7
Crowded housing	9	8	7	6	7	7
Cost burden greater than 30 percent	15	21	24	27	28	28
Cost burden greater than 50 percent	6	11	9	11	12	12
Severe problems	8	12	10	11	12	11
Very-low-income renter households with children[b]						
Number of households (in millions)	4.2	5.1	5.9	6.7	6.5	6.2
Percent with						
Any problems	79	83	76	75	77	82
Inadequate housing[a]	18	18	18	14	13	15
Crowded housing	22	18	17	14	17	17
Cost burden greater than 30 percent	59	68	67	67	68	74
Cost burden greater than 50 percent	31	38	36	38	38	41
Severe problems	33	42	33	34	32	28
Rental assistance	23	23	29	28	29	30

[a] Inadequate housing refers to housing with "moderate or severe physical problems." The most common problems meeting the definition are lacking complete plumbing for exclusive use, having unvented room heaters as the primary heating equipment, and multiple upkeep problems such as water leakage, open cracks or holes, broken plaster, or signs of rats.

[b] Very-low-income households are those with incomes at or below one-half the median income in a geographic area.

Note: Data are available for 1978, 1983, 1989, 1993, 1995, and 1997 (1978 data based on 1970 Census weights; 1983 and 1989 data on 1980 weights; 1993, 1995, and 1997 data on 1990 weights). Moderate or severe physical problems: See definition in Appendix A of the American Housing Survey summary volume, American Housing Survey for the United States in 1993, *Current Housing Reports, H150/93, U.S. Census Bureau, 1995. Cost burden: Expenditures on housing and* utilities are greater than 30 percent of reported income. Severe problems: Cost burden is greater than 50 percent of income or severe physical problems among those not reporting housing assistance. See Office of Policy Development and Research, U.S. Department of Housing and Urban Development. (1998). *Rental housing assistance —the crisis continues: The 1997 report to Congress on worst case housing needs. Washington, DC: U.S. Department of Housing and Urban* Development.

SOURCE: U.S. Census Bureau and the U.S. Department of Housing and Urban Development, Annual Housing Survey and American Housing Survey. Tabulated by the U.S. Department of Housing and Urban Development.

TABLE 29

Percentage of Low-Birthweight Births by Detailed Race and Hispanic Origin, Selected Years 1980–1998

LOW BIRTHWEIGHT (LESS THAN 2,500 GRAMS, ABOUT 5.5 POUNDS)

Race and Hispanic origin	1980	1985	1990	1991	1992	1993	1994	1995	1996	1997	1998
Total	6.8	6.8	7.0	7.1	7.1	7.2	7.3	7.3	7.4	7.5	7.6
White, non-Hispanic	5.7	5.6	5.6	5.7	5.7	5.9	6.1	6.2	6.4	6.5	6.6
Black, non-Hispanic	12.7	12.6	13.3	13.6	13.4	13.4	13.3	13.2	13.1	13.1	13.2
Hispanic[a]	6.1	6.2	6.1	6.2	6.1	6.2	6.2	6.3	6.3	6.4	6.4
Mexican American	5.6	5.8	5.5	5.6	5.6	5.8	5.8	5.8	5.9	6.0	6.0
Puerto Rican	9.0	8.7	9.0	9.4	9.2	9.2	9.1	9.4	9.2	9.4	9.7
Cuban	5.6	6.0	5.7	5.6	6.1	6.2	6.3	6.5	6.5	6.8	6.5
Central and South American	5.8	5.7	5.8	5.9	5.8	5.9	6.0	6.2	6.0	6.3	6.5
Other and unknown Hispanic	7.0	6.8	6.9	7.3	7.2	7.5	7.5	7.5	7.7	7.9	7.6
Asian/Pacific Islander	6.7	6.2	6.5	6.5	6.6	6.6	6.8	6.9	7.1	7.2	7.4
Chinese	5.2	5.0	4.7	5.1	5.0	4.9	4.8	5.3	5.0	5.1	5.3
Japanese	6.6	6.2	6.2	5.9	7.0	6.5	6.9	7.3	7.3	6.8	7.5
Filipino	7.4	6.9	7.3	7.3	7.4	7.0	7.8	7.8	7.9	8.3	8.2
Hawaiian and part Hawaiian	7.2	6.5	7.2	6.7	6.9	6.8	7.2	6.8	6.8	7.2	7.2
Other Asian/Pacific Islander	6.8	6.2	6.6	6.7	6.7	6.9	7.1	7.1	7.4	`7.5	7.8
American Indian/Alaska Native	6.4	5.9	6.1	6.2	6.2	6.4	6.4	6.6	6.5	6.8	6.8

VERY LOW BIRTHWEIGHT (LESS THAN 1,500 GRAMS, ABOUT 3.25 POUNDS)

Race and Hispanic origin	1980	1985	1990	1991	1992	1993	1994	1995	1996	1997	1998
Total	1.15	1.21	1.27	1.29	1.29	1.33	1.33	1.35	1.37	1.42	1.45
White, non-Hispanic	0.86	0.90	0.93	0.94	0.94	1.00	1.01	1.04	1.08	1.12	1.15
Black, non-Hispanic	2.46	2.66	2.93	2.97	2.97	2.99	2.99	2.98	3.02	3.05	3.11
Hispanic[a]	0.98	1.01	1.03	1.02	1.04	1.06	1.08	1.11	1.12	1.13	1.15
Mexican American	0.92	0.97	0.92	0.92	0.94	0.97	0.99	1.01	1.01	1.02	1.02
Puerto Rican	1.29	1.30	1.62	1.66	1.70	1.66	1.63	1.79	1.70	1.85	1.86
Cuban	1.02	1.18	1.20	1.15	1.24	1.23	1.31	1.19	1.35	1.36	1.33
Central and South American	0.99	1.01	1.05	1.02	1.02	1.02	1.06	1.13	1.14	1.17	1.23
Other and unknown Hispanic	1.01	0.96	1.09	1.09	1.10	1.23	1.29	1.28	1.48	1.35	1.38
Asian/Pacific Islander	0.92	0.85	0.87	0.85	0.91	0.86	0.93	0.91	0.99	1.05	1.10
Chinese	0.66	0.57	0.51	0.65	0.67	0.63	0.58	0.67	0.64	0.74	0.75
Japanese	0.94	0.84	0.73	0.62	0.85	0.74	0.92	0.87	0.81	0.78	0.84
Filipino	0.99	0.86	1.05	0.97	1.05	0.95	1.19	1.13	1.20	1.29	1.35
Hawaiian and part Hawaiian	1.05	1.03	0.97	1.02	1.02	1.14	1.20	0.94	0.97	1.41	1.53
Other Asian/Pacific Islander	0.96	0.91	0.92	0.87	0.93	0.89	0.93	0.91	1.04	1.07	1.12
American Indian/Alaska Native	0.92	1.01	1.01	1.07	0.95	1.05	1.10	1.10	1.21	1.19	1.24

[a] Persons of Hispanic origin may be of any race.

Note: Excludes live births with unknown birthweight. Low-birthweight infants weigh less than 2,500 grams at birth, about 5.5 po unds. Very-low-birthweight infants weight less than 1,500 grams, about 3.25 pounds.

Trend data for births to Hispanics and non-Hispanic whites and blacks are affected by expansion of the reporting area in which an item on Hispanic origin is included on the birth certificate as well as by immigration. These two factors affect numbers of events, composition of the Hispanic population, and maternal and infant health characteristics. The number of States in the reporting area increased from 22 in 1980 to 23 and the District of Columbia (DC) in 1983-87, 30 and DC in 1988, 47 and DC in 1989, 48 and DC in 1990, 49 and DC in 1991-92, and all 50 States and DC from 1993 forward. Trend data for births to Asian/Pacific Islander and Hispanic women are also affected by immigration.

SOURCE: Centers for Disease Control and Prevention, National Center for Health Statistics, National Vital Statistics System. Ventura, S.J., Martin, J.A., Curtin, S.C., and Mathews, T.J. (2000). Births: Final data for 1998, National Vital Statistics Reports, 48 (3). Hyattsville, MD: National Center for Health Statistics.

TABLE 30

Percentage of 6th- through 12th-Grade Students Who Participated in Volunteer Activities and Their Total Hours of Service Participation in Regular Community Service During the Curent School Year by Selected Student, Household and School Characteristics, 1996 and 1999

| Characteristic | Any participation | | Once or twice | | Regular service | | | | | | | |
| | | | | | 10 or fewer hours | | 11 to 34 hours | | 35 to 80 hours | | More than 80 hours | |
	1996	1999	1996	1999	1996	1999	1996	1999	1996	1999	1996	1999
Total	49	52	23	24	7	7	8	8	6	7	5	6
Grade												
6 to 8	47	48	24	25	8	8	7	7	4	4	3	3
9 to 12	50	55	23	24	6	6	8	9	7	8	7	8
Gender												
Male	45	47	23	24	7	6	7	7	4	5	5	5
Female	53	57	24	24	7	8	9	9	7	8	6	7
Race and Hispanic origin												
White, non-Hispanic	53	54	25	27	8	8	9	9	6	7	5	6
Black, non-Hispanic	43	47	21	21	5	6	5	8	6	6	6	6
Hispanic[a]	38	39	17	20	6	4	6	6	3	4	6	5
Other race-ethnicity	50	53	23	22	—	10	10	—	7	9	—	—
Language spoken most at home												
English	50	53	24	25	7	7	8	8	6	7	5	6
Other	32	33	17	16	—	—	—	—	—	—	—	—
Parents' highest level of education												
Less than high school graduate	34	37	18	19	—	5	—	4	—	4	—	5
High school graduate/GED	42	45	20	22	6	6	7	6	5	5	5	5
Vocational/technical school or some college	48	50	23	24	7	6	8	9	5	6	5	6
College graduate	58	62	29	28	7	9	7	10	8	8	7	7
Graduate or professional school	64	65	29	29	9	10	11	10	9	9	6	7
School type												
Public, assigned	47	51	23	24	7	7	7	8	5	6	5	5
Public, chosen	50	48	22	21	7	6	9	8	6	6	5	8
Private, church-related	69	72	28	31	9	8	13	13	10	12	8	9
Private, not church-related	57	68	28	29	—	—	—	—	—	—	—	—
School size												
Under 300	48	53	23	27	9	8	9	6	4	6	4	5
300–599	50	50	25	24	7	7	7	8	5	5	5	5
600–999	48	51	21	24	8	7	8	7	5	7	5	5
1,000 or more	49	54	24	24	5	6	7	9	7	8	6	8
School practice												
Requires and arranges service	56	59	27	28	7	7	9	10	7	7	7	8
Arranges service only	52	54	25	25	8	8	8	9	6	7	6	6
Neither requires nor arranges service	30	29	14	13	4	4	5	3	3	3	3	—

— = not available

[a] Persons of Hispanic origin may be of any race.

Note: Because of rounding, detail may not add to totals. "Ungraded" and home-schooled students were not included in this analys is.

SOURCE: U.S. Department of Education, National Center for Education Statistics, National Household Education Survey.

TABLE 31

Racial and Ethnic Composition: Percentage of U.S. Children under Age 18 by Race and Hispanic Origin, Selected Years 1980–1999 and Projected 2000–2020

Race and Hispanic origin	1980	1985	1990	1991	1992	1993	1994	1995	1996	1997	1998	1999	Projected		
													2000	2010	2020
White, non-Hispanic	74	72	69	68	68	67	67	67	66	66	65	65	64	59	55
Black, non-Hispanic	15	15	15	15	15	15	15	15	15	15	15	15	15	14	14
Hispanic[a]	9	10	12	13	13	13	14	14	14	15	15	16	16	21	23
Asian/Pacific Islander[b]	2	3	3	3	3	3	4	4	4	4	4	4	4	5	6
American Indian/ Alaska Native[b]	1	1	1	1	1	1	1	1	1	1	1	1	1	1	1

[a] Persons of Hispanic origin may be of any race.
[b] Excludes persons in this race group who are of Hispanic origin.

SOURCE: U.S. Census Bureau, Current Population Reports. Estimates of the population of the United States by single years of age, color, and sex; 1900 to 1959 (Series P-25, No. 311); Estimates of the population of the United States, by age, sex, and race: April 1, 1960 to July 1, 1973 (Series P-25, No. 519); Preliminary estimates of the population of the United States by age, sex, and race: 1970 to 1981 (Series P-25, No. 917): *Methodology and assumptions for the population projections of the United States: 1999 to 2100* (Population Division Working Paper No. 38); and unpublished vintage 1997 tables for 1980-98 that are available on the Census Bureau website.

TABLE 32

Reading Achievement: Average Scale Scores of Students Ages 9, 13, and 17 by Age and Child and Family Characteristics, Selected Years 1980–1996

Characteristic	1980	1984	1988	1990	1992	1994	1996
Age 9							
Total	215	211	212	209	211	211	212
Gender							
Male	210	208	208	204	206	207	207
Female	220	214	216	215	215	215	218
Race and Hispanic origin							
White	221	218	218	217	218	218	220
Black	189	186	189	182	185	185	190
Hispanic[a]	190	187	194	189	192	186	194
Age 13							
Total	259	257	258	257	260	258	259
Gender							
Male	254	253	252	251	254	251	253
Female	263	262	263	263	265	266	265
Race and Hispanic origin							
White	264	263	261	262	266	265	267
Black	233	236	243	242	238	234	236
Hispanic[a]	237	240	240	238	239	235	240
Parents' education							
Less than high school	239	240	247	241	239	237	241
Graduated high school	254	253	253	251	252	251	252
Some education after high school	271	268	265	267	270	269	270
Age 17							
Total	286	289	290	290	290	288	287
Gender							
Male	282	284	286	284	284	282	280
Female	289	294	294	297	296	295	294
Race and Hispanic origin							
White	293	295	295	297	297	296	294
Black	243	264	274	267	261	266	265
Hispanic[a]	261	268	271	275	271	263	265
Parents' education							
Less than high school	262	269	267	270	271	268	267
Graduated high school	278	281	282	283	281	276	273
Some education after high school	299	301	300	300	299	299	297

[a] Persons of Hispanic origin may be of any race.

Note: Data on parents' level of education are not reliable for 9-year-olds.

The reading proficiency scale has a range from 0 to 500:
   Level 150: Simple, discrete reading tasks
   Level 200: Partial skills and understanding
   Level 250: Interrelates ideas and makes generalizations
   Level 300: Understands complicated information
   Level 350: Learns from specialized reading materials

SOURCE: U.S. Department of Education, National Center for Education Statistics, National Assessment of Educational Progress (NAEP), *1996 Trends in academic progress.*

TABLE 33

Serious Violent Juvenile Crime Rate: Number and Rate of Serious Crimes Involving Youth Ages 12 to 17, Selected Years 1980–1998

Characteristic	1980	1985	1990	1991	1992	1993	1994	1995	1996	1997	1998
Rate per 1,000 youth ages 12–17											
Total	34.9	30.2	39.1	39.9	44.4	51.9	47.0	36.3	35.5	30.7	26.5
Number of serious violent crimes											
Total (in millions)	3.8	3.4	3.5	3.7	4.0	4.2	4.1	3.3	3.3	3.0	2.8
Number involving youth ages 12–17 (in thousands)	812	652	785	811	925	1,108	1,031	812	805	706	616
Percentage involving youth ages 12–17	21.3	19.4	22.4	21.8	23.2	26.4	25.0	24.7	24.7	23.2	22.2
Percentage of juvenile crimes involving multiple offenders	61.4	61.4	61.1	60.7	57.9	55.2	56.8	54.5	53.1	53.4	52.9

Note: The numerator is the number of violent crimes (aggravated assault, rape, and robbery) reported to the National Crime Victimization Survey for which the age of the offenders was known, plus the number of homicides reported to police that involved at least one juvenile offender perceived by the victim (or by law enforcement in the case of homicide) to be 12 through 17 years of age. The denominator is the number of juveniles in the population. Aggravated assault is an attack with a weapon, regardless of whether or not an injury occurred, or an attack without a weapon when serious injury resulted. Robbery is stealing by force or threat of force. Because of changes made in the victimization survey, data prior to 1992 are adjusted to make them comparable with data collected under the redesigned methodology.

SOURCE: U.S. Department of Justice, Bureau of Justice Statistics, National Crime Victimization Survey, Federal Bureau of Investigation, Uniform Crime Reporting Program Supplementary Homicide Reports.

TABLE 34

Youth Neither Enrolled in School Nor Working: Percentage of Youth Ages 16 to 19 Who are Neither Enrolled in School Nor Working by Gender, Race, Hispanic Origin, and Age, Selected Years 1984–1999

Characteristic	1984	1985	1990	1991	1992	1993	1994[a]	1995[a]	1996[a]	1997[a]	1998[a]	1999[a]
All youth ages 16–19												
Total	12	11	10	11	10	10	10	9	9	9	8	8
Gender												
Male	9	9	8	9	8	8	8	8	8	8	8	7
Female	14	13	12	13	12	11	11	11	11	10	9	9
Race and Hispanic origin												
White, non-Hispanic	10	9	8	8	8	7	7	7	7	7	6	6
Black, non-Hispanic	19	18	15	17	17	15	14	14	15	14	13	13
Hispanic[b]	18	17	17	16	17	16	16	16	16	14	14	14
Youth ages 16–17												
Total	5	5	5	5	4	4	4	4	4	4	4	4
Gender												
Male	4	5	4	4	3	4	4	4	4	4	4	4
Female	6	6	5	5	5	5	5	5	5	4	4	4
Race and Hispanic origin												
White, non-Hispanic	5	5	4	4	3	3	3	3	3	3	3	3
Black, non-Hispanic	6	6	6	7	6	6	5	6	5	6	5	5
Hispanic[b]	11	10	10	9	9	9	9	9	8	8	8	9
Youth ages 18–19												
Total	18	17	15	16	16	15	15	15	15	14	13	13
Gender												
Male	14	13	12	13	13	13	13	12	13	12	12	11
Female	21	20	18	19	19	17	17	17	17	15	13	14
Race and Hispanic origin												
White, non-Hispanic	14	14	12	13	12	11	11	11	11	10	9	9
Black, non-Hispanic	32	30	23	27	28	25	25	24	25	23	21	21
Hispanic[b]	25	24	24	23	24	23	24	23	23	20	19	20

[a] Data for 1994 and subsequent years are not strictly comparable with data for prior years, because of major revisions in the Current Population Survey questionnaire and data collection methodology and because of the inclusion of 1990 Census-based population controls in the estimation process.

[b] Persons of Hispanic origin may be of any race.

Note: The figures represent an average based on responses to the survey questions for the months that youth are usually in scho ol (January through May and September through December). Results are based on uncomposited estimates and are not comparable to data from published tables.

SOURCE: U.S. Bureau of Labor Statistics, Current Population Survey.

TABLE 35

Youth Victims of Serious Violent Crime: Number and Rate of Victimizations for Youth Ages 12 to 17 by Age, Race and Gender, Selected Years 1980–1998

Characteristic	1980	1985	1990	1991	1992	1993	1994	1995	1996	1997	1998
Rate per 1,000 youth ages 12–17											
Total	37.6	34.3	43.2	40.7	38.8	43.8	41.3	28.3	30.3	27.1	24.6
Age											
Ages 12–14	33.4	28.1	41.2	37.8	37.6	38.0	3.45	26.7	24.9	23.5	20.4
Ages 15–17	41.4	40.3	45.2	43.6	40.1	49.9	48.5	30.0	35.8	30.7	28.6
Race											
White	34.1	34.4	37.0	40.1	35.2	40.0	38.0	25.5	27.7	27.6	24.2
Black	60.2	35.2	77.0	48.0	54.3	71.5	63.0	44.5	43.4	30.4	31.0
Other	21.7	28.8	37.3	25.0	48.7	17.6	27.5	23.7	31.2	9.7	11.7
Gender											
Male	54.8	49.8	60.5	60.7	49.8	53.9	51.5	39.0	40.4	33.1	32.2
Female	19.7	18.2	24.9	19.6	27.2	33.1	30.6	17.0	19.7	20.8	16.5
Number of victimizations of youth ages 12–17											
Ages 12–17	877,104	742,815	866,272	825,895	809,118	933,762	905,544	633,301	687,638	622,302	569,935

Note: Serious violent crimes include aggravated assault, rape, robbery, and homicide. Aggravated assault is an attack with a we apon, regardless of whether or not an injury occurred, or an attack without a weapon when serious injury resulted. Robbery is stealing by force or threat of force. Because of changes made in the victimization survey, data prior to 1992 are adjusted to make them comparable with data collected under the redesigned methodology. Victimization rates were calculated using population estimates from the U.S. Census Bureau's Current Population Reports. Such population estimates normally differ somewhat from population estimates derived from the victimization survey data. The rates may therefore differ marginally from rates based upon the victimization survey-derived population estimates.

SOURCE: U.S. Department of Justice, Bureau of Justice Statistics, National Crime Victimization Survey, Federal Bureau of Investigation, Uniform Crime Reporting Program, Supplementary Homicide Reports.

APPENDIX B

Children's Development Resources on the World Wide Web

Children's Development Resources on the World Wide Web

Web site	URL	Description
Adventure Bonding Parenting Page	http://imageplaza.com/parenting/	The Adventure Bonding Parenting Page contains useful hands-on advice Ilustrated through humorous stories for parents on how to raise confident, independent children.
American Academy of Child and Adolescent Psychiatry	http://aacap.org/	The American Academy of Child and Adolescent Psychiatry web site includes hot topics, access to the AACAP journal and information for families. Included in this information for families are current, pertinent parent articles, questions and answers about child and adolescent psychiatry, and a list of the symptoms and mental illnesses affecting teenagers.
American Academy of Pediatrics	http://www.aap.org/	The American Academy of Pediatrics web site is the largest web site and the largest professional association of pediatricians containing information for both physicians and families. This information includes how to celebrate holidays safely, news briefs, and ongoing information about topics like immunizations and basic development.
American Medical Association	http://www.ama-assn.org	Kids Health at the AMA web site contains information for parents, including nutrition, safety/accident prevention, guidelines for developmental stages, infections and immunizations, emergencies/first aid, and the behavior and emotions of children.
AtHealth Mental Health - Parenting	http://www.athealth.com/consumer/newsletter	Parenting is an online newsletter presented by AtHealth Mental Health that includes information about child development and parenting issues in diverse family situations. The newsletter includes information on later-life parenting, at-risk parents, and widowed or divorced single mother families.
Child and Family Research and Development Program	http://www.childsvoice.org/	The Child and Family Research and Development Program web site provides parenting tips including managing the moods of your child, establishing safe boundaries, and the development of social skills.
Child Development Institute	http://www.cdipage.com	The Child Development Institute's web site contains information and products related to child development, child psychology, parenting, learning disabilities, and family relationships
Child Development Tracker	http://www.women.com/family/tracker	The child development tracker is a year-by-year guide to child development for parents of one-year-olds to parents of twelfth-graders.
Child Development	http://idealist.com/	The Child Development web site focuses on early childhood development with emphasis placed on classical theorists. This web site also contains an e-mail community and bulletin board for parents and teachers.
Connect for Kids	http://www.connectforkids.org/	Connect for Kids is a web site that has the intention of making good parents into great parents through its feature articles, reference room, and suggestions that can be implemented in the home, community, and school.
Developmental Studies Center	http://wwwdevstu.org/	The Developmental Studies Center's web site is targeted at educators, and includes current research, workshops, and materials that help educators foster children's intellectual, ethical, and social development.
Early Child Development (Presented by the World Bank)	http://www.worldbank.org/children/index.htm	The Early Child Development web site offers access to child development journals and reports along with data and statistics. In addition, there is a chart of the child development stages, a listing of requirements for healthy child development and a listing of the ten myths of early childhood development.

Children's Development Resources on the World Wide Web [CONTINUED]

Web site	URL	Description
Early Childhood Care and Development (Presented by the Consultative Group on Early Childhood Care and Development)	http://www.ecdgroup.com	The Early Childhood Care and Development web site addresses the global needs of children from infancy to age eight. It provides information about young children and health care, parent education and involvement, and language issues in education and gender issues.
EarlyChildhood.Com	http://www.earlychildhood.com/	EarlyChildhood.Com contains information and resources relevant to both teachers and parents, including current articles on child development, a child-care locator, a guide to buying educational toys for children, and a message board designed to promote discussion among parents and teachers.
Full-Time Parents	http://www.fulltimeparents.org	Full-Time Parents is a support group and employment service for parents looking for work at home or trying to find a flexible job in order to get the most quality time with your child.
I Am Your Child	http://www.iamyourchild.org	The "I Am Your Child" web site is designed to assist parents in promoting their child's healthy development and school readiness. It provides information including principles of brain development, a discussion on child-care options with suggested questions to ask potential caregivers, and a "Tip of the Day."
IndiaParenting.Com	http://www.indiaparenting.com/	IndiaParenting.Com is an educational web site that is targeted at Indian parents but contains a lot of useful information and advice for parents of any ethnicity. Issues covered in this web site include sex education, manners and discipline, teen issues, and advice on how to instill confidence in your child.
Kid Source Online	http://www.kidsource.com	Kid Source Online is a web site geared toward parents that addresses current issues through book reviews and articles on education, parenting, and health and safety. In addition, it also includes daily e-mail parenting tips, a topic of the month, and a list of company recalls.
KidInfo	http://www.kidinfo.com/	KidInfo is an extensive web site for kids, teachers, and parents. It offers homework help for kids, lesson plans, tips on cooking, shopping, and travel for parents.
KidsHealth (Presented by the Nemours Foundation)	http://www.kidshealth.org/Foundation	KidsHealth focuses on nutrition, health, fitness, and emergencies for children, teens, and parents.
Learning Network-Parent Channel	http://www.familyeducation.com/	The Parent Channel located on the Learning Network contains information for parents on family activities, school help, entertainment, and family finance. In addition, parents can also participate in message boards, receive e-mail newsletters, and get expert advice.
National Academy for Child Development	http://www.nacd.org/	The National Academy for Child Development is an international organization of parents and professionals. Its web site includes a listing of recommended products, recent research in child development, and current articles for students and professionals.
National Institute of Child Health and Human Development	http://www.nichd.nih.gov/	The National Institute of Child Health and Human Development web site provides information on many topics including current research in child development, epistemology, statistics, prevention, news, and events.
National Institute on Early Childhood Development and Education (Presented by the Office of Educational Research and Improvement/ U.S. Department of Education)	http://www.ed.gov/offices/OERI/ECI/	The National Institute on Early Childhood Development and Education web site explores and allows access to current research (speeches, projects, and publications) in child development and education.

Children's Development Resources on the World Wide Web [CONTINUED]

Web site	URL	Description
National Network for Child Care	http://www.nncc.org/	The National Network for Child Care web site provides relevant information on the health and safety of children, quality child care and education for children with special needs. In addition, it also provides a brief overview of a child's physical, intellectual, and social/emotional development from infant to school age.
National Parenting Center	http://tnpc.com	The National Parenting Center web site provides information on current parenting-related articles, "seal of approval" reviews of products and services available to children and parents.
Parent News	http://www.parentnews.com /	Included in this web site is current news, family facts, supplemental homework assignments, and movie reviews from doctors, psychologists, and educators.
Parent Soup	http://www.parentsoup.com/	Parent Soup is an extensive web site about parenting that contains useful tools, online communities, chat rooms with experts and daily polls.
ParenthoodWeb	http://www.parenthoodweb.com/	ParenthoodWeb provides information and tools for parents including kids health tips, family safety, product recalls, recipes, chat rooms, downloadable coloring pages, and E-cards.
Parenting Q&A	http://www.parenting-qa.com/	Parenting Q&A is a web site for all parenting questions. The answers can be found through a database of previously asked questions or e-mail correspondence, which are answered by experts.
ParentingDoc	http://www.parentingdoc.com	ParentingDoc provides parenting information and advice for the most common parenting and child-rearing problems. ParentingDoc also discusses challenges that parents face and gives parents the opportunity to participate in bulletin board discussions with experts.
Parents Edge	http://www.parentsedge.com	Parents Edge is an educational resource that explores current issues in parenting, and offers advice on homework, reading and math skills, and Internet learning for children.
Parents.Com	http://www.parents.com	Parent.Com is an online magazine that provides information on a variety of topics, including child development, pregnancy, health, safety, fun, and travel.
PediaNet	http://www.pedianet.com/	PediaNet provides information on immunizations and product recalls, tools such as a prescription guide, doctor locator, and a growth development indicator.
Pediatric Development and Behavior Homepage	http://www.dbpeds.org/	The Pediatric Development and Behavior Homepage provides access to clinically relevant information and educational materials about the developmental, learning, and behavior problems of children for professionals, students, and parents.
Positive Child Development Guide	http://www.growinghealthykids.com/	The Positive Child Development Guide is an online guide to the life transitions that children face from the prenatal stage to adulthood. The web site provides healthy child and youth development strategies for parents.
ProTeacher	http://www.proteacher.com	ProTeacher contains child development theories, research and resources including learning styles and special needs for elementary school teachers and counselors.
Schubert Center for Childhood Development	http://www.cwru.edu/artsci/schubert/	The Schubert Center for Childhood Development is a web site of Case Western Reserve University, which supports research in child development, as well as in areas of mental illness and mental retardation.

Children's Development Resources on the World Wide Web [CONTINUED]

Web site	URL	Description
Zangle.Com	http://www.zangle.com/	Zangle.Com is a web site that provides information for parents, including advice for children with special needs, stepfamilies, divorce, health, safety, behavior, and education.
Zero to Three	http://www.zerotothree.org/	The Zero to Three web site provides information for both parents and professionals including tips of the week, developmental milestones, choosing quality child care, leadership development and resource lists.

INDEX

DATE DUE

MR 24 '04			
MAR 1 7 2004